"Therefore both writers and readers of history should not pay so much attention to the actual narrative of events, as to what precedes, what accompanies,
and what follows each. For if we take from history the discussion of why,
how, and wherefore each thing was done, and whether the result was what
we should have reasonably expected, what is left is a clever essay but not a
lesson, and while pleasing for the moment of no possible benefit for the
future."

Polybius, *Histories*. Book 3, nr. 31

"The ultimate goal of the Atlantic nations should be
to develop a genuine Atlantic commonwealth, in which common institutions
are increasingly developed to address common problems."

Dean Acheson, 1961 *Report to President Kennedy*

"When all is said and done, Great Britain is an island;
France the cape of a continent;
America another world."

Charles de Gaulle, *War Memoirs*

Atlantis Lost

American Studies

AMERICAN STUDIES publishes monographs and edited volumes on American history, society, politics, and culture. The series is a forum for groundbreaking approaches and areas of research, as well as pioneering scholarship that adds new insights into relatively established fields in the study of America.

Series Editors:
Derek Rubin and Jaap Verheul,
Utrecht University

PUBLISHED IN 2009
Derek Rubin and Jaap Verheul (eds.)
American Multiculturalism after 9/11, Transatlantic Perspectives
ISBN 9789089641441

Atlantis Lost

The American Experience with De Gaulle, 1958-1969

Sebastian Reyn

Amsterdam University Press

Coverillustration: 02 June 1961 [Paris Trip Book, page 73] "President Kennedy leaves with President De Gaulle at the conclusion of their talks at Elysee Palace, June 2, 1961." [U.S. Department of State]. Photograph in the John F. Kennedy Presidential Library and Museum, Boston.
Cover: Neon, design and communications, Sabine Mannell, Amsterdam, the Netherlands
Design: JAPES, Amsterdam, the Netherlands

ISBN   978 90 8964 214 1
e-ISBN   978 90 4851 211 9
NUR   697

Contents

Acknowledgments

Every book is an odyssey of the mind. My odyssey stretched out over fifteen years of intermittent work and I am grateful for having learned so much along the way. Its length in time, I feel, allowed for ideas to mature. Both de Gaulle and Uncle Sam conjure up powerful images and associations. A book of this sort therefore lends itself to taking one side or the other and to ready-made conclusions and worn-out clichés. This I was determined to avoid. Now that I have reached my destination on my own account, I am resigned to the verdict of the reader.

While an odyssey such as this one is largely solitary, it could not have been completed without the help of others. In particular, my wife Gioia has been an indispensable source of support and a sound judge of all that has been written in these pages. As she has had to share most of the burden, this book is dedicated to her. I furthermore thank my father for setting the example of thoroughness in academics, although I cannot claim to understand his mathemical field of research. I thank my mother for her stubborn belief that issues beyond academia continue to be far more important.

I thank Professor Alfons Lammers of the University of Leiden for his encouragement in the early years of this project, before Professor Henk Wesseling of the same university took over. I am much obliged to both. I also thank Professor John L. Harper of the Johns Hopkins University and Professor Alan Henrikson at the Fletcher School of Law and Diplomacy for their early-on advice.

This book would have been impossible without access to the documentary wealth from American archives. The dedicated staffs of the various presidential libraries administered by the National Archives and Records Administration have not only helped me during my research visits, but they have also responded promptly and liberally to my many requests from the Netherlands for additional documentary material. They have furthermore been of assistance in declassifying some material. In much the same vein, I thank the Roosevelt Study Center in Middelburg (The Netherlands), which owns an impressive collection of research material. Researching at these great institutions was made possible by grants from the Reiman-De Bas Fund (administered by the Bernhard Fund), the Netherlands Organization for Scientific Research (NWO), the John F. Kennedy Library, and the Roosevelt Study Center. I also acknowledge the great service provided by the State Department's Office of the Historian by providing online access to an increasing number of volumes of the The *Foreign Relations of the United States* series, as well as the similar service provided by the University of Wisconsin through its digital collections. In the Netherlands, whenever I had trouble finding an article or a book, Peter de Zeeuw of the Netherlands Ministry of Defense never failed in his efforts to assist me.

Lastly, I would like to thank my present and former colleagues at the Ministry of Defense in the Netherlands for their tolerance of and interest in my academic hobby. Jacques de Winter and Lo Casteleijn have generously allowed for extra leave. Along with Jan Geert Siccama and Arnout Brouwers, they have also taken precious time to comment on parts of this study. More generally, I have benefited from my contacts with them in ways that I hope are reflected in the following pages.

For reasons of readability, I have made use of English translations of French texts whenever these were available.

Introduction

How does one take the measure of a statesman the size of Charles de Gaulle? The Frenchman was without doubt one of the giants of his time. He saved his country from eclipse in 1940 and from civil war in 1958 almost by force of personality. His political life was enveloped by a unique sense of national mystique. The quasi-mystical attitudes and feelings surrounding his mission – to restore France to a position of greatness – were an unalienable part of his larger-than-life political persona and of his political philosophy. To many he was the General, le Grand Charles, the man of June 18th, the miraculous reincarnation of Jeanne d'Arc, Georges Clemenceau, *and* Louis XIV: rarely ever just de Gaulle – a brigadier-general of the French army who, animated by an adamant loyalty to his country, turned into a remarkably effective and strong-willed political leader in times of extraordinary crisis.

Among Americans, too, de Gaulle's Olympian stature summoned a respect that devolved to few other foreign leaders. Walter Lippmann, America's foremost commentator on foreign affairs, confessed that, "having been one of his American admirers since June of 1940, when he raised his flag in Britain and summoned the French to go on with the war, I cannot pretend to write dispassionately about General de Gaulle."[1] Cyrus Sulzberger, a long-time European correspondent of the *New York Times* who often visited de Gaulle, thought of him as the "last of the giants" in an "age of mediocrity."[2] He was voted *Time*'s man of the year in 1958. "He has given Frenchmen back their pride, swept away the miasma of self-contempt that has hung over France since its ignominious capitulation to Hitler in 1940," the news weekly judged.[3]

De Gaulle's popularity among Americans probably reached a peak in April 1960, during a state visit to the United States. The symbolic value of his rendez-vous with President Dwight Eisenhower, his wartime companion, was easily recognized. The historic achievements of the French president and his efforts to extricate France from Algeria were dwelled upon in a spate of well-disposed press reports. Senators and congressmen regaled the visiting statesman with a standing ovation as he spoke, in an address to a joint session of Congress, of his country's dedication to the cause of liberty. "Despite changes of fortune, the Americans and the French feel for one another a friendship now two centuries old, and still as much alive as ever," de Gaulle stressed. "France, for her part, has made her choice. She has chosen to be on the side of the free people. She has to be on that side with you."[4] His ensuing tour of American cities was the jubilant cortège of an old comrade-in-arms, with large crowds gathering along streets and on squares to catch a glimpse of the General's statuesque appearance. New York even bestowed on him the honor of a Broadway ticker parade, with the bells of Trinity Church ringing the Marseillaise in the midst of an estimated one million onlookers. At the end of his journey through America, de Gaulle volunteered to the mayor of San Francisco that it had been "le plus agréable" of his life.[5]

But American opinion about de Gaulle was not always this unequivocally positive. President Franklin Roosevelt's hostility to the World War II leader of the Free French has become something of a legend. De Gaulle's popularity in the United States during the early years of the Fifh Republic was moreover at an artificial zenith. The implications of his dissenting views on the transatlantic relationship were not yet visible in 1960 and seemed of minor importance compared to the Cold War showdowns with the Soviet Union. But during the remainder of the 1960s, in particular after 1962, de Gaulle's policy of "independence" and "grandeur" made him the culprit of successive crises within the Western alliance. In 1963, after de Gaulle's veto of British membership of the Common Market, the American public had already become evenly divided on the question of France's dependability; by July 1966 – after France's announcement of its withdrawal from NATO and with de Gaulle openly courting Moscow – the majority of Americans stopped viewing France as a dependable ally and many described de Gaulle as "power-hungry," "egocentric," and "overly nationalistic."[6] President Lyndon Johnson received thousands of letters from infuriated citizens urging him to stand up against the General. They wanted to see diplomatic contacts with France reduced to the very minimum; they planned to set up a campaign to discourage American tourists from going to France; they urged Johnson to demand that France pay off its remaining war debts to the United States instantly; a retired colonel of the Air Force announced his decision to destroy or return the "Croix de Guerre avec Palme Vermeille" that de Gaulle had personally awarded him for his valor in World War II.[7] Characterizations of de Gaulle had thus deteriorated from proud to obstinate, from solemn to haughty, from visionary to acting mainly in narrow self-interest.

Most Americans came to understand that de Gaulle's return to power in May 1958 had signalled an important change in the Franco-American relationship. Even as many of the policies of the Fifth Republic were arguably a continuation of those of the Fourth, the change was more than one of style.[8] De Gaulle brought France, as Michael Harrison put it, "the novelty of resolute leadership and the pride of an ambitious program,"[9] with important implications for the Franco-American relationship and – more broadly – for European integration and the Western alliance. During his eleven years as president of France, de Gaulle was both America's staunchest Cold War ally – in particular in the Cuban missile crisis of October 1962 – and its greatest detractor within the alliance. Besides his achievements in bringing political stability to France and his check on

European integration, his "loyal" opposition to the superpower made him one of the outstanding political figures of the 1960s. When Jean-Baptiste Duroselle, a noted French historian, decided to count how often the political leaders of his day were mentioned during a conference on American-European relations in 1965, de Gaulle finished well ahead of his competitors. In those circles, he observed, de Gaulle had become an "obsession," and exasperation over his nationalist policies had produced a new and bizarre branch of learning: "Gaullology."[10] Duroselle had ample reason to conclude that this score was evidence of damnation mixed in with admiration. Apart from the mesmerizing quality of his leadership, the depth of his political vision, and his undeniable achievements, de Gaulle's size can therefore also be measured by the degree of controversy he evoked. "Être grand, c'est soutenir une grande querelle," he had quoted from Shakespeare's *Hamlet* in *Le fil de l'épée* (1932).[11] In the 1960s, his greatest quarrel would be with the Americans.

* * *

Sifting through the documentary wealth available at the US presidential archives three to four decades later, I was struck by the strong sentiment that de Gaulle and his policies provoked among American officials. Since de Gaulle sought to reduce American military, political, and economic might in Western Europe, it was probably inevitable that he was seen by policymakers in Washington as a difficult – or adversarial – ally. From the documentary record, however, he comes across as much more: an irrational, vainglorious leader possessed by a *folie de grandeur* who endangered the fundamental achievements of postwar American foreign policy. Many officials seemed to wear their distaste for Gaullism as an albatross around their necks. They appeared to denounce Gaullist foreign policy ever more strongly because it ran counter to their own ideas about the transatlantic relationship and of the place of the United States therein. Apart from the man himself, I became intrigued by the American perception of de Gaulle.

France in the 1960s clearly presented the United States with problems unlike those posed by any other European ally. De Gaulle's challenge to American leadership could hardly be more overt, since it was a mainstay of the political views he laid out in his writings, speeches, and press conferences (which he turned into virtual *pièces de théâtre*). Unease about de Gaulle's policy of independence in fact appeared to be an important determinant of American policies towards Europe, confirming Walt Rostow's reminiscence that "a good deal of European and Atlantic policy was [...] taken up with coping with de Gaulle's enterprises in ways which permitted the EEC and NATO to survive."[12] Policymakers in Washington also often seemed consigned to a state of uncertain anticipation about de Gaulle's next move. "Our working situation in Gaullist France is not unlike that in the Soviet Union where we have to look to the small, symbolic actions to identify significant policy trends," one White House staff member observed (even though the Central Intelligence Agency had de Gaulle "taped").[13]

This is not, therefore, a study of French foreign policy during de Gaulle's presidential tenure but of the United States' response to this policy. It looks at one of the most turbulent episodes in this bilateral relationship from the receiving end of de Gaulle's politics of grandeur. It is particularly concerned with understanding this response in the context of American approaches to the transatlantic relationship after World War II. Based on the American documentary record, it attempts to answer three broad questions: How did Americans *interpret* de Gaulle's policy of "independence" within the larger framework of their ideas about the transatlantic relationship? How did consecutive administrations actually *deal* with the challenges posed within this framework by de Gaulle's "independent" foreign policy from 1958 to 1969? Did de Gaulle's policy of "independence" *modify* American policies towards Europe and the Atlantic alliance?

⋆ ⋆ ⋆

One should, of course, have solid reasons for adding to the already massive body of scholarly literature on American postwar diplomacy and on the Franco-American relationship. I am nonetheless convinced there is reason to add a pebble of my own to this ever rising mountain.

To begin with, this book examines in more depth than most studies how consecutive American administrations dealt with the Gaullist challenge on a number of defining issues; it will, as a result, also advance some alternative conclusions. Although the chapters are arranged in chronological order, the aim has not been to provide a chronological account but to highlight the evolution of the disagreement with France over the transatlantic relationship by focusing on key areas. This book thus does not, for instance, contain separate chapters of the United States' dealings with France in the context of the Algerian conflict (or of the broader issue of decolonization), the Berlin crises of the late 1950s and early 1960s, or the war in Vietnam. This is not to argue that these issues were unimportant to the bilateral relationship. Neither are they ignored, as the reader will find out. But they are considered less central to the aims of this book, which concentrates on the American experience with de Gaulle in the context of the *transatlantic* relationship.

In addition, this book responds to the need for a monograph that explains the American reception of de Gaulle's policies and assesses their implications for American foreign policy.[14] Such a monograph has been lacking, despite the wealth of both primary and secondary material. It is important for at least three reasons.

First, whereas de Gaulle's anti-Americanism has been given ample attention (and has often been overstated), the anti-Gaullism among American policymakers largely stands to be examined. De Gaulle was the first postwar European leader to seek less rather than more American involvement in Europe. De Gaulle's willful search for independent French – and, by extension, European – policies vis-à-vis the United States set him apart within the Western alliance. However, while this remains the crux of *l'affaire de Gaulle*, the American attitude towards this self-willed European leader and his pretension to an international role of weight was an equally defining part of the dispute. What made it so difficult for many Americans to disregard de Gaulle's abrasive style, to accept his fundamental allegiance to the Cold War alliance, and to assess his, at times remarkably clairvoyant, propositions about world politics at face value? Why was it not possible to find common ground with the one European leader who appeared ready to assume more responsibility? What made him unpalatable as the harbinger of a resurgent Europe?

Second, a historical examination of the American experience with de Gaulle is not merely important in the context of the history of the bilateral relationship but also in that of US foreign policy. During the Fourth Republic, American policymakers were still overwhelmingly concerned about the deleterious effect on the Western alliance of supposed French weakness; the Fifth Republic's foreign policy redirected their concerns towards a Europe that was regaining its strength and composure. De Gaulle brought the question of how to cope with a resurgent Europe to the fore in a way that could not be ignored in the United States. How Americans responded is indicative of how they approached all of Europe after World War II. This is only compounded by the fact that no debate between Atlantic allies has matched the range and the depth of the Franco-American dispute from 1958 to 1969. The study of the American experience with de Gaulle therefore will tell us more about postwar American views of Europe than a study of American attitudes toward any other European country. The French, John Dos Passos already wrote in *Journeys Between Wars* (1938), "embody a stubborn, unfanatical, live-and-let-live habit of mind, a feeling in every man and woman of the worth of personal dignity that is, for better or for worse, the unique contribution of Western Europe to the world. [...] It's easy to forget how central the French people are in everything we mean when we say Europe."[15]

Third, in so far as the American experience with de Gaulle *has* been reviewed, I find there to be sufficient reason to add my own perspective and findings. Historians who have examined the American documentary record have often chided the United States for its dismissive attitude towards de Gaulle. They have attributed this attitude on the part of American policymakers to an overriding reluctance to share power or, worse, to a combination of hubris and blinding parochialism. Assessments of this type are to be found particularly in the work of the French historian Frédéric Bozo and his American colleague Frank Costigliola.

Bozo's assessment of the American reaction to de Gaulle is determined by his chief contention that the latter's foreign policy was "truly a grand design." He argues that the "existential" crisis within the Atlantic alliance in the mid-1960s above all reflected "ongoing transformations of the power relations that under-pinned the international system" – in other words: Europe was reemerging, the Cold War was abating, and de Gaulle was simply the champion of an adjustment of the Cold War alliance to these new realities. De Gaulle's objective, Bozo finds, "was not so much to weaken NATO as to transform the Western group of nations, if not somehow to *reinforce* transatlantic ties." (emphasis added) Yet American policymakers were stuck in their preconception that de Gaulle was a French nationalist with anachronistic notions of grandeur. Their policies were "reactive" and "devoid of a truly constructive vision to pit against de Gaulle's design." Only eventually did the United States feel compelled to adopt "a more constructive and dynamic approach" – a reference to the Johnson-led revitalization of the alliance in the wake of the French withdrawal from NATO in 1966. Of the two strategies for Europe, however, Bozo finds the one put forward by de Gaulle clearly superior and largely faults the United States with a single-minded focus on dominating the Western alliance.[16]

Costigliola's *France and the United States* (1992) is equally critical of American policies with regard to France. It portrays the Franco-American relationship as one between, on the one hand, a hegemon systematically engaged in unilateral power politics and, on the other hand, a particularly difficult client that resents taking orders and consistently questions the wisdom of the schemes in which it is asked to cooperate. Irked by persistent diatribes among American politicians and officials against "those damn French" and what he regards as their insensitivity to French concerns and interests, Costigliola finds that most of the blame for the querulous nature of the Franco-American relationship lay in Washington.[17]

While Bozo dispels interpretations of de Gaulle as a narrow-minded national-ist, Costigliola exposes the behavior of consecutive administrations toward France as domineering and belittling. Both call attention to a persistent American reluc-tance to share power with its European allies and to a general lack of understand-ing in American policymaking circles of de Gaulle and his vision. Both are largely justified in this regard. The documentary record strongly suggests that the United States was at least partially responsible for allowing the transatlantic dialogue to degenerate into a Franco-American quarrel. It is true that many American policy-makers habitually castigated de Gaulle as a narrow-minded nationalist obsessed with grandeur. They found his opposition to American leadership hard to swal-low. They found his pretension for a distinct role for France hardly justified given its modest national resources. They tended to set de Gaulle apart from his politi-cal environment, narrowing down their differences with him to a confrontation between, on the one hand, the United States and most of its allies and, on the other hand, "one elderly ruler in Europe." This attitude of ridicule and reprehen-sion failed to do justice to the quality of de Gaulle's strategic vision. It also made it inherently more difficult for consecutive American administrations to come to terms with this vision in a more constructive way.

Yet the story of how Americans reacted to de Gaulle cannot be satisfactorily explained by a supposed small-mindedness or a singular attachment to power on the part of American policymakers. Nor is it true that American policymakers all exhibited this attitude, or exhibited it in the same degree. There were also important philosophical differences between the various administrations with regard to de Gaulle. It is therefore time for a genuine effort to put American attitudes towards de Gaulle in perspective. A preoccupation with exposing the manipulative ploys and the almost childlike recriminations on the US side provides us with too little insight into the rather more complex American experience with de Gaulle.

While I have no reason – or desire – to exonerate Americans where criticism is due, this book makes an effort to understand the American disposition toward de Gaulle in the historical and political context in which American policymakers believed they operated. It hopes to find added value by explaining their experience in the context of longstanding American attitudes towards Europe, of the distinct traditions that have historically shaped US foreign policy, and of conceptions of the transatlantic relationship that prevailed in the United States during the early decades of the Cold War. This aspect of the book is necessary in order to gain deeper insight into the variety of responses in the United States to de Gaulle; in addition, it will help us understand some of the less tangible, but no less important, changes in American foreign policy as a result of the de Gaulle experience.

Washington and Paris had important interests that go a long way in explaining why they often clashed, and these will certainly be discussed. But there was much more at play. I have come to agree with the political scientist Philip Cerny, who has written that the Franco-American conflict of the 1960s was "the accumulation of a series of divergences which were not so significant in themselves, but which became crucial when set in the context of the conflict of paradigmatic perspectives."[18]

Perusing the extensive documentary record, I began to realize in particular that US policymakers were imbued with certain notions about Europe – and the American relationship to it – that prejudiced their assessments of de Gaulle. Behind the differences on a range of topics lay a fundamental disagreement about the nature of the transatlantic relationship. To de Gaulle, there certainly was historical solidarity between the United States and France, but there could be no bonds which would tie both sides of the Atlantic permanently together; in the final analysis, the Atlantic alliance was to him a temporary expediency to stave off a specific threat. Many Americans, in contrast, had come to view the transatlantic relationship in ideological and organic terms. The Cold War had transformed their mental map of the Atlantic Ocean, changing it from a geographical and mental barrier into a *mare nostrum*. "With the development of the Atlantic Community," the American political philosopher Louis Halle typically observed in 1957, "it has become instead of a broad wilderness separating two worlds or two hemispheres, a lake which makes close neighbors of all who live on its shores."[19]

Was there one predominant conception of the transatlantic relationship in the United States during the early decades of the Cold War, one that has influenced American policymakers in thought and in action? Amid the huge diversity of views, I was struck in the course of my archival research by persistent and widespread references to the transatlantic relationship as an evolving Atlantic "community." This more encompassing notion of a "community" was furthermore elaborated in an avalanche of policy papers, historical studies, political treatises, and citizen's initiatives. The Atlantic community, or slight variations thereof, was the catchword in the American political discourse from the late 1940s until the late 1960s to describe the transatlantic relationship. It implied that the Atlantic alliance was much more than a security response to a temporary exigency. It had unmistakable ideological and cultural connotations. Organizations with transatlantic membership, such as NATO and the OECD, were seen as the expressions of an underlying reality and the harbingers of growing Atlantic unity. The notion of an Atlantic community indeed had all the characteristics of a foreign policy paradigm. As a result, there seemed to me to be some truth in the observation of two American policymakers in 1965 that "for almost twenty years America's major foreign policy has been sustained on a nightmare and a dream. The nightmare was the Soviet threat in Europe [...]. The dream was an 'Atlantic Community.'"[20]

Diplomatic historians have traditionally shied away from giving much weight to the idea of an Atlantic community in explaining US policies towards Europe during the Cold War. Because of its admitted vagueness, it is indeed tempting to argue that this notion had a mostly rhetorical or even propagandistic function. The Norwegian historian Geir Lundestad, for instance, has flatly stated that "the deepest reason" for the absence of more Atlantic integration "was quite simply that there was virtually no interest in the United States in anything that would reduce American sovereignty."[21]

The concept of the transatlantic relationship as an evolving community of like-minded nations was nonetheless an important and influential characteristic of the perspective of the postwar generation of American policymakers. The Atlantic community idea served as a beacon in their view of the evolving world system, perhaps something akin to a mental map.[22] In this perspective, the institutional development of organizations such as NATO and the OECD not only seemed logical but also just the beginning of something more permanent and more desirable. The idea of an Atlantic community was more than a hyperbolic restatement of Cold War solidarity. The prevalence of the notion indeed reflected the fact that the transatlantic relationship had become the object of high-strung expectations among Americans after World War II. It was also one premise for the activist American support for European integration and unity from the late 1940s to the mid-1960s, for within an Atlantic community any European entity that might be created would likely be agreeable to US interests and ideals. What is more, Atlanticism was to most American policymakers the peacetime alternative to US isolationism and European nationalism. In this light, they regarded de Gaulle as a dangerous obstructionist: his foreign policy appeared to awaken ghosts of the past.

This is far from saying that all Americans in the early decades of the Cold War unequivocally subscribed to the notion of an Atlantic community or meant the same thing by it. On the contrary, its emergence as an idea in US foreign policy is to be explained in part by its ability to wed the conservative and the liberal traditions of American foreign policy and their essentially different approaches to Europe. Postwar American foreign policy can be seen as an uneasy yet reasonably effective synthesis between these two traditions, embodied by a bipartisan foreign policy establishment that determined the broad outlines of this policy. On the one hand, the idea of an Atlantic community could be supported from the conservative perspective as the extension of the Anglo-American strategic partnership to Western Europe; on the other hand, liberals tended to lend support to the Atlantic community as a scaled-down version of Wilsonian one-worldism in the context of the Cold War. The idea of an Atlantic community, in addition, incorporated the fundamental ambivalence felt towards Europe, making it a kind of compromise between the tendency to limit US engagement in Europe and the inclination to reform it. Under the pressure of the Cold War, the notion of an Atlantic community thus helped to bridge important differences within the internationalist segment of the American political community. This, in turn, also helps to explain both the pervasiveness and the ambiguity that has led diplomatic historians to neglect its function.

* * *

Charles de Gaulle never supported the American vision of an Atlantic community. For this, de Gaulle's attachment to his triptych – France, the nation-state, Europe – was simply too deeply entrenched. While he judged strong transatlantic ties necessary given the Soviet menace, he never came to view the United States as an intrinsically "European" power. From his perspective, the idea of an Atlantic community was at odds with his objective of a "European" Europe – the creation of a self-sufficient equilibrium between the states and the peoples that inhabited the European geographical space. And its popularization was an attempt to rationalize or – worse yet – transform ties arising from temporary necessity into permanent institutional bonds that would submerge French power and identity in a larger entity dominated by the United States.

In addition, while de Gaulle was a proponent – perhaps even an exponent – of Franco-American solidarity, he did not think that the French and the Americans belonged to the same "community" as a fellowship of interests, least of all a community affecting the identity of the participants and their degree of adhesion. Nor did de Gaulle believe that transatlantic security was indivisible, as was often asserted in the context of the Atlantic alliance. His doubts about the value of the American security guarantee were buttressed by his reading of the United States' late war entries in 1917 and 1941, only after having been attacked first, and by the flexible wording of Article V of the North Atlantic Treaty at the Senate's insistence. These doubts were further enhanced by the Soviet acquisition of nuclear weapons shortly after the signing of the Treaty. For a few months after the first Soviet atomic explosion in July 1949, de Gaulle remarked that "le Pacte [Atlantique], dans son contenu et sous sa forme actuels, perdrait, pour l'Europe, une grande partie de son efficacité. En tout cas, la nation doit être prévenue que rien n'oblige, ni ne prépare, les Etats-Unis à participer largement à la défense directe et immédiate de notre continent."[23]

As importantly, de Gaulle objected almost from the outset to the extensive military organization that was being built on top of the Treaty after General Eisenhower's arrival as NATO's first Supreme Allied Commander Europe (SACEUR) in January 1951. De Gaulle objected to a security system in which, as he wrote in his memoirs, "an American generalissimo with headquarters near Versailles exercised over the old world the military authority of the new."[24] He had rather hoped that the United States would be prepared to help restore France's political and military power on the European continent in the spirit of the Truman Doctrine and under the banner of the North Atlantic Treaty. However, instead of assisting France to become the military stronghold in Western Europe against the Soviet menace, the United States sought to maintain control of the European allies through NATO's integrated military command system and gave priority to paving the way for German rearmament. Washington moreover refrained from fully supporting French policies in Indochina and Africa.

As a result, de Gaulle turned into an early critic of NATO. He publicly called for a "reorganization" of the Atlantic alliance for the first time on March 10, 1952. These comments actually prefigured his September 1958 memorandum proposal for a global security organization (see chapter one), as he posited that the alliance should be given global coverage in order to respond to the increasingly global communist threat. He also sought to prevent the institution of an American-German axis "under the cover of the Atlantic Pact and the European army," presaging the Franco-German Treaty of Reconciliation of January 1963 ("un accord direct entre la France et l'Allemagne à la fois sur les sujets qui les ont toujours divisées").[25]

Most importantly, as de Gaulle stressed in December 1954, "le système appelé l'OTAN" amounted to the abandonment of the sovereignty and the spirit of the nation:

> Elle [France] place ses armées, ses bases, ses communications, directement sous une autorité qui n'est pas la sienne. Elle est dans une situation de dépendance qui met, en fait, sous contrôle étranger toute action militaire et, par

extension, toute action politique qu'elle entreprend dans des territoires qui lui sont, pourtant, rattachés [...] Elle laisse à d'autres le monopole des armes atomiques sans lesquelles un État ne peut être que subordonné. [...] Si ces conditions n'étaient pas, de fond en comble, révisées, comment intéresser la nation à sa propre sécurité et, par suite, à son propre destin?[26]

It is for this reason that, in July 1957, de Gaulle confided to Cyrus Sulzberger of the *New York Times* that he wanted NATO "seriously modified":

As it is, the alliance is completely unsatisfactory. America has taken everything. America has taken all the commands. America has all the responsibility. And America provides all the force. This is not sensible for an alliance. Look at Russia, Russia's satellites have proven valueless. I would insist upon a repartition of the responsibility and the authority of the alliance. The alliance must be something spiritual as well as physical. And it cannot be spiritually viable unless there is some sort of shake up.[27]

In February 1958, in addition, only months before his return to power, he gave a preview of things to come:

I would quit NATO if I were running France. NATO is against our independence and our interest. Our membership in NATO is said to be for the reason of protecting France against a Russian attack. But I don't believe that the Russians will attack at this time .... NATO is no longer an alliance. It is a subordination. ... After France has regained her independence, perhaps she will be linked with the Western countries in formal alliances .... But we cannot accept a superior, like the United States, to be responsible for us.[28]

For almost eleven years following his return to the helm in May 1958, de Gaulle's vision would be France's vision. During these years, his dedication to France and the primacy accorded to the nation-state would continue to be the salient features of his policy. But de Gaulle was much more than a French nationalist whose sole preoccupation was the protection of the French national interest or the amplification of his nation's glory. He was a strategic thinker of unusual acumen, one who actively sought to use French influence to resolve the outstanding political issues of the day. "Perhaps the most striking and authentic feature of this Gaullist grand design was the considerable feat of uniting an attractive and often logical view of the emerging international order with a pivotal role for France," Michael Harrison has reasonably judged. "The coincidence of French national interest with a transformed global system and a revised East-West settlement in Europe brought French diplomacy unprecedented attention in the 1960s and gave it a universal appeal unmatched in the postwar era."[29]

De Gaulle defined a response to the European "question" that had been posed by a history of continental conflict. This response was inevitably different from the American one, as it was informed above all by French history and by de Gaulle's singular determination to reinstate France as a great power. De Gaulle's European "question" was also different from the one that had vexed US foreign policy. What Americans tended to define broadly as the "European" question posed by chronic and internecine war, was to de Gaulle – as to most Frenchmen – above all the "German" question, which, as World War II drew to a close, increasingly became overshadowed – albeit not entirely substituted – by the emergence of the two superpowers. De Gaulle's European "question" might therefore be formulated as follows: how to safeguard French security and influence in a Europe susceptible to German domination *and* to maintain a measure of independence and freedom of action in relation to the Soviet Union as well as the United States?

In addition, resolving this question was in de Gaulle's analysis a European matter. The nation-states of Europe would have to find a *modus vivendi* among themselves if continental peace was to endure. When de Gaulle talked of European unity, he either referred to this continental *modus vivendi* defined by the equilibrium between these nation-states or, in a narrower sense, to the ensemble of Western European nations headed by France. In his view, the resurgence of "Europe" hinged on strengthening the position of France as the leader of the Western European grouping of states vis-à-vis the Soviet Union *and* the United States; in this grouping, moreover, France – not Germany – would have to be the dominant nation-state (at least in military and political matters). France distinguished itself from the other great powers, de Gaulle stressed, because it had "no ambition of extending ourselves beyond the soil where we are sovereign; because our present frontiers are sufficient for us as they are [unlike the Germans]; because we presume neither to convert nor to dominate anyone, either ideologically, politically, or economically [unlike the Americans or the Russians]."[30]

In de Gaulle's European equilibrium, the Anglo-Saxons would play a largely subsidiary role. There was, in de Gaulle's view, no question that France had to side with the democratic powers of the West as long as the threat of Soviet domination existed. In this regard, France under de Gaulle would be as steadfast an ally as the United States could have hoped for. But de Gaulle had no interest in being swallowed up in an evolving Atlantic community dominated by the Americans. In his vision of the European equilibrium "from the Atlantic to the Urals," the United States would be requested to take a back seat. De Gaulle's policy of independence and grandeur would do much to restore French self-awareness in a world in which France could no longer count on being in the first rank by force of numbers. This policy, however, inevitably set France on a course of conflict with its much more powerful American ally. "My only international rival is [cartoon hero] Tintin!" de Gaulle quipped to André Malraux towards the end of his life. "We are the little fellows who refuse to get taken by the big ones. No one sees this, because of my height."[31]

Chapter One

Organizing the West: Eisenhower, Kennedy, and de Gaulle's "Tripartite" Memorandum Proposal, 1958-1962

De Gaulle never lost sight of his aim to restore France's position of eminence in world politics, not even as it teetered on the brink of civil war over Algeria. On September 17, 1958, he threw down an unusual gauntlet, merely three months after having resumed the reins of power and eleven days before a new constitution was approved by the French people. He wrote a secret memorandum to President Dwight Eisenhower and British Prime Minister Harold Macmillan proposing a shake-up of the Western alliance. De Gaulle advocated a new "security organization" in which the United States, Great Britain, and France would make "joint decisions on political questions affecting world security" and draw up "strategic plans of action, notably with regard to the employment of nuclear weapons." De Gaulle was thus in effect demanding a say in America's global policies and a veto over the use of American nuclear weapons. He furthermore suggested that the world be carved up among the three nations in "theaters of operations," which were to be "subordinated" to the new organization. The memorandum furthermore issued a veiled threat to NATO, since de Gaulle wrote that France "subordinates to it [the new security organization] as of now all developments of its present participation in NATO [...]."[1] In essence, as de Gaulle observed in his memoirs, he proposed that "the alliance should henceforth be placed under a triple rather than dual direction, failing which France would take no further part in NATO developments and would reserve the right [...] either to demand its reform or to leave it."[2]

De Gaulle's "tripartite" memorandum is well known.[3] What is less known is the extent to which it preoccupied diplomatic relations between Washington, London, and Paris. For much of the 1960s, French diplomats encouraged the notion that the United States had never replied to de Gaulle's memorandum (until the United States Senate set the record straight following France's withdrawal from NATO).[4] Eisenhower's written reply of October 20, 1958, was in fact only the beginning of an elaborate correspondence and a prolonged series of diplomatic contacts. While the gist of the initial reply was unmistakably negative, Eisenhower recognized that de Gaulle had raised fundamental questions about the Western alliance that could not be ignored. He was furthermore concerned with the repercussions of a complete rejection for French participation in NATO. In the end, Eisenhower failed to come to terms with de Gaulle on the organization of the Western alliance. But it was a conclusion arrived at after much private questioning.

What is less known too is that de Gaulle's insistence on a tripartite organization did not end with Eisenhower's departure from the White House, for he made a purposeful effort to warm the incoming Kennedy administration to his tripartite design for the Western alliance. De Gaulle only seems to have truly abandoned this effort in the course of 1962, with the resolution of the Algerian conflict in May, Kennedy's unilateral handling of the Cuban missile crisis in October, and the Anglo-American summit meeting at Nassau (on the Bahamas) in December. De Gaulle's "memorandum diplomacy" thus coincided with what is often considered to be the first phase of his foreign policy, during which France still pursued its security policies within the framework of the Atlantic alliance and, as Edward Kolodziej put it, strove for "big power status through cooperation and cooptation."[5]

Eisenhower's ultimate inability to come to terms with de Gaulle set a precedent for later administrations. It set the stage for a political row that would come to shake the Western alliance to its very foundations. De Gaulle's decision in 1966 to withdraw France from NATO, which had been foreshadowed in the September 1958 memorandum, revived the question whether the United States could not have given his "tripartite" proposal more serious consideration. What were the principal reasons for Eisenhower's and Kennedy's disinclination to go along with de Gaulle's proposal? What concessions were they prepared to make in order to preserve French cooperation within NATO? Could a *quid pro quo* have produced a bilateral understanding on the organization of the Western alliance? Or were de Gaulle's demands simply too high?

Eisenhower, De Gaulle, and the End of the Fourth Republic

The Fourth Republic's Colonial Woes

"For at least two years before he became his country's president," Eisenhower wrote in his memoirs, "I had often remarked [...] that only General de Gaulle's accession to power could save France."[6] Eisenhower had not always looked so favorably upon de Gaulle's return to politics, as we will see, but in 1958 it was greeted in Washington with a degree of relief and even of "relative alacrity."[7] This is to be largely explained from the deep concern in Washington with the disarray and irascibility of the politics of the Fourth Republic. By 1958, of course, France was deeply enmeshed in the war in Algeria. The battle with the *Front de*

Libération Nationale (FLN), the Algerian rebel movement, had been exacting an increasingly heavy toll since it had begun in the mid-1950s; by 1957, the Algerian rebels were expanding the scope of their insurgency to France itself. Ominously, the war was also eroding civilian authority over an army thirsting for victory after its defeat in French Indochina in 1954 and the humiliating withdrawal from the Suez Canal under American pressure in December 1956.[8] While de Gaulle kept a purposely ambiguous and largely taciturn pose, a cabal of faithful Gaullists was working feverishly to nudge the Fourth Republic to its end. As Henri Guillemin noted, "the Gaullist strategy consisted of allowing the political class to see the threat of violence and therefore to side with him, and to let the soldiers believe he was their man."[9] By May 1958, de Gaulle thus seemed to many the only alternative to civil war and the only one capable of bringing the French army back into the fold.

It is important to note that the Fourth Republic's demise was attended by particular acrimony and exasperation in the Franco-American relationship. To some extent, the demise was even precipitated by developments in this relationship, for the government of Félix Gaillard had been brought down in April 1958 in part by his concurrence with an Anglo-American mediating mission that was seen by many Frenchmen as yet another Anglo-Saxon attempt to interfere in national affairs.[10] More generally, few issues had indeed been a more constant source of terse disagreement between the United States and the Fourth Republic than how to deal with the world beyond Europe. Washington feared in particular that France's repressive colonial policies in Africa and Asia played into the hands of communism. "We have to be spokesman for those wanting independence or we will be licked," John Foster Dulles once remarked.[11] In Indochina, the Eisenhower administration had initially backed the French struggle against the Viet Minh while pressuring Paris to give Vietnam autonomy. Following the French military defeat at Dien Bien Phu and the Geneva Agreements of 1954, however, it had elbowed the French out of the way in order to back the anti-French and anti-Communist Diem. "France is creating a vacuum in the world wherever she is," John Foster Dulles remarked; the United States "had to fill that vacuum ... [or] we could lose Europe, Asia and Africa all at once."[12]

The nefarious impact of colonial issues on relationships within the Western alliance surfaced even more clearly in the Suez Crisis. The debacle of the Franco-British military intervention in October-November 1956 to recapture the Suez Canal after its nationalization by Egypt's Gamal Abdel Nasser contained particularly harsh lessons for Paris. Eisenhower's public condemnation and the United States' stance in the United Nations Security Council left the French with a defining sense of betrayal. The Suez Crisis persuaded many in France that it needed to become more independent from the United States and Great Britain.[13] Most Frenchmen put the blame for their *déconfiture* on the Americans rather than the British (who had quickly buckled under American pressure), the Soviets, or the

Egyptians. Following the crisis, one American diplomat serving in France recalled, "everywhere we went we were immediately attacked [...] about this treacherous and stupid policy of ours."[14] The lack of American support in France's colonial troubles generally engendered ill will towards the idea of building an Atlantic community; or as Alfred Grosser has observed, it created "misunderstandings and disputes of such importance that the term 'Atlantic Community' was pronounced by Frenchmen with rather bitter irony."[15]

As early as 1955, the Eisenhower administration had privately concluded that France could not win the war in Algeria.[16] It was moreover thoroughly displeased with the ever-growing diversion of French troops from NATO to North Africa. By the end of 1957, France's Algerian predicament was beginning to undercut the Cold War alliance in political ways as well. On November 14, 1957, after American and British arms deliveries to the newly independent Tunisia had become public, Eisenhower recorded in his diary that the Gaillard government threatened "the most dire things such as a complete breakup of the Western Alliance."[17] One day earlier, he had expressed his apprehension about the deterioration in the Franco-American relationship to John Foster Dulles in equally dire terms: "it gets thicker and thicker – if the French suddenly drop out of NATO we are out of Europe."[18] "If the French exhaustion occurs," Dulles observed upon the fall of the Gaillard government in April 1958, "there may be a government in France which depends upon Communist support and it may be disposed not only to allow North Africa to come under Communist domination but to be negative toward NATO and the organizations of Western European unity ...."[19]

Eisenhower and The Fourth Republic as Europe's "Weak Sister"

The Fourth Republic's wear and tear in the relationship with Washington was not confined to colonial issues but was also evident in the realm of intra-European politics. Historians are wont to point out how the Fourth Republic, despite its weak international position and dependence on American aid, was able to defend its autonomy in the postwar years and how American attempts to forge it into a more cooperative ally were botched by a steady French reluctance to conform.[20] France's remarkable economic recovery in the decade following the war deserves mention, too, causing something of a "reversal of fortune" with Great Britain.[21] Yet, notwithstanding these assessments of its strength and resilience, the Fourth Republic was more typically perceived by American policymakers as a fickle ally within the Cold War alliance – or, as Ambassador Douglas Dillon put it, its "weak sister."[22]

France's perceived weakness was the more disconcerting because French leadership in Europe was considered to be imperative, in particular with regard to European integration and Franco-German reconciliation. "The best chance and hope seems to us to be under French leadership," Dean Acheson told Robert Schuman in September 1949. "It doesn't work for us to take the lead. We are too far away."[23] France did take the lead in establishing the European Coal and Steel Community in 1951 following the Schuman proposals of 1950. But the frenzied politics of the Fourth Republic continued to be a cause for concern in Washington, drawing the United States ever further into European politics. "Is the Western alliance doomed because of a rotten core?" mused Acheson in 1953, shortly after his departure from the State Department.[24] His anxious foreboding only seemed to be confirmed when, in August 1954, the French National Assembly rejected the proposal for a European Defense Community – and German rearmament with it – despite heavy pressure from the Eisenhower administration. After the votes were counted, the Communists in the Assembly jumped up to sing the *Marseillaisse*, promptly joined by the Gaullists in a rare demonstration of unison.

Eisenhower's personal assessment of the Fourth Republic was similar to that of most American policymakers. As SACEUR, he had been particularly annoyed with France's fears about German rearmament and its refusal to bring French troops from overseas to Europe. He had come to the conclusion, as he wrote to President Truman in February 1952, that:

> at the very bottom of all their [the French] 'backing and filling,' their seemingly contradictory statements and actions, is an instinctive, inbred fear of Germany and the Germans. With a growing realization of the severity of their economic crisis, occasioned partly, although not wholly, by the Indo-China war, they have to accept a slower rate of military preparation than originally planned. This, in turn, makes them fear that in any collective venture in Europe, be it political, economic, military, or all three, Germany would completely dominate.[25]

The practical difficulties which "a badly divided Western Europe" posed for organizing an effective defense against the Soviet Union persuaded Eisenhower, first as SACEUR and later as president, to support the idea of a European army put forward by the French Prime Minister Pleven in the summer of 1951. Initially Eisenhower had thought of the idea as including "every kind of obstacle, difficulty, and fantastic notion that misguided humans could put together in one package." He feared the plan would create "more antagonism than friendship" and that its failure would finish all attempts to re-establish German military strength, which was indispensable to reaching the goal of forty divisions considered necessary for the defense of Western Europe against a Soviet attack. But he shifted to a more favorable position in response to the practical problems he encountered as SACEUR in organizing European defense. Faced with the problem of manning the Norwegian army, he wrote to Secretary of Defense George Marshall in the summer of 1951:

It is easy to see that if Norway were merely a part of a West European political unit, the [manning] problem did not exist. In Italy there are almost 3,000,000 unemployed. Such examples are multiplied every day. Because of the great efficiency, economy, and general progress that could result from a more effective union of these separate countries, I recently decided to intervene in the plan for developing a 'European army.'

Such an "amalgamation of European resources and strength," Eisenhower believed, would provide the framework for German rearmament "on a basis acceptable to other European countries" and at the same time strengthen support in the United States for NATO.[26]

While in Europe to set up NATO, Eisenhower thus became an increasingly adamant and impatient supporter of European unification. A United States of Europe, he wrote in his diary in November 1951, would "instantly ... solve the real and bitter problems of today... So many advantages would flow from such a union that it is a tragedy for the whole human race that it is not done at once."[27] But Eisenhower also believed that political unity was not a prerequisite for the establishment of a European army. He rather believed that the reverse was true: that political unification would ultimately follow from a European army. "I am certain that there is going to be no real progress towards a greater unification of Europe except through the medium of specific programs of this kind," he had assured Marshall. [28] Yet the European Defense Community (EDC), for which Eisenhower "swore, prayed, almost wept,"[29] did not come about precisely because of the national political realities he was so impatient with. A few months after the EDC's defeat, Eisenhower informed Churchill that he wholeheartedly agreed with his allusion to France's "tyrannical weakness." He further explained his discomfort to his speechwriter Emmet Hughes: "I simply cannot understand why the peoples of Western Europe, and particularly of France, do not see that, unless they unite militarily and economically, they are doomed."[30]

In American eyes, France was thus a weak and unreliable ally, a vital but vulnerable link in the alliance, unable to govern itself or to come to terms with issues facing it in the wider world. Even as consecutive administrations looked to France to lead the continental allies toward greater cooperation and integration, the experiences with the Fourth Republic meant that its endeavors to gain recognition as a major power never met the full approval of the United States. This was no different for Eisenhower. For even before the fall of Dien Bien Phu on May 7, 1954, he wrote his friend Alfred Gruenther, his successor as SACEUR:

Her [France's] politics in Europe have been nothing but confusion; starts and stops; advances and retreats! She wants still to be considered a world power, but is entirely unready to make the sacrifices necessary to sustain such a position. ... she is bound to be shown up, as in Indo-China, as incapable of doing anything important by herself.[31]

The contrast with the American attitude toward Great Britain was evident. The Suez Crisis had severed the "special relationship," but only temporarily. When Prime Minister Harold Macmillan visited Washington in October 1957, he found Eisenhower and Dulles prepared to seek an amendment to the Atomic Energy Act of 1946 – also known as the McMahon Act – in order to aid the British nuclear deterrent (even as the United States discouraged France's nuclear effort).[32] Great Britain was furthermore granted a confidential agreement on achieving policy co-ordination between Washington and London. Eisenhower outlined this agreement as follows:

> Mr. Macmillan and I nominated our respective Secretaries of State for Foreign Affairs to consult together and to agree on particular areas of policy or on specific problems of a character that cannot be easily dealt with through normal channels. In such cases they were directed to establish working groups of American and British officials with the composition varied according to subject and including representation from all interested Departments and Agencies of the two Governments. The main objective of these working groups will be to facilitate the processing of problems where the main responsibilities are Anglo-American in character or where prior concert of Anglo-American policy would contribute to the more effective functioning of the multilateral organizations to which they both belong. Similarly, there will be occasions when it would be desirable, after Anglo-American discussions, to make an approach to particular friendly governments with a view of concerting action with them also.[33] [emphasis added]

In addition to being an ardent supporter of European unity, Eisenhower clearly saw NATO and the Atlantic community in part as an extension of the Anglo-American partnership. One year after the Suez debacle, the atmosphere between Washington and London had become so friendly again that *The Times* reported that "in terms of the Anglo-American alliance, participants in the talks have known nothing like them since the war-time conferences of Cairo and Casablanca."[34]

"Ike" and De Gaulle

From mid-1957 onwards, American diplomats gradually became more interested in a return of de Gaulle. The American embassy in Paris, distressed with the political instability in France, believed his return was becoming increasingly probable and even necessary. Embassy officials therefore made sure to keep in touch with the Gaullist camp.[35] This is far from saying that de Gaulle's return was doctored in Washington or that it was unambiguously desired. Yet, as the years passed and the Fourth Republic's problems grew larger, de Gaulle was increasingly given the benefit of the doubt: the prospect of a headstrong but more stable ally at least seemed more alluring than that of a chronically unstable Fourth Republic increasingly given to bouts of anti-Americanism. Eisenhower, too, took this view.[36]

As allied supreme commander during World War II, Eisenhower had had his share of confrontations with de Gaulle. His sharpest clash with the Frenchman occurred in December 1944, when Eisenhower ordered French troops to withdraw from Strasbourg three weeks after it had been liberated and just one day after de Gaulle had paid his first visit there. Eisenhower had sound military reasons for his decision: he was concerned about consolidating the long allied front after the Germans launched their Ardennes offensive. But de Gaulle, believing that a French retreat from Strasbourg would be nothing less than "a national disaster," furiously disagreed and threatened to remove the French troops from Eisenhower's command. This in turn caused Eisenhower to state that ammunition, food, and other supplies for de Gaulle's forces would then be withheld. It ultimately took Winston Churchill's personal intervention to resolve the conflict. At the British prime minister's urging, Eisenhower backed down and Strasbourg was held. But the experience caused him to complain to General George Marshall that "next to the weather [the French] have caused me more trouble in this war than any other single factor."[37]

Yet Eisenhower never exhibited the degree of antagonism toward de Gaulle found in President Roosevelt and other Americans. He managed to preserve a practical working relationship with him during the war, taking the Frenchman's intransigence with equanimity and even a measure of understanding. When visiting Paris in September 1944, for instance, Eisenhower deliberately stopped by de Gaulle's headquarters first "as a de facto recognition of him as the provisional president of France"; de Gaulle, he recalled, never forgot the gesture.[38] Eisenhower also said that "it was my influence, more than anybody else's, that got the French the sector in Germany [...]."[39] Eisenhower's stance toward de Gaulle was, to be sure, induced by the "military realities" of the war. These advised him that de Gaulle controlled the French resistance, that an allied occupation of France would be a waste of manpower, and that French troops could be used in the continuing battle with Nazi Germany.[40] But in addition to proving himself to be, as Raoul Aglion put it, "a better diplomat than many officials and statesmen" in his relationship with de Gaulle, Eisenhower also developed respect for de Gaulle's force of personality.[41] De Gaulle in turn extended his sympathy to the "generous-hearted" American commander.[42]

While the war experience thus probably encouraged Eisenhower to consider de Gaulle's return to power as a solution to France's political instability by the mid-1950s (as earlier mentioned), it would be wrong to conclude that his opinion of de Gaulle was unambiguously positive. On the contrary, the archival record shows that he had not always welcomed the idea of de Gaulle's return to power. As SACEUR in the early 1950s, Eisenhower repeatedly made clear that he did not consider de Gaulle's reinstatement as the solution to France's woes. He did not like de Gaulle's criticism of NATO and his opposition to the European Defense Community. In March 1952, Eisenhower wrote President Truman that "if General de Gaulle came to power, the government headed by him would presumably be reasonably stable [...]" but also that "he has so blatantly attacked NATO and American policy and position that [...] I don't know what would be the results of such a development."[43] Although he increasingly believed the French were in need of "a sort of evangelical uprising, following a Billy Sunday or a Pied Piper,"[44] he emphatically did not seek to cast de Gaulle in this role. A few months before the EDC's defeat, Eisenhower explained himself to General Gruenther:

> I believe the difficulty is largely a matter of spirit; unfortunately there is no one in sight who seems to have the capability of reversing the trend toward pessimism, defeatism and dejection. ... The only hope is to produce a new and inspirational leader – and I do not mean one that is 6 feet 5 and considers himself to be, by some miraculous biological and transmigrative process, the offspring of Clemenceau and Jeanne d'Arc.[45]

By the mid-1950s, however, de Gaulle's return had nonetheless become an increasingly attractive prospect from the perspective of the Eisenhower administration. Although de Gaulle reentered the political arena with the reputation of a supporter of an Algérie française, he had told the American embassy in May 1956 that assimilation of Algeria with France was in his view no longer possible and that a loose federation would be the best possible solution (failing which Algerian independence would be inevitable).[46] Washington's growing vexation with the partisan politics of the Fourth Republic, in addition, was making de Gaulle's criticism of the Fourth Republic easier to associate with. At age sixty-seven, de Gaulle moreover seemed to have become more moderate in his views. His physique had changed with time, "conveying wisdom rather than intransigence." His voice had softened. In personal encounters, he was more genial and relaxed.[47] As the Paris embassy wrote in June 1958, "there is some evidence that with passing years he has mellowed and may take in his stride things which in the past might have created troubles between us."[48]

If the Eisenhower administration greeted de Gaulle's return to power in May 1958 with a benevolent sense of relief, however, it was not without an element of concern. At the State Department, in particular, it was feared that de Gaulle would chart an independent course in the East-West conflict. "Anybody who considers that he alone can save his country may someday decide that he is the only one who can save the world," one senior State Department official estimated. "His old concept of France serving as the 'bridge' between East and West may not be entirely extinct."[49] It was also believed that de Gaulle's longstanding distrust of the Anglo-American relationship would lead to a greater insistence on a more significant and formalized role for France within the Western alliance. Although he was not expected to "willingly break up NATO," demands for nuclear cooperation and a resumption of "Big Three" meetings were clearly seen to be in the offing.[50]

The anxiety at the State Department about de Gaulle's intentions was in part also due to his relative silence during the years of seclusion in his country home in eastern France, at Colombey-les-Deux-Eglises, where he wrote his *War Memoirs* (whose three volumes were subsequently published in 1954, 1956, and 1959). It was fostered, too, by the presence of self-appointed and not always reliable spokesmen for the General. How confusing French assessments of de Gaulle's intentions could be was evidenced on May 21, 1958, when two conflicting reports reached the State Department. In one report, the French Ambassador Hervé Alphand told Dulles that de Gaulle was not anti-American but anti-European and that he would leave NATO intact but would try to reverse the process of European integration. In another, more accurate preview, a member from de Gaulle's entourage told the American embassy in Paris that de Gaulle strongly favored the movement towards European unity (even though the "modalities for achieving this would be different") but that France would have some suggestions to make in the Atlantic alliance and would expect to be heard.[51] Predicting de Gaulle was thus hazardous business. As Deputy Undersecretary of State Robert Murphy, not an admirer of de Gaulle, wrote in the margins of one estimate of de Gaulle's intentions: "I feel that at present there are so many points in de Gaulle's thinking and purposes about which we can only speculate with in some cases little of a solid nature to base an opinion."[52]

But at the highest levels of the American government, de Gaulle's return to power was received with positive excitement. "Everything turned out extremely well," a keyed-up Dulles told Alphand, repeating himself several times.[53] It was felt that Eisenhower's wartime bonds with de Gaulle could be cultivated to keep the General on board. There is little doubt that Eisenhower himself believed he could develop a meaningful relationship with his colleague. There was no one, he said after reading a *Life* editorial by C.D. Jackson on de Gaulle in the late spring of 1958, that he had had "more satisfying and revealing conversations" with and that "in view of some of the constructive steps he took in North Africa as early as 1943, there may be a great deal of hope that he can stabilize relations between France and Algeria ...."[54] As Eisenhower knew all too well from personal experience, de Gaulle could be a difficult ally. But as long as he continued to "tread the path of statesmanship and conciliation," Eisenhower wrote to Paul Hoffmann in June 1958, de Gaulle deserved the full support of the United States.[55]

Omens of Dissension: The Summer of 1958

Notwithstanding the uncertainty in official Washington, de Gaulle proved remarkably expeditious in laying down the fundamentals of his policies regarding the Western alliance. Indeed, within the span of four months, the contours of his design acquired definition – a feat that is all the more remarkable given the challenges posed by the Algerian conundrum and the constitutional reform of the French state. These fundamentals did not – or at least did not yet – include an independent policy of rapprochement towards the Soviet Union or a break with the European integration movement, as had been feared. On the contrary, de Gaulle proved firm in his approaches toward Khrushchev (especially when the latter precipitated the Berlin crisis in November 1958). And in December 1958, the French government ordered the accelerated implementation of the provisions of the Treaty of Rome, despite de Gaulle's reservations about its supranational aspects and the lowering of industrial tariffs. "In this poor world," de Gaulle explained in his *Memoirs of Hope*, "which deserves to be handled gently, we had to advance step by step, acting as circumstances demanded and respecting the susceptibilities of war."[56]

De Gaulle's policy toward the Western alliance in the initial years of his presidency consisted of three interconnected building blocks. First, de Gaulle accelerated the development of an independent French nuclear force, allocating more money and effort to the program. On July 22, 1958, de Gaulle signed a resolution setting a target date for the first experimental atomic explosion in the first quarter of 1960. As importantly, he gave the French nuclear effort a clear political payload by making it a mainstay of his policy of independence vis-à-vis the superpowers.[57] Meeting with his cabinet on June 17, 1958, the first cabinet meeting devoted to defense matters, de Gaulle decided that atomic weapons would only be allowed on French soil on the condition that these weapons were under French control and that France was involved in their strategic planning. Upon arriving in office, he furthermore put an end to discussions on nuclear cooperation with Germany and Italy, which had been commenced in the latter days of the Fourth Republic.[58]

Second, de Gaulle made a bid to orchestrate his European concert of nations. On June 29, 1958, he declined Prime Minister Macmillan's urgent pleas to end the stalemate in the negotiations to associate the Common Market with a larger European free trade zone. This reflected his determination that Great Britain should not be allowed to become a power in continental Europe where it would compete with France. De Gaulle's first meeting with Chancellor Konrad Adenauer on September 14 and 15, 1958, conducted at his private residence in Colombey-les-Deux-Eglises, stood in striking contrast with the Franco-British encounter. The French leader succeeded in finding common ground with the chancellor, captivating him personally, and was able to establish a close relationship from which he aimed to "weave a network of preferential ties with Germany."[59] Keeping the British at bay and tying the Germans closer to France, the fundamentals seemed thus in place for a "European" Europe, centered around France and ready to assert its voice in the councils of decision.

And third, de Gaulle began to put forward the idea of a tripartite organization of the Western alliance. When Macmillan paid a visit to Paris in June 1958, de Gaulle told him that he gave much significance to the issue of global policy planning between the three major allies and would like to get the Standing Group involved. His conversation with Dulles on July 5, which we will review in more detail later in this chapter, served a similar purpose.[60] During these early meetings, the September 1958 memorandum was in fact in gestation.[61]

If the contours of the Gaullist design emerged soon, the gist of the American response was also established early. On June 9, 1958, Eisenhower and Dulles met with Macmillan to discuss their attitudes towards the new government in Paris. Stressing that de Gaulle could not be treated as if he were "like God" and should not be allowed to endanger "our highly successful relationships," Eisenhower summarized their agreed stance: "We would undertake a tripartite relationship with de Gaulle in those areas where there exists an historical basis for it, such as in the Summit preparations and the re-unification of Germany. Otherwise, we will deal with the French through bilateral arrangements and, when appropriate, through NATO."[62] In other words, there was no willingness on the part of the Eisenhower administration to accord France an elevated status within the Western alliance just because de Gaulle had resumed the reins of power.

A few days earlier, on June 4, Eisenhower had instructed Secretary of State Dulles to visit Paris in order to establish relations with de Gaulle and probe his views.[63] Shortly before his departure, on July 3, Dulles conferred with Eisenhower on his upcoming rendezvous. They agreed that de Gaulle, being "all that stands between France and chaos, or a popular front at least," was entitled to general support from the United States. But on two important issues, American support could not be extended. In the nuclear realm, French Ambassador Alphand had suggested to Dulles that "it would be very helpful if the Secretary could say [to de Gaulle] that cooperation with France in this field would be possible once France demonstrated that she had a stable government."[64] Eisenhower told Dulles to convey to de Gaulle a "readiness ... to see what could be done by [a] liberal interpretation of existing authority." Yet it was clear that the Congressional Joint Committee on Atomic Energy (JCAE) would not permit any substantial cooperation with France by amending the Atomic Energy Act of 1946 within the foreseeable future. The president moreover revealed no sympathy with respect to the second question, for he discarded as "completely unrealistic" an idea that de Gaulle had raised with the SACEUR, General Lauris Norstad,[65] namely that of drawing up "world nuclear plans" in a tripartite organization.[66] In essence, Dulles's task was to assure that the new leader in Paris supported American strategies; or, as a high

State Department official wrote in a preparatory note, the meeting would provide "a unique opportunity to convince the man who will govern France for the next two years [sic] as to the validity of our policies."[67]

Dulles left Washington later that day. The conditions for his encounter with de Gaulle were adverse, in particular because of the concurrence with the signing of the British-American agreement on nuclear cooperation (which followed the amendment of the Atomic Energy Act).[68] The French newspaper *Combat* voiced the opinion of many Frenchmen that the amendment embodied "the creation of an Anglo-U.S. atomic directorate" and "can only make more apparent and more burdensome the hegemony of the English-speaking peoples at the heart of the Atlantic Alliance."[69] Anglo-American preponderance and French dependence thus hung heavy in the air when Dulles arrived in the French capital. "I remembered," wrote André Malraux, "seeing John Foster Dulles [...] drive through the gates of the Hôtel Matignon in an enormous car, like a Roman proconsul entering some city of the east."[70]

It is worthwhile to consider Dulles's conversation with de Gaulle in some detail, for on few occasions were conflicting world views so amicably exchanged as during the first conversation between the grim American apostle of freedom and the incarnation of French grandeur. Both given to long-winded explanations of the global forces at play, Dulles began with an expansive monologue on the universal aspirations of the Soviet Union and the increasingly global nature of the Communist threat. The Soviets had proven adept, he said, in exploiting the divisions in the world at large, drawing Nasser into their orbit, supporting Algerian rebels, inciting unrest in Latin America, Indonesia, and Southeast Asia. From the Kremlin, Dulles argued, ferment was orchestrated around the world. Soviet aggression was real but elusive, putting Western attempts to counter it at a disadvantage. Having set ambitious industrial development policies, Soviet leaders moreover could command a growing array of human and material resources. In contrast, the West seemed to have lost its "spiritual fervor." Dulles: "It was the dynamic opposed to the quiescent."

Dulles then addressed issues that the launching of the Sputnik, just nine months earlier, had brought to the fore. Emphasizing that the alleged "missile gap" was rapidly being closed, he tried to assure de Gaulle that the United States would not hesitate to use its strategic force in defense of the West. To make this commitment apparent to friend and foe, the United States was prepared to consider a NATO force equipped with tactical nuclear weapons that could be used "without having to depend on a US political decision." While Dulles was careful not to take issue with France's nuclear program, this plan would – pending a French decision – include French forces.[71]

In conclusion, Dulles effectively forestalled any proposal de Gaulle may have had in mind concerning a formalized tripartite directorate. He stressed that the political consultations within NATO should be extended in order to preserve allied cohesion and effectiveness in peace time: "NATO must ... evolve into a political association as well as a military alliance." An upgrade for France, however, would be undesirable in the light of the formal egalitarianism in the Western alliance. There exists *de facto* leadership for Great Powers in a coalition, Dulles explained; but their leadership should not be formalized since this could break the coalition apart.

The secretary's long exposition was followed by de Gaulle's only slightly more to-the-point monologue which revealed his fundamental difference in outlook. In response to Dulles's analysis of communist behavior, de Gaulle emphasized the nationalist rather than universalistic ambitions of Russian leaders. He perceived a continuous line from the Czars to Khrushchev. De Gaulle admitted that the Soviet Union used the artificial separation of Party and Government to disclaim responsibility for Soviet actions, "much as you do [with] the American Congress." But he played down Soviet strength in the light of the persistent nationalism in Eastern Europe: "Russia had not conquered its satellites." De Gaulle reiterated his determination to build a national nuclear force, even if it might take twenty-five years. Responding to Dulles's plan for the deployment of NATO tactical nuclear weapons in Europe, de Gaulle professed that France had no interest in these weapons if they would be subjected to the control of the SACEUR or the United States. In such a case, he explained, "the disadvantages of having nuclear weapons on French soil were not equalized by France playing a role in their use." De Gaulle flatly stated that all nuclear weapons on French soil, even those stockpiled and assigned to American forces, should fall under French control. De Gaulle was equally insistent that France be accorded a greater influence in world strategy, otherwise "it would not throw itself enthusiastically into the effort of defending the Free World." He stated his dissatisfaction with NATO, indicating that its area coverage was particularly insufficient on the southern Mediterranean flank. "France," he said, "was currently torn between Africa and Europe and this situation was reflected in NATO." The area of coverage, therefore, had to be extended to the Middle East and Africa, and NATO command structures consequently had to be revised.

In their brief ensuing conversation, Dulles did not take issue with de Gaulle but focused on the situation in Lebanon where the General had warned against the implications in the Middle East of any Western intervention.[72] In their private tête-à-tête in the afternoon, responding to de Gaulle's statement that the French would become effete if they did not think of themselves as a great power, Dulles said that France could only hope to be seen as a great power once it had proven to be stable.[73] The discrepancy in views could not be more clearly exposed: while de Gaulle reasoned that France needed to think of itself as a great power in order to achieve political stability, Dulles believed that France could only be accorded such status once it had proven its political stability. While de Gaulle valued the domestic value of a foreign policy of grandeur, the American secretary of state was above all concerned with its impact on the solidity of the Cold War alliance. De Gaulle had not explicitly pressed for a formal directorate or for American nuclear assistance, but his fundamental difference in outlook on the Western alliance had become clear.

Despite their friendly phrasing, de Gaulle's words were the most forceful thus far coming from a European ally. Dulles cabled to Washington that his five hours with de Gaulle revealed "no sharpness at any point" despite some "differences of emphasis"; de Gaulle, he emphasized, had pressed neither for American nuclear assistance nor for a tripartite directorate.[74] But this report understated the extent of their differences. "It was an important meeting and Dulles talked to me about it on several occasions," Ambassador Alphand, a participant in the meeting, recorded. "He had told de Gaulle that the world was divided in two blocs, the good Western liberals and the wicked Communists. He was astonished when de Gaulle replied that he was quite mistaken... ."[75] The significance of the meeting was that it revealed fundamental disagreements about the transatlantic alliance right at the outset of de Gaulle's presidency. With regard to the tripartite idea, Dulles had tried to close the door before de Gaulle could open it. Back in Washington a few days later, Ambassador Alphand disclosed that, prior to the meeting, de Gaulle had been "much more legalistic in his concept of the tripartite relationship."[76] The day after, however, the General told André Malraux that "either there is a West, with a common policy towards the rest of the world or else... But there will be no West."[77]

On nuclear matters, too, it was clear that the United States and France stood far apart. On July 9, the State Department informed Alphand that "one explosion would not be enough" to qualify France for American assistance under the McMahon Act.[78] Washington hoped that the enormous expense of developing a nuclear force would eventually persuade the French to abort their independent program. Despite de Gaulle's apparent disinterest in a NATO nuclear force, the multilateral nuclear framework that Dulles had outlined was elaborated during the summer of 1958. "It is conceivable," wrote Acting Secretary of State Christian A. Herter to the Chairman of the Atomic Energy Commission John McCone, "that, as the costs and difficulties of a national program become more apparent to General de Gaulle, he may wish to discuss such a concept with us."[79]

Besides Dulles's conversation with de Gaulle in July, American decisions in other parts of the world in the summer of 1958 did not bode well for the Franco-American relationship either. Indeed, they would provide the immediate rationale for de Gaulle's September memorandum. The potential implications for European security of US involvement in remote places were at the time clearly manifested in Lebanon and the Formosa Straits. On July 15, ten days after de Gaulle had warned against an intervention and Dulles had assured him that the United States had no such intention, Eisenhower sent marines into Beirut to support the pro-

Western President Camille Chamoun.[80] The operation was highly offensive to de Gaulle, since French interests in a vital region were wholly ignored. Although Paris had been warned that some action in the region would be taken, it had not been consulted.[81] In Paris, Dulles had said that French participation in case of military action in Lebanon would be undesirable because of French ties with Israel and the ongoing Algerian war. But could de Gaulle be expected to accept such a behest? The American expedition was moreover closely coordinated with the British, who a few days later undertook military action of their own to assist the weakened government of King Hussein in Jordan. Given that, in their meeting on June 29, Macmillan had agreed with de Gaulle that their approach should be coordinated, informal agreements with London or Washington on a consultative framework must have appeared insufficient to de Gaulle.[82] It must have strengthened his determination to shake the Anglo-Saxon club out of its habit of deciding issues of the West without consulting France.

The handling of the crisis over two tiny islands in the Formosa Straits had a similar effect. The crisis over Quemoy had really begun in September 1954, when Communist China shelled this offshore island, killing two Americans and raising the threat of an invasion. The Eisenhower administration had then debated whether to apply the policy of massive retaliation and bomb the mainland of China. Eisenhower decided to let the United Nations deal with it and signed a mutual defense treaty with Nationalist China (now known as Taiwan) in December 1954. After shelling intensified in early 1955, this time with the inclusion of Matsu, the Senate passed the Formosa Resolution which authorized the president to do whatever was necessary to protect Formosa and the Pescadores – but not Quemoy and Matsu. Trouble over Quemoy and Matsu flared anew in August and September 1958, when the islands were shelled again. The Eisenhower administration responded by sending the Seventh Fleet to the area. Dulles even urged Eisenhower to seriously consider the use of tactical atomic bombs, but the latter decided against it.[83]

The United States' handling of the crisis in the Formosa Straits was among the clearest examples of Dulles's brinkmanship. To Paris, it underlined that the United States could precipitate a nuclear conflict, which could implicate France, over regions where French interests were not directly involved. De Gaulle was not alone in casting a doubtful eye on American positioning in the Far East. The British, mindful of their vulnerable position in Hong Kong, were also concerned.[84] The strife over Quemoy and Matsu showed how American decisionmaking in even remote corners of the planet, through the diplomatic use of the nuclear weapons arsenal of the United States, could be detrimental to the security interests of its Western allies. According to Foreign Minister Couve de Murville, de Gaulle's memorandum proposal was in large part a reaction to such "systemic interventionism" by the Americans.[85] At the least, US decisions in the Near and the Far East during the summer of 1958 would reinforce de Gaulle's demands for a more balanced Western partnership in world politics.

De Gaulle's "Tripartite" Proposal

On September 25, 1958, Ambassador Alphand met with Dulles to deliver de Gaulle's memorandum to President Eisenhower. (A copy of the memorandum was delivered to the British Foreign Office in London for Macmillan.) After a quick reading, Dulles imparted to Alphand that the message raised "very major problems."[86] The French ambassador could not have agreed more. "The sending of this *poulet* will not contribute to advancing things," he had just written in his diary.[87] The final text, dated September 17, had been handwritten by de Gaulle on the basis of longer drafts prepared by his diplomatic counsel Jean-Marc Boegner and Foreign Minister Maurice Couve de Murville.[88] It read as follows:

Recent events in the Middle East and in the straits of Formosa have contributed to show that the present organization of the Western Alliance no longer corresponds to the necessary conditions of security as far as the whole of the free world is concerned. The sharing of the risks incurred is not matched by indispensable cooperation on decisions taken and on responsibilities. From this the French Government is led to draw conclusions and to make several propositions.

1. The Atlantic Alliance was conceived and its functioning is prepared with a view to an eventual zone of action which no longer corresponds to political and strategic realities. The world being as it is, one cannot consider as adapted to its purpose an organization such as NATO, which is limited to the security of the North Atlantic, as if what is happening, for example, in the Middle East and Africa, did not immediately and directly concern Europe, and as if the indivisible responsibilities of France did not extend to Africa, to the Indian Ocean and to the Pacific, in the same way as those of Great Britain and the United States. Moreover the radius of action of ships and planes and the range of missiles render militarily outdated such a narrow system. It is true that at first it was admitted that atomic armament, evidently of capital importance, would remain for a long time the monopoly of the United States, a fact which might have appeared to justify that decisions on the world level concerning defense would be practically delegated to the Washington Government. But on this point, also, it must be recognized that such a fact admitted originally no longer is justified by reality.

2. France could, therefore, no longer consider that NATO in its present form meets the conditions of security of the free world and notably its own. It appears necessary to it that on the level of world policy and strategy there be set up an organization composed of: the United States, Great Britain and France.

It would be up to this organization, on the one hand, to take joint decisions on political questions affecting world security and on the other, to establish and if necessary, to put into effect strategic plans of action, notably with regard to the employment of nuclear weapons. It would then be possible to foresee and organize eventual theaters of operations subordinated to the general organization (such as the Arctic, the Atlantic, the Pacific, the Indian Ocean), which could if necessary be subdivided into subordinate theaters.

3. The French Government considers such a security organization indispensable. It (the French Government) subordinates to it as of now all developments of its present participation in NATO and proposes, should such appear necessary for reaching agreement, to invoke the provision for revising the North Atlantic Treaty in accordance with Article 12.

4. The French Government suggests that the questions raised in this note be the object as soon as possible of consultations among the United States, Great Britain and France. It proposes that these consultations take place in Washington and at the outset through the Embassies and the Permanent Group.[89]

It would be wrong to seek the reasons for de Gaulle's tripartite proposal exclusively in his personal convictions and experiences. Tripartite designs for the Western alliance were part and parcel of the Fourth Republic's foreign policy, too, reflecting the same desire to be treated as a major power with global interests.[90] French demands for institutionalized great power status within the Western alliance actually go as far back as the negotiations over the North Atlantic Treaty. After a hard diplomatic battle, France then gained a place in the potentially powerful Standing Group, the executive arm of NATO's Military Committee that consisted of the American, British, and French top military officials.[91] French officials persistently tried to make the Standing Group – rather than the Supreme Allied Headquarters in Europe (SHAPE) – the central organization within the alliance for military strategic planning.[92] In April 1950, prompted by the looming loss of French military dominance over West Germany in the European Defense Community, Prime Minister Georges Bidault furthermore pressed for an "Atlantic High Council of Peace" within NATO, with a secretariat and permanent seats for the United States, Great Britain, and France.[93] In 1951, Prime Minister René Pleven twice raised the matter with Acheson, arguing for a "three-power consultative body (with Britain) to coordinate policy on a worldwide basis."[94] Especially after the Suez debacle in 1956, the government of the Fourth Republic had consistently voiced complaints that NATO only covered the North Atlantic region and did not serve French interests in the Mediterranean and the Middle East.[95] Consecutive French governments thus strove to strengthen France's position within the Western alliance by formalizing participation in some kind of tripartite formula with the United States and Great Britain. As Prime Minister Mendès-France wrote in 1954: "The fate of France is indissolubly tied to that of the Western world; its place is within the Atlantic Alliance. But on equal footing and not with an inferior rank."[96]

But no French government had ever put the tripartite idea forward in such forceful and candid terms. First, de Gaulle had explicitly linked French participation in NATO to American and British preparedness to accept his proposal, whereas his predecessors had been careful to stay within the bounds of the alliance. Second, by proposing an organization that would jointly decide on political matters that affected the security of the Western alliance and by implying a French veto over the US nuclear arsenal, de Gaulle's memorandum went well beyond demanding an extension of the Anglo-American "special relationship" to France. It would completely overhaul the relationships between the Western allies built up since the late 1940s. De Gaulle essentially proposed to replace the United States with a tripartite organization as the hub of the free world. This would not necessarily preclude a preponderant role for the United States given its superior resources, but it would certainly impose substantial limitations on American decisionmaking.[97]

De Gaulle's proposal was moreover consistent with his strongly-held belief that nation-states rather than multilateral institutions were the real actors in international politics, and that each nation responded to a calling of its own – France's calling being to lead continental Europe. It is noteworthy that, as late as 1959, he was still putting the finishing touches on the last volume of his war memoirs. As leader of the Free French during the war, de Gaulle had found that only intransigent opposition or unilateral action could gain France access to vital decisions made by the Big Three. Did he want to avoid being in the same dependent position with respect to the United States and Great Britain as during the war? This interpretation was certainly encouraged by Ambassador Alphand, who told American and British officials that de Gaulle really wanted to revive the Big Three relationship by which Roosevelt, Churchill, and Stalin "had consulted and planned on a world-wide basis" – the difference being, of course, that France would replace the Soviet Union.[98]

De Gaulle's memorandum obviously raised many questions that could not be answered by a closer reading. Most importantly, the proposed relationship between the tripartite organization and NATO was not entirely clear from the memorandum, which instead emphasized arrangements for non-NATO areas. Since de Gaulle had mentioned the Atlantic as one of the theaters of operation, he most likely envisioned NATO to be, as Macmillan called it, the "European branch" of the tripartite organization. De Gaulle's dislike of NATO was understood. But even as he had emphasized the inadequacies of NATO, he had not made any specific proposals with regard to NATO itself. There was the reference to Article 12, which permitted a revision of the North Atlantic Treaty after a period of ten years, but what changes in the treaty – if any – he envisioned was left unclear. There was also the veiled threat that continued French participation in

NATO was contingent on the establishment of the tripartite security organization. The choice that de Gaulle seemed to be offering the United States was between persisting in its unilateral conduct of foreign affairs or bring American policies into line with those of France and Great Britain.

Other questions surfaced as well. In connection with the idea of carving up the world in "theaters of operation," would each of the three powers be assigned special responsibility for specific areas? What, then, was the relation of de Gaulle's proposal to the war in Algeria? Did he seek the support of the United States? There was also uncertainty as to whether de Gaulle's mention of joint "strategic plans of action" indeed meant that he demanded a French veto over the use of American – and British – nuclear weapons. Or did de Gaulle implicitly ask for US assistance to the French nuclear program? The organizational aspects of de Gaulle's proposal were also subject to speculation. Would the tripartite organization have a staff and a secretariat? Was it to be part of the existing structures of the Atlantic alliance, for instance by building on the existing Standing Group or creating a parallel political standing group? All these matters could be discussed, as de Gaulle had proposed, by the representatives of the three powers in Washington. But the Eisenhower administration, as we will see, was understandably wary of entering into any discussions.

Eisenhower Responds

What did de Gaulle precisely have in mind with his proposal? How serious was he? It is fair to say that the Eisenhower administration was perplexed by de Gaulle's maneuver – and in private conversations, megalomania was soon named the prime motivation for his demands.[99] The proposal for what soon came to be called a world directorate – or *directoire* – was so extraordinary as to render it all but dead upon arrival. The rejection was instinctive because the complications were immediately apparent. The US military was reluctant to engage in the military planning de Gaulle seemed to want.[100] The other European allies were predictably dead set against any notion of an inner circle that would decide matters. De Gaulle had shown the memorandum in strictest confidence to NATO Secretary General Paul-Henri Spaak on September 24, who then told Dulles three days later that the French plan could usher in "the end of NATO."[101] The other allies, who were only familiar with the general contents of the memorandum, also found ways to make known their dismay.[102] Italy was particularly sensitive because of its position in the Mediterranean close to the Near East and Africa, regions that in de Gaulle's plan would presumably fall under French influence.[103] The Dutch, Danes, Norwegians, and Turks resented the inequality implied in the French proposal. And, perhaps most importantly, Chancellor Adenauer was distressed about the French proposal.[104] On his trip to Bonn, Macmillan found Adenauer feeling betrayed since de Gaulle had made no mention of his memorandum during their meeting just days earlier.[105] Macmillan himself, like Dulles, believed it was highly unfortunate that Paris had allowed either the contents or the existence of the proposals to be known.[106] Like Dulles, he also wondered whether de Gaulle could not be persuaded to rewrite his proposal so that it would be less offensive.[107] This, however, was wishful thinking.[108]

Washington and London were thus left to come up with a response. Eisenhower's and Macmillan's disposition toward the tripartite idea was decidedly cool, but they were also cautious and confused. "The best course to follow [is] to sit quietly and not exaggerate the situation," the American president told Ambassador Manlio Brosio of Italy.[109] As far as Macmillan was concerned, the idea of systematic tripartite coordination was certainly not as offensive as it was to Eisenhower, for he had no interest in arousing French hostility in view of the Free Trade Area negotiations with the Common Market.[110] Although the French had made clear that the memorandum was not linked in any way to the Free Trade Area discussions and Washington had warned London not to mix the two issues, the linkage would remain important in British deliberations.[111] Believing that some form of informal or symbolic tripartitism would probably have to be developed to appease Paris, London thus encouraged Washington to be forthcoming.[112]

French diplomats in Washington believed that the Eisenhower administration would not be prepared to consider de Gaulle's proposal for a tripartite organization seriously. "We knew from the start that he [Dulles] was not interested in the idea," Charles Lucet of the French embassy said. "He never said so frankly and clearly ... said it was necessary to study it, but we had the impression he was not really interested."[113] Yet, like de Gaulle, Dulles had often lamented the "inadequate" organization of the free world in dealing with the global communist threat. As a private citizen in May 1949, when the North Atlantic Treaty was being discussed in Congress, he had testified that its limitation to Europe would lead to Soviet aggression in other places – and the outbreak of the Korean War barely one year later seemed to confirm this analysis.[114] As secretary of state, the effectiveness of the Western alliance remained a constant concern for Dulles. Throughout the 1950s, in particular against the backdrop of the wars of national liberation, there was a widespread belief that political diversity was rendering the West inferior in comparison with the more tightly dominated Eastern bloc. The Soviet system also appeared better geared than democratic societies towards harnessing the economy for military purposes. Dulles was therefore not averse to adaptations to the Western alliance that in his view could make it more effective and cohesive. In May 1956, as secretary of state, he had discussed with Eisenhower the idea of a "political body" overarching the various organizations in the Atlantic region; the latter, however, made clear that he would rather give priority to European political integration, which he hoped would lead to a "genuine third force comparable to the United States or to the Soviet Union."[115] And in December 1957, at a NATO ministerial meeting, Dulles had suggested that the organization should establish liaisons with other defense groupings such as SEATO.[116]

Even de Gaulle's suggestion to have a say in nuclear decisionmaking was not as far-fetched as is often believed – perhaps not even as far-fetched as he himself might have believed. In December 1955, Dulles told Eisenhower that he had come to believe "that atomic power was too vast a power to be left for the military use of any one country." He suggested that the United States might consider calling together the forty-two nations with which it had security treaties, placing before them a proposal for an international group that would decide "when and how to use atomic weapons of defense – always reserving of course the right of the United States, in the event that it was directly attacked, to use whatever means it had." Eisenhower was interested in the idea and Dulles developed it in a long memorandum in early 1956. He suggested the establishment of regional groups, along the lines of NATO, "to study and plan the means whereby nuclear weapons could most effectively be used to deter armed attack and to preserve peace in each region." Although nothing came of the idea, Dulles's concern did not disappear, as he frequently expressed it to Eisenhower.[117]

Pressures to improve Western coordination were thus not the exclusive domain of de Gaulle. As Dulles said to the British ambassador in Washington, "some positive response" to de Gaulle's initiative had to be found.[118] He acknowledged that de Gaulle had put his finger on a weakness in the position of the West vis-à-vis the East. But Dulles also confessed to be at a loss in a letter to NATO Secretary General Paul-Henri Spaak: "I doubt that the answer [to the worldwide nature of the communist threat] is to be found in General de Gaulle's suggestion; or in attempting to make NATO into a means of reincarnating Western dominance of the world. I do not clearly see how we should move."[119]

Spaak himself, a resourceful politician, tried hard to induce Washington to respond in a serious and forthcoming manner to the French proposal. Speaking to the Atlantic Treaty Association in Boston on September 27, he addressed the issues that de Gaulle had broached in his memorandum (although reasons of secrecy obliged him not to make specific mention of the document, which de Gaulle had shown him just a few days earlier). The themes he sounded were strikingly similar to those of de Gaulle:

> This is the moment to ask a vital question: Is NATO, with its present composition, spirit, and machinery, still the right answer to the threat which communism represents for the free world? ... Is it sufficient, at the present time, to construct a solid military barrier along the Elbe, on the eastern frontier of the free world, if the free world is to be outflanked politically, militarily, and economically in the Middle East and Africa? ... The concept of a military Atlantic Alliance restricted to a specific geographical area, adequate in 1949, is ... no

longer so in 1958. A common policy, probably of worldwide scope, must be added to it. And it must be done at once.[120]

Although Spaak's analysis then diverged from that of the French leader – he argued that NATO offered ample potential for the needed adjustments – the Belgian diplomat perceived that de Gaulle's proposal had to lead to some substantial changes. Spaak's political instincts and temperament advised him to leap forward. In keeping with the recommendations of the Three Wise Men in 1956, he argued for a considerable expansion within NATO of political consultations (which in his view could represent an "innovation, even a revolution, in diplomatic practice") and of cooperation on non-military matters. In a letter to de Gaulle a month later, in which he declared his opposition to a three-power directorate, Spaak stressed that French concerns could be addressed by firmly establishing the principle of prior consultation.[121] He simultaneously urged the United States to respond to de Gaulle's memorandum proposal by significantly expanding consultations within NATO on military strategy and on areas outside the treaty area.[122]

Independent of Spaak, the continental European allies found ways to make clear their own objections to a tripartite alliance system in which France would speak for them. In particular, the protestations of the West German and Italian governments carried weight in Washington. They made clear that the establishment of a three-power "directorate" superseding NATO would politically demoralize the existing alliance system. The reaction from America's non-European allies to a tripartite management of world affairs or a formal extension of NATO's area of coverage was equally likely to be adverse. The risks of a blunt denial, however, were equally daunting. As Eisenhower explained to the Italian ambassador in Washington, he had to tread carefully. Preserving French cooperation in the framework of NATO was simply too important to justify an extemporaneous rejection, and de Gaulle's character meant that his threats had to be taken seriously.[123]

Eisenhower, true to his delegating style, did not closely monitor the process of drafting an official response to de Gaulle's memorandum. This was mainly the responsibility of the State Department which, staying in close touch with the British embassy in Washington, tried to come to terms with the ideas contained in the memorandum after a brief preliminary reply had been sent to Paris on October 2.[124] On October 9, 1958, Dulles received a memorandum from his European affairs office whose recommendations he approved the next day. Its basic conclusion was that rejection of de Gaulle's proposal was unavoidable. Given the serious objections from the Defense Department and the Joint Chiefs of Staff, none of de Gaulle's proposals in the military field were acceptable; as far as military circles were concerned, bilateral military planning with the British was already burdensome. De Gaulle's preference for a tripartite "political standing group" was equally undesirable because of the reaction of other allies, both within and out-side of NATO. However, as a flat rejection could draw a drastic reaction from de Gaulle, it was in "the political field where we must find a counterproposal or counter-suggestion sufficiently substantive to prevent a major explosion on his part with the concomitant loss of French active participation in NATO ...." No suggestions were made and it was estimated that none would really satisfy de Gaulle; their principal role would be to "allay the effect of our negative reaction." This was also to be the aim of the initial tripartite discussions in Washington that de Gaulle had suggested. Such informal discussions would be a "much better means of thrashing out the problem with the French than ... a relatively negative written reply"; they would represent a step in the French direction, give an oppor-tunity to dilute French objectives in a more general survey of world problems, and help condition the French to the Anglo-American view.[125]

Hence the only initial concession that Washington was willing to make was to discuss the plan. On October 13, Eisenhower decided that lower-level informal talks in Washington, such as de Gaulle had requested, should indeed be allowed to take place. But as he made his decision, the president stressed the importance of explaining to the allies that these meetings would be "for the purpose of dis-cussing the plan and [were] not the beginning of carrying into effect" the French proposals. He was also not prepared to conduct talks within the Standing Group.[126] As a matter of fact, Eisenhower and Dulles remained highly ambivalent about going ahead with preliminary talks, and in the week before the response was finally transmitted to Paris they seriously questioned their decision. They were extremely concerned lest a pattern for trilateral consultations would be es-tablished or de Gaulle's proposals would receive public exposure; this could cause the consternation among the NATO allies they were determined to avoid.[127] "By far the best development," Dulles told Ambassador Caccia on October 17 in a burst of wishful thinking, "would be the withdrawal of the de Gaulle letter." The British ambassador, however, insisted that de Gaulle could not be left in the cold. Since the United States and Great Britain could not satisfy de Gaulle on the sub-stance of the letter, he argued that they should at least agree to talk about the form.[128]

Eisenhower's official reply to de Gaulle's memorandum was transmitted to Paris on October 20. De Gaulle considered the response to his proposal evasive, since it ignored the French proposal for a new security organization as well as its references to joint nuclear and military-strategic planning.[129] What was clear was that it amounted to a rebuttal. Eisenhower's reply left little doubt about Washing-ton's disinclination to overhauling the Western alliance and its reluctance to en-gage in discussions with Paris on the basis of de Gaulle's proposal. He reasoned that the existing system of alliances and multilateral and bilateral arrangements, which obviously centered on the United States as their mainstay, already served the purpose of dealing with the "world-wide nature of the threat." If anything, this system needed strengthening, not basic reform. Eisenhower particularly stressed the significance of a growing "habit of consultation" within NATO "over the past two years" (which could be read as a reference to the Three Wise Men's report of 1956 but also to the Suez Crisis). He supported a broadening of this consultative practice, but the letter made clear that he would not agree to any inner councils: "I do not believe that we can afford to lose any of this developing intimacy among *all* the members of NATO and the closer bonds it forges." (emphasis added) On the contrary, the letter implied that adoption of de Gaulle's tripartite proposal would sap the life out of NATO and the other Cold War alliances. "We cannot afford to adopt any system which would give to our other allies, or other free world countries, the impression that basic decisions affecting their own vital interests are being made without their participation." In addition, Eisenhower foresaw "very serious problems, both within and outside NATO, in any effort to amend the North Atlantic Treaty so as to extend its coverage beyond the areas presently covered."[130]

Only with the utmost reluctance and circumspection did the United States agree to enter into discussions with the French via a tripartite ambassadorial committee (instead of the Standing Group). Eisenhower assigned Deputy Under Secretary of State Robert Murphy to the task of chairing the upcoming meetings with the French and British ambassadors. Murphy was the third highest official in the State Department, a man "who could handle a lot of fires" and who had operated a great number of arduous diplomatic missions for Eisenhower and Dulles. He had also inherited from the war days a personal rapport with his then British counterpart Harold Macmillan. From the French point of view, however, the choice was mainly significant in other respects. He was seen as a "diplomatic fixer" rather than a "policy man." More importantly, Murphy was known to de Gaulle as Roosevelt's man who had maintained relations with the Vichy authorities in North Africa. Murphy had prepared the "Darlan deal" that enabled the allies to take Northern Africa without much resistance from French forces. He had also been present at the Casablanca conference of 1943, at which the US president persuaded de Gaulle to shake the hands of his rival General Giraud. And Murphy had headed the "good offices" mission in the Franco-Tunisian crisis that contributed to the fall of the Gaillard government in early 1958. Among the Americans who appear on the pages of de Gaulle's *War Memoirs*, Murphy was the one most often portrayed in an unfavorable light.[131] The diplomat's own recollections of de Gaulle, published in 1964, were in kind:

> In Algiers ... I formed an opinion of de Gaulle as an ardent French patriot, but I never regarded him as a close friend of my country. I did not find that he then was a great admirer of American military and political sagacity. He knew little of the United States or of Americans, and it seemed to me that he was cynical in his appraisal of how the United States could be "played" vis-a-vis the Soviet

Union and Europe for the benefit of France. In his references to Britons and Americans, de Gaulle termed them "the Anglo-Saxons" which, curiously enough, was Hitler's terminology.[132]

If Eisenhower's slight concession had opened the door for de Gaulle's memorandum diplomacy, the chances of a meeting of minds were practically nil.[133]

De Gaulle's Memorandum Diplomacy under Eisenhower

Uncertain Beginnings: The Berlin Crisis (Winter of 1958-1959)

Before the first "exploratory" tripartite meetings were held on December 4 and 10, 1958, the parameters for discussing de Gaulle's memorandum proposal shifted in two important respects. First, the Eisenhower administration had thus far assumed that de Gaulle desired an amendment of the North Atlantic Treaty in order to widen its area of coverage. The impracticality of this proposition had figured prominently in Eisenhower's official reply and was also brought up as a main concern in discussions with French diplomats.[134] Washington was, however, soon told that de Gaulle had no intention of extending the geographic responsibility of NATO. He merely wanted to establish a tripartite arrangement for areas beyond NATO's confines, particularly in the Middle East and Africa. Hence, in spite of the memorandum's explicit reference to invoking Article 12 of the Treaty, NATO itself would not be directly discussed.[135] Was de Gaulle scaling down his demands? Dulles was puzzled and now suspected that all the Frenchman wanted was the public restoration of French grandeur. "Anything which will bring about this result, he will accept," he told Murphy. "If we ask him just what his program is, he will be hard put to come up with something."[136]

The second shift that would have a bearing on tripartite consultations was not generated in either Washington or Paris, but in Moscow. On November 10, Khrushchev announced that the Soviet Union intended to sign a peace treaty with East Germany. This, the Soviet leader argued, would terminate the rights of the United States, Great Britain, and France to maintain a military presence in West Berlin – and soon enough Soviet troops were indeed harassing American trucks on the *autobahn*. Khrushchev's bluster significantly affected tripartite relations. For one, it persuaded de Gaulle to moderate his demands on the United States for the time being. On December 15, he acknowledged to Dulles that the crisis had significantly altered the situation since he had issued his tripartite proposal. "It was ironic," said de Gaulle, "that the Berlin situation, in which France felt solidarity with the US, should happen at just the moment that various manifestations of US policy were giving displeasure to France." He assured Dulles that he did not want to exploit the Berlin situation in order to force American concurrence with his tripartite scheme.[137] While he continued to express his misgivings about NATO and his intention to "rectify" the situation some day, the crisis over Berlin also compelled him to admit that, as he wrote Eisenhower in October 1959, "it is not advisable at this time to change the present organization of the defense of continental Europe."[138]

At the same time, however, the Berlin Crisis caused the three western allies with special rights in the city to consult more often and intensely than they otherwise would have. Moreover, Eisenhower's respect for the French leader grew in the course of dealing with Khrushchev in 1958 and 1959, as a result of which he became more determined to find some common ground with de Gaulle on his tripartite proposal. And while de Gaulle said he did not want to exploit the situation, his invariably firm stance during the Berlin Crisis helped to cement his close relationship with Chancellor Adenauer of Germany. In some ways, at least, the Soviet leader had unconsciously blown some life into tripartitism.

Yet the first tripartite meetings in December 1958 showed above all that a meeting of minds – if at all possible – was still far away. On December 4, Ambassador Alphand played down the organizational implications of "a system of organized consultation with a regular schedule" and explained that, in the French view, the existing Standing Group should play a role in this respect. Murphy, however, countered that the original French proposal "went far beyond the concept of informal consultation"; since it seemed to involve drawing up "common policies and common programs of action," it "would call for a large organization with a large staff."[139] At the next meeting, on December 10, Alphand – on de Gaulle's personal instructions – merely asked his American and British counterparts to agree on two "preliminary" questions:

Is it possible or not to establish a program of common action related to world problems [...] with such a program to be so constructed as to restore the initiative to the West and not let it be or appear a prerogative of the East? Is it possible or not on the military level for the three to act strategically in common in case of military conflict anywhere in the world? ... An example would be the decision whether or not to use nuclear weapons.

Without agreement on these principles, Alphand maintained, there would be no basis for discussing the details of the French proposal. Murphy and Caccia nonetheless kept insisting on knowing the details of a tripartite mechanism before agreeing to anything.[140] It was clear that Washington was not about to discuss the tripartite proposal on French terms. The talks were now effectively stalled.

Dulles's subsequent conversation with de Gaulle on December 15 failed to bring the two sides any closer. The atmosphere was notably less friendly than their first meeting in early July. The United States had abstained the day before in a United Nations Security Council vote on a resolution calling for Algerian inde-

pendence. This had greatly angered de Gaulle and undoubtedly cast a shadow over his efforts to attain American political support for his Algerian policies in the framework of any system of tripartite policy coordination. He told Dulles that French participation in NATO would not be increased under his watch, dashing hopes that French military units returning from Algeria would in the future be assigned to NATO.[141] Less than a year after de Gaulle's return to power had been hailed in Washington, Franco-American relations were clearly at a new low. Eisenhower responded to his secretary of state's dismayed report: "It does seem that our friend should cease insisting upon attempting to control the whole world, of course with partners, even before he has gotten France itself in good order."[142] A few days earlier, Eisenhower had told the National Security Council of his conviction that de Gaulle was infatuated with prestige and that all he desired was achieving the status of which he was deprived in World War II: to be a member of the Big Three.[143] In his view, de Gaulle was simply asking too much for France and was making his demands largely out of personal reasons.

The tripartite talks chiefly continued because Dulles was concerned with the French "sit-down strike on NATO" during the NATO meetings in Paris and hoped that some progress would help preserve French cooperation.[144] De Gaulle, for his part, did not insist on answers to his "preliminary" questions and seemed to be satisfied as long as regular tripartite talks were held.[145] But the two sides did not get any closer. Ambassador Alphand insisted that the Standing Group should discuss strategic plans, including on the use of nuclear weapons. He also stressed the importance of military planning with respect to "theaters of operation" (particularly in the Middle East and North Africa): "Who will be the commander? How will the forces be divided? Should the wartime commander be the inspector in time of peace? How would planning for these areas be connected to NATO planning?"[146] Yet the State Department continued to effectively stall any progress. As Murphy assured the US Joint Chiefs of Staff: "the United States had not agreed to military talks with the French on any other than an ad hoc basis and ... the [State] Department was trying to eliminate any strategic discussions from the talks, trying especially to ensure that the talks did not proceed in a NATO context."[147] The question was above all whether de Gaulle would resign himself to the infeasibility of his tripartite proposal. The State Department's strategy to this effect seemed to be working, for de Gaulle did not return to his tripartite proposal during his last meeting with Dulles before the latter's death in May.[148] Nothing, however, could have been further from the truth.

Reprisal against NATO (Spring and Summer of 1959)
On March 6, 1959, Paris informed Washington that the French Mediterranean Fleet would be withdrawn from NATO. The French decision had been anticipated, and its military implications were not significant. Yet, as Acting Secretary of State Herter complained to Alphand, its psychological and political repercus-

sions were harmful, in particular given that allied unity was still being tested in Berlin.[149] Foreign Minister Couve de Murville, who informed the American embassy in Paris of the decision, emphasized that it was entirely connected with the Algerian situation.[150] French diplomats similarly refuted claims that de Gaulle's decision, which was taken against the counsel of his political and military advisers, was tied to American reluctance to discuss his tripartite proposal. Yet de Gaulle himself confided to NATO Secretary General Spaak that the two issues were clearly linked. Because no progress had been made in the tripartite talks in Washington, he explained, "it was necessary to take the questions directly to NATO."[151]

Any remaining doubts as to whether the issues were linked would be dispelled on May 1 by Michel Debré in a blunt exchange with Secretary of State Herter. The French prime minister made clear that the French refusal to permit the deployment of nuclear warheads for nine American air force squadrons based in France – a question considered particularly urgent in the context of the Berlin Crisis since NATO was in a high state of readiness – was connected to lack of progress with regard to the tripartite memorandum. In addition, Debré declared that "atomic cooperation" was of "extreme importance" to France and that it sought cooperation with the United States "both in the field of the peaceful uses and military uses of atomic energy." The exchange was significant, too, because Debré linked the tripartite proposal to American political support in the Algerian war. Debré:

> Whether we like it or not, France has as much a future in Algeria and the Mediterranean as in Europe. [...] France must square her responsibilities in Europe with those in Africa. The events of May, 1958 in Algeria were caused in large part by the feeling of frustration in Algeria regarding lack of understanding on the part of France's allies, and the lack of a common Western policy for Algeria. ... it [is] difficult to imagine either French military or civilian authorities giving strong support to the Atlantic Alliance unless that organization and its principal members gave support to French interests in the Mediterranean and Africa.

When Herter deplored the fact that these issues were all linked in the French view, Debré "frankly" replied that "these problems are linked because they are all related to the French national security."[152]

Debré's unusually candid exposition thoroughly displeased Herter and Eisenhower, the more so since the French prime minister had emphasized he had discussed his message at length with de Gaulle beforehand. In a long and important handwritten letter to Eisenhower on May 25, de Gaulle further clarified the "spirit and the substance" of his decisions. The significance of this letter, which echoed many of the themes of the September 1958 memorandum, was that – like Debré –

de Gaulle connected the withdrawal of the French Mediterranean fleet and the refusal to authorize NATO's atomic stockpile on French soil to the unaccommodating American response to his tripartite proposal. In addition, the letter made clear that de Gaulle had in fact unilaterally set out to implement parts of his design. De Gaulle explained that, following the withdrawal of the French Mediterranean fleet from NATO, he was setting up "a French command of the Mediterranean, having as its area of responsibility the whole of that Sea as well as North Africa" and that he would be prepared to discuss with "either Washington and London or with NATO [...] the conditions under which we could cooperate in this area ... ." Likewise, another French command would be charged with "the defense of Black Africa" – and de Gaulle declared himself to be quite willing to cooperate along the same lines in the Indian Ocean and the Pacific as well. De Gaulle moreover made clear that his demand for a veto over the American nuclear arsenal had been serious, linking it to the United States' refusal to assist France in its own nuclear effort as well as to France's refusal to authorize the presence of American nuclear weapons on French soil:

Obviously the question would appear quite differently if you had made it possible for us to take advantage of your own achievements. But America intends to keep her secrets, vis-à-vis France. This compels us to discover them ourselves and at tremendous cost. On this point, however, we have nothing other to express than regret. This is not the case insofar as America reserves to herself the total decision to use or not to use the nuclear weapons which she has. ... If there were no alliance between us, I would agree that your monopoly on the opening of atomic war would be justified, but you and I are tied together to such a point that the opening of this type of hostilities either by you or against you would automatically expose France to total and immediate destruction. She obviously cannot entirely entrust her life or her death to any other state whatsoever, even the most friendly. For this reason, France feels it is essential that she participate, if the case were to arise, in any decision which might be taken by her allies to use atomic missiles or to launch them against certain places at certain times. Until she has been able to conclude with the United States and with Great Britain the agreements which seem necessary to her on this subject, she cannot consent to such projectiles being stored on her territory and used from there unless she herself has complete and permanent control over them.[153]

The overriding concern over the standoff with the Soviet Union over Berlin imposed on the United States a posture of "calm but cold dignity" toward de Gaulle's conduct.[154] But privately Eisenhower examined the deadlock of the tripartite affair with growing uncertainty. During the spring and summer of 1959, the potential implications of de Gaulle's intransigence were much on his mind.

"We may be witnessing a beginning of a crumbling of NATO," he observed during one of his meetings with his advisers on the French problem.[155] He was gravely concerned, as he explained at another meeting, that "other NATO nations will finally become weary with de Gaulle's attitude and lose enthusiasm for the organization."[156] Since Eisenhower was persuaded that "the people dealing with de Gaulle ... were not sufficiently acquainted with his temperament,"[157] he began musing about his own wartime relationship with the Frenchman in an attempt to look for clues. On several occasions he recalled the "Strasbourg incident" of December 1944, during which he had clashed with de Gaulle. But Eisenhower realized the circumstances were different in 1959. "Unless we are prepared to deal with him this way, on a matter in which he is in a disadvantage," he said to Macmillan shortly after the French announced the withdrawal of their Mediterranean fleet from NATO, "there is no point in trying to be tough with him."[158] Eisenhower moreover cherished little hope of influencing a man whom he imputed with a "Messiah complex," viewing himself as "a cross between Napoleon and Joan of Arc," and thinking only in terms of "Glory, Honor, France." Sensing that de Gaulle was going to cause "great difficulties" for the Western alliance, "the question we must face is whether we can accommodate to those difficulties sufficiently to sustain the NATO concept."[159]

Could de Gaulle be accommodated? On August 18, 1959, Eisenhower discussed his options in an extensive review of American policy toward France. The Joint Chiefs of Staff had recommended that support could be given to France in Algeria in order to gain French cooperation in NATO. This option, however, did not appeal to Eisenhower whatsoever.

> How could we say that we support the French and still not damage our interests? The whole of our history ... is anti-colonial, and the French action in Algeria is interpreted by the rest of the world as militant colonialism. To support the French would be counter to everything we have done in the past. ... To stand up with the colonial powers would be to cut ourselves from our own moorings...

The president equated de Gaulle's behavior with that of Khrushchev on Berlin. Both were trying to force concessions from the United States, but, added Eisenhower, "we were not going to be blackmailed ... by de Gaulle or anyone else."[160]

On only one issue was Eisenhower willing to be more forthcoming. On former occasions he had already expressed sympathy for the French decision to build a nuclear force. "In fairness to de Gaulle," Eisenhower had confessed to Lauris Norstad in June 1959, "we would react very much like de Gaulle if the shoe were on the other foot."[161] He felt that the rigid legislation on nuclear assistance, for which he felt contempt, had "handcuffed" the White House in maintaining good relations with America's allies.[162] On August 18, he spoke along similar lines: "It was as if we had been fighting wars with bows and arrows and then acquired pistols. Then we refused to give pistols to the people who were our allies even though the common enemy already had them." But Eisenhower could do little to satisfy French needs in this respect. He could complain about the Congress and its watchdog, the Joint Committee on Atomic Energy, but he could not force a change in legislation. In the absence of a better option, Eisenhower therefore requested the urgent development of a multilateral approach to the nuclear affairs of the Western alliance that could help accommodate the French as well as carry congressional approval.[163]

On de Gaulle's tripartite proposal, the American position remained the same. Eisenhower's correspondence with de Gaulle in March and June had carefully evaded the issue, postponing discussions on the subject to his planned trip to Europe in the autumn.[164] The tripartite exchanges in April, which focused on African affairs, followed the fruitless pattern of earlier meetings; Alphand's pleas for joint contingency planning were again fended off.[165] A proposal by Spaak to expand consultation procedures by establishing a NATO machinery for developing common action programs toward other areas was also dismissed because of "greatly varying degrees of interest of NATO countries in these areas and because of effect in other areas of common NATO programs."[166] Yet the end of de Gaulle's memorandum diplomacy was not yet in sight.

Extending the "Special Relationship" to France
Although de Gaulle's bluff had not succeeded in bringing a fundamental change in the American attitude, the crisis of the spring of 1959 did bring home to Washington that more had to be done to pacify de Gaulle. Indeed, Eisenhower would use the occasion of his consultations in Europe prior to Khrushchev's American visit at the end of September to propose an extension of the "special relationship" between the United States and Great Britain. In his meeting with de Gaulle on September 2, he declared his willingness to accord all its attributes to France: consultation prior to the use of American nuclear weapons (except in the case of a surprise attack on US territory); a study of problems of world strategy with the intention of fostering agreement on decisions; a direct telephone line with Paris (there already existed one with London); ad hoc tripartite committees to discuss specific problems arising outside the NATO area. The conditions were that France would not insist on a formalization of these informal arrangements and that any tripartite arrangements would not concern the affairs of NATO, "on which an established machinery exists." In addition, Eisenhower had to tell de Gaulle that, to his regret, Congress barred him from furnishing assistance to the French nuclear weapons program.[167]

This surely was as serious an approach as could be imagined under the circumstances. Eisenhower's earnestness is evident, too, from his decision to inform both Adenauer and Macmillan beforehand of his move.[168] The meeting at Rambouillet castle certainly helped to solidify the personal relationship between Eisenhower and de Gaulle. The American president had been welcomed in France by large crowds. De Gaulle furthermore made several gestures that gratified him. The Frenchman explained, "in great confidence," that "if occasionally sharp words were spoken or strident voices were raised," these should be judged from France's difficult adjustment to the fact that she was a nation in decline.[169] Eisenhower was also the first foreigner to whom de Gaulle outlined his plan for offering self-determination to the Algerian people (two weeks before he appraised the public). And just before Eisenhower's departure, while standing on the lawn of Rambouillet, de Gaulle confided to the American president that France would test its first nuclear device in March 1960 in the Sahara desert and that a preliminary explosion had already been successful.[170]

Yet a meeting of minds on the tripartite issue did not occur. When Eisenhower referred to the congressional laws that prohibited a transfer of American nuclear material and knowledge to France, de Gaulle replied: "The McMahon Law! I changed the Constitution of France when I found it was no longer valid."[171] They also had expressed their widely divergent views of military integration under NATO. After the meeting, the tripartite consultations in Washington continued as usual, without any noticeable impetus coming from the September meeting of the heads of state.[172] Eisenhower's overture obviously fell short of the French proposal of the previous year, but tactical considerations may also explain de Gaulle's non-responsive attitude. He may in particular have decided to wait for the first French nuclear explosion to bolster his position. This would at least explain why, on October 6, he wrote to Eisenhower that with regard to his demand for joint decisions regarding the use of nuclear weapons "...there is reason to expect that the successful development by France of French atomic armament in the fairly near future will facilitate matters for us."[173] Or perhaps the preparations for a summit with Khrushchev convinced him not to press the issue, for in the same letter to Eisenhower he admitted that "it is not advisable at this time to change the present organization of the defense of continental Europe."[174] In the same vein, he notified Herter that, for the time being, "France would neither add nor subtract from its present effort and attitude" with regard to NATO.[175] Despite Eisenhower's attempt at rapprochement, the tripartite issue nonetheless continued to hang like the sword of Damocles over the Western alliance.

In addition, the fundamental differences of view between them also became more apparent during this time. De Gaulle first of all angered Eisenhower by putting the United States on the same moral plane as the Soviet Union in a press conference on November 10:

> Who can say ... whether some sudden advance in development – particularly in the field of space rockets – will not provide one of the two camps with such an advantage that its peaceful inclinations will not hold out? Who can say

whether, in the future, if basic political facts should change completely, as has already occurred on the earth, the two powers that would have a monopoly on nuclear weapons might not make a deal with each other to divide the world between them. Who can say whether, should the occasion arise – while each side might follow a policy of not hurling its devices at the principal adversary, so as not to be threatened by it – who can say whether the two rivals might not crush others? One can very well imagine, for example, that on such a terrible occasion, Western Europe might be destroyed from Moscow and Central Europe from Washington. And who even can say whether the two rivals, as a result of some unforeseeable political and social upheaval, will not come to the point of uniting? In truth, France, by equipping herself with nuclear arma-ments, is rendering a service to the equilibrium of the world.[176]

Eisenhower's reaction on November 17 was indignant and he demanded a reas-surance from the French president that he did not consider the United States as operating on such a "low moral plane." De Gaulle, however, reiterated his basic argument and pointed out the belated entries of the United States in two world wars.[177]

The rather philosophical debate between Eisenhower and de Gaulle on the im-plications of military integration under NATO was moreover stirred up by the latter's well-known address at the École Militaire on November 3. Eisenhower had already discussed the issue in some depth during his visit with de Gaulle in September. The US president had then contended that NATO was precisely geared towards balancing national political needs and esprit with the military need for centralized command in wartime. "I believe the American forces in Europe," he had moreover argued in a subsequent letter, "while serving in their own national uniforms and under their own flag, feel also a considerable – and a growing – attachment to their collective force and to the North Atlantic Commu-nity."[178] This, predictably, failed to impress de Gaulle.[179] As he explained to the cadets of the École Militaire, "integration" under NATO undermined national and military morale and had outlived its day.[180]

De Gaulle's public remarks again proved to Eisenhower that the tripartite issue had to be addressed in order to preserve French cooperation in NATO. During the summit meeting of Western leaders at Château Rambouillet on December 20, 1959, he tried to break the impasse for a second time. In his conversations with de Gaulle and Macmillan, Eisenhower put forward the idea of a machinery in one of the three capitals – preferably London – provided that this happened on a "clandestine basis" and that there was "no connection to NATO." Each country, Eisenhower suggested, should contribute one or two "competent" men of "good judgment" and "reasonably high rank." In addition, there would be some person-nel to handle political, military, and economic matters. Both de Gaulle and Mac-millan expressed their satisfaction with this suggestion.[181] However, like Eisenhower's suggestions in September, the implementation of his offer to institutionalize tripartite talks at a higher level stranded on the different conceptions entertained in Paris and Washington about the scope and the form of a tripartite coordinating mechanism.[182] "I am quite astonished at the atmosphere of formality with which the French seem to view the matter and the difficulties they see of putting the simple plan into action," Eisenhower wrote Macmillan on February 18, 1960. "Just where it jumped the track I do not know."[183]

France's first explosion of an atomic device in the Saharan Desert one week earlier – and a second a month and a half later – also failed to bring the hoped-for change in the official American attitude toward the French nuclear deterrent. On the eve of the first explosion, Eisenhower actually heightened French expectations of a policy change by publicly airing his frustration with the restrictions imposed by Congress. The JCAE, however, quickly responded that the Atomic Energy Act would be upheld in spite of the evident progress the French were making. When Foreign Minister Couve de Murville and Ambassador Alphand asked Herter on April 15 "whether France with its two atomic explosions and industrial capabilities could not be considered to be qualified within the terms of the [American] law," the latter thus replied that Congress would not consider France qualified in spite of Eisenhower's displeasure with the situation.[184]

Unexpected Impulse and Sudden Death

Ironically, it was not de Gaulle's extensive visit to the United States, from April 22 to 29, 1960,[185] but the failure of the summit with Khrushchev one month later that brought France and the United States somewhat closer on the tripartite issue. Immediately after Khrushchev's intransigent stance on the U2 spy-plane affair (he demanded a public apology from the American president), de Gaulle greatly impressed Eisenhower by assuring him that "no matter what happens, France as your ally will stand with you all the way."[186] Eisenhower also greatly appreciated the Frenchman's skillful handling of an extremely awkward situation.[187] Was it this sentiment of union in the hour of confrontation that prompted Eisenhower to say that he favored closer cooperation between the three Western powers at the "top governmental level"? At any rate, Eisenhower's desire to have more frequent tripartite meetings seemed genuine enough for de Gaulle to finally seize on the moment. He recalled his memorandum of September 1958 and reviewed the unsatisfactory tripartite arrangements established to date; he forcefully argued that two years ago crises had occurred in the Middle East, before that at Suez, and today in Berlin, that tomorrow another crisis could erupt, and that all the while there was no organizational machinery in the Western alliance to respond effectively. Soon, therefore, he would submit "specific proposals" to Eisenhower and Macmillan, in the "spirit" of his 1958 memorandum but developed with "greater precision."[188]

It was, interestingly, Macmillan who first followed up on the seeming revival of interest in tripartitism with specific proposals. During the meeting in Paris, the prime minister had been notably more responsive than Eisenhower to de Gaulle's exhortations.[189] Macmillan's responsiveness was inspired at least in part by his growing conviction that Britain's sliding position in the world made a rapprochement with Paris – and, in particular, the European Economic Community – unavoidable. On May 25, he preempted anything de Gaulle might have had in mind by proposing a system of tripartite consultations that was in essence an elaboration of Eisenhower's earlier suggestions. Macmillan suggested that the foreign ministers of the three countries should meet regularly – "about every two or three months" – and that each would designate a trusted official to prepare the agenda "with the approval of the Heads of Governments." Eisenhower's response was supportive and he immediately assigned Undersecretary of State for Political Affairs Livingston Merchant to the task of preparing tripartite consultations between the foreign ministers.[190] In de Gaulle's view, however, Macmillan's proposals fell short of his aims. Although he expressed satisfaction at the procedures for political consultation, he emphasized that basic French demands regarding joint strategic decisions and military planning were still not incorporated and, as usual, suggested that the members of the Standing Group lay the groundwork for arrangements in this field.[191] Macmillan's proposal moreover breathed the same informality – and hence noncommittal nature – of Eisenhower's earlier proposals. The British prime minister had made clear he did not want to establish a "formal Secretariat" and emphasized that tripartite meetings should not "upset the susceptibilities of other Governments."[192]

De Gaulle's memorandum diplomacy had now arrived at an important crossroads. He had been offered all that could be offered without provoking a reaction from the other allies that would undermine NATO in a different way.[193] The question was now whether de Gaulle could be given meaningful satisfaction in the strategic field without a major dislocation of NATO, too. De Gaulle's reply to Macmillan's bid made clear that his demands had not changed since his original memorandum proposal, causing a high State Department official to admit that "...frankly we were puzzled as to how to proceed on our French problem."[194] Eisenhower, however, was not yet ready to abandon his efforts to accommodate de Gaulle. His determination to give the French requests in the strategic field careful scrutiny opened up the last cycle of his effort to come to terms with de Gaulle's tripartite proposal. He had not shed his reservations on implicating NATO institutions, such as the Standing Group, in tripartite strategic consultations, out of fear of seeming to endorse an "inner directorate."[195] Eisenhower was nonetheless pondering hard if he could find "some way [by which] we could really get outside of this standing group into a real tripartite discussion of strategic and military questions in return for which de Gaulle would get on with NATO."[196] On June 30, Eisenhower inquired with Macmillan whether military talks could not be staged in Washington to which the French could assign their representative to the Standing Group while they would delegate another high military official. "This may not be the organized strategic planning on a global scale, including the question of the use of nuclear weapons anywhere, which he [de Gaulle] appears to want," wrote Eisenhower. "It is, however, a definite move forward in the field of military consultation which may in the end strengthen our alliance."[197]

On August 2, 1960, Eisenhower indeed made these concessions in a letter to de Gaulle. For the first time, he agreed to tripartite discussions on military-strategic issues.[198] The American president was as close as he ever came to accepting de Gaulle's tripartite design. De Gaulle, meanwhile, believed the time was ripe for a passionate reiteration of his original tripartite proposal. Was he perhaps contemplating the unfavorable implications of a change of rule in Washington after the presidential elections later that year? At any rate, writing to London and Washington on August 9, he made an urgent appeal to convene in September in order to agree on the tripartite plan he had set forth nearly two years ago. To Eisenhower:

My dear Mr. President, my dear friend, I feel that we – you, Mr. Macmillan, and I – hold in our hands an opportunity, which is at the same time a definite opportunity and a very temporary one, to organize a true political and strategic cooperation of our West in the face of the numerous and dangerous threats that confront us. We can do this all the better because, with respect to the basis of the problems, our views and our intentions are still quite close. If we three together were to confront this problem shoulder to shoulder, it seems to me that we could work out a joint plan for organizing our united action on world problems and for reorganizing the Alliance.[199]

It seems that de Gaulle indeed cherished some hope that this time he could reach an understanding with the American president. He strongly urged Macmillan to persuade Eisenhower to agree to a meeting in September.[200] Be that as it may, de Gaulle's move was not received well in Washington, for as Secretary of State Herter said in a conversation with Eisenhower, "it always comes down to de Gaulle never agreeing with anyone else but wanting everybody to agree with him."[201] Eisenhower's own reaction was indecisive and he did not respond until nearly a month later. "In talking to me," he laid down in a memorandum, "he [President de Gaulle] had always been so hazy in propounding his theories that apparenty I have never been able to respond adequately." Eisenhower seemed to realize that he could not accommodate de Gaulle as long he was not prepared to honor the latter's demand for joint political and military decisions. De Gaulle truly envisaged a tripartite organization – not the United States or NATO – to act on behalf of the West. Such an organization would not only undermine the loyalty to NATO of the other allies, most importantly of West Germany, in Eisenhower's view a system by which the French and the British would be able to veto American policies would also amount to "a committee for inaction rather than for action."[202]

In mid-August, Livingston Merchant traveled to London to confer with Macmillan on de Gaulle's proposal. He conveyed Eisenhower's impression that the possibilities for accommodating de Gaulle were now exhausted. The American president had not yet decided on how to respond to de Gaulle's letter, but an impulsively organized summit meeting in September, as de Gaulle had suggested, would surely upset the other European allies. In addition, it could unnecessarily provoke the Soviet Union, especially since the meeting would inevitably be interpreted in connection with the delicate problem of Berlin. Merchant and Macmillan hence agreed to bargain for time with de Gaulle by playing up the importance of a meeting of the foreign ministers on September 23 (which had already been planned).[203]

This was indeed Eisenhower's position when he finally replied to de Gaulle on August 30: he agreed in principle to convene with Macmillan and de Gaulle but final decisions were to be postponed until after the meeting of the foreign ministers, at which occasion de Gaulle would also be invited to submit the memorandum he had promised at the Paris Summit. It was, however, the remainder of his lengthy letter that was most significant, for in it Eisenhower placed himself irrevocably opposite to de Gaulle. In fact, in a far more outright and candid manner than in his first reply of October 1958, Eisenhower rejected the thrust of de Gaulle's views and forcefully argued the primacy of NATO in American foreign policy.

Eisenhower first of all explained that NATO should be considered as the expression as well as the precondition of the "historic shift" in the American attitude towards Europe after World War II. The United States had not sought to dominate Europe, but had rather responded to urgent pleas from European countries to commit itself to their security. While NATO had thus become the cornerstone of US foreign policy, de Gaulle's public criticism of America's domineering ways and his equally public skepticism of its nuclear security guarantee could ultimately usher in a revival of American isolationism. As in his original reply of October 1958, Eisenhower moreover extolled the virtues of the alliance system in dealing with a global menace, emphasized the political sensitivity of the other allies, and pointed to American efforts to expand liaisons between the various defense groupings as a way of improving coordination in the global contest.

> Given the facts of the situation today I must confess that I cannot see how the three of us can so organize, as you suggest, a "real political and military cooperation" if that cooperation implies lessening or subordinating of America's close working relationship with other nations and other alliances or if it implies a reorganization of NATO whose effect would be to remove American forces from Europe.

Eisenhower then proceeded to rebuff de Gaulle's thesis on the obsolescence of military integration and the inherent national nature of defense.

> I frankly must confess that I cannot understand completely your reasoning. It seems to me that to return to a prewar system of alliances, that is to say, a coalition of powers whose military efforts are not closely joined together, would diminish greatly the effectiveness of a Western alliance. The revolution in military strategy and military technology makes it more, not less, essential that nations integrate their military efforts. National forces fulfilling national missions each on its own soil could well result in a completely ineffective defense force. ... any such policy would compel the return of American troops to this hemisphere.

In the same vein, the US president revealed his private distress over the withdrawal of the French Mediterranean Fleet in the spring of 1959, since it caused "a major breach in the NATO wall of solidarity" – and he noted that in many other areas France had also withheld its cooperation. He felt strongly that the French government – since it had publicly as well as privately stressed the need for reforms – bore a responsibility towards the members of NATO to come up with concrete proposals: "Otherwise, does not the continual stress on the supposed inadequacies of NATO merely weaken it further?" Eisenhower also refuted the alleged lack of "unison" in Western policies on the Congo to which de Gaulle had referred in his letter of August 9. Arguing that intensive consultation had indeed taken place, he wrote: "If despite this process our positions remained somewhat apart, I doubt that any more formal or elaborate tripartite arrangements at whatever level could have altered this." Then, in closing, the American president adroitly pointed out a basic contradiction in de Gaulle's memorandum diplomacy and posed searching questions:

> I must confess, dear General, that I cannot quite understand the basic philosophy of France today. On one hand, France rejects the concept of close union needed to make effective the alliance's defensive forces, stating that such action takes from France the essential attribute of national identity. At the same time France proposes a close union of itself, the U.K. and the U.S. to work out common plans and policies with all the implications of the veto and of imposition of decisions on others which this suggestion holds. These two proposals appear to me incompatible. Additionally, I am sure our NATO partners would find them unacceptable.
>
> The role which France would want to play in a special tripartite relationship is also unclear to me. Do you envisage France speaking in this forum for the other continental members of the Alliance? Do you believe that it would be

wise to diminish the close relationship of my government with that of Chancellor Adenauer, a relationship which has since the war served to draw the Federal Republic firmly to the West? These questions puzzle me.[204]

Eisenhower's letter of August 30, 1960, marked the true end of his efforts to accommodate de Gaulle's demand for tripartite management of the Western alliance. A summit meeting of the three leaders, as had been proposed by de Gaulle, never occurred. De Gaulle did not respond in writing to Eisenhower's rebuttal of his arguments but chose to underline his differences with the United States in public. In a press conference on September 5, 1960, he spoke again of the need for reforming an alliance in which the United States was the dominator and, as in his original memorandum proposal of September 1958, referred explicitly to Article 12 of the North Atlantic Treaty. Stressing the inherent national nature of defense, he defended his decisions – taken over a year ago – on the French Mediterranean fleet and NATO's atomic stockpile on French soil. He even partially unveiled his tripartite proposal as he urged the three Western powers to cooperate on a political and strategic level in the world.[205] The Franco-American stalemate on the organization of the West was complete.[206]

On September 27, Eisenhower indicated to the British prime minister, who had come to New York to address the United Nations and found the president "rather ill and tired," that his ideas on improving relations with Paris were exhausted; on every approach from his side, "de Gaulle simply clams up."[207] The sole area where Eisenhower still cherished hopes of finding common ground with de Gaulle lay in the development of a multilateral nuclear scheme in which France could benefit from American advanced nuclear technology and know-how. Eisenhower was still resentful of the congressional restrictions imposed on his authority. The last stretch of his public career was therefore in considerable part devoted to making a "friendly gesture" to de Gaulle in this area and leaving a well-defined policy behind for the next administration to pursue.[208] Yet there is little doubt that Eisenhower had reached the end of the road in his efforts to come to terms with de Gaulle shortly before his departure from power. If his personal rapport with the General – going back to World War II and, despite their differences, enhanced during the two and a half years of their presidential overlap – had served to attenuate fundamental differences, John F. Kennedy's election to presidency would soon only widen the gap. But even Kennedy's arrival did not denote the definitive end of de Gaulle's memorandum diplomacy.

Memorandum Diplomacy under Kennedy

Even in the Cold War era of bipartisan foreign policy, many of the United States' policies were substantially modified when one administration made way for another. These modifications were bound to be more marked if the changeover was between a largely conservative administration and a largely liberal one, when an entire cohort of policymakers at the top- and mid-level was replaced. The new policy crowd had lingered for years in the margins of power, where it could develop a range of alternatives to the policies of the administration-in-office. While the new crowd obviously inherited the policies from the old one, it was usually also driven by a different set of concerns and predisposed to use dissimilar methods. As new policies were being introduced and international relationships were being reassessed, established policies inevitably got lost in the transfer.

De Gaulle undoubtedly realized that the discussions between Washington, London, and Paris on his tripartite proposal could easily fall by the wayside with the advent of the Kennedy administration in January 1961. This fate was only made more likely by their informal and guarded nature, which made it easy to overlook their significance for the future of French participation in NATO. The prospect of a transition of power in Washington may indeed have motivated de Gaulle to press Eisenhower and Macmillan for a hastily convened summit conference in September. An agreement between the three heads of state about some kind of tripartite arrangement would have established a clear marker, which the next administration would not be able to ignore.

Given Eisenhower's refutation in his letter of August 30, it is noteworthy that de Gaulle did not abandon his diplomacy for acceptance of his tripartite design when Kennedy came to office. In February, Prime Minister Debré invited an American embassy official over for dinner "to impress on us his strong feeling of [the] need for [a] coordinated US-UK-French position on international problems" and that such an arrangement would "tend to mitigate strains within NATO." Debré showed himself flexible on how tripartitism was to be achieved: "the important factor was that we had consultation and agreed positions."[209] Likewise, Ambassador Alphand was instructed to impress the importance of tripartite policy coordination upon the new administration.[210]

Most importantly, in March 1961, de Gaulle sent his confidant Jacques Chaban-Delmas, then president of the French National Assembly, as his emissary to Washington to press the tripartite issue. Chaban-Delmas, who had seen de Gaulle shortly before he left and had been fully expected by the American side to carry a message from the Elysée, put the idea before Kennedy in forceful terms. Since de Gaulle had "put the French political house in order" and "a vigorous administration" had taken office in Washington, he argued, the circumstances were now favorable for agreeing on an effective policy coordination mechanism between the Big Three of the Western alliance. Apart from parts of Africa and Asia, Chaban-Delmas implied that in any tripartite arrangement France would expect to bear particular responsibility for Western Europe, since it actively supported the goal of a united Europe and thus could serve as "a natural channel for the coordination of policies on the continent in the same way in which the United States and the United Kingdom are the natural channels for the coordination of policies in other geographical areas." Chaban-Delmas underscored that a failure to come to an agreement along these lines would, in the French view, set the West irreparably on the road to losing the Cold War. "Four or eight years from now it may be too late to proceed with such changes in methods, and thus to reverse the flow of events which, according to General de Gaulle, has been consistently favoring the Communists during the last eight or ten years," said Chaban-Delmas. What was required of the new administration was a genuine commitment to grant influence to its most important European allies, and thus to resist the "temptation" instilled by the predominant position of the United States within the Western alliance that "major decisions belong to the United States alone."

Chaban-Delmas even twice impressed on Kennedy the importance of his personal commitment to consultation and that the choice was his – as if determined to leave an indelible impression on the new incumbent. Interestingly, however, like Debré and Alphand before him, he played down the institutional formality that had been characteristic of de Gaulle's original proposal. He did not talk of a new security organization. Nor did he spell out de Gaulle's disapproval of NATO or issue warnings about reducing France's contribution to the alliance. "President de Gaulle," assured Chaban-Delmas, "is not against any channel of policy or any organization, and the President will find him a partner very easy to get along with, *once a policy of consultations is inaugurated*." (emphasis added) In the same vein, he underlined that "consultations should be carried out without irritating the sensitivities of the other Western nations and therefore on an informal basis." Nor did he restate de Gaulle's demand for a veto over the US nuclear arsenal or ask for American assistance to the French nuclear force. What mattered, Chaban-Delmas emphasized, was the coordination of policies when they are being conceived – and "not belatedly at the level of their implementation." Hence what de Gaulle seemed to be asking for through his emissary was what Eisenhower had already seemed prepared to offer: an extension of the informal strategic partnership between the United States and Great Britain. Did de Gaulle lower his demands to make them more palatable to the incoming administration?[211]

One month later, in April 1961, de Gaulle again called attention to his tripartite proposal when Dean Acheson stopped by in Paris. Upon Kennedy's request, the elder American statesman had undertaken a tour of European capitals in order to explain the policies of the new administration. De Gaulle's discussion with Acheson, however, must have confirmed to the Frenchman that Chaban-Delmas' mission to revive the tripartite proposal under the new administration had been in vain. Acheson stressed that the Kennedy administration strongly believed the political consultation process within NATO should be intensified and extended to geographical areas beyond the treaty's territory; multilateral approaches, he added later in the conversation, were more efficient in harmonizing policies than bilateral ones. To this, de Gaulle responded that he did not think NATO – being a military alliance – was the appropriate forum and that it would be more important for the three major western powers to intensify their consultation. Revealing the chasm that separated him from his American interlocutor, de Gaulle went on to observe that the United States had "the curious tendency to wish always to act as a member of some sort of group, whereas a state must have its own policy and ... the purpose of diplomacy was to bring divergent views of states into accord."[212]

The truth was that the Kennedy administration was even less inclined than its predecessor to accommodate de Gaulle's tripartite demands. Merely days after Kennedy's inauguration ceremony in January, Assistant Secretary of State for European Affairs Foy Kohler informed Dean Rusk of the Eisenhower administration's handling of de Gaulle's tripartite proposal and suggested that, since the regular tripartite discussions held at the ambassadorial level had obviously not satisfied de Gaulle's demands, "perhaps these discussions might be terminated." Kohler expressed many of the same concerns that had helped to determine Eisenhower's response to the tripartite idea: the potentially fierce reaction among the other NATO allies to what would seem a tripartite "directorate" governing their affairs; the incompatibility of any formal tripartite mechanism with the network of multilateral alliances that the United States had woven around the world; and the adverse implications for America's standing in Africa and Asia of what could easily be construed as some revamped colonialism.[213] Because French Ambassador Alphand emphasized to Rusk the importance de Gaulle attached to enhancing the tripartite discussions on the basis of his September 1958 memorandum, Rusk reluctantly declared himself willing to continue with the tripartite talks in Washington. But his response to Alphand's insistence also made clear that the Kennedy administration would not accord these discussions the priority considered necessary in Paris.[214]

It was above all the overall gist of the Kennedy administration's foreign and security policies that made it even less prepared than its precursor to accommodate de Gaulle. The Kennedy administration was uncommonly apprehensive about a resurgence of German nationalism, which encouraged it to reinforce the formal egalitarianism of the alliance, to downgrade the special relationship with Great Britain, and to disclaim French aspirations to speak for Europe. The State Department moreover became peopled with influential adherents to Jean Monnet's idea of European federal unity. These "Europeanists" regarded de Gaulle as their principal adversary. They fervently believed that the United States should prod the European allies along the way towards political integration. In yet another way, the Kennedy administration developed policies that were sharply at odds with de Gaulle's tripartite proposal. Fearing the loss of strategic control in the event of a war with the Soviet Union (or the threat thereof), it introduced a strategy of managed escalation and centralized control. There was virtually no sympathy within the Kennedy administration for the French nuclear effort and, in April 1962, Kennedy reaffirmed the American policy not to provide nuclear assistance to France.[215]

The Kennedy administration's initial approach to the tripartite issue was based on the assumption that de Gaulle "sees grandeur in very personal terms" and that his diplomacy was chiefly designed to achieve equality with Great Britain. In preparation of Kennedy's visit to Paris in late May and early June 1961, the State Department thus counseled that the new president extend "the same intimate relation ... in formulating world-wide policy" to France and "convince the General that he was getting the same opportunity to influence U.S. world-wide use of nuclear weapons *as he believes the British have*" (emphasis added). It was understood that de Gaulle would not give up his independent nuclear policy, yet the State Department hoped that "...the more of the special British status we can chop away, the less power the General may be disposed to invest in his own program."[216]

While the newly arrived Kennedy administration was assuming a notably reluctant stance towards de Gaulle's tripartite demands and the French nuclear program, Macmillan was moving in the exact opposite direction. He had been mulling over strategies to counter the seemingly deteriorating position on all fronts of the West vis-à-vis Soviet-led Communism and, in particular, to reposition Great Britain – and the European Free Trade Area of which it was the principal member – in relation to the thriving Common Market. In the summer of 1960, after much agonizing, his cabinet had already decided to apply for British membership of the Common Market, but the road was still littered with snags. During the Christmas holidays, Macmillan arrived at conclusions that would guide him throughout 1961 and which, taken together, he would half-jokingly call his "grand design."[217] In order to advance the British bid, Macmillan believed that the only way to assuage French opposition was by giving France great power status, which meant "putting real life into Tripartitism" and persuading the United States "to give the French some help in their nuclear plans."[218] In December 1960, Macmillan pondered in a memorandum for his ministers:

> Can what we want and what de Gaulle wants be brought into harmony? Is there a basis for a deal? Britain wants to join the European concern. France wants to join the Anglo-American concern. Can terms be arranged? [...]Are there offers which we could afford to make? And could we persuade the Americans to agree? [underlining in the original][219]

Realizing that Great Britain had little to offer on its own account and was therefore highly dependent on the Kennedy administration, Macmillan tried to draw in Kennedy and act as an intermediary between Paris and Washington to bring about the deal he had in mind. In January 1961, the British prime minister first paid a visit to de Gaulle at Rambouillet. In his diary, Macmillan recorded that de Gaulle, whom he had found "relaxed" and "friendly" during their six hours of private conversations, had seemed "genuinely attracted by my themes – Europe to be united, politically and economically; but France and Great Britain to be something more than European Powers, and to be so recognised by the United States... ."[220] Back in London, Macmillan proceeded to update Kennedy in rather optimistic terms, noting that the Frenchman ultimately had agreed on "exploratory Anglo-French discussions [...] to see if a plan could be agreed."[221]

The next building block in achieving Macmillan's "grand design" was his visit in early April to Key West and Washington to meet with Kennedy, his first encounter with the new president. Macmillan informed Kennedy of his government's decision to apply for British membership of the Common Market, which Kennedy did not hesitate to support. But he also impressed on the Americans that "a partnership in the nuclear field" would be necessary to maintain the unity of the Atlantic alliance – and he did not fail to report to de Gaulle that Kennedy had shown some interest.[222] Macmillan followed up his visit to the United States with a detailed exposition of his "grand design" in a letter to Kennedy at the end of April. He reasoned that British admission to the Common Market was important to the Western alliance as a whole, since "further political and economic division in Europe [between the EFTA and the EEC] will weaken the cohesion of the Atlantic Community, which must be the core of Western unity." Macmillan argued strongly that influencing de Gaulle was the key to British membership and that he and Kennedy "should be ready to go a long way to meet de Gaulle in certain fields of interest to him." This, Macmillan wrote, would entail a reform of NATO and a readiness to engage more seriously in tripartite consultations. In addition, he daringly proposed that Great Britain provide assistance to the French nuclear program, "whether by provision of technical information and 'know how' or by provision of war-heads," provided that the French nuclear force would not be independent but a "contribution to a joint Western deterrent."[223]

Whether tripartitism indeed had a future now depended above all on Kennedy's visit to Paris from May 31 to June 2 (prior to his encounter with Khrushchev in Vienna). By that time, Washington had already made clear to London that it would remain opposed to providing assistance to the French nuclear program.[224] Meanwhile, de Gaulle had remained skeptical both of the American willingness to share power within the Western alliance and of the depth of Great Britain's desire to become part of the European project. Despite the new administration's lip service to intensifying consultation with its allies, Kennedy's first months in office did not bode well. The first serious exchange of letters between Kennedy and de Gaulle had above all revealed their different perceptions on the situation in Congo.[225] In April, Kennedy – "still somewhat fumbling and over-eager," as de Gaulle wryly commented in his memoirs – had endorsed an ill-advised invasion of Fidel Castro's Cuba by Cuban exiles supported by the Central Intelligence Agency. Even in the opinion of Kennedy's favorite wise man Robert Lovett, the Bay of Pigs invasion was a "shocking example of what not to do as well as how not to do it" and "one of the worst disasters – not necessarily in scale but in the completeness of its failure."[226] What is more, Kennedy had not bothered to inform either Macmillan or de Gaulle of his intentions.[227]

Beyond the pressing problem of Berlin, Kennedy and de Gaulle thus differed on a range of issues. De Gaulle bore out his fundamental misgivings about NATO. "France will not tear down or demolish NATO now in an international crisis," he said. "But NATO cannot go on as it is indefinitely and France wants to reaffirm this."[228] He strongly cautioned Kennedy about the dangers of intervening – albeit with "military advisors" – in Laos or Vietnam.[229] De Gaulle said that no French soldier would ever again set foot in Southeast Asia; it is "a bad terrain militarily, politically and psychologically to fight a war." And to Kennedy: "I predict that you will sink step by step into a bottomless military and political quagmire, however much you spend in men and money. [...] I tell you this in the name of the West." And on Congo, too, their views continued to differ (in particular on the question whether the United Nations could play an effective role in resolving the crisis, as Kennedy believed). The Americans, de Gaulle concluded in his memoirs, "could not conceive of their policy ceasing to be predominant or of ours diverging from it. Basically, what Kennedy offered me in every case was a share in his projects." De Gaulle realized that "having taken stock of one another, we continued on our road, each carrying his burden and marching towards his own destiny."[230]

The two presidents also discussed the tripartite issue at some length. Although neither Chaban-Delmas nor Debré or Alphand had emphasized the nuclear aspect of the French memorandum proposal in their contacts with the Kennedy administration, de Gaulle began by highlighting the need for coordinating the use of nuclear weapons "by the three countries in the West who would have them." De Gaulle:

> These weapons are of a world-wide scope and might be used in the off-shore islands, in the Far East or even Cuba. It was not the affair of NATO to decide the use of nuclear weapons but a tripartite affair [...]. One day there should be a tripartite plan in this sense.[231]

Kennedy proved himself to be as forthcoming on tripartite consultations as Eisenhower had been when he had offered an extension of the special relationship.[232] French Ambassador Alphand had made clear during discussions in Washington that de Gaulle hoped his American counterpart would prove to be susceptible to his ideas.[233] Kennedy also had been given word on the eve of the visit that de Gaulle was primarily interested in the "problem of consultation and joint decision" and that the Frenchman expected Kennedy to come forward with proposals.[234] Kennedy indeed extended to France the guarantees that Eisenhower had given the British on consultations regarding "the use anywhere in the world of nuclear weapons, unless an attack were so imminent that our survival was at stake."[235] He also proposed that Secretary of State Dean Rusk work out a mechanism for tripartite consultations and a "common mil[i]t[ary] gr[ou]p to study such quest[io]ns as B[erli]n, Laos, Cuba."[236] De Gaulle responded favorably to Kennedy's willingness to enhance tripartite consultations, and Alphand has recalled that "great hopes were raised at the time that this problem of tripartite cooperation could be solved."[237] But Kennedy had stopped short of going along with tripartite nuclear planning. His accommodating pose proved to be too noncommittal to give de Gaulle much to hope for in the follow-up.[238]

The discussions between Kennedy and de Gaulle in Paris thus did not bring Macmillan's "grand design" closer to reality. De Gaulle had explained to Kennedy that he refrained from asking the United States for assisting the French nuclear effort, since "no one believes that any country will place its atomic weapons in the hands of others."[239] In addition, de Gaulle underscored to Kennedy his abiding reservations regarding British membership of the Common Market. While London strove for membership of the Common Market, the Frenchman argued, it had not at heart chosen to be "part of the European reality." De Gaulle made it clear that he considered this ambivalent attitude insufficient for accession; for Great Britain, de Gaulle stipulated, it was "either/or, either full, or none." Adding insult to injury, de Gaulle further chipped away at Macmillan's efforts to strike a comprehensive deal with his observation that the British "always try to play the part of a broker within any group within which they participate – even at times between the U.S. and the French."[240]

Despite Kennedy's concurrence with enhanced tripartite consultations, very little came of it.[241] General James Gavin, the American ambassador in Paris who frequently found himself at odds with the State Department, deplored the corrosion of the tripartite relationship. "To use a simile," he cabled to Kennedy, "what was at first in the form of an equilateral triangle has now distorted its shape to an isosceles triangle with de Gaulle way out at the apex with indications that he will continue to go further out unless drawn back in by the initiative of the US."[242] Gavin urged Kennedy to restore the balance lest de Gaulle decided to break free. His urging, however, was not heeded in Washington. De Gaulle's last correspondence to mention his tripartite proposals occurred in January 1962.[243] To this, Kennedy did not respond.

Yet it was Kennedy's handling of the Cuban Missile Crisis in October 1962 and his summit meeting two months later with Harold Macmillan on the Bahamas that probably put a definitive end to de Gaulle's memorandum diplomacy. Kennedy's deft handling of the missile crisis won him praise from most quarters and is still seen as his crowning foreign policy achievement. The president had risen to the occasion and had proven that, in spite of his young age, "at the moment of supreme danger ... a man of superior character and intelligence was at the helm."[244] It had redeemed Kennedy after the utter failure of the Bay of Pigs invasion and his awkward first meeting with Khrushchev in Vienna in 1961. But Kennedy's handling of the crisis also showed the hollowness of US assurances that it would consult the European allies during an international crisis. The need to consult the allies on a matter that could deeply affect their security was little more than an afterthought in the frantic deliberations in the White House. Roger Hilsman, the State Department's director of the Bureau of Research and Intelligence, put it this way:

> We were able to bring it off in Washington which was a near miracle, if we had tried to introduce several other capitals with all the punishing and pulling hostilities in those capitals, it's hard enough to get an effective coherent policy between our hawks and doves and everything else in the American government; if you had the French government and the British government with all their hang ups and de Gaulle's hang ups we would never have done it, it's as simple as that.[245]

It was Dean Acheson who pointed out to Kennedy that, since the allies had not been consulted on the course of action, they should at least be informed "in an impressive way." The colorful story of Acheson's subsequent visit to Europe and, in particular, of his furtive meeting with de Gaulle is well known. "Have you come from the President to inform me of some decision taken by your President – or have you come to consult me about a decision which he should take," de Gaulle asked the veteran diplomat upon his arrival. Acheson admitted that he had come to inform de Gaulle of a decision that Kennedy had already taken. After a brief discussion of the situation and having poured over, with the eye of a soldier, the aerial photographs of the missile sites Acheson had brought along, de Gaulle then said: "You may tell your President that France will support him in every way in this crisis."[246] Following Acheson's furtive visit to the Élysée, Ambassador Bohlen therefore had reason to report that "there is nothing [...] that we could complain about in regard to the attitude of the French government."[247]

De Gaulle's loyal stance during the Cuban Missile Crisis appears to have been premeditated. It had been foreshadowed, for instance, in a conversation he had had with Bohlen's predecessor James Gavin during the Berlin Crisis in September 1961. "If the state of affairs turns from bad to worse we will enter a catastrophe," de Gaulle had then said. "If such a catastrophe occurs, France will enter it together with the United States .... I say this on behalf of France, and I can vouch for France."[248] Kennedy's handling of the Cuban Missile Crisis, however, above all underscored to him that the United States was inclined to act unilaterally when the chips were down. Most Europeans, in fact, felt uncomfortable with the idea that their security was at stake over the presence of Soviet missiles on an island in the Caribbean, while this presence admittedly did not alter the strategic balance. They also sensed that the Cuban Missile Crisis was moreover in part caused by Kennedy's obsession with Fidel Castro's regime.[249] Robert Kennedy's secretly negotiated deal with Soviet Ambassador Dobrynin to remove American Jupiter missiles from Turkey and Italy furthermore caused concern that European security was being traded off for US security.[250] The lack of any serious consultation with the European allies on all of these aspects seemed to support the appropriateness of de Gaulle's insistence on a formal mechanism. On November 15, the embassy in Paris reported that de Gaulle had imparted to Prime Minister Macmillan that the Cuban crisis "had made him even more convinced of the correctness of the proposal he made in September 1958 to establish a directorate in NATO."[251] But the crisis must also have convinced de Gaulle once again of the futility of trying to persuade the Americans to accept his proposal, as he did not return to the issue again.

In addition, Kennedy's summit meeting with Macmillan in Nassau, on the Bahamas, from December 18 to 21 underlined to de Gaulle that he had not been able to break into the "special relationship" with his tripartite proposal. During this meeting, Macmillan accepted Kennedy's offer to provide Polaris missiles for a future British nuclear force which, together with equivalent American units, would be merged into a multilateral NATO nuclear force. This outcome was the result of a rare act of improvisation in international diplomacy, prompted by McNamara's abrupt decision to discontinue the Skybolt air-to-ground missile program on which the future British nuclear force depended. Intent on bailing Macmillan out of a politically dire situation at home, Kennedy offered to jointly build submarines armed with Polaris missiles. He also granted the British prime minister that – in a time of "supreme peril" – Great Britain would still be able to use its nuclear weapons unilaterally, thus leaving intact the notion of an independent British nuclear deterrent. While Macmillan left the Bahamas much relieved, the deal took de Gaulle, as well as other European leaders (such as Adenauer), by surprise.

Kennedy's subsequent offer to assist the French nuclear force in the same way – a makeshift attempt to mollify de Gaulle after the Anglo-American showing of unison – is widely known. Less well known is that, in the aftermath of the Nassau meeting, the Kennedy administration also considered the establishment of a "NATO Executive Committee" consisting of the United States, Great Britain, France, Germany, and one smaller country on a rotational basis. The idea, which was drawn up by Walt Rostow, was that this committee would be charged with "political crisis management before hostilities." Rostow surmised that de Gaulle would be interested in such a mechanism, since the Frenchman had often expressed his concern with finding better ways to coordinate the policies of the Western alliance. He also thought that, in the wake of the Cuban Missile Crisis, such a proposal would be generally welcomed by the European allies and that an executive committee would be a necessary addendum to the projected NATO multilateral nuclear force (MLF).[252] Kennedy indeed included the proposal in a letter to Adenauer on 12 January 1963. The establishment of "some executive mechanism," he argued to the German chancellor, would facilitate "swift consultation in times of crisis" and "make it possible to concert our views in regions beyond the NATO area."[253]

In some respects, the idea of a NATO Executive Committee came close to de Gaulle's original tripartite proposal, but there were important differences that made an agreement along these lines with Paris highly unlikely. First of all, membership of the executive committee would not be restricted to the United States, Great Britain, and France, the only countries that in de Gaulle's view could claim to have – as Kennedy's letter to Adenauer put it – "major world-wide interests and capabilities" as well as the only states within the Western alliance with a nuclear capability. Second, the arrangement would not involve the coordination of the use of US nuclear weapons. And third, decisionmaking would clearly remain the privilege of the North Atlantic Council in the American proposal.

The Kennedy administration never seriously put the idea forward in its communications with Paris and there is no record of it being proposed in NATO. The record thus suggests that Washington considered it at best a ploy to mitigate the negative reactions to the Nassau Agreement and to establish a dialogue with France. In this latter regard, despite the allied solidarity manifested by de Gaulle in the Cuban Missile Crisis, the breach between Washington and Paris had already become too deep to bridge. A few days after the Nassau meeting, French Foreign Minister Couve de Murville had told the American embassy that it was "now too late for de Gaulle's idea [of] tripartitism."[254]

The end of de Gaulle's memorandum diplomacy came, then, in 1962. The end of the Algerian war with the signing of the Evian Accords (in April); Kennedy's unilateral decisionmaking in the Cuban Missile Crisis in October; the Anglo-American meeting at Nassau in December – all these developments ushered in a more assertive phase in Gaullist foreign policy. De Gaulle shifted away from the triumvirate proposal toward a bilateral defense relationship with West Germany, leading to the signing of the Treaty of Reconciliation in January 1963. He shipwrecked Macmillan's grand design by vetoing British membership of the Common Market. When asked in 1963 whether he was interested in reviving his memorandum proposal, de Gaulle therefore replied that since the United States had preserved its "freedom of action," France had chosen to do the same.[255]

Conclusion

In some respects, Franco-American relations during the early years of the Fifth Republic rested in an *état de grâce*. The new stability of French politics, de Gaulle's personal stature, the fact that French policy towards Algeria was in flux, and the robust performance of the French economy had caused a remarkable improvement in American public opinion of France.[256] De Gaulle's jubilant tour of American cities in April 1960 was the most agreeable journey of his life, he volunteered to the mayor of San Francisco.[257]

Yet de Gaulle's popularity in the United States was at an artificial zenith, since his dissent was still largely hidden from the public eye. De Gaulle's tripartite memorandum of September 1958 confronted the Eisenhower administration with a formidable dilemma: both outright rejection and unqualified acceptance would have endangered NATO. On the one hand, de Gaulle made it clear that rejection would compel him to ultimately withdraw France from the military organization of the alliance. On the other hand, if Eisenhower had accepted de Gaulle's memorandum proposal, he would have concurred with a complete overhaul of the Western alliance – and this would have implied dismantling NATO as well. As the memorandum's reference to Article 12 suggests, the North Atlantic Treaty of 1949 would probably have to be revised in order to extend its geographic scope to much of the non-communist world. In order to establish a "triple rather than a dual direction" of the Western alliance,[258] such a revision would also be needed to establish the tripartite organization.[259] This organization would by implication supersede or perhaps even replace the North Atlantic Council. In addition, at the military-strategic level, the Standing Group rather than the American-dominated SHAPE would be the nucleus of the system. This group – composed of American, British, and French officers – would draw up joint plans for the employment of nuclear weapons, thus substantially firming up the US nuclear security guarantee to Europe and the more flexible mutual defense arrangement in Article 5 of the Treaty as well as reducing the potential for unilateral American action elsewhere in the world that could adversely affect European security. In de Gaulle's view, in this alliance organized on a tripartite rather than a multilateral – if American-dominated – alignment, France would obviously represent the interests of continental Western Europe. As the main military and political power in Western Europe, it would virtually be on a par with the superpowers; its nuclear weapons would give it a guaranteed edge over Western Germany. While Great Britain could presumably assume responsibility for the security of Northern Europe, the United States would be repositioned in a more distant role as an ally of ultimate recourse.[260]

The idea of full American acceptance seems so fictitious that the case is often overlooked. When Secretary of State Dean Rusk explained to Chancellor Adenauer in June 1962 that he saw the Atlantic community as "a nexus of interlocking special relationships reaching around the globe, including the Inter-American system, the Commonwealth, French associations in Africa and the welcome development of German interests outside Europe," this conception did not seem on the face of it all that different from de Gaulle's proposal to coordinate Western policies based on traditional spheres of influence, except that it involved no tripartite directorate and allowed a German role in it.[261] Acceptance of the tripartite design would have offered the United States at least one important benefit: the costs and responsibilities of the global containment of communism might have been shared more evenly. As France and Great Britain would have assumed principal responsibilities in designated parts of the world, it would presumably have allowed a reduction in expenditures for the United States. Eisenhower's overriding concern with balancing costs and commitments would thus have been addressed. America's overextended political commitments, too, could perhaps have been prevented or its implications have been attenuated. What, for instance, would have happened in South Vietnam if the problem had been dealt with on a trilateral basis and if de Gaulle's ideas for a neutralization of the area were incorporated?

The sheer audacity of de Gaulle's proposal for reorganizing the Western alliance and his unwillingness to compromise his vision nonetheless made it exceedingly difficult for Washington to come to terms with the demands contained in it. Compelled to preserve French cooperation in NATO, Eisenhower tried to find a middle ground where France, like Great Britain, could find some pride in being regarded as a major power in the West without uprooting the multilateral alliance system. "I really did try to meet his desire and need for some kind of world position and prestige," he reminisced in 1964. "I was offering him everything it was possible to offer [...]."[262] Eisenhower's search for a middle ground continued up to the end of his tenure and preoccupied him more than is commonly understood. Kennedy, too, gave ample attention to the tripartite issue during his first year in office, even as the gist of his policies ran counter to de Gaulle's vision. But a middle ground did not exist.

Although the United States thus never came close to agreement with de Gaulle on his proposal, it would be wrong to conclude that it was wholly unresponsive. In particular, Eisenhower took the threat to NATO seriously enough to struggle to come to terms with his wartime comrade. Both Eisenhower and Kennedy ended up extending the "special relationship" with Great Britain to France. Macmillan also encouraged Washington to be responsive to de Gaulle's proposal, hoping that this would mollify the latter's opposition to British membership of the European Economic Community. The United States was not prepared to engage in any substantive tripartite coordination of global security and strategic issues, least of all with regard to the employment of nuclear weapons. A French veto over the use of American nuclear weapons was out of the question. Both Eisenhower and Kennedy were, however, prepared to extend assurances to France that had been given to Great Britain: that Washington would consult Paris prior to the use of nuclear weapons anywhere in the world "unless an attack were so imminent that our survival was at stake."

With regard to coordinating policies towards areas beyond the NATO treaty area, Washington was prepared to engage in a series of informal discussions at the ambassadorial level, although their inconclusiveness understandably did not satisfy de Gaulle. More importantly, Eisenhower and Kennedy were prepared to extend the attributes of the "special relationship" to France on an informal basis.

Their offers in this area were not without substance, and they would have required some organizational arrangements. To be sure, Washington was not prepared to accord joint decisionmaking authority to any tripartite formula, nor was it prepared to lend unqualified support to French policies in Algeria as part of a tripartite deal as was suggested by some French spokesmen (in particular Debré). It should also be noted that the American overtures to de Gaulle fell short of the "special relationship" with Great Britain in at least one important respect: the United States was not prepared to provide the nuclear assistance to France that it provided to Great Britain. Eisenhower would have had no qualms about providing nuclear assistance to an independent French nuclear force but much to his chagrin found Congress in his way; Kennedy, as we will see, was firmly opposed to any such assistance. Moreover, since French views were bound to be less in accordance with the United States as those of Great Britain, the benefits of informal consultation were of less value to de Gaulle. If anything, the unilateral behavior of the United States in a range of crises – from Lebanon and Quemoy and Matsu in the spring of 1958 to Cuba in the fall 1962 – undoubtedly confirmed to de Gaulle the inadequacy of informal arrangements in order to influence American policies. Only with regard to Berlin, where formal treaties guaranteeing the position of France existed, was there a working tripartite relationship. One of the ironies of this history is that the management of the Berlin standoff persuaded Eisenhower to become more accommodating toward de Gaulle while it caused de Gaulle to lay his tripartite demands to rest. Another is that while de Gaulle tried to break into the Anglo-American combine, Washington was increasingly given to downgrading its special relationship with Great Britain and to urging it to join the continental European movement. Yet another is that when de Gaulle seemed to be lowering his demands to make them more acceptable to the incoming Kennedy administration, this administration was even less inclined than its predecessors to go along with any tripartite designs. The unanswered question, of course, is whether Paris and Washington would have been able to come to agreement if Richard Nixon had won the election of 1960.

Apart from extending the "special relationship" to France, the United States put much stock in enhancing the process of consultation within NATO in order to accommodate the growing restiveness of European allies. The problem with this approach in responding to de Gaulle's tripartite memorandum was that enhancing consultation was never a credible alternative to power-sharing. In particular, the Kennedy years showed that power-sharing could not be achieved through an agreed set of arrangements. These years provided plenty of evidence that Washington, particularly in times of crisis, viewed consultation as too cumbersome or at best as an instrument to mobilize allied support for American positions. The obvious lesson was that power-sharing could only occur in the context of a diffusion of power away from the United States. This diffusion would not be the result of US policies, but of the relative decline of the United States and the growing assertiveness of its allies. This diffusion of power is what de Gaulle, who obviously did not care to participate in the fiction of consultation within NATO, tried to achieve with his unilateral policy of independence. If anything, the United States' unilateral conduct during the Cuban Missile Crisis as well as the permanence of the Anglo-American special relationship evidenced by the Nassau meeting shortly thereafter probably finally persuaded de Gaulle that his tripartite proposal was leading nowhere.

What principal reasons caused Eisenhower not to accept de Gaulle's memorandum proposal? The so-called "Algerian interpretation" of the tripartite memorandum – namely that it was mostly intended to garner American support for France's Algerian policies – should be discounted as having influenced the US response in any important way.[263] Even though the memorandum proposal was considered among French elites as an instrument to compel Anglo-American support for French policies in North Africa, an interpretation that was instilled in particular by Prime Minister Debré and General Ely, there is no evidence that such an interpretation was prevalent in Washington. It certainly had little impact on Eisenhower's – or Dulles's – assessment of de Gaulle's proposal. It is true, as we have seen, that in August 1959, Eisenhower rejected the recommendation from the Joint Chiefs of Staff to support France in Algeria in order to gain French cooperation in NATO. This decision, however, was not connected to Eisenhower's rejection of the memorandum proposal. On the contrary, Paris was generally insistent that Algeria was an internal affair and would not tolerate any foreign interference. The Eisenhower administration had moreover understood that the proposal was linked to much broader issues than the Algerian conflict.

The principal reason for rejecting de Gaulle's tripartite proposal was that it threatened to disrupt an alliance system to which the United States had devoted considerable resources and political prestige. This system had served American interests well, since it allowed for US predomination while spreading the defense burden over more shoulders and upholding the egalitarian veil of a coalition. De Gaulle's tripartite conception of the Western alliance did not correspond with American notions about the Atlantic community as a scaled-down world community. The reactions from other European capitals – in particular Bonn and Rome – made clear that the Atlantic alliance would have faced serious internal unrest if the United States had gone along with de Gaulle's tripartism. Would Adenauer's policy to integrate Germany into the Western alliance have remained the guideline for German foreign policy? NATO Secretary General Spaak's warnings that West Germany and Italy would never agree to de Gaulle's tripartite proposal were daunting enough. "Rather than submit to a global directorate from which they would be excluded, they would reclaim their total political independence," he noted.[264] In the predominant American view, too, the political unity of the Western bloc might well have been dissolved rather than achieved through de Gaulle's tripartite proposal. Moreover, at a time when the East-West standoff in Berlin already strained allied unity, could one expect the United States to add further to uncertainty? Stability and unity of purpose in the Western camp were a natural concern for the hegemon. Furthermore, the drawing up of strategic plans, determining when and where and by whom nuclear weapons would be fired, would have hampered the strategic flexibility that is necessary in preserving an essential range of choices for national decisionmakers.

In explaining the American response, one also does well to consider Eisenhower's and Dulles's personal commitment to NATO. Eisenhower, it is true, felt that Europe's dependency on the United States should come to an end sooner rather than later. He insisted in December 1958 that,

> we will not always be the permanent foundation stone of the whole NATO alliance. Our original contribution of divisions and other forces to NATO was supposed to be temporary in character. Now we seem stuck with it permanently. We should ask when the hell these other people are going to do their duty. We have to get tougher with them .... These other NATO powers cannot go on forever riding our coattails.[265]

But Eisenhower's adhesion to the principles underlying NATO was unwavering. As the first SACEUR, he had played a vital role in the establishment of the organization in the early 1950s, and he kept in close contact with his successors and friends Alfred Gruenther and Lauris Norstad. As a military expert, he was moreover persuaded, in contrast to de Gaulle, that modern technology had made old forms of military cooperation inadequate. The range of new weapons, the speed with which they could travel, and their immense destructive power made the integration of military forces under a central command in wartime necessary.[266]

Other considerations, to be sure, contributed to Eisenhower's aversion to the tripartite idea. Particularly concerning the so-called Third World, where he saw much at stake, he had developed very little confidence in the sagacity of the European colonial powers. They failed in his view to adjust their attitude to the movement toward national independence. "Should we try to dam it [this movement] up completely," Eisenhower wrote Winston Churchill in 1954 in a particularly forceful attempt to persuade the British prime minister, "it would, like a mighty river, burst through barriers and could create havoc. But again, like a river, if we are intelligent enough to make constructive use of this force, then the result far from being disastrous, could rebound greatly to our advantage, particularly in our struggle against the Kremlin's power."[267] Eisenhower believed strongly that the American tradition was anti-colonialist and that the United States should sympathize with the drive for independence on the part of "dependent peoples." At a time when the United States was attempting to forge alliances of a different kind with the new states, de Gaulle's plan was hardly opportune. What, for instance, would be the reaction of the African and Asian countries to a Franco-British-American organization where Western policies and strategic plans for the Third World were decided? Would such an organization not be open to charges of neo-colonialism? As Eisenhower noted in one of many letters on the subject of Asia:

> This administration has been arguing that no Western power can go to Asia militarily, except as one of a concert of powers, which concert must include local Asiatic peoples. To contemplate anything else is to lay ourselves open to the charge of imperialism and colonialism or – at the very least – of objectionable paternalism.[268]

Evidently, de Gaulle's global tripartitism was not in keeping with Eisenhower's circumspect approach to building relations with the Third World.

The obvious excessiveness of de Gaulle's demands was a further disincentive for a positive American reaction; de Gaulle as much as admitted it himself. Despite de Gaulle's public assertions that France was reborn, it had mostly the characteristics of a nation in decline rather than of one experiencing rebirth. In the early 1960s, France was still deeply enmeshed in the Algerian conflict, prone to civil war and *coup d'états*. At various times, the General himself narrowly escaped death. In addition, the *force de dissuasion*, on the basis of which de Gaulle justified many of his claims, was still in its infancy; not until March 1960 would France explode the first atomic device and it would take many years before a substantial strike force was built. Given the legacy of defeat in World War II and the weak reputation of the Fourth Republic, how could French requests to be treated as a major power truthfully be acknowledged? Eisenhower's earlier cited cable to Dulles in December 1958, in which he remarked "that our friend should cease insisting upon attempting to control the whole world [...] even before he has gotten France itself in good order," makes clear that this was inconceivable.[269] "I was willing to recognize de Gaulle as an important world figure," Eisenhower later explained, "but he didn't have any means of exercising real world power."[270]

Finally, of course, the United States was hardly prepared to cede control over the Western alliance. "The trouble with de Gaulle was that he always returned to his September 1958 letter on the *directoire*," Douglas Dillon once said. "On this, de Gaulle really wanted the form and not the substance... ."[271] However, American jibes that de Gaulle was most of all interested in the appearance of influence – that he, as Eisenhower put it, solely thought in terms of "Glory, Honor, France" – were missing the point.[272] The reverse is probably closer to the truth: that the United States was only prepared to give France the appearance of influence while keeping the substance to itself. In the straightforward wording of one National Security Council document, American policies with regard to France generally amounted to "seek[ing] maximum French support for U.S. positions and objectives."[273] The tripartite meetings of the ambassadorial group in Washington, too, were mainly viewed as helpful in conditioning the French perspective to American views – not as venues for tripartite coordination.[274] The United States' prime concern was thus to gain greater control over French policies rather than to concede any control over American policies.

Could a quid pro quo have produced an understanding between Washington and Paris on the organization of the West? Certainly Eisenhower had no qualms about aiding the French nuclear force. He was, however, paralyzed by Congressional opposition to any agreements that might have ensued in the nuclear field. "I could have reached a satisfactory agreement with de Gaulle on the atom thing except for the law," Eisenhower complained in retrospect.[275] It is moreover doubtful whether de Gaulle, given his determination to preserve the independence of the French nuclear force, would have attenuated his demands as part of a trade-off involving American assistance to the French nuclear program. In contrast to his willingness to help out in the nuclear realm, Eisenhower was not prepared to give France a blank check on Algeria in return for French cooperation in NATO. As we have seen, his anti-colonialism and keen sensitivity to public opinion in the Third World impeded a deal of this kind. The truth of the matter is that Eisenhower was unable to strike a deal that could have satisfied both leaders to a sufficient degree. De Gaulle was not interested in anything but the accord he had proposed: a revamping of the Western alliance along tripartite lines in return for a more cooperative attitude within a sustained – albeit reformed – NATO. "It was all or nothing with him," Eisenhower concluded in 1964; "he wanted it at the top, all the way like Cicero and Pompey and Caesar."[276] Yet Eisenhower could only offer informal arrangements in response.

De Gaulle's rigidity has reinforced an impression that he was never actually interested in achieving the proposed reforms, and that he staged this *coup de théâtre* to set him free to execute his first priority – to withdraw France from NATO. John Newhouse, for instance, believed that de Gaulle purposefully sabotaged any chances of acceptance by showing the memorandum to Secretary General Spaak and leaking the contents to the other allies.[277] Wilfrid Kohl, too, argues that the proposal was "in essence a tactical ploy."[278] Elizabeth Sherwood draws a similar conclusion and quotes Couve de Murville who told her that "we never expected the United States to accept" the proposal.[279] Others have argued that de Gaulle's memorandum diplomacy must be accorded legitimacy on its own terms. Clear answers will possibly never be furnished, but with some justification the memorandum can be seen as more than a tactical ploy. Acceptance of tripartitism would have realized the Gaullist design in important ways: it would have gained France recognition from its allies as a nuclear power and as the supreme power in Western Europe, one whose vested global interests had to be taken into account. In spite of his rigidity, by making his proposal in secrecy, Philip Cerny has noted, de Gaulle indicated that "the negotiated *result* and not the memorandum itself, was meant to provide the symbolic reference point."[280] De Gaulle realized his demands were hard to swallow for Washington, but his memorandum diplomacy from 1958 to 1962 suggests that he held out some hope that the United States would eventually come around to his view. De Gaulle's passionate plea with Eisenhower and Macmillan in August 1960 and his overtures to the Kennedy administration as it took office suggest that he did not preclude the possibility of a positive outcome. All in all, Michael Harrison probably gave the most accurate description by presenting de Gaulle's memorandum diplomacy as the General's search for the "easy route to grandeur."[281]

"Our biggest argument as presidents came out of this idea [...] to have a publicly proclaimed triumvirate," Eisenhower said upon retirement about his relationship with de Gaulle. *New York Times* journalist Robert Kleiman judged that the United States should have been more receptive to de Gaulle's proposal and thus bore at least partial responsibility for de Gaulle's later intransigence. However, it is hard to conceive that either Eisenhower or Kennedy could have gone along with such fundamental changes within the Western alliance. This alliance had been developed for almost a decade with a great infusion of US resources and political capital and served American interests in the context of the Cold War rather well; the disadvantages connected with a sudden change of policy – specifically, the effects on America's stature with most of its other allies in the world – would almost certainly have outweighed the potential benefits. Eisenhower could moreover hardly have agreed to a design that would have conditioned American power to the visions of de Gaulle, the leader of a country that appeared weak and unstable and commanded relatively few resources of its own. If de Gaulle was indeed "asking for the moon"[282] with this tripartite proposal, it was also because he was asking too much for France.

Chapter Two

Whose Kind of "Europe"? Kennedy's Tug of War With de Gaulle About the Common Market, 1961-1962

In August 1954, efforts to establish a European Defense Community (EDC) foundered in the French National Assembly. This was a severe setback for the cause of European integration, but it was not its downfall. The American supporters of European integration, too, continued to support its advancement in other areas; as Eisenhower wrote to his friend Walter Bedell Smith in September 1954: "We cannot sit down in black despair and admit defeat."[1]

By January 1961, when Kennedy assumed the American presidency, the European integration movement had reinvented itself around the European Coal and Steel Community (ECSC), which had become operational in 1953. In the wake of the EDC's rejection by French parliamentarians, most supporters of European integration had understood that it first had to be pursued in the economic realm; economic integration, they had judged, might then – through some kind of bottom-up process – pave the way for political and possibly military integration. The integration movement had been rekindled at the Messina conference in June 1955 by the foreign ministers of France, Germany, Italy, the Netherlands, Belgium, and Luxemburg, despite an atmosphere of gloom. It had reached a new milestone with the Treaty of Rome in March 1957, establishing the European Economic Community (EEC) and European Atomic Energy Agency (EURATOM). Importantly, the "Six" had also confirmed the political aspiration of their cooperation, as the Rome Treaty had declared their determination "to lay the foundations of an ever closer union among the peoples of Europe."[2] By contrast, the rival European Free Trade Association (EFTA) of seven other European countries (often referred to as the "outer Seven"), established in January 1960 at the initiative of the British government, had never been able to take on a life of its own.[3] In fact, as Kennedy entered the White House, Prime Minister Macmillan was already actively preparing the grounds for British membership of the Common Market.[4]

There is little doubt that the support of consecutive American administrations was vital to the European integration movement; this support was also actively solicited by its leading proponents (the likes of Jean Monnet and Paul-Henri

Spaak). From the standpoint of its immediate self-interest, the United States might have been expected to prefer dealing with divided European governments that could be played off against another. Instead, a more enlightened concept of self-interest prevailed in Washington. In the reigning liberal mood of the age, the United States stood out in the eyes of both European and American supporters of European integration as a model for the advantages of federal union; it was no coincidence that Jean Monnet named his high-level lobby group for European integration the "Action Committee for the United States of Europe."

However, it is equally important to realize that, as Kennedy took office, the Common Market's future development was still very much undecided (in spite of the detailed provisions of the Rome Treaty). Would its economic policies be influenced more by free market liberalism or by state-led economic planning (as in the French tradition of *dirigisme*)? Would the Common Market be open to trade with the United States and other nations and be a beacon for free trade, or would it develop into a protectionist block impermeable to outsiders? Moreover, by choosing the formula of an "ever closer union," the Rome Treaty had presented integration as an unending process. Would the Six extend their cooperation into the political and military realm? If so, what would be the orientation of the resulting entity in world politics and, in particular, vis-à-vis the United States and the Soviet Union? Would "Europe" be a more effective partner alongside the United States, as most Americans hoped, or would it manifest itself as a "third force" given to political neutralism in the Cold War? American attitudes with respect to the movement toward European unity would clearly be determined by the answers to these questions.

Both Kennedy and de Gaulle entertained serious reservations about the Common Market, albeit for entirely different reasons. Both were determined to shape its future development to suit their diverging purposes. In fact, the Common Market became the main trophy in their tug of war about the future of "Europe" – and its very political and economic development would depend at least in part on the outcome of this tug of war. While their conflict focused on Great Britain's bid for membership of the Common Market and on trade liberalization, it took place in the context of sharply differing conceptions of Europe. Together with their disagreement over military-strategic reform, these differing conceptions were the main reasons for the crisis of January 1963 (which will be the subject of the next chapter). This chapter will analyze how, in the face of de Gaulle's European conception, the Kennedy administration tried to influence the development of the Common Market prior to de Gaulle's resonating denunciation of Kennedy's Grand Design in January 1963.[5] It argues that, in addition to Jean Monnet's remarkable influence on American policymakers at the time, Kennedy's policies toward Europe cannot be understood without considering their interrelationship with de Gaulle's plans for Europe. In addition to averting American decline, Kennedy's notion of an Atlantic "partnership" was designed to nip de Gaulle's aim of a "European" Europe in the bud.

The European State of Play in 1961

Macmillan and the Common Market

By the summer of 1960, as we have already noted, the Macmillan government had come to the agonizing conclusion that Great Britain had little choice but to begin negotiating to join the Common Market. We have seen, too, that Macmillan – pursuing a "grand design" of his own – tried to act as an intermediary between Washington and Paris in order to facilitate British membership, and that Kennedy gave his support without hesitation during their first personal encounter in April 1961 (the background to which will be discussed in the remainder of this chapter).[6] Four months later, on August 10, 1961, Great Britain finally gave formal notification of its wish to join the EEC. Reluctance was still evident in the announcement of the British government that its negotiators would need to take account of "the special Commonwealth relationship," "the essential interests of British agriculture," and "the other members of EFTA." Macmillan moreover publicly emphasized the economic motivations for joining the Common Market, thereby willfully disregarding the political implications of membership. In essence, he wanted Great Britain to join the Common Market without subscribing to the Rome Treaty's goal of "ever closer union"; in addition, he was determined to defend British economic interests to the bone. A British delegation led by Edward Heath arrived in Brussels in November to begin negotiations on Britain's entry. They were bound to be exceedingly difficult, but at last they had begun.

The road toward Great Britain's application for membership had been tortuous and painful, as is well known.[7] Notwithstanding Winston Churchill's stirring orations for a united Europe – even for a "United States of Europe"[8] – in the aftermath of World War II, London had from the outset stayed aloof from the European integration movement. Victory in World War II had set it psychologically apart from the continental European states as a nation vindicated, possessed with a vibrant national personality, and ensnared by global rather than regional interests. The experience of emerging victoriously from the war "was the defining experience, at different levels of consciousness, of every British leader for half a century,"[9] and it pervaded decisionmaking in London for decades to come. It is also important to recall that in the early 1950s, the relative decline of the British economy in the postwar decades had yet to make itself felt. Between 1947 and 1950, for instance, British exports rose some sixty percent in volume; in 1953, the British economy was still exporting more than twice as many manufactured goods as France and fifty percent more than West Germany.[10]

As a result, the British government was in some ways strangely disconnected from developments on the European continent. British officials had been surprised and dismayed by the French-led proposal for the ECSC in May 1950 (the "Schuman Plan"), which merged France's and Germany's coal and steel resources – the raw materials of industrial economies and war – into one pool. London continued to keep a distance from the ECSC despite its success, which – as British diplomat Oliver Franks once wrote – "cost us the leadership of Europe which we had enjoyed from the end of the war until May 1950."[11] Great Britain also did not participate in the EDC plan (named the "Pleven plan" after the incumbent French prime minister), which would have created a single European army with a single executive and a European defense minister answerable to a common assembly to be shared with the ECSC; this time it was only spared from exclusion by the French National Assembly's rejection of the plan. For the longest time, the British Foreign Office did not believe the Rome Treaty was going to happen. After it had been signed in March 1957, it continued to treat it largely as a trade issue to be left to the Treasury. The event had all but escaped the attention of Macmillan, who made no mention of it in his diaries.[12] And in his first meeting with de Gaulle after the latter's return to power, on June 29, 1958, Macmillan – perhaps hoping that de Gaulle's own antipathy to European integration would play in his favor – exclaimed that:

> the Common Market is the Continental System all over again. Britain cannot accept it. I beg you to give it up. Otherwise, we shall be embarking on a war which will doubtless be economic at first but which runs the risk of gradually spreading into other fields.[13]

But when the permanence of European integration had become obvious in the late 1950s and the twinges of British decline were increasingly making themselves felt, Macmillan had been compelled to seek some kind of association with the Common Market. His initial plan to dissolve the Common Market into a much larger free trade area – much like "a lump of sugar in an English cup of tea" – dissipated in late 1958.[14] The subsequent creation of EFTA was hardly more successful. By 1960, despite serious reservations, Macmillan was moving towards a negotiated entry into the Common Market. While the British government initially believed that its economy could hugely benefit from EFTA by importing cheap goods from the Commonwealth and then selling them freely within the EFTA area, the realization soon sank in that the Common Market was more successful economically and that Great Britain itself traded more with the Common Market countries than with the EFTA countries. By 1961, the British gross national product had already fallen much behind West Germany's, and West Germany had replaced Great Britain as the United States' main European trading partner.

The British shift toward the Common Market had also been caused by the deeply ambivalent and increasingly deprecatory attitude of the United States toward the "special relationship." In 1958 and 1959, the British government had tried to have the United States bring pressure on France in particular in favor of the EFTA. However, British diplomats ran into a fundamental lack of sympathy in Washington for its hesitancy towards European integration: "They blame us for standing aside."[15] President Eisenhower was strongly supportive of the Common Market and, in a meeting with advisers in April 1960, labeled the EFTA as "nothing but a counter-irritant to the Common Market." He regarded a "U.S. of Europe to be the possible salvation of the world and requested that we explore encouraging the Common Market to take in additional countries." Eisenhower thus urged the Macmillan government to join the Common Market, warning that "if a strong U.S. of Europe should emerge along with a strong U.S. of America, the British would be left out in the cold."[16] London thus had every reason to fear that a united Europe, or perhaps even West Germany, would usurp the privilege of being Washington's first ally. As Macmillan noted in his diary in July 1960:

Shall we be caught between a hostile (or at least less friendly) America and a boastful, powerful "Empire de Charlemagne" – now under French, but later bound to come under German control? Is this the real reason for "joining" the Common Market (if we are acceptable) and for abandoning (a) the Seven (b) British agriculture (c) the Commonwealth? It's a grim choice.[17]

The choice was gradually forcing itself upon Macmillan and his government. But Great Britain's chances of being accepted as a member of the Common Market ultimately depended on France – and hence on de Gaulle – rather than on the United States.

De Gaulle and the Common Market

When de Gaulle resumed the levers of power in the spring of 1958, most supporters of European integration feared that he would disengage France from the Rome Treaty, for none of the moves toward European unity of the Fourth Republic had met with his approval.[18] The notion of ceding state sovereignty to supranational institutions was clearly at odds with de Gaulle's article of faith that nation-states were the only realities and the sole legitimate depositories of political and moral authority. This belief was central to his entire political philosophy, together with his conception of France and its international role.[19] It had been the main inspiration for his opposition to the ECSC, the EDC, the EEC, and EURATOM; the Europe of the Communities obviously had no place in his vision on European unity, which would be based on the cooperation between nation-states and not on their integration in some kind of supranational entity. As he never tired of belittling the Rome Treaty in conversations with its proponents as "your little treaty of commerce,"[20] his intrinsically hostile views of European integration would hang like a sword of Damocles over the Common Market's head as long as he was president of France. His *Memoirs of Hope*, too, published after his resignation from the presidency in 1969, attest to his unrelenting distaste for the "doctrine of supra-nationalism" as "France's submission to a law that was not her own." Its pages bristle with disparaging remarks of the community's institutions and its supporters, deriding the latter as "myth mongers" and "so-called executives installed at the head of common institutions by virtue of the delusions of integration" and "surrounded by all the trappings of sovereignty" yet "helpless when it came to making and enforcing decisions." Somewhat paradoxically, they also make clear that he continued to view the Europe of the Communities – an "artificial motherland, the brainchild of the technocrats" which "carried all the hopes and illusions of the supra-national school" – as an acute threat to French sovereignty. He argued that French negotiators – "caught up in the dream of a supra-national Europe" – had already sold out the nation's interests to foreigners when they helped to establish the ECSC, EURATOM, and the EEC. With regard to the latter, the French agricultural interest had been particularly neglected.[21] "It would, therefore, be necessary to obtain it *en route*, or to liquidate the Common Market," he stated bluntly. Moreover, "while the Community was taking shape, I was obliged on several occasions to intervene in order to repel the threats which overshadowed our cause."[22]

De Gaulle nonetheless accepted the Common Market upon returning to power. In spite of his critique that French economic interests had been sold out by the Fourth Republic, de Gaulle recognized that the Common Market was in reality quite beneficial to the French economy. In his *Memoirs of Hope*, he particularly valued the modernizing influence of the Common Market:

> I was concerned with international competition, for this was the lever which could activate our business world, compel it to increase productivity, encourage it to merge, persuade it to do battle abroad; hence my determination to [practice] the Common Market, which as yet existed only on paper, to support the abolition of tariffs between the Six, to liberalize appreciably our overseas trade.[23]

Although this reading suggests that he supported trade liberalization, the fact that the guidelines for establishing the common external tariff encouraged high tariffs probably spoke in favor of the Common Market as well; de Gaulle was not driven by any strong desire to fully expose the French economy to the rigors of the open world market. French overseas dependencies furthermore profited handsomely from the creation of a European development fund. In other ways, too, such as in the area of social policy, France retained important privileges. Despite de Gaulle's objections to supranational institutions, he was sufficiently pragmatic to accept the Commission's proposals as his own so long as they promoted French economic interests.[24] In addition, by gradually forcing acceptance of a common agricultural policy among the Six, he could hope to make France – not Kansas – the granary of Europe. In sum, his government pressed harder and more successfully for the internal progress of the Common Market than any other member country.[25]

But de Gaulle had powerful political reasons, too, for leaving the Rome Treaty intact. Domestically, he had – for the time being – a clear interest in avoiding open conflict with supporters of European integration as long as France was still torn by the Algerian conflict and the Fifth Republic's constitution had not been fully accepted. His pragmatic approach to the Common Market helped to lay many minds to rest, whereas his larger view of European unity – and of France taking a lead role – held out great attraction to many parts of French society. Practical acceptance of the Common Market, based on a strict interpretation of treaty obligations and a narrow conception of the Commission's political author-ity, was thus fully compatible with his program of fostering domestic political unity.

As importantly, in the foreign policy realm, de Gaulle recognized that the Six provided a promising jumping board for realizing his encompassing vision of European political unity and for buttressing France's policy of grandeur. For all his talk of independence and his willingness to go it alone, de Gaulle understood that France, given its size, would need the concurrence of other states with its international vision in order to play a role of international consequence and ac-claim. He was therefore determined to use the composition of the Common Mar-ket bequeathed by the Rome Treaty in order to achieve his larger goal of reinstat-ing France as a world power and of a "united" Europe as an independent "voice" vis-à-vis the superpowers. One important difference with Europeans of a federal-ist persuasion, the likes of Jean Monnet, was that de Gaulle wanted to build Euro-pean unity by making the nation-state the basic entity of an expanding confedera-tion of like-minded and interested states through a process of "systematic rapprochement" – and hence not by transcending the nation-state through a process of ongoing integration.[26] Another difference was that he charged the movement toward European unity with a rather different political vocation. Whereas integra-tionists were generally pro-American in the sense that they looked to the United States for political inspiration, military protection, and financial nourishment, de Gaulle introduced the vague but pervasive notion of "Europeanism" – in essence, acceptance of the French view of "Europe" as independent from both super-powers – as the French litmus test for all aspirants to the Common Market's membership.

At the onset of the 1960s, political – and indeed military – cooperation between the Six could still be made to fit the consuming aim expressed in de Gaulle's war memoirs of persuading "the states along the Rhine, the Alps, and the Pyrenees to form a political, economic, and strategic bloc" and "to establish this organization as one of the three world powers."[27] While the Cold War dictated an alliance with the United States for the foreseeable future, there was no question that the cooperation between European states he had in mind could ultimately replace the Atlantic alliance as the guarantor of peace on the European continent. France's aim, he reiterated in May 1960, was:

> to contribute to building Western Europe into a political, economic, cultural and human group, organized for action, progress and defense...[...] If the Atlantic Alliance is necessary at present for the security of France and the other free peoples of our continent, they must, behind this shield, organize to achieve their joint power and development.[28] [emphasis added]

De Gaulle, Adenauer, and the Fouchet Plan

De Gaulle also accepted the Common Market with an eye on Germany. Paris and Bonn would, in his view, have to form the critical axis around which the other continental European states would revolve. Germany thus had to be tied to France for political as well as economic reasons, on terms favorable to France. The Common Market was the answer, because it established a grouping of continental European states in which France could have the upper hand. Moreover, the Common Market could function as an obstacle for any independent German rapprochement with the East. Without the Common Market, de Gaulle feared that at some point Russia – not France – would provide Germany with cheap agricultural products in exchange for German industrial equipment. "As long as Adenauer is in control there," de Gaulle reasoned in early 1961, "there will be no deal between the Germans and the Russians. But later – I don't know. I am not so sure. There are important factors pushing the Germans toward Russia and the Russians toward Germany. ... That is why we must have a strong Common Market."[29]

One cannot discuss Franco-German relations in the early 1960s without recognizing the pivotal importance of de Gaulle's personal relationship with Adenauer.[30] His renowned first encounter with the German chancellor, at his tranquil country home in Colombey-les-deux-Églises on September 14 and 15, 1958, had laid the basis for their extraordinary personal rapport.[31] "Ich bin dahin gefahren mit sehr schwerem Herzen," Adenauer later explained to a political associate; "Ich habe da erkannt, dass er wirklich ein ganz anderer Mann ist, als wir uns vorgestellt hatten."[32] Much has been made of the shared influence of their Catholic milieus, Adenauer's Rhineland predilection for things French and his mistrust of the British, the bonding outlook inured by old age (Adenauer was 82 years old), and so on. Without this genuine rapport at the personal level, de Gaulle certainly would not have been able to weave the "network of preferential ties with Germany" that would culminate in the Franco-German Treaty of Reconciliation of 22 January 1963. (It also helps to explain why, after Adenauer's handover to

Ludwig Erhard in the fall of 1963, Franco-German relations took a turn for the worse.)

However, it is equally important to understand that this first meeting between the "General" and "der Alte" had the character of a political transaction from which each gained his due. De Gaulle – "with what magnanimity!" – was wholeheartedly prepared to mend fences with France's "erstwhile aggressor," thus going a long way in satisfying Germany's psychological hunger for international respectability. "Diese Stunde war das Ende einer alten französischen politischen Tradition, das Ende des [...] In-Schach-Haltens, das heisst der Schwächung Deutschlands mit Hilfe verschiedener Methoden..."[33] In addition, he recognized Germany's right to reunification and – at least for the time being – respected Adenauer's fealty to the Atlantic alliance given the Soviet threat and the vital importance to Germany of the American nuclear security guarantee. In return, de Gaulle asked of Adenauer, as he put it succinctly in his memoirs, "acceptance of existing frontiers, an attitude of goodwill in relations with the East, complete renunciation of atomic armaments, and unremitting patience as regards reunification."[34] De Gaulle thus gained Adenauer's general acceptance of four elements of his vision designed to ensure French military and political hegemony in Western Europe and to lay the groundwork – to be pursued later – for a détente with the Communist bloc prior to German unification. In addition, de Gaulle assiduously sought to garner Adenauer's support for his view of European cooperation. France would implement the Rome Treaty, de Gaulle assured him, but French requirements on agriculture would still need to be accommodated and any British advances to the Common Market "must be turned down as long as Britain remained economically and politically what she was."[35] De Gaulle's exposition also foreshadowed his initiative two-and-half years later to supplant the Common Market with an intergovernmental system of political cooperation between the Six. Adenauer, in turn, made clear that "Germany on the whole is unfavorable to the agricultural Common Market and anxious to give satisfaction to Great Britain," but he qualified this – no doubt to his host's satisfaction – by stating that "nothing is more important than that the union of the Six should succeed... ." And while Germany "had drawn distinct advantages from the mystique of integration," Adenauer concurred with de Gaulle that "there could be no question of submerging the identity of our two nations in some stateless construction."[36]

De Gaulle had thus succeeded in seeing eye to eye with Adenauer early on. He would continue to cultivate their close personal as well as political relationship to great effect throughout the latter's chancellorship.[37] From 1958 to 1962, de Gaulle would furthermore exploit the Cold War crises over Berlin to cement this relationship further and to gain Adenauer's support for his European policies. From the outset of the crisis, in November 1958, de Gaulle made sure that he appeared to be a more dependable ally than the Americans or the British. Paris had immediately assumed a hard line with the Soviet Union, which helped to calm down Adenauer's anxieties about deals being made over his head and contrasted in particular with Macmillan's eagerness to negotiate; in return for de Gaulle's firmness, Adenauer agreed to end negotiations with Great Britain on Macmillan's free trade zone at the end of 1958.[38] In early 1961, de Gaulle also scored high marks in Bonn for his continuing firmness amidst considerable anxiety about the direction that the newly arrived Kennedy administration would take with regard to Germany.[39] After the East German regime had begun sealing off the eastern sector of Berlin by building a wall in August 1961, de Gaulle called on the West not to yield to Soviet pressure[40] and in his end-of-the-year message he publicly criticized American and British contacts with Moscow. To Adenauer, de Gaulle's stance contrasted favorably with the Kennedy administration's considerably more muted response.[41] There is reason to believe that this stance persuaded Adenauer, in the course of his visit to France in July 1962, to consent to de Gaulle's insistence on drafting a bilateral Franco-German treaty of cooperation designed to bring his conception of European unity closer to reality.[42]

But de Gaulle first tried to advance his plan for European unity on a wider base than his relationship with Adenauer. The swift pace by which the tariff cuts of the Rome Treaty were being implemented in 1958 and 1959 and the impending resolution of the Algerian question had opened the avenue for de Gaulle to come forward with proposals for European political unity.[43] He first discussed his ideas generally with Italian Prime Minister Amintore Fanfani in June 1959,[44] but the drive for creating a "European" Europe out of the Six truly began in earnest in the summer of 1960 – in other words, just when the Macmillan government was coming around to the idea of British membership of the Common Market.[45] Between July and September, de Gaulle invited the government leaders of the Six – one by one, Adenauer first – to Paris, "so that France could present her proposals in a setting commensurate with the subject."[46] On September 5, 1960, de Gaulle apprised the public of his concept of European political unity in one of his majestic press conferences. He first set himself apart from the ruling doctrine of European integration and the community organizations, which lacked political legitimacy and efficacy and worked "on the basis of [supranational] dreams," declaring that Europe could only be built on the basis of the "reality" of the nation-state. Then he went on to outline his own proposal for achieving European unity:

To arrange for the regular cooperation of the States of Western Europe in the political, economic and cultural spheres, as well as that of defense, is an aim that France deems desirable, possible and practical. [...] It will entail organized, regular consultations between the governments concerned and the work of specialist bodies in each of the common domains, subordinated to those governments. It will entail periodic deliberations by an assembly made up of delegates of the national parliaments. It must also, in my view, entail as soon as possible a solemn European referendum, in order to give this new departure for Europe the popular backing which is essential to it. If we set out on this road [...] links will be forged, habits will be developed, and, as time does its work, it is possible that we will come to take further steps towards European unity.[47]

De Gaulle thus introduced a novel political instrumentality for regional cooperation and an alternative avenue for the future development of European cooperation. Such organized cooperation between European governments would be qualitatively different from the still predominant federalist idea of progressive integration between the Six through the establishment of supranational institutions. However, this system of organized consultation would not be free of commitment: withdrawal was not an act to be taken lightly, nor were third states to be placed on an equal plane with those within it. The diplomacy of the participating states would be disciplined to search for a common position of the confederation relative to third parties.[48]

When de Gaulle presented his ideas to the other government leaders of the Six, their responses were prejudiced by concerns about the implications for their ties with the United States and by a preference to involve Great Britain in the discussions about a political union. In particular the Dutch and the Belgians, de Gaulle wrote disdainfully in his memoirs, had been "orientated far less towards the Continent than towards America and England, and above all anxious to see the latter join the Six on no matter what terms."[49] The truth of the matter was that they also had little desire to subordinate their views to those of Paris in a political union that was bound to be dominated by France, in particular if Adenauer's Germany allied itself with it.[50] This is also why they rushed to the defense of the communitarian method as the preferred way to political unity.

So when, on February 10 and 11, 1961, only weeks after Kennedy's presidential inauguration, the heads of government and foreign ministers of the Six met in Paris, France's proposals for a confederation ran into strong opposition, in particular from the Dutch led by their Foreign Minister Joseph Luns. This meeting only produced a commission, chaired by the Frenchman Christian Fouchet, which was charged with developing proposals for a union of states. On July 18, 1961, reconvening in Bonn, the heads of government of the Six nonetheless agreed on a system of regular political consultation and cooperation, and the Fouchet commission was now requested to prepare a draft treaty for a European political union. In the process of negotiation, de Gaulle had conceded important language ensuring the primacy of the Atlantic alliance and guaranteeing the authority of the communities on the basis of the Rome Treaty. Yet, by the fall of 1961, he had made important headway in achieving his plan for a "European" Europe.

Meanwhile, the Macmillan government had notified its wish to join the Common Market. De Gaulle's biographer Jean Lacouture has wryly suggested that Harold Macmillan's outcry in his encounter with de Gaulle in June 1958 helped to convince the Frenchman of the political advantages of the Common Market, for "if his British neighbours were so very much alarmed by it, it must be of benefit to the Continent."[51] While de Gaulle was careful enough not to reject British membership out of hand, he was extremely reluctant, preferring to keep the British at bay. The Belgian historian Pascaline Winand stated that "de Gaulle's veto of British entry into the Common Market was very much in the cards as early as 1961";[52] his memoirs suggest that his concurrence with British membership was never in the cards. De Gaulle never left much room for doubt that, in addition to finding economic terms acceptable to France, British membership hinged on London's willingness to share his conception of a "European" Europe. This implied, too, that London would have to abandon its "special relationship" with Washington.

Monnet on the Potomac

Kennedy's European Inheritance

Upon taking office, the Kennedy administration inherited a strong legacy of support for European integration from previous administrations – a legacy that goes at least as far back as World War II. "Like the little girl in the nursery rhyme, a European union, from the point of view of our long-run economic interests, can be either very, very good, or horrid," concluded one State Department analysis in the fall of 1943.[53] American planning for the postwar period, however, generally looked favorably on the idea of economic unification of Europe, which was thought to help restore markets for American products and to contribute to the hallowed goal of trade liberalization. Early on during World War II, American postwar planners envisaged a Europe-wide customs union regulated by a single regional authority strong enough to withstand demands from national governments and to serve as the single interlocutor for non-European states, including the United States and the Soviet Union, on economic issues; they also made ambitious plans for monetary unification and for agricultural reform. The resurgence of European economic nationalism was also dreaded for its political implications. American postwar planners believed that European economic and political cooperation – or even, as Dulles put it in 1941, "the political reorganization of continental Europe as a federated commonwealth" – was necessary to forestall the resurgence of nationalism and to integrate Germany in a stable pan-European framework. While official support for European unification remained more muted, in part because Roosevelt did not want to alienate the Soviet Union and Secretary of State Cordell Hull prized worldwide trade liberalization as the panacea above all, the ground for the United States' postwar record of support for European integration was prepared during the war years. [54]

In the immediate aftermath of the war, grand schemes of European integration were put on the back burner of American diplomacy. But in 1947, as economic reconstruction in Western Europe became bogged down in a reluctance among Europeans to allow Germany to regain its industrial strength and the Soviet Union tightened its iron grip on Eastern Europe, American policymakers felt compelled to relaunch their search for the "creative peace" that would transcend nationalism in Europe. Looking for ways to make more efficient use of Western Europe's economic resources, their willingness to try supranational approaches grew. The notion that Europe's economic and political integration was in the United States' strategic interests became part and parcel of American policy planning. It was harnessed by a favorable body of opinion voiced in leading newspapers and by politicians from both parties. Washington was, in addition, increasingly prepared to give US diplomacy an activist role in prodding the Europeans, who were reluctant to cede national sovereignty, to adopt the new approaches that were seen to be required to lift the European economies out of the "morass of bilateralism and restrictionism."[55] The European Recovery Plan – popularly known as the Marshall Plan – was engineered to enforce cooperation between the countries receiving American aid. It provided, in the words of a Dutch participant in the negotiations, "the first stimulus to European integration and cooperation," eventually leading to the establishment of the Organization of European Economic Cooperation (OEEC) in 1948.[56] Continuing American pressure on the European capitals to forge a "single market" and liquidate tariffs also led to the creation in 1950 of the European Payments Union as a first step toward free intra-European trade and monetary cooperation.[57] On a wider plane, the Marshall Plan must be regarded as spearheading an unparalleled drive on the part of the United States to transform the political, economic, and even social make-up of Europe in the context of the Cold War. The economic and political integration of Europe was not only perceived as being in agreement with the strategic interests of the United States, it was also befitting the enlightened character of the United States' postwar policies and seemed to extend the American model based on federal institutions and the modernizing concept of "growth."[58] This mindset, both munificent and self-aggrandizing, helped the United States to overcome its initial reservations with regard to the ECSC and support its creation in 1949 as well as the follow-on plan for an EDC. The EDC failed; however, "the least one can report," wrote the *New York Times* in 1956 "is that a permanent-looking layer of American customs has spread itself across the old Continent in the last ten years, to the consternation of the elite, the delight of the masses, and the solid satisfaction of the vendors."[59] Upon the signing of the Rome Treaty, Acheson voiced the cheerful consensus within the American foreign policy establishment that "the success of the movement toward unity in the West of Europe is no longer in doubt," adding that "only the rate of progress is undecided."[60]

Given this heritage, the Kennedy administration was bound to be supportive of the European integration movement. In fact, many of Kennedy's European policies found their origin in the closing years of the Eisenhower administration. The Bowie Report, prepared for Secretary of State Christian Herter in 1960 by a group of officials gathered by Robert Bowie from all corners of the administration, deserves particular mention.[61] This report sought to develop answers to the wide range of political, economic, and military issues that were expected to hassle the Atlantic community in the 1960s. It is best known for its development of the idea of a multilateral nuclear force, but its scope was considerably wider than that. It foretold many of the economic and trade policies of the Kennedy administration. Fearing that the Soviet bloc would surpass the West in terms of economic strength by 1970, for instance, the report pressed for much closer transatlantic coordination of economic and trade policies in the framework of the Organization for Economic Cooperation and Development (OECD) – established in 1960 as a follow-up to the OEEC – and the General Agreement on Trade and Tariffs (GATT). In addition, it took a positive view of the overall economic implications of the Common Market, provided that the Six would be prepared to "reduce the common external tariff on a multilateral non-discriminatory basis" (foreshadowing, in fact, the Trade Expansion Act). The report made clear that, in order to secure American economic interests and continuing political support for European integration, the Common Market needed to be seen as a step towards free trade, at least across the Atlantic, not as a step away from it.

The Bowie Report also displayed the almost instinctive preference among Americans for the communitarian approach to European integration, both for political reasons – integration was thought to reduce the potential for a European return to nationalism – and for reasons of efficiency. At the same time, it expressed strong encouragement of Great Britain's membership of the Common Market, at a time when the Macmillan government was only just beginning to seriously consider this prospect; EFTA was sadly devoid of political content and British adherence to it, Bowie feared, could weaken the cohesion of the Atlantic alliance. While Bowie considered an Atlantic confederation or union with common institutions as out of reach for the time being, he kept it in view as "an ultimate goal" of American foreign policy.[62] More importantly, however, his report marked the emergence of the idea of a "partnership of equals" between the United States and the emerging Common Market. The partnership idea took account of the success of the Common Market in the late 1950s, the impracticality of urgent calls for an Atlantic "Union" by people like Clarence Streit, and the desire to influence the direction of the European integration movement. It offered the perspective of a more balanced transatlantic relationship, too, for without European integration, "equal influence on common policy is out of the question, whatever the forms or fictions."[63] In sum, the Bowie Report underlined that the European integration movement was viewed in Washington in the 1950s and the beginning of the 1960s as a largely congenial contribution to transatlantic policy coordination and the Common Market as a constituent part of growing and significant promise within the Atlantic community.

The Bowie Report was given an attentive reading in official Washington and its recommendations resonated in reports prepared for the incoming Kennedy administration. The influential Stevenson Report, for instance, which was in reality prepared by a task force assembled by George Ball, reiterated the need for breaking down transatlantic trade barriers and for the establishment of an Atlantic partnership.[64] In a follow-on report on foreign economic policy, Ball stressed the positive contribution of the Common Market, where "beyond economic unity lies the long-term prospect of political union on the continent."[65] The so-called Acheson Report, submitted to Kennedy in March 1961 and approved by him in April, did not explicitly endorse Bowie's idea of a partnership of equals, speaking rather of "an Atlantic commonwealth, in which common institutions would increasingly be developed to meet common problems." However, Acheson did express strong support for European integration as a step toward a "genuine" Atlantic community, "in which common institutions are increasingly developed to address common problems." With regard to British membership, moreover, he found that "the U.K. should not be encouraged to oppose or stay apart from that movement by doubts as to the U.S. attitude or by hopes of a 'special' relation with the U.S." and that "over time, the U.K. might become convinced that its position apart from the continent did not constitute a promising base of power – particularly if the U.S. was dealing ever more closely with growing strength on the continent." The Acheson Report moreover adopted 1970 – the year when, according to Bowie, the Soviet economy would surpass that of the West – as the year by which "a more tightly knit Atlantic commonwealth" must be achieved.[66]

The Americans and Jean Monnet – The Other Special Relationship

The Kennedy administration's support of European integration would take on fresh intensity and focus not just as a result of the abovementioned policy reports but also because of those who were chosen to serve on it. Kennedy's European policies would in particular be shaped by a generation of mid- and high-level officials at the State Department who felt a strong personal commitment to the European integration movement and were determined to use their time at the helm to further its cause. The history of the so-called Europeanists in the Kennedy administration stands out as an example of the overriding influence that a relatively limited number of officials – equipped with energy, ability, and sense of purpose – can exert on an administration's policy. Operating, according to one of its exponents, J. Robert Schaetzel, as a "loosely knit group, allied in its support of European union, sensitive to Europe's objectives and problems, and tied by close friendship to the Europeans involved," they were to become the driving force behind Kennedy's vision of an Atlantic partnership.[67] The Europeanists differed in particular with those, like Adlai Stevenson and Chester Bowles, who sought to shift the focus of American foreign policy toward the underdeveloped world. They distinguished themselves from others who continued to view Europe as the single most important area of interest and foreign policy activity for the United States by the wholeheartedness of their dedication to the European integration process and the precedence they gave to building up the Common Market.

The Belgian historian Pascaline Winand has emphasized the differences within the Kennedy administration between, on the one hand, the Europeanists (devotees to the cause of European integration) and, on the other hand, the Atlanticists and the Internationalists (both of whom sought to dilute European integration within an Atlantic or an international framework). While this distinction is helpful, it is important to stress that there was broad support within the Kennedy administration for European integration as well as broad agreement that European unification should take place within an Atlantic framework. As Winand readily concedes, "most Europeanists agreed with Atlanticists in the field of defense, where Atlantic integration was still the preferred approach."[68] But in other areas, too, the goals of European and Atlantic unity were seen to be compatible. As George Ball made clear to French Foreign Minister Couve de Murville in May 1962, the United States was prepared "to develop the Atlantic institutions as rapidly as possible to make it practicable for Europe speaking with one voice and America to work ... toward the achievement of common goals."[69] Ball was thinking in particular of remaking the Organization for Economic Cooperation and Development (OECD) from "a body that could collect statistics, make studies, and formulate ground rules for cooperation" into "an effective machine for common transatlantic decision and action... ."[70] In addition, he and other Europeanists consistently advocated the establishment of an Atlantic parliament.[71]

The European vision of a whole generation of American policymakers cannot be understood without the extraordinary personal influence of the "founding father" of the European integration movement: Jean Monnet. The story of Monnet's influence on Washington policymakers and his ability to associate influential Americans with his epoch-making European project remains unique. So great was Monnet's influence in Washington, that, in the words of Ernst van der Beugel, "the history of American policy toward the process of European unification cannot ... be explained without recognition of Monnet's influence... ."[72]

From an early age, as a scion of a relatively well-to-do brandy-making family from Cognac and as an investment banker, Monnet had developed an extraordinary personal network of international connections. These connections, it is fair to say, were particularly strong within the Anglo-Saxon world. This was in part the result of the practical, internationalist outlook common among the inhabitants of the Cognac region. As Monnet explained in his memoirs, "the people of Cognac were not nationalist at a time when France was." And:

> The power of Great Britain was universally respected and very impressive to a young Frenchman who was ready to regard that country and its Empire as the natural place for him to work. Between Cognac and London, there were direct links that by-passed Paris. [...] At Cognac, one was on equal terms with the British: in Paris one was somewhat under their influence.[73]

In 1905, at age sixteen, Monnet's father had sent him off to work with a wine merchant in the city of London for two years in order to learn the English language and way of life. He went on, at age eighteen, to travel extensively throughout North America to visit clients and to develop a retail network. His first encounter with the United States was a transformational experience that produced lessons for a lifetime. The young Monnet was instinctively drawn by the optimism and the level of mutual trust between people on the frontier and was struck by "the dynamism of a world on the move," which stood "in contrast to the static balance of the old Europe." He observed little order in American society, but it did not put him off as was the case with many other European travellers: "I became convinced that there could be no progress without a certain disorder, or at least without disorder on the surface." His American experience also taught him that resistance to change led nowhere: "Where change was accepted, expansion was ensured." As importantly, he learned to understand the value of the distinctively American skill of managing change. "The United States had retained the dynamism of the Western pioneers," he wrote in his memoirs. "But to that they had added organization. To organize change – that, I saw, was necessary, and it could be done."[74]

Monnet's association with the Anglo-Saxon world was reinforced in the remainder of his business career. In the mid-1920s, he was recruited by the American investment bank Blair and Company to work for its French subsidiary; in 1936, he moved to New York as an investment banker. As an international banker, Monnet negotiated loans to aid the recovery of Poland, Romania, Yugoslavia, and Bulgaria in what John McCloy later termed "the forerunner of the Marshall Plan."[75]

His links expanded into the political realm mostly as a result of his various appointments as government envoy during the war. In 1914, still only in his mid-twenties, he persuaded French Prime Minister René Viviani that France and Britain needed to coordinate their war effort much more closely, and was consequently sent off to London to put words into action. Throughout World War I, he worked energetically to establish joint organizations such as a Conference of Ministers of Commerce, an Allied Wheat Executive, and an Allied Military Transport Committee – all of which prefigured the establishment of the ECSC more than four decades later. In 1938, after the Munich conference had raised the prospect of a new war with Germany, French Prime Minister Edouard Daladier sent him on a secret mission to President Roosevelt to ask for American aircraft for France. In 1939, Monnet went on to resume his World War I task of coordinating supplies as the chairman of the Anglo-French Coordinating Committee, a position which he had defined as that of an "Allied official" with "an Allied rather than a national point of view."[76] In 1940, in a last-minute attempt to keep France in the war, he persuaded Churchill to propose a political union between Great Britain and France to the government of Prime Minister Paul Reynaud. When this failed, Monnet placed himself at the disposal of the British government. He was sent to Washington as a British official to help pave the way for the Lend-Lease Act of March 1941, which effectively ended the neutrality of the United States.[77] Monnet's role during World War II in eliciting aid from Washington, both for Great Britain and for France, was so crucial that Lord Halifax, the British ambassador to the United States, called him "one of the real architects of our victory," and John Maynard Keynes estimated that his efforts shortened the war by a year. After the war, he masterminded the modernization of the French economy during the diffi-cult reconstruction years as the head of the *Commissariat-général du plan*. With its emphasis on growth, productivity, and statistical analysis, the "Plan Monnet" in essence sought to emulate the economic dynamism of the United States.[78] "The French," he reasoned, must adopt "the psychology of the Americans," which en-tailed "the disposition to change constantly."[79] Monnet earned his place in his-tory as the founding father of the ECSC; what is less well known is how strenu-ously he tried to convince the British government to join it.[80] His Anglo-Saxon orientation is clear, too, from his decision to name his high-level lobby group for European integration – established in 1955 to re-launch the European movement following the EDC's downfall – the "Action Committee for the United States of Europe."[81] It is fair to say, as historian John Gillingham has done, that "the Uni-ted States was both the most decisive influence on Monnet's life and the main source of his power."[82]

There is no doubt that Monnet had his own "special relationship" with the bipartisan policymaking establishment in Washington that shaped American for-eign policy after World War II.[83] Some of his most important and intimate friend-ships, such as the one with John McCloy, originated as far back as to his banking days in the 1920s or even, as in the case of John Foster Dulles, to the days imme-diately following World War I, when Woodrow Wilson came to Europe to garner support for his League of Nations.[84] In the crucible of World War II, these friend-ships deepened and he developed new ones to boot. Power brokers such as Harry Hopkins, Henry Stimson, Felix Frankfurter, Robert Lovett, Averell Harriman, and journalists including Walter Lippmann, James Reston, and the Alsop brothers: they all became part of Monnet's web of influence and regularly consulted Mon-net about organizing the war effort or about the political situation in France.[85]

During these years, Monnet also developed a close working relationship with Dean Acheson which later on turned out to be instrumental in overcoming Acheson's initial qualms about the ECSC as "the damndest cartel I have ever heard in my life."[86] After the war, he was able to develop similar ties with Eisenhower.[87] Moreover, a whole group of mid-level American policymakers – Robert Bowie, J. Robert Schaetzel, David Bruce, and others – became intimately involved through Monnet with his European projects.[88]

Monnet's special relationship with the American foreign policy establishment cannot be explained solely from his effortless command of the English language or his affable demeanor. Monnet was very much his own man, a far cry from the archetypical French bureaucrat. He cherished a positive view of the United States throughout and, in many respects, operated on similar wavelengths with his American counterparts; for this reason, too, "it was in the United States that he found his closest friends and his most important relationships... ."[89] Monnet was both intensely pragmatic and visionary, which enabled him to view crises as practical opportunities to shape the course of events; "in his life and spirit," Jacques Van Helmont has observed, "change was inscribed as the supreme law" and "he accepted the disorder that followed."[90] Monnet's optimism and dedication to action "were in a way more American than European," remarked Henry Owen, yet another American friend.[91] As is more common in the United States than in Europe, he operated on the boundary between business and government, bringing a can-do mentality and managerial quality to government affairs. Although he had had "neither the help nor the limitations of university or a *grand école*,"[92] he very much fit the professional and personal mold of many of his Ivy League-bred friends from New York's business community and Washington's law firms. As he wrote in his memoirs, he visited them regularly because he wanted to base his judgment on "the wisdom of practical men" who "cannot afford to make mistakes – bankers, industrialists, lawyers, newspapermen."[93] To the many Americans who befriended him, Monnet was the European of the new mold who responded to their own hopes and aspirations: he was practical, forward-looking, pro-American, self-effacing, and, above all, capable of rising above the narrow historical and mental framework of the European nation-state. In their eyes, Monnet was the embodiment of the "good" European. His integration movement seemed to provide a coherent and forward-looking method to resolving the European Question that had befuddled US diplomacy for so long. It provided an opportunity to reconstruct Europe – or, at least, its western part – in ways consistent with America's fundamental interests and beliefs. Monnet saw himself as a "citizen of the Western world," one of his closest European collaborators stated; "he could not conceive that Europe and the United States could develop divergent futures... ."[94] A few years before his death in 1979, the European Council declared him "Honorary Citizen of Europe." Yet there is some justification, too, in seeing him as a first citizen – along with the likes of Dean Acheson, John McCloy, Walter Lippmann, and Clarence Streit – of the Atlantic community.

It is important to note that Monnet's circle of American friends was limited in one important respect. He was particularly well connected with those Americans who were both internationalist and liberally inclined (regardless of whether they were Republican or Democrat) and who were orientated towards Europe, many of them representatives of the East Coast Establishment. They – like Monnet – felt most strongly that the European nation-state had discredited itself as a result of two world conflagrations. Throughout his life, Monnet pioneered supranational solutions to solve supranational problems, which tied in neatly with the "one world" program of Wilsonians and later – in the context of the Cold War – with building up the Atlantic community. Although he has been ascribed the traits of a French peasant,[95] Monnet was cosmopolitan in the true sense of the word: not bound by local or national prejudices and at home in all countries and places. As Van Helmont observed, "he saw the future globally."[96] As a young man working for the League of Nations, he had lamented that those who had drawn up the League Convenant had been "careful to avoid setting up a genuine authority independent of the member states, or even a first nucleus of autonomous international power."[97] In the early stages of World War II, when Monnet's relentless pressure on Washington officials to dramatically increase the United States' military production raised suspicions in some quarters, in particular with Secretary of the Treasury Henry Morgenthau, McCloy rushed to the defense of his long-time friend: "As for [Monnet's] national loyalties, they are unimportant whatever they are. I know you can depend on his loyalty to the main task."[98] Given the war-torn and divided state of Europe, uniting Western Europe through the pooling of resources and markets became Monnet's abiding goal after World War II, as well as his lasting legacy. But the scope of his vision was considerably larger than that of merely promoting the Europe of the communities. "European unity is the most important event in the West since the war," wrote Monnet once, "not because it is a new great power, but because the new institutional method it introduces is permanently modifying relations between nations and men."[99] If nothing else, the closing words of his memoirs reveal Monnet as a true believer in the world community:

Have I said clearly enough that the Community we have created is not an end in itself? It is a process of change, continuing that same process which in an earlier period of history produced our national forms of life. [...] The sovereign nations of the past can no longer solve the problems of the present: they cannot ensure their own progress or control their own future. And the Community itself is only a stage on the way to the organized world of tomorrow.[100]

The Frenchman was, in many ways, as his British-Swiss co-worker and biographer François Duchêne put it, truly the "first statesman of interdependence."[101]

Given Monnet's near symbiotic relationship with the American foreign policy establishment, it is hardly surprising that when he came to Washington in March 1961, "he found a president surrounded by a battalion of his friends."[102] Monnet had already been consulted by Robert Bowie in 1960 as he was preparing his influential policy report. Together with his Dutch collaborator Max Kohnstamm, he also contributed his views about an Atlantic partnership to the Stevenson Report prepared for the presidential candidate by Ball.[103] Monnet was also quick to dust off his old friendship with Acheson once it became clear that Kennedy was seeking the elder statesman's advice, and he assiduously tried to make his influence felt in the drafting of the Acheson Report.[104] But the weight of Monnet's influence with the new administration was not just determined by his acquaintances at the top level. It was perhaps even more important, as The Economist observed at the time, "that in the lower levels of the administration, where cables are drafted and commanded, there are enthusiasts for the pure milk of M. Monnet's doctrine who make even Mr. Ball – and perhaps even M. Monnet himself – appear as moderating influences."[105]

There is no question that the Europeanists within the Kennedy administration were spearheaded by George Ball, first as the vigorous undersecretary of state for economic affairs and then – after Bowles left his post in November 1961 – the department's number two.[106] Ball's influence within the Kennedy administration is often perceived as one consequence of Secretary of State Dean Rusk's hands-off management. It is true that Rusk allowed Ball to wield his scepter over the European offices of the State Department with remarkable independence, which caused Ball to characterize Rusk in his memoirs as "my self-contained leader."[107] But it is equally true that Ball and the other Europeanists would not have been given such leeway if most American policymakers had not been inclined to encourage the integration movement in Western Europe. To the great majority of them, the American example underscored the validity of the federal approach, the importance of the rule of law, and the benefits of free trade, a large single market, and private enterprise. The predominant reading of European history was one laced with internecine warfare, narrow-minded nationalism and mercantilism – and the integration movement seemed to provide an escape from this sorrowful history. In addition, many American policymakers took it as self-evident that there could be no fundamental conflict of interest with a unified Europe even as there undoubtedly would be differences of view. As Schaetzel made clear, "partnership as a goal was not in dispute; it was only a matter of whether the Europeans could make sufficient progress to convert the objective of partnership into reality."[108]

Monnet's personal influence on George Ball is well documented. Their collaboration became particularly important when Ball joined the State Department;

indeed, many of the Kennedy administration's European policies cannot be understood without Ball's connection with the Frenchman. Ball had befriended Monnet during World War II. He then became a close collaborator of the Frenchman in the 1940s and 1950s, when his law firm, whose European offices he had set up in Paris, represented the interests of the ECSC. (Ball edited a journal, *France Actuelle*, devoted to promoting American investments in France.) Ball deeply admired Monnet for his grasp of modernity – he described Monnet as the "preeminently modern man" – and for his ability to view crises as opportunities to affect change in the desired direction. Like Monnet, Ball appreciated the value of personal networks. Most importantly, Monnet had turned Ball into an ardent advocate of the European integration movement, to which he would devote a large part of his considerable energy as a public servant. "Though hacking our way through the trees by different paths," Ball explained about his association with Monnet, "we usually came out at the same clearing in the forest, and on one point we were unanimous – that the logic of European integration was inescapable."[109]

Monnet's other personal relationship that carried much weight with the Kennedy administration was the one with Dean Acheson. Acheson had remained a staunch supporter of European integration after his State Department years. Like Monnet, Acheson anticipated that the ECSC, EURATOM, and the Common Market would eventually be supplanted by a political community which in turn could serve as a building block for the wider Atlantic community.[110] Although their correspondence had languished during the Eisenhower years, Monnet lost no time rekindling their old friendship once Acheson had been appointed the most senior foreign policy adviser to the incoming Kennedy administration. As we will see, they would cooperate closely during the Kennedy years to promote the idea of an Atlantic partnership.[111]

In general, the Europeanists in the Kennedy administration operated on Monnet's wavelength in a number of important ways. First, they embraced Monnet's view that European integration was an inexorable process; they tended to agree in particular with what Walt Rostow once called the "Monnet sequence," which presupposed that economic integration would eventually be followed by political union and a resolution of the nuclear question.[112] Second, they shared Monnet's aversion to "intergovernmental debating societies" and his belief in the conditioning power of institutions. His community method of integration, they felt, held out the promise of replacing traditional notions about national sovereignty and political legitimacy. It moreover tied in to the notion prevalent at the time that "the European nation state as presently constituted is too small economically, too weak militarily and too ineffective politically for the modern world."[113] One Policy Planning Council memorandum early in the Kennedy presidency, for instance, proposed that the United States should try to convince de Gaulle that "Europe has no future as a congeries of archaic nation-states compared to what it might have as an integrated power complex," and that Washington would welcome "a quasi-independent Europe on these terms."[114] Third, they believed that Great Britain had to join the Common Market sooner rather than later. Fourth, they believed that a unified Europe should be accommodated within a transatlantic framework. In addition, the Europeanists believed that considerable responsibility rested upon the United States to urge Europeans toward the goal of unity. Their historical task was to further the cause of European integration and the wider Atlantic community. "To a visitor," David Howell, a British journalist of the *Daily Telegraph*, observed during these years, "the Washington administration gives the impression of being prepared to go to almost any lengths to see Europe united, with Britain included, and speaking with one voice, economically, politically and militarily. ... It struck me as being ... like Rome at the time of Diocletian, the first emperor to realise that the Empire was too unwieldy to be ruled from Italy and that a separate although allied centre of power must be created in the East to keep the edifice together."[115]

Monnet vs. De Gaulle

If, in the eyes of the Europeanists, Monnet stood symbol for the "good" European, de Gaulle was his antithesis. Monnet's personal relationship with de Gaulle was hampered, too, by a fundamental incompatibility of views and personalities, an incompatibility that was only moderated by their ability to act pragmatically in the face of great challenges. Monnet's views were shaped by his experiences in international business; de Gaulle was groomed in the army's conservative cult of nationhood. For Monnet, the state was a passing phenomenon ill-equipped to deal with the pressures of globalisation; for de Gaulle, it was the alpha and omega of political life. Whereas Monnet spent much of his energy in World War I and II on coordinating the allied war effort in the most efficient way possible, de Gaulle was above all concerned with protecting national self-determination against his more powerful allies. "If one were to try to list all the divergences in the thinking and action of the two men, one would never finish," Marjolin once declared.[116] While they shared a complete devotion to their lifelong causes, each man – one a man of influence, the other of power – was on a mission of his own.

Their most important differences revolved around two questions: first, the relationship between the nation-state and the movement towards European unity and second, the relationship of a unified Europe to the United States. Their differing views on these two questions would to an important degree shape the debate in the 1950s and 1960s about European unification – so much so that, as Marjolin stated, Monnet and de Gaulle came to embody "two great currents of thinking" about Europe.[117]

To be sure, neither de Gaulle nor Monnet could afford to ignore the other – and they had proven at times to be sufficiently pragmatic to combine forces, both against the background of France's near-mortal crisis in the mid-twentieth century and in order to further their respective long-term goals. Initially, the pressures of war forced them into collusion, in particular after the Torch landings in North Africa in 1942 made it increasingly urgent for the Allies to sort out which Frenchman should be considered the spokesman for his country. Harry Hopkins had persuaded President Roosevelt to send Monnet to Algiers as a political adviser to General Henri Giraud. Monnet's contribution to easing Giraud into transferring control to de Gaulle's Free French in the Comité Français de Libération Nationale (CFLN) in June 1943 – often overlooked – was crucial.[118] Monnet also carefully worked his contacts within the Roosevelt administration in order to secure American recognition for the CFLN and for de Gaulle's follow-on provisional government, established in May 1944 (only weeks in advance of D-Day), as the de facto government of France.[119] This was anything but easy: if he was able to bring most of the government machine around, President Roosevelt and his Secretary of State Cordell Hull – to Monnet's growing exasperation – persisted in their anti-de Gaulle attitude and their reluctance to cede control over France's civil administration until the reality on the ground in the wake of the liberation decided matters.[120] During this confusing time, in the spring and summer of 1944, Monnet served on de Gaulle's provisional government (GPRF) as minister responsible for supplies – the only government position he ever held. Monnet's collaboration with de Gaulle was extended to the immediate aftermath of the war, as they sought to deal with the daunting task of postwar reconstruction. Visiting the United States in August 1945, de Gaulle – greatly impressed with the signs of prosperity and industrial prowess around him – asked Monnet to engineer the modernization of the French economy with the infusion of American dollars, a request that led to the Monnet Plan.[121] In sum, de Gaulle's and Monnet's ability to work together during the war and its immediate aftermath in spite of their differences was vital to the national resurrection of France.

De Gaulle, although he owed Monnet a great deal, nonetheless continued to suspect him as an "inspirer" and "the mouthpiece of the foreigner" who worked for American rather than French interests.[122] The jibes in de Gaulle's *Memoirs of Hope* against the "myth mongers" who spread the "supra-national doctrine" and the "so-called executives installed at the head of common institutions by virtue of the delusions of integration" were clearly aimed at Monnet and his sympathizers. There is reason to believe that de Gaulle viewed Monnet's Action Committee for the United States of Europe, financed in part by the Ford Foundation, as "almost a subversive organization."[123] "Il fait un très bon cognac," de Gaulle was prepared to say to Monnet's credit in a conversation with Eisenhower in 1962. "Malheureusement, cette occupation ne lui suffit pas!"[124] As for Monnet, his dogmatic pragmatism, his disinclination to engage in personal attacks, and his self-chosen role of acting as a broker of ideas among those who held power caused him to be less open in his denunciations of de Gaulle. Yet, as a representative of the democratic or "republican" tradition in France, Monnet was naturally wary of the ventures of military men into politics; as René Pleven stated, he "had made up his mind that the General would never share power with anyone."[125]

Monnet's influence undoubtedly colored American perceptions of de Gaulle. Since he knew how to operate within the French bureaucracy, he was the preferred conduit of American officials for influencing official French positions. "When things were pretty sticky with the French," one American top official recalled, "we'd go talk to Jean Monnet and somehow they'd ease up a little bit after that."[126] He was also often the chosen interlocutor when Washington tried to make sense of French politics, which naturally included explanations of de Gaulle's behavior. During World War II, Acheson for instance professed, "Monnet gave me fascinating glimpses into General de Gaulle, who was as yet only a controversial mystery to me."[127] After the war, too, he often relied on Monnet for advice on how to overcome the nationalist stubbornness of de Gaulle.[128] Monnet's view about working around the imperviousness of the General was indeed similar to the attitude of, in particular, the Kennedy and Johnson administrations. "You do not negotiate with de Gaulle," Monnet once pressed on the journalist Don Cook. "What you must do is to arrange conditions, set up hard facts, realities that he must take into account in making decisions."[129] Perhaps most importantly, the mere presence of Monnet as an exemplar of the "new" Europe emphasized to Americans that de Gaulle still stood for the "old" Europe. With some exceptions, as a traditional statesman de Gaulle never earned more than grudging respect among American officials, whereas Monnet was genuinely admired as a leader for being in the vanguard of modernity.

George Ball would develop a particularly adversarial relationship with de Gaulle, whom he habitually censured for belonging to the era of Louis XIV (the Sun King).[130] The notion that de Gaulle was an agent of Europe's atavistic nationalist past was prevalent in official Washington. Ball recalls that National Security Adviser McGeorge Bundy was "the only fellow that had some independent views. I always suspected and used to accuse him of being a Gaullist, and he had a different appraisal of the General from mine."[131] Yet Ball's antagonism towards de Gaulle was particularly vehement. According to Dean Rusk, Ball "considered de Gaulle a major obstacle to everything he stood for."[132] This antagonism was instilled in part by his intellectual affiliation with Monnet. In his memoirs, Ball left no doubt about how he divided his sympathies: "I have no doubt that, of the two, Jean Monnet was the greater." Whereas Ball praised Monnet as a "superlative architect" with a durable vision of Europe, de Gaulle was merely a "superb actor" leaving "only legends and transient playbills – nothing permanent that affects the lives or sensibilities of future generations." To those who admired de Gaulle for being unusually clairvoyant, Ball retorted that the French leader's "great weakness" was that he "habitually faces backwards, seeing the centuries that are past, not the future that is to come."

I saw de Gaulle as a twentieth-century Don Quixote, seeking to preserve old forms and restore old patterns, always trying to push a modest-sized nation into the front rank alongside superpowers organized on a continent-wide basis – in total disregard of this century's requirements of scope and scale. [...] His whole life was dedicated to prove that a "leader's genius," when combined with "the people's virtue," could somehow "reverse the verdict of number" – that he could somehow make France a superpower in spite of itself. [...] Monnet never indulged in such whimsical fantasy; he was a twentieth-century man, in contrast to de Gaulle, the brilliant anachronism who disrupted Europe by undertaking a tour de force beyond the reach of his extraordinary abilities.[133]

Given the sweeping character of his condemnation of de Gaulle, Ball's personal conversations with the Frenchman during his State Department years were surprisingly civilized and good-humored. In the mid-1960s, Ball moreover would find himself largely in agreement with de Gaulle's analysis of the war in Vietnam.[134] Yet their fundamental disagreement about Europe was sufficiently clear to both that de Gaulle once greeted his American interlocutor in the corridors of the Elysée palace exclaiming: "Monsieur Ball. Not you again!"[135]

Washington and the Fouchet Plan

Given Monnet's sway over American perceptions of European unification and of de Gaulle, it is not surprising that many State Department officials were distrustful of de Gaulle's proposal for a political union laid out in the fall of 1960 and then discussed among the Six at the Paris summit meeting of February 1961, just as the Kennedy administration was moving into office.

The State Department's concern was both fanned and laid to rest through the machinations of like-minded allies. Prior to the Paris summit meeting, Dutch Ambassador Jan Herman van Roijen in Washington warned Secretary of State Dean Rusk that de Gaulle's proposal for a political union risked splitting NATO. De Gaulle's plan, Van Roijen explained, was to ultimately establish an "inner grouping" under French leadership that would "develop common policies in advance of NATO meetings, which would then be communicated to NATO." The Dutch government was particularly concerned that "Adenauer would accept the French view" and believed that a statement by the incoming US administration on the fundamental importance of NATO would help to bring the Germans to roost.[136] Rusk subsequently sounded out German Ambassador Wilhelm Grewe, who responded that a number of developments, "particularly recent actions by President de Gaulle," had made the situation "ripe for such open and strong [American] leadership." The German ambassador even suggested, on a strictly personal basis, that Dean Acheson be put forward as successor to Paul Henri Spaak, who had announced his resignation as NATO's secretary general.[137] Shortly thereafter, the State Department instructed its ambassador in Bonn to impress Adenauer – "prior to his departure to Paris" – with President Kennedy's commitment to NATO and to announce that the new administration intended "to move vigorously to sustain and improve the unity, safety and well-being of the Atlantic Community, making full use of all available instruments."[138] As for Dean Acheson, while political custom made him ineligible, as an American, for the post of NATO's secretary general, Kennedy did ask him to prepare a policy report – the Acheson Report – on strengthening the Atlantic community; in April, after its recommendations had been approved, Kennedy moreover dispatched the elder statesman as his personal envoy to Europe – and to Germany in particular – in order to underscore his determination to revitalize NATO.[139]

In sum, there is little doubt that the Kennedy administration's early activism was in part prompted by de Gaulle's proposal for a European political union and the perceived need to influence its fate. A broad outline for intergovernmental cooperation was accepted by the Six, and the Fouchet commission was charged with developing concrete proposals. But de Gaulle's proposal for a confederation had been far from accepted at the Paris summit; "the doubts and misgivings were considerable," de Gaulle wrote in his memoirs, and "they all had to do with America and England."[140] After the Paris summit meeting, the State Department hence assessed that

> ... [the] evolution of de Gaulle's proposals for political consultation has been healthy and that [the] other five countries, through their vigorous reaction to possible less desirable features, have been able to divert essentials into constructive channels. This development is one which should be judged intrinsically and independently of de Gaulle's possible motives as to [the] role France might play, since [the] other five can clearly be relied upon in their own interest to achieve [a] relative balance among the Six.[141]

This position also reflected Jean Monnet's characteristically pragmatic attitude toward de Gaulle's proposal. When Foreign Minister Couve de Murville first outlined the proposal to him in the summer of 1960, Monnet was pleasantly surprised that de Gaulle had decided to come forward with anything of the sort and ignored his continuing jibes at the European Communities. "What mattered, in my opinion, was that he had taken a political initiative, and given it some solemnity," Monnet judged. "I only hoped that it would not turn into a great dispute."[142] For the remainder of the year, he thus sought to seize on the momentum caused by the French initiative and to develop common ground with de Gaulle. In November 1960, Monnet tried to generate support within his Action Committee for his design to use the idea of a European confederation proposed by de Gaulle as a stepping stone toward federation. In this context, he proposed regular meetings of a council of heads of state as well as of councils of foreign, defense, and education ministers. He envisaged these meetings would be prepared by "permanent organizations"; given NATO's primacy in the defense realm, the defense council would have to be limited to "defense cooperation in its technical and logistic aspects."[143] Monnet clearly refused to be a prisoner of a formula, agreeing with Ball that it "was a matter of letting the thing evolve" in the right direction – even if de Gaulle was the author of the initial movement.[144]

Towards the end of 1961, as the draft treaty was being negotiated by the Fouchet committee and most countries – with the exception of the Dutch – appeared to be in favor, the official attitude of the United States was still largely supportive. In early November, the State Department instructed its European diplomatic missions that it would favor any effort "to maintain momentum toward integration" and it was not opposed "in principle" to efforts by the Six "to develop common policies and closer ties in [the] defense field."[145] As the negotiations progressed, the concerns grew. In late November, for instance, Spaak informed American diplomats of his view that the draft treaty was "retrogressive" in comparison with the Rome Treaty because it did not offer the prospect of political integration.[146] Yet an agreement among the Six that was acceptable to the United States still seemed possible at the end of the year.

The second official draft, circulated in January 1962 by Fouchet, finally exposed the rift between federalists and confederalists, between Atlanticists and Gaullists. This draft bore the marks of de Gaulle's personal intervention. It was rid of its references to the Atlantic alliance. It called for a subordination of all economic and defense policies to the Union of States. The establishment of community organizations was not guaranteed as in earlier drafts, nor was a clause for a revision of the political treaty after three years – on which federalists had pinned their hopes – maintained. The new draft stipulated that membership in the communities would not necessarily entail membership in the Union of States, hence providing an instrument for keeping Great Britain at bay. De Gaulle had rescinded on concessions made earlier by the Quai d'Orsay. "The big question is ideology," he explained to Cy Sulzberger of the *New York Times* in early 1962. "States make the decisions, not supranational commissions with their fictions. States are the reality; the rest is fiction."[147] In the end, de Gaulle clearly did not want to settle for a negotiated solution that would have substantially compromised his European vision.[148]

De Gaulle's sudden reversal to old positions sharply raised concerns in Washington and elsewhere about the course of the negotiations about the treaty. After a conversation at the Elysée in early 1962, the American ambassador to France, James Gavin, surmised that de Gaulle wanted to transform the Six into a "strong military bloc" in which France would have the leading role. Fearing that Adenauer was being lured into the Gaullist camp, Gavin alerted Washington with his recommendation that "our relations with Germany should be such ... that whenever she is confronted with a choice between aligning herself with France or the US, she should choose the US."[149] De Gaulle's interference in the negotiations alarmed the British government, too. Upon the presentation of the second draft, Edward Heath, the British negotiator for membership of the Common Market, aired his concern that a European foreign and defense policy would not be consonant with the Atlantic alliance and suggested that Great Britain be involved in discussions on the political future of Europe prior to being admitted to the Common Market. Although Heath also came out in favor of the intergovernmental model proposed by de Gaulle, his pronunciations further galvanized Dutch and Belgian resistance to de Gaulle's European political union. On April 17, 1962, the foreign ministers of the Six convened in Paris to discuss a compromise draft submitted by France, Germany, and Italy. The meeting ended in disagreement when Foreign Ministers Luns of the Netherlands and Spaak of Belgium made clear that their governments would not sign a European political treaty until Britain could participate in the negotiations as member of the Common Market.[150] The Fouchet talks thus came to an end.

De Gaulle came to blame the British for making a resolution among the Six impossible. He was wont to point out, too, the internal contradiction in the Dutch and Belgian desire for British membership as well as a supranational Europe. Their position, however, was rather straightforward: either Great Britain joined the Common Market, in which case The Hague and Brussels were prepared to accept something less than supranational integration, or Great Britain did not join, in which case they would continue to insist on the supranational method in order to protect their interests against Franco-German domination. And in the background there was always the United States, which was strongly supportive of Monnet's federalist approach and always careful to protect the transatlantic link (or, in the parlance of the time, the Atlantic community). As Rusk told Ambassador Alphand in May 1962, the Gaullist idea that Europe should act as a third force independent of the superpowers touched a "very sensitive nerve" in the United States.[151] In a press conference on May 15, de Gaulle reiterated his view that states – not supranational organizations – were the sole viable building blocs for European unity. Integration meant that Europe would have no policy of its own and could "be subjected to the power of some outside force." Europe was condemned to "a kind of hybrid" in the absence of a country powerful enough to federate the continent under its aegis. "Such a federating country might exist," he added, "but it would not be European."[152]

Persuading Kennedy, 1961

Kennedy's Skepticism
John F. Kennedy had reached the presidency without deeply-held views of European integration or the future of the Common Market. If anything, as Arthur Schlesinger Jr. has observed, Kennedy "felt that Europe would work toward unity

in its own way. As for the character of this unity, he did not think nationalism altogether a bad thing. He knew that the United States would not lightly renounce its own sovereignty; this made him a bit skeptical of rigid supranational institutions in Europe. [...] he was not tied to Monnet's formula's – or to those of anyone else."[153]

As the son of Joseph P. Kennedy, a multimillionaire Irish-American businessman who had served FDR as ambassador in London from 1938 to 1940, Kennedy had had quite a bit of personal exposure to Europe – and in particular to the electrifying life of British aristocracy in London (which he enjoyed to the fullest). In the summer of 1937, he had also followed in the footsteps of other scions of America's wealthy by taking a grand tour of Europe. While in Europe during these prewar years, he had developed an active interest in foreign affairs and a feeling for the different "personalities" of nations. There is no doubt that the charged political atmosphere on the war's eve had caught his imagination. During his father's stint as ambassador, he had been granted privileged treatment from American diplomatic missions on his numerous trips throughout Europe. This had given him the opportunity to talk about the gathering storm in Europe with diplomats like William Bullitt in Paris, Anthony Biddle in Warsaw, and Charles Bohlen in Moscow. When the war finally broke out in September 1939, his father had sent him to Glasgow to handle the more than two hundred American citizens whose British cruise ship had been torpedoed by a German submarine. As a result of such experiences, at age twenty-two, Kennedy could give a firsthand account of how Europe had spiraled into war. Upon the end of the war in 1945, Kennedy, still only in his late twenties, had made a trip to Germany, visiting Hitler's *Adlernest* near Berchtesgaden. The breathtaking beauty of the place, mounted high in the Bavarian Alps, impressed him so that it even instilled a measure of awe for its reviled former inhabitant: "He has the stuff of which legends are made."[154] For the young and impressionable Kennedy, Europe was a riveting scene of political drama, national cultures, and engrossing personalities. It had whetted his appetite for international diplomacy and had introduced a dose of foreign policy realism.[155]

Upon his return to Harvard University in 1939, Kennedy had turned his European experiences and his privileged position as ambassador's son into a thesis on Neville Chamberlain's appeasement policy at the Munich Conference, which was subsequently published as *Why England Slept* (1940). It can be – and has been – read as a defense of his father's support for Chamberlain's policy of appeasing Hitler.[156] Yet, with his fascination for the conduct of foreign affairs and having matured as a politician in the early years of the Cold War, Kennedy had escaped his father's isolationist leanings. He unambiguously embraced the United States' international commitments in order to ward off communism.

As senator, however, his attention had become directed towards the underdeveloped world rather than towards Europe. He had felt that the perspective of the

American foreign policy establishment was far too Europeanist.[157] In *The Strategy of Peace* (1960), a compilation of his speeches on international affairs, Kennedy situated the majority of the "areas of trial" in Asia, the Middle East, Africa, and Latin America. During his days in the Senate, he had displayed much more active interest in Africa and Asia than in Europe. His most notable senatorial speech on foreign policy was the one in July 1957, in which he censured US official support for France's Algerian policies and called for Algerian independence – for which he earned the condemnation of Dean Acheson and others for undermining an important European ally. "The strongest force in the world is the desire for national independence," President Kennedy once explained. "That is why I am eager that the United States back nationalist movements, even though it embroils us with our friends in Europe."[158] On the enduring power of nationalism, his basic view was hence closer to that of de Gaulle than of Monnet. The fate of European integration had not occupied his mind, nor had he ever talked of a creating an Atlantic partnership.

Kennedy's view of the Common Market, however, was influenced not by his political views but rather by his acute sensitivity to the economic and financial computations of power – and in this area he would often echo his father's conservative opinions.[159] The United States was still by far the most economically potent nation in the world, but its relative position was seen to be in decline in the early 1960s. In his first State of the Union address, Kennedy offered a bleak picture:

> We take office in the wake of seven months of recession, three and one-half years of slack, seven years of diminished economic growth, and nine years of falling farm income. Business bankruptcies have reached their highest level since the Great Depression. Since 1951 farm income has been squeezed down by 25 percent. Save for a brief period in 1958, insured unemployment is at the highest peak in our history. [...] Nearly one-eighth of those who are without jobs live almost without hope in nearly one hundred especially depressed and troubled areas. The rest include new school graduates unable to use their talents, farmers forced to give up their part time jobs which helped balance their family budgets, skilled and unskilled workers laid off in such important industries as metals, machinery, automobiles and apparel. [...]
>
> In short, the American economy is in trouble. The most resourceful industrialized country on earth ranks among the last in the rate of economic growth. Since last spring our economic growth rate has actually receded. Business investment is in a decline. Profits have fallen below predicted levels. Construction is off. A million unsold automobiles are in inventory. Fewer people are working – and the average work week has shrunk well below 40 hours. Yet prices have continued to rise – so that now too many Americans have less to spend for items that cost more to buy.[160]

Kennedy viewed the Common Market above all against the background of America's economic problems. He was particularly concerned – to the point of being obsessed – with the deteriorating US balance of payments. "Next to the nuclear problem," Walt Rostow recalled, "the balance of payments ... worried him more than anything."[161] And if others in his administration tried to mute his concern, Secretary of the Treasury Douglas Dillon would be there to remind him that "we simply cannot ignore the basic disciplines of the balance of payments except at our own peril."[162] The international economic system at the time hinged on a fixed dollar-gold exchange rate of $35 per ounce and the American pledge to redeem foreign dollar holdings with gold (as agreed in 1944 at the Bretton Woods conference). This system extended enormous benefits to the United States because it had turned the dollar into a reserve currency. But it had an obvious Achilles' heel: it was dependent on the continued credibility of the American capacity to convert dollars into gold. It had been feasible only because, after World War II, the United States owned the bulk of the world's gold stock and ran a huge trade surplus. So when the American gold stock dwindled from $22 billion in 1950 to $17 billion in 1960, the value of the dollar came increasingly under pressure. In November 1960, less than a month before the presidential elections, these developments had forced a rise in the price of gold in the private market to $40 per ounce. Moreover, in spite of a continuing trade surplus, the annual US balance-of-payments deficit had turned sharply upward from $1.2 billion in the early 1950s to $3.4 billion by the end of decade. Since this deficit was in considerable part caused by foreign military expenditures and foreign aid, the United States was, in the provocative words of David Calleo, beginning to feel the pinch of its "imperial burden."[163]

To any observer at the time, the deterioration of the American economic position obviously contrasted with the remarkable economic resurgence of Western Europe, epitomized by the German *Wirtschaftswunder*. Throughout the 1950s, growth rates in West Europe of more than five or six percent compared favorably with the 3.5 percent growth rate of the US economy; gross domestic product per capita grew even twice as fast in Europe. By 1960, Western European countries were managing growing balance-of-payments surpluses and expanding gold stocks, and were well on their way to exporting, collectively, as much as the United States.[164] One result of Europe's economic recovery was that American policymakers increasingly looked to the Common Market to solve the United States' monetary woes.[165] This was further encouraged by the belief that European economic growth was to a considerable degree made possible by American leniency. European economic growth, Walter Heller (chairman of the Council of Economic Advisers) explained to Kennedy in the spring of 1961, had been made possible by an "aggressive development of export markets," low defense expenditures, and easy access to American technology and management expertise.[166] Given the protectionist leanings of some members of the Common Market, especially France and Italy, and the protectionist nature of the Common Agricultural Policy that was being devised, there was a real concern in some circles in Washington of a commercial "Fortress Europe." If high tariff walls were indeed erected around the expanding European market, American multinationals might even increasingly be tempted to move plants into Europe rather than keep their production in the United States.

Upon entering office, Kennedy's support of European integration was thus not firm. It was certainly much less solid than either Eisenhower's or Dulles's support had been. That his administration would nonetheless come out strongly in support of the Common Market and propose an Atlantic partnership was due to George Ball's formidable position at the State Department and the informal influence on the administration of Dean Acheson and Jean Monnet. Despite his former affiliation to Adlai Stevenson, Ball was able to develop an effective relationship with Kennedy. As presidential candidate, Kennedy had been impressed with Ball's economic foreign policy advice in the Stevenson Report. It was Ball who consistently advised Kennedy to support the emergence of an economically and politically competent Common Market as part of a program to counteract America's economic woes. The disadvantages of the Common Market's common external tariff for the US economy, he argued, would be more than offset by the increased volume of trade across the Atlantic and by negotiating lower tariffs. The economic relationship between the United States and Western Europe, said Ball in one of his first appearances on Capitol Hill, was "no longer a relationship of the weak to the strong, of the followers to the leader," but rather "something far healthier – the relationship of the strong to the stronger."[167] Ball was remarkably effective in overcoming the skepticism of the president. Kennedy learned to appreciate him as a man who "gets things done" and gradually came to rely on Ball for most economic and trade matters.[168]

Ball, on the other hand, did not have as high an opinion of the president. Initially, this was in no small measure due to his intense dislike of Joe Kennedy, whom Ball despised as a "rabid isolationist" and "capitulationist" whose "isolationist frog-croaking" had been a "debilitating influence when our civilization was fighting for its life." A close reading of Senator Kennedy's foreign policy statements had somewhat reduced this unease after the election, but Ball continued to consider Kennedy's concept of America's world role "muddy." As president, too, he did not consider Kennedy "profound in his analyses or his judgment." Ball rather thought of Kennedy as "intensely pragmatic" – which, in this case, was not a compliment – and, to his disappointment, found it "very hard to keep a discussion going within the framework of any large policy."[169] Ball was, in addition, seriously concerned with Kennedy's "obsession" with the balance of payments, fearing the residual influence of the older Kennedy. "Those of us struggling to keep the problem in perspective were apprehensive whenever the President was planning to go to Hyannisport for a weekend," and when Kennedy returned "we braced ourselves for a sermon on gold and the hellfire awaiting us." Ball was particularly fearful that Kennedy's preoccupation with the balance of payments would cause a shift in commercial policies "toward restrictions and protectionism."[170] Kennedy was clearly not as doctrinaire a free trader as Ball, and he was certain to adjust uncomfortably to the mainstream liberal consensus in support of free trade.[171]

As part of his effort to get Kennedy's support for his ideas about free trade and European integration, Ball carefully orchestrated meetings for the newly elected president with members of his personal network. The most important of these was Jean Monnet, with whom he continued to consult on major policy initiatives while at the State Department. When Monnet came to Washington in March 1961, Ball arranged meetings for the Frenchman with key members of the new administration and with the president himself. Monnet's schedule is testimony to the informal influence he wielded in American foreign policy circles, even after the change of administrations. In one afternoon, he met separately with Dean Acheson, Walter Lippmann, McGeorge Bundy, Joseph Alsop, and Theodore Sorenson. Monnet's informal get-together with Kennedy early in his presidency appears to have been highly effective. The American president took a genuine liking to the Frenchman and gained admiration for his European project. Importantly, he began to take interest in the notion of an Atlantic partnership between the United States and the Europe of the Communities.[172]

The concept of an Atlantic partnership, François Duchêne wrote, was "a licence [for Ball and Monnet] to develop the Community in cohabitation with America."[173] The partnership was also designed to ensure that the Common Market would follow a transatlantic rather than a Gaullist course. In order to persuade Kennedy to continue the enlightened policies of his predecessors in support of European integration, they would at a minimum have to ensure that European economic integration would work to America's economic advantage as well. In the military realm, moreover, the cooperation of the Six could only be supported if it would not interfere with the objective of centralizing strategic control within NATO. In the final analysis, Ball was only able to enlist Kennedy's support for an Atlantic partnership with a united Europe because he had provided an attractive, action-oriented foreign policy vision with which Kennedy could manage America's relative decline. Kennedy – and Rusk – gave Ball and the Europeanists at the State Department considerable leeway to expound their beliefs and to turn them into policy. Kennedy would also be prepared to lend his voice to the supporters of European integration. "In the sequence that began with de Gaulle's return to power in 1958," Walt Rostow observed, "the brief period of Kennedy's presidency was for Monnet an interval of hope, touched with a strand of magic."[174] Although Kennedy would never be as much on board as Eisenhower had been, his administration was poised to nudge the Europeans toward greater unity within the transatlantic framework.

Squaring the Atlantic Circle

While the prospect of an Atlantic partnership was alluring and soon graced with the epithet of being Kennedy's Grand Design for Europe, its achievement required a highly complicated balancing act on the part of the new administration in the international as well as the national realm. For one, it banked on the emergence – not the actual existence – of a politically unified and pro-American Europe. Its achievement therefore depended in large measure on the willingness of the European countries to move towards the same objectives. The partnership idea also assumed a readiness in Washington to cede power to Europe in the process of rebalancing relationships within the Atlantic community. Moreover, in order to avoid upsetting the politics of engineering the Atlantic partnership, Washington needed to display an unusual diplomatic aptitude to steer clear of the hazards of intra-European politics and an extraordinary sensitivity to changing moods and positions in the European capitals. The Kennedy administration had to tread carefully within the European political landscape in order not to offend a traditional apprehension in certain circles to American interference. And if this were not enough, the administration also needed to persuade its critics in the US Congress that it was not selling out American political and economic interests in pursuit of a chimera.

The sine qua non of Kennedy's Atlantic partnership program was Great Britain's prospective membership of the Common Market. At his first meeting with Prime Minister Macmillan, on April 4, 1961, Kennedy had unhesitatingly expressed support for Great Britain's intention to apply for membership of the Common Market.[175] While Macmillan – as we have seen – had been anxious to extract Kennedy's assurance, it is hard to see how Kennedy could have withheld that support. He had merely followed in the footsteps of his predecessor and acted in accordance with the unanimous advice of Ball, Acheson, Monnet, Bowie, and others. Moreover, de Gaulle had already accepted Macmillan's plea for exploratory discussions in February. At the same time, however, the Kennedy administration's support for British membership would take on an added significance since it was charged with turning the Atlantic partnership into reality. Above all, as Dean Rusk explained, "we hoped that if Britain joined the Common Market, it would take into Europe that special relationship with the United States."[176] Kennedy thus had done more than to assure Macmillan; he had actually heightened Washington's stakes in a successful British application. Britain's presence in the Common Market was expected to offset the potentially "anti-American flavor" of the movement toward European unity as a result of de Gaulle's European policies and his skillful strengthening of his political rapport with Adenauer's Germany. In addition, Macmillan's logic that Great Britain's membership of the Common Market would strengthen the Atlantic community as a whole strongly resonated in Washington. "We cannot hope to succeed in drawing the Western countries more closely together [in an Atlantic community] if in Europe there's a continuing dichotomy between the Six and the Seven," the British prime minister posited in an important letter to Kennedy on April 28.[177] This logic was indeed similar to Ball's – and Monnet's – belief that striving for European unity served Atlantic unity as well.

While de Gaulle – and Adenauer – repeatedly raised their concern that British entry would weaken the political cohesion that a continental grouping could muster, Ball argued that British membership would actually make it easier for a political Europe to act in unison. "So long as the United Kingdom remained outside the Common Market," Ball reasoned, "it was like a giant lodestone exerting uneven degrees of attraction on individual member states of the Six, and even on individual factions within those member states."[178] Dutch and Belgian resistance to de Gaulle's plans for political cooperation among the Six indeed provided a case in point. Ball also argued that France would not on its own be able to keep Germany strapped to the Common Market forever. A post-Adenauer Germany, he believed, would at some point be tempted to seek a deal independently with the Soviet Union on its reunification. "If Britain remained aloof," Ball hypothesized to Edward Heath in March 1961, "such men as Erhard and Strauss ... might exploit the "division of Europe" as an excuse for breaking free from the Six, but if the British should wholeheartedly join the Six, the Community could furnish the glue to bind Germany irrevocably to the West."[179] It was probably in this vein, too, that Kennedy wrote to Macmillan: "Although the success of the Six has been striking, we doubt if the weights and balances will be right without your great influence at the center."[180]

To make the Grand Design for an Atlantic partnership between the United States and the Common Market come together, the Kennedy administration had to reconcile the array of political forces in Europe and the United States on at least three accounts.

First, there was an obvious need to reconcile de Gaulle – and in his wake Adenauer – to the implications of British membership, both for the continental European economy and for de Gaulle's plan to build a European political entity that would take a more independent stance vis-à-vis the superpowers. Rather than going along with Macmillan's plan of offering de Gaulle nuclear aid and tripartite policy coordination, Washington hoped to facilitate French acquiescence by urging London to fully accept the Rome Treaty, including its political provisions, and to enter negotiations without posing conditions. American officials showed little patience for understandable British concerns about severing economic ties with the Commonwealth and the EFTA. They often did little to hide their annoyance about what they perceived as British foot-dragging. "The pleasure at our decision [to apply for membership]," British ambassador in Washington, David Ormsby-Gore, thus reported, "is not ... accompanied by any enthusiasm for smoothing our path into the Common Market by bringing pressure on the Six in regard to the interests of the Commonwealth and the EFTA countries."[181] Indeed, as Kennedy wrote to Macmillan on May 22: "We [the United States] cannot help thinking that if you are once safely and strongly in the Common Market, you will be in a very good position to protect all of the interests which so legitimately give you concern at present."[182]

More problematic from the American perspective was how to assuage de Gaulle's apprehension about the political implications of British membership of the Common Market for his plans for European political cooperation in the areas of foreign policy and defense. The reason, of course, was that American support for British membership was precisely motivated by the – often implicit – aim of ensuring that any future European political entity would take the transatlantic alliance as its main point of reference. We have already noted that de Gaulle informed Kennedy, during one of their meetings in Paris in early June, of his continuing reservations regarding Great Britain's membership of the Common Market as long as it refused to be part of "the European reality," a mental change which he did not expect to occur anytime soon.[183] Adenauer also remained extremely skeptical about the authenticity of Great Britain's change of heart with regard to European cooperation. When, in May 1961, Ball tried to persuade him that the Macmillan government was prepared to reverse "several hundred years of policy toward the Continent," the German chancellor "vigorously" retorted that Churchill and Eden had said exactly the same to him in the early 1950s, after which they established the Western European Union "which has been in a state of rigor mortis ever since." According to Adenauer, "Macmillan will never join in any serious move toward European unity" and he, together with de Gaulle, "had [therefore] decided that they could not wait for the British."[184] There was not much the Kennedy administration could do to take away the impression that Great Britain would act as an agent for American views and interests in a united Europe, as it contained a kernel of truth.

Second, there was a clear incongruity between, on the one hand, support for Great Britain's membership of the Common Market and, on the other hand, the longstanding American commitment to the federalist approach towards European unity. Ball and other US officials consistently put pressure on London to fully accept the provisions of the Rome Treaty.[185] When they impressed on their British counterparts that London had to accept the political implications of membership, they therefore did not mean to argue – as de Gaulle did – that Great Britain had to loosen its ties to the United States but that it had to accept the integration method enshrined in the Rome Treaty. Yet the Kennedy administration could not ignore the edge that Great Britain's entry into the Common Market would give to the confederalist camp. In his letter to Kennedy of April 28, 1961, Macmillan left no doubt about his predilection for the intergovernmental method. He even suggested that his government's volte face with regard to the Common Market was induced by the diminishing of the federalist tide. "At one time the federalists seemed to have won the day and we did not feel able to go along with them," he explained. "Then with de Gaulle's return to power it looked as if the confederalists were in the ascendant and that is much better for us."[186] Kennedy's reply underlined that he was only prepared to deal with the "significant" economic disadvantages of Britain's membership if it produced the political upshot of strengthening European and Atlantic unity. "A customs union alone would be a source of economic difficulty for us, without compensating political advantage, and we should be most reluctant to see such a result."[187] The dilution of European integration in the short term as a result of British membership was considered a price worth paying only in the belief that Monnet's inexorable European logic would again take hold in the long term.[188] American support for the ostensibly contradictory aims of European political integration and British membership of the Common Market was one of the paradoxes that characterized the postwar bipartisan foreign policy synthesis between liberalism and conservatism.

Third, there was the imperative – felt strongly not only by Kennedy, but by parts of the administration and in Congress as well – to reconcile British membership of the Common Market to the interests of the American economy. Kennedy's residual ambivalence about supporting the European project was undoubtedly deepened by the economist John Kenneth Galbraith, who had been one of his tutors at Harvard University and with whom he kept up an animated correspondence after he had appointed Galbraith as his ambassador to India. In one of his letters to Kennedy, in July 1961, Galbraith seriously questioned the wisdom of American support for European unity:

> There is another possible view which is that modern industry with its ever increasing scale requires larger and larger trading areas. And access to markets is now more important than protection from competitors. Social security and modern fiscal policy provide the cushioning effect on national economies which were once provided much more imperfectly by tariffs. ... market access is now the thing. This the Common Market provides for Europeans. So viewed the ECE [sic] is not a unique act of political creation. It is an accommodation to the facts of modern economic and industrial life. ... It is a reflection of a trend and Europeans are on the trend and we are not. They are developing market access at our expense. ... Still we say fine. Let us get Britain and the rest of Europe in. Thus we build up Europe against the Bolshevists. In fact we are building up Europe, which is already economically powerful, against the United States.

Adding that he had "never been worried about the Pope running the government" but that he was "genuinely bothered about St. Francis," Galbraith urged Kennedy to defend American interests and "to find a tolerable association with the Common Market":

Ahead and required will be some hard and clear-headed trading with our allies. We cannot continue to think first of Europe and forswear any steps that might upset the present equilibrium or de Gaulle.[189]

Aroused by such alternative advice (and by conversations with his father), Kennedy pointedly expressed his unease about sacrificing American economic interests on the political altar of European unity to the State Department. On August 21, following the Macmillan government's formal membership application, he asked Ball in a National Security Action Memorandum for a "realistic" study of the economic implications for the United States. "If it [the expansion of the Common Market] should have an extremely adverse effect upon us a good deal of responsibility would be laid upon our doorstep."[190] In typical fashion, Ball responded to Kennedy's concern with a detailed memorandum merely two days later, explaining that the "situation is well in hand" and that American commercial interests were being protected. State Department studies, he pointed out, had shown that the "net effect" of further European integration and the expansion of the Common Market would be "to expand rather than diminish United States industrial exports," primarily because of the higher economic growth rates they would engender. The implications for American agricultural exports were less clear, since the common agricultural policy was still being negotiated among the Six; however, "British adherence [to the Common Market] should tend to reduce the level of protection – and hence of discrimination – since Britain is committed to low food prices for its consumers." The real pinch to US trade interests, clarified Ball, would occur if Great Britain succeeded in extending its preferential ties with Commonwealth countries to the Common Market. For this reason, Ball assured, American diplomats were making their opposition to such extension abundantly clear to the Europeans. "From the long-range point of view," Ball concluded, "there is only one appropriate course for the United States to follow – that is to work toward bringing about a progressive reduction in the level of the common external tariff of the Common Market." Such trade liberalization, he moreover believed, had to be pursued on a worldwide basis, not by forming a "cabal of the industrialized countries against the rest of the world." Ball:

> The proper road to the defense – and, indeed, the advancement – of our trading interests is to pursue liberal trade policies ourselves and to insist that the Common Market do likewise. This means that we must be in a position to reduce our own tariffs on a reciprocal basis.[191]

In responding to Kennedy's anxiety about the Common Market in the summer of 1961, Ball was hence anticipating the presentation to Congress in January 1962 of the Trade Expansion Act (TEA), which had already been foreshadowed in the Bowie Report and, in 1964 and 1965, would make possible a new round of multilateral tariff negotiations (known as the Kennedy Round). In doing so, he was making full use of a unique window of opportunity: the fact that the 1934 Reciprocal Trade Agreements Act was due to expire in the summer of 1962. The expiration of this act was already posing the question to American policymakers whether they should seek to amend it or introduce a new one. Ball was clearly in favor of a new approach. The Reciprocal Trade Agreements Act had made it extremely difficult to realize substantial tariff reductions, primarily because it had forced American trade negotiators to engage in a convoluted process of item-by-item haggling. The new bill, Ball felt, would have to facilitate a far more robust approach to trade liberalization, one which would also offset the negative implications of the emergence of the Common Market for the American economy. It would in particular have to lend the president the authority in negotiations with the Common Market to lower tariffs by fifty percent across the board and even to eliminate tariffs on products where the United States and the Common Market accounted for more than eighty percent of world trade.

George Ball used the remainder of 1961 to convince Kennedy to face down the predictable resistance to his free trade revolution in Congress and among industrial and agricultural interest groups. Ball also carefully crafted the Trade Expansion Act so that it would encourage British accession.[192] More than anyone else, he deserves the credit for converting Kennedy to trade liberalization as the answer to America's economic decline and the Common Market's emergence. The Kennedy Round remains significant in the history of tariff-cutting diplomacy because for the first time tariffs were reduced across the board on a linear method. It was also the first round in which the European Economic Community negotiated as a single actor. "My task, as I saw it, was to stand like Horatio at the bridge and forestall any British deal that would either seriously dilute the political significance of the Community or discriminate against America," Ball wrote in his memoirs.[193] And in the background there were always the likes of Acheson or the indefatigable Monnet – the "inspirer" as de Gaulle aptly called him – in order to help move things forward on both sides of the Atlantic. As Miriam Camps wrote, "there was a 'Monnet effect' on Ball and then a 'Ball effect' on Kennedy and then a 'Kennedy effect' on Macmillan."[194]

Kennedy's concern for the effects of the Common Market on the American economy thus made the Trade Expansion Act of 1962 of pivotal importance to the Atlantic partnership program. It was considered of great importance, too, in order to prevent the Common Market from developing into a protectionist bulwark under French leadership. The multilateral tariff negotiations that would ensue would furthermore provide an opportunity for the European community institutions to strengthen their position, as they would lead the negotiations on behalf of the membership countries. Last but not least, the Trade Expansion Act was designed to accommodate the emergence of the Common Market within the larger framework of the Atlantic community. As Ball stated in one congressional hearing, the new bill would "constitute a necessary instrument for strengthening the bonds between the two sides of the Atlantic."[195] And when Kennedy presented the new bill in January 1962, he could rightfully say: "As NATO was unprecedented in military history, this measure is unprecedented in economic history."[196]

The Atlantic Partnership on the Rise

The Interdependence Speech, July 4, 1962

1962 was the year in which Kennedy stepped onto the European center stage. The grand introduction of the TEA in January, the failure in April of de Gaulle's plan for a political union along intergovernmental lines, the lack of progress in Great Britain's negotiations with the Common Market, the ebbing away of the Berlin Crisis of 1961 – all of these factors encouraged the Kennedy administration to take initiative in shaping the European debate about the Common Market's future. While in 1961 the Kennedy administration had been careful not to upset the European political process by imposing itself, in 1962 it increasingly felt that American leadership was necessary to prod the Europeans down the road of political integration.

The administration's Grand Design for the Atlantic community culminated on July 4, 1962 – American Independence Day. Speaking at Philadelphia's Independence Hall, Kennedy used the occasion to insert his vision of an Atlantic partnership into the political debate. The choice of time and location was significant – and the words spoken would have an exceptional resonance in the history of the transatlantic relationship. Kennedy had expressly wanted to steer clear of the humdrum patriotic quality of Independence Day speeches.[197] Instead, he had wanted to respond to the forces of globalization and talk about the transatlantic relationship and the Common Market. Kennedy therefore presented the "effort for *interdependence*" as the wave of the future, an effort which, said Kennedy, already had inspired the American Constitution and which was now "transforming the world about us." Then he turned to the movement towards European unity in what was the main message of the speech:

> That spirit [of the effort for interdependence] is today most clearly seen across the Atlantic Ocean. The nations of Western Europe, long divided by feuds far more bitter than any which existed among the 13 colonies, are today joining together, seeking, as our forefathers sought, to find freedom in diversity and in unity, strength.
> The United States looks on this vast new enterprise with hope and admiration. We do not regard a strong and united Europe as a rival but as a partner. To aid its progress has been the basic object of our foreign policy for 17 years. We

believe that a united Europe will be capable of playing a greater role in the common defense, of responding more generously to the needs of poorer nations, of joining with the United States and others in lowering trade barriers, resolving problems of commerce, commodities, and currency, and developing coordinated policies in all economic, political, and diplomatic areas. We see in such a Europe a partner with whom we can deal on a basis of full equality in all the great and burdensome tasks of building and defending a community of free nations.

It would be premature at this time to do more than indicate the high regard with which we view the formation of this partnership. The first order of business is for our European friends to go forward in forming the more perfect union which will someday make this partnership possible.

A great new edifice is not built overnight. It was 11 years from the Declaration of Independence to the writing of the Constitution. The construction of workable federal institutions required still another generation. The greatest works of our Nation's founders lay not in documents and in declarations, but in creative, determined action. The building of the new house of Europe has followed the same practical, purposeful course. Building the Atlantic partnership now will not be easily or cheaply finished.

But I will say here and now, on this Day of Independence, that the United States will be ready for a Declaration of Interdependence, that we will be prepared to discuss with a united Europe the ways and means of forming a concrete Atlantic partnership, a mutually beneficial partnership between the new union now emerging in Europe and the old American Union founded here 175 years ago. All this will not be completed in a year, but let the world know it is our goal.

In urging the adoption of the United States Constitution, Alexander Hamilton told his fellow New Yorkers "to think continentally." Today Americans must learn to think intercontinentally.[198]

Kennedy's Philadelphia speech hence followed up on Robert Bowie's advice in the fall of 1960 to strive for a "partnership of equals" between the United States and the emerging Common Market. It turned Acheson's counsel in the spring of 1961 – to seize every opportunity to move toward "a genuine Atlantic commonwealth" – into something akin to a foreign policy program. The speech spelled out, at the highest political level,[199] the route towards "progressively closer association" within the Atlantic community: first, the Europeans would have to make decisive progress toward unity, and then the United States would be prepared to engage in a "concrete" Atlantic partnership between "equals." With its emphasis on "interdependence" and on cautioning the eventual Atlantic partnership "not [to] look inward only, preoccupied with its own welfare and advancement" but "to cooperate with all nations" and "serve as a nucleus for the eventual union of all free men – those who are now free and those who are vowing that some day they will be free," it came as close as any presidential speech to expounding the liberals' vision of the Atlantic community as a scaled-down world community.[200] And although it fell short of calls for a "true Atlantic community" with common institutions, issued by Clarence Streit's Atlantic Union committee during its Paris conference in January 1962, Kennedy's readiness to project the example of the American Constitution onto Europe and his call on Americans "to think intercontinentally" could be taken as a step in that direction.

Kennedy's Philadelphia speech carefully avoided taking sides in the European debate between federalists and confederalists, reflecting Kennedy's own pragmatism on the issue. In fact, in its opening phrases, the speech skillfully weaved the themes of national independence and interdependence together in one fabric of historical evolution. In a reference to the massive drive for decolonization after World War II and to the nations behind the Iron Curtain whose independence was still suppressed, Kennedy also stated that the "doctrine of national independence [...] remains the most powerful force in the world today." This part of the speech could also be read as a helpful nod to de Gaulle's political philosophy and as an affirmation of the Evian agreement on Algerian independence signed in March 1962. Yet, Kennedy above all stressed that any struggle for national independence would have to be amplified by a political effort that recognized the inherent interdependence of nations in an era of globalization. Most importantly, Kennedy unabashedly held up the federal model enshrined in the American Constitution as a beckoning example to Europe.

In fact, both the prominence of the Atlantic partnership idea and the example of federal union in the Philadelphia speech were testimony to Jean Monnet's extraordinary influence on the administration's European policies. In April, Monnet had paid a three-week visit to Washington during which he, together with Acheson, put together an Action Committee resolution that was subsequently handed to Ball, Rostow, Owen, and Schaetzel, and which had a great impact on Kennedy's Philadelphia speech.[201] Eight days before the speech, on June 26, Monnet tried to shape the response in Europe to Kennedy's proposal in advance, issuing a statement that his Action Committee for the United States of Europe, "which groups the vast majority of political parties in our six countries, as well as the free and Christian trade unions representing ten million workers, considers that only through the economic and political unification of Europe, including the United Kingdom, and the establishment of a partnership between equals of Europe and the United States can the West be strengthened and the conditions created for peace between East and West." The statement furthermore predictably favored the community approach as the "new method of collective action" and appeared to jab at de Gaulle's nationalism by declaring that "any other course would involve our separate countries in profitless adventures and preserve that spirit of superiority and domination which not so long ago led Europe to the brink of destruction... ."[202] It is therefore easy to see how the Philadelphia speech, only three months after the failure of the Fouchet Plan, had to be interpreted by de Gaulle as tugging Europe away from his vision of a "European" entity freed of America's tutelage and consisting of independent nation-states.[203] Kennedy's suggestion that the United States and a politically integrated Europe could develop "coordinated policies in all economic, political, and diplomatic areas" was a far cry, too, from de Gaulle's September 1958 memorandum proposal for tripartite policy coordination. "In retrospect," François Duchêne concluded, "Kennedy's partnership speech was the high-water mark of the ideology of integration."[204]

While Kennedy laid out a vision for the Atlantic community that could only be realized in a more distant future, the Philadelphia speech could not of course be detached from the political requirements of the day. For one, the allure of an Atlantic partnership certainly helped to garner support in Congress for the Trade Expansion Act put forward by the administration.[205] More importantly, the Philadelphia speech had to advance a key component of the Grand Design: British membership of the Common Market. It impressed on London that the United States was indeed transferring its special relationship with Great Britain to a progressively more unified Europe, thus encouraging the Macmillan government to join the Common Market without much ado. It furthermore had to convince a reluctant de Gaulle that the United States favored a strong Europe with which it would be prepared to cooperate on the basis of full equality – in other words, that British membership was not favored by Washington as a Machiavellian ruse to keep Europe under America's wing.

The negotiations between Great Britain and the Six were reaching a difficult and sensitive stage in the summer of 1962. They had not really begun until early 1962, primarily because France had refused to discuss agricultural matters with Great Britain until the Six had reached agreement on a common agricultural policy.[206] In February, France had furthermore opposed Heath's proposal that Great Britain be given a four-year exemption from this policy. The negotiations about Great Britain's preferential ties with Commonwealth countries, which London wanted to keep in place as much as possible, proved similarly difficult. The key concern for de Gaulle and Adenauer, however, was the effect British membership would have on the political identity and cohesiveness of the Six, a concern that was only exacerbated by the possibility of more EFTA countries joining once Great Britain was admitted. De Gaulle's opposition to British membership was not categorical, but his priority lay with building a "European" Europe – which could be much better achieved in tandem with Adenauer – and he did not think the British would be ready to join in such a venture (and hence would try to block it). Meeting Macmillan in late November 1961 at Birch Grove, de Gaulle had emphasized the obstacles on the road to British membership. "It is the timing that seems to worry him most," British Ambassador Sir Pierson-Dixon to France concluded after this discussion. "He would rather that we had come in earlier or left it till later. ... our inclusion will dilute the purely European conception which de Gaulle would prefer. King Alfred does not easily fit in with de Gaulle and Charlemagne."[207]

In the course of 1962, Macmillan was growing increasingly pessimistic about de Gaulle's disposition.[208] He also felt strongly that Kennedy's and McNamara's campaign against independent national nuclear forces, and in particular the French *force de frappe*, was in effect undercutting the British membership bid, because it upset de Gaulle and reduced the possibility of a deal in the nuclear realm with which de Gaulle could be enticed. In early June, in an important meeting at Château de Champs, Macmillan appears to have offered British-French nuclear collaboration as part of "some European deterrent" in an utmost attempt to persuade de Gaulle of his "European" credentials.[209] After de Gaulle had said that he gave priority to Franco-German rapprochement and that "even with the best will in the world on your part and no matter what promises you make, you are just going to change things in our little club," Macmillan also had argued that de Gaulle's understanding with Bonn could only be "ephemeral":

> This depends on the continued life of a very old gentleman in Bonn .... And if he were not here tomorrow, goodness knows what might happen to your Franco-Teutonic alliance. Goodness knows what bypass the German people might take in their effort to reunify East and West Germany. Maybe that effort will take the form of some kind of alliance with the East. I say to you that the real guarantee of the continuation of the Franco-Teutonic alliance, of the new Franco-Teutonic friendship, the real guarantee against German adventures to the East, the real guarantee of the progress of the Common Market and of continental Europe, economically and politically, is to accept us, Great Britain, as part of your political and economic complex, a real part and not just something that is aside but friendly.[210]

This was essentially the argument that George Ball had been making earlier to Edward Heath in March 1961. Macmillan had succeeded in making an impression on his French counterparts. "La Grande-Bretagne est décidée à tout faire pour entrer dans le Marché commun," Couve de Murville reported in the French cabinet on June 6. De Gaulle, too, appeared to recognize the change in Great Britain's attitude towards Europe since the 1950s. "L'Angleterre de Kipling est morte," he said to Alain Peyrefitte.[211] As for Macmillan, he appeared to indeed have felt that it was now or never: either the West would unite or it would falter. As he confided "with great intensity" to C.D. Jackson:

> I am 68 years. De Gaulle is over 70. Adenauer is over 80. We three old men must make this work because if we three don't make it work, the next genera-

tion of politicians and leaders will not succeed because they have not been through what we have been through and cannot possibly appreciate the full and total importance and urgency of this whole question.[212]

De Gaulle's disposition towards Great Britain's membership application nonetheless remained negative. He did not believe that Macmillan was sufficiently ready to assert Great Britain's independence from the United States and continued to dislike the inevitable changes that would occur in the power relationships within the Six if Britain were to join.[213] Yet he had not made up his mind and also indicated that the British probably would have to be admitted to the Common Market at some point. In spite of Macmillan's privately growing pessimism, there was hence still room for optimism in mid-1962. Progress seemed to be made in negotiating the agricultural and the Commonwealth issues. Macmillan, still seeking common ground between Paris and Washington, reported to Kennedy that his meeting with de Gaulle at Château de Champs had yielded "fairly satisfactory discussions" (he did not mention his overture in the nuclear realm, if indeed he had made one, perhaps dissuaded by McNamara's Athens speech a few weeks earlier).[214] On the French side, too, there was a feeling that substantial progress was being made.[215]

From the vantage point of Washington, the political situation in Europe looked manageable with some tactful diplomacy and seemed to be moving step by step in the right direction. In June 1961, after his visit to Paris, Kennedy had told congressional leaders of his doubt that de Gaulle wanted the British in the Common Market: "He appears to believe that they will not make the necessary political commitment, and in any case de Gaulle prefers the present situation in which he is the dominant figure."[216] By July 4, 1962, however, de Gaulle had lost the initiative within Europe with the failure of the Fouchet Plan, and buoyancy about the prospects of British membership and the future relationship with the Common Market had taken over in Washington. Two weeks before the Philadelphia speech, on June 18, Secretary of State Rusk left for Europe to assess the political situation in the major capitals. His briefing papers stressed that de Gaulle's policies presented the "principal current obstacle to our objectives" in Europe, but also that the French leader highly depended on his ability to continue to "seduce" Adenauer into supporting him: "Chancellor Adenauer is the key to the situation."[217] Rusk's reports of his meetings with European leaders must have contributed to the air of confidence in Washington about the feasibility of the administration's Grand Design for an Atlantic partnership. After having had his meetings in Paris, Rusk confidently cabled to Kennedy that "France will not offer any overriding political objection" to British membership of the Common Market, even as there was a sense of regret that "the presence of Anglo-Saxon Islanders" would modify the European project.[218] As for the German chancellor, Rusk added in another cable, he "repeated the view I have heard in Paris that the entry of Britain, Norway, Denmark, and Ireland into the Common Market would change the entire character of Europe"; Rusk nevertheless concluded that there was "general support in Bonn for UK accession and the confident expectation that the present negotiations will succeed... ."[219] And in London, the American secretary of state found Great Britain's chief European negotiator Heath "confident that negotiations are in good course and will be successfully concluded within [a] reasonable time period."[220]

The way thus seemed open for a positive speech about Europe by the American president on Independence Day. Five days after Kennedy had delivered his riveting speech, Walt Rostow reported after a trip to Europe that Jean Monnet had "not been more cheerful or in better form for a long while," and that he was convinced that de Gaulle and Adenauer had accepted British membership. Moreover, de Gaulle had pulled Monnet aside at a reception for Adenauer, telling his French antagonist that the views expressed in Monnet's Action Committee's statement of June 26 and his views were "not far apart."[221] After the Philadelphia speech, Kennedy's – and Monnet's – conception of an Atlantic partnership thus clearly seemed on the rise. However, America's chief diplomats underestimated de Gaulle's political audacity – his preparedness to go against the grain – as well as the tenacity with which he would hold on to his European vision, in which there was no place for the United States except as an ally of last resort. Enthused in no small measure by Monnet's activism, they also had no clear view of the effect of American policies and pronouncements on key European leaders. In addition, they had not resolved the tension between the call for an equal Atlantic partnership and the campaign against national nuclear forces. As a result, they unknowingly put at risk what they wanted to achieve.

After the Interdependence Speech

In the summer and fall of 1962, Kennedy seemed to come to grips with his foreign policy and make important progress in his European policies. After a series of congressional hearings and a number of concessions to the textile industry, the Trade Expansion Act passed the Senate on September 19, 1962, giving the president authority to decide on a comprehensive reduction of tariffs with the Common Market.[222] It was celebrated as an important victory for the Kennedy administration, which hailed the TEA as "the most important piece of legislation affecting economics since the Marshall Plan."[223] Looking back on those years, Dean Rusk still called it "a revolutionary act, the most far-reaching act since about 1933."[224] With the TEA in place and European integration on track, the way indeed seemed open for a more balanced economic transatlantic relationship – one in which European growth would act as an engine for the American economy and thereby help remedy the balance-of-payments problem that concerned Kennedy so.

The launching of the Atlantic partnership initiative also changed the context of the American campaign against national nuclear forces in one crucial respect: it increased Kennedy's willingness to consider relinquishing US control over a future European nuclear force. More specifically, it cast the proposal for a multilateral nuclear force (MLF) in a new light. In the context of the Atlantic partnership program, the MLF proposal thus became charged with the added motive of encouraging European political integration.

Prior to his appointment as ambassador to France, Charles Bohlen had discussed the MLF proposal with Kennedy several times, telling the president that "the whole scheme was somewhat a fraudulent one" unless the United States showed a greater willingness to cede control over it "if and when there was a European authority."[225] There is reason to believe that Kennedy had taken Bohlen's observation to heart and that it was on his mind as he spoke about an "equal" Atlantic partnership with a "united Europe [...] capable of playing a greater role in the common defense." [226] The July 4 speech was understandably opaque about the defense aspects of an Atlantic partnership, let alone the nuclear aspects of defense. However, in a press conference one day later Kennedy clarified that "a European nuclear force [...] is a matter that Europe should consider carefully" and that the United States would "be responsive to any alternate arrangement they wish to make."[227] Although Kennedy hastened to add that no European proposals had been forthcoming, Ambassador James Gavin encouragingly reported from Paris on July 6 that "there [are] certainly many in France who are beginning to think along these lines."[228]

On September 27, 1962, with Kennedy's approval, McGeorge Bundy indeed took the notion that the MLF could one day develop into a truly European force one step further in a speech in Copenhagen entitled "Building the Atlantic Partnership". Referring to the Kennedy administration's campaign against national nuclear forces, which had been shifted into higher gear by McNamara at the May 1962 NATO meeting in Athens, Kennedy's national security adviser added: "It would be wrong to suppose that the reluctance we feel with respect to individual, ineffective, and unintegrated forces would be extended automatically to a European force, genuinely unified, and multilateral, and effectively integrated with our own necessarily predominant strength in the whole nuclear defense of the alliance." And: "If it should turn out that a genuinely multilateral European deterrent, integrated with ours in NATO, is what is needed and wanted, it will not be a veto from the United States which stands in its way."[229]

Bundy's Copenhagen speech was a significant add-on to the Atlantic partnership program, since it added specificity to the still rather vague partnership concept and dealt with the ultimate question of nuclear weapons. His remarks were also significant because they appeared designed to lead the Europeans down the road of political integration by putting a reward on their achieving "full" political unity. It was soon clear to European capitals that the Kennedy administration was serious about this element of the Atlantic partnership, for George Ball reiterated the points Bundy had made in Copenhagen at a NATO Parliamentarians Conference in November.[230] In addition, an American briefing team led by Gerard Smith of the State Department and Admiral John S. Lee of the Pentagon "convinced many allies that we were now in earnest about the MLF," presenting elaborate studies on the project to the North Atlantic Council in the fall of 1962.[231]

In 1962, with Kennedy's Atlantic partnership speech, the enactment of the Trade Expansion Act, and the reworking of the MLF proposal, the United States was once again urging the Europeans to integrate after the demise of the European Defense Community in 1954. As a result, the administration was setting itself up for a similar disappointment once the unwillingness of European leaders to relinquish national sovereignty would surface. The Kennedy administration was careful enough not to engage in Dulles-type warnings of "agonizing reappraisals." With regard to the MLF, it stressed that the United States did not consider the matter urgent – since the American nuclear security guarantee provided a sufficient deterrent – and that the initiative had to come from the Europeans.

Yet Ball and other Europeanists increasingly saw the MLF, as British Labour Party leader Denis Healey aptly put it, "as the grit in the oyster, round which the pearl of European unity would form."[232] In October, a State Department instruction – approved by Kennedy – to the newly arrived Ambassador Bohlen stated that "our policy in the nuclear field reflects our basic objective in Western Europe: to work for an ever closer partnership between an increasingly integrated Europe and the US." American support for "politically divisive national nuclear programs" such as the French *force de frappe* obviously did not fit in with the Atlantic partnership. The conviction that the further integration of Europe was inexorable instead encouraged a certitude about the future course of events:

> Time will be required for European-minded groups in France, which favor the multilateral over the national approach, to continue to grow in strength; for the repercussions of continuing progress toward European integration to make themselves felt; and for the difficulties, costs, and limited advantages of a national program to become more widely appreciated. ... Through this transitional period, we should bear in mind that the nuclear issue is one on which we and the French have agreed to disagree, and we should have both the tact to avoid reopening this difference and the patience to await the verdict of history upon it.[233]

Yet the success of Kennedy's Grand Design hinged in large measure on de Gaulle's willingness to play his part. The key to de Gaulle's conduct, as Rusk had been briefed before his June visit to Europe, was Adenauer. The German chancellor had shown interest in the American MLF proposal in his meeting with Rusk in June.[234] But the year 1962 is above all notable for showcasing the acme of Franco-

German rapprochement since Adenauer's first meeting with de Gaulle at Colombey-les-deux-Églises in September 1958. From July 2 to 8, Adenauer paid de Gaulle a highly symbolic official visit and traveled through France in the first major tour of the country made by a German head of government since World War II. During this visit, de Gaulle proposed a bilateral treaty of systematic cooperation between France and Germany now that the Fouchet Plan had failed; Adenauer consented, believing that "it would be better than making Great Britain the arbiter of Europe."[235] A few months later, in early September, de Gaulle made an equally symbolic state visit to West Germany, the first in modern times by a French head of state, where he talked glowingly of Franco-German friendship before enthusiastic crowds. Meanwhile, de Gaulle was holding off a meeting with Kennedy in the United States, telling Ambassador Gavin on his farewell call on the Elysée that he was concerned such a meeting would end "on a negative note" for lack of specific achievement.[236]

The outcome of the Cuban Missile Crisis of October 1962 added to the Kennedy administration's confidence in its crisis management abilities, but it had a poisonous effect on its relations with the European allies, who – including Macmillan – had not been consulted about how to handle it. If anything, Kennedy's self-contained handling of the crisis showed that an Atlantic partnership of equals was still a distant prospect. Dean Acheson, too, was unhappy with Kennedy's performance, both because he thought the young American had not been tough enough with the Soviets and because he had not given sufficient weight to the interests of his NATO allies. Briefly after the crisis, he wrote a letter to Jean Monnet carping about weakness in the West, de Gaulle's anti-British bias, the mediocrity of world leadership, the tardiness of European integration, and the never-ending crisis atmosphere in the Atlantic alliance that made a broader "Atlantic Community" seem unrealistic. On November 23, 1962, however, Monnet responded with characteristic optimism:

I am not pessimistic as to the conditions of the world. It is inevitable that Europe and the United States move on different wavelengths. They are different... The way to get this [Atlantic] partnership is for Europe first to get unified and for this, England should be part of it; then Europe and the United States should deal jointly with problems that neither of them can solve by themselves, such as monetary stability, aid to underdeveloped countries or agricultural surpluses. As the interests will become more and more unified, the political view will become more and more common. [...] I think that if we want men to unite, we must unite their interest first and for this it is necessary that they accept to act according to the same rules administered by common institutions. I know this may appear to be a long process, but a change in the attitude of men is necessarily a slow process. I think this is what we are doing and in fact this is what is happening.[237]

Monnet assured his old American friend "to have no doubt [...] that Great Britain will be a part of the European unity fairly soon."[238]

Moreover, even as Secretary of State Dean Rusk generally preferred to stay on the sidelines of intra-European politics,[239] members of his department engaged in energetic "backstage" work on behalf of Great Britain's membership bid. When Prime Minister Georges Pompidou told Ambassador Bohlen on November 5, 1962, that Great Britain's desire to join the Common Market posed problems that could be "more easily dealt with if there was not too much haste," the latter replied that a delay was undesirable for the political problems it would cause the Macmillan government.[240] More importantly, the department's Europeanists – led by George Ball – actively worked their relationships in Europe to create the circumstances for positive decisions among the Six on British membership, in particular by trying to strengthen the working relationship between the European Commission and the British government. On December 8, ten days before Macmillan would meet Kennedy for an important summit at Nassau on the Bahamas, Ball arranged for Walter Hallstein to come to Washington to discuss the prospects of completing the negotiations on British membership at an early date. Ball left no doubt in the mind of the chairman of the European Commission that the American government considered early British entry as a matter of supreme importance. A few days later, Ball informed Kennedy:

> I think Hallstein was impressed with the seriousness that we attached to a quick conclusion of these negotiations and I feel we have paved the way for some work backstage that can give the negotiations a helpful shove. Meanwhile, you will be in a position to advise the prime minister at Nassau that we have struck a blow on his side.[241]

Conclusion

Kennedy's approach to the Common Market is in part inevitably the story of how he sought to offset the United States' relative decline. The sense that America's global position *was* deteriorating was not limited to the military domain. It was pervasive in the economic realm, too. Kennedy was acutely aware of this – and he hoped that a more integrated and wealthier Europe could provide part of the answer to American woes.

The story about Kennedy's policies with regard to the Common Market, however, was not about economics alone. These policies had an important political gist, too. Most American policymakers, in particular those in the State Department, were more concerned about the implications of Gaullism writ large in Europe than about the US balance of payments. De Gaulle's oft-stated desire for independence from the superpowers – to establish a united Europe as a "third force" in world politics – portended little good. "It was the elementary, fundamental question of whether the Europe that we wanted to build up would be European or Atlantic," Couve de Murville wrote of the Franco-American divergence about the Common Market.[242] The Kennedy administration's response to de Gaulle's Fouchet Plan was pragmatic, but only because it counted on the pro-Atlantic forces among the Six to ensure that any political union would recognize the primacy of NATO and keep Europe from drifting into neutralism. The specter of a resurgent nationalism in Europe after de Gaulle's return to power in France, too, had caused concern. From Washington's vantage point, it made Jean Monnet's credo of interdependence and supranational institutional development the more compelling – a credo to which in particular liberally inclined Americans already had been instinctively drawn. In sum, the primary aim of American policymakers was not to keep the European allies in a state of dependency in the exercise of hegemony, as some historians have suggested.[243] It was rather to exercise control over Europe's destiny in order to avoid losing Western Europe in the Cold War and to foil a repeat of Europe's nationalist past through the extension of liberal American values of federalism and free trade.

The Kennedy administration judged de Gaulle's European policies in particular for their impact on Germany, even more so than the Eisenhower administration had done. Germany had been the linchpin in Europe's disastrous wars. It was the apple of discord in the Cold War. Its democratic record was considered still too young and the German political mind too unsettled to instill much confidence about its future direction. The Kennedy administration was determined to inoculate German politics against the influence of Gaullism. De Gaulle's stirring declarations during his September 1962 visit to Germany – on various occasions he exclaimed to German crowds that he considered Germans a great people ("*ein grosses Volk*") – and his address to the Führungsakademie of the German Bundeswehr raised eyebrows on both sides of the Iron Curtain for resuscitating the dreaded German militarism.[244] (In American eyes, the French nuclear weapons program and de Gaulle's justification for it was already certain to whet the German appetite for nuclear weapons.) De Gaulle's assiduous attempt to forge a privileged partnership with Germany also introduced new risks to America's Cold War diplomacy: either Germany would be tempted to break free from its exclusive pact with an inferior France to strike a separate deal with Moscow about its unification, or France would seek to negotiate a deal with Moscow without the involvement of the "Anglo-Saxons" on the basis of its claim to speak for continental Western Europe and thus for Bonn. Adenauer's courtship with de Gaulle, albeit an important contribution to Franco-German reconciliation, was therefore looked upon in Washington with more than a little disquietude. The German chancellor obviously held the key to the balance of power in Europe. Adenauer consistently sought to balance Germany's vital requisite for American protection with his desire for political reconciliation with a former arch enemy and an inclination for deepened European political cooperation. But could he – or any of his successors

– be relied upon to always strike the right balance, especially if France and the United States were to increasingly find themselves in opposition to each other? As Ambassador Gavin noted with foresight, if it ever would have to come to a German choice between the United States and France, the United States had to be in a position to decisively influence that choice in its favor as long as the Cold War had not yet been won. De Gaulle's successful rapprochement with Adenauer's Germany made it imperative, too, that Great Britain join the movement toward European unity.

Should Kennedy have supported British membership of the Common Market as strongly as he did? He was, of course, following in the footsteps of his predecessor. Yet Great Britain's entry bid in August 1961 was conceived under adverse circumstances. The Six were still negotiating among themselves, and in particular France and Germany were still seeking to accommodate their diverging economic interests within the Common Market. Great Britain was moreover a reluctant bidder, trying to preserve as much as possible of its imperial legacy, the Commonwealth, and the special relationship with the United States. Macmillan also faced weak domestic political support for his volte face decision to seek Common Market membership, both from right-wing Conservatives and left-wing Socialists, as well as condemnation from the Commonwealth and the EFTA countries. Great Britain was, as Couve de Murville explained to Kennedy after de Gaulle's veto in 1963, "still subject to a conflict between its relations with the EEC, with the Commonwealth, and with the United States."[245] This French analysis was, in fact, similar to the prevailing view of Great Britain in the United States, which had been put into words by Acheson in his contentious West Point speech in early December 1962.[246] Even George Ball had doubts about the timing of Great Britain's application, even though he strongly supported it out of principle. In the summer of 1961, Ball recalls in his memoirs, he had been bothered that "events lacked synchronization":

> With Britain finally in the position where, with encouragement, it was prepared to join Europe, it might not have the chance. [...] Did Britain wish to face a European coalition hostile to its interests, or a group of European nations working closely with the United States that did not include Britain? To avoid these dangers, Britain must try to become the leader of Europe. But no British government could publicly admit that it hoped, by taking the leadership of the Community, to regain leverage lost through the shriveling of empire; that would stir resentment among the continental powers. Nor did Britain wish to turn its back on those tattered vestiges of empire that were the sole remaining residue of the Commonwealth – or, in other words, the former white dominion. [...] Had Britain joined the Schuman Plan at the outset, it could have taken the laboring oar in drafting the Rome Treaty that created the EEC, and the peoples of Western Europe might today be combining their en-

ergies in a broader framework that could give real meaning to the concept of an Atlantic partnership.[247]

The British had missed the boat in the 1950s, however, and by the early 1960s de Gaulle was sailing away with it under his own flag.

There was nonetheless a strong consensus within the Kennedy administration that Great Britain should join the Common Market and any move toward European political union at the earliest possible moment. A deepening division within Western Europe between the Six and the Seven was seen as too damaging in the context of the Cold War, a concern that was also much on Macmillan's mind when he made the decision to apply for membership. Great Britain's entry was necessary, too, to provide a sufficient counterweight to de Gaulle's aspirations to use the Common Market as a launching platform for his foreign policy ambitions. It was furthermore viewed as necessary in order to tie Germany permanently to the West, something that France alone would not be able to accomplish. British membership was sure to strengthen the Common Market's orientation on free trade as well, which served American trading interests and would help to alleviate the balance-of-payments problem.

American support for British membership of the Common Market was surely also encouraged by the fact that Jean Monnet ("Mr. Europe") was adamantly in favor of an early entry. Monnet's active support helped to overcome any qualms among American supporters of European integration about the consequences of British membership for the integration method. In the long run, they reasoned, the European integration movement would resume its relentless course anyhow, as it was the most rational way forward for European countries. American policymakers often assumed that Monnet and his co-workers represented the aspirations of the vast majority of Europeans, while they denied such legitimacy to de Gaulle. This was, however, more a hopeful reflection of their convictions of what arguably needed to happen in Europe than a realistic assessment of European political sentiments, which were still far more tied to the nation-state. European integration, as Alan Milward has argued, got underway because it was a politically acceptable – albeit somewhat deceitful – method for Europe's nation-states to resurrect themselves after World War II.[248] American policymakers were nonetheless not so much out of touch with European political reality as anticipating a new, more desirable reality, one which would ensue from the "inexorable" process of economic and political integration at the expense of the European nation-state. In a conversation with Kennedy in May 1962, André Malraux observed that the American president was "more sure of the idea of Europe than the Europeans were."[249] While Kennedy himself above all hoped that the Atlantic partnership program would alleviate the US balance-of-payments problem, this new political reality in Europe was the main trophy for the movers and shakers of the Grand Design – the likes of George Ball and the Europeanists at the State Department.

Most historians are wont to point out that Kennedy's Grand Design illustrated the chasm between rhetoric and reality characteristic of many of Kennedy's policies. Rather than as evidence of hypocrisy, however, it is more instructive to view the Grand Design as an expression of longstanding ambiguities in the transatlantic relationship. The signing of the Rome Treaty in 1957 and the subsequent emergence of the Common Market had caused a rethink in Washington of what was meant by an Atlantic community. Due to Monnet's remarkable influence, the Kennedy administration finally came up with the notion of an Atlantic "partnership" as a way to render political support to European integration while giving the semblance of equality within the evolving transatlantic relationship and retaining a measure of control. By 1962, "partnership" had become the buzz word replacing "community" in official documents and speeches.[250] However, because it was a rehash of the same conservative and liberal notions about American foreign policy, Kennedy's design for an Atlantic partnership was riddled with the same internal contradictions. On the one hand, it relied on the traditional Anglo-American strategic partnership to ensure the Atlantic orientation of the Common Market. On the other hand, it openly sought to promote the supranational ideal of European integration and transfer the "special relationship" from Great Britain to a politically integrated Europe. As Great Britain was always unlikely to further the cause of European integration, Kennedy's Grand Design was charged with goals that were clearly at odds with another. Moreover, neither of these goals was acceptable to the one European leader on whom the design's success in the final analysis depended – Charles de Gaulle.

Kennedy's Atlantic partnership was a reflection of enduring American ambiguities towards Europe, too, because it was an uneasy compromise between aloofness from and engagement with Europe, between the preparedness to grant Europe a measure of autonomy and the desire to retain control. This aspect of the Grand Design might have worked if the Kennedy administration had been more successful at applying its rhetoric of equality to its behavior vis-à-vis the European allies. However, the Kennedy administration was unable to put equality into practice, as its failure to consult the European allies in the Cuban Missile Crisis showed all too clearly. It did not resolve the contradiction between, on the one hand, asking the European allies to carry more of the burden and, on the other hand, strengthening American control over the defense of the West. The difficulty with Kennedy's Grand Design for Europe was that "the devolution of power and authority to a United Europe [...] was never spelled out in the defense realm."[251] In the realm of military strategy, the Kennedy administration tried to shore up the notion of full integration rather than of equal partnership. The drive for military integration was also central to the American proposal for a multilateral nuclear force, even as Kennedy administration spokesmen in the fall of 1962 came to hint that the United States might relinquish its veto over such a force if Europe became politically integrated. The idea of a European alternative to the

American nuclear deterrent based upon British and French nuclear forces, which appears to have occupied Macmillan's mind, never received serious consideration from the Kennedy administration, since it was at odds with the centrality of command deemed necessary in the nuclear age and with the priority given to halting the proliferation of nuclear weapons. Macmillan's strategy to use the "special relationship" to persuade the United States to grant France the attributes of a great power and strike a nuclear deal with de Gaulle was thus never more than a blimp on Kennedy's radar screen. (It remains doubtful, at any rate, that American nuclear assistance would indeed have swayed de Gaulle as long as the strains attached meant that the *force de frappe* would lose its independence, much less that Congress would have given its approval to any nuclear deal with France.)

The Europeanists at the State Department believed that the United States had to be prepared to apply its leadership if needed to prod the Europeans towards greater unity. However, they may have done themselves a disservice by fighting Monnet's battles. Miriam Camps, for example, observed that by "becoming overidentified" with the European proponents of political integration, the United States made them vulnerable to "Gaullist taunts that they are simply stooges for the American 'federator.'"[252] De Gaulle's biographer Jean Lacouture moreover judged that Kennedy's Philadelphia speech hardened de Gaulle's attitude toward Great Britain, since the Atlantic partnership idea posed "a significant challenge to de Gaulle's 'European Europe'" and made the British "seem like courtiers of the American President." The speech, Lacouture wrote, thus became "the first act of a drama in which the young, powerful god who could lay down the law and a septuagenarian mortal whose pride was as great as his weakness confronted one another."[253] The pressures caused by America's relative decline combined with the advent of a more activist administration thus had caused one of the lessons of the EDC's defeat for American diplomacy to fall by the wayside. This lesson was that it was best for the United States not to seem overbearing, a position that at the time had also been encouraged by leading pro-integrationist figures in Europe.[254]

The success of Kennedy's Atlantic partnership program ultimately hinged on de Gaulle, who was at the apex of his power at the end of 1962 because of the resolution of the Algerian war, the abatement of the Cold War after the Cuban Missile Crisis, his victory in the French elections of 1962, and his waxing alliance with Adenauer. "In 1962, despite storm warnings from de Gaulle, the general Atlantic mood was optimistic, with attention directed to avoiding hazards in the way rather than questioning whether it was the right one – or whether America and Europe should both be on the same road," J. Robert Schaetzel recalled.[255] In 1963, Kennedy would get stuck in the quagmire of intra-European politics. The most debilitating incongruity of Kennedy's Grand Design was therefore the one that was most often overlooked: that it was engineered to counter de Gaulle's conception of a European "Europe" while being wholly dependent on de Gaulle's concurrence for its accomplishment.

Grand designs are most often engineered by statesmen in order to resolve essential yet conflicting requirements of a nation's foreign policy. However, the contradictions in Kennedy's Grand Design would prove too great to warrant its success, let alone to withstand the General.

Chapter Three

The Clash: De Gaulle's Rejection of Kennedy's Atlantic Partnership, 1962-1963

By the spring of 1962, the political and military-strategic differences between Kennedy and de Gaulle had brought about a significant deterioration in their bilateral relationship – and word of this was increasingly making it to newspapers and editorials. Prominent journalists and columnists such as Joseph Alsop (of the *New York Herald Tribune*) and Cyrus Sulzberger (of the *New York Times*) were writing that "in the whole history of the Western alliance there has been nothing like the present remarkably ugly relationship between France and the US."[1] Walter Lippmann's considerable esteem for de Gaulle also suffered as the anti-Anglo-Saxon gist of the Frenchman's policies became increasingly clear; "my present mood," he wrote in a letter to British journalist Barbara Ward Jackson in May 1962, "is to take an increasingly strong stand against de Gaulle, designed especially to detach his German satellite – and I hope and believe Jean Monnet and his friends will eventually come out on top."[2]

The Franco-American quarrel turned into a veritable transatlantic crisis in January 1963, when de Gaulle scuttled Kennedy's Grand Design for an Atlantic partnership by vetoing British membership of the Common Market and rejecting the multilateral nuclear force (MLF) proposed by the United States. De Gaulle's challenge to the Atlantic partnership idea was also much reinforced by his signing of a bilateral treaty with West Germany – the Franco-German Treaty of Reconciliation. De Gaulle's "thunderbolt"[3] of January 1963 certainly marked a watershed in Franco-American relations during the Cold War. Franco-American differences over the transatlantic relationship could still be papered over by diplomats during the first four years of de Gaulle's presidency; in early 1963, however, they reached full public view and would be impossible to ignore henceforth. But the clash of 1963 was to have much wider implications than for the Franco-American relationship alone. For one, it would deeply affect American long-term policies toward Europe.

At Loggerheads On All Fronts (Spring of 1962)

Before we delve into the run-up to the clash and the clash itself, it should be noted that the friction between Washington and Paris in 1962 resulted at least in part from serious differences over the handling of the Cold War crisis over Berlin (which had flared up after the grim Kennedy-Khrushchev meeting in Vienna in June 1961 and had reached its nadir with the erection of the Berlin Wall in August 1961). We have already noted how de Gaulle used the successive crises over Berlin to build up his relationship with Konrad Adenauer and to gain German support for his European policies. From December 1958 onwards, de Gaulle postured as the more dependable ally in the West, assuming a hard line with the Soviet Union and hence allaying Adenauer's anxieties that France would seek to make a deal with the Soviet leadership without Germany having a say. Paris consistently resisted Western initiatives for negotiations with the Soviet Union over Berlin. In early August 1961, too, French Foreign Minister Couve de Murville objected to Secretary Rusk's proposal of a meeting of foreign ministers of the Western alliance in Paris for an early initiative.[4] The French position was that negotiations with the Soviet Union would be possible only in an atmosphere of relaxation between the East and the West; in other words, détente had to precede negotiations. Concessions would only breed new demands. Moreover, de Gaulle did not believe that Khrushchev would risk a war over Berlin.

The Kennedy administration's attitude, meanwhile, was marked by a mixture of vigor and forbearance. The propensity to fuse muscular energy and cautious diplomacy had been manifest as early as in Kennedy's Inauguration Address ("let us not fear to negotiate"), and it would shape Kennedy's policies – and in particular his management of crises – as well. On the one hand, many of these policies were driven by the New Frontier's cult of toughness and dynamism, which viewed foreign policy challenges primarily as "battles that must be won."[5] On the other hand, there was a paradoxical readiness to negotiate with the enemy when the chips were down. In each of the Cold War crises, while he publicly assumed a hard line, Kennedy carefully sought out opportunities to seek a negotiated solution with Moscow.

In the case of Berlin, this mixture of vigor and forbearance brought Kennedy into conflict with de Gaulle and, to a lesser extent, Adenauer. For one, the Kennedy administration viewed the Berlin Crisis as an opportunity to put its new strategy of flexible response into practice and to ride roughshod over the European reluctance to accept this strategy as NATO's own. On July 24, 1961, Kennedy decided to send "as many as six additional divisions" to Europe in order to strengthen NATO's conventional defenses.[6] But he had done so clearly expecting the European allies to do their part as well, for on July 20 he asked de Gaulle to similarly beef up France's conventional forces in Germany.[7] De Gaulle, however, refused to play along. Mostly as a result of the French refusal to bring in additional conventional forces, NATO's contingency planning on Berlin hardly amounted to anything, thus leaving Kennedy's flexible response strategy with respect to Berlin dangerously exposed. "The heart of our problem with the French is that they are playing a lone hand," McGeorge Bundy noted in October 1962.

The French military build-up is surprisingly feeble and can hardly carry conviction of French seriousness to Khrushchev. Even when the French had four divisions committed to NATO, their contribution was lower, proportionately, than might have been expected of so central a power. Now it is clear that the French only plan to have two divisions in Germany, holding the rest in France as "National M-Day Forces." If France proposes to play a full role in the defense of Berlin and the defense of Germany, these targets are absurdly low. If France means to leave these matters to the United States, then at a moment of crisis, the United States may have to act alone.[8]

Second, in contrast to de Gaulle, Kennedy had comparatively few qualms about making concessions to Moscow if this would avert a war with the Soviet Union, or even about recognizing East Germany. "We have recognized many worse governments," he remarked shortly after the Ulbricht government began erecting the Berlin Wall.[9] In the same letter to de Gaulle in which he had asked for strengthening France's conventional posture in Germany, Kennedy had already advocated the development of a strategy "to explore all reasonable avenues for settlement."[10] On August 24, Kennedy asked de Gaulle to agree to negotiations with the Soviet Union over Berlin, arguing that "the necessary complement to the military build-up is a clear willingness to negotiate."[11] Again, de Gaulle chose a different position. On August 30, NATO Ambassador Thomas Finletter informed Kennedy that among the allies "the unanimous opinion, except for France, is in favor of immediate steps looking forward to negotiations on the substance..."[12] In truth, of course, Adenauer was also deeply reluctant to engage in discussions with the Soviets, fearing that Kennedy would make unwarranted concessions on the Oder-Neisse line and on Berlin.[13]

The Berlin experience of 1961 and 1962 caused considerable frustration inside the Kennedy administration with de Gaulle's rigidity and contrary military policies. American officials were particularly irritated with what they perceived as de Gaulle's shameless and irresponsible exploitation of the US nuclear security guarantee. "General de Gaulle believes we are in Berlin and that if the Soviets disturb us we will shoot," Rusk complained to Adenauer on August 10, 1961. "This is not an adequate position in the sixties when we are considering a nuclear war."[14] Kennedy, too, was increasingly aggravated by de Gaulle's refusal to negotiate, complaining at one point to Barbara Ward Jackson that he felt that with de Gaulle and Adenauer "it's like trying to run across a plowed field, every time you move, your feet get heavier."[15]

Kennedy's irritation with de Gaulle's intransigence culminated in the spring of 1962 – and André Malraux became its unwitting brunt. On May 11, 1962, Kennedy received de Gaulle's minister of culture – and a living legend on his own account for his adventurous lifestyle and novels and the man who served as de Gaulle's "cultural *force de frappe*"[16] throughout the 1960s – in the White House Cabinet Room. Their conversation was truly remarkable not only for the bluntness with which Kennedy took aim at de Gaulle and his policies, but also for the degree in which it brought to light their fundamentally opposite views of the American presence in Europe. Pressing for France's agreement to British membership of the Common Market, Kennedy began by brushing off Malraux's claim that "if England really wished to join the Common Market, nothing could prevent her." He rather believed de Gaulle was deeply opposed to British membership for political reasons and "apparently preferred a Europe without Great Britain and independent of the United States – a powerful force which France would speak for," and that this view brought "France and the United States into conflict." Kennedy made abundantly clear, too, that he was tired of de Gaulle's – and Adenauer's – unbending position on Berlin, whereas the United States would carry the military burden of defending Western Europe if it came to war. He deplored that "some Europeans seem to regard our presence in a more sinister light, as a kind of unwarranted interference in their internal affairs." Sensing "latent, almost female, hostility" in France and Germany towards American dominance in Europe's security affairs, Kennedy pointedly remarked that if there was a French-German axis "he would be glad to let it try to handle the Berlin affair." Time and again, Kennedy demanded explanations from Malraux about de Gaulle's behavior. "We find it difficult to understand the apparent determination of General de Gaulle to cut across our policies in Europe." And: "What is the reason that we always wound up in such sharp disagreement?" The only reason Kennedy could find was that, "deep down inside, General de Gaulle did not want the Americans in Europe." He added, on a more menacing note, that "General de Gaulle should make no mistake: Americans would be glad to get out of Europe." During the conversation, Kennedy would repeatedly return to the theme that de Gaulle's policies risked re-awakening America's innate isolationism. "It has now cost us about $1,300,000,000 to maintain our forces in Europe and the savings on these forces would just about meet our balance-of-payments deficit." In sum, by the spring of 1962, Kennedy evidently was fed up with de Gaulle's obstructionism and anti-American taunts: "We feel like a man carrying a 200-pound sack of potatoes, and other people not carrying the same load, at least in potatoes, keep telling us how to carry our burden."[17]

Diplomatic contacts between Washington and Paris would remain querulous for much of the spring. Malraux's report of his conversation with Kennedy was received in Paris with similar infuriation. On May 16, de Gaulle retorted in a conversation with Ambassador Gavin that the United States "should not be mixed up in Western European difficulties and should keep itself apart only bringing its weight to bear in case of necessity."[18] This in turn prompted Kennedy to instruct Gavin that:

> when you see him [de Gaulle] again, I hope you will spell out our inability to accept the notion that we should stay out of Europe's affairs while remaining ready to defend her if war should come. We cannot give this kind of blank check. ... We shall not hesitate to make this point to the Germans if they show signs of accepting any idea of a Bonn-Paris axis. General de Gaulle really cannot have both our military presence and our diplomatic absence, and you should make this point with emphasis.[19]

When Gavin did so, de Gaulle icily replied that he did not fear American isolationism, "but exactly the opposite, that [the] U.S. will play a somewhat excessive role in European affairs," and he warned that America's "excessive leadership" in Europe would "only contribute to [a] breakdown within [the] Alliance." In his report to Washington, Gavin underscored that he had "never seen de Gaulle in a more unfriendly and tense state of mind," adding his conviction that "if there ever has been need for an agonizing reappraisal of our policy vis-à-vis Europe certainly it is now."[20] Whatever Gavin had in mind, de Gaulle professed to Secretary Rusk a few weeks later that he did not see how the bilateral relationship could be improved. According to the Frenchman, it "was best for each of us simply to play his own game and live with the situation."[21] Kennedy indeed played "his own game" by proclaiming his plan for an Atlantic partnership in his Philadelphia speech soon thereafter – thus doing exactly what de Gaulle did not want: inserting American power and ideas into European politics. However, it was an illusion that each could play his own game without it ending in conflict. By the spring of 1962, the Franco-American crisis of 1963 was clearly in the making.

The Fateful Meetings of December 1962

Other factors contributed to the upcoming crisis as well. For one, the political resolution of the Algerian conflict with the March 1962 Evian agreement and the proclamation of Algerian independence in July 1962 enabled de Gaulle to concentrate on his policy of independence vis-à-vis the United States. For another, the National Assembly elections of November 1962 resulted in one of de Gaulle's greatest political victories over the remaining vestiges of the Fourth Republic, which finally gave him "a bit of peace" on the domestic front to pursue his foreign policy ambitions.[22] Moreover, Kennedy's failure to consult the European allies in handling the Cuban Missile Crisis of October 1962 and his summit meeting in December 1962 with Harold Macmillan at Nassau – which will be discussed later in this chapter – put a definitive end to de Gaulle's memorandum diplomacy since September 1958. Rather perversely, the Cuban Missile Crisis also enabled de Gaulle to distance himself more easily from American leadership, since it had given him the occasion to attest to the firmness of his solidarity with the United States when the chips were down in the Cold War.

However, the Franco-American crisis of 1963 was in the end forced to a head by a decision in the fall of 1962 that seemed unrelated to Franco-American differences: Robert McNamara's cancellation for budgetary reasons of the US Air Force's Skybolt missile program. As we will see, the chain of events that followed this apparently innocuous decision led to an unintended reaffirmation of the Anglo-American strategic partnership at the Nassau summit and, subsequently, to a makeshift infringement on the independence of the French nuclear deterrent. To de Gaulle, this course of events confirmed his already strong suspicion that Great Britain was far from politically ready to join his European project but once admitted to the Common Market would rather act as a conduit for American strategic interests. In addition, it induced him to disavow publicly the American proposal for a multilateral nuclear force (MLF) that had been held out to him in the wake of the Nassau summit.

The Skybolt – or GAM-87 – was an air-to-ground missile that had been under development by the US Air Force since 1958 and was intended to become operational in 1964 or 1965. Its long range – 1000 miles, as compared with the 500 miles of its precursor, the Hound Dog missile – was designed to extend the range of American strategic bombers in response to improvements in Soviet air defenses. From the initial stage of its development, the British had been actively interested in the Skybolt missile as an alternative for their Blue Streak missile; as a result, the Skybolt was from the outset designed to be compatible with Great Britain's V-bombers. Meeting with Prime Minister Macmillan in March 1960, Eisenhower had agreed to sell the missile to Great Britain "in 1965 or thereafter" in return for the use of the Holy Loch submarine base in Scotland by US Polaris submarines. Macmillan had subsequently canceled the troublesome development of the Blue Streak missile and had staked the future of the British nuclear deterrent largely on the Skybolt. [23] Yet, the future of the Skybolt had remained uncertain: its technical feasibility was as yet unproven and, as a result, it proved a natural target for budget exercises in Washington. The advent of an American administration less prepared to accommodate Great Britain's wish for extending the lifespan of its national nuclear deterrent had merely added to the uncertainties. So McNamara's decision to halt the program was merely self-evident in American eyes when the estimated costs of procuring the Skybolt missile had risen from $1.4 billion to $1.75 billion in 1962 (on top of earlier increases), the Skybolt program increasingly compared unfavorably with other missile programs (such as Polaris and Minuteman), and the conviction took root that bombers at some point would be phased out anyhow as a means of delivery. In fact, his decision was entirely in accordance with the Acheson Report of April 1961, which had advised that "it would be desirable if the British decided to phase out of the nuclear deterrent business" and that "if the development of Skybolt is not warranted for U.S. purposes alone, the U.S. should not prolong the life of the V-Bomber force by this or other means."[24]

McNamara's cancellation of the Skybolt program evidently would cause the Macmillan government grave – potentially even fatal – political problems. This was recognized within the Kennedy administration, too, as these problems were aptly summed up by the State Department at the request of the White House in late October. The Skybolt's cancellation, the State Department judged, would "put in jeopardy not only Bomber Command but a vital element of British defense philosophy" and "call into question the whole concept of the independent British deterrent." It would amount to "an unmitigated political blow to the Conservatives" and "to the image, both public and private, of Tory competence in these two fields [defense and dealing with the Americans]." It even risked irreparably damaging the "special relationship," as "the British would certainly feel let down – hard." While the State Department neither questioned McNamara's decision nor the United States' policy of unfriendliness toward national nuclear forces (including Great Britain's), there was a measure of trepidation about its implications for a strategic partnership that had been so vital to the Cold War alliance. "If we were to appear to be "double-crossing" our oldest and closest ally – and it might well appear this way – it would be a serious blow to our whole alliance system."[25] Informing the British government about the plan to cancel the Skybolt program thus required a great deal of tact. After having received Kennedy's approval on November 7, McNamara first informed British Ambassador David Ormsby-Gore and then Defense Minister Peter Thorneycroft of his intentions. He also volunteered to go to London to discuss the alternatives prior to making any final decisions.[26] In spite of this, the Kennedy administration was ill-prepared for the intensity of the British reaction. As Thorneycroft recalled, the unilateral cancellation of the Skybolt "went deeper than defense policy and went to the very root of any possibility of the British trusting America in defense dealings again."[27] Nor did Washington have a clear view of the ramifications if, for fear of a complete breakdown of the special relationship, the British were nonetheless granted a deal to keep their nuclear deterrent alive. As Deputy Secretary of Defense Roswell Gilpatric recalled, "no one foresaw [...] the chain of events that followed."[28]

In the crucible of the crisis produced by McNamara's cancellation of the Skybolt program, the nuclear weapons issue and Great Britain's bid for membership of the Common Market were hurled together in a way that undercut Kennedy's design for an Atlantic partnership. In December 1962, in the time span of one week, Macmillan successively met with de Gaulle at Rambouillet and with Kennedy at Nassau – and both issues were on the table. Neither meeting was decisive in bringing about the crisis of 1963, yet their combined effect spelled disaster for

Kennedy's hopes of de Gaulle playing his part in bringing about the Atlantic partnership that Kennedy had put in the offing in July 1962.

Macmillan's meeting with de Gaulle at Rambouillet on December 15 and 16 took place under a rather worse constellation than their June meeting at Château de Champs. In June, Macmillan had impressed de Gaulle with the depth of his commitment to join the Common Market. Yet British negotiators had proved much less flexible in negotiating the terms of entry in subsequent months; meanwhile de Gaulle's political position – domestically as well as internationally – had become steadily stronger. After the Philadelphia speech, the Kennedy administration moreover had cranked up the pressure on the Six to admit the British, which de Gaulle resented. The Rambouillet meeting between de Gaulle and Macmillan not only ended on a sour note, but also in a state of considerable confusion about what the two elder statesmen had discussed in private. The British prime minister certainly informed de Gaulle of his Skybolt quandary and he would also claim to have told de Gaulle that he would ask for Polaris submarine missiles if Kennedy would stick to the cancellation of Skybolt.[29] De Gaulle at the time confirmed that Macmillan mentioned Skybolt, but he later denied to Adenauer that Macmillan had told him of his intention to ask for Polaris missiles. Whatever happened precisely, it was clear that the gulf between the two had never been so wide. De Gaulle had approached the meeting as if it were a trial of whether Macmillan was prepared to sever Great Britain's close ties with – and dependency on – the United States. The Skybolt affair proved to him that the British government was at the mercy of Washington and that it was applying for membership of the Common Market as America's pawn. Great Britain's devotion to the special relationship was only underscored by the fact that Macmillan did not take up on de Gaulle's suggestion that France and Great Britain develop a missile together, possibly through reviving the Blue Streak missile. In his talks with Macmillan, de Gaulle made his reservations about British membership of the Common Market clear in a way that left little doubt about his negative disposition. Immediately after the meeting, British diplomats were convinced that "only a bloody fool" would think that de Gaulle would agree to British membership of the Common Market anytime soon. It is not entirely clear whether Macmillan, too, gloomy and angry at de Gaulle's attitude, had given up all hope.[30]

The Nassau conference between Kennedy and Macmillan from December 18 to 21 stands out as a most confusing one. In Ball's damning estimation, it was "one of the worst prepared summit meetings in modern times."[31] Kennedy and Macmillan had been scheduled to discuss a wide range of topics, but their meeting was completely overshadowed by the topic of Skybolt. In preparing for the meeting, Kennedy agreed with McNamara that the decision to cancel the Skybolt program was definite, regardless of the problems this posed for the British. Yet Kennedy also understood that he could not leave Macmillan empty-handed. Three alternatives were therefore discussed in Washington prior to the meeting: 1) the

British could finance the remainder of the Skybolt program for their own use; 2) they could be offered the shorter-range Hound Dog missile as an interim solution; or 3) they could be offered Polaris missiles for use aboard submarines. However, with regard to the latter option, to which Macmillan probably referred in his meeting with de Gaulle, the State Department considered it essential that Great Britain would only be granted missiles if it agreed that they become part of a NATO-owned multilateral nuclear force. On November 24, Rusk sent McNamara a letter explaining his concern about the political fallout in Europe if the United States would supply Great Britain with Polaris missiles without strings attached: "Their [the Europeans'] resentment [of the Anglo-American special relationship] has been kept within bounds so far by indications that this relation would not be extended beyond the V-bombers (which are obsolescing) into the MRBMs [medium range ballistic missiles] which are clearly the next phase in Europe-based nuclear deterrence." According to Rusk, "the political costs of continuing to deny MRBM aid to France would be significantly increased," and American assistance to "nationally manned and owned British MRBMs would almost certainly eventually lead to German demands for equal treatment." He also feared that the provision of Polaris missiles would endanger Great Britain's chances of being admitted to the Common Market.[32] The MLF had already moved closer to the center stage of American diplomacy in the wake of Kennedy's Philadelphia speech about an Atlantic partnership. Now it was also being put forward as a useful device to defuse the potential political fallout in Europe of the Skybolt crisis.

On December 16, the division between the Pentagon and the State Department came clearly to the fore as Kennedy met in the Oval Room with his advisers to prepare for his encounter with Macmillan. McNamara proposed the sale of Polaris missiles to Great Britain without demanding that these would eventually be included in a multilateral force. Giving priority to prodding the Europeans to beef up their conventional forces, he reasoned that "there is no way in which we can persuade the Europeans to buy and pay for both a multilateral force and a full compliance with NATO conventional force goals." However George Ball, representing the State Department, argued that any arrangement that would continue to grant the British a national nuclear capability would have major political repercussions in Europe and go against the grain of America's non-proliferation policy. Kennedy thus found himself in the horns of a daunting dilemma. On the one hand, the political consequences for the Macmillan government would be grave if he decided against helping Great Britain. On the other hand, if he did help Macmillan he would risk the retribution of the continental European allies – and this could have serious repercussions for Britain's bid for the Common Market. At the end of the discussion, he decided that the meeting should be planned on the assumption that the United States would offer Polaris missiles to Great Britain on the condition that the eventual force would be committed "to a multilateral or multinational force in NATO" and that the British would beef up their conventional forces.[33]

Given this prelude, it is not surprising that the meeting at Nassau began in an atmosphere of considerable mistrust and uncertainty. The core question was whether Kennedy would allow for a continuation of the national British deterrent or insist on its gradual dissipation in a multilateral arrangement. He began by suggesting to Macmillan that the British could continue the development of the Skybolt missile for their own purposes. Although he had rejected Rusk's suggestion to help the British finance the further development of Skybolt in an earlier meeting,[34] Kennedy did offer to share in the costs – a deal which he had worked out with British Ambassador Ormsby-Gore aboard the airplane en route to the Bahamas. The British prime minister, however, was no longer interested in the Skybolt missile since it had been exposed as too expensive and technically flawed; "the lady," he said, had been "violated" in public. Macmillan moreover accepted the American view that the bomber would sooner or later become obsolete as a means of delivery for nuclear weapons. Nor did Macmillan see much use for the Hound Dog missile as an interim solution because the introduction of this missile would require major adaptations to British bombers. The discussion therefore quickly focused on the provision of Polaris missiles for British submarines, which in Macmillan's view "were more suitable for an island like Britain, which also had a great naval tradition."

In the remainder of the meeting, Kennedy, strongly seconded by Ball, pressured Macmillan to commit the Polaris missiles to a mixed-manned multilateral force and tried to strip the British nuclear force of as much independence as possible. Macmillan, however, was adamant about preserving the independence of the British nuclear force: "The UK does not want to be a clown, or a satellite." He insisted that Great Britain absolutely needed to preserve the right to withdraw its submarines from NATO command for reasons of national interest. He also resisted any pressure for mixed-manning of a NATO nuclear force: "The crews must feel that they are the 'Queen's sailors' until a supranational organization comes into being." Macmillan acknowledged that his position in respect of having a nuclear deterrent was not much different from de Gaulle's. "I do not believe," he posited, "that the Atlantic partnership will ever succeed or be built up except on pooling of equal pride and honor." Macmillan and his Foreign Minister Lord Home furthermore took issue with Kennedy's statement that the provision of Polaris missiles would "shake the European allies" and undercut Great Britain's negotiations with the Common Market. As for the European reaction, Macmillan said that there would be "frankly, absolutely none." Lord Home chimed in by saying that the proposal for a multilateral force had almost no appeal in Europe. Since there was "not a single ally in Europe that would allow Germany to have its finger on the trigger," the Europeans would be satisfied "to see the United States, Britain, and France cooperate in a nuclear force if the Europeans knew about the deployment, targeting, etc." Macmillan also cast doubt on Germany's interest in "having one of fifteen sailors." As if this fierce defense of British sovereignty were not enough, Macmillan warned that he would feel compelled to overturn the historic Anglo-American strategic partnership. If he could not get Kennedy's agreement on a substantial measure of independence for his nuclear force, "we would have to undertake an agonizing reappraisal of our military and political policies." After much haggling over precise language, Macmillan finally succeeded in preserving the right to withdraw British nuclear forces from NATO "where H.M.G. may decide that supreme national interests are at stake."[35]

At the end of the turbulent summit at Nassau, the strategic partnership between the United States and Great Britain thus had once again won the day. Notwithstanding the cancellation of Skybolt, Kennedy had granted the British nuclear force a new lease on life with the provision of Polaris missiles for British submarines, albeit that this new lease was concealed by the concomitant endorsement of a multilateral nuclear force.[36] As so often is the case, personal relationships had mattered a great deal in bringing about this result. British Ambassador David Ormsby-Gore's intimate rapport with Kennedy had been of particular importance. On the eve of the Nassau meeting, it was Ormsby-Gore who had convinced Kennedy of the seriousness of Macmillan's political predicament and of the need for Britain to maintain an independent nuclear deterrent.[37] Resistance to Macmillan's escape clause had come mainly from George Ball and the Europeanists at the State Department. They had pressed relentlessly for phasing out the British deterrent, as well as for Great Britain's unqualified entry into the Common Market (which entailed signing up to the objective of political integration). They had, in fact, endeavored to reverse a long history of special links between Washington and London – a mainstay in American foreign policy since the 1800s – in order to advance the cause of European integration. Together with the Marshall Plan, American support for European integration since 1947, and Kennedy's call for an Atlantic partnership in July 1962, the State Department's attempt at Nassau to force Macmillan into ditching the British national nuclear deterrent was a culminating point in the long campaign to reconstruct Europe. A buoyant George Ball certainly viewed his success in foisting the multilateral formula on Macmillan at Nassau as an important political and personal victory. Like Monnet, he felt that by the end of 1962, great strides were being made toward the goal of an integrated Europe and hence toward an Atlantic partnership. In its communications with European allies after Nassau, the State Department conveniently ignored the escape clause Macmillan had been given. Believing they had been given a presidential mandate to pursue their program, the Europeanists had few inhibitions to ratchet up the pressure on the European allies to accept the multilateral formula for an allied nuclear force.[38] They had not, however, achieved full victory. The joint endorsement of the multilateral force was only ostensibly the main result of the Nassau summit, given prominence largely for reasons of public diplomacy. It would not have gained Kennedy's public support if he had not felt obliged to off-set politically the provision of Polaris missiles to Great Britain.[39] As importantly, the Europeanists could claim victory only if the one European leader who could still abort their plans would choose to go along with the flow of events they had fostered.

The Treacherous Road from Nassau to Paris

The Next Problem: France

As Richard Neustadt has observed, neither Kennedy nor Macmillan was able to keep his mind on de Gaulle at the Nassau conference – and their neglect of "French hostility" to their respective foreign policy designs was one of the key explanations for "the Nassau story."[40] Of the two, Kennedy had been more atten-tive to the potential fallout of an Anglo-American deal in Europe. Although he had wanted to spare Macmillan a political fiasco, his attendant concern about an adverse reaction in Germany and France to Great Britain's preferential treatment had made him press the British prime minister to accept the multilateral formu-la.[41] Macmillan, by contrast, had focused on preserving the independence of the British deterrent. He had not fully informed Kennedy about the gist of his meet-ing with de Gaulle at Rambouillet just a few days earlier. His priority was simply to get Kennedy's promise to substitute Polaris for Skybolt. Given de Gaulle's in-transigence at Rambouillet and weakening domestic support for the membership bid, Macmillan may have already concluded that British membership would not come about soon anyway. This would at least help to explain his single-minded-ness in extracting a promise from Kennedy on Polaris. It would also throw light on his apparent disinterest – astonishing given his avid earlier attempts to broker a nuclear deal involving Washington and Paris – in getting the United States to extend nuclear aid to France and his nonchalance about the possible fallout of the Nassau deal in Europe.

Kennedy had ultimately given in to Macmillan's insistence on preserving a na-tional nuclear deterrent. It was quite clear to his delegation at Nassau that this meant a gesture had to be made toward Paris as well, or else Great Britain's pros-pects of Common Market membership would inevitably suffer. Although Ade-nauer would also have to be taken along, de Gaulle posed by far the most difficult diplomatic hurdle in the aftermath of the Nassau meeting. Prior to the meeting, Ambassador Bohlen had warned against the provision of Polaris missiles to Great Britain because of the possible repercussions for Great Britain's entry negotia-tions.[42] In addition, the State Department had consistently emphasized that any arrangement would have to be multilateral in order to avoid the notion that the Anglo-American special relationship was still in force.[43] At Nassau, the potential repercussions of the Polaris deal with Macmillan had been pointed out to Kennedy by Assistant Secretary of State for European Affairs William Tyler, who had calculated that de Gaulle would view the Nassau agreement as "confirmation of his claim that the United States was more interested in dominating Europe than in encouraging Europe to be really an independent and entirely self-reliant entity."[44] Mainly in order to limit any political damage to the British membership bid, it was therefore decided that the Polaris offer should be extended to France. On December 20, Kennedy cabled a letter to de Gaulle about his agreement with Macmillan and stated that he would "consider a similar agreement with you, should you so desire."[45] Yet, as George Ball acknowledged in his memoirs, "our offer to the General would inevitably appear as an afterthought – and the General was not one to wear anyone's cast off clothing."[46]

Whether an afterthought or not, one of the peculiar consequences of the Nassau agreement with the British was that, all of a sudden, the question of aiding the French nuclear program had posed itself in full force. In the course of finding a way to meet Macmillan halfway, the Kennedy administration had actually veered away from the strict non-proliferation policy expounded by McNamara in the spring of 1962 towards a more lenient policy of pooling the existing British nuclear deterrent under the NATO banner together with a future French deterrent and designated American nuclear forces. However, the question of what kind of assistance the United States would be prepared to give France and on what conditions was still unanswered. Presumably the offer would be similar to the one offered to the British. But what did "similar" mean? Would France be granted an independent deterrent or would it be requested to partake in the mixed-manned multilateral force that had been proposed by the State Department? Would the United States be prepared to go as far as furnishing warheads? In the confusion after the Nassau summit, the entire range of possibilities for nuclear cooperation with the French would be reconsidered.

The Front Lines in Washington

Preparations for the Nassau summit had already clearly brought to the fore the division between the State Department and the Pentagon on alliance nuclear policies. The State Department's Europeanists were fervent supporters of the idea of a *multilateral* nuclear force. They did not like the rival concept of a *multinational* force, which merely envisaged the coordination of national nuclear forces. Such an arrangement would connote that the United States would recognize a French national deterrent as a valuable asset to the defense of the West. In addition, a multinational setup could not be extended to Germany without granting it the national nuclear capability that the whole concept of a NATO nuclear force was supposed to prevent. In order to counteract German sensitivities about being discriminated against, the State Department was also strongly in favor of manning the nuclear forces with soldiers from different nationalities. "We have been able to find no other way than mixed manning to reconcile authentic German participation with denial of a national capability to Germany," Rostow wrote to Rusk during the Nassau conference. "Mixed manning is, therefore, at the heart of our position on a multilateral force."[47] However, there was strong opposition within the Pentagon to such a mixed-manned multilateral force, which was seen as militarily insignificant and squandering resources better spent on conventional forces. Assistant Secretary of Defense for International Affairs Paul Nitze, who was also at Nassau, was a particularly vocal opponent of a multilateral arrangement. Nitze rather preferred a series of bilateral coordination arrangements between the United States and Europe's nuclear powers, much like "spokes in a wheel." As a consequence, he was also not averse to aiding the French nuclear effort.[48]

After Nassau, the disagreement between the multilateralists of the State Department and the multinationalists at the Pentagon continued unabated. The summit's ambiguous outcome – the result of Kennedy's insistence on a multilateral formula and Macmillan's insistence on an escape clause – gave both sides reason to believe they had won the day. The Pentagon placed priority on the buildup of European conventional forces. It was concerned that the multilateral force would use up the funds that could otherwise be used to strengthen conventional capabilities. For this reason, the Pentagon wanted to implement the Nassau agreement quickly and at a minimum cost to the British. It also wanted to come to a rapid resolution of the issues with the French. In a meeting with Rusk on the implementation of the Nassau agreement, McNamara argued that, if France was willing to commit nuclear forces to a NATO multilateral force and accept satisfactory command and control arrangements, "we should be prepared to supply submarines and war heads... ."[49] He hoped that this would save Paris money, which could then be invested in conventional forces. The Pentagon also contended that this might induce a more cooperative attitude on the part of de Gaulle: "we must realistically face up to the fact that the only avenue toward achieving cooperation with our Allies is by our demonstrated willingness to cooperate through our own actions." The Europeanists at the State Department, however, believed that extending the Nassau agreement to France would be a mistake and also did not favor a swift implementation of the agreement with Great Britain. Behind this position was the expectation that the high costs of maintaining an independent deterrent would eventually compel Great Britain to join a truly multilateral scheme. The State Department also foresaw a long dialogue and did not want to prejudice the outcome by the nature of initial contacts with the French. It was playing for time to allow the "inevitable course of European multilateralism" take hold in London and Paris.[50]

The Europeanist view on post-Nassau strategy was laid out in a lengthy paper drafted at the State Department by Walt Rostow in the weeks after the summit. Presenting the post-Nassau period as a "complex transitional process," Rostow viewed the establishment of a mixed-manned multilateral force as vital to the cause of European unity and Atlantic partnership. The MLF would ensure that "European nuclear forces be targeted and controlled to the maximum extent possible on a unified basis, with maximum acceptance of U.S. doctrine concerning the role and use of nuclear weapons." It would also reduce the feeling of discrimination in Germany; failure to do so, it was estimated, would mean that Germany's Western oriented government would "sooner or later make way for a government which is committed to more nationalist approaches, including a German nuclear program and also the exploitation of its powerful East-West bargaining leverage." In addition, the MLF would help resolve the tension between granting European allies a finger on the trigger and the goal of European integration: "One cannot simultaneously work for European integration while spreading about and embedding in concrete the power of national European governments to trigger a nuclear war which would engulf the whole Europe Community." The paper thus deplored that Great Britain had been allowed to hold on to its national nuclear force at Nassau and urged that the United States would henceforth "seek to transform the image of the multilateral mixed-manned force from association with third-class Alliance citizenship to its being the wave of the future."[51] In this context, too, the report considered it essential that "the possibility of the mixed-manned force evolving into a European force (linked to NATO and SAC) not be excluded at this time."[52]

There is evidence of considerable wishful thinking in Rostow's paper as to the attractiveness of the multilateral formula to the European allies. There was the hopeful expectation that the British would eventually relinquish the independence of their nuclear force: "The unavoidably high cost of that deterrent will be one of the factors which may incline the U.K. over time to participate in a genuine multilateral mixed-manned force." The paper also prognosticated that "if Britain successfully enters the Common Market ... Britain may, in the course of the 1960s, come to accept wholeheartedly the hard facts of interdependence and the case for full multilateralism." However, Rostow was forcibly less confident in predicting the development of French attitudes. "There are strong undercurrents in France which already are prepared for a truly multilateral solution [...], but it is still to be established whether de Gaulle is interested in moving at all in the direction of interdependence." Yet, even as the paper recognized that "we have not the slightest evidence that de Gaulle is prepared to bargain a radical change in his basic policy towards Europe and the Atlantic Partnership against equality with Britain in its nuclear relationship with the United States," it still rather naively concluded that

the central task in the post-Nassau period in our policy towards the French is ... to find out if de Gaulle is prepared to enter into dialogue with us over the full range of our current cross-purposes; and, in particular, whether he is prepared in any serious way to throw his weight behind a truly multilateral force

(European or NATO) and to contribute positively to its creation. [...] the costs to U.S. interests of de Gaulle's present policy are such that we should be prepared to establish [...] any opening the Nassau agreement may provide to alter the present thrust of those policies, and to end the decorous cold war between Paris and Washington. [...] It is out of the counterpoint between European separatist impulses and the hard facts of interdependence that the President's concept of an Atlantic partnership must be brought to life.[53]

At the White House, meanwhile, there was a more pragmatic view much less committed to the multilateral nuclear option. Prior to the Nassau summit, David Klein of the White House staff had written a memorandum to McGeorge Bundy because he found himself "out of sympathy with some of the theology that has evolved on the question of our relations with de Gaulle, and particularly the impact of our nuclear policy on these relations." Although he subscribed to the view that de Gaulle's cooperation could not be purchased, Klein believed that the American position "has been too often and too dogmatically reiterated" and that "one of the first and most useful things we can do now ... is to take the nuclear question out of the immediate forum of debate." Not only would this help to ameliorate relations with Paris in the short run, but Klein also asked whether "in the long run, don't we really want to leave ourselves some alternatives and freedom of choice?" Against this background, Klein suggested that de Gaulle be invited to visit the United States soon after Kennedy's planned meeting with Macmillan: "With the President's Cuban and elections accomplishments clearly on the record, and de Gaulle's election victory to his credit, both sides are probably in the best position in years to get together for such discussions."[54] Following the Nassau summit, the White House staff continued to resist the State Department's strong predilection for the multilateral approach in nuclear affairs.

However, the MLF enthusiasts at the State Departments clearly had the wind behind them after the Nassau summit, partly because the Anglo-American agreement on designating nuclear forces to a multilateral force required a lot more staff time to be devoted to the project.[55] In early January, moreover, Deputy Secretary of State George Ball was sent to Europe to explain the gist of the Nassau agreement to the North Atlantic Council and a number of European capitals. As was his wont, he emphasized the multilateral aspects of the agreement, and his presentation to the North Atlantic Council on January 11 amounted to a strong sales pitch for the mixed-manned multilateral force. Ball stressed that the national nuclear forces of Great Britain and possibly France would have to be assigned to the same commander as the proposed mixed-manned force – SACEUR – and that they could only be used according to the Athens guidelines.[56] The Nassau meeting's aftermath was thus at least as confusing as its run-up. The British, on the one hand, plausibly emphasized that Macmillan had safeguarded the independence of the British deterrent with his proviso. The Americans, on the other hand, led by Ball, chipped away at this independence whenever they could, putting great stock in Macmillan's promise to make the British Polaris force "available for inclusion in a NATO multilateral nuclear force," together with "at least equal U.S. forces."[57] In his investigation into Nassau on behalf of Kennedy, Richard Neustadt characterized Ball's position as follows:

> The British formula was worth supporting if it made life bearable for the Tories while they did their work of bringing Britain into the EEC. It was worth offering the French since a negotiation might entangle them in such a way as to assure complaisance toward the British at the coming round of talks on the EEC. But once the British had got into "Europe", we should modify that formula as fast as possible, and work our way back to the safe ground of a "truly" multilateral solution – MLF.[58]

Ball's incurable persistence in casting intra-European and transatlantic relations in a multilateral mold clearly puts them in the camp of American foreign policy liberals. His considerable pragmatism about the road to be traveled made his attitude also vintage Monnet. But pragmatism alone would not be sufficient to overcome the shortcomings of the Polaris proposal as viewed by France and the fundamental incompatibility of views between Washington and Paris.

The Mixed French Reaction

By some tortuous way, McNamara's cancellation of Skybolt and Kennedy's ultimate lenience with Macmillan had resulted in an offer by the United States to provide Polaris missiles to Paris – thus breaking with Kennedy's policy of categorical non-assistance to the French nuclear weapons program. Just how far the Kennedy administration was prepared to go in assisting the *force de frappe* was not clear; it was still making up its mind. What was clear, however, was that any American assistance would come with strings attached. "The key," said Dean Rusk during one of the Nassau follow-up meetings, "would be a sufficiently fundamental change in French policy."[59]

In the weeks following the Nassau summit, Washington largely remained in limbo about de Gaulle's response. On the day de Gaulle received Kennedy's letter sent from Nassau, he ordered his chief of staff Etienne Burin des Roziers to inform the American embassy that he was "very impressed" with its contents and needed time to "reflect on it."[60] There was a mixed range of signals. Some exchanges gave Washington the impression that de Gaulle was not averse to exploring the matter seriously. De Gaulle's written reply to Kennedy's letter was, in the words of McGeorge Bundy, "somewhat better than we might have expected and obviously leaves room for much more discussion."[61] Upon hearing of the American offer, French Ambassador Alphand nevertheless judged that it would be politely rejected in Paris.[62] A few days after the Nassau meeting, Couve de Murville moreover indicated that the Anglo-American deal had not been well received and had made it difficult for France to concur with Britain's entry into the Common Market. The French foreign minister told American diplomats that the "fact that Macmillan went to Nassau at this juncture proves [that] Macmillan [had] not yet decided to be really European but is still holding on to Great Britain's special relationship with the US" and that "any arrangement which envisaged [a] close linkage [between] UK-Europe-US would result in all involved becoming Americanized." Couve de Murville also made clear that the American offer of Polaris missiles did not fit well with the French nuclear program.[63] Many years hence, Burin des Roziers summed up French awkwardness with the American offer in the weeks after the Nassau summit as follows:

> we were offered Polaris rockets to launch nuclear warheads we didn't have. [...] Thus, on a technical level, this proposal was of no immediate relevance for us. More importantly, the project called for these Polaris rockets to be made available to Great Britain, and eventually to France, as part of an international force over which we had no control. This international force, like NATO, would be under American command. Granted, there was a clause stating that in grave circumstances (in case of national survival), we could use this force. But de Gaulle said he couldn't quite see how, in an apocalyptic case of nuclear war, we would be able to separate our nuclear power from this international force.[64]

Yet, it was at the time still unclear to Washington how de Gaulle would ultimately react to the offer. In the aftermath of the Nassau meeting, the Kennedy administration sought to whet de Gaulle's appetite for American military assistance and hoped that a deal could be struck with France on the basis of the Nassau declaration. The most important objective was to draw the French into a serious dialogue on nuclear issues and to buy much needed time to work out the details of a co-operative arrangement. McGeorge Bundy, for instance, feared above all that "a dialogue may be cut off before it begins by those on both sides who prefer to nourish their suspicions of each other."[65] Against this background, too, Rusk advised that Kennedy invite de Gaulle to Palm Beach, albeit not before the latter had had his planned meeting with Adenauer on January 21.[66] In addition, Kennedy hosted French Ambassador Alphand and his wife for New Year celebrations at Palm Beach, using the relaxed ambiance to explain his thinking and to impress on the French not to reject the offer out of hand but to further discuss the matter.[67]

The Kennedy administration in particular tried to arouse de Gaulle's interest by purporting that the Nassau offer represented a "major turning point" in American policy towards France. On January 1, the State Department instructed Ambassador Bohlen to convince the French president that the United States was now prepared to recognize France as a nuclear power and to put an end to the exclusive nuclear relationship with the British. At the same time, Bohlen had to make clear that American assistance for the French nuclear program would not come free of charge. The United States would only be prepared to revise its attitude "on the understanding that the French themselves revise their policy to accept the multilateral principle," which was considered necessary to avoid a German quest for a national nuclear force. The type of assistance the United States would be prepared to give France was deliberately left vague.[68] Dissatisfied with the State Department's rigid attachment to the multilateral formula, Bohlen actually exceeded his instructions – though not, as Neustadt put it, "White House intent" – by stating that "no possibilities were excluded" and "all relationships were open for discussion."[69] In their conversation on January 4, an "extremely amiable" de Gaulle indeed left Bohlen hopeful about the course of events. Although de Gaulle observed that the American offer was of "very little immediate practical value" to the French nuclear program; and although he reiterated his opposition to multilateral arrangements and declined to meet with Kennedy anytime soon, he also imparted that he did not want to close the door on future discussions. After this meeting, Bohlen concluded that de Gaulle "definitely had decided that the advantage to France in the Nassau offer is not sufficient to bring him to any degree of commitment to the multilateral idea," but also that "he was holding back with a view of having us make the next move of a somewhat more concrete nature, particularly on the question of submarine construction and possibly the question of warheads."[70] In early January, de Gaulle thus still appeared resolved to find out what the United States had in store for him at the end of the road. And as long as he was entangled in nuclear negotiations with the United States, Bohlen judged, he could not "be beastly to the British."[71] Kennedy's Grand Design for an Atlantic partnership still seemed within grasp.

The General Says "No"

De Gaulle's "Thunderbolts" of January 1963

In little more than one week, de Gaulle issued what George Ball would aptly call the "thunderbolts" that struck at the heart of Kennedy's Grand Design for an Atlantic partnership.[72] In his seventh press conference as president of France, on January 14, 1963, de Gaulle rejected British membership of the Common Market anytime soon and dismissed the American proposal for a multilateral nuclear force. In a long exposé, he first expounded that Great Britain did not fit in with the Six, economically as well as politically, and de Gaulle's own goal of a "European" Europe:

England is, in effect, insular, maritime, linked through its trade, markets, and food supply to very diverse and often very distant countries. Its activities are essentially industrial and commercial, and only slightly agricultural. It has [...] very marked and very original customs and traditions. In short, the nature, structure, and economic context of England differ profoundly from those of the other States of the Continent.

[...] the entry first of Great Britain, and then of those other States [belonging to the EFTA], will completely change the series of adjustments, agreements, compensations, and regulations already established between the Six, because all these States, like Britain, have very important traits of their own. We would then have to envisage the construction of another Common Market. But the 11-member, then 13-member and then perhaps 18-member Common Market that would be built would, without any doubt, hardly resemble the one the Six have built.

Moreover, this Community, growing in that way, would be confronted with all the problems of its economic relations with a crowd of other States, and first of all with the United States. It is foreseeable that the cohesion of all its members, who would be very numerous and very diverse, would not hold for long and that in the end there would appear a colossal Atlantic Community under American dependence and leadership which would soon completely swallow up the European Community. This is an assumption that can be perfectly justified in the eyes of some, but it is not at all what France wanted to do and what France is doing, which is a strictly European construction.[73]

Having thus dealt a blow to the immediate prospects of British membership,[74] de Gaulle went on to roundly reject the US offer of nuclear assistance based upon the Nassau agreement and stressed his fundamental opposition to nuclear integration in the context of the multilateral force:

France has taken note of the Anglo-American Nassau agreement. As it was conceived, no one will be surprised that we cannot subscribe to it. It truly would not be useful for us to buy Polaris missiles when we have neither the submarines to launch them nor the thermonuclear warheads to arm them [...]. But also, it does not meet with the principle [...] which consists of disposing in our own right of our deterrent force. To turn over our weapons to a multilateral force, under a foreign command, would be to act contrary to that principle of our defense and our policy. It is true that we too can theoretically retain the ability to take back in our hands, in the supreme hypothesis, our atomic weapons incorporated in the multilateral force. But how could we do it in practice in the unheard moments of the atomic apocalypse [...]. In sum, we will adhere to the decision we have made: to construct and, if necessary, to employ our atomic force ourselves.[75]

The hope that France could somehow be drawn into the Nassau arrangement or at least be pinned down in protracted discussions about its future nuclear deterrent thus vanished from one moment to the next. De Gaulle's press conference of January 14 stands out as a nadir in the history of American-French confrontations during the Cold War. He had struck an unmitigated blow at Kennedy's design for an Atlantic partnership. He had rebuffed Great Britain's membership bid of the Common Market and the multilateral nuclear force. He had forcefully restated his objection to the supranational Europe favored by the likes of Monnet, which had been seen by the Kennedy administration as the indispensable constituent of "equal" partnership. And he had publicly denounced the American goal of a "colossal Atlantic Community" – under whatever guise.

The effect of de Gaulle's press conference was much compounded by the ceremonial signing of the Franco-German Treaty of Reconciliation at the Elysée palace, at the conclusion of Chancellor Adenauer's two-day official visit to Paris on January 22. The treaty provided for the coordination of the two countries in foreign affairs, defense, information, and cultural affairs, and wove a fabric of regular meetings between the heads of state, ministers, and chiefs of staff. It stipulated that "the two Governments will consult each other, before taking any decision, on all major questions of foreign policy [...] with a view to achieving as far as possible a similar position." In addition, the treaty arranged for much closer defense cooperation, such as in defense doctrines, armament policies, and training and exchange of personnel. However, it did not contain explicit references to NATO's primacy in European security affairs.[76] Within a matter of weeks, de Gaulle had thus boldly placed his bid for controlling Europe's destiny.

Initial Reactions

De Gaulle's press conference of January 1963 had truly been, as one French newspaper stated, a "conférence de choc" – and today it is difficult to overestimate the vehemence of reactions at the time. Press reactions throughout Europe concluded that de Gaulle was claiming French hegemony over Europe.[77] It is important to recall, too, that a press conference given by de Gaulle was hardly an ordinary event. "It was," as John Newhouse observed, "rather, a piece of theater, a happening, an event of sometimes capital importance – a ritual with all the panoply and pomp of a royal ceremony, but few royal heads of state performed so brilliantly or to such effect as this plebiscitary monarch."[78] In other words, as much as the words, it was the manner that counted.

The man who had lost the most was Macmillan. He had staked his political fate on the membership bid, and de Gaulle not only left him empty-handed but humiliated. "This man [de Gaulle] has gone crazy – absolutely crazy," an exasperated British prime minister exclaimed to Kennedy in a phone conversation on January 19. "The real simple thing is he wants to be the cock on a small dunghill instead of having two cocks on a larger one."[79] To a friend, he wrote that "I do not remember going through a worse time since Suez."[80] In a pique, he concurred with the Foreign Office's advice to cancel an official visit by Princess Margaret to Paris. On January 28, he mourned in his diary that "all our policies at home and abroad are in ruins."[81] But Macmillan was hardly alone in his dismay. De Gaulle's proclamation had caused a row in most of Western Europe. The supporters of European integration, who by and large had been in favor of British membership, were in an uproar; Couve de Murville, for instance, recalled that he had never seen Monnet in such a rage as after de Gaulle's press conference.[82] In Rome, Macmillan found the Italians "angry and alarmed" and bent on revenge against de Gaulle.[83] In France, too, many feared that de Gaulle was isolating the country from its European partners and irresponsibly picking a fight with the Americans. Former Prime Minister Paul Reynaud, for instance, wrote in Le Monde in a state of puzzlement: "France isolated, the Entente cordiale ridiculed, the irritation, if not the enmity of the United States towards us, when it is their presence in Europe that guarantees our liberty, the Common Market, the motive-force of our expansion, threatened with splits. And why?"[84]

In the United States, too, the atmosphere after de Gaulle's press conference was one of bewilderment and anger. From the vantage point of Washington, de Gaulle's reprisal was almost irrational, as it was perceived to go against the grain of European public opinion. "Tell me, ye gods," one Washington official reportedly lifted his hands to the skies, "how is it possible for one lonely, elderly ruler of a small country to frustrate the desires and aspirations of 250 million other Europeans?"[85] Rather than his positions, however, it was de Gaulle's bluntness in expressing them that had caught the administration by surprise.[86] Charles Bohlen, who had been in touch with a number of French ministers prior to the conference, observed that the views expressed by de Gaulle were well-known per se, but admitted surprise at the "frankness and brutality" with which they had been put forward. In particular, with regard to the Nassau agreements, de Gaulle had gone "considerably farther in the direction of complete rejection than had been anticipated," reported Bohlen[87] Of all American officials, George Ball felt particularly dressed down. On January 14, he was in Bonn to solicit Adenauer's support for the MLF. The preceding days he had been in Paris, where he had been informed by a befriended French journalist of the preparations at the Elysée for the press conference. When Ball confronted Couve de Murville about this, however, the latter denied it, so he had left the French capital believing the sky was clear.[88]

The Franco-German Treaty on January 22 equally distressed Washington; as George Ball later wrote, "I can hardly overestimate the shock produced in Washington by this action or the speculation that followed, particularly in the intelligence community."[89] The fact that Adenauer had kept the United States wholly in the dark raised serious concerns. Consecutive administrations had been highly supportive of Franco-German reconciliation as indispensable to ending Europe's history of internecine conflict. But the lack of any reference in the treaty to NATO (while it did include important provisions for bilateral military and political coop-eration), the latent anti-Americanism expressed in de Gaulle's press conference, and his known aspirations to negotiate a separate deal with the Soviet Union to end Europe's division gave the treaty a highly ominous ring in Washington. Was this the beginning of a Franco-German bloc that would act independently from the Western alliance, notably with regard to the East-West conflict? Would Ade-nauer be prepared to support de Gaulle in pursuing a deal with Moscow without the consent of the United States? Was he trying to loosen the shackles on Ger-many of military integration within NATO? Did he support de Gaulle's dismissal of Great Britain? From Kennedy's perspective, de Gaulle was evidently on a cru-sade to force the allies to choose between France and the United States.[90] And Adenauer, it was felt, had made a serious mistake by appearing to take de Gaulle's side. Germany would therefore have to bear the brunt of the American response.[91]

In the weeks following the press conference, there was still some hope that the other members of the Common Market could pressure de Gaulle into refraining from cutting off membership negotiations with Great Britain. For many, Mon-net's attitude that "nothing is quite an accomplished fact so long as it is not accepted" and his statement to the press that "whatever General de Gaulle may have said, the negotiations for British membership of the Common Market could be concluded very rapidly" provided a rallying theme.[92] Considerable pressure was brought to bear by the Kennedy administration on the German government in particular to take a stance against de Gaulle. But the hope vanished as Couve de Murville, in a dramatic meeting of foreign ministers in Brussels on January 28, declared the negotiations with Great Britain suspended as far as France was con-cerned and the Six were compelled to go along.[93]

De Gaulle's assault on key building blocks of the Atlantic partnership program had been so sudden and comprehensive that the Kennedy administration was temporarily swept off its feet. It simply had lost the initiative in Europe to de Gaulle, a highly discomforting thought given his views. There was moreover con-siderable speculation about what de Gaulle still had in store for the United States. The State Department was infested with "wild rumors" that de Gaulle's next move would be to try to negotiate, with Adenauer's acquiescence, a European settle-ment directly with Moscow. "We looked at all possibilities of a Paris-Bonn deal with Moscow, leading toward a Soviet withdrawal from East Germany to be fol-lowed by some form of confederation between the two parts of that severed coun-try," Ball recalled. "That would, of course, mean the end of NATO and the neu-tralization of Germany."[94] Kennedy was also bracing himself for an escalation of the confrontation with France, and asked Ambassador Bohlen whether de Gaulle had indeed begun a "systematic campaign to reduce American influence and presence on the continent."[95] Kennedy certainly believed that there were a num-ber of areas in which another move by de Gaulle against American interests was possible and asked what could be done about them.[96] He was in particular concerned that the French would open an attack on the dollar, "to indicate their power to do something if nothing else," and therefore ordered the Treasury Department to prepare for all contingencies.[97]

French Ambassador Hervé Alphand, meanwhile, had become something of a *persona non grata* in Washington. He had spent a large part of his career in the United States, serving as France's highest diplomatic representative in Washington from 1958, and had become profoundly attached to his American environment, but now he was confronted with hostility and incomprehension in many quarters. The status of an unswerving ally that de Gaulle had gained only just over two months earlier in the Cuban Missile Crisis seemed all but lost. "L'ennemi numéro 1 pendant quelque jours aux État-Unis n'est pas Khrouchtchev mais de Gaulle," Alphand wrote in his diary. "Il y a des grands froids dans les dîners. Le Président me fait comprendre par son frère Bobby que, pour le moment, il est préférable que je ne le voie pas. Toutes choses [...] sont tournées contre nous." Interestingly, the French ambassador held the British, in particular his colleague David Ormsby-Gore, responsible for orchestrating the anti-French campaign by nurturing rumours that de Gaulle was truly planning a reversal of alliances. "Ils se conduisent comme des enfants furieux," he judged. "Il est vrai que rien n'est pire pour un Anglais que de ne pas être accepté dans un club."[98] In the French view, the British were exploiting the Anglo-Saxon club to which they still belonged to blacklist the French in Washington. However, Alphand could not ignore the fact that it was de Gaulle who had posed a wilful – and potentially fatal – challenge to the overarching theme of Kennedy's European policies: the Atlantic partnership program.

Holding the Line Against Gaullism

The Debate within the Kennedy Administration

The initial anxiety within the Kennedy administration about a possible reversal of alliances in Europe lessened with the passage of time as well as French and German denials that anything of the sort had been mooted. However, the notion that Gaullism was on the rise in Europe was seen as a political threat of almost equal dimension, since this would reintroduce the specter of nationalism in European politics and of European neutralism in the Cold War that American postwar policies had been designed to keep at bay. There is little doubt that, from the vantage point of Washington, Gaullism was gaining influence in early 1963. "De Gaulle may in fact attract more European support than he had before," the Central Intelligence Agency analyzed in February 1963. "Public opinion in France, and to a lesser extent throughout Western Europe, is increasingly receptive to his thesis that Europe, with its growing economic strength, ought to wield political and military influence comparable to, and independent of, the US."[99] Ambassador John Tuthill cabled from Brussels that the Chairman of the European Commission, Walter Hallstein, also believed time was on de Gaulle's side and that his nationalist views could spread "like a mist" over Europe. Tuthill also reported that the prominent Dutch Commissioner for Agriculture Sicco Mansholt "said that one had to recognize that de Gaulle has pulled the switch with the result that the locomotive [of European integration] is proceeding down a different track than had originally been envisaged."[100] The Europeanists at the State Department tended to interpret every French move as part of an elaborate Gaullist plan to wipe out American influence on the European continent. After a European trip in the spring of 1963, for instance, Walt Rostow informed Kennedy that the French, in anticipation of trade negotiations with the United States, were trying to "nail down the EEC to positions which were unacceptable to us" and concluded that this "is simply a version of the general French strategy of making their prediction of U.S. withdrawal from Europe come true via French policy."[101]

In the midst of all this dismay at the turn of events, Dean Acheson was rapidly being moved into a position as the elder statesman most capable of reversing the trend. As he wrote to his friend John Cowles, publisher of the Minneapolis Star and Tribune, on January 31, he had been busy "hand-holding, encouraging, advising, and prodding on both sides of the Atlantic as General de Gaulle lowered the boom with such a resounding thud." There is no question that Acheson, too, judged the situation in the West to be extremely serious after de Gaulle's mutiny against American leadership and the Atlantic community. "This threat is greater than that of last October [the missile crisis] and it can't be handled with a blockade – or with band aids."[102] Following de Gaulle's "thunderbolts" of January 1963, the United States suddenly found itself holding the line against Gaullism instead of progressively building an Atlantic partnership.

In the tumultuous weeks and months following de Gaulle's January 14 press conference, three schools of thought sprang up within the Kennedy administration on the question of dealing with de Gaulle – and their interplay would continue to shape American policies toward France and Europe through the mid-1960s.

First of all, there was the indignant response to de Gaulle's rebuff of the Europeanists at the State Department and their powerful patron Dean Acheson. This response was amplified by the large body of American public opinion that took offense at de Gaulle's criticism of the United States' role in Europe. Since the Europeanists had been the prime movers of Kennedy's Atlantic partnership program, the vehemence of their response is easily understandable. More importantly, they regarded de Gaulle's nationalism as a serious threat to their epoch-making European project and their design for an Atlantic partnership, based on liberal ideas of free trade and multilateralism. Failure of this project would risk bringing back the nationalist demons of Europe's past, most of all in Germany. It would also bring on a perilous weakening of Western unity in the global struggle against Soviet communism. Above all, however, de Gaulle had posed a potent challenge to their basic views of Europe and of the transatlantic relationship – views that had shaped America's postwar attitudes towards Europe to an important degree.

As at the onset of the Cold War in 1947, the State Department's Europeanists believed that only the self-confident infusion of American power and ideas could provide the necessary antidote to an ominous drift in European politics. Throughout the spring of 1963, they pressed Kennedy to engage in a broad political counteroffensive in Europe in order to check the malicious influence of Gaullism and raise European morale. In May, for instance, Walt Rostow urged Kennedy to task the USIA and CIA to orchestrate a campaign of "counter-psychological warfare ... to assure that French arguments are systematically countered in the European press and through other avenues of communication with the European elite."[103] In June, shortly before Kennedy's visit to Germany, George Ball gave the president a "hard-boiled appraisal" of the state of European affairs. While Ball was careful enough to counsel that the United States must keep a distance from the "anti-Gaullist cabal," his memorandum left no doubt whatsoever about his hostility to de Gaulle's "abrupt assertion of old-style competitive nationalism expressed in a new-style rhetoric":

Unquestionably, Europe is in a mess, and it is not going to get out of this mess quickly. Never, at any time since the war, have European voices been so discordant, European opinions so confused, European Government so lacking in direction. Never, at any time since the war – and this is the main point – has Europe been in graver danger of back-sliding into the old destructive habits – the old fragmentation and national rivalries that have twice brought the world to disaster in the past. [...]
In this environment of impuissance and nonfusion, de Gaulle's interjection of competitive nationalism [...] is a mischief and a danger. In facing this danger, we must never forget – or let others forget – that the General's brand of nationalism can work in only one direction. It can push Europe back to its old fragmentation, can reinstate old rivalries, revive old grievances. But it is a destructive force. It cannot build anything, since nationalism motivated by a desire for dominance or hegemony, no matter how deceptively decked out, is the negation of internationalism and supranationalism.[104]

Ball feared the political implications of de Gaulle's "counter-revolution of nationalism" in a number of respects. He reasoned that de Gaulle's authoritarian politics was undermining the vitality of French democracy to the extent that it paved the way for a future Communist takeover:

Each week de Gaulle's France grows perceptibly more absolutist, while the French people have packed off on a political holiday – an Indian Summer of political irresponsibility. By destroying the whole structure of parties except the Communist party, the General has eliminated the institutional means for resisting Communism.

Ball moreover felt that the "contagious infection of resurgent nationalism" – more specifically, de Gaulle's pursuit of an independent nuclear force and his "assault" on the Common Market institutions – was endangering German loyalty to the West at a particularly sensitive time, since Adenauer was about to leave from the scene and hand over the chancellorship to Ludwig Erhard. "In those changed conditions a Germany not tied closely and institutionally to the West can be a source of great hazard," he prophesied. "Embittered by a deepening sense of discrimination and bedeviled by irredentism, a Germany at large can be like a cannon on shipboard in a high sea." [105]

Dean Acheson's view of the crisis of 1963 largely coincided with that of Ball. As before, Kennedy had called on the elder statesman to sort out his policies in a time of crisis and, in late January, had asked for his analysis of the unraveling of the Grand Design and of the measures to be taken to regain ground. Acheson produced a sixteen-page memorandum for Kennedy that would form the basis for American policies in the first half of 1963. Acheson concurred with the view that de Gaulle had not revealed fundamentally new attitudes, but stressed that "the very revelation of these attitudes is a change in substance; just as the act of declaring war is a change, even after a considerable period of intense hostility." His prescription for dealing with the crisis and for staving off a Gaullist Europe centered on Germany. Acheson was highly critical of Adenauer's compliance with de Gaulle's designs: "what was surprising about Adenauer was that he acted so submissively in signing a treaty of Franco-German rapprochement and unity in effect as an acceptance of de Gaulle's anti-American, anti-Atlantic policy." He advised Kennedy to put maximum pressure on Bonn to make a clear choice be-tween the United States and France. "Germany wants the best of all worlds," he judged. "To allow this is not in American interests." Worried about the popularity of the Franco-German treaty in Germany, Acheson in particular recommended that the "first aim of policy should be to prevent ... early ratification" and the "next aim should be to use the treaty to rebuke both Adenauer and de Gaulle ...." And in order to bait Germany out of the Gaullist camp, Acheson proposed that the United States announce a stabilization of American troop levels in Europe, further develop the idea of a multilateral nuclear force with German participation, strengthen bilateral military ties with Germany, and strongly restate support for the goal of German reunification. The Gaullist tide, Acheson believed, must be stemmed by an unambiguous German choice in favor of the United States. [106]

The second school of thought – embodied by Charles Bohlen, the ambassador to France and one of America's most seasoned diplomats – took a more stoic view of de Gaulle. Assuming that little could be done to alter de Gaulle's views and that the Europeans – including the Germans – could not be forced to make a stance against France, Bohlen argued time and again that the United States had no better option than to proceed calmly with its existing policies as circumstances permitted and patiently await de Gaulle's disappearance from the political scene. He cautioned against getting into a divisive debate with de Gaulle, favoring a dispassionate attitude to Gaullist taunts.

Bohlen had particularly strong reservations about pushing the MLF on the Europeans as long as the United States was not prepared to give up control over the use of its nuclear weapons. Looking back on the January debacle, he came to believe that Ball had been the worst person to sell the Nassau agreement to the European allies and that his meeting with Couve de Murville and presentation to the North Atlantic Council on January 11 had prompted de Gaulle to lash out against the MLF in his press conference.[107] "If we intend to leave present presidential authorization for use of this weapon as it is, then I believe the multilateral force will soon be exposed as a fraud," he cabled to President Kennedy in February.[108] Bohlen reiterated this view in a long, personal letter to McGeorge Bundy on March 2. He added that in his opinion very little could actually be done to improve relations between Washington and Paris. "I see no prospect for any real dialogue developing between the President and de Gaulle." Furthermore:

> It seems to me that [...] the difficulty of our policy in regard to Europe is that we have not fully adjusted to the fact of European recovery. I do not mean only the economic and financial recovery, but also the moral and spiritual vigor that seems to have accompanied this process, coupled with a very serious but nonetheless real line of thought to the effect that the danger of a Russian attack (particularly after the Cuban crisis) has greatly diminished and, in fact, is non-existent in the eyes of many Europeans.

Bohlen therefore suggested that it would be better "to leave Europe alone politically and [...] unchanged militarily" and "not continue to press the Europeans hard for an increase in conventional forces" or for a multilateral formula that did not accord them genuine control over nuclear weapons.[109] In sum, Bohlen counseled a far more passive stance in Europe in response to de Gaulle than either Acheson or Ball.

The third school of thought – dominant among those members of the White House staff who dealt with Europe – adopted Bohlen's pragmatism, but was more inclined than Bohlen to admit that American policies were at fault and to seek ways to find common ground with de Gaulle. Senior members of the staff, in particular McGeorge Bundy and David Klein, felt out of sympathy with what they considered the Europeanist "theology" at the State Department. They not only doubted the wisdom of picking a fight with de Gaulle, since this could deepen the crisis, but they also believed that some of de Gaulle's grievances were quite legitimate. They took a rather more skeptical view of the MLF proposal put forward by the State Department. They had, in addition, a less exalted view of America's role in Europe and were less alarmed by the nature of de Gaulle's nationalism or its potential effects on Germany. Their views were buttressed by the analyses and commentaries of fellow Harvard University academics Henry Kissinger, Stanley Hoffmann, and Richard Neustadt, all of whom took a more considerate view of de Gaulle. Neustadt's response to J. Robert Schaetzel, Ball's collaborator at the State Department who was about to mount an attack on de Gaulle's policies in a published article, typified the more detached view at the White House:

> Are we supranationalists? Are we consistently committed heart and soul to United Europe as conceived by the Action Committee before January 14? Are we really convinced that but for de Gaulle's press conference the movement toward that goal was steady, sure, and certain of success? ... By we I don't mean you. I mean the American government in all its acts and voices as seen and heard by the intelligent, informed European readers of your article.[110]

Arthur Schlesinger Jr., serving as Kennedy's special assistant also believed that, as he wrote Ball in February, "de Gaulle's policy is not just one man's arbitrary and wrong-headed effort to turn back the clock of history" but rather reflected "contemporary moods and needs in Europe." It was only natural, Schlesinger emphasized, that a resurgent Europe would seek independence, in economic, political, and military fields. De Gaulle's policy of independence thus sprang "from valid psychological sources," and the United States had to take account of this. Schlesinger even suggested that de Gaulle's rebuff of the Grand Design had been provoked by assertive American policies that denied Europe a measure of independence. "In a sense, it is we who have been trying to turn the clock back when we act as if Europe were in the dependent condition of 1948-49."

However, Schlesinger did not think that the United States should leave the field open to de Gaulle. On the contrary, he argued that the Kennedy administration should begin a "serious, but quiet, counterattack against the Gaullist conception of Europe" by forging a progressive coalition with the emerging European center-left. In many European countries, Schlesinger reasoned, there was a "new and surprisingly ardent pro-Americanism on the part of the center-left, arising from the fear that a de Gaulle-Adenauer Europe will be restrictive, conservative, and undemocratic." This provided the Kennedy administration, given its liberal profile and youthful magnetism, with an opportunity to undercut de Gaulle's position in Europe:

In some way, the notion of independent Europe must be married to that of a democratic Europe, a New Frontier Europe, a Europe in which the people make the decisions, a Europe des peuples rather than a Europe des pères. [...] If we can figure out ways of tapping the social and political emotions involved in the idea of a democratic Europe, we may be able to begin to put de Gaulle on the defensive and expose him where his ideas are truly regressive – not in his concept of an independent Europe, but in his concept of an authoritarian Europe.[111]

Schlesinger's advice may not have persuaded Ball, but it did influence the preparations for Kennedy's visit to Europe in June. During this trip, the American president above all sought to connect with the people rather than with the governments – "Ich bin ein Berliner!" – and to project an image of youthful idealism.[112] When read with the rise of the New Left and the events of May 1968 in mind, which ultimately drove de Gaulle from office, Schlesinger's words also have a prophetic ring. By then, however, the Vietnam War had caused many European progressives to turn their back on the idea of the United States as a beacon.

Forcing a Choice on Bonn

The Ball-Acheson school dominated the Kennedy administration's response to de Gaulle's rebuff in the first half of 1963, largely because its activist posture enabled Kennedy to regain the political initiative in Europe. While the administration's official response was one of equanimity, its dismay with the turn of events forced by de Gaulle's coup de théâtre could not be concealed. As the unofficial spokesman of the administration, Acheson in particular would publicly take aim at de Gaulle and urge the United States to press on with its policies. De Gaulle could slow things up, Acheson admitted, but he could not alter the main course of events. While it was not possible "to persuade, bribe or coerce de Gaulle from following a course on which he is set, the power of the U.S. to shape the inevitable for de Gaulle is immense," he stated in public.[113] As he explained to his friend Louis Halle in March, "it seemed important to put de Gaulle in proportion."[114]

As Acheson and others had counseled, however, the administration's counter-offensive revolved around Germany. Kennedy had been impressed with Acheson's forceful memorandum, which had urged him to turn the heat on Bonn in no uncertain terms – and he consequently instructed that "any discussion we have on ... Germany should include Dean Acheson."[115] Washington understood that if de Gaulle were successful in locking Germany into his camp, this would amount to a geopolitical landslide against the Atlantic community and American influence in continental Europe.

At the same time, the Kennedy administration recognized that Germany was the Achilles heel of de Gaulle's strategy, since it depended far more for its security on the United States than on France. Adenauer was moreover severely criticized in

Germany for his willingness to sign the Franco-German treaty under the circumstances. His designated successor Ludwig Erhard was known to be far more oriented toward the United States than France and a registered proponent of liberal economic policies. After Couve de Murville had ended British membership hopes in Brussels, for instance, Erhard fumed that the ratification of the Franco-German Treaty had to be put off. And while Foreign Minister Gerhard Schroeder felt impelled to employ his diplomatic skills to take the edge off Erhard's anger, he was no enthusiastic supporter either of an exclusively Franco-German entente. "Calm down Mr. Erhard, the treaty will be ratified, but simply not put into practice," Schroeder said; all that had to be done was "to defuse any hint of it against the Atlantic partnership."[116]

In the wake of de Gaulle's "coup" of January 1963, the Kennedy administration thus staged a vigorous diplomatic campaign to compel Bonn to distance itself from de Gaulle. The Franco-German treaty was the first target. On Acheson's advice, the German government was pressured to delay the Bundestag's ratification of the treaty, and John McCloy – the highly regarded former high commissioner to occupied Germany – was brought in to put pressure on Adenauer to this effect.[117] The domestic opposition to Adenauer's easy acquiescence to de Gaulle's designs was, in fact, already strong and there was an overwhelming consensus that Germany could not afford to alienate the United States. Heinrich von Brentano, the caucus chairman of the Bundestag and a former foreign minister, and Gerhard Schroeder soon began to collaborate on a preamble to be included in the German treaty of approval that would express Germany's continuing commitment to NATO, European integration, and trade liberalization – thus going against what de Gaulle had meant to accomplish with the treaty.[118]

The American diplomatic campaign to check Gaullism hinged, in addition, on the MLF proposal. Paradoxically, the proposal thrived under the circumstances brought about by its rejection by de Gaulle. Washington valued it above all as a bait to keep Bonn from engaging in an exclusive relationship with Paris. Aligning Germany more firmly with the United States in the military realm would remove the sting of French nationalism. It is moreover useful to recall that the prospect of Franco-German nuclear cooperation or of a German nuclear *Alleingang* was less far-fetched in the minds of American policymakers than it often appears in hindsight. "It is no good saying that Germans do not want atomic weapons," Ball noted in the above-mentioned memorandum to Kennedy. "Even if that were true today – and the evidence is confusing – what Germans will come to demand in a competitive Europe is power and equal treatment."[119] The MLF proposal was viewed, too, as the only device still available to Washington to salvage the Grand Design, since it seemed to offer the potential of bringing the European Community and Great Britain together even if the latter remained outside the Common Market and of providing an avenue for linking Europe with the United States.[120]

Of course, what was presented publicly as the pursuit of the common good was in reality also a fight against political evil. In Rostow's view, German support for the MLF could bring "definitive defeat" to de Gaulle's ambitions for "an enlargement of French power via intimate military association with Bonn."[121] The view that the MLF was the United States' strongest trump card in the tug of war with de Gaulle over Europe was prevalent in those days. The yearning to debunk de Gaulle as the spokesman of Europe even encouraged some American officials to suggest that the United States should go beyond Nassau by holding out the prospect of relinquishing its veto over the MLF and express stronger support for a European nuclear force. This would, they believed, help to undercut de Gaulle's ability to present the French nuclear program as the only way to achieve a European-controlled nuclear force. John Tuthill, the American ambassador at the European communities, for instance, suggested that the United States promote the cause of European integration and British admission by holding out the promise of assisting in the development and manufacture of a nuclear weapon "as a European community enterprise"; this would have the political benefit, he argued, of "strengthening the position of those who oppose de Gaulle's conception of both Europe itself and its future relationship with the US... ."[122] Yet another official believed that Washington could "deflate de Gaulle as the champion of a pure Europe" by proposing that the Western European Union (WEU) – the one European organization that comprised Great Britain and the Six – be used as a vehicle for a European nuclear force.[123] Ball and Rostow also were in favor of hints that the United States would be prepared to allow the MLF to evolve into the nuclear arm of a politically integrated Europe, both in order to "dramatize" its willingness to treat Europe as an equal partner and to provide a counterweight to de Gaulle.[124] The MLF, as Henry Kissinger observed, had thus evolved into "an attempt to implement the Grand Design without France and, if necessary, against it."[125]

In early 1963, State Department officials swarmed off to elicit consent for the MLF in Europe. Only days after de Gaulle's press conference, Kennedy asked Livingston T. Merchant, a former ambassador to NATO and strong supporter of the MLF, to head an American mission to open official talks with the European allies on the MLF. While Kennedy impressed upon him that the MLF was not to be pushed on the Europeans, his reservations were obscured from European eyes by the fervor of his diplomats.[126] The establishment of Merchant's office within the State Department enabled the MLF proponents to minister most aspects of the MLF negotiations with little interference, with Ball acting as their guardian in the higher councils.[127] The Policy Planning Council, headed by Walt Rostow and invigorated by Robert Bowie and Henry Owen, also took to elaborating the case for the MLF. The Europeanist view of the MLF was expounded by Robert Bowie in International Organization in the summer of 1963. Bowie argued that, apart from unifying the Western deterrent, any solution to the problem of nuclear control should "foster the progress and vitality of European integration and Atlantic partnership" and – since "obviously, various tendencies are contending for the ultimate outcome" – influence the orientation of the European movement in Europe. Bowie: "The multilateral force should foster European integration by bringing together the Five and the British into an integrated nuclear effort, open to France when she is ready to join."[128] The White House, meanwhile, preferred not to apply the brakes on the MLF enthusiasts under the circumstances brought about by de Gaulle. "If we had made no proposal designed to meet the nuclear ambitions of Europe," McGeorge Bundy reasoned, "[then] indeed we would have left General de Gaulle a free field. And the charges of American monopoly and insensitive domination would have been redoubled in strength."[129] The idea of nuclear sharing enabled Washington to assert American leadership in the face of a policy vacuum in Europe after de Gaulle's rebuff. It was the straw Washington had to cling to in order not to lose more ground.

President Kennedy's trip to Germany, Ireland, Great Britain, and Italy from June 23 to July 2 was the crowning element of his diplomatic campaign to counter the Gaullist foray in Europe. While lacking in concrete achievements, the trip was a hugely successful exercise in public diplomacy. Kennedy was received by large and enthusiastic crowds everywhere he went. The German leg of this trip, with a weighty policy speech on the Atlantic partnership in the historic Paulskirche in Frankfurt and a roaring speech in Berlin, was even triumphant. In Berlin, three-fifths of the city had turned out to greet him, "clapping, waving, crying, cheering, as if it were the second coming," and the crowd had responded very strongly to his words – to the point of reaching a public hysteria that frightened Kennedy.[130] In Paris, of course, the sensation of Kennedy's trip was looked upon warily. His Germany visit, as Foreign Minister Couve de Murville later wrote, was the most effective move that Kennedy could have made to outdo de Gaulle.[131] De Gaulle himself acknowledged the setback in France's bilateral relationship with Germany by declaring that "treaties are like young girls and roses; they do not last long" on July 2, on the eve of his last visit to Adenauer as chancellor.[132] The American embassy in Paris, too, reported that there was widespread disenchantment in Paris with the follow-up to the Franco-German Treaty.[133] And in several meetings with American officials, the otherwise affable Couve de Murville bitterly complained that US policies were forcing Germany to choose between France and the United States.[134]

The Kennedy administration's diplomatic campaign to hold the line against Gaullism had thus reached its objectives by mid-1963. The Bundestag's decision in May to attach a preamble to the Franco-German treaty restating Germany's overriding commitments to NATO and the European communities had already reduced it, in Ball's words, to "the final act in a love affair between two old men."[135] De Gaulle was unable to establish a similar personal rapport with Chancellor Adenauer's successor, Ludwig Erhard, who was a devout Atlanticist and free-trader. He had overestimated the ability and the willingness of German polity to distance itself from the United States. He had thereby overplayed his hand. As McGeorge Bundy later told Jean Lacouture in response to the French thesis that Britain would have been America's Trojan horse in Europe:

> A Trojan Horse? But it was in Bonn, not in London. The links of the Germans with us were much deeper and more indissoluble that those with the British. De Gaulle may have succeeded in distancing Macmillan or even Wilson from us. But not Erhard or Kiesinger, who constantly reminded us that, for them, the Atlantic Alliance had primacy over every other consideration.[136]

However, it would be wrong to conclude that de Gaulle's bold affirmation of his independence from the United States in early 1963 had changed *nothing* in the transatlantic relationship.

The Grand Design in Limbo

The efficacy of the American diplomatic campaign in Europe in the first half of 1963 could not conceal that de Gaulle had transformed the political landscape in Europe and that Kennedy's Grand Design for an Atlantic partnership lay in shambles. Since Great Britain would not become a member of the Common Market for the time being, it would have to influence the political outlook of the Six as an outsider instead of an insider, giving de Gaulle obviously more leeway to develop European political cooperation in directions less amenable to the United States. De Gaulle's veto of British membership had also significantly reduced the Trade Expansion Act's potential to lower trade barriers between the United States and the Common Market in the upcoming negotiations within the GATT. And as Gaullism appeared to have resuscitated nationalism in continental Western Europe, those within the Kennedy administration who had vested their hopes in the "inexorable" process of European integration now feared the impact of nationalist counter-revolution and the dissipation of their vision of an Atlantic partnership between the "new union now emerging in Europe and the old American Union" (as Kennedy had stated in Philadelphia).

To make matters worse for those such as Ball and Acheson who favored assertive American leadership in Europe, US diplomacy shifted to a less assertive stance in mid-1963, when the sting of the Franco-German treaty had been removed and the shock waves of de Gaulle's press conference gradually began to ebb away. The shift from activism to aloofness is most evident in Kennedy's decision to go easy on the MLF proposal once reluctance among the European allies to engage in the project had come to the fore. Although he had allowed the State Department to approach the European allies, Kennedy had always remained deeply skeptical about the project and had never fully committed himself. After Nassau, he had learned his lesson of caution in the hypersensitive area of nuclear politics. Even as he instructed Livingston Merchant before his mission to Europe in February, he had expressed his "deep concern" that "the United States might be tying itself too closely to a project that might fail." According to the minutes of that meeting:

> He [Kennedy] said it was his impression that the British were not for it; the French were clearly against it; and the Italians did not have a deep-seated interest in it. The Germans reportedly were interested, but once they realized how little they were getting for their money, they might look at it differently. Moreover, he wondered whether the multilateral force would have any real attraction unless the United States was prepared to give up its veto, and at this point he saw no justification for relinquishing the veto.[137]

Kennedy believed that the drive for the MLF should come from Europe rather than from the United States, and he doubted that the Europeans were seriously interested given the considerable costs and the domestic political complications of participating in a nuclear force as well as the inevitably adverse reaction from Moscow. He was also wary of getting pinned down on a complex treaty commitment that would be difficult to get through the Senate. Kennedy certainly gave the Merchant mission no leeway to suggest to the European allies that the United States would be prepared to sacrifice control over the MLF.[138] As Arthur Schlesinger rightly observed, Kennedy "considered that, as long as the United States retained its veto (and he never mentioned renunciation as a possibility, though other members of his government did), the MLF was something of a fake. Though he was willing to try it, he could not see why the European allies would be interested in making enormous financial contributions towards a force over which they no real control."[139]

Given Kennedy's skepticism about the MLF, it is hardly surprising that when the European lack of enthusiasm came to the foreground, he decided to go easy on the proposal. Great Britain's continuing resistance to definitively join its nuclear forces with the MLF – in spite of strong American pressure – posed particular problems, since it threatened to reduce the project to an American-German affair.[140] With Kennedy's European tour in late June in the offing, his National Security Adviser McGeorge Bundy wrote an important memorandum that strengthened the president's resolve not to stake US prestige on the project. One week prior to Kennedy's departure for Europe, Bundy argued strongly for a "sharp change in planning for political discussions of the MLF in Europe." Bundy's sobering judgment was that the French were hostile, the British opposed, and the Italians divided; the Germans, meanwhile, merely went along with developing the proposal because they wanted "to keep the Americans happy." Bundy hence urged a toning down of the MLF campaign. "Only among the passionate pro-Europeans like Monnet is there real sentiment for the MLF," Bundy concluded, "and this sentiment itself is conditional upon a clear offer to abandon the veto at an early stage if a genuinely European force becomes practicable." The MLF proposal, he further explained, had risen to prominence primarily because the Europeanists at the State Department were "passionate believers in the MLF as a means of blocking national deterrents, General de Gaulle, and all other obstacles to European unity" and had "pressed the case more sharply and against a tighter timetable, at every stage, than either you or the Secretary would have chosen."[141] Kennedy indeed took to heart Bundy's advice to go easy on the MLF. He disregarded pressure by the MLF supporters within his administration to make his European trip a deadline-setting event.[142] And upon his return from Europe, he had Bundy instruct Secretary of State Rusk to avoid "any impression that the United States is trying to "sell" the MLF to reluctant European purchasers."[143]

Kennedy's step on the brakes of the State Department's MLF campaign was also inspired by his increasing interest in 1963 in negotiating a limited ban on nuclear tests with the Soviet Union. The call for a ban on nuclear tests had originated in the mid-1950s, after the radioactive fallout of an American nuclear test near Bikini had caused casualties among Japanese fishermen. Eisenhower had pursued the matter with the Soviets, after initially having defended the unfettered continuation of nuclear tests, but the U2 affair had aborted these initial talks in 1960. Kennedy had taken an active interest in a test ban treaty, both as a presidential candidate and as incoming president. He feared that without such a ban, the number of nuclear powers might grow to ten or fifteen in a matter of years. So once it became clear that the Cuban Missile Crisis had bolstered his position vis-à-vis Khrushchev, Kennedy believed the time was ripe for new initiatives in this area – and he knew that Khrushchev was interested in agreements that put the Soviet Union and the United States on the same level. On June 10, Kennedy issued a call for a test ban treaty in a speech at American University; in July, American, British, and Soviet negotiators initialed a Limited Test Ban Treaty (LTBT), and the treaty was subsequently signed on August 5.[144] The drive for the LTBT made it incumbent upon the White House not to burden negotiations with Moscow with contentious plans to involve allies in the nuclear defense of the West. Kennedy moreover hoped he could somehow persuade de Gaulle to sign up to the treaty as well. Theodore Sorenson affirms that the American president was willing to go a long way toward drawing in de Gaulle and that he even considered giving nuclear assistance to France to this end.[145] On July 19, Kennedy indeed informed Averell Harriman, his chief negotiator, that he wanted to keep "the road open for appropriate US-UK nuclear cooperation with [the] French if they adhere to test ban [...]."[146] And on July 24, in a letter to de Gaulle, Kennedy offered to help find alternatives for nuclear weapons tests in the air, under water and in space if France abandoned its refusal to sign the test ban treaty.[147] Even as Bohlen reported from Paris that Kennedy's offer had failed to win over de Gaulle, in part because the latter doubted that Kennedy would be able to deliver on his promises, pressing for the MLF against his wishes did not seem opportune in this context.[148]

In other ways, too, the Kennedy administration's plans for reforming the Western alliance had run into the ground by the summer of 1963. Persistent American pleas for strengthening conventional forces as part of the new flexible response strategy had still made very little headway in Europe.[149] Once again, France appeared in Washington's view to be by far the biggest obstacle to adapting the strategy of the alliance. Throughout 1963, French representatives at NATO were resisting the further development of MC 100/1, the Military Committee's strategic reappraisal that was to underpin NATO's new force goals. In November 1963, the French finally stated their outright opposition to the principles contained in MC 100/1 of "flexibility of response" and "limited tactical nuclear warfare" and insisted on preserving the alliance's "trip-wire" strategy, thus effectively blocking its further consideration. France's obstructionism within NATO was immensely frustrating to American officials, who believed they were just beginning to achieve consensus among the allies. They tended to dismiss French objections as insincere. McNamara, for instance, argued that France, too, would want to respond initially with conventional forces in the event of Soviet aggression despite its official attachment to the doctrine of automatic nuclear retaliation. "I am convinced," the American secretary of defense confided to Cyrus Sulzberger, journalist of the *New York Times*, in December 1963, "de Gaulle doesn't believe his own strategy but is using it only for internal reasons and ... to apply pressure against the allies in order to increase French political ascendancy."[150] Fearing that de Gaulle was putting nearly everything in NATO on hold, the Americans were increasingly looking for ways to circumvent the French – establishing a pattern that would become stronger over the years.[151] There were, however, important limits on how much could be achieved within NATO without French involvement. In December 1963, NATO Secretary General Dirk Stikker informed McNamara that he thought that a discussion of MC 100/1 should be avoided "for a very long time."[152] The Pentagon's concern that de Gaulle's nuclear program was depleting France's defense budget at the expense of its conventional forces was moreover legitimate.[153]

In addition to the stalemate within NATO, the steady progress toward European unity on which the Kennedy administration had reckoned with the announcement of the Atlantic partnership program appeared to have run into serious trouble by mid-1963. De Gaulle's blunt rejection of Great Britain's bid for membership had left a thick residue of mistrust among the Six. France was only able to get the Common Agricultural Policy by threat of boycotts. De Gaulle's aversion towards European integration would ultimately lead to the "empty chair" crisis of 1965, when France refused to carry out the stipulations of the Rome Treaty regarding the introduction of majority voting and the role given to the Commission. British membership, meanwhile, seemed further off than ever, even as the foreign ministers of the Six agreed in July 1963 to resume contacts with Britain within the framework of the Western European Union. The whole debacle finally cost the skin of Harold Macmillan, the European leader to whom Kennedy had felt the closest. On October 18, he resigned as a result of bitter disagreements within his Conservative Party. But it would be a mistake to believe that Britain's chances of Common Market membership would have improved under a new government. "There is no sign that in the foreseeable future he [de Gaulle] will change his attitude towards England, and certainly if the Labour Government is returned to power this question will be further pushed off," Bohlen reported from Paris in August 1963. "He will continue to view movements towards the so-called Atlantic Community as attempts by the United States, through the process of 'integration,' to establish its control and hegemony over Europe."[154]

In sum, 1963 is the year in which it became clear that the United States did not have the power to impose its designs on Europe against the willful opposition of the man in the Elysée, even as it did have the power to stifle de Gaulle's designs for a "European" Europe. From mid-1963 onwards, therefore, Kennedy's Grand Design for an Atlantic partnership rested in a state of limbo.

Washington's Changing Perspective on Europe

"We have been very generous to Europe, it is now time to look out for ourselves," President Kennedy said to the National Security Council on January 22, 1963. "We have to get tougher about this. We must keep our economic house in order."[155] Kennedy's statement, one week after de Gaulle's press conference, summarizes the subtle but crucial shift in Washington's attitude to the movement toward European unity from strong support to guarded ambivalence as a result of the events of 1963. Kennedy was particularly adamant that his administration stop the "continual hemorrhage" as a result of the negative balance of payments and that Europe should pick up more of the defense burden. He believed the time had come to put US national interests first. The aftermath of de Gaulle's "coup" of January 1963 thus reveals the shallowness of Kennedy's personal commitment to his administration's fervently promoted Atlantic partnership program, confirming suspicions long held by its main proponents.[156]

We have already noted that Kennedy feared there were a number of areas in which another move by de Gaulle against American interests was possible and that he was in particular concerned that France would open an attack on the dollar. In the wake of de Gaulle's press conference, there was also a heightened concern about the Common Market's Common Agricultural Policy. In this area, as in others, French and American interests were clearly contrary. France tended to view the Common Market as the exclusive outlet for its increasingly efficient farm production, whereas the United States was determined to defend its position since World War II as a major supplier of agricultural goods to Europe. The French argued that the United States gave its farmers similar protection, that Europe was under no obligation to provide a market to American farmers, that the revolution in mechanization and modern farming which hit the United States a generation ago, producing a tremendous expansion of yields at lower costs, had just begun in Europe – a historical accident that had given the United States an abnormal share of European markets. However, given that one-third of American commercial agricultural products – mostly wheat, flour, feed grains, and poultry – was exported to the Common Market, the US Department for Agriculture was intensely troubled by the rapid development of the Common Agricultural Policy at the expense of American farmers. Secretary of Agriculture Orville L. Freeman therefore pressured Kennedy to take a firmer approach. In a strong letter to Kennedy on February 9, 1963, he warned that "a new spirit of regional isolationism in Western Europe" had gained strength with de Gaulle's assertion of French interests. Interestingly, Freeman based his plea for a firmer stance on a much broader plane than agricultural interests:

> This regional isolationism strikes at the very core of the partnership that has been developing between the United States and Western Europe. It threatens mutual defense arrangements, it threatens political rapprochements, it threatens trade and commerce. It threatens American agriculture which looks to the Common Market as the leading dollar buyer of its export products, and thereby threatens the international monetary position of the United States because of this impending loss of dollar revenue.
>
> This tragic division within the U.S.-European partnership may represent a clash of opposing visions of the future. One vision, as typified by the Monets [sic] and the Schumanns [sic] – and this is the vision with which we are allied – is that of a united Europe, fostering Free World economic interests, actively strengthening the Western Alliance's stand against communism. The other vision, typified by de Gaulle, is that of opportunism – the opportunity for a small group of European nations to emerge as a new, independent world force, with apparent total disregard for ties that in recent years have successfully bound the Western nations together.[157]

There is ample reason to believe that Kennedy was more susceptible to such warnings after de Gaulle's rebuff of the Atlantic partnership. There is evidence, too, that he took an increasingly detached view of the desirability of trade liberalization in general, which was the key assumption in the Trade Expansion Action of 1962, and that he was less willing to sacrifice American interests on the high altars of free trade and European integration. The episode even seems to have caused something of a reconsideration on Kennedy's part of the desirability of British membership of the Common Market, in particular if that meant that

American agricultural exporters would suffer because the Commonwealth countries would gain access to the European market. On November 20, 1963, just two days before his assassination, Kennedy told Undersecretary for Agriculture Charles S. Murphy that he was "not so stuck on the Kennedy Round of negotiations and that if we could not get a good bargain ... we should make no bargain at all"; in a striking admission, he even wondered if "we had not made a mistake in encouraging the creation of the Common Market" and thought it "probably was fortunate for us that Britain had not gotten into it."[158] In sum, the documentary record strongly suggests that Kennedy entertained serious doubts about the official European policies of his administration – and that these doubts had become stronger after de Gaulle had put the Grand Design on hold.

The implications of de Gaulle's mutiny against American predominance in Europe were not limited to the personal views of Kennedy, they also affected broader American perceptions of Europe in at least four ways.

First, de Gaulle had made it substantially more difficult for American policymakers to accept a key assumption of the Europeanists: that the sort of European economic and political integration advocated by Monnet's Action Committee for the United States of Europe was inexorable and that de Gaulle should therefore be treated as the anachronistic representative of the old Europe of virulent nationalism and internecine war. As a result, the Kennedy administration's Grand Design for a future Atlantic partnership between the United States and a politically integrated Europe gradually appeared an increasingly intangible vision. Even as the Fouchet Plan for European political union had been rejected in early 1962 and the American diplomatic campaign of 1963 had been effective in bringing Germany back into line, de Gaulle was bound to leave a lasting mark at the expense of the Communities. Dean Acheson admitted as much, despite his insistence that the United States should not hesitate to assert its power in Europe to turn the political dynamics against de Gaulle's rebellion. "Monnet and his people can help: they are good at organizing support for a new idea when the opponent is ignorance or inertia," he professed in April 1963. "But they cannot lead against de Gaulle. They have no power base."[159] De Gaulle himself certainly felt confident about the degree of support for his foreign policy. "Il me semble," de Gaulle wrote to his old associate Michel Debré following his July press conference, "que les Français ont décidément et profondément choisi l'indépendance."[160] In addition, as a French journalist with good contacts in the Elysée informed Washington, de Gaulle believed that in the long run his vision would prevail elsewhere in Europe as well:

He [de Gaulle] knows perfectly well that he is isolated in Europe. But he doesn't care because in due course, he is convinced, his European partners will understand that the type of Europe he is proposing is the only one which can stand up to both Russia and the United States and negotiate with the United States, on equal footing, the close cooperation in which he eventually believes. But this Europe, as he sees it, can only be established once France has regained her power. If England had been allowed into the Common Market at a period when France was not yet strong enough, she would have dominated the association, destroyed its spirit, opened the door to American penetration. Only a strong France can avoid all this.[161]

One ramification of the crisis of 1963 was that the assumption that there was one vision – Monnet's vision of increasing integration and waning national sovereignty – that was bound to prevail over all others was no longer tenable. De Gaulle's foreign policy could no longer be simply thrust aside as a nationalist rearguard action against the tidal wave of modernity and interdependence. There were now two equivalent but very different visions of the future of Europe, each with important domestic and international support; and the outcome of their thrashing about was uncertain. Hence, Washington could not ignore that the "nationalist counter-revolution" long feared by Europeanist officials at the State Department had indeed transformed the political outlook in Europe. This was bound to affect American policies in important ways.

Second, the overwhelmingly constructive treatment the European integration movement had enjoyed in the United States since the late 1940s evolved towards a position of ambivalence. We have already seen how George Ball had to put to rest Kennedy's fears – and those in Congress – that British membership of the Common Market would hurt American economic interests, and protecting these interests in case of British admission was a consistent occupation for American diplomats. We have also seen that fears of European protectionism were reinforced as de Gaulle demanded that French economic interests would be heeded within the Six, in particular by collaborating in the development of the Common Agricultural Policy after the Rome Treaty. In 1963, Monnet – albeit still widely admired and a beacon of practical wisdom for Ball and others – stopped being the pivot around which US policies in Europe were developed. De Gaulle's *conférence de choc* had done much to strengthen American premonitions that the Common Market might evolve into an inward-looking bloc under French control rather than an increasingly potent and like-minded partner of the United States in the global struggle against communism. Hence, with the trade negotiations of the Kennedy Round in the offing, Washington was adopting a notably tougher stance toward the Common Market. With de Gaulle firmly in control of French foreign policy and determined to shape the Six to his liking, not even the Europeanists at the State Department could resist the policy drift. The hardening American position was, for instance, reflected in a memorandum from Ball to Kennedy on the eve of a visit by Walter Hallstein, the Chairman of the European Commission. "Our consistent support for the European Community has been postulated on our assumption that the Community would be outward-looking and that the Common Market and the United States had a common interest in increased trade, lower barriers, and economic cooperation," Ball stressed. "The continuance of our policy of support will depend – to a considerable extent – on a demonstration by the Community and its member countries that this assumption is still valid."[162] De Gaulle had introduced a degree of uncertainty in American policymaking circles about the future character of the Common Market that previously did not exist.

Third, there was an increasing tendency in the American policymaking community after mid-1963 to disregard de Gaulle's deviant positions rather than to take them head on, to try to isolate France within Europe by simply forging ahead with American policies as if there were no de Gaulle, to make the point that France could always "resume" its "empty chair" once it had come to its senses (which presumably would be after de Gaulle's departure). The main proponent within the Kennedy administration of showing calmness and composure in response to de Gaulle's program of diminishing American influence on the European continent was undoubtedly the seasoned Charles Bohlen. In August 1963, the US ambassador in France wrote a long analysis of French foreign policy for Kennedy, in which he described the fundamental notions guiding de Gaulle. "I feel," Bohlen impressed on Kennedy, "that the United States should accept the permanence of these factors without necessarily seeking to modify our own attitudes. I say this because under present circumstances there is not the slightest possibility of any opposition to de Gaulle within France arising, and while it is true that he is a man 73 years old I think we have to look forward to at least a minimum of two, and possibly a maximum of nine, years to his continuance in power."[163] Bohlen's call for stoicism in the face of de Gaulle's provocations was influential with Kennedy and Rusk, and later also with Lyndon Johnson.[164] De Gaulle's minimalist attitude on nuclear sharing as well as on other NATO issues was moreover already isolating France as the black sheep of the Atlantic alliance. By the end of 1963, it was becoming common practice for American diplomats to try to circumvent de Gaulle, to ignore French objections, and to proceed with affairs as business as usual whenever possible. Meanwhile, the relationship between Washington and Paris increasingly assumed the marks of a dialogue of the deaf.

Lastly, the events of 1963 gave encouragement to those in Washington who argued that the United States should not continue to place its major bets on European integration but should rather attempt to play on intra-European divisions in order to maximize its influence. Such an approach, which would become a hallmark of the European policies of the Nixon administration, would be more attuned to the limitations of American power in Europe, which had been exposed by de Gaulle, as well as to its resident potential for controlling bilateral relationships. It included a shift away from emphasizing the further development of multilateral institutions within the Atlantic community, which had been a key element of Acheson's advice to Kennedy in the spring of 1963. This more detached – or realist – view of the state of European affairs and its implications for US foreign policy was, for instance, laid out in April by the Director of the State Department's Bureau of Intelligence and Research, Thomas L. Hughes. Hughes stressed that the dissipation of the dream of European unity actually worked to the advantage of American diplomacy:

> De Gaulle is not likely to be able to organize Europe according to his wishes. Europe is today a group of independent political entities of which the three strongest, in particular, form a sub-balance of power within NATO. Their relations with each other and with the United States are in constant flux. This fact precludes the establishment of a united Europe for the foreseeable future. But is also offers certain advantages to the United States. One feature of this situation is that as one state moves into disagreement with specific American policies – and each does so from time to time – the others tend to move nearer the US. [...] It should be possible for us ... to maximize our own attractiveness as leader of the alliance against any European challenger by exploiting the preference of many in Europe for the more distant and more powerful contender for this role.

Against this background, Hughes thought cooperation with de Gaulle still feasible and desirable after January 1963 and he argued for an "alliance of the possible" between the United States and France.

> Such cooperation presupposes ... that we lower our sights somewhat, at least as regards France during de Gaulle's tenure. Satisfactory solutions to all disagreements between the United States and France do not seem possible, nor will we be able to harmonize our policies on many important issues. Indeed, we are faced by a French attempt, not to break up the Western alliance, but to reduce American political influence in Europe. De Gaulle has powerful cards in this competition and can do serious damage not only to our concepts of alliance structure and policy but also to our national interests in such matters as trade policy. At the same time the natural divisions within Europe can be turned to our advantage .... We may thus be able to walk a very difficult and careful path, doing some business with de Gaulle on specifics, avoiding exacerbation of differences on longer term goals, and exploiting intra-European divisions to prevent de Gaulle's leading Europe along paths unacceptable to us.[165]

While Hughes did not occupy a position of great influence within the Kennedy administration, the logic of his analysis and his *divide et impera* prescription for US diplomacy was powerful enough by itself – and hence it does more to explain actual American diplomatic maneuvering in Europe than any reading of public policy statements. As we will see, a similar line of reasoning would moreover come to characterize Henry Kissinger's thinking about Europe.

The Aborted Relationship: Kennedy and De Gaulle

On November 22, 1963, on a campaign visit to Dallas, Texas, Kennedy was assassinated in full daylight. "Le président Kennedy est mort comme un soldat, sous le feu, pour son devoir et au service de son pays," declared de Gaulle upon hearing the horrendous news. "Au nom du peuple français, ami de toujours du peuple américain, je salue ce grand exemple et cette grande mémoire."[166]

The gulf of perceptions between the United States and France that had opened up during Kennedy's aborted presidency had inevitably strained his personal relationship with de Gaulle. In many ways, Kennedy had thought of the General as most Americans did: irritating, intransigent, insufferably vain, inconsistent, and impossible to please.[167] "What can you do with a man like that?," he had often asked in quiet exasperation; at other times, annoyance clearly had gotten the upper hand as he would talk of "that bastard de Gaulle."[168] Walt Rostow recalled:

> He hated de Gaulle's having a whip hand over him – getting our protection free; hurting us wherever he could; and piling up a gold surplus at our expense, via our NATO outlays in France. [...] This sense of weakness in dealing with a nation we were protecting violated something personal in the President. [...] He would come back to it time and time again – the image of de Gaulle sitting there sassing him from his little pile of gold.[169]

Kennedy could not understand why so obviously a great man took such seemingly petty positions. After a long telephone conversation with de Gaulle in December 1961, for instance, having failed to persuade him to agree to discussions with the Soviet Union on Berlin, Assistant Secretary of State William Tyler had been struck by Kennedy's "puzzled mood as to how he could get General de Gaulle to understand that what he wanted him to do was something that was really in the interest of the West..."[170]

Yet, Kennedy had also genuinely admired de Gaulle and had been fascinated with the historic figure he had cut out. Aware that he was still only a "novice" in world politics, as de Gaulle would put it in his memoirs, Kennedy had paid due respect to the outstanding quality of de Gaulle's political stature. Whereas his personal relationship with Konrad Adenauer had always remained standoffish,[171] his personal contacts with de Gaulle were invariably courteous and respectful. At a glittering white-tie dinner at Versailles Palace during his visit to Paris, he had drawn the French president on his recollections of great men like Churchill and Roosevelt.[172] There is reason to believe that his admiration for de Gaulle's courage and stamina had been enhanced, too, by the various assassination attempts on the latter's life against the backdrop of the Algerian war.[173] From the outset, Kennedy had admired de Gaulle's policy of extricating France from Algeria.[174] His offer of support to de Gaulle during the attempted putsch of the generals in April 1961, only a few months after Kennedy had assumed office, designed to counter rumors of American involvement, had also been borne out of an authentic desire to help de Gaulle in this historic endeavor.[175] Kennedy had deeply admired de Gaulle's "faculty to lead ..., to visualize a goal and set sail for it," a family friend recalled.[176] Kennedy's fascination for de Gaulle was in some ways perhaps the envious admiration of a consummate pragmatist who continually examines his goals and changes his tactics for a leader who appeared certain of his goals and unwavering in his determination to achieve them. One is indeed tempted to conclude that had Kennedy written *Profiles in Courage* (1955) about international instead of American statesmen, he would have devoted a chapter to the life of the Frenchman.

Kennedy's interest in de Gaulle was undoubtedly reinforced by his susceptibility to matters of style and intellectual brilliance, as there is much evidence that the Frenchman had caught his imagination in this respect. He was known to be impressed with the rhetorical skills de Gaulle displayed at his stately press conferences.[177] Moreover, while Kennedy had not cherished deep feelings for any foreign country (with the exception of Ireland), Bohlen has recalled that, "possibly through the influence of Jacqueline, his wife, he had a certain feeling for France, he liked the quality of French thought, he liked the sort of élan and being in the audacity of some of the thought, and the kind of cool 18th century quality of French thinking."[178] De Gaulle, of course, came as close as anyone to the embodiment of the French culture of intellect. In addition, however, he was a brilliant and highly effective politician – a modern kind of philosopher king. One might argue that the Kennedy mystique of Camelot – the comparison of the Kennedy White House with the legendary place where the wise and virtuous King Arthur held court in medieval times – had in a sense opened him up to the mystique that de Gaulle had created about himself.[179] Theodore Sorenson's characterization of Kennedy as an "intellectual," for one, could be applied to de Gaulle as well:

> He meditated, but on action, not philosophy. His was a directed intelligence, never spent on the purely theoretical, always applied to the concrete. He sought truth in order to act on it. His mind was more critical and analytical than creative...[180]

And in November 1962, after de Gaulle had won his stunning election victory, Kennedy had asked for an analysis of his political techniques. He was – "as a political man" – interested in the lessons to be learned.[181]

Hence, in addition to feeling strangely out of sympathy with many of the official policies of his administration, Kennedy had privately felt uneasy with the sad state of affairs in the American-French relationship following de Gaulle's press conference. He had never settled on one policy. In the course of 1963, his attitude had in fact come to be guided by all three schools within his administration on the question of dealing with de Gaulle. In the first half of 1963, he gave the "Ball-Acheson school" leeway, mostly motivated by tactical considerations; later in the year he shifted to the "Bohlen school" and "McBundy/Klein school" out of a desire to normalize relations. Kennedy constantly tried to find ways of reengaging with de Gaulle. According to McGeorge Bundy, "he never gave up on de Gaulle."[182] In the view of one chronicler of the Franco-American relationship, the effort to reach a common understanding had preoccupied Kennedy even to an "unfortunate degree."[183] He would certainly ask everyone who was acquainted with the General – his ambassadors Gavin and Bohlen, Cyrus Sulzberger of the *New York Times*, and André Malraux – to elucidate the motivations behind his policies.[184] "If I can put all that effort in the Russians," he once explained to Schlesinger, "I can put some of it into the French."[185]

Kennedy's premature death has left us with the tantalizing but ultimately unanswerable question whether a meeting of minds was still possible after the clash of 1963. There is some reason to believe that Kennedy, who always kept himself open to new arguments, had come to understand de Gaulle's policies better, that he was willing to admit that the French president may have been right on some issues and that his own State Department was part of the problem. Schlesinger, for instance, believes that he "could never rid his mind of the thought that, if this or that had been done differently, it might have been possible to avoid the impasse of 1963."[186] For this reason, too, Kennedy had asked Richard Neustadt to undertake his study of the crisis of January 1963. Kennedy often sought to arrange a reunion with de Gaulle after their get-together in Paris in June 1961. "L'entente de l'Occident," he stated to Ambassador Alphand, "ce sont les bonnes relations entre le Général et moi-même."[187] A meeting with de Gaulle had indeed been rescheduled for February 1964 at Hyannis Port. And three weeks before his assassination, Kennedy "rather happily" told his former ambassador to France, James Gavin: "Well, I am going to see the General in the next few months, and I think I will be able to get something done together."[188] Shortly after his assassination, Paris press editorials claimed that Kennedy secretly had decided a few days before his death to establish entirely new relations with de Gaulle and that a dossier on this project, which the new president would find on his desk, now had the "sacred value of a last will."[189]

Such a dossier did not exist and, in hindsight, a true meeting of minds appears improbable given divergent interests of the United States and France and the policy context in which Kennedy had to operate. De Gaulle, moreover, was bound to have kept a purposeful distance. "Au fond," Alphand explained in his diary about de Gaulle's refusal to meet Kennedy, "il ne veut pas être confondu avec ses voisins, de l'Est ou de l'Ouest européen...et pour le remplacer il envoie *La Joconde*, avec André Malraux."[190] However, had Kennedy lived longer, he is likely to have tried to normalize relations with France. If so, he would have had to abandon altogether the politics of confrontation with de Gaulle favored by Acheson and Ball. There is reason to believe that he was poised to do so by the fall of 1963. For when McGeorge Bundy prepared Lyndon Johnson, as Kennedy's hapless successor, for a meeting in December 1963 on an impending confrontation with the French in NATO over military-strategic issues, he wrote: "President Kennedy had decided – I think rightly – to damp down this controversy and he never had a chance to say so to Rusk and McNamara."[191] In the same vein, Bohlen has claimed that Kennedy – "just before his assassination" – accepted his thesis that little could be done to bring sense to de Gaulle.[192] Alas, it was an uneasy conclusion which he had privately re-examined often.

Conclusion

The clash of 1963 between Kennedy and de Gaulle marked a turning point in the postwar transatlantic relationship. It was the first time the United States found itself in such clear and comprehensive opposition to the policies of a major Western European ally, and – accustomed to the self-evidence of American leadership in the Cold War – it was simply caught off guard by this. It was also the first time that the disagreement was about the extent and the nature of American involvement in Europe. De Gaulle was the first European government leader to reveal that this involvement was not unambiguously desired in Western Europe. His aim, stated in private and in public, to keep the United States at bay in order to achieve a "European" Europe, broke with more than a decade in which European leaders had generally emphasized the importance of American involvement in Europe in order to ward off the Soviet threat and help reconstruct the European economies. This helps to explain why the distress at the state of affairs in 1963 was more severe on the American than on the French side. Americans found de Gaulle's objections to their involvement in Europe hard to grasp and even harder to appreciate. Senator William J. Fulbright's despair with de Gaulle, expressed in a television interview in November 1963, was illustrative of American public sentiment: "I really don't know what he means when he professes his dedication to friendship with the United States and so on and yet what he does and says in other connections seems to be directly contrary to this."[193] Indignation and frustration with de Gaulle's deviation within the Western alliance also pervaded the ranks of officials. Before 1963, differences with de Gaulle still appeared manageable with the right mix of policies; in early 1963, however, Gaullism became an albatross around the neck of those within the Kennedy administration who had placed their hopes in European integration and the Atlantic community. As Dana Durand, a researcher at a Washington think tank, remarked in a paper for McGeorge Bundy in early 1964:

The U.S. government has been engaged in what might be called a reverse ca-
nonization of Charles de Gaulle, elevating him to a stature of a virtual political
demon. This effort has its supporters in certain private sectors, here and in
Europe. But without official prosecution, it would hardly have attained the
proportions of a damnation. The irony of these proceedings lies in the fact
that the prosecutors obviously admire de Gaulle's overtowering stature and
respect his dignity and force, in short, acknowledge that he is probably the
outstanding personality of this era. The damnation is not one of hatred for a
fallen saint of evil, but of sorrow for one who has erred and wandered wilfully
from the path of righteousness and could be brought back to it if only he
would listen to sage councils.[194]

The question of who is to blame for the clash of 1963 has preoccupied many, and
the answers have predictably varied. By contrast, there is no question that Harold
Macmillan was the biggest loser at the end of the day – and he paid the highest
political price as a result. He had had the highest stakes on the table, and in 1963
he lost the most important of them: British membership of the Common Market.
His "grand design" of the winter of 1960-1961, which had sought to construct a
deal between the Americans and de Gaulle that would make British membership
palatable to Paris, had ended in an unmitigated foreign policy disaster. The obstacles posed by de Gaulle proved too high and the Americans were too reluctant
to play the role allotted to them (in particular in the nuclear realm). Macmillan
has come in for strong criticism, in particular in hindsight, for his inability to
choose "Europe" over the "Empire" and the "special relationship."[195] However, it
is hard to see how any British leader could have severed ties with the United
States and the Commonwealth to the extent that de Gaulle considered necessary.
American support for the British membership bid moreover depended on the expectation that the "special relationship" would persist and – through the good
offices of London – be broadened to Europe. In the final analysis, Macmillan's
"grand design" was above all the tragic victim of the incompatibility of the "grand
designs" of de Gaulle and of Kennedy.

De Gaulle generally has been held chiefly responsible for the clash, in particular in the United States and Great Britain. There certainly is reason to believe that
he had used his press conference of January 14 to bring the issues about the
future of Europe to a head. Many years later, Couve de Murville said that he believed the press conference had been unnecessarily provocative and that he had
advised to tone it down.[196] De Gaulle indeed could have allowed the negotiations
with Great Britain to come to a less abrupt and rambunctious end, or have chosen
the gentler course of writing to Macmillan and Kennedy to apprise them of his
intentions. De Gaulle, however, had wanted to give a demonstration of his conception of Europe and of his power to promote it and block competitive designs.
The resolution of the Algerian conflict, his election victory in the fall of 1962, the

abatement of the Cold War after the Cuban Missile Crisis – all these factors had enabled him to assert French independence from the United States. In the Council of Ministers of December 19, 1962, after his meeting with Macmillan at Rambouillet, de Gaulle had decided against British membership of the Common Market, and had subsequently ordered Alain Peyrefitte, his Minister for Information, to arrange his next press conference on January 14 in order to settle the issue.[197] Since de Gaulle had made this decision before the results of the Nassau meeting between Kennedy and Macmillan had become known, "Nassau" cannot therefore be blamed in isolation for de Gaulle's veto. There is moreover much evidence that de Gaulle had long believed that he would have to veto Britain's application in the end, even as he gave negotiations the benefit of the doubt.[198] Macmillan, as we have seen, might have understood – as some British diplomats certainly did – that his exchange with de Gaulle at Rambouillet had sounded the death knell to his European ambitions. The outcome of the Nassau meeting therefore probably only strengthened de Gaulle's resolve to end Macmillan's membership bid; it furthermore gave him the opportunity to do so under the banner of resisting the Anglo-American "directorate" over Europe.

None of this, however, absolves Kennedy of the incongruities in his Grand Design for an Atlantic partnership, of the chasm between the stated policies of his administration and its actual conduct towards the European allies, and of the makeshift character of his foreign policy. The Nassau meeting, including its run-up and its aftermath, symbolized the often erratic manner in which the major foreign policy decisions of the Kennedy administration came about. There had been no prior consultation with the French or any of the other allies. At the regular NATO ministerial meeting, just one week prior to the conference, the United States had given no indication that it attached new importance to the MLF.[199] All of this created the impression in Paris that Washington and London were attempting to manage the Western alliance from the high ground of their special relationship; many French officials actually came to believe that they had long before cooked up the Nassau agreement.[200]

The offer to extend the Nassau arrangement to France, borne out of the improvisational proceedings of the summit, was moreover not well thought through. It did not suit the technical requirements of the French nuclear program. The improvised nature of the offer left American officials essentially empty-handed when approached by French diplomats about the details of the arrangement.[201] There was thus never a real dialogue in part because Washington had not made up its mind over what it had actually put on offer. What was clear was that both the provision of American equipment and know-how and the inclusion of the French deterrent in a NATO multilateral force would have undercut the independence of the French nuclear deterrent. The offer also dangerously bypassed de Gaulle's well-known antipathy to NATO. When Kennedy asked Macmillan at Nassau whether he thought the Polaris offer should be extended to France, the British prime minister therefore volunteered that de Gaulle "probably would not want it."[202] Presumably, France might have pried the same escape clause from the United States as Great Britain, as Kennedy seemed to have suggested to Alphand.[203] However, Washington never made a secret of its strong preference for multilateral solutions – if not at the time, then in the more distant future. If anything, "Nassau" confirmed that the United States would not hesitate to exploit an ally's state of dependency in order to bring other nuclear forces in the Western alliance to heel. If Macmillan had been able to resist the pressure, this he could do only by capitalizing on the special relationship. It is unlikely that de Gaulle could be made to believe that he or any of his successors could have counted on similar clemency in Washington. In sum, it is hard to see how the administration's post-Nassau stratagem of deliberate vagueness in order to tie France down in negotiations could have worked and a rebuff of the multilateral force by de Gaulle could have been avoided.

The German historian Oliver Bange has nonetheless argued that the American offer to France was genuine.[204] Yet the sincerity of the Kennedy administration, too, is to be seriously questioned. Although it did its best to impress on de Gaulle that the offer was serious, the Kennedy administration made clear that this would have required him to revise France's positions with regard to NATO, the *force de frappe*, and the European integration process in fundamental ways. This was obviously a long shot, in particular since the Kennedy administration was never in the position to promise assistance in the development and fabrication of warheads. In the absence of such a policy reversal, however, France under de Gaulle "does not constitute a reliable partner" and thus would not be eligible for nuclear assistance, in the words of Rusk in a post-Nassau meeting.[205] "We were unenthusiastic about this offer to France," Rusk later admitted. "President de Gaulle was quite right that we would probably have asked for conditions that [he] would not have been willing to accept."[206] Bundy has, in addition, acknowledged that the Polaris offer was extended to Paris mainly for pragmatic reasons in the public relations sphere:

> The French problem was daunting, given the distance between the preferences of Washington and Paris that had been clear for more than a year. But for Kennedy the next choice was clear. He must make it plain to de Gaulle that he was now prepared to consider a program of assistance to France comparable to what he was ready to provide for Great Britain. Such an offer he would make, and if it were rejected by de Gaulle then at least it would be clear that the decision to go it alone was French.[207]

The crisis of January 1963 that wrecked the Kennedy administration's Grand Design was therefore in part a crisis of its own making.

Besides de Gaulle's strong-willed policy of independence and the contorted history of "Nassau," Kennedy's clash with de Gaulle was prompted by the assertiveness of his own European policies, in particular by his ambitious attempts to shape allied strategies and the movement toward European unity. From de Gaulle's point of view, vetoing British membership of the Common Market was in large measure a defensive move – as was his rejection of the MLF.[208] From his perspective, the Kennedy administration, with Ball and McNamara as its prime movers (albeit in different areas), had in reality moved from practicing an accommodating hegemony to a stifling hegemony. The crucial year in this respect was 1962. The Kennedy administration's European policies had then become much more overbearing by reinvigorating the campaign against national nuclear forces, introducing the flexible response strategy in NATO, and launching the Grand Design for an Atlantic partnership. In all fields – the political, the military and the economic – Kennedy was trying to make Europe more responsive to America's needs. In a sense, Kennedy revealed the American "will to power cloaked in idealism" that de Gaulle had already distinguished in Franklin D. Roosevelt in 1944. De Gaulle's abrasiveness must be judged against this background as well.

Assessments of Kennedy's achievements as leader of the Free World have varied widely. On the one hand, he was a highly effective politician because of his youthful energy, his self-deprecating wit, his sense of style – all of which made him seem, in the eyes of Europeans, more "European" than American.[209] His two presidential journeys to Europe, in particular his last one in June 1963, showcased his talents for public diplomacy. Kennedy has also deservedly received high marks for his handling of some of the most dangerous crises of the Cold War. He was perhaps the greatest political talent of his time, who – in the measured words of de Gaulle – "had it not been for the crime which killed him, might have had the time to leave his mark on our age."[210]

On the other hand, most historians have found sufficient reason to mark the gap between myth and reality in Kennedy's foreign policies, between the rhetorical flourish of his speeches and the rather less high-minded quality of his day-to-day policies.[211] This judgment can certainly be applied to Kennedy's European policies. His intellectual curiosity and the decidedly cerebral bent of the people in his administration clearly did not stand in the way of prizing appearance over substance. What particularly emerges from the history told above is that Kennedy was hardly wedded to the policies of his administration. JFK never fully embraced the Grand Design for an Atlantic partnership he so eloquently proclaimed but was construed by others within his administration and intimate outsiders such as Acheson and Monnet. If anything, he was vying for control over Europe's destiny rather than for partnership. He was a consummate pragmatist who revealed a cool detachment in almost every sense and continually expressed unease with the perceived generosity of American policies. What emerges, too, is that his perennial doubts about official wisdom had surprisingly little effect on the gist of his administration's policies, which continued in the postwar bipartisan foreign policy mode. If Kennedy imposed restraint on the State Department's Europeanists, it was for tactical reasons; he rarely gave them the feeling he doubted their sagacity. Even as he strengthened the White House staff and proved relatively adept at crisis management, he was hardly in control of his administration's policies. This can be seen to have contributed to the deterioration in Franco-American relations during his presidency, for while the State Department's anti-Gaullism never dominated the White House, it had a great impact on day-to-day relations and mutual perceptions.[212] For all the innuendo of action, Kennedy could thus boast of few foreign policy achievements in his European policies.

To apportion blame, however, is not to tell the whole story. For the clash of 1963 above all brought to light the incongruity of American and French ideas about Europe and the transatlantic relationship. The clash of 1963, Couve de Murville rightfully wrote in his memoirs, "fut le plus grave, parce qu'elle allait vraiment au fond des choses, je veux dire parce qu'elle portait sur la nature même des rapports entre Amérique d'une part, l'Europe d'autre part et en premier lieu bien entendu la France."[213] In hindsight, therefore, the 1963 clash has assumed almost an aura of inevitability about it as a clash of perceptions.

It is important to note, too, that the clash revealed the limits of American power in Western Europe more clearly than any other event in the history of the transatlantic alliance had done (save perhaps the demise of the European Defense Community in 1954). De Gaulle effectively scuttled Kennedy's design for an Atlantic partnership. For one, he steered the European movement away from its focus on Monnet's idea of a "United States of Europe," which had had such strong resonance in American policymaking circles after World War II. The European protagonists of integration and the Atlantic partnership were no less dismayed at this turn of events than their American sympathizers. "The press conference of 14 January 1963 marked a turning-point in the life of the European community," Paul-Henri Spaak assessed in his memoirs. "After that, the trust, the spirit of cooperation that had prevailed during the first few years were not to exist in the same way."[214] Monnet likewise reflected that "by its manner no less than its content, it [de Gaulle's press conference] marked a turning-point in relations between France and the other countries of the West."[215] For another, de Gaulle's veto of British membership changed the anticipated course of events in significant ways. Had he failed to block Britain, the movement toward European unity might have been more responsive to American influence, the Franco-German relationship might have been far less central to its further development, the Common Agricultural Policy might not have been created, the domestic British view of "Europe" might have been far more positive, and transatlantic trade relations might have been more in sync. De Gaulle's veto even undermined Kennedy's achievements on the domestic front. Most importantly in this regard, the Kennedy administration had fought hard to ensure the passage of the Trade Expansion Act (TEA) of 1962, which it hailed as historic but whose value much depended on Great Britain's actual entry into the Common Market. Without British membership of the Common Market, however, the TEA turned out to be a watershed with – as William Diebold Jr. put it – "some dry sides": rather than fulfilling its potential of breaking with the past, trade negotiations would henceforth continue to follow "a familiar kind of watercourse and as time passed the flow has not continued to increase in force, depth, or breadth. The stream has not run dry, but it has become narrower, stonier, and twistier."[216]

Within NATO, finally, de Gaulle went beyond his dismissal of the MLF by using his veto power to frustrate the reform of the alliance's military strategy on which Kennedy had campaigned, and which required the European allies to substantially reinforce their conventional forces.[217] The mere coming into being of an independent French nuclear force moreover established a radically altered strategic reality for the United States. "It must be recognized that if France is capable of creating a nuclear conflict by forcing the United States to come to its aid, the power of deciding on war and peace no longer belongs in the last analysis to Washington," Walter Lippmann perceived in 1962. "The 'force de frappe' is a stratagem which commits the United States while reserving to continental Europe, in the first instance, all nuclear initiative."[218]

Yet the main point made here is that the clash of 1963 was a watershed because it served as a catalyst to change Washington's perspective on European affairs. This perspective had been dominated since the late 1940s by policymakers – from Acheson to Dulles and Ball – who held out high hopes for the "inexorable" process of European integration within the supportive framework of the Atlantic "community." The United States had at various times gone to great lengths to advance the cause of European integration. Following in the footsteps of Truman and Eisenhower, Kennedy had even held out the prospect of a partnership between equals. De Gaulle, however, had turned the Atlantic partnership into a chimera with his thunderbolts. Until January 1963, American officials could still indulge in the idea that he might have had his reservations against NATO and European integration, but that he lacked the determination or the political strength to go beyond his declaratory policy; there was a pervasive belief, not confined to the State Department, that "de Gaulle's France cannot significantly postpone or delay the pace of major European developments, including integration and multilateralism."[219] After January 1963, American officials could no longer underestimate de Gaulle's tenacity and political courage. "His emergence in full control of a strong, rich, prosperous, untroubled France was always possible but never really expected," one memorandum admitted.[220] Yet, de Gaulle *was* in full control. Rather than Monnet, moreover, he had now emerged as the harbinger of a resurgent Europe. In the wake of de Gaulle's manifestation of his political will and clout, Washington's stance toward European unity was hence beginning to shift from one of adamant support towards one of inherent ambivalence and caution, and, if necessary, one of exploiting Europe's enduring political divisions.

Chapter Four

The Demise of the Last Atlantic Project: LBJ and De Gaulle's Attack on the Multilateral Force, 1963-1965

On November 22, 1963, the burdensome tasks of the American presidency were placed on the shoulders of a man who, very much to his own dismay, had remained at the periphery of power for some three years. For Lyndon Johnson, the vice presidency had become a depressing straitjacket from which there seemed no escape – "not worth a bucket of warm spit," as his fellow Texan John Nance Garner ("Cactus Jack") once famously said.[1] Within a matter of hours, however, he was thrust into the full dimensions of the presidency under circumstances unimagined. Upon taking the presidential oath, it was incumbent on Johnson to provide leadership not just to his country but to the entire "free world." Few people were as qualified for the harrowing task as Johnson, who was dyed in the wool of American politics and had reason to consider Kennedy his political junior. But since he had obtained the presidency in the wake of tragedy, Johnson was still very much working in Kennedy's shadow. With memories of the brutal murder in Dallas still afresh, he had little choice but to pose as the faithful executor of the murdered president's policies. "Let us continue," he therefore pledged in his first presidential address to the Congress. "And now, the ideas and the ideals which [Kennedy] so nobly represented must and will be put into effective action."[2]

The American project for a multilateral nuclear force (MLF) within NATO seemed only one case in point – and it is on the ups and downs of this project during the Johnson years that this chapter will focus. Johnson had not been made aware of Kennedy's reservations about the project. He rather assumed that his predecessor's personal support was as strong as the official record. In 1964, the State Department's Europeanists even transformed the MLF into the spearhead of his transatlantic policies and a test of American leadership in Europe. They presented the establishment of a multilaterally owned and operated nuclear force as far and away the best approach to giving the European allies – above all Germany – a say in the nuclear defense of the West. To them, the MLF also presented a last opportunity to salvage the Atlantic partnership from de Gaulle's nationalism and to strengthen the institutional bonds within the Atlantic community. Yet, in spite of the considerable political weight the United States consequently seemed to attach to the project, it failed to make the passage to reality. In December 1964, in one of the first instances in which Johnson would assert himself vis-à-vis his foreign policy apparatus, he decided to let the MLF wither on the vine.

Relatively little effort has been made by historians to explain the ups and downs of the MLF project as part of the Franco-American conflict about the transatlantic relationship.[3] However, the convoluted history of the MLF during the Johnson years deserves consideration as part of this study for more than one reason. First, the extent to which de Gaulle was responsible for pulling the rug from underneath the project has not been sufficiently recognized. De Gaulle had remained steadfastly opposed to the MLF since his press conference of January 14, 1963, even as France was not being required to participate. He saw the MLF above all as Washington's instrument to strengthen its grip on European security affairs and particularly on German political loyalties; its realization, regardless of whether France would be required to participate, was hence wholly incompatible with his own views of Europe and the transatlantic relationship. The circumstances that led Johnson to allow the MLF's ultimate demise to a large extent originated in threats that were coming from Paris. As we will see, American officials not only underestimated the depth of de Gaulle's opposition, but also his power in preventing its realization.

Second, although the MLF did not come into existence, the story of its pursuit usefully informs us about the views of those American policymakers who gave it such adamant support. In the political context of the day, the MLF acquired great symbolic value as the American trump card in the competition against de Gaulle's designs. The MLF was supported above all by those Europeanist officials at the State Department – the likes of George Ball, J. Robert Schaetzel and Walt W. Rostow – who regarded de Gaulle's nationalism as a mortal danger to European integration and to the multilateral development of transatlantic ties; these officials, as before, received strong support from like-minded wise men of American foreign policy such as Dean Acheson and John McCloy.

Third, the fact that, in spite of the State Department's strenuous efforts, the MLF would be relegated to the transatlantic boulevard of broken dreams greatly weakened the hold on transatlantic policies the Europeanists and their outside supporters had enjoyed. The MLF crisis at the end of 1964 turned out to be the trigger for Johnson to impose a policy of restraint toward de Gaulle on those within his foreign policy apparatus who had consistently wanted to force a showdown. Henceforth, Johnson's priorities – not those of the Europeanists at the State Department – would dominate American policies toward France and the European allies. The demise of the MLF was hence attended with important changes in the making of Atlantic policy.

LBJ and De Gaulle

The jarring transfer of leadership created problems of legitimacy for Johnson that could not easily be dispelled. Johnson was acutely sensitive to his extraordinary predicament, for he told Doris Kearns:

> I took the oath, I became President. But for millions of Americans I was still illegitimate, a naked man with no presidential covering, a pretender to the throne, an illegal usurper. And then there was Texas, my home, the home of both the murder and the murder of the murderer. And then there were the bigots and the dividers and the Eastern intellectuals, who were waiting to knock me down before I could even begin to stand up. The whole thing was almost unbearable.[4]

Most citizens, senators and congressmen, government officials, journalists and commentators clearly could not instantly place their trust in someone who came to power by mere accident. At best, Johnson could count on the benefit of the doubt, some initial credit to work with.

In American foreign policy circles, in particular, Johnson did not have the appeal Kennedy had come to enjoy. It was not so much the lack of experience in world politics, for Johnson had more practical experience than Kennedy had had at the outset of his presidency.[5] Nor could his official track record seriously be a source of concern. Johnson was bred in the domestic liberal politics of FDR's New Deal. He had proven himself to be a committed internationalist who felt entirely comfortable with the bipartisan foreign policy consensus of the postwar period. As the Senate's majority leader, Johnson had helped to safeguard this foreign policy consensus against the isolationist tendencies in the Republican Party.[6] As vice president, Johnson had repeatedly gone on record as a firm supporter of the Atlantic alliance. If anything, his speeches suggested that he had thrown himself in with the activists of the Kennedy administration. On April 16, 1961, speaking in Paris, he had heartened the partisans of Atlantic and European unity by following almost literally the advice contained in the Acheson Report concerning the progressive strengthening of the Atlantic community:

> No single nation has enough influence and power to maintain this spacious environment of freedom. The coalition of the peoples and the nations of Western Europe and North America is indispensable to this end. ... To the United States it is of prime importance to maintain and strengthen the coalition, both for its cohesion and power within the Atlantic area and its capacity for constructive action outside that area. If that cohesion and capacity are to be enhanced, vigorous measures will be required in the political, military, and economic fields. ... Progress toward an integrated European community will help

enhance that capacity and thus to strengthen the Atlantic Community. ... Our end goal ... should be a true Atlantic Community in which common institutions are increasingly developed to meet common problems.[7]

And on November 8, 1963, in a speech in Brussels, he had again placed himself in the avant-garde that wanted to strengthen transatlantic ties and remake Europe. Speaking about the MLF, he said that it would be only a "first step" toward a "greater European voice in nuclear matters." Johnson had made it clear that the US veto would become negotiable and he had hinted that the MLF could be converted into a European deterrent, if that was what a united Europe later wanted. "Evolution of this missile fleet toward European control, as Europe marches toward unity, is by no means excluded," he had said, voicing a greater commitment to the idea than Kennedy at the time.[8]

It was, however, the absence of an instinctive interest in international diplomacy and the parochial mindset associated with his home state Texas that disquieted many. He was, a friend once volunteered, a "nationalist" in the sense that his first interest concerned national affairs.[9] There is little evidence that Johnson learned anything about international relations from his trips.[10] "Johnson was generally impatient with the niceties of diplomacy," Louis Heren wrote. "He accepted the existing [...] arrangements, such as NATO, as a politician would accept a coalition of local and state political forces."[11] His Texas drawl and Hill Country anecdotes easily led people to believe that his conception of the world was about the size and shape of the Lone Star state. His background and aversion to academics and intellectuals even created something of a cultural discord with an important part of his foreign policy apparatus.[12] Johnson's political style and personal conduct were simply too different for comfort from those of the cosmopolitan and suave Kennedy. By the time Kennedy began to prepare for his re-election in 1964, Johnson was nearly immobilized by the prospect of never being able to escape from the margins of power. "Every time I came into John Kennedy's presence, I felt like a goddamn raven hovering over his shoulder," he later explained. "Away from the Oval Office, it was even worse. The Vice Presidency is filled with trips around the world, chauffeurs, men saluting, people clapping, chairmanships of councils, but in the end, it is nothing. I detested every minute of it."[13] On his trips, he had indeed often behaved as an unhappy, brooding, at times irascible man – and stories about the Texan venting his rage on embassy officials on his foreign travels had found their way to Washington.[14] Even as "continuity" would be the key word after the takeover, the presence of Johnson's overbearing personality at the helm constituted a significant change; and "as the months wore on," Ball wrote, "the imprimatur of LBJ was stamped on almost everything we did – and our method of doing it."[15] As Senate majority leader, Johnson had been an undisputed master of politics in Washington, who had carried or stymied bills in the Senate almost by sheer force of personality. "I spent years of my life," Kennedy once explained, "when I could not get consideration for a bill until I went around and begged Johnson to let it go ahead."[16] But the "treatment," Johnson's intimidating trademark handling of fellow senators, was hardly appropriate at the level of government leaders and foreign ministers.

Apart from Khrushchev, de Gaulle was probably the most important foreign leader – and certainly one of the most intractable – with whom Johnson would have to cope upon his assumption of the presidency. The Frenchman was among the most eloquent and generous in paying homage to the deceased president. With "perceptible emotion," he had imparted to Dean Rusk that he had always had the greatest admiration and respect for Kennedy and that his death had elicited among the French a sense of a deep personal loss. "I am here," said de Gaulle, "because I have been sent by the people of France."[17] De Gaulle's spellbinding presence as the world leader with the greatest prestige and experience in the front rank of the official mourners worked like a magnet on the assembled media. He was the only allied leader of World War II still politically active. In the space of a few months, all the West's ranking political chiefs except de Gaulle had moreover departed the political scene in non-elected transfers. The funeral proceedings further enhanced his stature. De Gaulle was the first of four government leaders to be received by Kennedy's widow Jacqueline at the end of the ceremony. He was also the first in a row of nine foreign leaders with whom Johnson would confer privately.

Johnson's mood in awaiting his personal rendezvous with de Gaulle had been edgy; he felt, as Ball remembered, "very awkward" and "ill at ease."[18] It was Johnson's first brush with presidential diplomacy. The circumstances of the funeral were obviously not conducive to any real diplomacy, bargaining, or deal-making; but they did make it incumbent on him to present himself to the community of world leaders as a confident and able leader who was fully qualified to assume Kennedy's place.[19] Johnson, urged his advisers, had to convey to the phalanx of foreign dignitaries, but especially to the General, an air of confidence.[20] American officials feared that de Gaulle would try to take the helm if Johnson failed to lay the groundwork for his leadership during the first months of his administration: "It may easily give de Gaulle the handle he needs for some new stroke at his January press conference. Such a stroke, given his nature, is almost bound to be framed as a challenge to US leadership and so to you."[21] Johnson had moreover read a cable from his ambassador in Paris, Charles Bohlen, only minutes before de Gaulle arrived at the State Department to pay his respects. De Gaulle, Bohlen had reported, had privately expressed serious doubts about the credibility of the American nuclear security guarantee; the French nuclear force, he had argued, was to be a trigger line to set off America's nuclear involvement in the event of a Soviet attack. Bohlen had urged Johnson to take the matter up with his guest.[22]

Johnson's conversation with de Gaulle in the evening of November 25, 1963, lasted only twenty-two minutes. The two men talked in as courteous a manner as the use of an interpreter would permit, downplaying the problems that had existed between their governments and referring to them as being "greatly exaggerated." When de Gaulle said that France knew perfectly well that it could count on the United States if it were attacked, Johnson felt that things were going his way and could "hardly suppress a smile."[23] De Gaulle stated his belief that France could count on the United States and affirmed that the United States would inversely find France at its side in times of crisis. Johnson promptly interjected that the French attitude in the Cuban Missile Crisis had provided sufficient proof of this. In his view, things could hardly be more amiable.[24]

The meeting was, however, yet to produce a hangover for Johnson. His advisers had urged him to renew Kennedy's invitation to de Gaulle to visit the United States in the spring of 1964.[25] Johnson indeed alluded twice to the prospect of a visit to the United States in 1964. De Gaulle first replied that Kennedy had paid him a visit in Paris and that he had "intended to return it." At the end of their conversation, while accompanying de Gaulle to the elevator, Johnson reiterated his expectation to see him in February. De Gaulle then replied that the details were to be discussed through the usual diplomatic channels.[26] Johnson was now confident that de Gaulle had agreed to visit the United States.[27] But it soon became clear that de Gaulle's equivocal reference to "diplomatic channels" meant that the whole visit did not automatically carry over to the new administration and had to be entirely renegotiated. Ambassador Hervé Alphand called on the State Department the following day to say that de Gaulle preferred Johnson to come to Paris[28] and yet another day later Paris issued a statement announcing that the two leaders had agreed that the conditions of their future meeting would be decided upon at the appropriate moment by the two governments.[29] The impasse was complete. De Gaulle had no intention of going to Washington,[30] and Johnson would certainly not break away from Washington before the presidential elections of 1964 had provided him with a vice president.[31] The two men would not meet again until Konrad Adenauer's funeral in April 1967; by the time of their next meeting, at Dwight Eisenhower's funeral in March 1969, they were both out of office.

Johnson hence failed to establish a personal working relationship with de Gaulle at the very outset of his administration. Soon after their meeting, the incompatibility of French and American foreign policy designs was further accentuated by France's recognition of the People's Republic of China in January 1964.[32] But they also had too little in common to help resolve outstanding issues. Johnson lacked the insoluble bond of common experience that Eisenhower had cultivated with de Gaulle. He also did not have the intellectual curiosity that had drawn Kennedy to de Gaulle. Johnson simply lacked the background and the inclination to establish a personal rapport with the cerebral French president. As he admitted after having left office:

When Chancellor Erhard came to my Ranch at Christmas in 1963, we knew very little about one another, but before he left we'd come to understand each other so fully that I knew no matter what issue came between us we'd be able to sit down and reason it out. This is what I wanted to happen with every leader I met and most of the time I was successful. President de Gaulle was the hardest to get to. I always had trouble with people like him, who let high rhetoric and big issues take the place of accomplishment.[33]

As for de Gaulle, while he consistently expressed admiration for Johnson in his regular meetings with Ambassador Bohlen,[34] there is sufficient evidence that he felt a much greater remoteness to the Texan than he had felt to Eisenhower and Kennedy – or later to Nixon.[35]

But it would be wrong to conclude that Johnson did not have a clear idea of how to deal with de Gaulle. Johnson felt the atmosphere between Washington and Paris had become far too hostile during the Kennedy years. De Gaulle had become a pet target of American commentators, officials, and semi-officials. Newspaper editorials mentioned him along with Khrushchev as the major obstacle to American diplomacy. Senator William Fulbright in a book and Dean Acheson and Robert Bowie in a number of articles and speeches had stated that de Gaulle's policies put at stake some of America's major postwar goals. There were also insistent stories about low-level State Department attacks against the French.[36] As vice president, Johnson had kept a distance from the verbal combat with the French – and, in his view, there was very little to gain from it. In marked contrast to Kennedy, he spent little time on his diagnosis of the General and the policies that would best serve American objectives. Soon after assuming the presidency, he therefore laid down his guideline for dealing with de Gaulle: "I made it a rule for myself and for the United States government simply to ignore President de Gaulle's attacks on our policies."[37] Johnson would display a remarkable consistency in this posture throughout his tenure. His relations with de Gaulle, he relished telling his aides, reminded him of his baseball adventures in younger days: he was feared as a power hitter and rival pitchers would try to throw their fast ball at him, but he would just lean back and let the ball go into the catcher's mitt.[38] Johnson refused to become too upset with de Gaulle; he did not want the Frenchman to think he had "pinked" him.[39] Not once did he criticize de Gaulle in public; Johnson told Cy Sulzberger he saw no point in "feuding with an old man."[40] He never denounced de Gaulle's personality or ability, nor did he tolerate subordinates making derogatory comments about the Frenchman.[41] Never did he give representatives of France's opposition parties, who came to elicit support from the White House with pro-American viewpoints, the impression that he preferred them over the General.[42]

Rusk has said that Johnson's attitude was imbued by a heartfelt solidarity with other government leaders.[43] If anything, however, it was a display of Johnson's tactical astuteness in dealing with other people. "Johnson had a feminine sense of what the world looked like to other people," Walt Rostow clarified. "He understood enough of what the world looked like to other men to know how to persuade them. But he knew there were people you couldn't persuade and de Gaulle was one of them."[44] Johnson's code of conduct moreover conformed closely to the advice he received from Charles Bohlen, his ambassador to France, who argued time and again that very little could be done to improve relations with Paris as long as de Gaulle was at the helm. Patience and restraint in dealing with de Gaulle would ultimately pay off, Bohlen assured in one memorandum: "It should always be borne in mind that de Gaulle cannot have very many more years of being in power, and the present indications are that a very large portion of the objectionable features of current French policy would disappear with his departure from power."[45] Bohlen's recommendations did not go unchallenged within the administration. They were criticized as overly meek by those who wanted to speak up to the General.[46] Johnson was at times also pressured to replace Bohlen as ambassador by commentators who believed his phlegm stood in the way of improving the relationship.[47]

Nonetheless, this was the line that Johnson took. Bohlen's assessment of de Gaulle was closest to his own instinct.[48] Like Bohlen, he believed that the United States had little leverage over de Gaulle and felt that an exchange of ugly words would only play in the General's hands. For the time being, he looked upon de Gaulle, as one commentator put it, as he would at "a recalcitrant Senate Committee baron for whom he did not, for the moment, have a handle and therefore had no reason to bother his head about."[49] He respected de Gaulle's monumental achievements. Johnson often volunteered that he viewed France under de Gaulle as an asset to the alliance and a great improvement over the unstable Fourth Republic. He did not want to quarrel with de Gaulle's preoccupation with the glory of France, he told French ex-premier Paul Reynaud in 1965, as long as he made no "attempts to cut my throat."[50] Time, Johnson thought, would eventually take care of the differences with France, for he was convinced that a France without de Gaulle would be more amenable. "And just remember", he told Sulzberger in 1965, "he is a lot older than I am and I am going to outlive him."[51] Johnson summarized his attitude toward de Gaulle most succinctly in his memoirs. Clarifying the background to his temperate response to France's withdrawal from NATO in 1966, he wrote:

> Many people expected me to denounce the French leader's move and to resist his disruptive tactics, but I had long since decided that the only way to deal with de Gaulle's fervent nationalism was by restraint and patience. He would not remain in power for ever, and I felt sure that the fundamental common interests and friendship of our two nations would survive. To have attacked de Gaulle would have only further enflamed French nationalism and offended

French pride. It also would have created strains among the nations of the European Common Market and complicated their domestic policies.[52]

In 1964, however, the battle within the Johnson administration about how to respond to de Gaulle's challenge to American leadership still had to be won.

The MLF Re-endorsed

Johnson's vice presidential record on the MLF was a deceptive yardstick. He had strongly supported the MLF in his Brussels speech only weeks before becoming president, hinting that the United States would be prepared to relinquish its veto over the MLF as Europe progressed towards political unity. But there is reason to believe that these statements largely originated in the State Department, which had routinely provided the material, rather than in his convictions.[53] Johnson had been an outsider within the Kennedy administration and had at no time been personally involved in the project. Yet his administration would stake American prestige on the project in its first full year to an extent that previous administrations had not. The State Department, in particular, would engage in what one observer at the time characterized as "a public relations campaign to gain official, political, and academic support [for the MLF], of an energy and ruthlessness unknown since Harriet Beecher Stowe [...]."[54] How did Johnson get so deeply committed to a project he cared so little for?

We have already noted that, given the accidental nature of his rise to power, Johnson had little choice but to elaborate on the policies of his predecessor with the people his predecessor had appointed. His unfamiliarity with the proposal's details moreover left him at the mercy of those who were keen to push their cause with the White House. In December 1963, McGeorge Bundy had tried to warn Johnson of a "tension which existed for many months between MLF advocates in [the] State Department and President Kennedy."[55] But Bundy's warning somehow failed to make an impression on Johnson, perhaps because it paled in comparison with Dean Acheson's outspoken advice to Johnson to continue working on the MLF.[56] In addition, a major objective of American foreign policy during the transition was to dispel any uncertainty in NATO about American leadership caused by Kennedy's death. Drastic policy reversals, such as ending the talks with allies on the MLF, were hence to be avoided. In his first meeting on the MLF in the White House, in early December 1963, Johnson therefore decided that he would return to the issue once these talks were more advanced and the political forces around the MLF had more clearly defined themselves.[57] In the meantime, administration representatives were to begin low-key consultations with congressional leaders. A congressional liaison officer was added to Livingston Merchant's staff at the State Department. Eisenhower, who had an active personal interest in the MLF and whose support could be useful in eliciting Republican support for an eventual treaty, was also brought into the fray.[58] Johnson simply proceeded with the matter where Kennedy had left it – and for several months the project advanced with little interference from higher levels.

Yet in the spring of 1964, circumstances began to call for a clear-cut presidential decision on the MLF. Under the auspices of the State Department, the discussions in NATO's Working Group in Paris and its Sub-Group in Washington had proceeded at a steady pace. Particularly the Washington branch, which produced an endorsement of the military feasibility of the MLF in March, was making sufficient progress as to justify further action at a higher level. [59] At the same time, the project appeared to have lost much of its political vigor. With the exception of Germany, the allies participating in the discussions had been diffident at best. The British stressed above all that they could not commit themselves because of impending national elections; the Italians meanwhile were preoccupied with the rapid alternation of governments in Rome. There was also a pervasive feeling among the allies that Johnson was not truly committed to the project. As NATO Secretary General Dirk Stikker observed, the MLF was generally regarded as "dead" for lack of political will.[60] The MLF supporters within the administration were naturally troubled by this state of affairs and were seeking a greater commitment from the White House in order to dispel European doubts.[61] Obviously, the time had come for Johnson to show his hand with regard to the MLF.

There was yet another development that demanded the White House's attention, one that lent new urgency to a prime rationale behind the MLF. In early 1964, reports about a secret rapprochement between France and Germany in the nuclear realm surfaced with increasing frequency. Influential circles in German politics, presumably disillusioned with the sluggish progress on the MLF, were reported to favor a closer alliance with France, which would be extended into the nuclear realm.[62] These reports were serious enough to cause Walt Rostow at the State Department to examine the possibility of Franco-German cooperation in producing missiles to be deployed in both countries, manned by bi-national crews and equipped with nuclear warheads under nominal French control.[63] Although American officials were – with reason[64] – generally skeptical that de Gaulle would be willing to cooperate with Germany in the nuclear realm, the mere idea that such backstage maneuvering was taking place set off alarms in Washington.[65] Many American officials believed that nuclear flirtations with France would merely heighten feelings of discrimination in the German polity, as de Gaulle would not grant the equal status it desired. "The 'Gaullist' elements in Germany could wax in strength at the expense of moderates – thus casting a long shadow over the Federal Republic's future and our own," Rostow argued. [66] The rumors of a Franco-German nuclear rapprochement strengthened the hand of those in the government who continued to believe in the MLF as a nuclear-sharing formula within NATO. The MLF proponents could at least point to the political need to acknowledge a German desire for a nuclear role within the Western alliance. As a result, the MLF again arrived at the fulcrum – and it was now up to Johnson to decide which way the balance was to tilt.

On April 10, 1964, Johnson convened with his foreign policy advisers at the White House to discuss the multilateral force. While Dean Rusk and Robert McNamara were absent, some prominent supporters of the MLF within the administration had found their way to the Oval Office: George Ball, Walt Rostow, Thomas Finletter, Henry Owen, and Gerard Smith (who had taken over Merchant's job at the State Department's MLF bureau in February). Of those present, McGeorge Bundy, Assistant Secretary of State William Tyler, and William Foster of the Arms Control and Disarmament Agency did not belong to the row of staunch MLF advocates. Only Foster would in the course of the meeting come to speak against the MLF, pointing out to Johnson that the project would stall talks on disarmament and non-proliferation with the Soviet Union. His official position, however, did not carry much weight; his argument was moreover offset by the fact that the MLF had always been presented as precisely a non-proliferation device. Bundy confined himself to an occasional remark of caution, referring to reservations with regard to the project in parts of the administration and stating that it would be unwise to force the MLF upon the Europeans. The initiative at the meeting thus unquestionably lay with the band of enthusiasts.

With his usual energy, Ball immediately took the lead in the conversation. He stressed the danger of perpetuating German discrimination and emphasized the need for giving the Germans a legitimate role, "on a leash," in the defense of the West. A charter on the MLF, he argued, could be signed by the end of the year if Johnson would give his fiat to the undertaking. Finletter, who was particularly vigorous,[67] stressed that the United States had to stop being "diffident" about the MLF. He reported that there was considerable doubt in European capitals with regard to Johnson's commitment. If those doubts could be dispelled by a display of American leadership, he believed, a sufficient number of countries would surely be ready to join the MLF. Ball and Finletter assured Johnson that the British, who had been the most reluctant participants in the negotiations, would also enlist if only the United States insisted: "The British would go back to the MLF if the US made clear that the MLF was the only alternative for them." Other allies, most notably Italy, would then follow suit, for they had linked their position to that of the British.

President Johnson did not take part in the discussion. He heard his aides out and in wrapping up the meeting formulated his resolutions:

1.   the Department of State broaden its discussions with Congress on the MLF and begin informal briefings on the committees concerned;
2.   the Europeans be told that in his judgment the MLF was the best way to proceed. The President also felt the MLF could satisfy the pride and self-

respect of the Europeans but warned against trying to shove the project down the throats of the potential participants;

3.   if possible, an agreement on the MLF be reached by the end of the year.[68]

There was an inherent inconsistency between, on the hand, Johnson's agreement to ratchet up the diplomatic campaign to reach agreement by the end of 1964 and to intensify contacts with Congress and, on the other hand, his admonition not to shove the project down Europe throats. In fact, the extent to which Johnson gave authorization to press the MLF idea became a point of bitter disagreement within his administration. The proponents readily believed that they had carried the day with the White House. The fact that Kennedy had not taken decisive action against the project in the fall of 1963 and had simply allowed his public record to testify of his continuing support had given them sufficient authority to continue their work on the MLF – and, as one scholar of the episode wrote, "like contemporary versions of Sisyphus, they slowly began to roll the rock back up the hill."[69] Now, the new king of the hill had refrained from pushing the rock back. As far as Johnson knew, Kennedy had staked out a public commitment to the project and had established the bureaucratic machinery to give force to that commitment.[70] What is more, he had even appeared to encourage the MLF proponents in their titanic effort. It was probably also the colloquial straightforwardness of Johnson's language, peppered with activism, which led the proponents to believe that they had gained solid presidential backing in achieving allied agreement on the MLF by the end of the year.[71]

Others – particularly within the White House staff – felt that the band of MLF supporters had deliberately misrepresented the measure of European support for the MLF in order to get Johnson's approval. Germany's craving for nuclear weapons was overemphasized and Britain's reluctance was belittled, they believed; the potentially adverse French reaction to an American diplomatic drive for the MLF was never mentioned. One member of the White House staff who was profoundly skeptical of the project's proclaimed virtues, complained some months later about the April meeting: "There was some chicanery – to the extent that the political facts of European life were not candidly and frankly stated. The theologians had a cause and were more interested in achieving an objective than stating a problem."[72] Members of the staff moreover believed that the State Department was overstepping its bounds by transforming what they perceived as Johnson's casual commitment into a full-fledged diplomatic campaign which staked Johnson's prestige on the MLF's establishment. Their disapproval of the "theologians" was justified to the extent that the zeal of the State Department's subsequent diplomatic efforts on behalf of the MLF was out of step with the shallowness of Johnson's personal commitment. But one should add that they had also neglected to inform Johnson of the potential pitfalls of the project and of Kennedy's private qualms.

In the final analysis, of course, Johnson himself was responsible for giving the State Department the impression that he strongly supported the MLF. He had certainly neglected the opportunity to impose a less zealous stance on his diplomats with regard to the MLF. Because he had no strong personal opinion on the MLF or any deep understanding of its history or complexity, Johnson too easily reverted to his talent as a compromiser: to the enthusiasts he pledged progress, to the cautioners he promised prudence. Philip Geyelin's account of Johnson's mindset at the time is instructive: "The President ... argued later that he had not meant to say much of anything; the truth probably is that he genuinely wasn't aware he had. There was no urgency then; his attention was turned elsewhere."[73] In contrast with Kennedy, Johnson was not given to independent political judgment in the international domain. Instead, he relied heavily on his foreign policy advisers. The State Department had put the matter before Johnson as if the fate of the project rested solely in his hands. His fiat alone would be enough to establish the fleet. The United States could apply its leadership to the cause with relatively little risk and later – possibly at the end of the year – reap the fruits of diplomatic success. In his perfunctory look at the MLF, Johnson thus gave an authorization that went beyond his own commitment and that would later see him engaged in a tough fight with a vital part of his bureaucracy.

It soon became clear that the band of MLF supporters needed little encouragement to double their efforts.[74] According to the new timetable, a formal agreement on the MLF was to be provided by the first day of 1965. This would be after the elections in the United States and Great Britain, and well before the German elections of mid-1965 could seize upon the issue. The tempo and the range of the MLF campaign picked up commensurately. Procedures were stepped up to canvass Congress, where opinion on the MLF was still largely skeptical.[75] Briefings of domestic and foreign newspapermen were arranged in order to generate favorable press comment,[76] with the important side effect that the MLF increasingly came to be regarded as a project on which the Johnson administration staked its prestige. In June 1964, Jean Monnet's Action Committee for the United States of Europe moreover endorsed the MLF as part of the Atlantic partnership concept and as a transitional arrangement until the unification of Europe had proceeded to the point where an "authority capable of controlling and administering the European contribution to joint defense becomes a practical reality."[77]

Most importantly, the European allies were notified of the American strength of purpose. Meeting with his NATO colleagues in The Hague in May, Dean Rusk stated that any doubt regarding the measure of American support to the MLF had been due only to a desire to obtain a genuine European reaction. "We have now had that clear response," Rusk said, "the force is seen as meeting real political and military need, and we intend to go ahead." Rusk moreover strongly challenged de Gaulle's rhetoric of national independence in the nuclear age. Absolute national sovereignty had become outmoded with the advent of nuclear weapons,

Rusk stressed; the United States "simply cannot understand the revival of the notion of absolute independence within the free world."[78] American officials could soon report that the military feasibility and the political virtues of the MLF had become better established in a number of European capitals and that "the climate for the MLF has markedly improved in recent weeks."[79] The MLF's revival, finally, was incontrovertible by the time Chancellor Erhard came to visit Johnson in mid-June. Their joint communiqué read that the United States and Germany were agreed that "efforts should be continued to ready an agreement for signature by the end of the year."[80]

The Surmountable British

In American deliberations on the MLF of this period, the French position was rarely mentioned or considered. The prevailing assumption in Washington was that it was of little relevance what France thought of the MLF – that it was its own business to be opposed to the concept. "The MLF could proceed without French acquiescence," Rusk volunteered in a meeting with NATO Secretary General Stikker, "as long as France was not required to be physically involved." The Johnson administration worked on the assumption that the French were "perfectly willing" to let the MLF go ahead without them so long as the MLF vessels would not moor at the harbors of France.[81]

The German government, meanwhile, had been America's most loyal ally on the MLF, which is hardly surprising given the project's stated aim of elevating Germany to the rank of allies with a voice in the nuclear defense of the West. Ever since George Ball had briefed Konrad Adenauer on the issue in early 1963, the MLF had been a touchstone of German policies in the alliance.[82] Adenauer's successor Erhard was a particularly firm supporter, primarily because he was keen on strengthening Germany's Atlantic ties in the wake of the clash of 1963. Although the State Department was wont to explain German interest in the proposal from a natural desire for control over nuclear weapons, the decisive benefit in the German view was that the MLF would tie the United States more closely to European security. There was furthermore no good reason for the German government to withhold support from a project undertaken largely on its behalf. The main argument of American supporters for the MLF was thus rather contrived. "Not only did the MLF derive directly from the American view of the German problem," Alastair Buchan, a well-connected British professor whose advice was often sought by Washington, remarked in a critical paper for the US government, "but the effect of making it an explicit and public proposal ... was to force the German government to play the role for which the State Department had already cast it, namely as a power eager for physical association with the control of nuclear weapons."[83] In any event, Erhard and his Foreign Minister Gerhard Schroeder were much the staunchest advocates of the MLF in Europe. In the summer of

1964, the German chancellor publicly stated that he supported the project "due to personal conviction," hence attaching his prestige and that of his government to its realization.[84] The political coalition with Bonn provided the MLF proponents in Washington with a crucial axis from which considerable momentum could be generated within NATO.[85]

But merely a consensus between Washington and Bonn was not enough to establish the MLF. An exclusively American-German deal would not be palatable to many sides. It would be interpreted as too overt an admission of Germany into the nuclear realm. A bilateral deal would also deviate from the original multilateral concept. At least one other ally of sufficient stature therefore had to participate in the MLF. Since France would not participate, it was obvious that Great Britain – the other nuclear power in Western Europe – held a pivotal position. British participation was also necessary to mollify Germany's real or imagined sense of discrimination. The American diplomatic effort in 1964 therefore focused on persuading a deeply reluctant London to commit itself.

It was generally understood that British reservations with regard to the MLF could not be easily dispelled. The response in Britain to the MLF had ranged from unenthusiastic to outright hostile.[86] The origins of this were not difficult to fathom, for they were not much dissimilar to the objections expressed by that other European nuclear power. "I do not believe," said Prime Minister Macmillan in 1963 in a House of Commons debate on the Nassau agreements, "that our Western alliance could really stand permanently if in this vital [nuclear] field the United States were given for all time the sole authority. We are allies. We must remain allies, but we must not become satellites. I can understand why the French government, who are a world power as well as a continental power, wish to develop their own nuclear force."[87] Yet the British government had not officially ruled out some kind of multilateral nuclear arrangement under NATO, one that also extended to Germany. After all, Macmillan had accepted at his Nassau meeting with Kennedy that the future British nuclear force was going to be assigned to a multilateral force. British diplomats had furthermore participated in the Working Group negotiations in Paris (albeit on a "no-commitment basis"). There was a pervasive sense in London that if the United States and Germany eventually agreed to establish the MLF, Great Britain could not afford to stand aside. The "special relationship" with Washington had to be safeguarded.

British reluctance to engage in discussions about the MLF was reinforced by the fact that two different concepts had actually been discussed at Nassau: the MLF, which would be multilaterally owned and mixed-manned, and a multinational force (MNF) that would consist of national nuclear forces assigned to NATO in a looser formula.[88] Following the Nassau conference, the United States had devoted its best minds to the development of the MLF proposal. The principal interest of the British, however, clearly lay with the MNF. In response to American pressure to accept the multilateral concept, the British drew up a variety of alternative plans that started from the notion of a multinational force but would include a small multilateral component.[89] State Department officials had little patience with British waywardness. In their view, it was essential that the MLF be all wrapped up before the "Gaullist" wing of the CDU stepped up its attacks against Chancellor Erhard in the run-up to the elections of 1965. Increasing the pressure to come to terms with the MLF proposal, American officials began telling their British interlocutors that the United States would proceed with the MLF regardless of the British position.[90] This raised the possibility that Germany – as the major or perhaps only European participant – would replace Great Britain as America's most trusted ally.

The prospect of a Labour Party victory in the British elections of October 1964, predicted by most insiders, considerably complicated negotiations about the MLF. Labour leaders much surpassed their Conservative counterparts in scorning the MLF, primarily because it was in their eyes a disguised proliferation device that could only antagonize the Soviet Union. Harold Wilson, the man most likely to be the next prime minister, had even acquired something of a record on this. "There are many signs," said Wilson in an interview with Cyrus Sulzberger of the *New York Times*, "that this [the MLF] could only whet the German appetite, if there is one. If you have a boy and wish to sublimate his sex appetite, it may not be wise to take him to a striptease show."[91] The party's stance on the issue was no better than that of its political standard-bearer. In the eyes of the strong left wing of the Labour Party, the MLF was pro-German and anti-Soviet, and this was precisely the wrong order. Party spokesmen also vaguely promised that a Labour government would divest Britain altogether of its independent nuclear capability once it came to power, in which case the plans for a multilateral force would be rendered rather circuitous. The Labour Party's standpoint did not significantly alter in the election year and its manifesto for the elections even called for "renegotiating" the Nassau agreement. Hence when Richard Neustadt was in London in June 1964, on envoy from the White House to gauge the Labour Party's MLF stance, most people he met mentioned the project along with a gamut of curses. Neustadt reported: "No member of the frontbench [of the Labour Party] is impressed with [the] MLF in its own terms; none really buys our line on Europe or on Germany; .... Moreover – more important – all the internal forces in their system press the other way, to put off the issue, or better still (were Johnson willing) to evade it altogether."[92]

Yet, in spite of all the sentiment against the MLF, a new Labour government was not expected to refuse participation in a project that had advanced as far as it had and that the United States had said it really wanted. Not prepared to abandon the "special relationship" when the chips were down, London would in all likelihood succumb to Washington's will in the final moments.[93] After his London visit, Neustadt concluded that a Labour government would most likely go along if the United States would take care "to ease the path for Wilson, pay him a good price, [and] leave him no possible excuse we can foresee for failing to proceed toward the MLF in company with us and with the Germans."[94] American officials were also generally optimistic about the chances of British concurrence because of de Gaulle's intransigence within NATO. Alastair Buchan observed in a lengthy analysis for McGeorge Bundy: "This France, under President de Gaulle, refuses even to discuss, so that any attempt in the next year or two to improve the political cohesion of the alliance by means of institutional arrangements rather than by the multilateralisation of forces, might risk either a French veto or an open break with France. ... There seems to be a disposition in Washington to assume that when Mr. Wilson has seen the limitations of the consultative approach, he will take Britain into the MLF."[95] In sum, combined American and German pressure along with a desire to curb de Gaulle was expected to bring the British around to the MLF.[96]

Indeed, when the Labour Party assumed governmental responsibility in October 1964, Harold Wilson saw himself confronted with a nuclear past he could not ignore. With an eye to the timetable, the United States increased the pressure on London to sign up to the MLF within a matter of weeks. Wilson had to come up with something, if only to strengthen his hand in the upcoming negotiations on the MLF charter. His cabinet quickly concocted a counterproposal to the MLF. Based on a pre-election alternative, it proposed an Atlantic Nuclear Force (ANF) to which the entire British deterrent would be committed for "as long as the alliance lasts" but which would be much more loosely defined than the American proposal for a multilateral force. [97] Wilson was keen to avoid any appearance of nuclear dissemination. With his four-vote majority in the House of Commons, he could not afford even the slightest defection in his party. In order to live up to his campaign promise – cherished in particular by the Labour Party's left wing – to dispose of Great Britain's "independent" nuclear force, the use of the ANF's nuclear weapons would be subject to the veto power of the United States, Great Britain, France (assuming it could be seduced to participate), and any of the other participating nations. Wilson was also opposed to a "European clause" in any treaty on a NATO nuclear force, since this would entail the disappearance of the American veto in the event of the unification of Europe. The British ANF proposal provided for a multilateral component, but this was clearly a lesser element of the force, mainly designed to gain the political approval of Washington and Bonn. The Labour government moreover preferred a multilateral force consisting of land-based Minuteman missiles instead of an expensive flotilla of surface vessels. The ANF proposal was thus also more in line with British economic interests.

On December 7, 1964, Harold Wilson traveled to Washington for his first encounter with President Johnson. The prime minister, anxious to establish good relations with his American counterpart, had arrived understandably fearful of the US response to his ANF plan. Both George Ball and Richard Neustadt had personally warned Wilson that the meeting could only be termed successful by the United States if he would give in on the MLF.[98] Wilson could not see how the ANF could carry the day with Johnson and how he could resist the MLF without incurring great damage to Anglo-American relations. The vulnerability of Wilson's position was recognized in Washington as well. McGeorge Bundy put it quite bluntly in preparation for the meeting: Johnson's position was strong and Wilson's was weak. Johnson had just won a landslide victory in the American presidential elections, was at the height of his popularity, and seemed intent on realizing the MLF before his credit with Congress ran out. The British prime minister clearly found himself in a position in which he could be made to accept vital elements of the MLF proposal.[99] That is, if Johnson put the screws on him.

But to Wilson's astonishment, his American host did not force the issue at all. Johnson got off to a furious start, censuring British economic policies and the trouble they were causing the United States. Yet once their private conversation turned to the issue of nuclear sharing, "with the Prime Minister [...] almost on the ropes," Johnson's tone changed. Wilson – still intimidated by Johnson's opening salvos – conceded considerable ground, stating that his only real objection to the MLF concerned the possible abandonment of the American veto in the event of European unity. He said he was not principally opposed to the formula of a surface fleet as envisaged in the MLF proposal. Johnson, however, declined the opportunity to squeeze out Wilson's obeisance to the MLF, stating that he "would not take any adamant position and had no intention to force the matter now." He merely handed Wilson a paper restating the American position on the MLF[100] and urged him above all to come to terms with Bonn on the way forward. The United States, Johnson said, would give careful consideration to anything the British and the Germans might work out, but he was not "going to put his feet in concrete."[101] The surprising outcome of the meeting was therefore that Johnson had let Wilson off the hook. Their discussion of the MLF was described in their communiqué as little more than an "initial exchange of views" and "a preliminary to further discussions among interested members of the alliance."[102] There were no commitments, no time schedules, no mention of agreements to be signed by the end of the year, just vaguely worded intentions. Johnson had not pressed his British counterpart into an agreement on the MLF, not even into a modified version of it using elements of the British ANF proposal. He had merely impressed on Wilson to hit it off with Bonn under his own steam.

The purport of Wilson's meeting with Johnson did not immediately dawn on the press. First appraisals even claimed that Johnson had been adamant and that Wilson was now "stuck" with the MLF; the influential *Times*, for instance, wrote that the meeting heralded the termination of the British national deterrent and termed it an "act of national abnegation, surely unprecedented."[103] In truth, American officials had impressed on their British colleagues that they did not want them to go around claiming that Wilson had killed the MLF.[104] American spokesmen continued to pay tribute to the multilateral concept and to encourage the British and the Germans to reach an agreement. It would not take long, however, before rumors emerged that the Johnson administration had substantially softened its stance on the MLF and allies were beginning to take note of the shift in the American position.[105] Less than two weeks after the Anglo-American summit meeting, James Reston of the *New York Times* reported in a front-page article the existence of a presidential directive to the effect that the United States did not seek an agreement on the MLF unless a true consensus in Europe was achieved.[106] The reporter's information, in fact, had come straight from the Oval Office and the document in question was National Security Action Memorandum 322 (which we shall discuss later).[107] As London and Bonn were considered unlikely to produce an agreement on their own account, the implication of Johnson's ruling was that the United States had virtually given up on the MLF.

Great Britain's opposition to the MLF, however stiff, had not been insurmountable. It was also not the principal cause of the MLF's demise. Andrew Pierre's assessment of the episode may well serve to buttress this argument:

> It is probable that an agreement of some type of an ANF/MLF arrangement could have been reached in December 1964, if Washington had insisted upon it. The British were caught between the possibility of a purely American-German accord on the MLF, or if this did not occur, the danger of a nuclear arrangement between a frustrated Germany and an ambitious France. Both were undesirable from London's point of view, since the former would weaken British influence in Washington and make Bonn its most intimate ally, while the latter was even more dangerous since it would increase Germany's nuclear knowledge, create the danger of an anti-Anglo-Saxon "third force" in Europe, and be a cause of valid apprehension for the Soviet Union. Despite continuing differences of opinion between Britain, Germany, and the United States over the make-up of an integrated nuclear force, an agreement could well have been forged between these countries plus Italy and some of the smaller European nations in late 1964.[108]

But Pierre's otherwise accurate assessment does not recognize the decisive role played by France – the only country in NATO that had consistently expressed opposition to the MLF – in American decisionmaking. Similarly, State Department officials had failed to take French sensitivities and – more seriously – the probability of an effective French counterattack into account as they pressed for the MLF. Their eyes fixed on the prize, their efforts had focused on London. France only appeared in their calculations as the bulwark of an outdated European nationalism which the MLF was supposed to check. They had, as a result, lost sight of an important political reality: that France could prevent the establishment of the MLF even though it would not participate and irrespective of the

British position. In the Elysée, a bomb under the entire project had been ticking. And Johnson had felt the need to dismantle it.

But this is getting ahead of the story. The remainder of this chapter will seek to answer the question how Johnson's sudden reversal on the MLF came about.

The Wide Range of French Opposition

To de Gaulle, the MLF was clearly an abomination. His foreign policy was predicated on the notion that defense matters were fundamentally and immutably tied to the legitimacy of the nation-state. It was why he had objected so strongly to the European Defense Community in the early 1950s. The case for national autonomy was in his view even stronger in the nuclear realm: the atom bomb could only be national in character and the independence of the *force de frappe* was hence an unassailable article of faith of Gaullist foreign policy. Since the MLF proposal sought to extend NATO's principle of military integration – worse than obnoxious in de Gaulle's view – to the nuclear realm, there was never much of a chance that he would support it. As long as the United States was not prepared to relinquish its veto (which de Gaulle believed would forever remain the case), the force would give the European allies only the appearance of control. In his vocabulary, nuclear "integration" was simply a chimera and the multilateral force a "farce." The MLF would be little more than "an American naval foreign legion."[109]

But de Gaulle also had serious objections to the MLF proposal even if France would not be required to participate. It would, first of all, strengthen America's hand in Europe's security affairs. For one, the MLF would cut off de Gaulle's ambition to have the French national deterrent play a central role in the nuclear defense of Western Europe. For another, the MLF would lessen the distinction between nuclear haves and have-nots in Europe, thus depriving France of its nuclear monopoly on the European continent (in particular vis-à-vis Germany). Germany's participation in the MLF would moreover irrevocably alter Bonn's relation with Paris and Washington, to the obvious advantage of the latter. In addition, the MLF would complicate efforts to seek détente in the West's relationship with the Soviet Union. In sum, the MLF was so sharply at odds with French views and interests that it was only natural that its prevention was an important objective of French foreign policy.[110]

The French had kept remarkably silent on the MLF since de Gaulle's rebuke of January 1963, thus fostering the impression that Paris would not try to block its founding. If anything, French spokesmen declared that France had simply decided not to join the MLF project because it could not afford both participation in the MLF and development of the *force de frappe*. They also refrained from censuring allies that did show interest. Until the spring of 1964, Paris even seemed to tolerate the possibility of German participation.[111] But French acquiescence was only guaranteed as long as the MLF was just one of many proposals, headed in no particular direction. The French view during much of 1963 and 1964 was that the MLF was a bathtub toy that would never float right side up. Yet when American pressure on behalf of the MLF increased following Johnson's April resolutions and raised the possibility that the MLF might come into being, the French position began to harden. De Gaulle's diplomatic drive in the second half of 1964 to thwart the MLF would turn out to be remarkably effective.

Paris, Bonn, and the Common Market

Franco-German relations had significantly deteriorated since de Gaulle and Adenauer had concluded the Treaty of Reconciliation on January 22, 1963. Having succeeded Adenauer in October 1963, Ludwig Erhard was manifesting himself as a staunch Atlanticist. He also came out strongly in support of the MLF proposal, primarily as a way to tie the United States more firmly to European security. De Gaulle's ideas about Europe and the transatlantic relationship were clearly wasted on him and his cabinet.[112] By 1964, the regular get-togethers between the German chancellor and the French president had become routine exercises that did little to contribute to mutual political understanding and agreement. The Franco-German entente had become a "fragile plant," as André François-Poncet put it in Le Figaro; it permitted a certain amount of useful homework but had on the whole been reduced to a dialogue of the deaf.[113]

But France remained well positioned to drive a wedge in the coalition between the United States and Germany on the MLF. Erhard's public endorsements tended to obfuscate that influential circles in Germany were not as favorably disposed toward the project. There was criticism that the MLF was rather expensive for a "loyalty demonstration" that offered no real control over Germany's nuclear defense.[114] More importantly, there were also doubts about the wisdom of advertising loyalty to Washington and alienating Paris. France's central position in the Common Market and its official policy of reconciliation with Germany were considered too important to justify such a course. The strongest criticism of the MLF therefore came from the "Gaullist" wing of the CDU/CSU, Erhard's own party. The German Gaullists reproached Erhard and his Foreign Minister Schroeder for "sacrificing" the alliance with France by giving unqualified support to American policies. "We Europeans should not place blind confidence in the reliability and trustworthiness of the Americans, who do not wish without more ado to let themselves be drawn into an atomic war," argued Franz Josef Strauss in true Gaullist style in June 1963. "So long as Europe has no nuclear weapons, Europe has no sovereignty."[115] German Gaullists like Strauss believed that the French nuclear deterrent could in the long run provide the nucleus of a European force. They hence also felt that the costs of the MLF would be better used toward furthering a truly European solution.[116] The fact that the MLF could prompt France to reappraise its policy of reconciliation with Germany clearly raised the possibility of undermining official German support for the proposal. Indeed, the inherent and consistent inability of Germany's Cold War foreign policy to choose between Washington and Paris was the real Achilles' heel of the MLF project.[117]

The first piece of evidence that the French were shifting from passive to active opposition to the MLF surfaced in the summer of 1964, after the Johnson administration had intensified its diplomatic efforts to obtain European approval. French spokesmen stopped excusing themselves for not taking part in the negotiations. At a West European Union (WEU) Assembly meeting in June, Jacques Baumel, the Gaullist leader in parliament, derided the MLF as "inefficient, riddled with contradictions, and ... merely an elegant attempt to solve a problem for which it was no solution at all."[118] More importantly, de Gaulle used his talks with Erhard in early July to convey a notably tougher stance on German participation in the MLF, briefly after the latter had agreed with Johnson that the MLF charter be readied before the end of the year. "Why does Germany want to join the MLF?" de Gaulle asked Erhard.[119] In his private conversation with Erhard, he reportedly also hinted at the need for a truly European nuclear force, describing the French force de frappe as a way station to such a force and suggesting that Germany might associate itself with it. When Erhard asked whether this meant that Germany would have a say over the force de frappe, de Gaulle apparently emphasized the "essential French nature" of the force. But he also pledged that French nuclear weapons would be used for Germany's defense.[120]

Whatever the credibility of these overtures, it was clear that de Gaulle was now pressing Bonn harder than before on the MLF. This certainly came as a rude surprise to Erhard.[121] Most German officials, like their American counterparts, had believed that the French would not object to German participation in the MLF. De Gaulle's July meeting with Erhard robbed them of this illusion. The full scope of French opposition would yet have to reveal itself, but some German circles were already assuming that it denoted the beginning of a tough French drive to head off German participation in the MLF.[122] Any doubts about how seriously de Gaulle regarded Germany's participation in the MLF were finally removed by his reproach of Bonn's Atlanticism at his semi-annual press conference on July 23, 1964. De Gaulle's warning was ominous enough to catch the attention of German foreign policymakers:

> One cannot say that Germany and France have yet agreed to make a policy together, and one cannot dispute that this results from the fact that so far Bonn has not believed that this policy should be European and independent. If this state of affairs were to last, there would be the long-run risk of doubts among the French people, of misgivings among the German people, and, among their four partners of the Rome Treaty, an increased tendency to leave things as they are, while waiting, perhaps, to be split up. ...[France] is now strong enough and sure enough of herself to be able to be patient, except for

major external changes which would jeopardize everything and therefore lead her to change her direction.[123]

The reaction in Germany was furious. De Gaulle's words emanated the dual threat of denouncing the Treaty of Reconciliation and breaking up the Common Market in the event Germany caused the "major external changes" he had in mind (such as by making the MLF possible). President Johnson's reaction the next day was temperate by comparison, as it emphasized that the United States was not trying to force anyone to choose between Paris and Washington.[124] The choice, however, was once again intruding itself upon Germany with increasing urgency.

Although Franco-German relations plummeted in the summer of 1964, French hostility towards the MLF would not come out into the open until the fall. The record suggests that French opposition was directly linked to the project's prospects of realization. From early October onwards, stories appeared in the French and German media on the possibility that the United States and Germany might take bilateral steps towards the MLF.[125] These stories stood in connection with a visit to Washington by Wilhelm Grewe, the German ambassador to NATO. Erhard was keen to have the MLF affair wrapped up well before the German parliamentary elections in September 1965, and he had become increasingly disturbed by delays in readying an agreement by the end of the year. The stoppage had been caused mainly by British ambiguity and, with Harold Wilson assuming office that month, British procrastination was expected to impede the MLF negotiations even more. Grewe was sent to Washington to deliver a letter to Johnson in which Erhard expressed his growing uneasiness with the state of affairs and urged the United States to keep to the intended time schedule. Erhard also suggested that, if necessary, Germany would be prepared to reach a bilateral agreement with the United States at the end of the year – to which others could then later add their signature.[126] At a news conference on October 6, Erhard furthermore added substance to the rumors by indicating that Germany was prepared to implement the project together with the United States. "We hope ... the doors will stay wide open for other European countries to join," but "a beginning has to be made," said Erhard. And asked specifically if he would consider entering the MLF without the other European allies, he replied: "I cannot give you a flat 'yes', but I cannot deny it."[127]

Grewe never received any clear message that the Johnson administration would seriously contemplate a bilateral deal with Germany on the MLF.[128] The official view in Washington had always been that at least one other major nation – i.e., Great Britain or Italy – had to participate. Johnson's reply to Erhard confirmed his intention to reach agreement by the end of the year, but he also underlined the importance of broad participation in the MLF.[129] At the State Department, however, there certainly was sympathy for a bilateral deal, primarily out of irritation with British foot-dragging. "It would be good to have the British in from the beginning," one diplomatic telegram had stated in June. "However, if [the] choice is between having them in at the beginning and a further year's delay, there is no question but that we want to avoid delay. Any hint that we would compromise on this point could involve us in greater difficulty with the Germans."[130] State Department leaks had also contributed to the rumor that a bilateral deal with Bonn was secretly being prepared. And when *Die Welt*'s Washington correspondent wrote a story about the "fiasco" of Grewe's visit, he was soon called in by an irritated Henry Owen of the State Department's Policy Planning Council, who stressed that the United States was set on moving ahead with the MLF regardless of the British: "The British have no choice – they must either knuckle under or watch the MLF go without them."[131] Readiness of this sort was thought to help bring the British around. But it also let a different cat out of the bag. Besides forcing the British closer to acceptance of the MLF, word of a bilateral deal between the United States and Germany on the MLF alarmed the French.[132]

It was soon becoming increasingly clear that de Gaulle could not be expected to accept the MLF without further ado. "There are indications," reported Bohlen from Paris on the day of Erhard's press conference, "that recent press reports re [garding the] possibility [of a] signature [of the] MLF soon have not been lost on French thinking on this subject." Adding: "[The] French appear never [to] have thought [that the] MLF would materialize and were correspondingly casual. Now, however, that concrete possibility looms their basic antagonism to [the] idea [is] becoming more active." Bohlen also cited friendly disposed French diplomats who speculated that de Gaulle might move drastically against NATO, the United States, and Germany because of the MLF. "We should anticipate [a] more active French anti-MLF campaign for future in spite of [the] public line of indifference," concluded Bohlen.[133] By the end of October, alarming reports from the embassy in Paris had indeed become numerous and French resistance to the MLF had become a principal concern in Washington.[134]

The potential implications of French hostility towards the MLF finally began to dawn on Washington. On October 20, the thrust of the French campaign to avert the MLF was revealed to the State Department in a call from Bruno de Leusse of the French embassy. In "...perhaps the most pronounced expression [of] French hostility to [the] MLF," Alphand's deputy highlighted the disruptive impact of the MLF on Franco-German relations. By joining the MLF and making their security dependent on a non-European power, he argued, the Germans would abandon their "European vocation." The MLF, it was implied, was bound to cause havoc with the spirit of European integration.[135] Paris appeared to be threatening that pressing ahead with the MLF could ultimately lead to the dissolution of the Common Market.

At this point it is important to note that the Common Market was already experiencing a crisis of its own and that this was affecting calculations in European capitals with regard to the MLF. In the fall of 1964, the Six had reached a deadlock over the common agricultural policy. The Erhard government had time and again blocked an agreement on the prices of cereals. With elections less than a year ahead, it was deeply averse to draw the anger of German farmers by lowering these prices. And since the Rome Treaty had not demanded a common agricultural policy prior to 1970, Bonn felt that it fully stood within its rights to refuse an agreement in 1964.[136] Yet de Gaulle, as we have seen, had made the early enactment of a common agricultural policy a priority in French foreign policy upon his return to power and was quite prepared to undo the Common Market if he did not get his way. With the Six thus drifting towards crisis, there was a widespread reluctance in European capitals to embark on new adventures that could further undermine Franco-German relations and the Common Market. Many Europeans, perceiving the MLF above all as an American challenge to de Gaulle's notion of a "European" Europe, were concerned that the MLF would provoke him into a more damaging retribution against the Common Market than his veto of Britain's membership in January 1963.[137] The Johnson administration's drive to reach agreement on the MLF by the end of 1964 thus seemed increasingly out of sync with political developments in Europe. As it turned out, the political state of affairs in Europe in the fall of 1964 would even enable de Gaulle to kill two birds with one stone.

The hope among officials in Bonn as well as in Washington was that Common Market issues and the MLF could be treated separately. Yet the conjuncture was not overlooked by Paris. France had valid economic reasons to stand firm on the moot point of the grain price, but de Gaulle also recognized the opportunity to link the impasse within the Common Market with his goal to scuttle the MLF. Both issues were presented by French officials as a defining test of the "Europeanism" of the Germans.[138] On October 21, de Gaulle's Minister of Information Alain Peyrefitte issued a warning that France would "cease to participate" in the Common Market if Germany continued to resist an agreement on common cereal prices by the end of the year.[139] Couve de Murville echoed this threat in a speech before the National Assembly a short while later and moreover linked it to Germany's support for the MLF.[140] It was the first of a couple of speeches by French leaders that presented both the MLF and the issue of agricultural prices as test cases for Germany's earnestness about achieving friendly relations with France. On November 5, Prime Minister Georges Pompidou denounced the MLF and the prospect of a bilateral American-German agreement as being directed against France. He left no doubt that Paris expected Bonn to concede on both issues, or else it would risk the split-up of both the Common Market and the Treaty of Reconciliation. "The agricultural common market must take shape, for without it the industrial common market will simply collapse," said Pompidou. And: "If the multilateral force were to lead to the creation of a German-American military alliance, we would not consider this as being fully consistent with the relations we have with the Federal Republic which are based on the Franco-German Treaty."[141] French officials even hinted that German participation in the MLF could compel Paris to seek an entente with Eastern Europe, which would present additional hurdles for the reunification of Germany.[142] Finally, in a speech in Strasbourg on November 22, de Gaulle added his weight to the French campaign by warning the Erhard government that it would "inflict a deep wound on a great hope" if it abandoned the Franco-German entente to become an "auxiliary" of the United States.[143]

The pressure on Erhard to concede on the MLF in order to mollify the French became almost unbearable. There was no longer any doubt that the MLF would irrevocably damage Germany's amity with France. De Gaulle struck Erhard where he was most vulnerable. In the German domestic political debate, the unproven virtues of the MLF were increasingly outweighed by a desire to prevent France's perennial animosity. When the "Gaullists" launched their first major attack in the Bundestag on Erhard's Atlanticist foreign policy in mid-October, Erhard had not yielded an inch. But he could not prevent a procession of concerned German politicians from making their way to Paris soon thereafter, when French leaders were beginning to lash out publicly against German participation in the MLF. In particular, Konrad Adenauer had found – at his advanced age – a new calling as the leader of the "Gaullist" wing in the CDU. On November 9, the patriarch of Germany's postwar politics left on a self-appointed mission to Paris in order to ease the growing Franco-German rift. His visit was a gala of Franco-German goodwill, during which Adenauer even solemnly declared that "we should thank God for having given us General de Gaulle."[144] Adenauer's mission gravely undermined Erhard's domestic position on the MLF. De Gaulle informed Adenauer of his deep-seated objections to the MLF, ranking it even above the common agricultural policy as the Franco-German issue on which there was little room for compromise. Upon his return, on November 11, the CDU voted in favor of postponing any commitment to the MLF until it could be given a "more European character" and be made less objectionable to France. Erhard and his Foreign Minister Schroeder were fiercely attacked for their Atlanticist predilection and for being too rigid with the French.[145] Even as Erhard persisted in his support for the MLF, the prospect that a treaty had to pass the German Bundestag in the face of French enmity had made his objective ever more controversial. De Gaulle's diplomatic harangue against the Erhard government had raised the possibility that the MLF would simply fall through for lack of support within Erhard's own party.[146]

De Gaulle had furthermore acquired leverage over Erhard because his threats of reprisal against the Common Market compelled other European capitals to press Bonn to pay a price in the nuclear realm. Walter Hallstein, the German chairman of the European Commission, also urged the MLF's deferral until after agreement was reached among the Six on the unified grain price.[147] Erhard, however, reluctant to link the issues, was even more reluctant to let go of the MLF. In late November, he made his sacrifice: he accepted the common agricultural policy and lower cereal prices in hopes of gaining French acquiescence on the MLF.[148] Yet, as Newhouse put it, de Gaulle might have been prepared to "let Erhard wriggle off the grain-price hook, at least until after the German elections in September, provided that the MLF was discarded."[149] Erhard's sacrifice was in vain. He had simply paid the wrong price and, as we will see, de Gaulle would hence get his way on both accounts.

De Gaulle's campaign against the MLF had thus transformed the Erhard government into an ally under duress. He had found an important weak spot in the Johnson administration's drive to garner European support for the MLF. Germany's alleged appetite for nuclear weapons moreover had been presented by the American advocates of the MLF as the prime rationale of the MLF. With Bonn showing signs of battle fatigue at the end of 1964, the premise on which much of the campaign had been built – and on which Johnson had decided to give his uncertain support – was rapidly changing.

NATO

Besides putting the future of Franco-German cooperation and the Common Market in doubt, de Gaulle issued strong warnings against NATO in order to stave off the MLF – and this posed dilemmas above all to the Johnson administration. In fact, de Gaulle's initial riposte to the establishment of the MLF was always more likely to take form against NATO than against the Common Market.[150] French disengagement from NATO, starting in March 1959 with the withdrawal of the French Mediterranean Fleet, was already long in evidence. In April 1964, all French naval personnel were withdrawn from NATO.[151] In early July, the Central Intelligence Agency furthermore informed the White House that, according to an unnamed high French official, de Gaulle was actively considering a "drastic step" against NATO.[152] And in November, de Gaulle notified Ambassador Bohlen of his intention to leave NATO in 1969 (i.e., as soon as the treaty allowed for it).[153] Suddenly, American insistence on the MLF raised the specter of prompting de Gaulle into an early withdrawal from NATO while giving him an opportunity to blame the Americans for trying to force the MLF down European throats.

Indications that the MLF could provoke a complete French withdrawal from NATO were abundant by November 1964. When Pompidou and Couve de Murville addressed the French National Assembly in early November, for instance, neither had been willing to affirm – in response to direct questions – that France would continue to participate in NATO.[154] The possibility of imminent French withdrawal was also inserted in diplomatic contacts between Paris and Washington; in a forthright telephone conversation with Dean Rusk, French Ambassador Alphand warned that the MLF would cause a "very serious situation" in NATO.[155] General Michel Fourquet, the chief of the French air force with good access to the Elysée, might have given the strongest expression of French hostility to the MLF. In a conversation with Charles Bohlen, Fourquet ominously stressed that the introduction of the MLF would "coldly stab NATO to death." Fourquet also reiterated the more widespread belief that the proposal had created – rather than responded to – a German nuclear appetite, and he underlined that in his view this was the United States' "main crime."[156] While Fourquet's statements were unusually harsh, they corresponded with the views of the French government. The Gaullist press, too, which was sponsored by government circles, was given to combining opposition to the MLF with blanket threats to NATO.[157]

Given the barrage of French threats to NATO at the end of 1964, historians have generally overlooked the fact that French attempts to stave off the MLF could have been at least as effective if they had strictly played by the rules of NATO – and potentially even be politically more rewarding to Paris. American officials had always rather easily assumed that the MLF would help cement the alliance more firmly and could be incorporated within the NATO framework without further ado. According to the concept, the MLF would be assigned to NATO and placed under the operational control of the SACEUR; the missiles of the fleet would then be targeted by the SACEUR in accordance with NATO-agreed strategies.[158] But the rule of unanimity within NATO meant that France could simply veto the MLF if it felt strongly enough about it, or at least prevent its absorption into NATO. While many in Washington and elsewhere may have felt that France had already withdrawn from NATO for all practical and political purposes by 1964, it was still a full member of the Atlantic alliance with blocking power over all decisions taken in the North Atlantic Council.

To be sure, because of France's persistent obstructionism, some had been advocating that the rule of unanimity be abandoned as the principle superseding everything else within NATO. In particular, Secretary General Dirk Stikker, who was privately chafing at French negativism toward NATO,[159] regarded this rule as a cardinal weakness since it made "NATO's chain of strength ... only as strong as its weakest link."[160] In the spring of 1964, he proposed that the alliance adopt a practice already in use within the OECD which meant that if a member disapproved of an action desired by the majority it could abstain while the others went ahead. Stikker actually sought to strengthen his case by arguing that such a formula was already being applied in practice to allied talks about the MLF; these discussions took place in a working group of eight nations which been meeting at the NATO headquarters in Paris but not as a NATO body (primarily in order to avoid French interference). "But it would be much easier," he explained in a conversation with Dean Rusk, "if the action [on the MLF] could be taken within rather than outside NATO and if it could be explained as a NATO action." Stikker's abstention – or constructive disengagement – doctrine got virtually no support, also not from Rusk.[161] But the quandary that troubled him was real and the rule of unanimity would inevitably threaten the MLF as soon as the French decided to shift from passive opposition to outright hostility – as they did.

In August 1964, Stikker was succeeded as NATO secretary general by the one candidate who was able to receive the endorsement from both the United States and France: the cautious Italian diplomat Manlio Brosio.[162] Brosio had been highly regarded as ambassador to Great Britain, the United States, and France. In contrast with Stikker, he wanted to be an impartial mediator within the alliance.[163] From the outset, he was above all concerned with the potentially disruptive consequences of the MLF. In Brosio's view, the American proposal simply elicited too much opposition in Europe. He was particularly apprehensive about de Gaulle's reaction; with his good contacts in the Quai d'Orsay and the Elysée, he had sensed earlier than most that French hostility toward the MLF was growing. In late September, paying his dues in Washington shortly after having taken over from Stikker, Brosio stressed that his "principal preoccupation" would be to assuage French hostility toward NATO and that he above all aspired to be an "honest broker" who would not take sides. While reassuring his American interlocutors that he approved of the MLF concept per se, he left little doubt that in his view de Gaulle might well exploit an agreement on the MLF as a "pretext for creating a major crisis in the Alliance [...]."[164]

Brosio had no desire whatsoever to question NATO's rule of unanimity. On the contrary, he clearly spoke out against any such modification in an address to NATO parliamentarians on November 16 – his first major policy statement as NATO's secretary general. Brosio stated that no ally had the right "to develop the structure of the Atlantic organization, or to effect in it modification calculated to radically alter its character in the direction of either more or less integration *without the full consent, unanimously proclaimed, of all its members.*" In addition, he argued that the MLF was subject to this provision since it was "manifestly a project with capital military and political implications." Brosio even seemed to be suggesting that setting up the MLF *outside* NATO against the wishes of any member state was incompatible with the terms of the treaty. He denied, one day later, that he had wanted to give the impression that it was legally impossible to establish the MLF outside NATO, but also reiterated that he preferred to see the MLF issue settled within the framework of the alliance and subject to the provisions of the treaty (and therefore to the rule of unanimity).[165]

According to one alert commentator, Edmond Taylor, Brosio's speech was "couched in prudent diplomatic language and delivered in such unemotional tones that many of his listeners, apparently including the press, did not immediately grasp its significance." However, in an article for *The Reporter*, Taylor rightly called attention to the fact that Brosio's stance had presented MLF proponents with a haunting dilemma. The undeniable implication of Brosio's reaffirmation of the rule of unanimity was that de Gaulle could block the incorporation of the MLF into NATO. The journalist revealed that proponents of the MLF in Washington and elsewhere could be faced with an entirely different situation than they had previously envisaged. Instead of forcing France to acquiesce in the project or withdraw from NATO, these proponents were themselves confronted with the possible choice of abandoning the project or setting it up outside NATO. This last option did not generate much enthusiasm even among the fiercest advocates of the MLF in the United States. "It would, in effect, mean creating a rump NATO alongside the legal one," Taylor observed. "Besides raising a host of technical difficulties, it would probably lead to the gradual withering away of the original organization." Brosio's address, Taylor pointed out, sent "widening ripples" through the alliance. Particularly in the smaller member states, it crystallized the diffuse opposition to the MLF:

> Observers here believe that the courageous position taken by the NATO secretary-general is certain to influence the attitude of several NATO governments that have never had much enthusiasm for MLF. Norway's Foreign Minister Halvard Lange stated in a press conference in London that his country would not participate in [the] MLF under any conditions, and it is expected here that Denmark and Iceland will take the same stand. There is a strong likelihood that Belgium and Luxembourg will do the same. Portugal, Greece, and Italy are also considered possible defectors. Thus Washington's strategy of isolating France as the only holdout at next month's ministerial meeting of the North Atlantic Council seems foredoomed to failure.[166]

Washington and the "Coming Crunch in European Policy"

By the end of 1964, a transatlantic crisis over the MLF – with France and the United States as the principal antagonists – began to seem inevitable. Because of de Gaulle's counteroffensive, the MLF was bereft of a solid political basis in Europe. Whatever political strength remained behind the MLF proposal seemed increasingly derived from Washington's position alone. This position was still one of strong support for the MLF. The Johnson administration had staked its prestige as leader of the alliance on the project. Its advocates at the State Department continued to control daily diplomatic actions. The clear impression in Europe was hence that Johnson was determined to force allied agreement on the MLF in time before the German elections of September 1965.

That a crisis was brewing in Europe was not lost on Washington. In the perception of the Europeanists at the State Department, however, it was above all a moment of truth. They fervently believed that Washington should not give in to de Gaulle's counteroffensive or to British foot-dragging. This was a crucial battle in the dispute over Europe's future, comparable to the debate about the Schuman plan in 1949 and 1950.[167] The Europeanists were quite ready to take de Gaulle head on. Rather than making the MLF less commendable, his opposition in their view underscored the urgency of counteracting European nationalism and weathering the storm. They also hoped that the MLF, once established, would offer a post-de Gaulle government an alternative to the expensive *force de frappe*. In addition, they remained willfully optimistic about the chances of securing an agreement by early 1965.[168] All that Johnson had to do was to show strength of leadership.

This attitude is revealed in particular in the memoranda drafted at the time by Walt Rostow as director of the State Department's Policy Planning Council. Reflecting on the "coming crunch in European policy," he wrote to Dean Rusk on October 12 following a visit to Europe:

> Everyone concerned, including the British and the French, now understands that the decision on the MLF will determine whether NATO moves forward in the next decade around a pattern of increasing Atlantic integration or whether NATO moves towards fragmentation. ... I believe that the underlying forces in Europe are sufficiently favorable for us to make this turn in the road with success; but we should not underestimate the likely noise in the system. ... Although the issues are more muted, I cannot help observing that the turning point of 1965 will be quite as important as that of 1947: we shall either solve the array of problems before us on an integrated basis or, should we fail, see a quite rapid phase of disintegration take hold in the Atlantic.[169]

In another memorandum one week later, Rostow gave evidence of the preoccupation with the German question so common among proponents of the MLF in the State Department. Any argument against the project withered next to the imperative nature of this question. Rostow:

> We are not supporting the MLF because it's fun or because we expect everyone involved will like it. We are supporting the MLF because it is the best among a series of unsatisfactory solutions to a problem which will not go away. ... At the core of the problem is Germany, as it has been at the core of every major initiative we have taken in Europe since 1945. On this most vital and treacherous of issues our objective is to solve the problem in the way most likely to permit moderate German politicians to survive and flourish. And that objective has been continuous for a generation.

In addition, Rostow characteristically stressed the importance of showing American leadership. The defeat of the European Defense Community in the French National Assembly in 1954, he argued, produced a relevant lesson: "We should not let the matter drag." There was moreover one significant difference with the EDC: "The United States is prepared to join the MLF. Properly handled, this fact can mean the difference between failure in 1954 and success in 1965."[170]

But the Europeanists could not prevent the MLF from coming under more critical review within the Johnson administration as the storm in Europe gathered strength. The approaching December deadline, too, was thrusting those parts of the bureaucracy into the decisionmaking process that were less convinced of the project's virtues. Rostow may therefore well have written his memoranda in recognition of the fact that the State Department's control over the MLF's destiny was slipping. The MLF project had developed into a question of bending ("surrendering" in the State Department's lexicon) or breaking ("standing firm"). And those in Washington in favor of bending were becoming more vocal. On October 31, there was some interagency discussion as to whether it would not be better to let the whole affair slide for two or three years: "Were we really sure whether we would be better off after the creation of an Atlantic force? Wasn't there more stability in the present situation than we gave credit for, since the Germans were not about to proliferate?" Although it was concluded that for the moment nothing was to be gained from delay, the fact that questions were beginning to be raised was important.[171]

The State Department's Arms Control and Disarmament Agency (ACDA) had been most consistent in its objections to the MLF proposal. It was above all interested in reaching agreement with the Soviet Union on a treaty stemming nuclear proliferation. Since Moscow castigated the MLF as a proliferation device and Soviet negotiators in Geneva named it the major obstacle to a non-proliferation treaty, the project greatly impaired their own ambitions.[172] The ACDA, however, did not carry great bureaucratic weight.[173]

In addition, many officials at the Pentagon were skeptical of the MLF's advertised benefits; only the US Navy considered the multilateral fleet a welcome extension. The project was considered expensive and complex whereas it would not add substantively to NATO's deterrent posture. The MLF also threatened to absorb scarce European resources to the detriment of the conventional reinforcements required for implementing the flexible response strategy in Europe. The Pentagon was also warier than the State Department of disruptive French moves against NATO.[174]

But the strongest resistance to the MLF resided within the White House staff. McGeorge Bundy was not opposed to the multilateral concept in principle and his record had led proponents to believe he was on their side.[175] But the nature of his office determined that he was above all concerned with guarding the president's options. He believed that it was his task to protect Johnson from getting into trouble over a project to which – as Bundy correctly sensed – he did not feel personally committed. In addition, Bundy was quite capable of independent judgment on foreign policy issues. Concerned with the lack of strong support in Europe, he had always remained skeptical of optimistic State Department reports on the MLF negotiations. If anything, Kennedy's "Nassau experience" had conveyed a lesson of caution to him, and he was firmly bent on preventing a repetition of events. McGeorge Bundy was therefore on his guard.

Bundy's private vigilance was fed by members of his staff. Particularly David Klein, a senior member of the staff and responsible for European affairs, frequently expressed misgivings about the way the State Department conducted the MLF negotiations, believing that it was overselling the project and losing sight of political realities at home as well as abroad.[176] In the same vein, Klein felt that the aforementioned Rostow memorandum on "the coming crunch in European policy" showed a "distortion in emphasis and context."[177] "Even at this late date," he had already argued to Bundy in a long memorandum, "I think it remains moot whether the MLF can really strengthen the Alliance."

> The obvious result [of the MLF] would be to replace NATO, a broader-based and perhaps less integrated organization, with a smaller grouping, more deeply integrated and less outward looking. Is such a development really in our interest? Do we want a narrower and more exclusive European Alliance? Would such a move be consistent with our desire for an expanding, outward looking Europe, bringing together its several parts? In other words, will the MLF contribute to an improved Alliance, to improved relations within Europe, and to improved coordination between Europe and the U.S.? This is by no means an obvious conclusion.

Klein also keenly observed that the administration's public profile on the MLF was far more specific and supportive than Johnson's commitment, and that this might end in political defeat for the American president. "The last thing we want to do is tie this MLF millstone around the President's neck."[178]

In November, largely as a result of the December deadline for negotiations and the increasing mayhem in Europe, the MLF once again came under review at the highest policy level after months in which the State Department had had virtual license. A clear position on the MLF also had to be prepared before Johnson's meeting with Prime Minister Harold Wilson at the White House in early December. It was high time to make the divided bureaucracy responsive to the need of preparing a cogent position. At Bundy's suggestion, Johnson brought his presidential authority to bear on the policymaking process. On November 14, National Security Action Memorandum 318 (NSAM 318) ordained that coordination within the administration was to be tightened up. More specifically, Johnson's directive stipulated that all American officials who traveled overseas to discuss the matter were bound by written instructions cleared in the White House, the State Department, and the Defense Department; in addition, only a few designated officials were authorized to discuss the MLF with the press.[179] Following NSAM 318, a committee was formed around George Ball and McGeorge Bundy to survey all aspects of MLF diplomacy and to come up with a coherent and unified position. Although it came to be called the Ball Committee – the group met at his office and he was also responsible for drafting its final report – it was really of interdepartmental reach. Richard Neustadt, for instance, who was closer to McGeorge Bundy than to the State Department, was brought in to direct its staff work. The essence of the committee's work was to hammer out a consensus within the administration on the way forward. Yet the objective remained to achieve what the president had officially said he wanted – to reach allied agreement on the MLF by early 1965 – without precipitating a political crisis or exposing him to a major policy failure.[180]

American diplomacy on the MLF had reached a new – and final – stage. Through the involvement of the White House staff, Johnson's priorities gained currency in the process and inserted a measure of caution. NSAM 318 moreover revealed that Washington was no longer exclusively worried about the delay the British were causing. "It is also obvious," it stated, "that we shall have to take careful account of the interests and purposes of France." [181] De Gaulle's anti-MLF campaign was beginning to have an effect in Washington; for safety's sake, the Ball Committee was charged with devising a fallback that would save Johnson's face in the event that the political risks of establishing the MLF within the foreseeable future became too great.

The Implacable French

When de Gaulle suddenly left no stone unturned to head off the MLF in the fall of 1964, this was perceived in Washington as a perverse change of course. In fact, both American and French officials did their best to appear as the righteous and aggrieved party. Alphand's phone call with Dean Rusk on November 13 was a case in point. The French ambassador strongly conveyed that Paris did not understand why the United States had "suddenly started to press [the] creation [of the] MLF" as a "top political priority." Whereupon Rusk replied that there had been no change in the American position since the proposal was first forwarded in 1961 – and that the United States had been led to believe that France was prepared to condone the membership of other allies. It was Paris, said Rusk in his "vigorous riposte," that had "misleadingly" changed its position.[182] In truth, the approaching hour of decision marked the end of a period in which France and the United States had failed to see eye to eye on the MLF.

Since French acquiescence in the MLF had been taken for granted, Washington had put little thought into dealing with the possible ramifications of French opposition. Paris's protestations suddenly confronted policymakers with difficult questions late in the day. Could de Gaulle still be persuaded to assume his former tolerant stance on the MLF? The nuclear realm offered the most obvious opportunities for striking a deal – but also the most elusive. Could recognition of the *force de frappe* as a valuable contribution to the defense of the West have persuaded de Gaulle to go easy on the MLF? Exploring the possibilities of accommodation between American and French views on the MLF, David E. Mark of the State Department's Intelligence and Research Bureau posed the question as follows:

> It goes without saying that Washington must again think through the terms it might be prepared to offer Paris for a modus vivendi of several years of duration (a genuine reconciliation is probably not in the cards during de Gaulle's reign). The major issue will be the degree to which the United States might be willing to recognize, and even to institutionalize, France's status as a very major power in the West. Would the U.S. now be ready to accept France as a nuclear power in its own right? [emphasis added] ...or would this be felt to be too incompatible both with having the U.K. move, through the MLF, toward giving up its independent nuclear force and with inducing Germany to abjure developing such a force ...?[183]

At a high-level interagency meeting on October 31, there was also some discussion in this direction. While it was agreed that little could be done to make the MLF per se more palatable to the French, McGeorge Bundy suggested that the Johnson administration be prepared to accept any kind of association with the future French *force de frappe* and that the MLF be made "plausibly open to the French."[184] Similar suggestions were indeed inserted in high-level contacts with French diplomats.[185] They would at the very least help to offset the notion that the MLF proposal was aimed against French influence in Europe and that the United States rather than de Gaulle was dividing the alliance. There is, however, sufficient reason to assume that the preparedness to adjust the multilateral formula in order to include the French was genuine. For one, the documentary record shows that Harold Wilson's proposal for a more loosely defined Atlantic Nuclear Force accrued some sympathy in Washington precisely because it provided more leeway for an arrangement that included the *force de frappe*.[186]

Trying to appease de Gaulle by allowing for coordination of the French deterrent with the MLF was nonetheless the wrong answer to the problem. De Gaulle had no interest in any association of the *force de frappe* with the MLF (or, for that matter, the ANF). This would simply be at odds with his overriding goal of retrieving French independence, since it created the impression that the *force de frappe* would be little more than an auxiliary force. It also would put de Gaulle's ambition to organize European defense around his nuclear deterrent at a greater distance. De Gaulle did not reject coordination with American or British nuclear forces outside the NATO context. But there was in his view no need to hurry. On the contrary, he believed it would pay off to wait until the *force de frappe* had become an operational reality, achieved by France alone.[187]

Besides hints at nuclear coordination, some thought was being given in Washington to making the MLF less offensive to de Gaulle by stripping the proposal of its wider connotations of promoting European and Atlantic integration. "The

MLF would appear to be more compatible with West Europe's current stage of political development and mood if the rationale for it were depoliticized," Thomas Hughes of the State Department's Bureau of Intelligence and Research for instance believed; if the MLF could be "divorced from the context of European integration and Atlantic Community building," this would "minimize its anti-French connotations."[188] In the same vein, Mark believed that "the matter does not seem entirely hopeless" if only Washington could persuade Paris that "the revised MLF, by itself, need not present insuperable obstacles to the pursuit by de Gaulle of his European vision.[189] Such recommendations, however, came several years too late. The MLF carried a heavy freight of political connotations that could not be instantly shaken off. Ironically, the more the MLF proponents argued that their project was of capital importance to the future of European integration, the Atlantic community, and Germany, the less acceptable it became to the one European capital whose consent was now being sought. "MLF seems to us to have become blown up as [a] political issue of far greater proportions," Bohlen and Finletter cabled the State Department on November 5, "in which de Gaulle believes that what is at stake is [the] entire military and political orientation of Germany, and indeed Europe, vis-à-vis [the] US."[190] And as de Gaulle explained to Rusk in December, France could never condone the acquisition by Germany – either directly or indirectly – of a nuclear capability.[191]

Most American officials realized that, in fact, not much could be done to defuse the French campaign against the MLF. The United States simply had very little leverage over de Gaulle. Some staff work was committed in late October to examine whether the MLF could be made more agreeable to the "reasonable elements" in France.[192] But de Gaulle did not have to fear domestic opposition to his efforts to foil the MLF; on the contrary, the opposition parties were equally unsympathetic to the MLF. "I have seen a lot of a material on the nature of the French problem in moving ahead with the MLF, but few ideas on how to deal with it," Klein wrote to Bundy. "Clearly, this is a tough one without much possibility of French give."[193]

This helps to explain why American diplomats put their minds above all to keeping the record "straight." They ardently tried to refute the belief that the absence of a Franco-American dialogue on the MLF was caused by a general American unresponsiveness to French ideas about the transatlantic relationship going back to de Gaulle's tripartite memorandum of September 1958. Eisenhower's assumed lack of a response to that memorandum was often cited in newspapers as a reason for French recalcitrance.[194] The air was also rife with insinuations that the United States had failed to inform France about its plans with the MLF and that the diplomatic channels between Washington and Paris were clogged up. Ambassador Bohlen was particularly thin-skinned about such allegations – and he repeatedly urged the State Department to issue a declaration listing previous efforts to explain the MLF to France.[195] While Bohlen did not get his way, there was a fair amount of feigned innocence on the American side.

The State Department's initiative to get in touch with the Elysée prior to Harold Wilson's visit to Washington in early December must be considered in the same light. The interface with de Gaulle was at the top of the agenda when President Johnson met with his foreign policy advisers on November 19 to discuss the MLF. The lessons of Nassau were still fresh in the minds of American policymakers, making it imperative to steer clear of another Anglo-Saxon deal without prior consultation of the French. The Ball Committee had conceived of a proposal to send a high-profile mission headed by John McCloy to Paris. Rather than a genuine effort at consultation, this proposal was an attempt at public posturing. For during the White House meeting, George Ball, with Rusk's support, stressed that the mission would serve to offset allegations that the United States was trying to isolate de Gaulle within NATO: "We should seriously make the point to him (in such fashion that it was understood publicly): 'We are not against you, but we don't know what troubles you, and we don't have proposals from you.'" Johnson's response to his foreign policy advisers, however, was profoundly skeptical – a herald of things to come:

> [...] this sort of emissary is just going to irritate de Gaulle. He's after bigger fish. He wants to talk to me and he wants to talk about things that are very important to him – assuming that he wants to talk at all. [...] de Gaulle might well conclude that there was no government operating in the United States, just bankers from New York. [McCloy worked with Chase Bank in New York.] De Gaulle is certainly not going to succumb to a bunch of errand boys. He might react the way President Johnson would if de Gaulle started sending French bankers as his personal emissary.[196]

In the end, Johnson authorized only Ball himself to visit Paris, where he had an entirely unproductive meeting with de Gaulle.[197] But the White House session had made clear to Johnson the narrow range of options once de Gaulle's active opposition to the MLF had come to the fore. If Johnson was indeed intent on getting allied agreement on the MLF by the end of the year, he would simply have to endure fierce and wide-ranging opposition from Paris. To de Gaulle's advantage, the potentially disruptive consequences of his wrath would hold more sway in the councils of decisions than the unproven virtues of the MLF.

LBJ Acts to Ease the Rift

The MLF was never at the hub of Lyndon Johnson's concerns. In 1964, he was absorbed with obtaining a popular mandate on his own account in the presidential elections in November, by the rapid escalation of the war in Vietnam, by the thorny issue of race relations at home, and by preparations for his Great Society program. The transatlantic nuclear project was but one of the smaller issues, to which he did not feel personally committed. "We are not going to be adamant in our attitudes," he volunteered at a press conference at his Ranch in late November 1964. "We are going to be cooperative and helpful, and we hope we can obtain a meeting of the minds of all our allies."[198] Johnson certainly never brought his presidential stature into play in order to persuade Congress of the MLF's virtues, disregarding Rusk's and Bundy's recommendations to this effect.[199]

Yet Johnson had allowed his name to be attached to the proposal. And with his diplomats embarked on an apparently unchecked drive for the MLF, it was reasonably assumed that it had found strong support – rather than benign indifference – at the top level. Most American diplomats, particularly those who conducted the MLF affair on a daily basis, had reasonably taken for granted that the president was intent on achieving the MLF. Johnson, unlike Kennedy before him, had never exhorted them to be reticent in their dealings with European governments. "I would have thought that Johnson took me off, if he was that cool about it," Rostow remarked many years later.[200] The truth was nonetheless that America's high-pressure diplomacy on the MLF originated in the strongly held views and singular pertinacity of the State Department's Europeanists and their supporters. The gap between the strength of their commitment and the weakness of Johnson's was bound to lead to a row within the administration as soon as European opposition grew.

Johnson's clash with a key part of his foreign policy bureaucracy came within a month after his landslide election victory against the Republican Barry Goldwater. Resistance to the MLF in Europe had become much more vocal since his April decision, mainly as a result of the French turnabout. The attitude on the Hill continued to tend towards the negative and, in the absence of an unambiguous European demand, the White House increasingly seemed bereft of a vital argument to guide an MLF treaty safely through the Senate. Johnson's officialdom, however, was still entirely geared towards establishing the MLF. Now that it was increasingly getting him into political trouble and he had finally won the White House under his own steam, the time had come for Johnson to assert control.[201]

Prime Minister Harold Wilson's planned visit on December 7 to Washington served as the catalyst to come to terms with the political situation. The Ball Committee was charged with preparing a position for Johnson. Getting Wilson's agreement on the MLF – or a variation thereof – was still its overriding objective. The committee therefore focused on the question of breaching the gap between London and Bonn on the MLF. The British and the Germans still differed vehemently on the precise formula and, in the words of American negotiators, even seemed to be on a "collision course." Responding to pressures from within the CDU party, Erhard was advocating a European clause in the MLF agreement to safeguard the possibility of a future European nuclear force developing from the

MLF; by contrast, Wilson – harangued by the Labour Party's left wing and cogni-
zant of his scant majority in the House of Commons – insisted on the US veto so
as to avoid any appearance of nuclear dissemination. Bonn strove for some form
of majority voting in the control body (although granting Washington a veto for
the moment); London, however, insisted on retaining an absolute veto. The
weight of American diplomatic pressure clearly lay on Wilson. Both Ball and
Neustadt traveled to London as special envoys, impressing on the prime minister
that the measure of success of his first meeting with Johnson would be entirely
dependent on his responsiveness to the MLF proposal.[202] The Ball Committee's
final recommendation to Johnson suggested some changes in the MLF formula to
fall in with British wishes but otherwise advised him to impose the force on Wilson. It stated bluntly that "in dealing with the British we must impress upon them
that the final scheme must be so arranged that their participation is on a parity
with the Germans and other Europeans rather than with the United States." In
submitting the committee's recommendation, Bundy stated that the latter's position was weak enough that he could be made to accept the MLF if Johnson insisted.[203]

Meanwhile, however, McGeorge Bundy was secretly preparing the ground for
the MLF's demise. Convinced that the State Department's political judgment was
affected by a good measure of wishful thinking, Johnson's national security adviser had been gathering information around the official channels. Henry Kissinger, for instance, wrote Bundy in late November that "...it is simply wrong to
allege that the future orientation of the Federal Republic depends on pushing
through the MLF." In Kissinger's opinion, Germany was also not stable enough
to become the "balance-wheel of our European policy." He moreover believed
that "the present State Department line is likely to fail and to fragment the Alliance still further" and that "many American officials abroad seem so committed
to their preferred solutions that I am not sure they can always distinguish their
wishes from reality."[204] Being in the White House, Bundy moreover had become
persuaded of the weakness of Johnson's commitment to the MLF. In his role as
the president's "guardian of options," he therefore felt that the regular channels
failed to provide Johnson with at least one important option – that of abandoning
the MLF.

On November 25, in a top-secret memorandum to Rusk, McNamara, and Ball,
Bundy finally declared himself against the MLF. "Against my own expectations of
two weeks ago," Bundy wrote, "I am reaching the conclusion that the U.S. should
now arrange to let the MLF sink out of sight. Whether this should be done quickly
or slowly is an important tactical question, but the overriding point which I wish
to suggest in this tightly limited group is that we should now ask the President for
authority to work toward a future in which the MLF does not come into existence." Bundy's principal argument was that the political costs of pressing on
with the MLF had become unacceptable; "the MLF is not worth it." Bundy

furthermore expressed his belief, "from my own conversations with the President," that Johnson did not feel committed to the project. Bundy acknowledged the embarrassment a sudden change in American policy would cause Erhard, but he was in no doubt that the German chancellor "would be glad to join [...] in a radical defusing of the MLF and a proposal for a completely fresh look at the nuclear defenses of the Alliance, with an ostentatious inclusion of France in this process of discussion."[205] Bundy's memorandum did not have an immediate impact on the preparations for Wilson's visit. George Ball, for one, was in Europe (London and Paris) at the time and would not learn of Bundy's change of heart until the eve of Wilson's visit. When Johnson began to turn his mind to Wilson's upcoming visit, the Ball Committee's memorandum was hence still the official recommendation. But Bundy had finally staked out his dissent from official policies in his secret memorandum.

In the afternoon of December 5, Johnson finally met with his advisers to discuss the situation. Instead of the routine briefing session that the State Department had in mind,[206] he had summoned his most senior foreign policy advisers – Rusk and McNamara – to the White House. David Bruce, the American ambassador to London whose judgment had been valued by President Kennedy, and Dean Acheson were also brought in. Vice President-elect Hubert Humphrey served as the liaison to the Senate. From the outset of the meeting, Johnson made clear his intense displeasure with the Ball Committee's recommendation. And thus began a weekend of heated debate in the White House. Johnson now controlled the arena, weighing the pros and cons of the MLF and scolding his counselors for having led him down a rocky path. "Mr. President," Acheson reportedly said as tension mounted and hard words were spoken, "you don't pay these men enough to talk to them that way – even with the federal pay raise."[207]

Johnson – at long last focusing his mind on the issue – realized that parts of his administration had been pushing the MLF as the centerpiece of his Atlantic policies, to which they had devoted massive energy and staked his political prestige. He discovered that American officials had been insensitive to the adverse political climate in Europe and that they had been acting in flat contradiction with his maxim that the United States "stop telling Europeans they have to do this or that – or else."[208] He stressed that he had never committed himself to achieving the MLF against all odds, even though he had been prepared to make a best effort to persuade the Europeans and Congress of its benefits. He chided his advisers for overestimating his political clout, for being inconsiderate of his political interests. In the course of this exchange, the official recommendation by the Ball Committee fell by the wayside.[209]

The discussion initially focused on Germany. What would happen, Johnson wanted to know, if he should decide against the MLF? Would the Germans then go off on their own? Would the MLF's demise lead to a German national nuclear capability? His aides responded that, within a decade or so, this could indeed be the case. Unless arrangements were made to trim down Germany's second-class status, the mere existence of the British and French national deterrents might provoke the Germans into developing one as well. Johnson took the point, intimating that he would take this course if he was a German leader. But then, as attention shifted from long-term objectives to more immediate political exigencies, the MLF moved into more treacherous waters. The conditions in Europe were outright adverse. With his four-vote majority and a militant left wing, Prime Minister Wilson was in a tight corner. The Italian government had dropped into a crisis once again – and Rome had informed Washington that it would be reluctant to sign an MLF charter at the end of the year. Above all, however, de Gaulle's vehement opposition to the MLF spelled political havoc.

Some of Johnson's advisers warned that pushing ahead on the MLF was likely to provoke a wide range of French countermeasures. De Gaulle's threats were certainly affecting the Common Market and NATO. Belgium, one of the allies in the MLF Working Group, had expressed qualms about forging ahead with the MLF without the consent of the French. France's hostility had already compelled Turkey, another participant, to withdraw its support.[210] Denmark and Norway never participated in the MLF negotiations; however, fearing a French attack on NATO, they began to speak out against the project. Most importantly, as we have seen, de Gaulle's antagonism had divided the German polity. The influential "Gaullist" wing within the CDU was exerting strong pressure on Erhard to assume a more accommodating stance toward France and stall the MLF. Should Johnson take de Gaulle head on? Could he responsibly incur the risk of being blamed for a French attack on NATO, for undermining Franco-German reconciliation, and possibly even for the disintegration of the Common Market? The stakes were unmistakably high. Some tried to persuade Johnson to avoid a confrontation, while others – in particular Acheson and Ball – stressed the need for unwavering leadership.[211]

Faced with such conflicting advice, Johnson looked for a familiar peg to hang his hat on. While the debate in the White House was continuing, influential senators were sounded out on Capitol Hill and the results were transmitted to the Oval Office without delay. Most senators – some of them seated on the powerful Joint Committee on Atomic Energy – proved as yet unconvinced of the project's virtues. They were generally reluctant to permit anyone to stand close to America's nuclear hardware if it did not serve a demonstrated good purpose. They might also have sensed that the public mood toward the MLF was turning negative.[212] Thus informed of the situation on the Hill, Johnson asked his advisers how they could expect him to sell a complex and controversial treaty obligation to skeptical senators if even the Europeans were so ambivalent about it. While conceding that the State Department had not yet undertaken a concerted effort to inform Congress about the MLF, primarily because it did not yet know exactly what it wanted Congress to accept, Ball and McNamara pointed out that a solid presentation after

Wilson's visit would probably remove most of the criticism.[213] But Johnson remained unconvinced; he had now entered territory on which he was far more familiar than any one his aides. He was far from convinced that Congress could be swayed to back the MLF. "His election [...] had been a defeat of Goldwater extremism and not a solid liberal mandate," he argued.[214] "I don't want to be a Woodrow Wilson, right on principle, and fighting for a principle, and unable to achieve it."[215]

Instead of a routine briefing, the White House meeting in preparation for Harold Wilson's visit thus had left the American position on the MLF in complete disarray. Johnson strongly felt that the recommendation to twist Wilson's arm on the MLF was sorely out of touch with political reality. It would set him on a track to political trouble soon after having won the White House in a landslide. Realizing the predicament he was in, Johnson was clearly searching for a way out. Another session therefore had to be arranged. But before the second session began one day later, on December 6, Johnson's still unformed resolve against the MLF was significantly stiffened by his national security adviser.

In the aftermath of the first meeting, Johnson had asked his aides why Kennedy had been "tentative" on the MLF, to which they had opaquely responded that there had been different reasons at different times. Early next morning, however, McGeorge Bundy decided to pull out the memorandum he had written for Kennedy in June 1963, and to which the late president had then reacted "very strongly and affirmatively." The pith of this memorandum had been that the MLF was not worth all the trouble if US diplomatic pressure was the only factor that could bring it about, that American diplomacy should switch from "pressure" to "inquiry" and remove any sense of a deadline. Bundy had also informed Kennedy that part of the problem was to be found within the administration, adding that "there would be a certain loss of face for the passionate MLF salesmen, but they are not the US government."[216] The impact on Johnson of reading McGeorge Bundy's memorandum to Kennedy is not difficult to fathom. Johnson had been largely unaware of Kennedy's reservations, despite Bundy's attempt in early December 1963 to inform him, and he had pursued the MLF in part as a matter of loyalty to his precursor. Had he known of Kennedy's disposition, he surely would not have treated the matter as casually. Johnson moreover could recognize in Bundy's old memorandum the situation and the people he was struggling with at that very moment. The dilemmas and the names were strikingly similar. Bundy's memorandum even seemed to indicate a way out for Johnson.

In addition to unearthing his memorandum to Kennedy, Bundy believed that the time had come to notify Johnson of the private qualms he had already expressed in his secret memorandum to Rusk, McNamara, and Ball. Together with the old memorandum, he therefore presented an "alternative view" on the MLF. Although Bundy claimed that he still favored "going ahead very hard with Wilson" and merely wanted to inform Johnson that "there is another side of the case," his memorandum presented the case against the MLF as effectively as anyone could have done. First among an array of contrary forces, Bundy called attention to the strength of French hostility:

> General de Gaulle's hostility is fixed and strongly supported by all French Gaullists. Tactically, the violence of French feeling can probably be somewhat moderated if you visit Paris and reason with him, but the underlying hostility of France will remain. It is true that the French propaganda now is preventive in purpose, but it will continue at least until ratification in all countries. The French will charge us with dividing the Alliance and blocking the future of Europe, and many who do not support de Gaulle will believe them. The Germans will be split by this French pressure and they, too, will show some tendency to blame us.[217]

It was the first time that French opposition was listed as a prominent reason by anyone on the American side to go easy on the MLF. De Gaulle's clamor had until then been accepted as inevitable background noise to the establishment of the MLF. Its political connotation – that it would provide an alternative for Europeans to the French *force de frappe* and a counterweight to the pernicious influence of Gaullism in Europe – had made it all the more difficult to accept that de Gaulle's opposition could be a reason at all to abandon the MLF. On the contrary, the stronger the French resisted, the more important the Europeanists at the State Department considered it to show leadership. In a way, therefore, McGeorge Bundy had broken a taboo. At the end of his memorandum, he stated that the "devil's advocate" would state the choice for Johnson this way:

1. If you go full steam ahead, you face a long, hard political fight, a major confrontation with de Gaulle, and a possibility of defeat or delay which would gravely damage the prestige of the President.
2. If you go half steam ahead, there will probably be no MLF, but it will not be your fault alone. You will have kept the letter and spirit of the Kennedy readiness to move if the Europeans wanted it. There will be trouble with the Germans, but nothing unmanageable. There will be plenty of opportunities for debate, discussion, and delay, and for gradual and ceremonial burial. Your wisdom, caution, and good judgment will have the praise of liberals, of military men, of the British, of the French, and of many Germans – and you will have freedom to make a different choice later if you wish.[218]

The effects of French opposition to the MLF would reveal itself to Johnson through other channels as well. In the morning of December 6, an urgent cable came in from the American ambassador in Bonn, George McGhee. McGhee reported in vivid terms on the crisis in the CDU, describing how those who feared open confrontation with France – Adenauer included – were frenetically trying to force Chancellor Erhard into stalling the MLF. According to McGhee, the very survival of Erhard's government was at stake.[219] His report was an obvious setback to the supporters of the MLF. Not only had the Germans been the only solid allies in Europe, but their inherent nuclear appetite had also consistently been put forward by the State Department as the main reason for the MLF. Yet now it appeared as if pushing ahead with the MLF would cause more problems with the Germans than renouncing it.

The same morning Johnson also talked to William J. Fulbright, chairman of the Senate's Foreign Affairs Committee. While Fulbright had not originally been adverse to the MLF, he now informed Johnson that he would not support it because of lack of European support and that any agreement would probably fall short of votes in the Senate. Fulbright had participated in the NATO parliamentarians' meeting in November, where the dearth of European support for the MLF and the ramifications of de Gaulle's counteroffensive had been dominant themes. It was at this meeting, too, that NATO Secretary General Manlio Brosio had restated the rule of unanimity within NATO.[220]

By the time Johnson met with his advisers for the second time, in the afternoon of December 6, he had made up his mind. At the outset, he simply announced that he was not going to sell the MLF to Harold Wilson; instead, a fallback position was to be prepared prior to his meeting with the British prime minister the next day. Johnson's newfound resolve took most by surprise and some – Ball, McNamara, and Bruce[221] – muttered objections, pointing out that a sudden policy reversal would be a blow to American leadership in Europe, leave the field open to de Gaulle, and – most ominously – have serious repercussions in Germany. But Johnson was bent on chucking the MLF. Significantly, he could rebut his advisers' protestations with the information that had reached him in the morning. When it was claimed that Fulbright supported the MLF, he snarled that the senator had just assured him of the contrary. When attention shifted to the possible repercussions in Europe, Johnson whipped out Bundy's memorandum and – to the consternation of George Ball and others – began to recite the arguments for backing down on the MLF on the very grounds of European opposition.[222] And Johnson had McGhee's message in hand when some of his advisers warned of a serious backlash in German national politics in the event the United States gave up on the MLF. He could now argue that Erhard's predicament would get worse, not better, if Washington continued to press the MLF. "If the Germans are going to have trouble with this," Johnson said, "what in the hell are we going to make all this fuss about."[223]

As he lectured his advisers, Lyndon Johnson was at long last riding his bureaucracy with a tight grip on the reins. It nonetheless still required some thought in order to define a fallback option that avoided the potential fallout of reversing a widely publicized commitment.[224] Johnson and his advisers were still searching for a method to toss the MLF back to Europe as Wilson paced across the White House lawn. In the end, Johnson simply assumed the "inquiry" stand that Bundy had suggested to Kennedy in June 1963. He would leave the initiative entirely with Wilson (after having first assailed him on some economic issues). Johnson knew that his British counterpart would be far from eager to discuss the topic. He would let him present his ANF proposal, then offer some polite comments to the extent that modifications were necessary to meet German demands, and finally encourage Wilson to sort it out with Erhard under his own steam.

This is indeed how Johnson's private conversation with Wilson came to pass.[225] The official meetings between American and British delegations in the three days of Wilson's visit were conducted in similar non-committal fashion. The differences between the MLF and the ANF were discussed, but without any serious attempt from either side to breach them. American officials were above all interested in managing the public presentation of the summit's conclusions. They were determined to prevent any one, including the British, from claiming victory for having killed the MLF; the opposite notion, that major steps had been taken toward achieving the MLF, was also to be avoided.[226] Washington in particular went out of its way to avert claims that French opposition had influenced Johnson's decision to go easy on the MLF; conversely, it was also exceedingly careful not to supply de Gaulle with the appearance of an Anglo-Saxon accord – and hence with a welcome excuse to lash out against NATO or the Common Market. If the final communiqué of the Anglo-American summit deserves consideration, it is therefore for its utter inconclusiveness and circumspection – or perhaps for its seemingly innocuous reference to the "legitimate interests of all members of the Alliance."[227]

The purport of the meeting was at first hidden from the public view, masked by the blandness of the communiqué, the apparent satisfaction of both leaders, and the continuing assurances from American officials that they still considered the MLF the best idea available to solve the nuclear-sharing problem within NATO. Initial press reports even suggested that Wilson had given in on the MLF, causing Bundy to warn Johnson that they "may lead de Gaulle to talk of another British surrender."[228] Wilson, astonished and relieved that Johnson had not twisted his arm on the MLF, declared that the meeting had been "completely successful" and evidenced a "total identity of view" between London and Washington. There had been "no theology," he said, referring to the State Department's pressure in the recent past.[229] Gradually it was dawning on the allies that there had been an important relaxation in the US stance on the MLF, if only for the sheer inaction of the Johnson administration which had pressed so hard for allied agreement on the MLF by the end of the year.

It was a rare leak by Johnson to the press that confirmed that the United States had withdrawn its active support for the MLF. Johnson had not been wholly comfortable with the state of affairs, even after his encounter with Wilson. First, he feared that London and Bonn would catch him by surprise and overcome their differences to strike a deal on an ANF formula with a strong MLF component.[230] This would then oblige him to resume the active pursuit of the MLF whereas de Gaulle's hostility would not have changed.[231] He would then also have to approach Congress without a clear European consensus. Secondly, Johnson had been seriously disturbed by the fact that a key part of his foreign policy bureaucracy had been so unresponsive to his political needs and could lead him into tight spots. In the course of the sessions in early December, Johnson had come down hard on his advisers and left them with unforgettable lessons. In Philip Geyelin's view,

> rough as some of the sessions [in December] apparently were, they were also instructive. Few who were there or heard about it would thereafter make any quick assumptions about what would be palatable and what would not, when presented to Lyndon Johnson. Few would come unprepared to present their case in minute and, if possible, irrefutable detail. And few would presume to speak for the President without being quite certain where he stood. It was a memorable object lesson in Johnson decisionmaking, a major development in the President's move towards mastery of the "processes," a significant turn in the U.S. approach to Alliance policy.[232]

Johnson nonetheless felt he had to take additional measures in order to secure the bureaucracy's responsiveness to his political needs. He was determined to establish tighter control over American foreign policy. Johnson was to act with remarkable efficacy in dealing with both of his concerns.

On December 17, Johnson summoned his foreign policy advisers to the White House and asked them to agree to an unambiguous presidential guideline concerning the MLF. National Security Action Memorandum 322 (NSAM 322) nailed down that future discussions on nuclear questions within the Western alliance were to be conducted by American officials in observance of strict rules. Elaborating on the theme of NSAM 318, the new directive ordained that all members of the American government refrain from exerting any amount of pressure on the European allies. In addition, it laid down what political requirements had to be fulfilled before Johnson would be willing once again to take the issue up. Any nuclear scheme could only have his support, NSAM 322 stipulated, if it was founded on solid agreement among principal European allies and after it had been fully discussed with France:

> I wish all American negotiators to avoid public or private quarrels with France, and to maintain in public and private the following position: We are interested in reducing our differences with France; we will never support any proposal

for a nuclear force which is in fact directed against France; we will not sign any agreement which does not contain open doors for France; nor will we make any agreement until after French opinion and French desires have been carefully and responsibly explored.[233]

Not only had Johnson thus decided against pushing the MLF, but NSAM 322 also reflected his resolve not to drive France into isolation.

The contents of NSAM 322 were publicly known before the ink had dried up – literally. The memorandum had come to Johnson's desk for signature as he was being interviewed by James Reston of the *New York Times*. The president permitted – deliberately or impulsively? – the reporter to set his eager eye on the memorandum.[234] Not surprisingly, its gist returned – apparently with White House approval – on the front page of next day's issue of the newspaper.[235] The impact of Johnson's press leak was profound. It made it well-nigh impossible for the avid proponents of the MLF to continue their pressure tactics under his banner. His reversal on the MLF now also dawned fully on Europe's capitals.[236]

The MLF had run its last course. NSAM 322 had sealed its fate. Johnson had virtually given de Gaulle a veto over the MLF; no nuclear-sharing plan discussed "in advance and detail" with France could have produced the latter's consent. De Gaulle had raised the price of the MLF by launching an attack on several fronts and unleashing a range of forces against the project. These hit the MLF where it was most vulnerable. A few months later, a British diplomat told the American embassy in Paris that de Gaulle had said to Hervé Alphand: "The MLF is dead. It is I who killed it. Yet I almost regret having done so since it would have permitted me to do sooner that which I intend to do."[237] Lyndon Johnson could no longer be blamed as the wrecker of the Atlantic alliance.

Conclusion

The MLF was never formally laid to rest. It was never murdered – no *corpus delicti*, no embarrassing funeral for one-time advocates to attend. NSAM 322 simply laid down that the United States would refrain from using strong-arm tactics to reach agreement on the MLF. American officials would still be allowed to assume an encouraging stance in anticipation of a unified European position on the MLF. Indeed, when signs of distress in Europe about the change in the American position filtered through to Washington,[238] the Johnson administration staged a measured effort to convey its continuing interest in a collective solution to the nuclear problem. The United States was not prepared to force a solution on Europe, but neither should its position be interpreted as "aloof" or "neutral." At a press conference on January 16, 1965, President Johnson expressed the "greatest of interest" in Anglo-German talks scheduled a week later as a follow-up to Wilson's December visit to Washington. "I strongly hope in these talks there will be progress that will allow us to move on to fruitful multilateral discussions." Johnson reaffirmed, in response to a direct question, that the United States was still "strongly in favor of a mixed-manned nuclear fleet."[239]

However, the pervasive and accurate feeling that there was no strong or active support for the MLF in the White House could not be dispelled with incantations. The contrast with the Johnson administration's pre-December 1964 record of activism in support of the project was all too obvious – and the fact that this activism was deemed essential inevitably fostered the belief that Johnson's decision to go easy on the proposal implied a withdrawal rather than a slight modification of policy. Support in those European quarters that had avowed interest in the MLF began to disintegrate under French pressure and Washington's inaction. As soon as the results of Johnson's crucial meeting with Wilson had been relayed to Bonn, Erhard – pressured by the Gaullist wing in his party – urged Johnson to have a "big pitch" with de Gaulle on the MLF.[240] In mid-January, the German chancellor further backtracked, as he asked that the proposal be put on hold until after German parliamentary elections in September 1965 – a move also designed to clear the ground for his meeting with de Gaulle on January 19. For a while, the Germans proved to be even more reluctant negotiators than the British.[241] As for Johnson, he did not publicly speak about the MLF again after his January press conference – and for the remainder of the year, the MLF would thus live on in a twilight zone of halfhearted pursuit. In December 1965, Johnson finally put the MLF to sleep when Chancellor Erhard paid his first visit to Washington after the parliamentary elections. In their carefully guarded private conversation, Erhard came down squarely on the side of a "hardware solution," but he found Johnson determined not to make any commitments.[242] A few weeks later, the German chancellor confided to Henry Kissinger, who was in Europe on one of his trips for the White House, that he had indeed sought a revival of the MLF in the weeks prior to his meeting with Johnson. He had noticed, however, that American interest in the question had considerably cooled and continued to do so "with every passing day." Kissinger reported:

> In Washington he had observed the following line-up: Ball was strongly in favor of German co-ownership; Rusk more moderately so; McNamara seemed at best indifferent and the President's attitude could be summed up as follows: "Ludwig, I will do anything for you but don't complicate my life by asking for nuclear weapons."[243]

The story of the MLF's ultimate demise under Johnson's watch is important to the subject of this study in a number of respects. The failure of the MLF has typically been explained from its conceptual flaws. Most importantly, it would not have given the Europeans genuine control over their nuclear defense while it would have required a major investment. The Italian statesman Altiero Spinelli thus hit the nail on the head when he said to Vice President Hubert Humphrey in January 1965 that the MLF was a "half attempt," and that as far as he was concerned "it would be better to have mixed-manning in the Pentagon, rather than in submarines or ships."[244]

Yet careful analysis also shows that French opposition was more significant in bringing about the MLF's demise than often has been recognized. "The French view [on the MLF] may be the clearest," McGeorge Bundy acknowledged in *Danger and Survival* (1988), "and it may have been decisive."[245] If it had not been for de Gaulle's active opposition, American pressure might have brought it off – and, backed by clear European support, Johnson would also have been in a much stronger position to convince the skeptics in Congress. In December 1964, Harold Wilson had fully expected that he had no choice but to concede to Johnson on the MLF. The Erhard government would probably also have pledged German participation if de Gaulle had not marshalled his German supporters on the domestic front against the project. As Bundy wrote: "The Germans initially supported the MLF, but only until they learned the strength of French opposition, and more because it was an American proposal than because of any strong German conviction."[246] The credible threat of a French attack against NATO had further raised the political price to LBJ of pushing ahead with the MLF. De Gaulle could have simply vetoed the MLF's incorporation into NATO as well, which would have left Johnson with the unenviable option of establishing the nuclear force outside NATO. In sum, de Gaulle held more trump cards than Johnson.

Second, the story of the MLF's demise made clear that the United States could not hope to isolate France within Europe. It showed, in particular, that the United States could not force West Germany to go *against* France on an important issue, just as de Gaulle had been unable to draw West Germany into his camp against American domination with the Treaty of Reconciliation in 1963. Already, the clash of 1963 had shown that Washington could ill afford to underestimate de Gaulle as a leader willing to go to great lengths to realize his vision; after the MLF's demise, Washington also could no longer underestimate his political clout in Europe – if only because of France's central role. As Patrick Gordon Walker, the British Foreign Secretary, volunteered to William Tyler in March 1965 in an unusually forthright frame of mind, the Johnson administration "had killed and buried not only the MLF but the ANF by the position we had taken since December."

> He said the only hope would have been for us to continue to press the Germans, instead of which we had told the Europeans that they should work things out among themselves. This they were incapable of doing, and it was clear that Erhard was not about to do anything which would expose him to pressure from de Gaulle. He said that Germany would finally have to choose between de Gaulle and the United States, and that unless we held the German

feet to the fire on this issue, we would be conceding the victory to de Gaulle.[247]

Lastly, Johnson's decision against the MLF marked significant shifts in the decisionmaking processes in Washington. It had made clear, as Alphand astutely informed de Gaulle, that Johnson was not the prisoner of the "zealots" ("zélateurs") in his administration.[248] Johnson's verdict on the MLF was therefore also a declaration of independence from those advisers – in particular Acheson and Ball – who had consistently and vigorously sought to use American power to promote transatlantic and European unity against the Gaullist tide. In particular, immediately following Johnson's victory in the 1964 presidential elections, Acheson had avidly tried to win "landslide Lyndon" over to his activist transatlantic agenda. In a series of memorandums in November and December, he had advocated the MLF (or a variation on the theme), the creation of a new Atlantic Assembly, and further progress on trade liberalization, all "solidly based on the principle that collective, not national, action is the key to progress." It was clear that he held high expectations:

> The United States is the most powerful nation in the world, the most concerned with the broad international public interest. Our President has had the greatest endorsement of any leader in decades. And yet our press is calling for the reconsideration of policies which we have been following for years, because Harold Wilson and General de Gaulle [...] do not like them. All that is needed is a clear lead from you to set things straight and get us started forward.[249]

But Johnson declined the honor of bringing about Acheson's Atlantic dream. On the contrary, having lost the MLF battle, the Europeanists were forced to the margins of Atlantic and European policymaking. While remarkably effective at dominating the gist of American foreign policy in the early 1960s, they had always had a limited power base in Washington (notwithstanding the support of grand old men of American foreign policy such as Acheson and McCloy). In the context of the MLF crisis, more pragmatic and realist foreign policy voices gained currency in the White House. Writing to Bundy, Neustadt hailed Johnson's decision with a dry wit that revealed that the battle had been as much between the activist Cold War liberals and the pragmatists within the administration as between the United States and de Gaulle:

> In my "professional" opinion as a President-watcher he not only made a free choice, knowing what he was doing, but the right choice for a President to make at this juncture. I'm impressed, and proud of him, and I'm not joining the chorus – which will swell for a while – of Achesonians (to-lead-is-to-lead)

or of British Foreign Office spokesmen. Those guys think rulers exist to be used. But we're the king's men, so to hell with that. The FO officials want an Anglo-German entente, for good reasons from our point of view, but if they have to use our king to make theirs move, their reasoning is flawed as fatally as that of our "cabal."[250]

Reflecting on Wilson's visit in a euphoric memorandum to Johnson, McGeorge Bundy had already reasoned that the preparatory meetings on December 5 and 6 had been "without doubt the most productive and useful two days that we have had in foreign affairs since President Kennedy went to Berlin." He hailed Johnson's refusal to act on the counsel of his advisers "a turning point in the process by which you take the effective command of a major issue of foreign policy" and the abolishment of the State Department's MLF office as the most "important or constructive administrative decision [...] in the last 18 months in that Department."[251] Following the MLF crisis of 1964, Bundy would feel much less inhibited to develop policy options to mollify de Gaulle that were independent of the State Department, complaining to President Johnson that its "views are so rigid that I doubt if we will get much from them."[252]

Disgruntled with Johnson's decision, the Europeanists in the State Department and their outside supporters were dismayed by the surge in pragmatism and realism in American foreign policy. "I know your theory," Acheson muttered to Neustadt at a next occasion. "You think Presidents should be warned. You're wrong. Presidents should be given confidence."[253] The surrender of the MLF came as a rude surprise for those who had envisioned "clear sailing."[254] The State Department had not fathomed that the president's commitment was so much weaker than the public record. The MLF supporters therefore felt the new guidelines had all of a sudden left them "emasculated."[255] And they reproved Johnson for failing to put his leadership to the cause. "Here you had a man," Finletter complained, "one of the most skillful handlers of Congress that ever existed in the United States, as President of the United States – just having won an overwhelming victory over his opponent – at the very peak of his power with Congress, and he never really asked them to do anything."[256] What the MLF supporters could not admit is that Johnson, by subsiding on the MLF, wisely prevented a repeat of the Nassau debacle.

It was the Europeanists' dexterity and their singular determination that had kept the proposal alive after Kennedy tried to quietly extinguish it. Now, they were decisively sidetracked. On the same day that NSAM 322 was made public through Reston's column, the MLF office in the State Department, from which the campaign had been orchestrated, was dismantled; Gerard Smith resigned as MLF coordinator and his staff was dissolved.[257] President Johnson refrained from acting vindictively towards the State Department, and some of the MLF supporters – Walt Rostow foremost – even climbed to higher ranking positions within the administration[258] But the White House would not allow them to breathe new life into the project. So when George Ball – opposed to "letting things drift" and leaving the initiative to de Gaulle, "who loves trouble" – prepared to make a speech on the MLF in February 1965, the White House intervened. Ball feared that "the long postwar battle to create an Atlantic community could easily be lost" if the United States stepped back from the batting plate. McGeorge Bundy, however, dreaded above all the "sound of divided trumpets within the administration." It was ten days before French Foreign Minister Couve de Murville would arrive in Washington and everyone – apart from the devout Atlanticists and Europeanists – was content with shelving the project at least until after the German elections. "If anyone is to restate our Atlantic nuclear policy," McGeorge Bundy therefore warned Johnson, "it ought not to be someone who is a devout partisan of a particular solution like George."[259] Restrained by the White House to speak up against de Gaulle, Ball volunteered in exasperation to NATO Ambassador Thomas Finletter: "You know, I can't do anything with the President. I'm sorry I just can't."[260]

The demise of the MLF and the marginalization of its supporters signaled an important shift in American foreign policy away from staking political prestige on the progressive realization of an Atlantic community, a "commonwealth" in which – as Acheson had counseled at the outset of Kennedy's tenure – "common institutions are increasingly developed to address common problems." After the clash of 1963, the MLF had come to embody the hopes of a whole generation of American officials whose liberal foreign policy beliefs centered on the intertwined objectives of European unification and the Atlantic community. In his memoirs, George Ball disingenuously asserts that he was never a fervent advocate of the MLF, belittling it as a "clumsy if not unworkable military concept" and "seeing it solely as a political instrument."[261] This does no justice to the importance the State Department's Europeanists – including Ball – and their sympathizers attached to the project. In the perceptive words of Wilson's Minister of Defense Denis Healy, they had vigorously supported the MLF as "the grain of sand round which the pearl of European unity would develop."[262] At the same time, it was to them, as Hammond has written, a powerful "tool designed to unite de Gaulle's opposition in Europe and embolden it within France" and supported by many "as a counterattack to de Gaulle."[263] Led by Acheson and Ball, the Europeanists had been the fiercest opponents within the American government of de Gaulle, contributing most vocally to his "damnation" and being most inclined to speak up against his "anachronistic nationalism." The MLF's demise was their biggest defeat.

As poignantly, the State Department's drive to enlist European – and in particular German – support for the MLF backfired against the greater goal of European integration. This is more than merely stating, as McGeorge Bundy has done, that "to try to make nuclear weapons an instrument of European unification was to ignore the basic reason for their existence in both Britain and France."[264] For as Miriam Camps has argued, de Gaulle's decision in 1965 to leave an "empty chair" within the Common Market in response to the planned introduction of majority voting in the Council of Ministers was motivated in part by "the French failure to shake the Germans on the defense issue during the summer and the autumn of 1964." Camps:

> [...] the real lesson [to de Gaulle] of the cereals prices "victory" at the end of 1964 was not that the Germans had yielded to the French on this point or had put loyalty to the Community above the interest of the German farmer, but that they had stuck to the MLF and were conceding on what they considered to be a far less important issue. [...] In this situation, it was entirely logical that General de Gaulle should have concluded that a "European Europe" was not a possibility; it was also entirely consistent that in those circumstances he should have wanted to limit the extent to which his hands were tied by commitments to his Common Market partners.[265]

The MLF crisis also denoted a turning point in the view of those Americans who had invested heavily in Europe and the transatlantic relationship since World War II. John McCloy, for one, censured Johnson's decision to "put the ball in the court of the Europeans" as a "real triumph" for de Gaulle. His dismay with the turn of events is indicative of the broader context in which the "wise men" of the Establishment judged Johnson's betrayal to their cause:

> One of the great objectives of United States foreign policy after World War II was the reorientation of Germany and Japan. Thus far, achievements have been made over the opposition of both de Gaulle and the Soviet Union. The United States does not want to make the same mistake as after World War I. Poincaré was wrong in 1919 and so is de Gaulle in 1965. ... The attempt of France to seek primacy in Europe at the expense of the Germans and the other Europeans; the attempt to revert to a system of European alliances; the axes of power concepts of the nineteenth and early twentieth centuries are simply not good enough as a basis for security in a nuclear world – it is toying with outworn concepts. ... The United States should take the risk of leadership to bring about lasting peace. I do not believe we can successfully "put the ball in the Europeans' court." They cannot handle it alone – they never have and I do not believe they ever will. The prospect of their doing so in the face of the competing designs of General de Gaulle without our help is almost nil.[266]

However, those – like McCloy, Acheson, and Ball – who believed the United States must incur the risks of leadership in order to face down de Gaulle's nationalism were not allowed to occupy the center stage of American policymaking ever again.

The MLF project was the last convulsion of the postwar era of American liberal activism in the Atlantic.

Chapter Five

De Gaulle Throws Down the Gauntlet: LBJ and the Crisis in NATO, 1965-1967

Having imposed restraint toward de Gaulle on his administration in the MLF crisis, Johnson could no longer be seen as the wrecker of the alliance. Yet the most severe transatlantic crisis of the Johnson years still lay ahead – and much would depend on how the Texan would deal with it. On March 7, 1966, de Gaulle informed Johnson that France would end its military participation within NATO. In addition, he requested the removal from France of troops not under French command. This chapter will examine Johnson's response to this blunt challenge to the postwar architecture of Western defense.[1]

De Gaulle's distaste for NATO, of course, was not new, nor was his distinction between the alliance and the organization (even though this distinction rarely occurred to Americans). De Gaulle stressed that he favored military alliance with the United States as long as there was a Soviet threat – and that France would therefore remain party to the North Atlantic Treaty. But NATO's integrated military structure did not fit his strong belief that a nation – certainly France! – must be in charge of its own defense.[2] De Gaulle also objected to the subjection of French armed forces to a system of military integration under American dominion. NATO was, in de Gaulle's unsentimental view of international relations, above all a tool for US hegemony. What is more, de Gaulle argued that the institutionalized character of the alliance codified the bipolar system in world politics and perpetuated the Cold War. NATO was certainly incompatible with de Gaulle's oft-cited aim of persuading "the states along the Rhine, the Alps, and the Pyrenees to form a political, economic, and strategic bloc" and "to establish this organization as one of the three world powers and [...] as the arbiter between the Soviet and Anglo-American camps."[3] While de Gaulle had been willing to admit that NATO had been useful when there had been a plausible threat of a Soviet military attack on Western Europe in the early 1950s, he had long since argued that events had overtaken NATO's usefulness. If anything, he considered NATO an impediment to the gradual political rapprochement with the Soviet bloc that would usher in an end to the Cold War and the creation of "a Europe from the Atlantic to the Urals."

In 1966, Johnson was forced to face the full implications of this vision. His anticipation of de Gaulle's attack on NATO and his reaction once it occurred will be assessed hereafter. It is important to note at the outset, however, that the NATO crisis was about much more than France's withdrawal from NATO. It was also about forging a more constructive relationship with the Soviet bloc in order to pave the way for a future European settlement, about finally resolving the nuclear sharing issue within NATO, and about bearing and sharing the financial and military burdens of defending the West. The interrelatedness of these thorny issues would put Johnson's qualities as a statesman to the test. His skillful performance in the NATO crisis would do little to polish his blazon as a foreign policy president, stained as it was by the Vietnam War. But it mattered much to the long-term viability of the Western alliance.

Toward a NATO without France

Waiting for De Gaulle

De Gaulle's hostility towards NATO was, as we have seen, well established by the time Johnson assumed the presidency. Before the General's return to power in 1958, he had volunteered to journalist Cyrus Sulzberger and others that he would withdraw France from NATO if he were in power. The threat of withdrawal had been inherent in his tripartite memorandum proposal to Eisenhower and Macmillan of September 1958. His important speech on national defense at the École Militaire in November 1959 had also amounted to a rejection of military integration. De Gaulle had had virtually no room for acting against NATO during the height of the Cold War and with France still entangled in the Algerian war; forcing an early break with the United States would also have undermined his ability to coax the other Western European nations into forming a strategic entity around France. Even so, he had withdrawn the French Mediterranean Fleet from NATO in March 1959; most of the Atlantic fleet followed in 1963. France had barred American nuclear weapons from its soil unless it could have a say over them, which in early 1959 had prompted the relocation of some 250 fighter bombers from France to Britain and Germany in the first withdrawal of allied troops from French territory. The French army divisions returning from Algeria after 1962 had not been assigned to NATO despite a requirement to do so. French officers had been withdrawn from NATO's planning staff and from certain exercises. In sum, the writing had been on the wall ever since his return to power.[4]

Following the resolution of the Algerian conflict and with the lessening of East-West tensions following the Cuban Missile Crisis, more decisive French moves against NATO began to become more likely. Kennedy's simultaneous drive to introduce the new American strategy of flexible response and centralized control over nuclear weapons within NATO probably only reinforced de Gaulle's resolve.

With the rejection of the Fouchet Plan in 1962 and the worsening of Franco-German relations after the departure of Adenauer, there was also less holding de Gaulle back. Warning signals about a French attack on NATO began to increase in the cable traffic between Washington and its diplomatic outposts in Europe from 1962 onwards. The previous chapter has already revealed that de Gaulle might have used the Johnson administration's MLF campaign as a pretext for withdrawal. In early January 1965, Charles Bohlen reported from Paris that it had become increasingly clear that de Gaulle's ideas on the reform of NATO "really involved a destruction of the existing structural organization of the Treaty." Friendly officials at the Quai d'Orsay had moreover confided to him that de Gaulle preferred to cease French participation in NATO at least before 1969, when Article 13 of the North Atlantic Treaty allowed for member states to leave the alliance upon a one-year notice.[5] In subsequent months, embassy reports were becoming increasingly frequent that de Gaulle was planning for drastic steps soon after the French presidential elections in December 1965.[6] In early May, for instance, he told Bohlen, in more explicit terms than ever before, that all forces and installations on French soil would have to be brought under French command before review of the treaty in 1969. De Gaulle also affirmed "very clearly and definitely" that when the treaty would be reexamined, "any form of integration would have to go."[7] Bohlen by then had come to believe that de Gaulle would terminate French participation in NATO between early 1966 and early 1968 and denounce the North Atlantic Treaty in 1968 or 1969, intending to replace it with "a series of bilateral defense arrangements with at least the US, the UK, and Germany."[8] At NATO, meanwhile, French officials ominously declined to approve the construction of a new building for SHAPE near Paris. And in early June 1965, anti-Gaullist sources at the Quai d'Orsay informed the American embassy that Washington would be well advised to develop contingency plans for a de Gaulle offensive soon after the December elections.[9] There was "stormy weather ahead," France's representative at NATO warned Thomas Finletter; de Gaulle "would move in hard and immediately on NATO" once he had won the presidential elections.[10]

Ever since de Gaulle's tripartite memorandum diplomacy had run into the ground in the early Kennedy years, Paris had not come up with new proposals for the reform of NATO nor did it seriously attempt again to find a middle ground with the material leader of the alliance – the United States. Pressed by American diplomats to come forward with proposals, French officials habitually retorted that it made little sense for France to formally present its ideas for discussion as long as the other members of NATO were opposed to substantial changes in the alliance. Instead, de Gaulle had resigned himself to changing unilaterally the French contribution to NATO and progressively making French abstention a fait accompli within the Western alliance. As Foreign Minister Couve de Murville explained to Cyrus Sulzberger of the *New York Times* in November 1964:

1. There is no use discussing reform of NATO so long as there is no agreement on the direction NATO should take. France wants less integration; everyone else wants more. Therefore the argument is hopeless from the beginning.

2. Also we have taken several moves already on our part which show which direction we want NATO to take. We have reduced our force commitments and at the same time have stressed our plan for an atomic force. We have therefore reformed NATO ourselves to the extent that we could. We have disintegrated as much as we could without danger.

3. But the atomic affair is most important. We have rearranged the French army without taking account of NATO's view. We have reduced the size of our conventional forces in order to be able to spend more on our atomic force.

Pressed why France had not at least drawn up a tentative plan for NATO reform, Couve de Murville added:

> What would be the point? No one in NATO, apart from France, dares to speak up to the U.S.A. And really, apart from France, Britain and Germany, the rest of the allies think the best thing is to leave everything to Uncle Sam and spend the least possible amount on defense.[11]

The most elaborate French statement on NATO reform hence appeared in the form of an article in the quarterly *Politique Étrangère* in the fall of 1965, which, according to a claim by the *New York Times* citing "qualified sources," had been submitted to de Gaulle for approval.[12] Its anonymous author echoed familiar Gaullist themes, arguing that NATO had outlived its usefulness and was an instrument of American foreign policy rather than of the collective security of its members. The article envisaged the "superposition" of two "systems" to replace NATO. First, it proposed that the Atlantic alliance be transformed into a general alliance with the United States, devoid of any military integration but allowing for strategic coordination (in particular of nuclear forces). Second, it suggested a Western European defense compact along the lines of the erstwhile European Defense Community. The integration of Western European forces would essentially be maintained, even be enhanced, but the number of partners to this integration would be reduced by one – the United States. This did not mean, however, that American forces would not be maintained in Europe as a symbol of the loose transatlantic alliance and that they could not somehow be linked with the forces of Western European nations short of full military integration. Nor did the author warmly endorse the concept of military integration, but rather thought such a system was necessary as a framework to contain German forces. The article thus tried to resolve a central conundrum of Gaullist foreign policy: how to restrain

Germany in a Western Europe rid of American dominance? The proposed system of military integration, moreover, would not include the nuclear forces of its members – France and, if it joined, the United Kingdom – nor would Germany participate in the direction of these forces. Germany would thus have to entrust its nuclear defense to France, without having a say over the *force de frappe*. In return, France would commit its nuclear forces to the defense of Germany.

The article was widely believed to reflect the thinking at the highest French levels, and, as such, it caught the attention of the State Department.[13] The French government, however, neither endorsed the article nor provided any detailed proposals along these lines for discussion among the allies. Nor did it fully reflect de Gaulle's thinking. In particular, its emphasis on integrating European forces was non-Gaullist. De Gaulle – as Bohlen had rightly surmised – was rather thinking about a web of bilateral agreements pledging mutual support in case of an outside attack. In early May 1965, he told a baffled Alphand that he not only intended to withdraw from NATO before 1969 but that he would even aim to scuttle the North Atlantic Treaty in order to replace it with a system of bilateral agreements between nation-states. And in another conversation with Alphand in July, de Gaulle reiterated his intention to propose "un accord bilatéral très simple" to the United States pledging mutual support in case of an attack on either one. Such an arrangement would hence include a mutual defense commitment along the lines of Article V of the North Atlantic Treaty. When Alphand protested that the Johnson administration would never agree to sign a bilateral agreement, de Gaulle remained sanguine: "Alors il n'y aura pas d'alliance formelle. Mais serait-elle nécessaire si vraiment la Russie et les États-Unis ont décidé de ne pas se faire la guerre?"[14]

These plots against NATO and the North Atlantic Treaty were thus tied in with de Gaulle's assessment that the Soviet Union no longer posed an acute military threat to Western Europe. They were also inextricably linked to his long-term vision of overcoming the division of Europe through an active policy of détente, entente, and ultimately cooperation with the East. As between NATO and the Treaty, de Gaulle consistently distinguished between the Soviet Union and Russia – the former the courier of a totalitarian and threatening ideology, the latter an integral part of any European equilibrium. Even with the Communist Party in power, de Gaulle had few hesitations to work towards a state of affairs in which France and Russia would be the two main pillars of European stability, keeping the Germans in check and the Anglo-Saxons at bay. As we have seen, de Gaulle's search for a mutually beneficial relationship with Moscow dates back to World War II. The emergence of the Soviet Union and the United States as victors over Germany, he had then feared, would either lead to a new war between these two superpowers or to a condominium in Europe. De Gaulle's quest to forestall a superpower struggle around the European stake, which he knew would come at the expense of French influence, was ultimately ineffective. What is more, Roosevelt's and Stalin's refusal to accept France as a great power with a say in the post-war order – and the resulting exclusion of France from the Big Three conferences at Yalta and Potsdam – left an indelible scar on his mind. His aims of ending the "Yalta system" – which in de Gaulle's lexicon stood for the division of Europe and the dominance of the superpowers – and bringing about a Europe "from the Atlantic to the Urals" were to remain at the heart of his foreign policy. De Gaulle's decision to withdraw the French military entirely from NATO in 1966, his simultaneous efforts at atmospheric improvement of relations with the communist world, and the construction of the French atom bomb were integral parts of de Gaulle's plan to end the Cold War and to reinstate France as a pillar of European security.[15]

In the 1960s, to be sure, de Gaulle was hardly original in pursuing a more relaxed relationship with the Soviet bloc. De Gaulle had even been the last of the Cold Warriors. Following the Cold War drama of the Cuban Missile Crisis of October 1962, Washington and Moscow had already embarked on the road towards détente. Johnson's commitment to improving relations with the Soviet Union and diminishing the threat of nuclear war was strong from the outset of his presidency, motivated in part by the example of his political hero Franklin Roosevelt.[16] De Gaulle's first public hint at changing course was only given in a broadcast on New Year's eve of 1963, when he announced his view that the gradual evolution of communist regimes in Eastern Europe would coalesce with a transformation of the Western alliance itself to pave the way for a Europe "toute entière."[17] This relatively late switch from intransigence to rapprochement vis-à-vis the Soviet bloc must be explained above all from developments in the all-important relationship with Germany. During the Berlin Crises from 1958 to 1961, de Gaulle's unyielding stance had helped to cement his crucial relationship with Chancellor Adenauer. It was moreover aimed at dissuading the German polity from striking a separate deal with Moscow in order to achieve German reunification; as Walter Lippmann once pointed out, "at bottom the hard policy is directed not against the Russians, but against those Germans who want to make an opening to the East."[18] In the course of 1963, it became clear that intransigence towards the Soviet Union was no longer producing these benefits in relation to the Franco-German relationship. De Gaulle's relationship with Adenauer's staunchly Atlanticist successor Erhard quickly soured. His aim to build Europe on Franco-German cooperation seemed increasingly forlorn. By the mid-1960s, de Gaulle "told any visitor who cared to listen [...] that the major problem was to keep Germany under control" and "was returning to France's traditional diplomacy of trying to balance off Germany with the Soviet Union."[19] In addition, with détente becoming increasingly popular in European circles, it was important for de Gaulle to ensure that the Soviet Union would regard France as the natural European interlocutor in discussing the future of Germany rather than a future German government.

From 1964 onwards, there was a notable increase in diplomatic contacts between Paris and Moscow. Visiting Moscow in January 1964, French Finance Minister Valéry Giscard d'Estaing reached agreement on negotiating a five-year bilateral trade accord; the accord, under which France extended $356 million in credits, was subsequently signed in October 1964. In May 1965, the Soviet State Committee for the Use of Atomic Energy and the French Atomic Energy Commission furthermore signed a two-year agreement on peaceful uses of atomic energy, arranging for exchange visits by scientists and technicians. And in October 1965, Couve de Murville paid a six-day visit to the Soviet Union, becoming the first Western foreign minister to visit the Soviet Union since Khrushchev's fall in October 1964 and the first French foreign minister to visit there since 1956. French contacts also increased with Poland. In September 1965, Polish Prime Minister Jozef Cyrankiewicz paid a visit to France, at the end of which both sides called for a normalization of East-West relations. One month later, Giscard d'Estaing signed a five-year agreement in Warsaw under which trade between the two countries would be increased by fifty percent in 1969.

In early 1966, the stage for de Gaulle's disengagement from NATO was set. On December 19, he had won re-election, albeit in two rounds.[20] In January, the crisis in the Common Market as a result of de Gaulle's empty chair policy was finally resolved with the Luxembourg compromise. The *force de frappe* was gradually becoming an operational reality with the deployment of the Mirage IV bomber. And de Gaulle was planning a state visit to Moscow in June 1966. The time was ripe for asserting France's independence from the United States by taking a drastic new step.

American Anticipation

Given de Gaulle's longstanding hostility to NATO, it is not surprising that the possibility of a French withdrawal came up in American diplomatic correspondence well before 1966. By 1964, in part because of the rising tension over the MLF, intimations from French sources that the Elysée was preparing a "drastic step"[21] against NATO were not uncommon. As a result, American officials began to ponder the implications of such a move by de Gaulle well before its actual occurrence.

In the spring of 1964, the State Department's Policy Planning Council – headed by Walt Rostow – began to secretly explore the possibility of a NATO without France. Interestingly, it broke with the routine assessment that French participation in NATO was indispensable. For most of the 1950s, France's military contribution had been considered essential in order to withstand a large-scale Soviet attack; its troops and its central geographic position offering strategic depth behind the potential frontlines in Central Europe made it so. A Policy Planning Council analysis of May 1964 noted, however, that the military value of French participation had declined in the 1960s for a variety of reasons. The increasing reliance within NATO on tactical nuclear weapons; the strategy of forward defense along the eastern frontier of Western Germany; the enhanced military contribution of West Germany, as a result of which France's troop contribution accounted only for roughly fifteen percent of NATO's combat forces by 1964; the reduced likelihood of a large-scale Soviet attack, even as the threat of an "unpremeditated conflict" in Central Europe remained real: all of these developments had made French military participation in NATO less important. The Policy Planning Council therefore concluded that from a military perspective "a NATO without France may be tolerable," despite the considerable hassle and the costs of relocating military lines of communication, infrastructure, and facilities.[22]

The implications of a French withdrawal would be mostly political, the Policy Planning Council believed. The defection of an important ally would naturally send a shiver through NATO. It would raise the specter of disintegration within view of the year in which the Treaty would be up for review – 1969. It might also weaken public support in the United States for NATO and for American troop deployments in Europe. Rostow's Policy Planning Council nonetheless stressed that a French withdrawal could well turn out to be beneficial on balance. It anticipated that NATO "pruned of its obstructionist member" would finally be able "to display a unity and a scale of activity" considered necessary to deal with the Soviet threat. Even American-French relations might paradoxically improve in the wake of a French withdrawal from NATO, for the potential for any further anti-American moves by de Gaulle would have been significantly reduced. The gist of this early policy exercise at the State Department was hence not only that NATO could do without France, but that its anticipated withdrawal might even be a blessing in disguise.[23]

It is also telling that the obvious alternative to a French withdrawal – "a NATO reorganized to suit de Gaulle's nationalistic tastes" – was never contemplated within the Johnson administration. The Franco-American disagreement over NATO had moved well beyond de Gaulle's unsuccessful tripartite memorandum diplomacy into a state of paralysis in which dialogue was entirely absent. In particular, in the State Department there was virtually no willingness to look at the issues from de Gaulle's perspective. On the contrary, US diplomacy had been geared towards containing the wicked effects of his nationalism for most of the 1960s, in particular in relation to Germany and the movement towards European unity.

The absence of a Franco-American dialogue on NATO also reflected the powerful advice of Charles Bohlen, the American ambassador to France. We have already observed in the previous chapter that Bohlen consistently discouraged attempts at seeking compromise. Bohlen fervently believed that de Gaulle could not be won over by concessions or flattery and had "an absolute fixation with independence." In his view, it would neither be in de Gaulle's style nor in the interest of the United States to seek a compromise over NATO. He considered it "extremely doubtful" that de Gaulle ever expected a positive reply to his memorandum proposal of September 1958; it was rather a tactical ploy to justify his premeditated actions against NATO. As importantly, Bohlen argued that French foreign policy was almost exclusively the creation of de Gaulle's political convictions, which led him to seek tension in France's rapport with the United States, and that it was not supported by the large majority of the French or by the government apparatus. Future French governments were likely to pursue more agreeable foreign policies, Bohlen reasoned. From the outset, his advice was thus to weather de Gaulle's provocations with equanimity and continue as much as possible with business as usual.[24]

Bohlen's sobering advice to President Johnson did not go unchallenged. Prominent old hands like Acheson and Harriman and strong-minded policymakers such as Ball believed that de Gaulle could be influenced if handled with firmness and determination. Sharing an inclination to speak up to the Frenchman, whose views they found incompatible to their own, they were utterly dismayed at Johnson's relatively passive attitude.[25] Others, such as Assistant Secretary of State for European Affairs William Tyler, rather disagreed with Bohlen's assessment that de Gaulle's foreign policy enjoyed scant domestic support and was "merely the product of his peculiar outlook and state of mind." Tyler sensed that many in France and in Europe, even those who had no sympathy for de Gaulle, "feel that he does reflect and give expression to a certain sentiment not only in France but in Free Europe as a whole [...]: a confused sense that it is possible, indeed natural and necessary, for Europe to have interests within the framework of an alliance with the United States which do not in all cases spring from a conception of the world identical with that held by the United States [...]."[26] Tyler's realistic assessment, which struck a sympathetic chord in McGeorge Bundy's White House staff, might have given reason for a look at NATO from the French perspective. Yet it went against the predominant grain of anti-Gaullism in American foreign policy circles. Bohlen's advice to ride out the "impervious" General moreover had the edge of providing an operational code of conduct that was closest to Johnson's own inclinations. It was, in addition, the most levelheaded about the potential for finding a middle ground.

By the fall of 1965, as de Gaulle began to prepare the public for the final showdown, the NATO crisis was unmistakably in the offing. On September 9, 1965, in his twelfth press conference, de Gaulle openly hinted at his determination to withdraw France from NATO's integrated military structure before 1969. He also dwelled on the "empty chair" crisis within the Common Market. From Washington's vantage point, "de Gaulle's juxtaposition of these two problems [...] was deliberate and designed to build up to a clear 'confrontation' between the economic, political, and security conceptions reflected by the United States and most Europeans (including many Frenchmen) on the one hand, and himself on the other."[27]

A few days before his September press conference, de Gaulle had apprised George Ball of his intentions with regard to NATO. De Gaulle had stressed that he did not want to break up the alliance and that "there would still be a *de facto* understanding for common defense even if no signed treaty existed," as Ball recalled in his memoirs. He had made clear, however, that he planned to withdraw France from NATO before 1969 and that he would not tolerate any foreign forces on French soil that were not under French command – and this included NATO itself. He would not make any proposals to this end about which there could then be negotiations among allies; instead, he would "lay down conditions in discussions between France and the United States that would not include either Germany or the United Kingdom."[28] In a follow-on meeting with Ball, Couve de Murville elucidated that de Gaulle would make his move against foreign troops on French soil in 1966.[29] And a few months later, as if de Gaulle's intentions weren't sufficiently understood, the French foreign minister derided NATO to American journalists as a "thingamagig [truc] at the end of Avenue Foch" which needed to be removed "from France's back."[30]

Ball had in point of fact already begun working with the Defense Department and the Joint Chiefs of Staff on plans in anticipation of a French withdrawal from NATO.[31] In the course of the ensuing interagency debate in the summer and the fall of 1965, there was little doubt that NATO could survive militarily without French participation, as the State Department's Policy Planning Council had already concluded in 1964. While the four French air squadrons and the missile units stationed in West Germany were considered valuable, the military significance of French army units was judged to be marginal. During one interagency discussion in August, Ball was asked whether "our objective, if necessary, would be NATO without France." Ball replied that "he had heard of no one in government who opposed this as our policy and that in his discussions with the allies, they favored it." The challenge as American policymakers saw it therefore was, in the apt words of Assistant Secretary of Defense John McNaughton, "how best to end up with a good NATO without France."[32]

As early as the spring of 1965, the Joint Chiefs of Staff had begun to develop contingency plans for an orderly withdrawal of American forces from France under the codename EULOC. The total American troop strength in France was approximately 28,700, mostly army and air force personnel.[33] American military installations in France primarily consisted of lines of communications (such as depots, supply centers, and pipelines) for the Seventh Army in West Germany and of operating bases of the American Air Force. The Pentagon's military planners looked at a range of actions – from partial withdrawal to complete relocation. On August 20, 1965, the Joint Chiefs of Staff finally sent a top secret message to the SACEUR as the American commander in Europe (US-CINCEUR) instructing him to prepare preliminary plans for the withdrawal of American troops from France.[34] The removal of American forces and installations was assessed as "militarily feasible, politically acceptable to our Allies and ourselves, and within a reasonable cost range."[35]

Interestingly, given this state of affairs, there was some discussion about whether the United States should withdraw American forces from France before de Gaulle made his move. There was some instinctive support for such a course of preemption, particularly within the State Department; Rusk, for instance, had requested that the option be considered.[36] Someone like Dwight Eisenhower also advised Ball that, since de Gaulle's objectives were clear, the United States should promptly remove NATO's headquarters to Brussels before de Gaulle could make any formal demands.[37] Such an American withdrawal, by seizing the initiative, was above all thought to counteract the presumed corrosive effects on the alliance of a wait-and-see attitude. In the end, however, the State Department decided against pursuing this option. A preemptive withdrawal might have been emotionally satisfying, if only for the dramatic effect of marking dissatisfaction with de Gaulle's policies. But cooler heads prevailed. Bohlen, for one, feared that an unprovoked withdrawal of American forces would merely strengthen de Gaulle's domestic position in the run-up to the presidential elections of December 1965.[38] It would only have played into the hands of de Gaulle and "simply save him trouble."[39] In June 1965, Chancellor Erhard moreover had told President Johnson that he wanted to avoid a confrontation with de Gaulle with a view to the German elections of September 1965.[40] Most importantly, a preemptive withdrawal would have incurred the risk of shifting the burden of blame for provoking a crisis from de Gaulle to the United States, not least in the eyes of the other European allies.

The most important issue for American policymakers to resolve was therefore whether the United States should agree to a bilateral treaty with France in view of de Gaulle's larger design to substitute NATO – or even the North Atlantic Treaty – with a series of interlocking bilateral defense arrangements. It was presumed that de Gaulle's alliance system, while lacking an integrated military structure, would provide for "periodic consultation on a political level and for more frequent, perhaps even continuous, contact among national defense authorities for the purpose of coordinating national defense plans." Moreover, "coordination of the French force de frappe with US and UK strategic forces could also be accomplished by such bilateral agreements, which might in addition provide for tripartite 'nuclear consultation' among the three."[41] American officials, however, were agreed from the outset that the bilateral set-up of the Cold War alliance favored by de Gaulle was not acceptable – and this had also been the purport of Ball's response to de Gaulle and Couve de Murville in September 1965.[42] They were not prepared to abandon a system which provided, in their view, "the most efficient method of utilizing the combined military capabilities of the members" and "the means for the quickest and most effective possible response in time of crisis." NATO moreover provided "the framework through which German rearmament can be controlled, and Germany can play its full role in the defense of the West."

It also facilitated "a degree of unity of political attitude and policy in the Atlantic area not otherwise obtainable." Most importantly, while de Gaulle could withdraw from NATO, he could not be allowed to turn back the clock of European history. "The central issue," the State Department counseled, "is whether there shall be a collective multilateral system between equal sovereign states employing integration only as needed in the interest of effectiveness, or a system of bilateral power politics involving all the dangers of the turn of the 20th century."[43] The ghosts of the past had to remain under control.

Bracing the Allies: The Select Committee

For most of 1965, with de Gaulle's withdrawal hanging like the sword of Damocles over its head and the September elections in Germany disallowing any major new initiatives, NATO was unmistakably in the doldrums. The Vietnam War was moreover consuming Washington to a rapidly increasing degree, this being the fateful year of America's escalating involvement in that war.[44] President Johnson meanwhile faced criticism for failing to provide leadership in what was seen by some as a period of dangerous drift, in particular after his decision to go easy on the MLF. As always, Dean Acheson was in the forefront of those who advocated urgent action in order to strengthen the alliance with Europe. Repeatedly at odds with "Mr. LBJ," Acheson wrote to a friend in July 1965 in a state of dejection:

> My guess about the Continent is that by the turn of the year de Gaulle will move to dissolve NATO and edge us out of Europe. We should not wait for him, but begin to act ... I would try for some agreement on [...] Central Europe and German unification, a quiet review of the relation of types of military power in Europe to political policy, planning for a step forward on international monetary arrangements and tariff agreements. These I would push so that de Gaulle will have to disclose a full policy of obstruction. He should not be permitted to choose the battle areas and win isolated (appearing) victories.

Acheson added, "Although I preach this crusade, I have no royal converts and a children's crusade would not be a crusade at all, not even a disaster. That would follow inaction."[45]

It is true that Johnson did not seek direct or public confrontation with France, as Acheson and others would have wanted; he did not want to incur the blame of having provoked a French withdrawal – and thereby a NATO crisis – through actions of his own. It would, however, be unfair to castigate the Johnson administration for complete passiveness in the face of de Gaulle's imminent attack. On the contrary, during the summer and fall of 1965, the United States made a concerted effort to give NATO a renewed sense of direction and purpose in order to brace it for the shock accompanying a French withdrawal. Measures "which do not involve basic structural reform in NATO and which are thus least subject to

French veto, will make NATO far less susceptible to de Gaulle's abrasions and increase its value for other members," the State Department observed in its policy review on France and NATO.[46]

The first of these was the introduction of a new five-year force planning system within NATO. The political importance of this system was, at least in part, that it would set force goals for 1970. This implied that the alliance would continue in its current form after 1969. For this reason, French Defense Minister Pierre Messmer was instructed to oppose it at a ministerial meeting in May 1965.[47] But France could not prevent talks about such a new force planning system to continue. There was, in addition, considerable pressure from the American side to put NATO's Allied Command Europe Mobile Force (AMF) on a more stable and financially sound footing. This force was plagued by the difficulty of getting NATO financing for its exercises. "It thus leads a hand-to-mouth existence," Harlan Cleveland, the American ambassador to NATO reported, "limping along from exercise to exercise to ad hoc solutions, dependent on French abstention rather than veto and on the case-by-case support of governments which are becoming increasingly reluctant." But the decision to give the force a higher priority was also fuelled by a desire to provide "visible evidence [of NATO's] continuing vitality," "to build a NATO project on a 'less than 15' basis" and "to extend the principle of interdependence, of integrated planning and action."[48]

The most important progress within NATO, however, was almost surreptitiously made in the sensitive realm of nuclear politics. The issue of nuclear sharing, which was closely linked to Germany's place within the alliance, was still unresolved after the MLF was left to drift in late 1964. Yet nuclear weapons had increasingly become an integral part of NATO's defensive posture as a result of the deployment of American tactical nuclear weapons in Western Europe since the late 1950s. By 1965, American nuclear warheads stored in Europe already numbered over 5,000, and this number was to increase even further. Nine NATO members owned a variety of delivery vehicles and had concluded bilateral agreements with the United States providing for information and training in the use of nuclear weapons. Two-key systems, other physical checks and electronic permissive action links ensured American control over the release of nuclear warheads, but the involvement of other European allies in their use had undeniably become an operational reality. This development, however, had not been appended by a consultative mechanism about nuclear matters at the political level. American officials were moreover still seriously concerned at how Germany's foreign policy orientation might in the long run be affected by de Gaulle's policy of independence and his actions against NATO.[49] German participation in NATO's nuclear defense certainly was considered a main issue by all major parties in the Bundestag elections of the fall.

On May 31, 1965, at a meeting of NATO defense ministers, Robert McNamara proposed a "select committee" of four or five member states to study ways in which allied participation in the planning and targeting of American nuclear forces and the exchange of information on issues of nuclear defense could be improved.[50] Although it was from the outset certain that France could not be persuaded to support its establishment, it was also clear that its opposition would not run as deep as that against the MLF (or the ANF).[51] Given the attention accorded to the issue in the run-up to the Bundestag elections, Paris was careful not to oppose categorically a German role in nuclear matters. De Gaulle could not count on being able to rally as broad an opposition against nuclear consultation within NATO as he had been able to do against the MLF.[52] The French reaction to NcNamara's proposal was therefore one of guarded opposition. On July 7, France rejected the proposal but indicated it would not object to other NATO member states proceeding without French participation.[53] In all, ten member states would participate in the discussions following McNamara's initiative; only France, Portugal, Iceland, Luxembourg, and Norway abstained.

When launching his initiative, McNamara underlined that Washington considered nuclear consultation within NATO as "additional to whatever action may be taken on the MLF or ANF forces."[54] Yet in the course of 1965 the "software" of consultation rapidly emerged as a suitable alternative to the "hardware" of the MLF. McNamara's initiative solved the pressing question: If not the MLF (or ANF), what? The promise of nuclear consultation in particular appeared credible enough to meet German political requirements; on election campaign, for instance, socialist leader Willy Brandt spoke out in favor of German participation in nuclear consultation mechanisms as opposed to hardware solutions. At the same time, it was considerably less controversial than the MLF, both on the congressional front and internationally, as it would shy away from giving other allies a finger on the nuclear trigger. McNamara's initiative even offered the Johnson administration a welcome opportunity to get the alliance moving again without precipitating a crisis. As the American embassy in Paris judged, nuclear consultation "as an alternative, rather than a supplement, to the MLF/ANF" had the advantage of "narrowing de Gaulle's area for diplomatic maneuver with respect to NATO" as well as that of a "fresh approach" to solving the nuclear defense issue within the West.[55]

As importantly, the significance Johnson was beginning to attach to negotiating a nuclear non-proliferation treaty with the Soviet Union also worked in favor of nuclear consultation instead of sharing nuclear hardware with the allies. The idea of such a treaty had been first put forward by Ireland in 1958. American interest in it revived as a result of China's first nuclear test in October 1964; India meanwhile was approaching a decision on nuclear weapons as well and there was a concern that Japan would be tempted to follow suit.[56] Secretary Rusk had by then already created an interagency committee under the chairmanship of Llewellyn Thompson, a former ambassador to the Soviet Union, to coordinate discussions about the proliferation of nuclear weapons. China's explosion furthermore prompted Johnson to establish a separate task force chaired by Roswell Gilpatric, a former deputy secretary of defense. The MLF/ANF was fiercely debated within the Gilpatric group, since the idea of sharing nuclear weapons with Germany was obviously anathema to the Soviet Union and the main obstacle to achieving a non-proliferation treaty. The Gilpatric group did not achieve consensus on this point, but its final report did note that a choice probably would have to be made at some point.[57] Given the sensitive political stage in the MLF affair at the time (see the preceding chapter), the State Department strongly objected to Gilpatric's recommendations and successfully insisted that they be kept secret. Regardless of this response to the Gilpatric report, the pursuit of a nuclear non-proliferation treaty increasingly preoccupied the Johnson administration.[58] American and Soviet officials began to explore its prospects. On June 15, 1965, the United States moreover proposed to resume negotiations in the Eighteen-Nation Disarmament Committee (ENDC) in Geneva, which had been adjourned in September 1964, in order to draft the treaty (as well as to broaden the 1963 limited test ban treaty to include underground tests); on August 17, the United States introduced its own draft. The possible establishment of the MLF and a German role therein, however, held up further progress, causing Johnson's disarmament negotiators William Foster and Butch Fisher to urge an official abandonment of the MLF and similar mixed-manned schemes in Europe.[59]

It was McGeorge Bundy who played a central role in the decisive shift in American policies from nuclear hardware to consultation in the latter part of 1965. As in December 1964, Bundy took it upon himself to break the bureaucratic logjam caused by the continuing advocacy of the State Department for the MLF. In October 1965, in a paper for President Johnson, he elaborated the case for a "fresh start" in NATO's nuclear sharing debate in the aftermath of the German elections. The United States, he urged, should now clearly decide against the MLF "or any other mixed manned weapons system." The policy of "calculated delay and indecision," which had been pursued in the light of the German elections, had outlived its usefulness. And even Germans were not pressing en masse for a revival of the MLF, "in view of its costs with France and its possible repercussions on the Common Market." Bundy hence declared himself unconvinced by admonitions from George Ball's offices at the State Department that only a hardware solution could in the long run satisfy the Germans: "I continue to think George's reporting reflects his own convictions at least as much as the situation." Bundy recommended that President Johnson instead shift his support firmly behind allied participation in nuclear policymaking along the lines of McNamara's proposal, the favorable response to which had left him "more encouraged about the prospect of a sensible answer than at any time in years." A shift toward consultation, he assessed, was "for the good of the Atlantic Alliance" – and it had the added advantage of making a non-proliferation treaty easier to accomplish.[60] When, on November 24, Soviet Ambassador Anatoly Dobrynin finally confirmed the Soviet leadership's interest in a non-proliferation treaty, Bundy was beginning to believe that "a real Johnson breakthrough" in the nuclear realm was in the making.[61]

American diplomats were by now indeed actively pushing NATO allies to approve McNamara's proposal for a "select committee" at the December meetings of foreign and defense ministers. Despite the generally favorable response to the initial proposal, Harlan Cleveland, who had succeeded Finletter as ambassador to NATO, reported that most allies were still fearful of provoking the French and of engaging in any action that could be perceived as divisive.[62] McNamara and Denis Healey, his British colleague, impressed on their German counterpart Kai-Uwe von Hassel that there were no plans in place for the selective use of nuclear weapons and there was an urgent need for effective procedures for political consultation in such an event. According to the diplomatic report, "the revelation that his colleagues representing nuclear powers were very dissatisfied with the present status of nuclear planning seemed to be a new and sobering thought to Von Hassel" and the German defense minister was "rather taken aback."[63] The American effort at getting agreement on McNamara's proposal was successful. At the meeting of NATO foreign ministers in mid-December, Couve de Murville tried to capitalize on fears of a crisis as he ventured to limit the Select Committee to a short-term existence. This attempt led to extensive skirmishing between the foreign ministers and Secretary General Manlio Brosio. In the end, however, France agreed to the establishment of the Select Committee without setting a deadline. In spite of Couve de Murville's "fancy footwork," France had wanted to avoid a row with its allies just days before the run-off presidential elections in France.[64] The MLF, meanwhile, was shelved in the course of the consecutive visits of Harold Wilson and Ludwig Erhard to Washington in December 1965. Erhard "came down squarely on the side of a 'hardware solution'," Johnson wrote to Wilson.[65] But the American president, as we have already noted in the previous chapter, remained uncommitted. And Wilson, as Bundy observed after having read the prime minister's reply, was "moving away from the common nuclear force just as fast as he politely can."[66]

After NATO's ministerial meetings of December 1965, American policymakers congratulated themselves on their ability to get "the Alliance moving again" despite French obstructionism. The establishment of the Select Committee and the new five-year force planning system indeed helped to brace the European allies for the crisis that was still to come. They had gotten accustomed to the notion that a NATO without France was a practical – if inconvenient – proposition. Since they were, as Cleveland reported, "increasingly willing to leave the French chair vacant and go ahead on moves to strengthen NATO," French leverage had been successfully diminished. As even Cleveland was to admit, however, the success of American diplomacy at the NATO conference table was overshadowed by the presence of "two ghosts at the feast" – the prospect of a French withdrawal from NATO and the escalation of American military involvement in Vietnam.[67]

LBJ and the Coming Crisis

President Johnson, meanwhile, stuck to the remarkably philosophical attitude to de Gaulle which had been his rule of thumb from the outset. On August 6, 1965, he even specifically ordered all American government agencies to "take special measures to prevent U.S. activities in France which could needlessly embarrass United States relations with France."[68] This order had been prompted by the diplomatic incident with France caused by four photo-reconnaissance passes of an American Air Force jet over the French nuclear production plant at Pierrelatte on July 16, 1965. There is reason to believe that de Gaulle personally did not take the matter up highly.[69] But the French government seized on the incident to bolster domestic support for his foreign policy of independence and forced the United States into a formal apology on July 22. "If this incident had not developed, another would and presumably will," Bohlen concluded. "Unfortunately, this one could not have been better designed to serve de Gaulle's purposes."[70]

Johnson's policy toward de Gaulle was as much one of judicious restraint as one of patience, that is, of riding out de Gaulle. This was predicated on the two-fold notion that de Gaulle had no serious public or political support in France or in Europe for his foreign policies and that, because of his advanced age, he would vanish from the political scene in the not too distant future. This notion was advanced, as we have seen, in particular by Bohlen. In February 1965, it was reflected in an assessment of the American embassy in Paris as follows:

> Despite the malign delight with which other members of the Alliance might regard an all-out confrontation, the stresses thus created for other members of the Alliance would be disruptive, and it is probably best to grin and bear it, keeping the empty chair available wherever we can. ... Our hope should always be that the temperature of nationalism will drop and France will return to a more accommodating disposition toward the United States.[71]

The concept of the forlorn General was encouraged, too, by Thomas Finletter, who believed that "Gaullist opposition [within NATO] is founded on the unique philosophy and the intellectual and moral power of one man [...]." Finletter therefore reasoned that "in a not distant future she [France] is going to come back into a cordial relationship with the US and with the Atlantic Community" and that "the important thing for present is not to create any difference with France which will be lasting."[72] Johnson's assertions that he was going to "outlive the General" were indeed of the same vein, and his resulting equanimity won out against the inclinations of those at the State Department, including Dean

Rusk and George Ball, who were inclined to allow their irritation with de Gaulle to shape policies.[73]

There is some evidence that Johnson's restraint in dealing with de Gaulle was also motivated by his appraisal of the domestic political scene. Whereas he was never able to overcome the innate prejudice held against him by the foreign policy establishment, Johnson was an undisputed master in the domestic realm. Many of his foreign policy decisions – including his decision to let the MLF wither (see previous chapter) – were therefore framed by his reading of the measure of support for a particular foreign policy in Congress. Johnson was not devoid of foreign policy convictions. On the contrary, he was deeply committed to upholding America's security commitments abroad, to improve relations with the Soviet Union, and to reduce the threat of nuclear war. But he was constantly concerned with maintaining sufficient public support for his foreign policy decisions. He was also determined to avoid strategic setbacks that could get him into trouble domestically; Johnson was acutely aware of Truman's fate, who was heavily criticized for having "lost China" when the communists took control in 1949.[74] With regard to NATO, Johnson was worried that American public support for it could diminish to the point where he would be forced to cut down US troop commitments. A war of words with de Gaulle, which could have easily gotten out of hand, did not fit in with his overriding objective to leave the alliance strengthened.[75]

Discussing European affairs at his ranch in Texas in early November 1965, Johnson asked for the advice of Douglas Dillon, who had just resigned from his post as secretary of the treasury. Dillon had previous experience with France as ambassador in the 1950s, and Johnson was thinking of sending him as his emissary to de Gaulle after the French elections.[76] Dillon's memorandum of January 1966 probably came as close as anything to formulating Johnson's policy of restraint toward de Gaulle and its future implications. After asserting that de Gaulle's views were impervious, Dillon wrote:

Policy toward de Gaulle cannot be considered in isolation. It is and must remain an integral part of our overall foreign policy. While it would be possible to devise a U.S. policy which could bring about an accommodation with de Gaulle, this would require the abandonment or modification of major U.S. objectives. Such a price is far too high to pay .... The U.S. should make no substantial concessions to de Gaulle, but should pursue whatever policies it finds appropriate, irrespective of his position. In arriving at decisions on overall U.S. policy, little weight should be given to Gaullist views. We should operate on the assumption that de Gaulle's leadership of France is temporary, and that he will be succeeded by a government more responsive to public opinion, hence more favorable to NATO, United Europe, and the United States.

Dillon, like Johnson, thus departed from the twofold notion that de Gaulle's designs were incompatible with those of the United States and, in addition, that the General was inherently unreceptive to American arguments. But the reality of his intransigence did impose important considerations of a tactical nature on Washington. In recognition of this, Dillon went on to map out a course of action for Johnson.

> While continuing firmly on our course in spite of de Gaulle's views, we should lean over backward to be polite and friendly to France, to de Gaulle personally, and to all French government officials. Backbiting, recriminations, attempts to downgrade the importance of France as a nation, or attempts at reprisals should be avoided no matter what the temptation. They cannot be effective, will only irritate de Gaulle and make him more difficult to deal with, and are likely to cause French public opinion to rally to his side against the United States.

In submitting the Dillon paper to Johnson, McGeorge Bundy stated that it represented, in fact, the position "you have sustained so skillfully for more than two years." Dillon extended the line of recommendation to predicaments that were soon to come:

> If de Gaulle insists on the removal of U.S. forces from French soil we should accede gracefully .... If France should decide to pull out of any active role of NATO, we should not replace our NATO tie with France by any bilateral agreement. Any such agreement would make it much more difficult for France to return to the fold at a later date and might set a pattern that could undermine the whole NATO structure. In the event of a French withdrawal, we should support the continuation of the NATO organization without France. ... it should be made very clear that there is an empty chair always ready and waiting for France should she decide to return.[77]

LBJ's Exercise in Restraint – Spring of 1966

De Gaulle Throws Down the Gauntlet
On February 21, 1966, at one of his regal press conferences, de Gaulle at last appraised the world of his decision to leave NATO by 1969. NATO, he underlined, had become obsolete because of the changes in the Communist bloc:

> Owing to the internal and external evolution of the countries of the East, the Western world is no longer threatened today as it was at the time when the American protectorate was set up in Europe [...].

He also reiterated his familiar claim that the acquisition of nuclear weapons with which the Soviet Union could hit the American homeland had undercut the credibility of the American nuclear security guarantee, on which the defense of Western Europe had hinged. In addition, the global involvement of the United States held important risks for Europe:

> ...conflicts in which America engages in other parts of the world – as the day before yesterday in Korea, yesterday in Cuba, today in Vietnam – risk, by virtue of that famous escalation, being extended so that the result could be a general conflagration. In that case Europe – whose strategy is, within NATO, that of America – would be automatically involved in the struggle, even when it would not have so desired.

De Gaulle moreover made clear that NATO's concept of military integration was at odds with his consuming aim of restoring France's self-assurance:

> France's determination to dispose of herself, a determination without which she would soon cease to believe in her own role and be able to be useful to others, is incompatible with a defense organization in which she finds herself a subordinate.[78]

These arguments were similar to those de Gaulle had marshaled against NATO and in favor of a new security organization in his memorandum to Eisenhower and Macmillan of September 1958. But there was – nearly eight years of policy divergence later – no longer the hope of potential agreement.

De Gaulle was, however, still far from precise about the timing and the manner of France's withdrawal in his press conference. On the contrary, his words created the impression that he was in no hurry and envisaged a measured extraction rather than a dramatic move:

> Consequently, without going back on her adherence to the Atlantic Alliance, France is going, between now and the final date set for her obligations, which is April 4, 1969, to continue to modify successively the measures currently practiced, in so far as they concern her.[79]

In late February, Washington was nonetheless receiving indications from a friendly high-level source at the Quai d'Orsay that a drastic move by de Gaulle against NATO and American forces on French soil was at hand.[80] These indications prompted George Ball – possibly in an attempt to deter or to moderate de Gaulle – to tell the new French ambassador in Washington, Charles Lucet, "in no uncertain terms" of the seriousness of the matter.[81] Even so, when de Gaulle finally "laid down his conditions" for continued participation in the Atlantic alliance in a brief handwritten letter to President Johnson dated March 7, the scope and the briskness of his action was unexpected.[82] Bohlen, who had been called in by Couve de Murville to receive de Gaulle's letter, reported to Washington that "the line taken was very hard – harder than what the Quai was trying to produce."[83]

After pledging allegiance to the North Atlantic Treaty, "unless events in the course of the next three years should change the fundamental elements of the relations between East and West," de Gaulle's letter to Johnson announced that France would completely cease its military participation in NATO and that it would ask foreign troops to leave French soil unless arrangements could be made that ensured French sovereignty:

> France intends to recover, in her territory, the full exercise of her sovereignty, now impaired by the permanent presence of allied military elements or by the habitual use being made of its air space, to terminate her participation in the "integrated" commands, and no longer place forces at the disposal of NATO.[84]

Reflecting de Gaulle's insistence on dealing with great powers rather than multilateral institutions, he sent similar letters to the government leaders of Great Britain, Germany, and Italy on March 9. And on March 11, the French government issued an aide mémoire to each member state of NATO detailing the logic behind the French move. All of these communications made clear that only the implementation of the French decision was to be subject to further negotiations with allies:

> Doubtless, it would have been conceivable for negotiations to be undertaken to amend the provisions in force by common agreement. The French government would have been happy to propose it, had it been given to believe that such negotiations could lead to the outcome that the French government itself has in view. Unfortunately, everything shows that such an undertaking would be doomed to failure, since France's partners appear to be, or assert that they are all advocates of maintaining the status quo, or else of strengthening everything which, from the French viewpoint, appears henceforth unacceptable.[85]

A follow-on aide mémoire, dated March 29, clarified that NATO headquarters and American forces were to be relocated from France by April 1, 1967.[86] Even given his well-known track record, de Gaulle was casting off NATO's – and ipso facto America's – yoke with unforeseen asperity.

Responding to De Gaulle

In Washington, the State Department was in the grips of indignant anger about de Gaulle's eviction notice. In his letter of March 7, de Gaulle had emphasized that France would remain party to the North Atlantic Treaty after 1969. But American diplomats were hardly in the mood to recognize this as evidence of de Gaulle's enduring loyalty to the Western alliance. They were rather given to the idea of renouncing France as a member to the North Atlantic Treaty now that it had ceased to participate in NATO. Such a radical countermove would at least refute the Gaullist assertion that a distinction could be made between NATO and the North Atlantic Treaty.[87] The notion of expelling France altogether even left its mark on Johnson's provisional reply to de Gaulle on March 7, which had been drafted by the State Department:

> I would be less than frank if I did not inform you that your action raises grave questions regarding the whole relationship between the responsibilities and benefits of the Alliance.[88]

De Gaulle's affirmation of his allegiance to the Western alliance paradoxically also gave cause to doubt his steadfastness as an ally. His letter of March 7 had stated that France would remain ready "to fight on the side of her Allies in the event that one of them should be the object of an *unprovoked* aggression". (emphasis added) The inclusion of the word "unprovoked" was not a meaningless slip, since it was also used by other French spokesmen. It moreover corresponded with de Gaulle's assessment that American involvement in other parts of the world would lead to conflicts which, as de Gaulle had said in his February 21 press conference, "by virtue of that famous escalation" could lead to "a general conflagration" at Europe's expense. Was de Gaulle defining a new curb on the allied solidarity enshrined in the North Atlantic Treaty? If so, was he thereby seeking to gain leverage over American policies beyond Europe or, vice versa, to create room for distancing himself from his allied obligations in case the Vietnam War expanded to a "general conflagration"? "An 'unprovoked' attack," Dean Acheson retorted during a Senate hearing, "is a slippery term, because an attack is usually the result of a quarrel and nobody knows who provoked whom [...]. Suspicion always arises when someone introduces a new and slippery phrase to loosen up their [sic] obligations."[89]

As usual, the White House staff took a more dispassionate view of de Gaulle's actions than the State Department. McGeorge Bundy had left the administration in late February,[90] but his role as President Johnson's watchman against the State Department's virulent anti-Gaullism was more than adequately assumed by the economist Francis Bator.[91] On March 7, Bator wrote to Johnson that forcing France to renounce the North Atlantic Treaty might satisfy "one's sense of elementary justice," but would be utter nonsense in every other respect. Any such countermeasure would be meaningless given France's geographic location in relation to the Soviet bloc and Germany. "It is like threatening to abandon Kentucky in the face of a land attack by Canada. It is hard to do unless one is prepared to throw in Ohio," Bator reasoned. Support for American leadership from the other European allies would moreover be solid only as long as "the provocation comes from Paris," Bator believed. A "cool approach" would even be preferable from a domestic vantage point; it would inevitably be criticized for "letting the French get away with murder," Bator argued, but also avoid the potentially more damaging charge that "our inflexibility helped to destroy NATO."[92] One day later, Bator put in his apprehension about contacts between exasperated State Department officials and journalists. It must be remembered, Bator wrote, that de Gaulle was a "lightweight jujitsu artist" who had "no real cards" to play with. "All his leverage comes from our over-exertions."[93] Walt Rostow, Johnson's pick as Bundy's successor, also did not share Ball's fury, although he certainly was – like Ball – a fervent anti-Gaullist. A perennial optimist, Rostow above all focused on the advantages of a NATO without France, as he had done in May 1964 as head of the State Department's Policy Planning Council. In a memorandum to Johnson on March 7, Rostow judged:

> There will be pain and anxiety in Europe in facing a NATO without France. If all we reestablish is a NATO – as it now is – without France, the organization could progressively weaken with the passage of time. On the other hand, if we use the occasion of French withdrawal to tighten NATO and move forward in specific fields leaving an empty chair for a French return, there may be psychological and political compensation for the setback.[94]

Despite these differences of opinion within the Johnson administration, there was agreement that rallying the allies around the NATO flag of military integration was in the first order of things to do. Involving the allies through consultations at NATO would be the best way to isolate France politically. It would also rebut de Gaulle's larger aim of reinstating the Western alliance on the basis of bilateral agreements between nation-states. Johnson's brief provisional response of March 7 therefore pointedly stated that the United States had shared de Gaulle's views with the other allies "to ask for their comment."[95] The following day, the American ambassador to NATO, Harlan Cleveland, was instructed to round up the other thirteen allies to see whether they could agree on a common declaration.[96] After more than a week of cajoling the European allies, who proved reluctant to confront de Gaulle, a short and rather bland statement indeed underlined the continuing importance of an "integrated and independent military organization" to which "no system of bilateral arrangements can be a substitute."[97]

The Johnson administration was, however, divided over a more substantive response to de Gaulle. In particular, George Ball wanted Johnson to speak up forcefully in defense of the pursuit of "integration" in international affairs against the forces of nationalism embodied by the General. When called up by journalists, Ball invariably assailed de Gaulle's distaste for NATO as "a kind of hallucination" and as evidence of an unhealthy longing for a disastrous past. This was a grave crisis, he stressed, because it concerned a clash between "conflicting views as to how one goes about organizing peace in the Western world and bring[ing] about a European settlement." The central objective of the United States in this crisis, Ball posited, was to ensure that the "Atlantic world" would continue on its course toward collective decisionmaking. Ball characteristically accused de Gaulle of trying to turn back the clock: "... the General is headed back toward 1914," he told Sevareid. "This is gravely dangerous," he added to Reston, because it "sets in motion opposition forces in other places. [...] As long as we have a divided Germany in the heart of an industrial complex of Europe, we are in real danger."[98] In an interview with André Fontaine, published in Le Monde on March 31, Ball similarly stood up for the principle of military integration and censured the French withdrawal from NATO as "a step backward toward the restoration of the old system of national rivalries."[99] De Gaulle's withdrawal decision was in Ball's view not so much lamentable in the light of the Cold War, for its military consequences were surmountable. It was deplorable because it went against Ball's own views and convictions as a liberal internationalist. France's departure from the NATO framework was above all a threat to the liberal postwar order in the Atlantic region to which he had devoted his life and had the potential of unleashing ghosts of the European past.

As so often when it came to European affairs, Ball found a forceful companion in Dean Acheson. On April 4, Acheson publicly assailed de Gaulle for going back to pre-1914 balance-of-power politics and for being motivated by a "strong medieval instinct" and a "strong resentment" over his wartime treatment by Roosevelt and Churchill.[100] "No landlord serving notice of termination of a lease upon an undesirable tenant could have been more brusque," he testified before the Senate.[101] Acheson had long tried to get Johnson to speak up to de Gaulle. In March 1965, concerned by the "reemerging nationalism" in Europe and the stalemate in NATO, he had pressed Johnson in vain to agree to a policy review. He had then made no secret of the fact that his proposal had been fuelled by disquiet about the impact of de Gaulle's policies on the Western alliance: "Can a place be found for her [France] in new NATO arrangements, without retarding integrated action by other interested countries? If not, how can de Gaulle best be isolated and frustrated in his opposition to such actions?"[102] In December 1965, concerned with the prospect of a French withdrawal from NATO, Acheson had been the driving force behind a statement of the Atlantic Council that urged Johnson to bring about a "fully integrated" Atlantic community with "joint political, economic, and military institutions."[103] Such advice was broad – "so broad that it states very little explicit policy," according to one official[104] – but its sense of mission about

NATO was vintage Acheson. In the wake of de Gaulle's withdrawal note, Acheson continued to advocate a strong response. As in the aftermath of the crisis of January 1963, he argued that de Gaulle was a man who "can and does in time recognize the inevitable and adjust his conduct to it. [...] The power of the US to shape the inevitable for General de Gaulle is immense."[105]

On March 16 and 17, 1966, President Johnson convened his advisers to discuss a more substantive response to de Gaulle's letter of March 7. Rusk, Ball, and Assistant Secretary of State for European Affairs John Leddy represented the State Department; Bohlen returned from Paris; Acheson was also brought in; Cyrus Vance and John McNaughton represented the Pentagon; Robert Komer, Bill Moyers, and Francis Bator of the White House staff were also present.[106] Johnson's advisers were clearly split into those who wanted to act vigorously against de Gaulle and those who strongly preferred to tread carefully and calm the waters. The State Department had prepared a reply to de Gaulle that would have amounted to a sharp rebuke. "This letter flings down the gauntlet to de Gaulle and commits us in effect to an opposite course," Komer jotted on his note paper. Unsurprisingly, Acheson briskly supported its towing line, telling Johnson that "as leader of [a] coalition, [you] must capture [the] propaganda initiative" and that "our pitch must be to strengthen it [the Alliance] by something new [...]."[107] Notwithstanding his longstanding advice to Johnson for phlegmatic responses towards French provocations, Bohlen also favored a tough reply to de Gaulle's withdrawal decision.[108]

Johnson, however, refused to be pushed into a public denunciation of de Gaulle. "Let's not gig de Gaulle," he responded to the State Department's clarion call to join the propaganda battle. "Let's avoid appearances of saying 'you're another' right back."[109] The president's disinclination to seek out confrontation with his French counterpart was moreover reinforced by advice from his White House staff. Following the first meeting, on March 16, Robert Komer questioned in particular Acheson's assertion that "the best way to stop de Gaulle is to beef up the alliance – make it more integrated rather than less." Komer advised against entering "a full-blown war" with de Gaulle over "more integration vs. less." He also warned Johnson that the "something new" Acheson considered necessary to reenergize the alliance,could well bring the proponents of the MLF back into business: "the lessons of recent history [...] suggest that we stop, look, and listen before flinging down the gauntlet to de Gaulle."[110]

Encouraged by Johnson's unwillingness to pick a fight with de Gaulle, the White House staff drafted an alternative reply, one which avoided "picking unnecessary fights" and "quoting de Gaulle on de Gaulle, putting the worst interpretation on what he says." Most importantly, this draft introduced the notion that "as our old friend and ally [...] there will always be an empty chair waiting for France."[111] Such an "offer of a golden bridge for the French nation," Bator tried to convince Ball, would give the letter a "gracious ending" and make clear that the

United States did not want to isolate France; in addition, it made a distinction between de Gaulle and France. Ball, however, was "rather disturbed" by Bator's draft, thinking that it had been "diluted to the point where it won't have anything like the impact it [the State draft] would have had in Europe."[112] During Johnson's second meeting with his advisers on responding to de Gaulle, on March 17, the new draft was assailed as too conciliatory – and the sentence added by the White House staff was removed. But the next morning Bator put it back in, albeit in a somewhat revised form. "I admit," Bator confessed to Johnson, "I am thinking what historians will say about this letter in 5-10 years – especially if things go wrong, and America is unfairly blamed by some Europeans for splitting Europe."[113]

On March 22, Ball handed Johnson's reply to de Gaulle to the French ambassador.[114] The letter reiterated American support for NATO, after having sought "the counsel of other Treaty members," and stated that the other fourteen members would continue to organize their collective defense through its integrated military structure. There was, however, no longer any hint in the letter of renouncing France as a member to the North Atlantic Treaty. On the contrary, noting de Gaulle's assurances on France's dedication to the Western alliance, Johnson stated squarely: "I respect that pledge." Upon Eisenhower's suggestion, the letter also implied that the United States was open to adaptations of NATO as required by "the needs of the hour."[115] The letter had remained the bone of contention between the State Department and the White House and some changes had been made at the urging of the former to sharpen the tone. Yet the final paragraph had remained unaltered:

> Indeed, we find it difficult to believe that France, which has made a unique contribution to Western security and development, will long remain withdrawn from the common affairs and responsibilities of the Atlantic. As our old friend and ally, her place will await France whenever she decides to resume her leading role.[116]

Johnson's position of temperance had now been clearly established, and it would continue to guide his public statements.[117] At the State Department, however, the bickering and the jibes at de Gaulle were unrelenting, spreading the notion that America's diplomats were on a different track in dealing with the NATO crisis.[118] In particular, Ball did little to hide his intense frustration with de Gaulle. On April 29, he delivered an address full of ominous hyperbole about the French withdrawal from NATO – and he even seemed to publicly criticize Johnson's muted reaction. Ball:

> Today there is a special temptation to pragmatism in our relations with Western Europe, where we are faced again with the reappearance of an assertive

nationalism that challenges the whole structure of our postwar arrangements. [...] our relations with Western Europe carry a heavy freight of history. [...] we cannot forget that jealousies, ambitions, and aggressions in Western Europe were responsible for the two greatest wars of modern history.

Ball described de Gaulle's Europe – "a continent of shifting coalitions and changing alliances" – as a "nostalgic evocation" that was inherently unable to provide a stable and peaceful European settlement. And if "Europe" indeed desired to play a role in the world, Ball pointed out, it had no choice but to organize itself "commensurate with the requirements of the modern age."[119] There is reason to believe that Ball's public taunt at de Gaulle as a man who represented Europe's calamitous past was the straw that broke the camel's back, for on May 4, Johnson instructed Rusk and McNamara that he wished "the articulation of our position with respect to NATO to be in constructive terms. [...] Our task is to rebuild NATO outside of France as promptly, economically, and effectively as possible."[120] Rebuilding NATO without France required a less confrontational stance toward de Gaulle than Ball's inclinations and persuasions permitted – adding further to the "increasing futility" of Ball's opinions within the administration.[121]

Negotiating the Terms of Separation

Johnson had thus marked the playing field by resisting the State Department's advocacy for a strong rebuke. The presidential exchange of letters between France and the United States of March 1966 set the tone. De Gaulle's decision could not be revoked; Johnson refused to be provoked.

But Johnson's reply was also just the beginning of drawn-out and complicated negotiations about the exact terms of separation. French participation in NATO's integrated military structure, American forces and allied facilities in France, and French forces in Germany were too entwined to be separated in one clean stroke. These negotiations still allowed for either firm or lenient approaches, and Johnson would have to involve himself on a number of occasions to determine the American negotiating stance. The line-up in Washington on these occasions would be a familiar one. The posse at the State Department, headed by Rusk and Ball and shored up by Acheson and McCloy (both of whom were intimately involved in the negotiations), continued to press for a hard line toward de Gaulle. Fearing that de Gaulle's preference for bilateral relationships would gain currency over the multilateral approach associated with the American-made postwar international order, it focused on defending NATO's integrated military structure and on imposing a heavy political and economic price on France for leaving it.

The White House staff, however, which now included Rostow as Bundy's successor, favored pragmatism and flexibility. A provocative negotiating stance, Rostow and Bator feared, would shift the blame for the crisis from Paris to Washington. They also believed that the "Fourteen" – i.e. all allies other than France – would remain united only as long as "our position vis-à-vis the French appear[s] to others as reasonable on its own merits." It was, in their opinion, imperative to "minimize the strain on German politics" and keep "the Franco-German rift to a minimum," above all by resolving the thorny issue of French troops in Germany as quickly and quietly as possible. Rostow moreover viewed the crisis as a window of opportunity to "make clear our commitment to an evolving constructive NATO, which can serve as a base for a policy of bridge-building to the East."[122] With Secretary of Defense McNamara a dispassionate participant in the discussions – the Pentagon simply wanted to adjust the posture and the organization as quickly as possible – the debate within the Johnson administration about the terms of separation was hence mostly waged between the State Department and the White House.

The first issue that had to be resolved in the withdrawal negotiations concerned the relocation of allied troops and facilities from France. The French government, in its aide-mémoire of March 29, had established April 1, 1967, as the date by which NATO's facilities – such as SHAPE, Central Europe Command, and NATO's Defense College – and all American troops and facilities had to be moved.[123] Deputy Secretary of Defense Cyrus Vance had already assured Johnson that the American military could indeed be relocated by March 1967 and that the costs, estimated at roughly $700 million, could be significantly reduced if the relocation was used to improve efficiency.[124] And in May, McNamara officially notified Johnson that he was ready to move American forces and facilities "as promptly as practicable."[125] George Ball nonetheless had been making preparations at the State Department for a "very hard line" in response to de Gaulle's requirement.[126] And Rusk was poised to ask de Gaulle whether by insisting that all American soldiers would have to leave France he also meant those soldiers who were lying dead in military cemeteries on French soil.[127] By late May, the State Department had consequently drafted "another tough U.S. note to de Gaulle."

Once again, however, Johnson foiled the confrontational designs of the State Department. Knowing full well that this would "raise hell over at State, where all, including Sect. Rusk, feel strongly about the clarity of the historical record," the president ruled against any delaying tactics.[128] Johnson was immovable: the American army was to have withdrawn from France before the deadline that de Gaulle had set. "When a man tells you to leave his house," he impressed on his advisers, "you tip your hat and go."[129] This would remain his basic attitude. At a meeting of the National Security Council in December 1966, McNamara said that ninety percent of American personnel would have left France by the deadline and that the remainder would follow by mid-summer. But Johnson insisted that the deadline be fully met:

Let us get out rather than be pushed out by de Gaulle. [...] If we cannot meet the French deadline for withdrawal, we should avoid a public fight about it if we can. [...] We should do our very best to comply with de Gaulle's request that we leave – even if it means putting men in inadequate housing during winter.[130]

In all, more than 60,000 people and 813,000 tons of material were removed from France within a year.[131] "For the record," the American military reported to Johnson, "we did meet the 31 March 1967 deadline. All operational units and headquarters were out of France and operational elsewhere by that date. All material and personnel that were scheduled to be out by 31 March were, in fact, out." Ironically, the American withdrawal from France – "one of the most unique politico-military operations of modern times" – thus ended on a note of pride.[132]

The second issue revolved around the status of France's military contribution to the Western alliance. De Gaulle was realistic enough to understand that NATO was not going to disappear only because France was retreating from it. Even from his damning perspective, NATO was moreover still indispensable as a framework for German rearmament; "a simple respect for General de Gaulle's intelligence," McGeorge Bundy therefore slyly noted during a congressional hearing, "suggests [...] that he has asked SACEUR to leave France only because he is confident that his example will not be followed."[133] As NATO was there to stay and France would continue to be party to the North Atlantic Treaty, a way had to be found to put military cooperation between France and NATO on a new footing.

Redefining the status of French forces in Germany certainly was the trickiest aspect of this issue. These forces comprised about 76,000 military, which included two army divisions, two wings of fighter aircraft, and two Nike missile battalions. On March 10, in its aide mémoire, the French government proposed to establish liaisons between the French command and NATO "as well as to determine the conditions under which the French forces, particularly in Germany, would participate in time of war, if Article 5 of the Washington Treaty were to be invoked, in joint military actions, both with respect to the command and to the operations themselves."[134] In its aide mémoire of March 29, Paris forced the issue to a head by ordaining that the assignment to NATO of French forces in Germany would end as soon as July 1, 1966.

There was little question within the Johnson administration that all American nuclear support for French forces would have to be withdrawn once they were withdrawn from NATO.[135] But the continuing presence of French forces on German soil posed much more difficult questions. It was "our toughest problem on the table," Bator informed Johnson, since "the terms on which they remain, or are withdrawn, will deeply affect French-German relations [...]."[136] The issue was potentially explosive in German politics. Without a new agreement, the continuing presence of French troops in Germany "would smell of occupation" if they were not part of NATO.[137] Most German politicians also objected to the diminution of the NATO framework, which had allowed for German rearmament. At the same time, however, there was a widespread wariness about alienating the French.[138] Strikingly, the question of French forces in Germany was hardly considered consequential from a military point of view. "The French forces are almost all reserve divisions, far back from the line, and not effectively trained, manned and equipped by U.S. standards," the American negotiating instructions judged; "in a completely 'unattached' condition and without the assignment of U.S. nuclear weapons [they] would have a minus military value if any."[139]

In early April, after a six-hour cabinet meeting, Chancellor Erhard rejected the French position that its troops in West Germany and assigned to NATO could remain there without a new agreement defining their legal status and their role "in the framework of the common defense of NATO."[140] Erhard hence took the position that France's withdrawal from NATO did affect its rights to station forces in Germany. These rights, Bonn argued, were based on agreements on the presence of foreign forces in Germany reached in October 1954, which had then assigned these forces to the SACEUR.[141] In an aide mémoire to France on May 3, 1966, the Erhard government moreover stated that "it makes an essential difference whether the foreign forces stationed on Federal territory are placed under a joint command in which the Federal Republic of Germany participates in an appropriate degree, or whether these forces are solely under the national command of their state of origin." It insisted that French troops could only stay if a new agreement were reached and "a satisfactory arrangement can be made for the military tasks of these forces and their functions within the framework of common defense."[142] According to the Erhard government, French troops in Germany would in some way have to fall under NATO command in time of war.

The State Department was, as was its wont, also preparing to take a very tough stance on the question whether French troops in Germany would be allowed to stay if they were not assigned to NATO. In mid-April, a trilateral working group – consisting of representatives of the United States, Great Britain, and Germany – was established in Bonn in order to develop a common position.[143] At the State Department's recommendation, Johnson picked John McCloy as his chief negotiator. McCloy was, of course, one of the "wise men" of America's bipartisan foreign policy establishment and a favored troubleshooter of both Democratic and Republican administrations; he was also a valid choice given his formidable reputation in Germany as the United States' former High Commissioner to occupied Germany from 1949 to 1952, when he had wielded near dictatorial powers over millions of Germans. But, as a staunch Atlanticist and Jean Monnet European, McCloy could above all be counted upon by those who wanted to take a very tough line with the French. The corporate lawyer from New York had, as we have seen in the previous chapter, been dismayed by Johnson's decision in December 1964 to back down on the MLF. He was also deeply concerned about the

crisis in NATO – and, fearing that the Johnson administration was far too absorbed with the Vietnam War, he was actively lobbying in Washington and elsewhere for action to halt the disintegration of NATO. After his appointment,
McCloy indeed immediately urged Erhard to be hard-hitting with de Gaulle, assuring the chancellor that the United States would support any position that "recognized the seriousness of the situation and provided an adequate response to
the French."[144] Once again, with the arrival of McCloy on the negotiating scene,
Germany had become the pivot of Franco-American differences.[145]

The trilateral working group indeed took a tough negotiating position in May
by "insisting that the French publicly undertake a commitment to assign these
troops to NATO when those members of the Alliance with troops in Germany
agree that a state of emergency exists." De Gaulle, assessed Rostow and Bator,
was "asked to give up a veto which he now holds [...] and to undertake a commitment formally tougher than [...] ours."[146] McCloy had also already agreed with
German Foreign Minister Gerhard Schroeder that if France had not reached a
new agreement with Germany before July 1, or had at least agreed to leave French
troops in Germany under NATO command pending a satisfactory arrangement,
French troops would be required to begin their withdrawal.[147]

In the White House, however, feelings were much less adamant than at the
State Department. Bator had already cautioned in March against "our natural tendency [...] to discourage any special bilateral arrangement, for fear of setting a
bad precedent in further fragmenting the Alliance." In his view, "there is a danger
that if we discourage them [the Germans] from trying to work out a deal with the
French, we will get the blame in Germany and the rest of Europe for driving the
French out."[148] And in May, Bator – now seconded by Rostow – judged that the
working group's position was at heart untenable and therefore should be seen as
little more than a negotiating ploy: "Nobody thinks de Gaulle will agree to this; it
is meant as an opening tactic from which we are willing to retreat. [...] we must
avoid being subject to the charge that we presented impossible conditions to the
French and that de Gaulle's negative response is justified."[149] As before, the
White House was above all determined to avoid becoming the culprit of the
NATO crisis by seeking confrontation with the French.

De Gaulle called the bluff. The working group's position had been conveyed to
France in a memorandum of the German government on May 3. In a succinct
reply on May 18, the French government simply discounted the legal aspects of
the case. Instead, it deftly raised the issue to a political plane by asking whether
"the Government of the Federal Republic desires the maintenance of the French
forces on its territory"; if not, France would be ready to withdraw its forces within
one year.[150] De Gaulle amplified this message by deciding to withdraw the French
fighter jet squadrons based in Germany. On June 13, he also stated to Bohlen that
"in truth [...] France did not really wish to keep her forces in Germany" and that

"objectively it would be better if the French troops were back in France."[151] In sum, de Gaulle was not going to be the *demandeur* in this crisis.

The French position put the onus back on the German government. The strongly Atlanticist Schroeder continued to favor a tough stance, insisting on a NATO framework for the continued presence of French troops. Erhard, however, much to McCloy's dismay, was reluctant to sacrifice French-German relations on the altar of NATO. On May 26, the German chancellor informed the Bundestag that West Germany "unequivocally" wanted the French forces to stay.[152] De Gaulle had won the day: his negotiating position was now significantly strengthened. Throughout June, NATO proposed a variety of arrangements for French forces in Germany, all of which were rejected by Paris.[153] When the French were making preparations to pull out forces from Germany, Erhard quickly came to terms with Paris on an interim agreement that allowed French forces to stay beyond July 1.[154] At the end of July, talks on a permanent arrangement reached a deadlock. American diplomats above all blamed Erhard's weakness for the state of affairs, since he had given de Gaulle the impression that Bonn "would never invite the French troops to leave."[155] In doing so, they closed their eyes to the fact that their diplomat-in-chief in the White House had had no desire to force the issue to a head either.

The status of French forces in Germany was finally resolved at the military level. Having reached a deadlock at the political level, the Erhard government decided to authorize the SACEUR, General Lyman Lemnitzer, to confer with the French chief of staff, General Charles Ailleret, about the extent to which French forces might be prepared to cooperate with NATO. German attempts, backed up by the United States, to issue instructions to the two generals concerning certain minimum assumptions on the nature of French military cooperation both in war and in peace – including the assumption that French forces would serve under NATO command if France should enter a war under Article 5 of the Treaty – were rejected out of hand by Paris. It took until the end of October before Lemnitzer was finally authorized to begin his talks with Ailleret without any preconditions.[156] Meanwhile, the French and the Germans had also engaged in bilateral discussions on a legal basis governing the status of French forces in Germany. Discussions continued without result until the Erhard government was replaced by the "grand coalition" of CDU and SPD headed by Chancellor Kurt Georg Kiesinger and Foreign Minister Willy Brandt in early December. Two weeks later, Brandt and Couve de Murville settled the issue with a simple exchange of letters. They circumvented the legal problem by stating that the agreements regarding the presence of foreign forces in Germany reached in October 1954 did "not rule out" the continued presence of French forces. In the end, no military or political conditions were attached to the continued presence of French troops on German soil – indeed, as one study noted, "a total victory for the French negotiating position."[157]

On most other issues connected with the French withdrawal from NATO, de Gaulle's intransigence equally won out. This was the case with regard to the possibility of a re-entry of American forces into France in the event of war or of an emergency such as the Berlin Crisis – a subject that Ambassador Bohlen discussed a number of times with Couve de Murville. De Gaulle, however, was immovable in his position that a re-entry would not be possible except after a declaration of war by France. Neither was he prepared to allow any American military stocks or equipment to remain in France, even under French custody, or for any American military personnel to remain on a contingency basis.[158]

On some other issues, the predilection in the White House to forestall "another public show" conspired with French military interests to devise a pragmatic way out.[159] France had, for instance, decided to put authorizations for overflights by foreign military aircraft on a monthly basis, which presented a hassle to the NATO allies who needed French air space. The resolution of this issue was possible because France had an interest in continued access to the early warning information provided by NATO's air defense system (NADGE), on which the credibility of the *force de frappe* depended. The bargain: the NATO allies would be permitted to continue their military overflights in return for continued French access to NADGE. The French were also prepared to permit the continued use of the Donges-Metz petroleum pipeline and certain telecommunications facilities in peacetime, provided that they were placed under French management. Although they could give no assurance that these facilities would be available in wartime, since France may decide not to participate in a war in which the rest of NATO is engaged, the White House concluded that it would be better to have "something less than an ironclad agreement than none at all."[160]

Re-inventing NATO

Institutional Adaptations

The French withdrawal from NATO caused changes in the organization of the alliance that still define it today. On July 1, 1966, all French military personnel withdrew from NATO's military headquarters. France, however, continued to be represented in the North Atlantic Council. SHAPE, with a staff of about 3,000, was relocated to Casteau in Belgium; AFCENT (staff of about 2,000) was relocated to Brunssum in the Netherlands; the International Staff (1,000) was moved to Brussels; and NATO's Defense College went to Rome. The Washington-based Standing Group – consisting of American, British, and French military representatives – was replaced by an International Military Staff located in Brussels. The most politically sensitive decision concerned moving the seat of the North Atlantic Council from Paris to Brussels. The Johnson administration insisted that the collocation of the political and military councils of the alliance was essential; the move, Washington pointed out, was also necessary because France had made clear that it might not support NATO in the event of war. Some allies were hesitant, but since France assumed a decidedly indifferent stance, agreement could be reached. Indications from a "sensitive" source at the Quai d'Orsay that de Gaulle had decided to request the Council to leave Paris after the legislative elections in March 1967 may also have contributed to the decision.[161] In early November 1966, the Council – with French acquiescence – broadened the responsibilities of the Defense Planning Committee (DPC), which had been set up in 1963 to oversee NATO's force planning, to handle all alliance matters in which France would not be included. One of its first decisions was to transfer the Military Committee from Washington to Brussels.

The short of all this was that NATO could continue to function without French military participation and that Brussels became its indisputable executive hub. On the eve of NATO Secretary General Manlio Brosio's visit to Washington in mid-November, the State Department concluded:

> The process of developing a new role for France in the Alliance [...] has caused less pain and disruption than might have been expected. The changes taking place can be characterized as pragmatic and evolutionary in nature. [...] France has been reasonably cooperative in accepting arrangements by the Fourteen for conducting that business of the Alliance in which France does not participate.[162]

At the NATO ministerial meeting of mid-December, the Johnson administration could therefore present the picture of a revitalized organization which had surmounted the crisis caused by France's withdrawal.

Solving the Nuclear Conundrum

More important than this institutional renewal was that the happenstance of France's withdrawal from NATO, the increased interest in negotiating a nuclear non-proliferation treaty with the Soviet Union, and the change of government in Germany produced a way out of the nuclear-sharing problem that had been haunting NATO since the 1950s.

In the wake of the French withdrawal, the White House staff feared that the State Department would try to breathe new life into the MLF or similar nuclear projects.[163] De Gaulle's move against NATO indeed galvanized the State Department once again behind a "hardware approach" to nuclear sharing as a way to tie Germany more firmly to the West. It tried in particular to get Johnson to pressure Wilson to be forthcoming to Erhard along the lines of his erstwhile proposal for an Atlantic Nuclear Force. Such attempts, however, were successfully aborted by the White House staff, where Bator had assumed the role of Johnson's watchdog.[164] National Security Action Memorandum 345 (NSAM 345) of April 22 quickly put an end to the State Department's efforts. Johnson instructed his advisers to come up instead with proposals to enhance the participation of the allies in nuclear planning. NSAM 345 placed particular emphasis on the establishment of "a permanent body of restricted membership within NATO with functions including both intensified consultation and the direction of U.S. and U.K. nuclear weapons and delivery vehicles assigned to NATO and/or collectively owned." While two alternative approaches were to be considered – "one of which assumes the creation of a 'NATO nuclear force' and one which does not" – it closed the door for the "MLF-ites" by stipulating that any "NATO nuclear force" would not consist of mixed-manned submarines or a surface fleet with nuclear weapons.[165]

By the fall of 1966, the Select Committee that had been established in December 1965 at McNamara's initiative was beginning to yield results. In preparation of the customary ministerial NATO meetings in December, it recommended the establishment of a ministerial Nuclear Defense Affairs Committee (NDAC) and a subordinate Nuclear Planning Group (NPG) for the purpose of consulting on nuclear policies. Membership of the NPG was the most difficult issue to resolve. Whereas the NDAC would be open to any ally, membership of the NPG would be limited to four permanent members – the United States, Great Britain, Germany, and Italy – and two members to be chosen for one-year terms on a rotational basis. Some allies – in particular Canada, Greece, the Netherlands, and Turkey – naturally resented the rotational formula, which forced them to vie for membership during the NPG's first year.[166] But the "Johnson breakthrough" in the nuclear realm that McGeorge Bundy had been hoping for in November 1965 was nonetheless close at hand. At a meeting of the National Security Council on December 13, 1966, McNamara asserted that the new nuclear consultation mechanisms would in particular meet the needs of the new German government, thus ending all talk of the MLF or ANF.[167] "If I could do things differently," McNamara later said, "I would have introduced the Nuclear Planning Group much earlier than I did as a means to draw the Europeans into nuclear affairs."[168]

The changes on the German domestic front in 1966 had been a decisive factor in improving the chances of a solution to the nuclear issue within NATO along the lines of McNamara's proposal. Having talked to a great number of German politicians and officials in early 1966, Henry Kissinger concluded that "outside the Foreign Office not a *single* leading German political figure – including the Chancellor – indicated any desire for the hardware solution" and "*every* significant German political figure believed that top priority should be given to improved consultation."[169] There were, however, still qualms about a non-proliferation treaty, which was interpreted as being primarily aimed against Germany. Many Germans underscored that their renunciation of nuclear weapons in 1954 had been conditional on the pledge of the Western allies to strive for German unification; if this renunciation were to be extended to Eastern Europe, these Germans pointed out, it would have to be accompanied by similar Soviet pledges. As Bator argued in a memorandum to Johnson in April 1966, in order to solve the nuclear conundrum the Germans had to take the "hardest" step "unilaterally to renounce collective as well as national ownership of nuclear weapons, and to justify this as an essential step toward non-proliferation, world-wide arms control, a European settlement, and unification."[170]

On December 1, Kurt Georg Kiesinger replaced Ludwig Erhard to become chancellor of the "grand coalition" between CDU/CSU and SPD. Willy Brandt, the charismatic vice chancellor and foreign minister, effected important changes in German foreign policy. During the election campaign, the SPD's new leader – Brandt had succeeded Erich Ollenhauer as party secretary in 1964 – had declared support for a non-proliferation treaty and avowed that with the SPD at the helm, Germany would not continue to insist on co-ownership or joint control of nuclear weapons. More importantly, Brandt sought to strike a decidedly more conciliatory tone with the communist bloc than either Adenauer or Erhard, both of whom had looked exclusively to the West for political sustenance. Reflecting the growing acceptance of East Germany as a fact of life, he argued in particular that it would be best not to ignore the other Germany's existence – which was the core of the Hallstein Doctrine that governed German foreign policy since 1955[171] – but to try to transform it through rapprochement (Wandel durch Annäherung). Brandt's anti-Communist credentials were impeccable due to his firmness vis-à-vis the Soviets as mayor of Berlin in the difficult years from 1957 to 1966, but he had increasingly come to believe in the benefits of an "open door policy in human and cultural contacts" with Eastern Europe.[172] His vision of rapprochement with East Germany – in particular at the societal level and economically – was becoming increasingly influential in German political circles (not just within the SPD). It appealed at the same time to those who favored peaceful coexistence of the two Germanys and relaxation of the Cold War, those who believed that Germans had morally forfeited the right to live in a unified state, those who hoped to speed up the demise of the East German regime from within, and those who wanted to forestall an economic collapse in East Germany because this would make reunification harder to achieve. From the American perspective, meanwhile, Brandt's arrival on the NATO scene in December 1966 made it both easier to solve the nuclear discord within the alliance and more pertinent to usher in a less confrontational approach to the Cold War. As Secretary Rusk cabled President Johnson from Paris:

One of the most important developments here has been Willy Brandt's reaction to non-proliferation. The present German government is ready to forget "hardware" and Brandt told me to forget the European clause. [...] Brandt made a major impression on NATO in demonstrating that the new German government will not be bound by the rigid theology of the Adenauer period and is prepared to probe the possibilities of better relations with Eastern

Europe, including the East Germans. This may not move us forward, but twenty years of hostile confrontation has not done so and I believe that we should give them a chance to find out whether another approach might produce more results.[173]

The new role given to the ministerial Defense Planning Committee had allowed for circumventing France when NATO's foreign and defense ministers met on December 14. In this format they agreed to the formation of the NPG and the NDAC for nuclear planning and consultation. Six months later, in May 1967, NATO's defense ministers also finally adopted flexible response as NATO's official strategy, "after six years of often acrimonious debate."[174] By this time, however, the attention of the alliance had shifted from strengthening the defense of the West to pursuing détente with the East.

Towards a Policy of Détente

Before Brandt laid the foundations of his Ostpolitik as foreign minister of the "grand coalition," de Gaulle – as we have seen – had already been looking for a systemic rapprochement with the communist bloc. In 1966, French contacts with the Soviet Union actually reached a peak. On March 29, Soviet leader Leonid · Brezhnev hailed Franco-Soviet relations at the opening session of the 23rd Congress of the Soviet Communist Party. In the spring and summer of 1966, Foreign Minister Couve de Murville paid subsequent visits to Bulgaria, Poland, Czechoslovakia, and Hungary. On May 31, the French carmaker Renault announced that it had agreed to rebuild the Moskvich car plant in Moscow, raising its production capacity from 90,000 cars annually to more than 300,000. On June 20, de Gaulle began an eleven-day visit to the Soviet Union at the end of which he agreed with his Soviet hosts to establish a "hot line" between Moscow and Paris. And in December 1966, Soviet Prime Minister Alexei Kosygin paid a return visit to France to conclude an agreement on Franco-Soviet collaboration in economic, scientific, and technological areas.

In the American media, de Gaulle's rapprochement to communist Eastern Europe and his visit to Moscow a few months after the French withdrawal from NATO heightened speculations about a reversal of alliances. But in American government circles an entente between Paris and Moscow beyond the pomp and ceremony of state visits and bilateral cooperation in strictly confined areas was considered remote.

In particular, the CIA stressed the limitations of Franco-Soviet conciliation in a number of reports on Franco-Soviet rapprochement. While the Soviet leadership was certainly pleased by the division in the Western camp and for this reason alone was quite ready to court de Gaulle, it was also – judged the CIA – very cautious and all the while kept "a watchful eye on Washington and Bonn." Moscow and Paris shared a fear of German ascendancy in Europe. They supported similar approaches to the most important unresolved border problem in Europe, being prepared to accept the Oder-Neisse rivers as the permanent boundary between East Germany and Poland, whereas Washington and Bonn always insisted that the eastern border of a reunified Germany should be determined in the framework of an overall settlement. But the issue of German reunification was also the main obstacle to a real entente. Moscow might have hoped to get de Gaulle's acknowledgment of the status quo of a divided Germany, for instance by officially recognizing East Germany. De Gaulle, however, was not prepared to break with the Western position in support of German reunification, although he clearly regarded it as a long-term objective. Moscow was moreover keenly aware that de Gaulle carried little weight as a mediator, recognizing that it would ultimately have to deal with the United States rather than France. In the CIA's view, the Soviet Union even feared that de Gaulle's attack against NATO would "result in a reduction of American influence to an undesirable degree."

> Although Moscow long has made the "Bonn-Washington axis" its bête noire, to some extent it welcomes the ties between the two capitals as a restraint on West German "revanchism". Despite their fears that the West German tail will somehow wag the American dog, the Soviets would not be likely to look with equanimity upon a total disintegration of NATO and an end to the American role in Europe.[175]

Paradoxically, the Soviet reaction to the French withdrawal from NATO was thus rather guarded.

So when de Gaulle departed for his state visit to the Soviet Union in June, Washington did not anticipate any breakthroughs – least of all a reversal of alliances. De Gaulle had also tried to lay American concerns to rest. Prior to his departure, he had discussed his visit with Ambassador Bohlen. De Gaulle was convinced that the Soviet Union was seeking a détente in East-West relations and that it was in the interest of the West to support this. However, he also recognized that Moscow wanted "some recognition of the two Germanys," and he assured Bohlen that he "would not take any official action that appears to confirm it." De Gaulle regarded his visit as mostly of symbolic significance. "The only thing that he might conceivably obtain in Russia was some indication of reunification as a very long range aim," Bohlen reported to the State Department.[176]

De Gaulle's ten-day visit to the Soviet Union indeed turned out to be an exuberant display of public cordiality notably short on achievement. The French president was frequently given opportunity to speak in public to large crowds and even delivered a statement on Soviet television. He was the first Westerner to be allowed to the Tyuratam site, in order to witness launches of a satellite and an intercontinental ballistic missile. For the most part, de Gaulle responded in kind. He referred to the historical ties between the two countries and hailed the achievements of the Soviet Union. At times, however, he ignored the sensitivities of his hosts by speaking of "Russia" instead of the Soviet Union and by describing France as "a country of freedom." More importantly, there was no serious discussion of outstanding East-West issues or any rapprochement with regard to Germany.[177] As Walt Rostow informed President Johnson after de Gaulle's encounter with Brezhnev: "It is clear that each of these men is trying to use the other; but basically there is little give in Moscow on the gut issue, namely German reunification."[178]

It should be noted that the Johnson administration was not at all averse to the notion of détente with the communist bloc, despite the war in Vietnam. On the contrary, there were few issues that Johnson was more interested in than in improving relations with the Soviet Union and diminishing the threat of nuclear war.[179] Rostow has even observed that Johnson saw the United States and the Soviet Union as "the two eldest children in a large family [...] with the responsibility for keeping peace and order in the family."[180] The idea of "building bridges" with Eastern Europe – albeit excluding the Soviet Union – had figured prominently in Johnson's speech in Lexington, Virginia, on May 23, 1964. "We will continue to build bridges across the gulf which has divided us from Eastern Europe," said Johnson. "They will be bridges of increased trade, of ideas, of visitors, and of humanitarian aid." Shortly after this speech, Johnson had instructed the State Department to develop specific programs to this end.[181] In 1966, the increasing popularity of the politics of détente in Western Europe combined with the need to take the wind out of de Gaulle's sails and to be seen as responsive to German desires made it the more incumbent on Washington to demonstrate support for a relaxation of attitudes towards the Soviet bloc. Besides proposals for nuclear consultation, NSAM 345 therefore asked for "constructive political, diplomatic, and economic initiatives addressed to Eastern Europe and the Soviet Union" and "other forward looking proposals that would increase the cohesion of NATO and the North Atlantic community."[182]

Successive American administrations had until then held that a settlement that arranged for the reunification of Germany had to precede détente with the Soviet Union. The reversal of this order to a détente-settlement sequence was the key to entering a new phase in East-West relations. There are indications that de Gaulle's decision to withdraw France from NATO and his overtures toward Eastern Europe helped Johnson to make the definitive shift towards détente politics in the summer of 1966. In the spring, most of his advisers came to agree that the president should give a substantive speech on American policy toward Europe – "so de Gaulle does not look like the wave of the future" – and that this speech should be held "not too soon after de Gaulle's return from Moscow nor during the August holidays in Europe."[183] Throughout the summer and early fall, the State Department and the White House worked frenetically on a major presidential policy speech. The groundwork for the speech was laid in NSAM 352 of July 8, in which Johnson "instructed that – in consultation with our Allies – we actively develop areas of peaceful cooperation with the nations of Eastern Europe and the Soviet Union" and, importantly, that "these actions will be designed *to help create an environment in which peaceful settlement of the division of Germany and of Europe will become possible*"[184] (emphasis added). The speech's principal objective, however, as Rostow underlined, was to manifest the United States' continuing interest in European affairs "at a moment when our noises tend to be Asian" and to express "a doctrine congenial in Europe" but "different from de Gaulle's [...]."[185]

Johnson's speech to the National Conference of Editorial Writers of October 7, 1966, incontrovertibly committed the United States to a policy of seeking relaxation in the Cold War relationship with the Soviet Union. The president argued that Europe's division could only be overcome if East and West "succeed in building a surer foundation of trust":

> We must improve the East-West environment in order to achieve the unification of Germany [...]. Our task is to achieve a reconciliation with the East – a shift from the narrow concept of coexistence to the broader vision of peaceful engagement.[186]

By stating his opposition to any change by force of existing borders in Europe, Johnson also very carefully meant to convey that in the American view this applied as well to the existing Oder-Neisse border between Poland and Germany. In addition, Johnson emphasized that he wanted to forge ahead on a non-proliferation treaty with the Soviet Union.

While the Johnson administration thus came out in favor of a détente in East-West relations, it was equally preoccupied with safeguarding NATO's relevance and military muscle. For it faced the following dilemma: how to engage in a more constructive relationship with the Soviet Union while avoiding the delusion that peace was just around the corner, which could beguile the Western alliance into letting down its defensive guard. It was in this vein that Walt Rostow, one of the principal advocates of détente politics within the Johnson administration, had counseled Johnson in June 1966. Rostow:

> [...] on East/West matters we wish to do as much as is sensible to do, but we must always remember that the limit on what we can do is largely set by changing attitudes in Moscow and Moscow's commitment to keep East Germany tightly as a satellite. It is the plug in their whole security and ideological system. That system is now changing; but we have no evidence other than that it will change slowly [...].

Johnson's national security adviser hence cautioned that the effort to improve relations with the Soviet Union should not tempt the United States into a "casual" approach to maintaining and strengthening the Atlantic alliance.[187]

Rostow's unease was undoubtedly fed by evidence of a slackening in defense efforts among the European allies. For one, this slackening rendered Kennedy's strategy of flexible response ever more chimerical. As an internal report on NATO's force levels assessed, the effect of détente on the alliance's military strategy and wherewithal was undeniable:

> The changes that have taken place in East-West relations in Europe have made it more unlikely than ever that NATO will make the effort to improve its conventional capabilities. Because of this, and because the underlying changes have affected us as well as Europeans, the U.S. should rethink its basic concepts of military strategy and the role of NATO military forces. [...] Europe thinks that US and USSR have neutralized each other's nuclear strategic forces. Just as importantly, Europe sees the Soviet Union going through a process of embourgeoisement which makes preposterous the idea of communist holy wars in Europe. [...] In this environment, the Europeans generally are no more concerned than they ever have been with the war fighting capability of NATO's forces.[188]

Détente, however, not only gave occasion to a weaker European defense effort. It also encouraged those in the United States who were looking for a reduction of American forces in Europe to try their chance. For this report was not merely a complaint about European credulity about the Soviet Union. It also posited that indeed "a case can be made for abandoning the effort to develop a NATO conventional capability sufficient to withstand a full-scale Warsaw pact conventional attack." This, in turn, would "permit the U.S. to withdraw some combat forces from Europe."[189]

Harlan Cleveland shared Rostow's apprehension that détente could gradually undercut the strength and the cohesion of the Western alliance. In November 1966, in a memorandum that was widely distributed at the top levels of government, the American ambassador to NATO declared that détente – albeit politically alluring – was in reality "dangerous business." Cleveland in particular stressed the need for the United States to retain firm control over the détente politics of the European allies. In this respect, he reasoned, Washington and Moscow were actually in the same boat. The two superpowers had a common interest in maintaining stability in Europe and in ensuring that "the guiding influence in defining a new 'climate of relations' is US-Soviet and not, say, French-Romanian." Cleveland's logic was illustrative of the United States' hard-edged approach to détente:

the US and the USSR have a common interest in seeing to it that the scope and the pace of change does not get out of hand – that Europe, West and East, does not revert to its hallowed tradition of separatism, violence and war – that the stability attained by the two "hegemonies" (forgive the expression) is not sacrificed to "East-West relations," which really have no important content except in a US-Soviet context. In short, the process of "détente" should, first of all, be within a framework acceptable to the US and the USSR – acceptable because of a perceived common interest in not abruptly or radically de-stabilizing the situation surrounding their perceived national strategic interests. [Cleveland believed that] – rather than abolishing the two alliances – both "blocs" should mutate in characteristic fashion and engage in mutually valuable intercourse until the time comes when it seems unimportant to keep open the old political sores.[190]

De Gaulle's independent search for détente and for an end to the Cold War hence did not fit in with the hegemon's approach. By implication, Cleveland believed that such self-regulating policies of European allies would lead to political instability which, given Europe's violent history, could only be more dangerous than the bipolar standoff of the Cold War.

This was the background to what one student of the period has aptly characterized as the "multilateralization of détente" in the so-called Harmel Report of December 1967.[191] At various times, one or the other ally had suggested a reappraisal of NATO's future, similar to the Report of the Three Wise Men in the aftermath of the Suez Crisis in 1956.[192] The time never seemed ripe, however, until the French withdrawal served as a catalyst. The practical necessity of adjusting to the French withdrawal combined with the political need to counter de Gaulle's condemnation of the organization finally provided a compelling rationale. A renewed consideration of NATO's purposes had moreover become the more desirable in view of the groundswell in support of détente and the short time remaining until 1969, the year in which member states were entitled to withdraw from the Treaty. NATO was seen by most Europeans as a Cold War institution *par excellence* – de Gaulle was hardly alone in this respect. In order to re-establish it as an instrument of Western policy commanding popular support, its military purpose of deterring the Soviet military threat had to be reconciled with the growing desire to "build bridges" with the opponent. So when, in the fall of 1966, Belgian Foreign Minister Pierre Harmel proposed a fundamental review of NATO's future tasks, this fell on fertile ground – and the North Atlantic Council agreed in December that it should be undertaken.

In November 1966, when Harmel first approached Washington about his initiative, it was agreed that the most important aim of the study would be to underscore the continued relevance of NATO "against the background of [the] French withdrawal and [the] approach of 1969."[193] The Harmel exercise is indeed often

RE-INVENTING NATO

credited for reinstating NATO's sense of purpose after France's dramatic withdrawal in 1966, primarily by resting its future significance on the "not contradictory but complementary" objectives of military security and détente. Speaking to his colleagues in the North Atlantic Council of December 1967, Harmel concluded that the study had "highlighted that the Alliance had developed stabilising effects vis-à-vis the outside world and amongst its own members." And Rusk declared that the exercise itself had reaffirmed the validity of NATO's political role: "[T]he most important thing had been the process of the Study itself involving intense consultations among governments."[194]

But the significance of the Harmel exercise for NATO does not point in one direction only. The Harmel Report itself, which was bland in its recommendations, had not come about with the close involvement of government leaders. President Johnson, for instance, as Rusk later clarified, "didn't take much interest in the Harmel exercise because it was not that sufficiently important."[195] More importantly, the exercise is, on closer scrutiny, also of interest for its revelation, "through the extensive and often heated process of developing the study," of the widely divergent views among the allies on core issues.[196]

As part of the Harmel exercise within NATO, four working groups were formed in the spring of 1967, each assigned to a broad topic and chaired by a rapporteur of certain repute. The first working group, on East-West relations, rapidly agreed that "détente management" should be a second rationale for the alliance since its first rationale – to provide an effective military deterrent – "was not sufficiently understood, especially by young people."[197] But beyond this rather general notion, which would form the core of the Harmel Report, views on how to pursue détente diverged considerably. Some members – such as Great Britain, Norway, Denmark, and Canada – insisted that the alliance *as a whole* develop initiatives toward a European settlement with the Soviet Union, which would truly have multilateralized the politics of détente. Yet France, protective of its independence from the United States, was determined to preserve its bilateral policies toward the Communist bloc, and it feared an erosion of four-power responsibility for Berlin. Regardless of Brandt's insistence that "the East/West discussions should go on within the framework of the alliance,"[198] the Harmel Report therefore fell short of proposing a new NATO machinery to deal with East-West relations. It merely noted – by way of compromise – that "both bilateral and multilateral contacts will be needed" to reach a European settlement and that "each Ally should play its full part in promoting an improvement in relations with the Soviet Union and the countries of Eastern Europe, bearing in mind that the pursuit of détente must not be allowed to split the Alliance."[199]

The second working group, on intra-alliance relations, was "racked with dissension."[200] It was chaired by Paul-Henri Spaak, the outspoken former NATO secretary general from Belgium, who had submitted a forceful and highly personal paper as the basis for discussions.[201] Besides taking issue with de Gaulle's foreign policy, Spaak advocated common NATO policies on a wide range of non-military issues as well as further progress towards European unity. His paper contained many references to the 1956 report of the Three Wise Men, which had already called for "a significant strengthening of political consultation" within NATO. The French delegate, Jacques Schricke, vehemently objected to Spaak's Atlanticist sermons right from the outset. As Spaak refused to change his paper, however, his working group broke up without approving anything.[202]

In the fourth working group, on developments beyond the NATO area, dissension was also rampant. The Dutch rapporteur of this group, Constantijn Patijn, an international law expert and former parliamentarian, provoked the wrath of France and "at least five other NATO members" by writing that "NATO's task beyond the Treaty area is [...] to devise common policies for its members."[203] For this purpose, Patijn came up with a number of institutional proposals in order to improve political consultations within NATO in respect of global issues, such as the establishment of a planning body, small groups to study specific problems, and a NATO group within the United Nations. He received strong support from American diplomats, causing some allies to fear that the United States was above all trying to garner European support for the war in Vietnam. But with his legalistic inflexibility and lack of political finesse, Patijn failed to bring about a consensus. "Professor Patijn is full of the best intentions," one report of the working group's proceedings observed, "an idealist unencumbered by an awareness of the practical functioning of the Alliance, professorial and unfortunately unteachable."[204]

Only the discussions in the working group on general defense policies, headed by the American diplomat Foy D. Kohler, produced little controversy. It broadened the term "security policy" to cover not only defense issues but also "realistic measures to reduce tensions and the risk of conflict including arms control and disarmament measures."[205] Yet it also emphasized the unremitting value of NATO's military strength and integrated defense model. Seeking to avert a slackening of defense efforts, it made the achievement of lower force levels and lower costs contingent on arms control agreements with the Soviet Union. Kohler's report actually planted the seeds for subsequent consultations on mutual and balanced force reductions (MBFR), which proved helpful in containing public pressure for cuts in defense budgets and denied Moscow the option of simply waiting for NATO allies to diminish their forces unilaterally.[206]

France, meanwhile, voiced predictable reservations throughout the Harmel exercise. In December 1966, Couve de Murville had agreed to it on the condition that it would not result in binding recommendations for enhancing political integration within the alliance.[207] Paris's qualms about the exercise become the more serious when the four working groups' reports, in particular those of Spaak and Patijn, began to take shape. By the fall of 1967, with the "political phase" beginning after the working groups had presented their reports, Couve de Murville warned Bohlen that France would be ready for a "showdown" on the final report.[208] Paris would not accept the final report if it recommended that NATO should assume greater political responsibility or come up with a common détente policy. Eugene Rostow and Cleveland subsequently informed NATO Secretary General Manlio Brosio that the United States preferred to "stand firm and to go ahead, on the basis of the open endedness and of the empty chair, leaving to France the responsibility of drawing the ultimate formal consequences."[209] Rusk added to Harmel that "we should not let ourselves be blackmailed."[210] Robert Bowie, on assignment from the State Department, stressed that "the French were already effectively out of the Alliance," adding that as far as Washington was concerned, "the Alliance would in no way be weakened if the French were totally out."[211] Washington thus gave the impression of being ready to risk French defection from the North Atlantic Treaty in order to get what it wanted in the Harmel exercise.

The diplomatic wrangling in the final stages of the Harmel exercise brought the negotiators – faced with a disappointing outcome – to a state of mind "verging on despair," causing Cleveland to remark that the "usual wells of sympathy for French obstinacy had run dry."[212] As importantly, however, the Harmel exercise showed that the most important European allies – Germany in particular – were unwilling to confront France. A detailed account by the CIA of the Harmel exercise summarized the positions of allies as follows:

> The West Germans particularly sought to avoid any provocation of the French as they did not want to risk what they already had – an Alliance that included France, plus a recognized and proven forum for consideration of the German problem. The British [...] were worried that a dispute over it would adversely influence their Common Market membership application. The Scandinavians, while seeking a new image for NATO, indicated that innovations were a lesser concern when compared to retaining France as a counterweight to Germany in NATO. Belgium, the Netherlands, and the US were the most determined to see the study through to a successful conclusion.[213]

France finally joined in approving the Harmel Report at the ministerial meeting of December 1967, but not until all references to common NATO policies were deleted. De Gaulle had no intention of relinquishing membership of the alliance altogether; for this reason, he accepted some NATO involvement in the politics of détente, along the lines recommended by the first and third working groups. But he was not ready to accept a deepening of the institutional bonds within the Atlantic community. Hence he blocked the phalanx of Atlanticists – the likes of Spaak, Patijn, and their American supporters – that wanted to use the French withdrawal from NATO's integrated military structure to deepen political integration within the Atlantic community. The United States ended up "seeking no new commitments by any ally and [did] not contemplate an 'integrated political command structure' in the Alliance."[214] It was content with NATO's more modest regeneration as – in Kohler's words – "a locus for consultation."[215]

The Harmel exercise was significant because, as one student wrote, it "reversed the slow process of disintegration that had beset NATO since the late 1950s and that came to the fore with de Gaulle's challenge to the raison d'être of the alliance."[216] It enabled NATO to reestablish itself as an organization devoted to détente as well as to defense, thus giving evidence of its abiding political and military functions and denying de Gaulle's thesis that it had become an anachronism. It provided the indispensable multilateral context for Germany's increasing desire for rapprochement with the East in the form of Brandt's Ostpolitik; as a result, it was "instrumental in the shift from the bilateral superpower détente of 1963 to the multilateral European détente of the 1970s."[217] In pursuing détente, the allies would moreover encourage the evolution – not the breakup – of the Communist bloc, recognizing both Moscow's security interests and America's attachment to stability in Europe. At the same time, the Harmel exercise reaffirmed the political adhesion of its members to the Treaty beyond 1969. None of the Fourteen wanted to get rid of the "O" in NATO. And the fact that France agreed to the Harmel Report signaled that the alliance could still be an effective forum for reaching common positions.

Yet behind the drape of allied solidarity and unity of purpose, the Harmel exercise also showed the limitations of the alliance – in particular to those who had held such high expectations. The exercise produced no drive for deepening integration across the Atlantic, nothing that came close to Acheson's earlier cited call for a "genuine Atlantic commonwealth, in which common institutions are increasingly developed to address common problems." Interestingly, "NATO" was not mentioned once in the Harmel Report. The exercise had also shown how difficult it was to get agreement within the alliance on a common approach to détente. Even with this agreement, bilateral contacts were to remain more important than multilateral approaches. Proposals for a permanent NATO body that would deal with East-West relations went nowhere. At the urging of the French, the Harmel Report had rather emphasized that "as sovereign states the Allies are not obliged to subordinate their policies to collective decision" and that allied consultation merely enabled an ally to "decide its policy in the light of close knowledge of the problems and objectives of others."[218] Such language was not far removed from de Gaulle's narrow conception of the Atlantic alliance and a far cry from the hopeful ideas of those who had been expecting NATO to manifest itself progressively as a forum for collective decisionmaking.

The Harmel exercise furthermore showed that there was virtually no European support for the coordination of policies beyond the treaty area through NATO. In a talk with Secretary General Brosio in September, Walt Rostow and Harlan Cleveland had still held their hopes out for "some kind of a body for permanent study of a common political strategy" for the Mediterranean and the Middle East – a proposal that was prompted by the Six Days' War in the Middle East in June 1967.[219] Although the Harmel Report mentioned the Mediterranean as an area posing "special problems" to allied security, it relegated the crisis in the Middle East simply to the sphere of the United Nations. Needless to say, there was no mention whatsoever of America's military exploits on behalf of the Free World in Vietnam. On the contrary, the report's language on allied consultations regarding issues beyond the treaty area is instructive for its utter elusiveness: "In accordance with established usage the Allies, or such of them as wish to do so, will also continue to consult on such problems [outside the North Atlantic area] without commitment and as the case may demand."[220] De Gaulle had been unable to gain acceptance from Washington for his September 1958 memorandum proposal, his opening gambit for coordinating the policies of the Western alliance beyond the treaty area. He had – as we have seen – then proposed a tripartite security organization for this purpose, which would have supplanted NATO. The Harmel exercise made clear that de Gaulle was not about to accept a NATO role in this area in the aftermath of France's withdrawal from the integrated military structure.

Finally, the Harmel exercise provides further evidence of a deep-seated reluctance among European allies to isolate France, even after its withdrawal from the integrated military structure and in spite of frequent irritations with the intransigence of the French positions. The British, for instance, "did not want to see a report that was unacceptable to the French" and aimed for a result "that was neither too difficult for the French to swallow nor so weak that it would undermine the Alliance."[221] The cautious Brosio preferred "a minimum agreement on détente with the French," leaving "the machinery to a later date." And German Foreign Minister Brandt agreed that "it would not be wise to have a clash with the French in connection with the Harmel Study."[222]

In short, the history of the Harmel Report is an ambiguous one. On the one hand, it revitalized NATO after the French withdrawal and established the Johnson administration's reputation as an effective and responsive manager of the alliance. On the other hand, it was another Gaullist victory over those who continued to regard the Atlantic alliance as an increasingly important framework for collective action and policy coordination.

The Trilateral Negotiations

The story of NATO's revival under Johnson's stewardship is not complete without considering the negotiations in 1966 and 1967 between the United States, Great Britain, and Germany about the costs of maintaining troops on the German front. France was not involved in these negotiations. But the specter of a further disintegrating NATO after the French withdrawal – and consequently of leaving the European field open to de Gaulle – made it all the more incumbent on Washington to resist strong pressures to reduce the American and British troop presence in Germany.

What was at stake? In the early 1960s, in order to help maintain their troop levels in Germany, the United States and Great Britain had negotiated a series of bilateral "offset agreements" with Bonn. These agreements provided for German purchases of American and British military equipment by way of compensation for the costs of maintaining troops in Germany; the local expenses of these troops caused a heavy foreign exchange drain for the United States and Great Britain, while they produced an important windfall in foreign exchange earnings for the German economy. In the mid-1960s, however, it became increasingly clear that the German government would have difficulty continuing its purchases of American and British military equipment on a sufficiently large scale. And by 1966, the Erhard government, struggling with a budget deficit resulting from deteriorating economic conditions and increased social spending, was determined to reduce the offset payments to its Anglo-Saxon protectors.

This caused serious problems for Great Britain in particular, which faced even greater financial problems than Germany. For the Wilson government, defending the pound and redressing Britain's large balance-of-payments deficit was a matter of life and death. In the summer of 1966, it therefore threatened to make significant cuts in the British army on the Rhine (51,000 military) if West Germany were to fail to continue its offset payments. In the United States, too, the level of American military forces in Europe was causing increasingly serious financial and political problems. The total foreign exchange cost of stationing American forces in Germany (210,000 troops of the American Seventh Army) was estimated at $800 million a year. The Johnson administration faced strong pressure in Congress to reduce substantially the number of troops given the persistence of the US balance-of-payments deficit and the growing prosperity of Western Europe. The costs of the United States' escalating military involvement in Vietnam were also beginning to make themselves felt. The increasing availability of airlift and sealift capabilities moreover made it feasible to redeploy troops to the United States without undermining the deterrent posture of the alliance. On August 31, 1966, congressional pressure culminated in a resolution submitted by Mike Mansfield (a Democrat from Montana), the majority leader in the Senate, along with 43 co-sponsors, calling for a substantial withdrawal of American forces from Europe.[223]

Whereas the crisis precipitated by de Gaulle and the European groundswell in support of détente were affecting the spirit and the political content – the "heart" – of NATO, the offset crisis was hitting the alliance in the wallet and was raising serious questions about NATO's economic sustainability (the "belly"). "Our allies face the difficult problem of not wanting to accept de Gaulle's solution," Under Secretary of State Nicolas Katzenbach wryly observed during a meeting of the National Security Council, "but not wanting to pay for a NATO solution."[224] What was truly at issue in the offset crisis, however, was the ability and the willingness of the United States and Great Britain to maintain their troop levels in Germany as well as Germany's ability and willingness to continue to pay for them.

The most urgent problem confronting Johnson was how to dissuade the British government "from rushing into troop cuts," which would "start an unraveling process in NATO" and "increase domestic pressure on us to follow suit."[225] In late August 1966, he therefore proposed to hold trilateral negotiations on the interconnected issues of troop levels, offset payments, and the force posture still required by the threat. British Prime Minister Wilson promptly agreed, after Johnson had offered him to have the Pentagon place orders for military equipment in Great Britain ($35 million) on the condition that he would make no changes to British troop levels until the conclusion of the trilateral negotiations. Johnson next forced Chancellor Erhard's hand during the latter's visit to Washington in late September. The negotiations began in earnest in October 1966 and would last until the end of April 1967.

The Johnson administration, however, was also divided on the question of drawing down military forces from Germany. As was to be expected, the State Department was extremely cautious about any troop withdrawals from Europe, as this would seem to weaken America's commitment to European security. The Joint Chiefs of Staff, in addition, underlined that there was no military justification for any withdrawal and that such a withdrawal would reduce the capacity to carry out the strategy of flexible response. Secretary Rusk ultimately recommended only a very limited withdrawal of American troops from Germany by "dual-basing" two of the three brigades of one army division and 162 of the 216 airplanes in three air wings (out of a total force of five-plus divisions and nine air wings with 662 aircraft). This would save the United States an estimated $100 million annually.[226] Secretary of Defense McNamara, however, differed with his chiefs of staff. He strongly favored deeper cuts in the American troop presence in Europe; he was moreover convinced that the Johnson administration would not be able to prevent Congress from imposing deeper troop cuts than even he considered wise.[227] McNamara therefore recommended the dual-basing of four of the six brigades of two divisions and 324 of the 432 aircraft in six air wings – twice the troop withdrawal that Rusk considered acceptable. This would save the United States twice as much: an estimated $200 million annually.

Johnson had asked the strongly Atlanticist John McCloy to represent the United States in the trilateral negotiations with Great Britain and Germany. "The choice of McCloy," as Eugene Rostow has pointed out, "was not simply window dressing, it was part of a policy of strengthening the hands of the people within the government who wanted to stay, and not to have any change [of troop levels in Europe] unless the Russians changed."[228] The elder statesman vigorously opposed McNamara's recommendation for deep cuts; Rusk's recommendation for a more modest withdrawal was in his view acceptable only if the United States could demonstrate that these troops could be redeployed quickly and pledged that no additional withdrawals would be contemplated except in case of a reciprocal reduction of Soviet forces. McCloy stressed that American troop withdrawals would not be consistent with the emphasis placed on conventional forces in the US-sponsored strategy of flexible response, especially since they might precipitate troop withdrawals by other allies as well and would certainly make it harder for the United States to prod them to do their part within NATO. More importantly, McCloy was opposed for political reasons having to do with the future of the Atlantic alliance. As one of the founding fathers of the United States' internationalist foreign policy following World War II, he was deeply concerned by the Mansfield resolution, which he believed sprang from isolationist sentiments.[229] Troop cuts would moreover encourage a dangerous political drift in Europe and, in particular, in Germany in the direction of a Gaullist-type nationalism. "There is a growing danger," he reasoned in a letter to Walt Rostow, "that Europe will drift back into a condition where the old struggle for leadership with alliances and counter-alliances and cross axes again become a pattern of history, while at the same time a widening of the distance between Europe and the United States develops." The Germans, he felt, were at risk of becoming "prey to a new form of nationalism patterned on Gaullism."[230] In November, with the negotiations barely underway, McCloy therefore strongly urged Johnson to decide against any appreciable troop cuts, "squeeze as much offset money as possible out of the Germans" and "be prepared to eat the difference."[231]

President Johnson, meanwhile, was wrestling with the fiscal implications of financing both his Great Society programs and America's involvement in Europe and Asia. In his view, the crisis in NATO was compounding the growing budget deficit of the US government. In a National Security Council meeting at the end of 1966, Johnson furthermore opined that the developments in Europe were fanning isolationism at home. Referring to Republican gains in the congressional elections of November, he said:

> Recent French, British and German actions make clear that they are looking inward. We can't get the American people to support our NATO policy when they see the actions taken by the French, British, and Germans. We are fast approaching a day of reckoning.[232]

As usual, Johnson was focused on the mood in Congress. In a discussion with McCloy in early March 1967, he repeatedly dwelt on the difficult situation on the Hill with regard to American troop levels in Europe – "I have dealt with those babies for 30 years" – and said he expected to have to withdraw at least two divisions. But Johnson was equally sensitive to the potential political impact of American troop withdrawals on NATO and Germany. Johnson had been regularly fed reports about German nervousness about American steadiness.[233] A substantial withdrawal would be perceived as a historic shift in US foreign policy, possibly leading to the unraveling of NATO. Like Vietnam, Johnson was not prepared to "lose" NATO. "I want to use all the influence I can to hold the Alliance together and to get the Germans to pay the bill," he therefore concluded.[234] Unlike Great Britain, however, the United States stopped short of issuing a threat to withdraw troops if the Germans failed to deliver.

The tripartite negotiations were completed on April 28, 1967. In the end, Washington reassured Bonn that it had no plans to reduce significantly the American troop presence in Germany. Bonn, in turn, proved prepared to assist in redressing the US balance-of-payments deficit. It agreed to continue its procurement of American military equipment and to initiate the Bundesbank's purchase of medium-term US government bonds; in addition, it agreed not to convert any of its large dollar holdings into gold. Similar arrangements were made for the British, although some help was needed from the Johnson administration to underwrite, through military purchases in Great Britain amounting to $40 million, that part of the British deficit that was not covered by Germany. The United States limited its troop withdrawal from Germany to the two brigades of Rusk's recommendation (using the "dual-basing" formula), and to the redeployment of 96 aircraft.[235]

France had no direct involvement in the trilateral negotiations. Yet the French withdrawal from NATO had played a crucial role in their successful resolution. It had, first of all, made it incumbent on the Johnson administration to overcome the offset crisis regardless of the fiscal implications. Second, de Gaulle's "eviction notice" of March 1966 had enabled the United States to reduce quietly the costs and number of overseas forces as well as to relay German concerns about the credibility of the American security guarantee by relocating some units from France to Germany. "I think it is fair to say," McNamara had confessed to the Senate in June 1966, "that in these relocations and reorganizations we hope to achieve, over a period of years, a situation substantially better than the status quo with respect to both U.S. expenditures and the balance of payments."[236] The resolution of the offset crisis contributed significantly to holding NATO together in the 1960s. Johnson and McCloy deserve most of the credit. They were able to broker an arrangement acceptable to all sides for spreading the financial burden of maintaining NATO's defensive posture. Ironically, their success had been made possible in part by the French withdrawal from NATO.

Conclusion

The French withdrawal from NATO was "probably the most serious event in European history since the end of the war," the otherwise cool, calm and collected Charles Bohlen impressed on the members of the House of Representatives.[237] General Lauris Norstad similarly insisted, in a Senate hearing, that "this is a crisis."[238] Yet the question remains: To what extent can one truly speak of a crisis as a result of de Gaulle's withdrawal notification?

The military repercussions of the French exodus from NATO were considered bothersome but surmountable. The French move against NATO had moreover been anticipated. The Franco-American dispute had evolved from the tripartite debate under Eisenhower via the open clashes under Kennedy into a "dialogue of the deaf" under Johnson. Thomas Hughes, the State Department's director of Intelligence and Research, had been one of only a few who had tried to define terms of agreement with France by making adjustments to NATO – but his views were hardly influential.[239] At the Pentagon, attitudes toward de Gaulle's views had also been less hostile than at the State Department.[240] In White House circles, too, critical voices of NATO could be heard that would have received a welcome hearing in the Elysée.[241] Yet there was by the mid-1960s no starting point left for a compromise that could have averted a French move. The damnation of de Gaulle by the foreign policy establishment, led by Acheson and McCloy, would furthermore have aborted any attempt to seek a middle ground. "Too many hard voices have been allowed to speak for Washington," Bernard W. Poirier, an American business consultant who had helped formulate Kennedy's defense policies, concluded in a letter to Walt Rostow. "The truth is we lost the original opportunity to revamp NATO by growling at every French suggestion to discuss changes to the treaty or its implementations."[242]

The dearth of American initiatives to reach a compromise with de Gaulle on NATO can be explained in the first place by the unattractiveness of such a compromise from the US vantage point. First, given its huge stake and investment in European security, the United States could hardly be expected to take a back seat in the alliance. Washington was determined to retain control over its military affairs. "In moments of crisis the vital need of the Alliance is political unity backed by American strength," McGeorge Bundy explained.

> To meet this need SACEUR [...] is indispensable. [...] Without an effective command – plainly responsive both to the alliance as a whole and to Washington as the center of strategic strength – there would be no instrument for measured response in any new crisis, and without that instrument we should lose a critical governor for peace.[243]

This American view of the central importance of the SACEUR and of an integrated command in wartime was incompatible with de Gaulle's insistence on national control over French forces and operations on French soil. De Gaulle would have no recurrence of his clash in December 1944 with General Eisenhower, who had ordered French troops to withdraw from Strasbourg three weeks after it had been liberated. As one diplomat at the Quai d'Orsay explained to Kissinger in early 1966:

The difficulty was not the peacetime but the wartime status of "integrated" units. According to present arrangements once forces were released to SA-CEUR, he could use them in any part of the NATO territory as he saw fit [...]. This was an intolerable situation for France. France not only wanted to have the right to release its forces in case of war; it also wanted to have a decisive voice in the conduct of military operations on its territory. It did not want re-treats which treated its soil as a pawn in some larger game.[244]

Second, any American concession involving an enhanced status for France within the alliance would have caused serious problems with the other allies, and most importantly with the Germans; as Eisenhower had learned after de Gaulle's tri-partite memorandum proposal, they were vigilant about even the hint of a direc-torate within NATO. Third, the existing arrangements served the United States and the majority of European allies rather well. Most European allies preferred a system in which the United States presided as the *primus inter pares* over the Gaul-list alternative of a European pillar in which the leadership would accrue to one or two European states. The American political position in Europe was hence strong. Fourth, France was hardly an indispensable ally both from a military and political point of view. Both Germany and Great Britain ranked above France in terms of their importance to NATO. Well before de Gaulle's withdrawal notification, the Johnson administration was therefore in a position to conclude that American interests were better served by a French withdrawal from NATO than by a NATO reorganized to suit Gaullist preferences. And fifth, any concession the United States would have been willing to make was at best uncertain to have satisfied de Gaulle to produce a compromise. "I honestly don't know," John Leddy confessed to Congress, "what alternate system there is that would provide the requisite security, that would continue to move in the direction of more cooperation rather than less, and would at the same time meet the fundamental concepts of General de Gaulle."[245]

The truth is that by 1965, the Franco-American relationship had already degen-erated into an implicit agreement to disagree. This was manifest in the persistent refusal on both sides to hold a presidential summit. Johnson was frequently pressed to arrange for such a meeting.[246] But the White House desisted. Nor was de Gaulle interested. "We have nothing to request," he volunteered to Sulzberger in July 1965.[247] A proposal by Senator Mansfield for a meeting between Johnson and de Gaulle was not well received in Paris, as Kissinger reported in January 1966, "particularly when Senator Mansfield said that de Gaulle and Johnson would make two beautiful figures together on the balcony."[248] As a result, John-son's first-ever meeting with de Gaulle in person was not until Adenauer's funeral in April 1967, some four years after assuming the presidency.

In a way, therefore, de Gaulle's move against NATO and the US troop presence in France merely brought the long malaise in Franco-American relations to a head; only the comprehensiveness and the briskness of de Gaulle's move had contained an element of surprise, fuelling emotional outrage among Americans. What is more, France's departure from NATO was seen by influential parts within the Johnson administration as a welcome window of opportunity for revitalizing NATO and for streamlining the American force posture in Europe. On the day of the French withdrawal, Walt Rostow wrote to Johnson with a sense of relief that "de Gaulle's cards consist in threats more powerful if they hang over us than if they are executed."[249] France's separation from NATO's integrated military structure was accomplished with relative ease, in no small part due to Johnson's resolve not to pick a fight with de Gaulle. The most sensitive issue – the arrangements for the continued presence of French troops on German territory – was finally resolved by giving in to de Gaulle's position. Johnson also used the circumstances of the French defection from NATO to resolve the question of nuclear sharing that had haunted the United States since the 1950s and to make some useful institutional adaptations. The French historian Frédéric Bozo has credited de Gaulle for being "indirectly responsible for the move to redefine the objectives and political legitimation of the Atlantic Alliance."[250] If anyone deserves credit for revitalizing NATO, however, it would have to be Johnson for his calm response and skillful alliance diplomacy. Under his leadership, the United States behaved – as Couve de Murville was to admit in his memoirs – like a "pouvoir responsable."[251]

The NATO crisis of 1966 was a crisis mainly in other respects. First and foremost, it was a crisis because de Gaulle's critique of NATO was compounded with a yearning across Europe for détente in the East-West relationship and with strains on the alliance resulting from the heavy financial burden of the Cold War military posture. In addition to responding to the French withdrawal from NATO, Johnson had to resolve complex questions on which the future of the alliance hinged: How to talk détente without undermining the military readiness of the alliance required by the Soviet threat or giving up the goal of German reunification? How to ensure the defense of the West without going bankrupt? In addition to relocating NATO's facilities from French soil, such questions required nothing less than NATO's political reinvention in the aftermath of the French withdrawal. Johnson was remarkably adept at overcoming this part of the crisis, for which he has belatedly earned his rightful credit.[252] Under Johnson's responsive and politically astute leadership, NATO showed more flexibility and resilience than either its critics or its friends had supposed.

Second, it was a crisis because de Gaulle's actions against NATO challenged the viability of the Atlanticist ideology of the alliance. While de Gaulle's decision to pull France out of NATO allowed Johnson to re-establish it as an up-to-date institution, the French withdrawal also brought out into the open in the most dramatic way a fundamental conflict of purpose within the alliance (regardless of the Harmel Report). Since the early days of NATO, the strain of liberal internationalism in American foreign policy had saddled the transatlantic relationship with an activist program of reform. This program had included strong support for the European integration movement and for British participation in it, the Marshall Plan, the proposal for a multilateral nuclear force under NATO, and efforts at trade liberalization across the Atlantic (such as in the context of the Kennedy Round). It had accounted for the "enlightened" character of postwar American foreign policy – and for some of its most substantial achievements and most notable defeats. It had also caused the transatlantic relationship to become loaded with soaring expectations about the future Atlantic community. These expectations were becoming increasingly unrealistic in the course of the 1960s, in no small part because of de Gaulle's obstructionism.

Following the rebuttal of Kennedy's Grand Design in 1963 and the derailing of the MLF campaign in 1964, the NATO crisis engendered by de Gaulle in 1966 contributed decisively to the shift in American foreign policy toward a more pragmatic – and hence less ideologically driven and less ambitious – approach to the transatlantic alliance. Or as Thomas C. Schelling, the economist and strategist from Harvard University, analyzed:

> Whatever he says to the contrary, President de Gaulle has challenged the alliance itself – not the mutual defense commitment of Article 5, but the developing community of Atlantic nations. He is not merely withdrawing from it, he is denouncing it. And, unfortunately, it is within his power to spoil the Alliance. [...] In a sense, the Alliance is dead. Or perhaps it is only the ideology of the Alliance that is dead. This Alliance did have a lot of ideology. It also had a lot of rhetorical theory and architecture – involving pillars, dumbbells, concentric circles, vertical and horizontal integration, and other metaphors and analogies that were meant to describe it. [...] It seems to me that we have reached the end of our architectural period in Europe, the period of integrated cohesive schemes supported by theories. We may be entering a more pragmatic period. There is more than disappointment; there will be a loss of morale on both sides of the Atlantic.[253]

To this one should add that there had always been a nagging concern within America's foreign policy establishment that a lack of forward movement in achieving transatlantic unity might give occasion to a relapse into a violent past. From the late 1940s onwards, lack of progress toward more integration was consistently thought to give nourishment to a latent European nationalism, most ominously in Germany. George Ball's strongly worded public reaction to France's military withdrawal certainly falls in this category:

> ... we have always recognized the danger that the European people, with reflexes conditioned by history, might from time to time be tempted to lapse into the habits of the past, to unfurl the dusty banners of other centuries, and to re-

create the conditions in which Europe might once again become the cockpit of the world.

Ball's reaction revealed the continuing ambivalence in American perceptions of Europe. The "new" Europe – personified by the likes of Jean Monnet and Paul-Henri Spaak – was enthusiastically supported, whereas the "old" Europe – personified above all by de Gaulle – brought back haunting memories. "If there was to be peace in Europe and in the world," Ball reasoned, "the old national rivalries had to be replaced by something more constructive."[254] But that "something more constructive" hardly resembled the state of affairs in 1966, with NATO in disarray and the European movement held hostage by de Gaulle's assertion of national prerogatives.

De Gaulle's nationalistic "atavism" was also held partly responsible for letting the genie of American isolationism out of the bottle, spearheaded by those in Congress – such as Senator Mansfield – who pressed for a significant reduction of American troops in Europe. Mansfield himself explained to the administration that he had introduced his resolution because "we are the only NATO country that is meeting its commitments" and because he felt the continued presence of American troops in Europe was no longer unambiguously desired by Europeans, and not because of financial reasons or the war in Vietnam.[255]

After the scuttling of the MLF in late 1964, Johnson's purposely unruffled response to de Gaulle's defection from NATO was another victory for the pragmatists over the Atlanticists. Johnson's attitude of restraint was a milestone in the evolution of US policies toward a more realistic conception of the Atlantic relationship. Despite the intimate involvement of Acheson and McCloy in responding to the NATO crisis, the Establishment was gradually losing its grip on the direction of American foreign affairs. The Vietnam War and the unstoppable advance of age also did their grinding work. It is not sufficient to note that Johnson deserves credit for leading the alliance into calmer waters, which he does. It is also important to recognize that Johnson's policy of restraint had not come about without serious clashes within his own administration – both over the issue itself and his style of leadership. "In acting as Chief of Staff for the NATO-France crisis," Dean Acheson wrote to Anthony Eden in June 1966, "I have found myself in the middle of a whole series of intra-USG [US government] vendettas – Defense vs. State, White House vs. State, JCS vs. McNamara, Gaullists vs. European Integrationists, and LBJ-turn-the-other-cheekism vs. DA-let-the-chips-fall-where-they-mayism."[256]

At one important White House meeting on responding to de Gaulle in May 1966, as David Bruce recorded, Johnson finally ignited the "Acheson powder magazine" with a "wholly intemperate attack on United States officials who had assailed President de Gaulle for his NATO stance." Acheson, backed by Ball, responded to Johnson's accusations with strong words of his own about the president's behavior, and "the fat sizzled in the fire for quite some time."[257] But there was more at hand than a spat of personalities. Acheson's argument with Johnson was also one about the intrinsic value of the transatlantic alliance in American foreign policy. While Johnson spent much more time on European issues than he is usually given credit for, from Acheson's perspective this was hardly enough. What Acheson wanted was strong presidential leadership in defense of the Atlantic community against the resurgent forces of European nationalism embodied by de Gaulle. What Johnson wanted was merely to "rebuild NATO outside France as promptly, economically, and effectively as possible."[258] Once he had accomplished this, his attention was once again diverted to more pressing issues, and in particular to the war in Vietnam. "Europe is forgotten," Acheson bitterly complained in a letter to his old boss Harry Truman, "and a good deal that you, General Marshall and I did is unraveling fast."[259] While this assessment was too bleak, there was truth in British Ambassador Patrick Dean's judgment in early 1967 that the United States was beginning to see itself "less as a leader of the Atlantic Community and more as the Atlantic-Pacific Power whose best interest lies in encouraging, but not being too closely enmeshed in, the development of collective regional endeavors in all areas of the world." The conjunction of the NATO crisis of 1966, the Vietnam War, and Johnson's desire for détente in the East-West relationship also ushered in a new era in the transatlantic relationship, with "less sentiment and more hardheadedness in the American attitude to Europe."[260]

The representatives of America's revered foreign policy establishment were thus deeply disillusioned with Johnson's leadership and with developments in the transatlantic relationship. Their heirs, many of whom had entered the Kennedy administration with grand ambitions about transforming the transatlantic relationship, were moreover being replaced by men of more pragmatic disposition as the Johnson years took their course. In September 1966, six months after de Gaulle's eviction message, Ball – already a maverick on Vietnam – quit the administration. "My job had lost its savor, and, as our involvement in the Vietnam nightmare had passed the point where I could significantly influence policy, it was time to resign," he explained in his memoirs.[261] Acheson's disillusion and Ball's departure marked the transition to a less ambitious era in the transatlantic relationship.

Chapter Six

Grand Designs Go Bankrupt: From Divergence to Accommodation, 1967-1969

If one had to pick a year in which the Franco-American relationship reached a nadir, it would no doubt be 1967. Following the withdrawal from NATO, de Gaulle capitalized on his newly achieved "independence" by seeking rapprochement with the Warsaw Pact countries. In 1967, France would also proclaim a nuclear strategy that made no distinction between the West and the East, issue high-profile statements on a range of issues across the globe that set France clearly at odds with the "Anglo-Saxons," and launch an attack on the American dollar as the linchpin of the international monetary system.

In all of these issues, French foreign policy was more openly than ever aimed at redressing a global balance of power that de Gaulle felt was tilted too heavily in favor of the United States. De Gaulle argued that, while there was an apparent military standoff between the United States and the Soviet Union, "the US was so much more powerful from the economic and financial point of view as well as in organization of its state that there was no comparison." In his view, the United States' hegemonic hubris had become more of a threat to peace than the ideological designs of the Soviet Union. "It was 'inevitable,'" he declared to Bohlen in the summer of 1967, "that so much power as that possessed by the U.S. sooner or later [...] would begin to influence the policy and conduct of any country."[1] By the fall of 1967, the CIA had come to believe that de Gaulle was "more concerned with [...] the dominant role played by the United States in Europe than with fears of Soviet hegemony" and might withdraw France from the Atlantic alliance altogether by 1969; de Gaulle, given his age, was judged to be "anxious" to present his successors with a fait accompli.[2]

It is therefore not surprising that de Gaulle's foreign policy by 1967 was seen as virulently and incorrigibly anti-American. His popularity among Americans dropped to new lows. In October 1967, Dean Acheson voiced his frustration at de Gaulle's grandstanding by lashing out against the French as "the most [...] selfish people in the [...] world" and "the greatest nuisance" in Europe.[3] And in December, asked what would happen if France were to renounce the North Atlantic Treaty in 1969, the former secretary of state bluntly declared that "France is worth nothing to NATO – absolutely nothing whatever – and NATO will be improved by the absence of this France rather than helped by it."[4] Acheson's emotive respon-sive to de Gaulle's independent posture was indeed reflective of the public mood at the time.[5]

The atmosphere was only marginally better at the level of heads of state, although it was obviously restrained by the demands of the office and President Johnson's determination to retain an attitude of politeness.[6] Johnson's reunion with de Gaulle at Konrad Adenauer's funeral on April 25, 1967 – der Alte had passed away at the respectable age of 91 – was a case in point, as it made painfully clear how little communication was possible between them.[7] In a mood of resig-nation, Johnson wrote to Dwight Eisenhower upon his return to Washington that "there does not appear to be a great deal of substance we can constructively say to one another."[8] If anything, their get-together in Bonn added an uncomfortable experience. Johnson's outgoing behavior, which often bordered on boorishness, had clashed with de Gaulle's aloof and solemn demeanor. Before entering the Bundestag, "when photographers urged a handshake, Johnson reached across [German president Heinrich] Luebke and clasped de Gaulle's hand," the Ameri-can embassy in Bonn reported. "Luebke stacked his hand on theirs. Johnson [and] Luebke smiled and [a] faint trace of [a] smile [was] reported on de Gaulle's face."[9] De Gaulle was visibly annoyed at being drawn into this show of political unity at the funeral of his German companion.[10]

And yet, in the last year of Johnson's presidency and the early days of Nixon's, a remarkable rapprochement took shape between Washington and Paris. For both, 1968 turned out to be an annus horribilis. It taught both the United States and France that they had outlived the means and the popular support required for their respective foreign policies. They hence moved toward a less confrontational relationship. According to Article 13 of the North Atlantic Treaty, any member state would be permitted to renounce membership of the alliance after the treaty had been in force for twenty years. April 4, 1969, passed without a ruffle in the water. Franco-American relations were better than they had been at any time dur-ing de Gaulle's tenure. This chapter will seek to chart and to clarify this note-worthy shift from divergence to accommodation.

The Pragmatic Beginnings of Franco-American Accommodation Under LBJ

At Loggerheads on All Horizons

In the course of 1967, de Gaulle took positions on a wide range of foreign policy issues that greatly strained the Franco-American relationship. His criticism of US military involvement in Vietnam reached a pinnacle. In the six-day Arab-Israeli War of June 1967, de Gaulle opposed the Johnson administration's continued support for Israel. He had explicitly warned Israeli Foreign Minister Abba Eban against initiating the war; once the attack occurred, he strongly condemned Israel as "the aggressor" in the conflict and aligned French diplomacy in the crisis with that of the Soviet Union.[11] De Gaulle's insinuations that the war could have been averted if only the United States had exercised its leverage over Israel did not sit well with American diplomats.[12] They caused Bohlen, in a telegram that betrayed his deepening sense of frustration with de Gaulle's criticism of the United States, to express "concern" about "the degree to which under de Gaulle's one-man rule personal and subjective prejudices have been translated into political action."[13] On November 27, in one of his more notorious press conferences, de Gaulle moreover appeared to add an antisemitic gloss to his criticism of Israel's behavior by typifying Jews as "an elite people, sure of itself and dominating."[14] From the American perspective, the General was once again stirring up Europe's ghastly past.

Shortly after the crisis in the Middle East, de Gaulle took his dispute with American dominance in world affairs across the Atlantic. With his riveting – and somewhat improvised but no less intentional – call for a "free Quebec" (*Québec libre*) during a rally in Montreal on July 24, his policy of independence stepped out of bounds. Canadian Prime Minister Lester B. Pearson had no choice but to denounce de Gaulle's statements for inciting separatism. The fervent response of the Québécois to his visit had rekindled in de Gaulle emotions he had experienced upon his re-entry of France as a liberator at the end of World War II. But his interest in promoting the cause of the French in Canada already had a long history, and he had made clear to his advisers prior to his departure aboard the warship *Colbert* that he would not be going to Quebec as a tourist but "pour faire l'Histoire."[15] Unruffled by the denunciation of his statements by the Canadian government and the often vehement criticism from many quarters (including in France), de Gaulle returned to France as if he had achieved a moral and political victory.[16] Half a year later, he told Cy Sulzberger of the *New York Times* that, in his view, the French Canadians were the "worst oppressed minority in the world, with the exception of the Arabs in Israel and the Tibetans in China."[17] It is important to note, however, that de Gaulle's statements on this trip were aimed less against Canada than against the United States. "The French part of Canada now intends to organize, *in conjunction with other Canadians*, means of safeguarding their substance and independence in contact with a colossal State that is their neighbour," he had said in another speech in the city of Quebec, one whose words had been more carefully weighed (emphasis added).[18] There is reason to assume that de Gaulle was prepared to go even further and "to promote an independent French-speaking republic in North America."[19] In addition to expressing support for the residue of French civilization in the New World and reinstating France as a power with global political connections, de Gaulle had sought to use the Canadian French in part as an avant garde in reducing the influence of the United States – the Anglo-Saxon powerhouse – in its own neighborhood.[20]

In the realm of nuclear strategy, de Gaulle's policy of independence was carried to its logical conclusion with the doctrine of "defense in all directions" (*défense tous azimuts*). This doctrine was articulated in December 1967 by General Charles Ailleret in an article in *Revue de défense nationale* and it accurately reflected de Gaulle's strategic thinking.[21] The *tous azimuts* doctrine categorically stated that the *force de frappe* should not be aimed at one single enemy but be able to strike anywhere in the world in order to deter "those who might wish, from whatever part of the world, to use us or to destroy us in order to assist in the achievement in their war aims."[22] It did not discriminate between NATO and the Warsaw Pact. And it clearly implied that the United States was to be considered a potential adversary, in particular since it might be tempted to seize control over French territory in case a war broke out in Europe.[23]

All in all, de Gaulle's policy of independence was carried to such extremes in 1967 that its support in France began to weaken. He was increasingly censured in French newspapers for having lost touch with political reality and, in particular in the context of the Mideast crisis and his visit to Quebec, for needlessly antagonizing France's allies. The General was "entering a sort of planetary drift, in strategic matters, the Near East or his relations with Western allies," his biographer Jean Lacouture has written. "The vision was still dazzling. But a new intemperance and sometimes a disconcerting distance from reality were perceptible."[24] Opinion polls moreover began to show that a majority of the French people – of all political colors (i.e. including Gaullists and Communists) – was opposed to the idea of leaving the Atlantic alliance altogether and wanted to preserve the link with America.[25]

Charles Bohlen, meanwhile, having served for more than four years as ambassador in Paris, had become deeply frustrated with de Gaulle's habit of chiding the Americans at every turn on any issue. De Gaulle had worn down the veteran US diplomat. He had begun his tour on a high, branded as the "right man on the spot" by *Time*.[26] His advice as a "very shrewd judge of the way Europeans judge us" – in McGeorge Bundy's words – had carried much weight within the Johnson administration.[27] Over the years, however, Bohlen's reporting from Paris was becoming noticeably more acidic about the General and more disheartened about the possibility of any accommodation between France and the United States – and hence less capable of nuance and less valuable. Walter Lippmann, for instance, after having spent an evening with the Bohlens in Paris in early 1964, judged that the American ambassador was too hostile to de Gaulle to be able to do an effective job.[28] In November 1966, Bohlen had concluded that de Gaulle, "who conducts completely single-handedly French foreign policy," had lost his "sense of timing and appropriateness," and was even beginning to show signs of mental instability:

It would seem that de Gaulle is suffering from two aspects of old age: (1) a progressive hardening of the prejudices – of which he had plenty, and (2) a growing indifference and even unconcern with the effect of his words on international and French public opinion. The fixation which he has always had in regard to the power and size of the United States has grown into a compulsive obsession. ... we now must definitely recognize that one of the motivating forces of de Gaulle's conduct of foreign policy is his anti-American obsession and I believe that we can expect that almost anything he says in the future will contain some uncomplimentary references towards the United States. ... It is perhaps too soon to state that de Gaulle is "becoming senile," but certainly the restraint which used to accompany his actions and characterize his words seems to be slipping very badly.[29]

In 1967, as the Franco-American relationship plummeted to new depths, Bohlen's reporting showed signs of exhaustion and resentment at de Gaulle's unrelenting public criticism of US foreign policy. He was relieved of his post in November 1967, leaving it the next February to become deputy undersecretary of state for political affairs. Bohlen's final assessment of de Gaulle's foreign policy upon leaving his post was illustrative of the cul de sac in which the bilateral relationship loitered in early 1968. "[...] De Gaulle's preoccupation with the power of the U.S. became an obsession," he wrote, and as long as the General remained in power there was no room for improvement. Interestingly, however, Bohlen was less concerned about the long-term orientation of French foreign policy than about the impact of de Gaulle's anti-Americanism on US foreign policy. "France is eternal and de Gaulle is not," Bohlen stressed in his last cable as ambassador to France, and the French were at heart sympathetic towards the United States. But de Gaulle's consistent opposition "cannot help but produce a feeling in the U.S. that the policy of France is indeed hostile to that of the U.S."

> It seems to me that the greatest problem in Franco-American relations now lies on our side of the Atlantic. There is no doubt that American public opinion is being badly affected by the policies and action of General de Gaulle, and I regret that I have found very little comprehension among leading French political figures, and with the General himself, as to the special importance this factor bears in the American Governmental structure and that an explosive American public opinion could very easily force a change in the present attitude of the American government towards France.[30]

In the concluding chapter of this book, we will return to the question of whether de Gaulle's policy of independence had much of an impact on American foreign policy. For now, we would note that Bohlen proved to be too fatalistic about the potential for an improvement in Franco-American relations with de Gaulle still at the helm. In the course of 1968, French public opinion became increasingly concerned with the implications of de Gaulle's relentless quest for independence and with his anti-American rhetoric. His Middle-East policy was far from popular, and in particular his statements on Israel drew heavy criticism. With his call for a free Quebec, de Gaulle clearly overstepped the boundaries of diplomatic decorum according to virtually the entire French press. In January 1968, the *New York Times* reported from Paris about "strong signs" that de Gaulle and his advisers were beginning to worry about the increasingly strong – even vitriolic – reactions to French policy statements in the Anglo-Saxon world, even from "thoughtful and normally soft-spoken commentators." There was, in addition, a growing perception among French businessmen that upsetting Americans was not good for business, or as an article in *L'Express* stated: "French industrialists today realize that they have a sales manager: General de Gaulle, magnificent for exporting to the Middle East, terrible for selling to the United States."[31] Most importantly, however, developments in a number of other areas conspired in 1968 to bring the United States and France closer before LBJ left the Oval Office in January 1969. The common feature of these developments in 1968 was that they made clear to both Washington and Paris that their respective foreign policy aspirations had reached a dead end, and that they stood to gain from an attenuation of their differences.

Vietnam – From Bombing to Negotiating

The Vietnam War was never central to the Franco-American relationship in the 1960s, nor did the Franco-American dispute over the war significantly affect its outcome. The row over Vietnam was nonetheless significant for a number of reasons. While discomfort and disaffection with the United States' military involvement in Vietnam were widespread in Western Europe, especially after 1965, de Gaulle was the only allied government leader to voice criticism openly. This criticism was all the more important because French influence was still felt in Vietnam, a former French colony, and because it lent authority to critics of the war in the United States. De Gaulle's criticism was also significant for underscoring the lack of active support from European allies for the war. Rather than assuring the European allies that the United States was faithful to its security commitments in the face of the communist threat, its military quandary in Vietnam damaged US authority in Europe. To many Americans, in turn, the absence of European support in Vietnam cast a sobering light over the significance of NATO – or the more abstract notion of an Atlantic community – to American foreign policy in other parts of the world. But one should note as well that by 1968 the conflict also provided an opportunity for rapprochement between the United States and France. De Gaulle responded favorably to Johnson's announcement of a partial bombing pause and simultaneous call for negotiations on March 31, praising it as "an act of reason and political courage."[32] Hanoi subsequently proposed (and the United States accepted) Paris as the site for preliminary talks. In the spring of 1968, the Vietnam War ceased to be a divisive issue between the United States and France.

De Gaulle was one of the earliest and most consistent critics of American policies in Vietnam.[33] His views had been shaped by the painful conclusion of the French colonial experience in Southeast Asia and elsewhere, which had taught him that superior military power could not achieve political victory over Third World nationalism and that it would be wiser to settle for a negotiated end to the conflict even if this meant accepting a setback (at least temporarily). This meant accepting the neutralization of Vietnam along the lines of the 1954 Geneva Agreements as the best possible outcome, even as this was widely understood to bring a communist government to power. In June 1961, de Gaulle had issued a private warning to President Kennedy against the quagmire the United States would find itself in if it decided to step up its military involvement.[34] While some evidence suggests Kennedy took de Gaulle's words of caution to heart and Washington had considered neutralization an acceptable solution to the Laotian crisis in 1962, Kennedy also feared that another setback would open him up to charges that he was too "soft" on communism.[35] When, on November 1, 1963, Diem, who had been sympathetic to the idea of a negotiated neutrality, was killed in a coup backed by the Americans, de Gaulle openly distanced himself from American policies in Vietnam for the first time.[36] By then, neither Kennedy nor Johnson was susceptible to de Gaulle's warnings. They were determined to prevent a communist takeover in South Vietnam. From 1963 onwards, as the United States progressively heightened the military stake in the conflict, the difference of opinion with de Gaulle became increasingly more public. In particular, after the Johnson administration took its fateful decision to escalate the number of troops in Vietnam in early 1965, de Gaulle's public opposition became openly antagonistic. Johnson's decision to bomb the North Vietnamese, he argued to Ambassador Bohlen, was only hardening Hanoi's negotiating stance and made negotiations on a political settlement virtually impossible.[37]

American officials feared the residual French political, economic, and cultural influence in South Vietnam, which tended to either bolster neutralist sentiments within the South Vietnamese leadership or raise fears that the United States might adopt neutrality as a solution. The impact of France's deviation on domestic and international public opinion also worried American diplomats.[38] "To the [Vietnamese] generals here, de Gaulle looks much bigger than he does to us," Ambassador Henry Cabot Lodge Jr. cabled from Saigon in early 1964.[39] Shortly thereafter he called the State Department's attention to "secret information indicating that there are persons purporting to be under the strong influence of the French government who are working directly against U.S. vital interests in Viet-Nam" and urged the State Department to request de Gaulle "to call off his dogs."[40] De Gaulle's position also undercut the Johnson administration's ability to build a domestic political consensus behind the military involvement in Vietnam. "The de Gaulle approach offers a faint glimmer of hope in a way to a solution at a cost to us somewhere commensurate with our national interests in Southeast Asia," Senate Majority Leader Mike Mansfield, for instance, wrote in one of his many letters to Johnson on Vietnam. "We should be prepared to listen most intently and with an open ear and mind to whatever the French may have to say on Vietnam."[41] And McNamara reported to President Johnson after a visit to Vietnam in March 1964 that "de Gaulle's position and the continuing pessimism and anti-Americanism of the French community in South Vietnam provide constant fuel to neutralist sentiment and the coup possibility."[42]

In particular in 1964, the United States tried to bring the views of the French more in line with American policies. In early June 1964, for instance, President Johnson sent George Ball on a mission to Paris to talk directly to de Gaulle in order to solicit his views on "any new blueprint that would assure the guaranteed independence of the nations of Southeast Asia."[43] Despite Ball's valiant effort at persuasion, de Gaulle was immovable. He stressed that Vietnam was a "rotten territory" where victory would continue to elude the Americans. "I do not believe that you can win in this situation even though you have more aircraft, cannons, and arms of various kinds," de Gaulle predicted. "The more the US becomes involved in the actual conduct of operations[,] the more the Vietnamese will turn against us [the United States]." De Gaulle predicted that the United States would sooner or later "come to the conclusion that we would have to make peace [...] with China and others in the area." He rejected the notion put forward by Ball that China was an expansionist power, pointing out that China moreover would not have the resources for an aggressive foreign policy for a long time. He talked of a "vast diplomatic operation" to bring the conflict to an end. "De Gaulle is merely waiting for events to come his way," Ball concluded, and "he probably envisages that some time in the not too distant future we will begin to consider seriously his suggestion of a conference."[44]

While important newspaper men such as Walter Lippmann, James Reston, and Cy Sulzberger, as well as congressmen like Senator Mike Mansfield, had come to support the "de Gaulle solution" for Vietnam by the spring of 1964, his views made no inroads whatsoever within the Johnson administration. Ball, incidentally, was the only prominent dissenter within the administration, but it cannot be surmised that his dissent had been motivated by de Gaulle. On the contrary, he chafed at de Gaulle's criticism, believing that the General merely wanted to cut down the United States and to build up France, and rejected the notion of granting the French a diplomatic role in achieving a solution.[45] If de Gaulle had any influence on Ball's Vietnam position, it was because the nationalist danger Gaullism represented to him made it all the more incumbent to avoid diversions from the European into the Asian theater.

Ball did return to Washington hoping that his exchange with the General would bolster his own position as opponent of America's growing military involvement in the Vietnam war. Yet he found Johnson "unwilling to listen" and rather preoccupied with drumming up congressional support for the war effort.[46] "Southeast Asia represents the most difficult of the postwar crises," Walt Rostow had written to Johnson in order to stiffen his resolve while Ball conversed with de Gaulle. "Neither President Eisenhower nor President Kennedy gripped it directly. The softer options have been about used up. And there it stands before you."[47] Two months later, in early August, Congress passed the so-called Tonkin Gulf Resolution, giving Johnson a blank check for further military action in Vietnam. In early 1965, after Johnson won his landslide victory in the presidential elections, the United States deployed the Marines to South Vietnam and began bombing North Vietnam. De Gaulle's cautionary counsel was thus thrown to the winds. Washington was even wary of sharing any information with Paris for fear of informing Hanoi.[48]

Rather than giving pause for reflection, American officials typically dismissed de Gaulle's criticism as self-serving. "The one cardinal interest that the French have in the Vietnamese matter is that of enhancing the prestige of General de Gaulle," Bohlen reported in 1965.[49] De Gaulle's views were also thrust aside as just one more illustration of the "obsessive" anti-American gist of his foreign policy. After one conversation at the Elysée, Bohlen even detected a "considerable measure of *Schadenfreude*" at America's toil.[50] There always seemed a reason not to take French qualms about the Vietnam policies of the United States at face value. Upon Johnson's decision in early 1965 to raise American troop levels in Vietnam substantially, for instance, Couve de Murville expressed his concern and pressed the case for negotiations with the North Vietnamese on a visit to Washington. Bundy believed that the French foreign minister "honestly does not think we can avoid defeat in South-Vietnam" and that "his worry is not pretense." In the same breath, however, he cast off Couve de Murville's concern as "a comforting conclusion for a Frenchman for obvious reasons."[51]

De Gaulle's frequent allusions to the hard lessons to be learned from the French experience in Southeast Asia indeed hardly impressed Americans. One internal review of the Johnson administration's foreign policy accomplishments typically stated that the Vietnam predicament was not the result of US policy mishaps but had been created "by generations of French mismanagement and the thrust of expanding communism from the north."[52] Most American officials resented de Gaulle's thesis that the United States was bound to fail where France had failed before. They were convinced that the nature of the American involvement in Vietnam and the reservoir of resources available to the United States simply could not be gauged in equal terms. Of all American officials, Secretary of State Rusk appears to have been singularly incapable of appreciating de Gaulle's position on Vietnam. He blamed de Gaulle for undermining Vietnamese morale and for undercutting the United States' quest for safeguarding Southeast Asia. Time and again, Rusk asserted that the US was making a stand in Vietnam since a failure to do so would directly affect the credibility of the American security guarantee to Europe.[53] But Rusk was hardly exceptional. In late June 1965, faced with advice from McNamara and Rusk to step up drastically again the military campaign in Vietnam, President Johnson asked McGeorge Bundy to compare the French experience in 1954 to that of the United States in 1965. Bundy reached the "comfortable conclusion" – to use his own words – that the dissimilarity was overwhelming and was heavily in favor of the latter:

> France in 1954 was a colonial power seeking to reimpose its overseas rule, out of tune with Vietnamese nationalism, deeply divided in terms of French domestic opinion, politically unstable at home, the victim of seven years of warfare [...]. The U.S. in 1965 is responding to the call of a people under Communist assault, a people undergoing a non-Communist national revolution; neither our power nor that of our adversaries has been fully engaged as yet. At home we remain politically strong and, in general, politically united. Options, both military and political, remain to us that were no longer available to the French.[54]

The haughty unresponsiveness of the United States to his words of caution annoyed de Gaulle.[55] In his discussion with Ball in June 1964, de Gaulle had suggested an international conference to begin the search for a negotiated solution; in 1965, French diplomats avidly engaged with North Vietnamese and Communist Chinese representatives in Paris and talked of a "concerted action" with the Soviet Union. When the Johnson administration nonetheless enhanced its military involvement in Vietnam, however, de Gaulle concluded that for the time being there was no basis for negotiations. This did not mean that he had given up on a negotiated solution but that he would be content to let the war unfold until it would dawn on the Americans that they could not achieve a military victory in South Vietnam. In order to facilitate future talks, de Gaulle quietly continued to cultivate French diplomatic channels in Hanoi, Beijing, and Moscow.[56] Meanwhile, he maintained his sharply critical stance towards the Johnson administration. On September 1, 1966, addressing a crowd of some one hundred thousand Cambodians in Phnom Penh, de Gaulle stressed that the United States was "more and more threatening for the peace of the world" and that only an American commitment to withdraw troops unilaterally from Southeast Asia could lead to peace talks. The United States, he said, would do well to follow the example France had given by extricating itself from the Algerian conflict under much worse circumstances.[57]

In early 1968, Lyndon Johnson finally buckled under the pressure of a war going awry – and it would bring him to accept Paris as the locale for talks with the North Vietnamese. As early as February 1965, Thomas Hughes, the State Department's director of intelligence, had concluded that "the question before the United States government is not *whether* France will play some role in this matter but only *how* it will play its role."[58] In May 1965, Hanoi had indeed tried to make contact with Washington via the Quai d'Orsay, prompting Bohlen to conclude that "Paris with some French involvement may be [the] only choice" as a locale for negotiations.[59] Reacting to de Gaulle's address in Phnom Penh in the fall of 1966, Johnson had first mentioned the possibility of scheduled *mutual* withdrawals. And in 1967, several North Vietnamese "peace feelers" were issued from Paris.[60] The large-scale Tet offensive launched by Vietcong and North Vietnamese forces on January 30, 1968, finally marked the political and psychological turning point in the Vietnam War. Even though the communist insurgents were successfully repelled, the offensive turned the tables of domestic public opinion against the Johnson administration. In a dramatic televised address to the American people on March 31, President Johnson finally felt compelled to declare a halt to the aerial bombing over most of North Vietnam and to call for negotiations. In addition, he surprised his countrymen by announcing that he would not stand as a candidate in the upcoming presidential elections.

On April 18, 1968, Couve de Murville declared that Paris would be available as the location for preliminary talks if the United States and North Vietnam so desired. The circumspectly worded French offer broke the deadlock between the two sides about the negotiation site. Both Hanoi and Washington had initially proposed a range of other capitals in Asia and Europe, on which they failed to agree.[61] President Johnson, to be sure, only accepted Paris with some reluctance. He feared that the French would throw in their lot with Hanoi during the talks. When Rostow informed him that the North Vietnamese had agreed to holding talks in the French capital, Johnson replied: "Well, I'd rather go to almost any place than Paris."[62] A few days earlier, at a regular Tuesday luncheon at the White House with Dean Rusk and Clark Clifford, the new secretary of defense, he had voiced similar sentiments, explaining that the French "are not in the least interested genuinely in peace."[63] One decisive advantage of Paris, however, was that all parties – including North Vietnam and China – had some form of diplomatic representation there. It was moreover politically palatable to all sides because France was an ally of the United States but one with manifest sympathy for Hanoi's position on the war. Paris also proved suitable to both Beijing and Moscow, allowing Hanoi to avoid a choice between the two. On May 3, Hanoi finally offered to meet in Paris and Johnson accepted. Ten days later, Averell Harriman and Xuan Thuy, the respective heads of the American and the North Vietnamese delegations, had their first encounter in the Majestic Hotel on the Avenue Kléber. Paris would remain the negotiation site until the Paris Peace Accords were signed in 1973 by the governments of North Vietnam, South Vietnam, and the United States.

Johnson's decision to accept Paris as the place for negotiations was widely interpreted as a victory for de Gaulle's policy of independence, an interpretation that was naturally encouraged by French spokesmen. More importantly, however, the choice for Paris inaugurated a period of Franco-American rapprochement, first on Vietnam and then on other issues. In early May 1968, the CIA judged that de Gaulle's favorable response to Johnson's call for negotiations had been primarily motivated by a recognition that "if France hoped to play some role in the talks, he must mitigate somewhat his uncompromising stand against US actions in Vietnam."[64] From the spring of 1968, the French indeed tempered their disapproval of American policies in Southeast Asia. As the host of the peace talks, the French government had no choice but to assume the cloak of impartiality, the more so since de Gaulle hoped to involve himself sooner or later in the diplomatic process as a mediator. Moreover, while the war would not end until 1975, the era of escalation shifted to an era of political negotiations and gradual military withdrawal – and there was thus much less to criticize from the French point of view. The day-to-day contact in the context of the negotiations with French experts such as Etienne Manac'h was also appreciated on the American side.[65] There was even an upsurge of sympathy among the French with the American plight in Southeast Asia as American troops began their withdrawal.[66] De Gaulle was convinced of the sincerity of the American about-face. In 1969, after having spoken to President Nixon, he even instructed the French embassy in Beijing to convince the Chinese of this and of Nixon's desire to improve the Sino-American relationship more generally.[67]

Johnson's decision to negotiate and to accept Paris as the locus for negotiation thus did much to remove Vietnam as an irritant in the Franco-American relationship. De Gaulle, however, was not allowed to revel long in his triumph. The beginning of the Vietnam peace talks on May 13, 1968, coincided with the outbreak of a student-worker revolt in the streets of Paris that would throw the country in sudden disarray and lead to serious economic trouble. One of the ironies of this history is therefore that de Gaulle's diplomatic *coup de théâtre* came on the brink of domestic catastrophe, an irony that was the more poignant given that de Gaulle's policy of independence was geared in no small measure towards strengthening domestic unity. Another is that just when de Gaulle's policy of independence appeared to have reached the pinnacle of success, it was beset by new and unanticipated problems to such a degree that this time it would be Johnson who would lend a hand to an ally in dire straits.

May – From Grandeur to Havoc
"I no longer find this very amusing," de Gaulle told François Flohic, one of his aides, on April 28; "there is no longer anything difficult, or heroic, to be done."[68] "France is bored," the title of one article in Le Monde famously ran.[69] These state-

ments have become noteworthy mostly in hindsight, as they belied the profound domestic crisis that followed.

In May 1968, the pendulum of France's political history experienced one of its violent swings from reverence of the state to revolt against it. Within a matter of weeks, a local student protest transformed into a nationwide challenge to de Gaulle's regime by the collective force of youth, labor, and opposition: on May 3, students of the Sorbonne university clashed with police, the beginning of ten days of street fighting; on May 12, communist and non-communist workers joined in a 24-hour sympathy strike; from May 14 to 22, wildcat strikes swept the country, bringing the economy to a halt with more than half of French workers on strike. De Gaulle's call of May 24 for a referendum on a vaguely worded program of educational and economic reform, which he coupled with the prospect of resignation in case of a negative result, failed to restore order. On the contrary, his address to the nation was followed by further rioting in Paris and in large cities in the provinces. The May crisis revealed the government as being badly out of touch with its citizenry and out of control of the situation. The French state, as Jean Lacouture observed, "was a great body that had lost its nervous system and whose circulation had seized up" – and for de Gaulle this was nothing short of a personal catastrophe: "The France that he had picked up, ten years before, lying by the wayside, half-dead, was now falling to pieces in his hands."[70] For the first time since 1958, de Gaulle looked despondent. On May 28, François Mitterrand declared his candidature for the presidency. Georges Pompidou, de Gaulle's prime minister, was bolstering his own position as semi-independent from that of the General. Finally, on May 29, de Gaulle had his legendary secret rendezvous in Baden-Baden with General Jacques Massu, the commander of the French forces in West Germany, and a number of other army leaders to ascertain the state of mind and the loyalty of the army to the government. The following day, on May 30, the General told the nation that, after having considered "all the eventualities, without exception," he had decided to dissolve the National Assembly and to have early legislative elections.

"The old man intends to slug it out," Walt Rostow wrote to President Johnson from Paris on May 30. "He threw down the gauntlet without [the] slightest sign of uncertainty."[71] The Johnson administration had already begun to explore the implications of de Gaulle's retirement, but underestimated the tenacity of the General.[72] Nicholas Katzenbach, Ball's successor at the State Department who also happened to witness the turmoil in Paris firsthand, noted that de Gaulle's "very tough" speech "clearly implied [a] threat to rule by decree if necessary [...]."[73] Algeria was no longer part of the calculation and a military coup was not in view, but on many other accounts France appeared to be where de Gaulle found it in the spring of 1958: on the brink of civil strife, with the army standing in the wings. De Gaulle's speech had "placed France on the knife edge of disaster," the CIA even assessed.

Over the short run, we believe that the government probably would succeed in restoring order and essential services, but only at the cost of poisoning political life for the indefinite future. The longer term outlook is therefore more ominous. The Gaullists have repeatedly violated and perverted their own constitution. They have treated even the moderate opposition with disdain and indifference. [...] Thus the stage has been set for a polarization of political forces in France [...]. Whatever the short term outcome France faces a period of unrest and, eventually even civil war.[74]

In his May 30 address, de Gaulle had issued a call for "civic action" to assist the government in countering the threat of "dictatorship, that of totalitarian communism."[75] Most American reporting, however, stressed that de Gaulle's authoritarian style, rather than any subversive communist plan, had brought about the crisis. The CIA, for instance, believed the crisis to be a logical response to the Fifth Republic's presidential system. Following the Third and the Fourth Republic, "the pendulum swung so far in the opposite direction that the Assembly was almost reduced to political insignificance." This encouraged the government to turn down "arrogantly" the views of the labor unions, students, and the opposition parties of the left on even minor issues, even after the setbacks for the Gaullists in the parliamentary elections of March 1967. Students, whose numbers had surged from 170,000 to over 600,000 in a decade, still labored under a rigid testing system developed by Napoleon and in the outdated and crammed facilities of old universities. Pleas for reforming the system received almost no hearing. "It was this widespread frustration with the unresponsiveness of the system [...] that gave depth and breadth to the massive protest movement [...]." And when Prime Minister Pompidou gave in to all the major demands of students on May 13, the lesson was clear to all those whose aspirations had been nipped: "the government could be more successfully challenged in the streets than in the National Assembly."[76]

The turn of events in France could not but inspire some gloating on the other side of the Atlantic. "If it weren't so serious – as the saying goes – one would be tempted into just a little fugitive satisfaction at the deflation of his imperial authority," the conservative commentator William F. Buckley Jr. opined. "Let's face it, human beings being, unfortunately, human, it is satisfying to a part of one's nature to see General de Gaulle's enormous nose being rubbed into his apparent inability to govern his own country."[77] Even the *New York Times*, whose reporters had often risen to de Gaulle's defense, declared in its editorial that,

the turmoil in France on the tenth anniversary of General de Gaulle's return to power seriously – perhaps irreparably – deflates the Gaullist mystique. A regime that has claimed order as its first achievement is shown to be presiding over disorder. A movement that boasts of being the wave of the future discovers that it, too, has its next generation in revolt. The "profound transformation" President de Gaulle repeatedly claims he has accomplished in France turns out to be not so profound after all.[78]

Official Washington studiously avoided any hint of vindictiveness, as was to be expected. But there inevitably was some private gloating over de Gaulle's problems. Sargent Shriver, the new American ambassador, who arrived in the midst of the student riots, made no secret of his sympathy for the young activists. Whereas Bohlen had focused on the traditional diplomatic issues of policy and strategy, the bright and breezy Shriver – married to Eunice Kennedy and formerly a driving force behind the Peace Corps – was a quasi-celebrity whose main assignment was to improve the atmospherics of the bilateral relationship through public diplomacy. On his first day at the embassy, he therefore decided to venture out to the Latin Quarter and ended up squatting down with the students on Boulevard St. Germaine. "I presented my credentials to the French students before I presented them to de Gaulle," he quipped.[79] Although Shriver's public demonstration raised more than a few eyebrows in diplomatic circles, old-hand Vernon Walters recalled that most American diplomats at the Parisian embassy, where he served as the military attaché at the time, sympathized with the rebellious youth and "some of them almost seemed to welcome these events as promising his [de Gaulle's] overthrow."[80]

This, of course, was not to be, nor was there going to be a "civil war" as the CIA prognosticated. De Gaulle's brinkmanship of May 30 put the forces of law and order back in control. Workers gradually returned to work in the ensuing weeks and the government took charge of the universities. On June 23 and 30, the Gaullists moreover won a massive election majority. Yet there was little doubt that the May Crisis had tarnished de Gaulle's standing in French politics and had important implications for his foreign policy. In the view of most American diplomats, the May Crisis was a welcome reality check after two years in which de Gaulle had taken his policy of independence to extremes. "France [...] may be returning to reality; important, as is her due, but not the false, inflated, imperious France that de Gaulle has sought," Shriver remarked at the height of the crisis, adding that this renewed sense of reality on the French side might offer a chance for improving the bilateral relationship.[81] After May 1968, it was considered much less likely that de Gaulle would denounce the North Atlantic Treaty in 1969. The seditious role played in the crisis by the French Communist Party – which de Gaulle had chosen to emphasize as he cast the die on May 30 – moreover shed a sobering light on his policy of détente, entente, and finally cooperation with the Eastern Bloc.

Perhaps the most important political consequence of the May Crisis was that de Gaulle could no longer pose as the executor of the unified will of the French people. Even as the General at long last emerged victorious, the personal mystique that had always surrounded him was no longer as compelling as before the crisis. De Gaulle had explicitly sought to unify the French around a foreign policy of grandeur. Most Frenchmen, however, seemed to believe that his preoccupation with French prestige abroad had instilled a wanton neglect of domestic issues. "May" showed that they were, at any rate, more concerned with their standard of living than with matters of foreign policy. As France returned to calm, it was clear to American officials that either de Gaulle or his successor would have to pay urgent attention to domestic concerns for the next couple of years. "Every sacred tree in France has been shaken beginning with university through trade unions to political parties, including communists and Gaullists," Shriver observed in the wake of the crisis. "Whoever governs France after elections will face battery of difficult internal problems, and it is solution – or non-solution – of these problems that will dominate French political scene for immediate future (as opposed to de Gaulle's 'politique de grandeur' which everyone, friend or foe, agrees can never be same again)."[82] As a result of the May Crisis, France was therefore likely to be a more tractable ally than it had been for years.

Another important consequence of the May Crisis was that it swept away the economic underpinnings of de Gaulle's policy of grandeur. On May 29, Katzenbach informed President Johnson that the crisis cost France an estimated $1 billion per week and that any settlement with labor would likely cause prices to go up and worsen France's balance of payments and trade balance.[83] De Gaulle's decision to buy off domestic discontent with higher wages indeed led to economic trouble. The French balance-of-payments deficit, previously headed for somewhere between $200 million and $300 million, was suddenly anticipated to reach between $500 million and $600 million. Higher wages also caused inflation, leading to a flight from the franc and a run on gold and the deutsche mark. The free-market price of gold rose to more than $40 an ounce. After years of hoarding gold, France was now forced to sell some of it to raise money in order to maintain the franc. By September, the French central bank had lost an "astounding" $3 billion in reserves.[84]

Whereas until May 1968, monetary issues had been a source of friction, de Gaulle's financial misfortune now set the stage for an unforeseen rapprochement between France and the United States. De Gaulle vowed throughout the crisis that he would not devalue the franc. It was, however, uncertain how long France could resist the pressure from the market given the hemorrhage of reserves – and by November the air was rife with speculation that the French central bank was reaching a breaking point. The United States, meanwhile, had powerful reasons to oppose a devaluation of the franc, in particular because it could set off a chain of events ultimately resulting in another attack on the dollar and a complete breakdown of the monetary system. As Secretary of the Treasury Henry Fowler advised President Johnson in early June 1968, the monetary system is in such fragile condition that even a mild devaluation could bring about massive fund movements [...]. Almost certainly, it would have an adverse effect on sterling, which is still very weak. [...] Should that happen, there would be repercussions on the dollar and, perhaps, general monetary chaos – with everyone trying to get out of currencies and into gold. Whether the monetary system, in its present form, could survive this series of steps is problematical. The U.S. might well have to cut the gold convertibility link to the dollar and float itself. And that would destroy the present system and probably badly cripple world trade.[85]

By early June, the Johnson administration therefore began working on plans in the strictest confidence to save the franc, the pound, and the dollar.[86] Above all, Washington was trying to dissuade any unilateral moves by the French and was similtaneously weighing in on Germany to revaluate the deutsche mark, since this would help to take off the pressure from the franc, the pound, and the dollar. It insisted on a multilaterally agreed currency adjustment, if any. In November 1968, fears of a unilateral devaluation by France reached a peak. On November 18, Walt Rostow hurriedly cabled Fowler, who had travelled to Europe, about "unverified reports that the French may unilaterally act to devalue the franc so substantially as to upset the world monetary system [...] because the German Government is un-willing to revalue the mark upward." President Johnson instructed the secretary of the treasury to take the matter up personally with Chancellor Kiesinger and to persuade him to "promptly contact President de Gaulle and urge no unilateral move until appropriate monetary authorities can convene and act on a multilateral basis."[87] A German concession in the monetary realm was considered crucial to head off a French devaluation, but the Germans proved extremely reluctant to do their part and refused to consider a revaluation of their own currency. On Novem-ber 19, Johnson informed Harold Wilson that "our tentative approach would be to work for something like [a] 10 percent German revaluation and [a] 5 percent French devaluation, with small corresponding moves by Italy and The Nether-lands."[88] One day later Rostow impressed on Johnson: "If we can hold the French – or hold them to a modest devaluation plus big short-term loans – the pound can be protected; and I'm still not sure that's impossible because de Gaulle has staked so much on a policy of 'no devaluation,' out of simple pride."[89]

On November 23, taking the market by surprise, de Gaulle indeed announced that "the parity of the franc will be maintained." One day later, in a national address, he furthermore announced draconic budget cuts in order to defend the currency.[90] De Gaulle's defiance of "odious speculation on the national currency" has been described as one more public show of his policy of independence.[91] It had been made possible, however, only by a $2 billion international credit pack-age, which had been agreed a few days before and in which the United States assumed a large part of the burden.[92] President Johnson's simultaneous message to de Gaulle, in which he expressed confidence in the franc and in France's economic policies, also helped to stabilize the market.[93] "The international monetary system is not a field for pettiness and retribution," Johnson wrote in his memoirs about his efforts to help de Gaulle avert a devaluation of the franc.[94] The American embassy reported that the latter was indeed very pleased with Johnson's willingness to come to the assistance of the franc.[95]

Johnson's handling of the franc crisis of November 1968 – a crisis that Lacouture has labelled the "monetary equivalent of May"[96] – thus greatly contributed to an improvement of the bilateral relationship near the end of his presidency. To be sure, this improvement was also aided by a commensurate deterioration of the Franco-German relationship. During the negotiations about the monetary crisis in Bonn in November, "the Germans to the end [had] refused to budge."[97] They did ultimately agree to measures to increase imports and reduce exports, but they did not revalue the deutsche mark.[98] Johnson's advisers instantly shared the view that de Gaulle's ensuing decision not to devaluate the franc "was in part politically motivated and a response to the hard-headed German tactics at Bonn."[99] At a National Security Council meeting on November 25, the bitterness between the French and the Germans over the monetary crisis figured prominently in the discussion. The sympathy, for once, was with de Gaulle. Fowler remarked: "The French, I think quite properly, feel that the Germans have not done as much as they could or should as partners in this operation."[100] Johnson's readiness to continue to help de Gaulle was moreover evidenced by his insistent probing whether more should be done to bolster the franc. His decision to come to the support of the franc in November 1968 despite his earlier differences with de Gaulle and the concurrent inability of Paris and Bonn to work out a deal to defend the French currency marked an important adjustment in the trilateral relationship. For the first time since 1958, the adjustment was in favor of American-French accommodation. This change was moreover reinforced by developments in the Cold War.

Cold War – From Détente With the East to Tripartitism Revisited

On the night of August 20, 1968, thousands of Soviet tanks occupied the streets of Czechoslovakia, followed by hundreds of thousands of Warsaw Pact troops. In Prague and other cities, Czech and Slovak citizens confronted the soldiers, denying them assistance such as the provision of food and water. They openly denounced the invasion and the Soviet leadership. Their non-violent struggle, however, stood no chance against the Soviet-led military machine. More than seventy Czechs and Slovaks were killed during the invasion and hundreds were wounded. The Czechoslovak leader Alexander Dubček was arrested and brought to Moscow, along with several of his colleagues. The crackdown sparked a wave of emigration, ultimately numbering 300,000 people, many of them highly qualified. It abruptly ended the so-called Prague Spring, the hopeful but brief period of political liberalization in Czechoslovakia that had begun with Dubček's rise to power in early January 1968. The invasion also led to the Brezhnev Doctrine, which established that individual socialist states had "limited sovereignty" within the "socialist commonwealth" – meaning that they risked military intervention if they strayed too far from the course charted in Moscow. And it sent a shiver through the West, reminding it of the repressive nature of the Soviet regime.

The Soviet-led military intervention in Czechoslovakia of August 1968 was a serious disappointment to Johnson, who had hoped to convince the Senate to ratify the Nuclear Non-Proliferation Treaty before the end of his presidency and to make significant headway in strategic arms control talks with Moscow.[101] Fearful of repeating the Hungarian experience of 1956 and intent on arms control negotiations with the Soviet Union, the Johnson administration had done very little in support of the Prague Spring.[102] The documentary record strongly suggests that the Johnson administration was caught off guard by the Soviet military intervention. Rusk and Rostow had affirmed to Johnson as late as July 24 that "real crisis [in Czechoslovakia] has subsided" and that "the Soviets will not move militarily against them."[103] When Soviet Ambassador Anatoly Dobrynin asked for a meeting at the White House to explain the ongoing military intervention, he found that – somewhat to his relief – the seriousness of the matter had not dawned on the American president.[104] The Johnson administration had been so fixated on arranging an arms control summit in Moscow with Alexei Kosygin that it simply could not imagine a Soviet-led military intervention. "The political costs the Soviets would have to pay was one reason we thought they would not move," Rusk explained a few days after Warsaw Pact soldiers crossed the border. "The 'Cold War' is not over," Johnson unhappily observed. "We have been disillusioned if not deceived."[105] Largely because of the Czech Crisis, Johnson was not to have the arms control accomplishment that would have ended his presidency on a more positive note.

Johnson's disappointment, however, was a mild affliction compared with de Gaulle's fate. For the latter, the crushing of the Prague Spring was little less than a foreign policy catastrophe. Although de Gaulle's visit to Poland in September 1967 had already been a cold shower on French aspirations and Franco-Soviet rapprochement had lost steam by mid-1968 for lack of interest on Moscow's part,[106] de Gaulle had been much encouraged by the political liberalization in Czechoslovakia. Taken together with the increasingly independent stance assumed by Nicolae Ceausescu's Romania, the course of events in Prague was bestowing a sense of inevitability to de Gaulle's sequence of détente, entente, and cooperation with Eastern Europe. In a late July press conference, he could still credibly describe the developments in Czechoslovakia as "but an episode in the inevitable process of gradually relaxing Russian control over the countries of the socialist bloc."[107] Added to the plausible notion that the United States, beset by Vietnam and its own domestic turmoil, was beginning to reduce its presence in Europe, the "policy of blocs" indeed appeared to be giving way to an emerging

Europe from the Atlantic to the Urals. It all read like "the beginning of a scenario that might have been written at the Elysée."[108]

In private, the French government had been rather fearful that the developments in Czechoslovakia would spiral out of control – more so, in fact, than the Johnson administration. De Gaulle was above all concerned that the quick pace of events would provoke the Soviets into a violent response. In particular, when Warsaw Pact troops engaged in a large military exercise in Czechoslovakia in the summer, the signs did not look good to Paris. "They are going too quickly, and too far," de Gaulle judged about the reformers in early July in a conversation with Jean-Marie Domenach, a French writer who had just returned from Prague. "The Russians will intervene, then, as always, the Czechs will give up fighting and night will fall once again over Prague."[109] Michel Debré, serving this time as de Gaulle's foreign minister, proved even less hopeful in late July. Four weeks before the invasion, he impressed on Undersecretary of State Katzenbach that "it was absolutely impossible for the Soviet Union to accept the course of liberalization in Czech because if this continued it would affect all other Eastern European countries and prove to be irreversible." Debré "did not think that it would be possible to reverse this course in Czech, other than by force." The French foreign minister "thought the Soviets were prepared to do this" and that "it was conceivable, but unlikely, that Dubček could avert the crisis by making major concessions to the Soviets."[110] Still, when de Gaulle's nightmare did turn into reality, without the Czech army or police firing a single shot on the invaders, it was, as de Gaulle's long-time aide Etienne Burin des Roziers recalled, "a very hard blow for him."[111] The Czech Crisis above all revealed the severe constraints placed on his grand design for ending the Cold War by the sheer repressive nature of Soviet domination and the persistent force of communist ideology. It served to re-energize NATO and ended talk in the United States of substantial troop cuts in Europe. And it "dispelled most of the remaining fancies about French influence on Soviet behavior."[112]

Although both Johnson and de Gaulle were inclined to play down the crisis and to continue their pursuit of détente with the Soviet bloc as best they could, the Czech Crisis at first seemed to only aggravate Franco-American differences. In the first official response to the Soviet-led incursion, the French government emphasized that it was yet another manifestation of the "politics of the blocs" that had been "imposed in Europe as a result of the Yalta agreements" and which France had been trying to overcome for years.[113] By hence blaming the Czech Crisis on the entire "Yalta system," de Gaulle appeared to implicate Washington as well as Moscow. This, in turn, caused Yalta veteran Averell Harriman – in one of his jabs for which he had earned the moniker "the crocodile" – to deliver a stinging rebuke in a radio interview:

I think that President de Gaulle has somewhat oversimplified history when he compared the Warsaw Pact and the domination of the Soviet Union in Eastern Europe with the free association of nations through NATO. [...] There is one thing which de Gaulle says which is true: that he was not at Yalta, and therefore his impressions have not been gained from a knowledge of what went on, but a lack of knowledge.[114]

Despite de Gaulle's recurring critique of the bipolar power configuration in Europe and the angry responses this drew from some Americans, there was a noticeable improvement in the atmosphere between Paris and Washington in the wake of the Czech Crisis. Majority opinion in France was far more condemnatory than de Gaulle of the Soviet Union. Many French officials, as Shriver reported, moreover believed that an "agonizing reappraisal" of French foreign policy was in order after the Soviet aggression; they exhibited a new willingness to cooperate with the United States.[115] In October, Henry Tanner of the New York Times reported, in an article that Shriver recommended to President Johnson, that "beneath the unruffled appearance of French diplomacy these days, there is a wide acceptance of the fact that the foundation of President de Gaulle's concept of foreign policy has been shaken if not destroyed by the Soviet intervention of Czechoslovakia." There were indications that, in Tanner's words approvingly cited by Shriver, de Gaulle had been "more deeply upset over the Soviet military intervention than he lets on publicly."

High ranking [French] officials concede the basic Gaullist assumption which emerged from General de Gaulle's visit to the USSR in June 1966 has been proved wrong by Czechoslovakia. This assumption was that the Soviets had moved far enough toward peacefulness and liberalism in international affairs to permit a western statesman to claim their friendship while at the same time encouraging the Poles, Czechoslovaks, Hungarians and others to demand national sovereignty. They now feel that liberalization in Eastern Europe will remain stagnant until "the heresy hits Rome," i.e. the USSR, and that is a long time off.[116]

Building on the genuine groundswell of goodwill towards the United States among French officials and the faltering promise of détente, the Franco-American relationship turned toward a more cooperative mode in the fall of 1968. According to Shriver, even de Gaulle realized that "with the Soviets on warpath this is not the time to be feuding with [the] US." On the eve of Foreign Minister Debré's visit to Washington in October, the first visit by a French foreign minister in two years, the American ambassador pressed the importance of using the new ambience to lay the groundwork for a fundamental improvement of the bilateral relationship once de Gaulle left the scene.[117] In fact, Walt Rostow had already asked the CIA in August to examine the possibilities for a rapprochement between the United States and France. Washington, to be sure, was under no illusion. "There are a number of ways in which Washington could accommodate Paris, particularly in economic, scientific, technical and financial matters," the CIA reported upon Rostow's request; however, "in [the] political arena, there is not a great deal which can be accomplished so long as Paris and Washington have differing conceptions both of world issues and of the roles each should play in international efforts."[118] Although French foreign policy showed signs of adjustment in the aftermath of the Czech Crisis, it was clear to both the CIA and the State Department that de Gaulle had not abandoned his basic objectives or fundamental principles.[119] Yet the circumstances for a substantive improvement in the relationship had never before been so advantageous during Johnson's term.

At least as important as the implications of the Czech Crisis in this regard was the increasing uneasiness in Paris with the reemergence of Germany as a power to be reckoned with. Bonn was, as we have seen, already quite prepared in 1968 to use its monetary clout and to withstand the pressure from its Western allies to revalue its currency. With the evolution of its Ostpolitik since late 1966, Bonn was also increasingly taking an independent line in international diplomacy.[120] Whereas France's policy of détente had become largely immobile by 1968, the United States' arms control initiatives and Germany's initiatives for an opening to the East were overtaking those of France in importance. Reports in the spring of 1968 that German Foreign Minister Willy Brandt had denounced de Gaulle in a speech as "power hungry" also did not help matters.[121] The reemergence of German influence could not but affect the French attitude towards its eastern neighbor. The days of Adenauer, during which Bonn often referred itself to de Gaulle's leadership, and Erhard, who was orientated on Washington, were quickly fading to make place for more self-possessed policies. In the wake of the Czech Crisis, de Gaulle not only refused to offer an unambiguous pledge of military support to Germany, but he also suggested that Germany's eastern policies had played a part in provoking the Soviet-led invasion. "The Russians were worried by the threat of a revitalized Germany joining with [the] Czech and perhaps even East Germany, plus the Chinese, in joint actions against Russia itself," de Gaulle explained to Shriver on September 23. "It was the spectre of China and Germany working together against Russia in the next five to ten years that was the real cause of their alarm and actions."[122]

Interestingly, the French reorientation on the West as a result of the Czech Crisis and the resurgence of German power accounted for an unforeseen revival of tripartitism in French diplomacy in the fall of 1968. The invasion of Czechoslovakia set off a hectic pace of meetings at NATO, with many allies declaring themselves to be in favor of enhancing the defense posture of the alliance and – at long last – raising their defense spending. After de Gaulle's first intimation to American sources in early January 1968 that France would not leave the North Atlantic

Treaty in 1969,[123] Paris on November 16 joined in an official declaration of the North Atlantic Council stating that "the French government considers that the Alliance must continue as long as it appears to be necessary."[124] De Gaulle, however, as was to be expected, was strongly opposed to proposals for strengthening NATO in response to the crisis. Instead, Washington was receiving indications that he was interested in reviving his memorandum proposal of September 1958. De Gaulle intimated as much in a discussion with Ambassàdor Shriver in mid-September.[125] During his Washington visit in October, Foreign Minister Debré also gave evidence of a renewed interest in a tripartite coordination of policies in his conversation with President Johnson, as he suggested that the major powers of the West should improve the regular coordination of their actions in Europe and the Middle East.[126] The State Departement's Director of Intelligence and Research, Thomas Hughes, furthermore believed that de Gaulle was considering some kind of tripartite nuclear cooperation in the wake of the Czechoslovak Crisis.[127]

At the same time, French diplomats – not least of all the "thoroughgoing anglophile" Debré[128] – were throwing out feelers for a Franco-British rapprochement, potentially even leading to French acquiescence in British membership of the Common Market. This renewed interest on the part of France in strong relations with Great Britain was without doubt inspired by a desire to compensate for Germany's growing political and economic weight on the European continent. It was highlighted in particular during the new British ambassador Christopher Soames' audience with de Gaulle on February 4, 1969. In the course of a long tête-à-tête, de Gaulle told Soames, whose standing with the General was undoubtedly enhanced because he was Winston Churchill's son-in-law, of his willingness to engage in secret talks with London about the possibility of a looser organization of the Common Market in order to suit British tastes as well as of increased political and defense cooperation between France, Great Britain, Germany, and Italy.[129]

Given that the Johnson administration was searching for ways to improve the relationship with France in the fall of 1968, these French overtures aroused interest. Any formal tripartite scheme obviously would not have been any more acceptable to the United States in 1968 than it had been in 1958, since it would have caused a confrontation with Germany and undermined NATO; at any rate, such a scheme was never officially put forward by the French government. Yet there was a willingness among American officials to explore other ways to improve structurally the bilateral or even the trilateral relationship. This was evident, for instance, in a remarkable conversation between Undersecretary of State for Political Affairs Eugene Rostow and French Ambassador Charles Lucet against the background of the franc crisis in late November 1968. Giving his personal view, Rostow not only supported a Franco-British entente in order to keep growing German influence in check but even hinted at the future possibility of Franco-American nuclear collaboration:

> Rostow said he had never been able to understand one aspect of French European policy, namely the assumption that France could indefinitely control or manage the Germans. As the Ambassador knew, we strongly favored the Franco-German rapprochement, and tried never to do or say anything to weaken it. That relationship was fundamental to any hope of a European future. But to us the natural and prudent way to organize Europe was on the foundation of the Entente Cordiale, which we could support on the basis of parity from the background [sic], within a strong NATO and OECD context. To Rostow, speaking personally, the political implication of the crisis was clear. Germany wished to assert its economic primacy.

We knew of course of French sensitivity to the thought that we treated Britain differently from France. [...] Rostow thought, speaking for himself, that in the right political setting, the issue of differential treatment of Britain and France, which was largely illusory, could be overcome, *even in the nuclear field*, without affecting NATO arrangements.[130] (emphasis added)

As it turned out, there would be no restoration of the "entente cordiale." De Gaulle's private conversation with Soames even turned into a venomous affair between London and Paris. The virulently anti-Gaullist Foreign Office led by Foreign Secretary Michael Stewart transfigured de Gaulle's words into an attack on NATO and Prime Minister Wilson decided, at the Foreign Office's insistence, to violate the diplomatic mores by informing Chancellor Kiesinger during a visit to Bonn in February *before* responding to de Gaulle.[131] The Soames affair certainly hindered Franco-British rapprochement for as long as the Labour government remained in power.[132] But the rapprochement between France, the United States, and Great Britain in late 1968 would be of enduring significance. Lord Ismay's oft-cited dictum about NATO – i.e., that it had been devised to keep the Russians out, the Americans in, and the Germans down – exercised its powerful logic on decisionmakers in Paris as well: from the French perspective, the Anglo-Saxons continued to be needed to keep the Germans in check and to keep the Soviets at bay. The events of 1968 forced a reorientation of French foreign policy towards the Western alliance and towards the removal (under Georges Pompidou) in May 1971 of the French veto of British entry in the Common Market.

The accommodation between the United States and France, meanwhile, would be taken further by the Nixon administration and would, as Rostow had envisaged, include covert collaboration in the nuclear realm. Johnson, however, deserves the credit for having laid the foundations, both by his consistent and sagacious policy of restraint in response to the Gaullist challenge and by the nature of his decisions in the course of 1968, the *annus horribilis* in both American and

French foreign policy. While he had been incapable of developing a meaningful personal relationship with de Gaulle, Johnson's constructive role was recognized in Paris as well. It was conveyed straight to the Oval Office by Michel Debré on October 15. The French foreign minister had been granted a meeting with the American president at the recommendation of Rusk.[133] Debré, speaking as de Gaulle's "interpreter," stressed that Johnson had been president "during one of the most difficult years since the last war" and would leave office "with our total admiration." Johnson responded in kind. He then invited Debré to join him in watching the lauching of the first Apollo test flight, part of the program to put a man on the moon. As they were seated side by side in two armchairs in front of the TV set, the American president towering over his guest, Debré turned, put his hand on Johnson's arm, and said:

> Mr. President, despite everything you hear, despite everything that people may say, we consider you to have been a very good friend of France.[134]

1969 – When "Great" Minds Meet: Nixon, Kissinger, and De Gaulle

Helped by the Vietnam debacle and the abhorrence many Americans felt for the domestic upheaval of 1968, Richard M. Nixon won the presidency by a small margin in the popular vote but a large majority in the electoral college.[135] It was a stunning comeback for the Republican. After having lost the presidential elections of 1960 (by a minute margin to John F. Kennedy) and the Californian gubernatorial elections of October 1962, he had all but vanished into the political wilderness. Yet now he had entered the realm of world leaders that he had coveted so fervently for eight lonely years. For all his insecurities, Nixon felt that this was his natural habitat.

By January 1969, de Gaulle was undoubtedly the leader with the greatest allure. The Nixon presidency's three-month overlap with that of de Gaulle was remarkable. Despite its brevity, it proved long enough to produce major changes in the dynamic of the Franco-American relationship, laying the groundwork for further improvements in the years after de Gaulle's resignation on April 27. The absence of dialogue that had been characteristic of the Johnson years made way for a genuine meeting of minds. Nixon and his foreign policy czar Henry Kissinger cherished an admiration for the General and his statecraft that was rare among Americans. Their quest to put US foreign policy on a realist footing and to adjust it to a decline in America's global position also greatly contributed to the newfangled Franco-American amity. After a year of dramatic setbacks and nearing the end of his political life, de Gaulle would finally be presented with the American interlocutor with whom a more fruitful relationship could be developed.

Sympathy for the General

Ever since they first met in April 1960, during de Gaulle's state visit to the United States, there existed an intimate rapport between the Frenchman and the Californian.[136] This was, to some extent, rather surprising. As Eisenhower's vice president, Nixon was a consummate career politician with strong ties to his party; de Gaulle was not only the contrary to a career politician in everything he did, but he intensely disliked party politics in his own country. Nixon's Quaker background had little in common with de Gaulle's Catholicism. There were undeniable differences between their personalities, too. Nixon was often painfully insecure and secretly manipulative, to which de Gaulle's supreme self-confidence and heroic record stood in sharp contrast. Yet from the outset they had caught each other's imagination as belonging to the sublime crop of wielders of statecraft.

De Gaulle perceived in Nixon a budding statesman of considerable intellect, which he probably thought a rare phenomenon in American politics. "In his somewhat curious post of Vice-President," de Gaulle recalled in his memoirs, "he struck me as one of those frank and steady personalities on whom one feels one could rely in the great affairs of State if they were to reach the highest office."[137] There is little doubt that de Gaulle would have preferred Nixon to succeed Eisenhower as president. When Nixon wrote de Gaulle a letter upon having lost the election, he replied affectionately and asked him to lunch should he visit Paris.[138] Nixon did so in June 1963, after he had lost the gubernatorial election in California, and again in 1967. At the first of these occasions, de Gaulle prophesied, in a toast on a patio behind the Elysée palace, that his guest "at some time in the future" would return to a "very high capacity" in American politics.[139] It was a remarkable morale booster from a foreign leader to someone whose political career had plunged to such depths that his obituaries had been written. He himself had announced after his rout at the Californian polls: "You won't have Nixon to kick around anymore, because, gentlemen, this is my last press conference."[140] De Gaulle might have foreseen more clearly than others that Nixon's role in American politics had not yet been played out because of his political qualities and that it would therefore be sensible to continue to invest in their personal relationship. There is certainly reason to assume that de Gaulle believed Nixon would return as the Republican candidate in the 1964 presidential elections; in January 1964, he privately declared an unambiguous preference for Nixon over the incumbent Johnson.[141] And in 1967, de Gaulle emphatically told Vernon Walters in private that he continued to believe that Nixon, having "crossed the desert" like de Gaulle had, would be elected president.[142] André Malraux once explained that de Gaulle furthermore felt a bond because "Nixon also had his 'period of exile.'"[143] So when Nixon at long last reached the presidency in 1969, Le Monde's André Fontaine had reason to write that "le général de Gaulle a trouvé l'interlocuteur américain qu'il souhaitait depuis longtemps."[144]

As for Nixon, his esteem for de Gaulle was near infinite. He did not share the distaste for Gaullism that was common within the bipartisan establishment that had dominated American foreign policy for two decades. There are no known Nixon statements denouncing the General or his policies, nothing that approximates the denunciations by the likes of Acheson, McCloy, and Ball, no hint of the frustration occasionally expressed by Kennedy or – to a lesser extent – Johnson. He had, to be sure, not always been an active admirer, and for a long time he probably shared the customary assessment of de Gaulle as vainglorious and obstreperous.[145] But ever since the commonplace assessment of the General was belied in their first personal encounter, he held nothing but the highest regard for the Frenchman. Nixon was obviously also much taken with de Gaulle's remarkable willingness to continue to see him during his years out of office and by de Gaulle's predictions – "years before it was even suggested in the American press" – that he would one day be elected to the White House.[146] In his book *In the Arena* (1990), he moreover described his conversations with de Gaulle as "among the most valuable ones I had during my public career" and cited profusely from de Gaulle's writings (in particular *Le fil de l'épee*).[147] His long chapter on de Gaulle in *Leaders* (1990) is not only a riveting tribute to a remarkable leader but a personal portrait filled with sympathy for a gentle giant: "Seldom has history seen a leader whose personality combined all the admirable qualities that de Gaulle's did."[148]

Nixon's high regard for de Gaulle was undoubtedly occasioned by the fact that the latter was a leader of the calibre to which Nixon aspired. His esteem was that of an aspiring statesman for a living epitome of statecraft – the last one still in office in 1969. Similar to de Gaulle, he was relatively uninterested in domestic policies, considering them "a bore" whereas "in foreign policy you have the fate of the country at stake."[149] They were both highly sensitive to the link between the psychology of the nation and its foreign policy. In a seminal speech to San Francisco's Bohemian Club in July 1967, Nixon had worrying questioned "whether America has the national character and moral stamina to see us through this long and difficult struggle"; in his memoirs, he makes clear that this concern was the motivating force behind his presidential campaign.[150] His foreign policy was hence partially charged with the domestic purpose of restoring the self-confidence of Americans and of keeping their isolationist instincts – particularly strong in liberal quarters at the time – at bay. Nixon's most urgent foreign policy test upon resuming the levers of power was, of course, that of extricating the United States militarily from Vietnam – a test somewhat akin to the one de Gaulle had faced with regard to Algeria ten years earlier. Nixon's call on "the great silent majority of my fellow Americans" to support his controversial decision to keep American forces in Vietnam notwithstanding large and increasingly violent protests was certainly reminiscent of de Gaulle's calls on the French people in times of crisis.[151] In some ways, Nixon even appears to have styled his political persona after the Frenchman. In the preface of the 1968 edition of *Six Crises* (originally published in 1962), for instance, Nixon wrote:

> Sometimes a nation is ready and a man is not; sometimes a man is ready and a nation is not; sometimes a nation decides that a man is ready for leadership and his is the right kind of leadership for the time. Only time will tell what course destiny will take in this watershed year of 1968.[152]

This sense of destiny and of the indivisible bond between a nation and a leader are at least as characteristic of de Gaulle as of Nixon. Nixon, like de Gaulle, had spent years as a statesman in frustrated abeyance before returning to the pinnacle of power. In addition, he yearned to be recognized as a writer-politician and an intellectual force in his own right – the hallmark of the truly great. In all of these respects, Nixon aspired to be – in the words of one scholar – "America's de Gaulle."[153]

It is important to note that the strength of the Nixon-de Gaulle relationship resulted from an ideological affinity as well. Both were politically conservative and internationally realist. They hence operated on similar wavelengths, even if they did not always agree. By American standards, Nixon was an unapologetic guardian of the national interest (certainly if one regards his more Wilsonian statements as little more than mandatory rhetoric to garner support, as Kissinger has suggested).[154] In his first annual foreign policy report to the Senate, in February 1970, the new president stressed that "our interests must shape our commitments, rather than the other way around."[155] He believed that without a clear view of the national interest, a foreign policy was bound to be mercurial and – as Vietnam showed – could easily go awry. This belief was accepted wisdom among realist students of international relations, but it was rather uncharacteristic for an American politician – let alone for one to be so open about it. "In a British or French state paper, such statements would have passed for truisms," Kissinger later wrote. "In America, it was unprecedented for a president to stake his policy on the explicit affirmation of the national interest."[156]

Nixon shared de Gaulle's axiom that a dominant executive was a prerequisite for an effective foreign policy. "We need a strong President to deal on an equal footing with strong leaders of other powerful countries," he wrote in *In the Arena*. "The alternative to strong Presidential government is government by Congress, which is no government at all."[157] This preference for a formidable executive and a relatively weak Congress, especially in the conduct of foreign affairs, was another hallmark of the American conservative political tradition. It also mirrored de Gaulle's convictions about the French constitution, which he put in practice with the foundation of the Fifth Republic. De Gaulle's grasp on French foreign policy was almost complete, and his long-term vision rendered it an uncommon consistency. Nixon likewise assumed office convinced that the conduct of foreign policy was a quintessential presidential function that should not be left to bureaucrats. During the Nixon years, US foreign policy would be formulated in – and in many cases even executed from – the White House (often in great secrecy). Not since the days of Franklin Roosevelt would the making of American foreign policy be so centralized. More than most other presidents, Nixon would meticulously prepare and time his speeches so that they would have the greatest possible effect. William Safire, William Bundy, and Cy Sulzberger have all emphasized that in all these respects Nixon followed the example of the contemporary statesman he most admired: "The model of de Gaulle was always with him."[158] Nixon, as Arthur Schlesinger Jr. has observed in The Imperial Presidency (1974), tried "to establish a quasi-gaullist regime in the United States."[159]

This operational mode was much encouraged by Nixon's recognition of the ever-changing balance of power between nation-states, rather than their cooperation within a multilateral framework, as the central regulating mechanism in world politics – another similarity with Gaullism. Whereas the predominantly liberal American policymakers of the 1950s and 1960s denounced balance-of-power politics as a dangerous anachronism in the nuclear age and evocative of Europe's past wars, Nixon was quite prepared to acknowledge – and even to promote – the existence of multiple military, political, and economic centers of power in the world. "Nixon did not accept the Wilsonian verities about the essential goodness of man or the underlying harmony among nations to be maintained by collective security," Kissinger explained. "In Nixon's perception, peace and harmony were not the natural order of things but temporary oases in a perilous world where stability could only be preserved by vigilant effort."[160] Like de Gaulle, Nixon entertained a geopolitical mindset rather than an institutional one. International stability would depend less on the regulated behavior of states in a multilateral framework than on an equilibrium based on the relative distribution of power within the international system. Nixon also diverged from thinking in strictly bipolar terms, believing that stability hinged on an equilibrium between the five great economic centers of powers in the world (albeit with the United States as its most powerful core) – or as he stated in an interview with Time magazine in January 1972:

> We must remember the only time in the history of the world that we have had any extended periods of peace is when there has been balance of power. It is when one nation becomes infinitely more powerful in relation to its potential competitor that the danger of war arises. ... I think it will be a safer world and a better world if we have a strong, healthy United States, Europe, Soviet Union, China, Japan, each balancing the other, not playing one against the other, an even balance.[161]

This multipolar world view was consistent with Nixon's policy of détente. The containment of the Soviet Union would remain the overriding objective of American foreign policy, but Nixon introduced sweeping policy changes towards this end. Despite his reputation as an anti-communist die-hard, Nixon had no qualms about pursuing détente in the relationship with the Soviet Union – yet another similarity to de Gaulle. Whereas de Gaulle viewed détente as a first step toward ending the division of Europe, however, Nixon viewed it above all as a way to strengthen the American position vis-à-vis the Soviet Union and to induce it to become less expansionist by ensnaring it in a multipolar web of interests. "The idea was to emphasize those areas in which cooperation was possible," Kissinger has elucidated, "and to use that cooperation as leverage to modify Soviet behavior in areas in which the two countries were at loggerheads."[162] Nixon pursued détente not because he shared liberal hopes of ending the Cold War by "building bridges" to the East, as Johnson had tried to do, but because he believed it served the interest of the United States to deal with the Soviet Union on a less antagonistic basis. His pursuit of détente would be utilitarian and devoid of illusions. In his memoirs, Nixon wrote:

> Never once in my career have I doubted that the Communists mean it when they say that their goal is to bring the world under Communist control. [...] But unlike some anticommunists who think that we should refuse to recognize or deal with the Communists lest in doing so we imply or extend an ideological respectability to their philosophy and their system, I have always believed that we can and must communicate and, when possible, negotiate with Communist nations. They are too powerful to ignore. We must always remember that they will never act out of altruism, but only out of self-interest. Once this is understood, it is more sensible – and also safer – to communicate with the Communists than it is to live in icy cold-war isolation or confrontation.[163]

The renewed consensus on containment was to find a more rational balance between goals and means, between interests and ideals, between confrontation and cooperation, between undifferentiated involvement and total disengagement.[164] In a multipolar world, the Soviet Union would no longer be the object of an American-led struggle by all free nations, but one of the players in a balance-of-power game still dominated by the United States as the most powerful nation. In addition, the multipolar vision allowed for a fundamentally different approach to China, which in Nixon's view had to be brought out of its largely self-imposed isolation into the global equilibrium if only to play it off against the Soviet Union in a game of "triangular" diplomacy.[165]

Nixon's vision of a multipolar world inevitably also affected the American position toward Europe. In his July 1967 speech, he had suggested that NATO was "obsolete" because "we live in a new world," and that priority be given to setting up a "new alliance, multilateral if possible, bilateral if necessary."[166] Addressing the North Atlantic Council in April 1969, twenty years after the signing of the Washington Treaty, Nixon called on NATO to tune in to the "real world," in which men are "driven by suspicion" and "take advantage of their neighbors" and which compelled a recognition of "the sometimes different interests of the Western nations."[167] Nixon also exhibited a greater willingness than Kennedy or Johnson to accept European autonomy.[168] While the Nixon administration would retain NATO in order to exert control over European security and to maintain a position of strength vis-à-vis the Soviet Union, it would otherwise move towards a position of aloofness. It no longer assumed, as the previous administrations tended to do (even though Kennedy, in particular, privately chafed at the assumption), that the United States and an integrating Europe shared all basic interests. This was least of all the case in the economic and the monetary sphere, where the Common Market was becoming an increasingly formidable competitor. But it was also true with respect to détente with the Soviet Union – where Brandt's Germany was pursuing an increasingly self-determining policy – or the myriad of foreign policy issues beyond Europe. The Nixon administration furthermore distanced itself from the intra-European debate between federalists and confederalists, abandoning the activist support that consecutive administrations had given to Jean Monnet and his followers since the late 1940s. It is telling that Nixon's voluminous memoirs contain no references to the European integration movement or its champions. As far as Nixon was concerned, the era of American generosity and tutelage toward Europe had come to an end. In a period of relative decline, Americans had to be far more attentive to their own interests. The Europeans, meanwhile, had to learn how to stand their own in a world of changing power relationships. Even as Nixon remained committed to NATO, his change of attitude toward Europe thus unmistakably generated a more amenable environment for Gaullist aspirations.

Nixon was instinctively far more attuned than his Democratic predecessors to the limitations of American power and more prepared to scale down his foreign policy ambitions accordingly. For any American president in the late 1960s, to be sure, the main foreign policy challenge would have been how to adjust to a decline in the global position of the United States. When Britain's Institute for Strategic Studies assessed in early 1969 that "it was largely accidental that the end of the American desire and ability to be the Universal [sic] and dominant power should coincide with the end of eight years of Democratic rule" and that this change was rather the result of "recent experience at home and abroad" which "had exhausted their [the Americans'] confident sense of purpose and ability," Nixon jotted in the margins: "Very important and accurate."[169] Yet Hubert Humphrey's response to America's relative decline – and certainly George McGovern's, if he had won the presidential elections of 1972 – would most likely have been intrinsically different.

Nixon's response to the relative decline of American power followed the internationalist precepts of the conservative tradition. He was determined to counter the rising isolationist mood among liberals in particular by providing a more realistic basis for America's interaction with the world.[170] He would also rely less on the costly, grand, almost architectural schemes of his Democratic predecessors for strengthening the Free World than on the "intelligent" manipulation of power and events. Under Nixon, US foreign policy would cede many of the more idealistic pretensions associated with internationalist liberalism. It would be disinclined to promote democracy abroad. Instead, it would conform to the sobering axiom of realpolitik: a policy of well-defined realistic objectives, a shrewd attention to detail, an inclination to pragmatism and moderation, an aversion to ideology, an emphasis on diplomacy paired with a willingness to use force if required by the national interest. His policy would be guided by long-range objectives, such as the normalization of relations with mainland China. But as Nixon explained in his memoirs: "I did not feel that there should be any single foreign policy priority. There were many priorities, moving in tandem, each affecting the others."[171] The Nixon Doctrine, based on Nixon's impromptu statements to the press during a visit to Guam in July 1969, bid farewell to the undifferentiated globalism that he thought had inspired the foreign policies of Kennedy and Johnson.[172] Nixon refused to be drawn into another Vietnam conflict because of the notion that conceding defeat in a regional conflict would adversely affect the entire calculus of power with the Soviet Union. In the final analysis, Vietnam was of peripheral interest to American security. The nascent strength of regional power centers compelled the United States to try alternative, less direct ways to influence world events and counterpoise Soviet expansionism. American foreign policy, Nixon believed, should concern itself with the orderly devolution of US power to incipient regional powers. The era had passed in which American policymakers would see Europe as a challenging building ground and the Atlantic community as a scaled-down world community.

Nixon's benevolent disposition towards de Gaulle was greatly reinforced by the looming presence of Henry Kissinger as his chief foreign policy adviser. The Harvard academic was at least as ardent an admirer of de Gaulle as the president. Born in Germany; a scholar of nineteenth century European balance-of-power politics (his dissertation had dealt with the Congress of Vienna); an acknowledged realist thinker about international relations – for all these reasons, Kissinger was well placed to assess de Gaulle and his views in their European historical and political context. He was, in the apt words of one biographer, a "European mind in American policy."[173] In the course of the 1960s, Kissinger had shown himself to be one of the most insightful commentators in the United States on the topic of de Gaulle. Together with Walter Lippmann and his fellow European and Harvard academic Stanley Hoffmann, he was one of the very few who were able to see things from de Gaulle's end. Kissinger's *The Troubled Partner-*

ship (1965), for instance, contained an analysis of Franco-American differences over the Atlantic relationship that still ranks among the most perceptive. What is more, Kissinger believed de Gaulle's strategic vision was clearly superior to that of the Americans: "The irony of the Franco-American rivalry is that de Gaulle has conceptions greater than his strength, while the United States power has been greater than its conceptions."[174] Kissinger was not devoid of criticism of de Gaulle. He castigated, in particular, his "abrupt tactics" and "imperious style."[175] Even so, Kissinger judged that de Gaulle's views were frequently closer to the "historical truth" than those that inspired American policies.[176]

Kissinger's *The Troubled Partnership* also deserves closer attention because it can be read as an antithesis to the views of George Ball, to whom the book contains many explicit and implicit references, and because it heralded the alternative approach the Nixon administration would follow. Kissinger not only took issue with Ball's – and many others' – belief that de Gaulle was an "anachronistic ruler obsessed with national prestige," he assailed the transatlantic policies of the Kennedy and Johnson administrations as illusory and too technocratic. Kissinger held America's traditional sense of exceptionalism and the unrealistic expectations often entertained about the world beyond America's frontiers responsible for the mood swings in the history of US foreign policy between isolationalism and activist internationalism. This foreign policy would have to be put on a more rational footing in order to provide a steadier and saner approach to international affairs. Kissinger was therefore determined to reconcile Americans with international political reality and with the notion that their foreign policy should put the national interest first.

In particular, American support for European unity along federalist lines, Kissinger argued, did not correspond to European political realities, which continued to revolve around the nation-state, nor was an integrated Europe necessarily in the American interest. In this respect, Kissinger clearly distanced himself from the views of Ball and the other Europeanists at the State Department – and by implication those of Jean Monnet as well. "It was always somewhat unrealistic," he thought, "to imagine that the methods by which economic integration had been achieved could be applied automatically to the political arena."[177] According to Kissinger, the blame for the European crises in the mid-1960s did not rest solely on de Gaulle's shoulders. By championing the federalist approach, the United States had contributed to the stalemate between European federalists and confederalists. He also disagreed with the thesis often put forward by Ball and other Europeanists that transatlantic cooperation could only be effective *if* the relatively small European nation-states merged into one political entity. What is more, such a centralized Europe would in Kissinger's view hardly be in the American interest. The alternative, confederal vision of European unity would have the advantage of granting the United States much more leeway: "a confederal Europe would enable the United States to maintain an influence at many centers of decision rather than be forced to stake everything on affecting the views of a single, supranational body."[178]

For all of these reasons, Kissinger counseled, the United States should no longer concern itself with the "internal evolution of a united Europe." Instead, it must focus on maintaining bilateral relationships with all European countries; in addition, it should "use its ingenuity and influence in devising new forms of *Atlantic cooperation*." In *The Troubled Partnership*, Kissinger explicitly built on the tripartite proposal de Gaulle had put forward in September 1958. He called for a "political body at the highest level for concerting the policies of the nations bordering the North Atlantic," suggesting that the North Atlantic Council be superseded by an "executive committee" for the development of common policies and strategies.[179] As importantly, Kissinger emphasized that the United States should be prepared to grant Europeans more autonomy. The formal allied consultation process to which the Kennedy and the Johnson administrations attached high importance tended to reduce the European allies to "advisors in an American decisionmaking process." Kissinger essentially agreed with de Gaulle's thesis that American dominance in the councils of decision was practically absolving the allies of their responsibilities and sucking the life out of the alliance. Rather than seeking to impose its views on the alliance, the United States should accept that its European allies held different views about world affairs. "A wise Alliance policy will not gear everything to the expectation that common positions can be developed on a global basis," Kissinger concluded; "it will also take account of the fact that the interests of Europe and America are not identical everywhere."[180]

Kissinger also intensely disliked the managerial style of American foreign policy, castigating the "bureaucratic" and "process oriented" way in which it was forged, which he considered unfit for agile statecraft and held responsible for stilted and unproductive exchanges with allies. "We [...] have expected our Allies to fit themselves into an overall-strategy essentially devised in Washington."[181] This American division-of-labor approach to the allies, "with relatively little concern for their history or tradition," he believed, failed to accommodate the legitimate need of countries to have a unique sense of purpose. France was a case in point: a great power that had experienced the devastation of two world wars, lost a colonial empire, and on occasion reeled on the brink of civil war. "For the greater part of his career," Kissinger empathized with de Gaulle, "he has had to be an illusionist. In the face of all evidence to the contrary, he has striven to restore France's greatness by his passionate belief in it."[182] Rather than exerting the power of comprehension, however, American diplomats indulged in crucifying de Gaulle for not fitting the American-made mold of the loyal European ally. "The problem for de Gaulle was not how to relate France to a division of labor," Kissinger understood, "but his conviction that before France could relate itself to anyone, it had to relate itself to itself, that it had to have some sense of its purpose."[183]

Kissinger reiterated many of the above views in other publications and in lectures in the mid-1960s.[184] In a long essay in 1968, with the presidential elections in the offing, he moreover presaged many of the Nixon administration's notions about the shift from strict bipolarity to increasing multipolarity, exploring its significance for the transatlantic relationship in particular. "Military bipolarity is a source of rigidity in foreign policy," Kissinger posited. "A bipolar world loses the perspective for nuance; a gain for one side appears as an absolute loss for the other." Therefore:

> Our deepest challenge will be to evoke the creativity of a pluralistic world, to base order on political multipolarity even though overwhelming military strength will remain with the two superpowers. [...] A more pluralistic world – especially in relationships with friends – is profoundly in our long-term interest. [...] Painful as it may be to admit, we could benefit from a counterweight that would discipline our occasional impetuousity and, by supplying historical perspective, modify our penchant for abstract and "final" solutions. [...] In the years ahead, the most profound challenge will be philosophical: to develop some concept of order in a world which is bipolar militarily but multipolar politically. [...] historically, stability has always coincided with an equilibrium that made physical domination difficult.[185]

In the emerging international environment, Kissinger evidently no longer found a use for the conceptions of Atlantic unity that had inspired a whole generation of American policymakers – the generation of Dean Acheson and the bipartisan foreign policy establishment that had created the postwar international system. Whether they liked it or not, in the new world their conceptions had lost their relevance.

> NATO is in difficulties because it has yet to adjust to the political multipolarity of the late sixties. [...] This state of affairs has been especially difficult for those Americans who deserve most credit for forging existing Atlantic relations. Two decades of hegemony have produced the illusion that present Atlantic arrangements are "natural," that wise policy consists of making the existing framework more tolerable. "Leadership" and "partnership" are invoked, but the content given to these words is usually that which will support the existing pattern. European unity is advocated to enable Europeans to share burdens on a world-wide scale.
>
> Such a view fails to take into account the realities of political multipolarity. The aim of returning to the "great days of the Marshall Plan" is impossible. Nothing would sunder Atlantic relationships so surely as the attempt to reassert the notions of leadership appropriate to the early days of NATO. [...] It is not "natural" that the major decisions about the defense of an area so poten-

tially powerful as Western Europe should be made three thousand miles away. It is not "normal" that Atlantic policies should be geared to American conceptions. In the forties and fifties, practicing unity – through formal resolutions and periodic reassurances – was profoundly important as a symbol of the end of our isolationism. In the decade ahead, we cannot aim at unity as an end in itself; it must emerge from common conceptions and new structures. [...] In the next decade the architectonic approach to Atlantic policy will no longer be possible.[186]

In addition, Kissinger shared the French view that NATO was hardly a suitable instrument for promoting détente, distancing himself from the main conclusion of the Harmel exercise of 1967. "A military alliance, one of the chief cohesive links of which is its integrated command arrangement, is not the best instrument for flexible diplomacy," Kissinger reasoned. "A diplomatic confrontation of NATO and the Warsaw Pact would have all the rigidities of the bipolar military world." Kissinger furthermore believed that "the major initiatives to improve relations between Western and Eastern Europe should originate in Europe with the United States in a reserve position."[187]

Kissinger thus did not see NATO as the harbinger of an evolving Atlantic community, nor did he believe that the United States should seek to promote such an evolution. His convictions as well as those of Nixon about the transatlantic relationship were a far cry from Acheson's earlier cited recommendation to Kennedy in 1961 that "the ultimate goal of Atlantic nations should be to develop a genuine Atlantic commonwealth, in which common institutions are increasingly developed to address common problems." If anything, their conceptions about both world politics in general and the transatlantic relationship in particular more closely resembled those of de Gaulle (rid, of course, of de Gaulle's dedication to France). The Nixon administration was from the outset poised to pursue policies that were much more palatable to de Gaulle than those of any previous – or for that matter subsequent – American administration. In sum, it is hardly a spur of the imagination to interpret "Nixingerian" foreign policy as Gaullism American-style.

There was no time to lose before imposing the new policy toward France on a restive foreign policy establishment Upon entering office, the Nixon administration found itself confronted with the nasty brawl in Europe over some of de Gaulle's statements about the future of Europe in the earlier-mentioned Soames affair. In his memoirs, Kissinger recalled:

Like old warriors of a battle whose memory sustained emotion and righteousness, all the American veterans of previous controversies with de Gaulle rushed into the fray. The new administration was deluged with proposals from inside and outside our government to seize the opportunity to reaffirm our commitment to a federal Europe and to reject de Gaulle's proposal [...] for a special directorate of the larger European powers. The new administration was being asked to pick up the fallen lance of its predecessor and tilt once more against the windmills of European dogma, to resume the acrimonious debate with France exactly where it had been suspended by our election. This we were determined not to do. [...][188]

Franco-American Accommodation Under Nixon and Kissinger

Given their views on world politics and their considerable regard for de Gaulle, it is not surprising that Nixon and Kissinger saw ample room for improvement in the Franco-American relationship upon their arrival at the helm. "I have had a friendly exchange with de Gaulle," Nixon scribbled on his papers for his first press conference as president of the United States. "I believe prospects for improved relations are good + will work toward that end."[189] The change of attitude in Washington was reciprocated in Paris. The spring of 1969 even witnessed a public information campaign by the French government, orchestrated from the Elysée, to boost relations with the United States. "This is the first time in history that the French have ever undertaken any publicity campaign to improve understanding between France and any other nation," Ambassador Shriver cheerfully reported on the nationwide operation, which included posters in cities, small advertisements in every major French newspaper and magazine, and a film for use in movie theaters. The cost of the campaign – estimated at between four and five million dollars – was "more than the cost of operating the U.S. embassy in France for one year, and yet it has not and will not cost the U.S. government anything."[190]

On February 23, only one month after his inauguration as president, Nixon left for an eight-day trip to five European nations: Belgium (for a visit to NATO), Great Britain, Germany, Italy, France, and the Vatican. The State Department had advised against a trip so soon after the inauguration. Nixon, however, was determined to make his own foreign policy. Before venturing into discussions with the Soviets, the North Vietnamese, and the Chinese, he wanted to demonstrate to the Europeans that their security continued to be of the highest priority in American foreign policy. He also wanted to "show the world" that he was "not completely obsessed with Vietnam" and to "dramatize for Americans at home that, despite opposition to the war, their President could still be received abroad with respect and even enthusiasm."[191] The impact of Nixon's early visit was, of course, heightened by Johnson's failure to visit Europe during his tenure (except for his attendance at Adenauer's funeral). His demonstration of humility and apparent willingness to consult with European leaders was indeed well received. "President Nixon's European trip," journalist Chalmers M. Roberts opined, "has written an end to the postwar era in which the United States sought to and did largely impose an American design on Western Europe."[192] From European quarters there was appreciation for "the pragmatic approach without fanfare."[193]

Nixon's visit to France was unquestionably the high point of the European trip.[194] De Gaulle bestowed the American president full honors. He greeted his guest at the airfield with ringing words of welcome – in English. There was a splendid state banquet at the Elysée. De Gaulle had even agreed to dine at Ambassador Sargent Shriver's residence, which, at the insistence of Nixon's staff, had been completely refurnished and rid of all the Kennedy photographs and Catholic paraphernalia.[195] Nixon had three long private conversations with de Gaulle totalling ten hours, covering the whole range of foreign policy issues. "The scope of our conversations was as vast as the acres of formal gardens we could see from our meeting place in the Grand Trianon Palace," Nixon later wrote.[196]

The records of the conversations between Nixon and de Gaulle demonstrate a like-mindedness and degree of mutual confidence that contrast significantly with similar records in the Kennedy and Johnson years. In their first meeting, in de Gaulle's office in the Elysée Palace, they agreed that the Soviet Union was no longer intent on "marching west" and that détente in the East-West relationship was – in de Gaulle's words – "a matter of good sense," even as Nixon underlined – and de Gaulle agreed – that "we should be hard and pragmatic in dealing with the Soviets."[197] Their second conversation, in the Grand Trianon palace in Versailles (once Louis XIV's retreat), ranks as among the most substantial of any ever held between the General and an American president, primarily because it made clear that US foreign policy had taken a direction that was far more congenial to de Gaulle and that the personal relationship between the two heads of state was a formidable one. Without delay, Nixon took de Gaulle in "great confidence" by informing him of his inclination to establish a limited antiballistic missile system in order to protect the American nuclear deterrent – but not American cities – against a nuclear strike by the Soviet Union, a subject of hot debate in Congress. He had been surprised, he said, when he had been presented with classified information that the Soviet Union had almost caught up with the United States in strategic missiles. Both sides still had a second strike capability, "which meant that a decision would have to be made in less than 20 minutes for something that could kill 60 or 70 million people," but a missile defense system was increasingly considered needed to safeguard the American deterrent in the future.

After having thus taken de Gaulle in confidence, establishing a statesmanlike relationship of trust, Nixon went on to give his view on the French nuclear deterrent and on the position of the United States toward Europe. The words of the new American president were a ringing endorsement of the views that de Gaulle had been expounding for years. "It was important for the good of the US," said Nixon, that not only France should have nuclear weapons but in a broader sense that in the economic, political, and military fields that the European community have independent power and existence. ... Things in Europe should be allowed to develop in their own way. Times had changed. [...] The period in which the US could effectively assert leadership [in Europe] is no longer here.

The Franco-American quarrels of the Kennedy and early Johnson years about nuclear proliferation and the future of Europe would clearly have no sequel under Nixon. De Gaulle, in turn, also assumed a position that seemed to go against the grain of earlier policies, for he pressed his American guest to maintain a significant troop presence in Europe regardless of the strong pressure in Congress to reduce it. "It would not be good," he warned Nixon, "if the idea arose that the departing US forces should be replaced with German units."[198] The spectre of a resurgent Germany – not only economically and financially but also politically and militarily – had by the late 1960s evidently become a more pressing concern for de Gaulle than that of American domination in Europe.[199] In addition, at Nixon's urging, de Gaulle agreed to appoint an expert to begin discreet talks between the two countries on addressing the woes of the international monetary system. And they quickly agreed that their future exchanges on the affairs of state "need not necessarily pass through the usual diplomatic channels," thereby bypassing the State Department.[200]

To be sure, the two presidents also had their share of differences. On the Middle East, for instance, their views diverged: de Gaulle argued for a solution to be imposed by the "Four Powers" whereas Nixon warned that Israel would never accept such a solution; the General opposed Nixon's suggestion of arranging parallel talks on the Middle East between the United States and the Soviet Union for fear of being shut out.[201] All the while, however, Nixon "made a good impression," Prime Minister Couve de Murville recalled; "we had the idea that he was taking things personally in hand in order to have a policy that would be much more satisfactory to us than the policy of his predecessors."[202] Foreign Minister Debré told his staff that "a new era of understanding and cooperation was now opening between France and the United States, and the Americans should seek to cooperate as closely as possible with us in every area where French and American interests coincide."[203] And de Gaulle volunteered to his aides that the Franco-American relationship could now enter an era of "much greater intimacy" because of his strong personal relationship with Nixon.[204] At the end of the discussions, he agreed to visit Nixon in Washington in early 1970.[205] Nixon had unmistakably succeeded in putting the Franco-American relationship on a new footing. "The new entente cordiale between the Presidents of France and the United States [...] would alone have made the European trip worthwhile," he assessed in his memoirs.[206]

Arguably the most important topic discussed during Nixon's visit to Paris was not the Soviet Union or the situation in the Middle East, not even Europe or the French nuclear program, but the interrelated issues of establishing a normal relationship with China and ending the war in Vietnam. Discussing these with de Gaulle had for Nixon even been the primary reason for embarking on his European journey. "President de Gaulle's cooperation would be vital to ending the Vietnam war and to my plans for beginning a new relationship with Communist China," Nixon explained, for he considered Paris the best place for opening "secret channels of communication" with Hanoi and Peking.[207]

In regard to both issues, de Gaulle had set policies that served as an example to Nixon. France, of course, had officially recognized China as early as January 1964 (much to the dismay of the Johnson administration). Nixon's discussions with de Gaulle in 1963 and 1967 also had helped to shape his views on dealing with China. "De Gaulle put it very directly" that "it was better to recognize China now when she needs you because of her weakness rather than to wait later when you have to recognize her," Nixon recalled. "Nobody said it better, and needless to say, it made an impression on me."[208] De Gaulle indeed reiterated the point in their 1969 meeting. In addition, he expressed the view that Soviet behavior was increasingly motivated by a fear of China: "They [the Soviets] are thinking in terms of a possible clash with China tomorrow. They cannot face both China and the West (the US in particular) at the same time. Thus [...] they may well opt for a policy of rapprochement with the West."[209] From July 1969 onwards, Nixon and Kissinger would avidly use the "Paris channel" – operated by the incomparable Vernon Walters – to relay secret messages to the Chinese leadership in Peking.[210] De Gaulle moreover instructed his new ambassador in Peking, Etienne Manac'h, to impress upon the Chinese that the new American president was serious about normalizing the relationship.[211] France thus played an important role in getting the new administration to engage China and the Soviet Union in the game of "triangular" diplomacy, which would become a hallmark of Nixon's foreign policy.

On Vietnam, too, Nixon paid tribute to de Gaulle. For a long time, as a contender for high office, Nixon had fiercely defended America's military involvement in Vietnam as a way to contain an expansionist China. As president, he dreaded the domestic political consequences of a "loss" of South Vietnam to Communism.[212] By early 1969, however, Nixon had concluded that the war had become – in his speechwriter William Safire's words – "a bone in the nation's throat" and that the United States had to disengage from it.[213] But he was also determined that the end of the war should be "honorable" and leave American international prestige and credibility intact.

On both accounts, Nixon seems to have taken de Gaulle's views seriously. When they discussed Vietnam in 1967, de Gaulle had advocated an early end to the war. "If I can do Algeria, you can do Vietnam," de Gaulle said.[214] In 1969, speaking to Nixon in the Elysée, the Frenchman again stressed that the United States should end the war and seek a negotiated solution with North Vietnam, but also that it should not depart "with undue haste" – or "*en catastrophe*." In addition, he underlined that the French withdrawal from Algeria had been far more difficult to accomplish than an American withdrawal from Vietnam:

> The US did not have a million settlers in Viet Nam. The US had not been in Viet Nam for 130 years as the French had in Algeria. Viet Nam was far from the US and not on its doorstep, the way Algeria was to France.

De Gaulle moreover suggested that for the United States to reach a settlement in Vietnam would be relatively painless because its predominant position in the world was not in danger: "its power and wealth was so great that it could do this with dignity."[215]

There is indeed reason to believe that Nixon sought to emulate de Gaulle's masterful but drawn-out retreat from Algeria, which ended in a political agreement with the rebels that avoided domestic disorder or international degradation.[216] Moreover, as was the case with regard to China, Paris proved a convenient site for contacts with the North Vietnamese, and French diplomats would serve as an important conduit.[217] In his conversation with de Gaulle in the Elysée on March 2, Nixon volunteered that he had decided to begin secret talks with the North Vietnamese and he asked de Gaulle to convey to Hanoi that he was serious about ending the war.[218] And when de Gaulle came to Washington for Eisenhower's funeral in late March, Nixon said that he now had a withdrawal plan and intended to begin secret talks with the North Vietnamese. De Gaulle, in turn, told the American president of his distinct impression that the North Vietnamese were prepared to engage in peace talks.[219] "In retrospect," Nixon wrote in *Leaders*, "I believe this meeting laid the groundwork for Kissinger's secret trips to Paris, which resulted four years later in the Paris Peace Agreement and the end of American involvement in Vietnam." Without French assistance, "the negotiations could not have been carried to a successful conclusion."[220]

The Franco-American relationship continued to improve until 1973, when tensions where rekindled by the Nixon administration's declaration of the "Year of Europe" and the Middle East War. Although de Gaulle's successor Georges Pompidou carried on along the Gaullist track, he was often preoccupied with domestic economic and social problems and far more prepared to cooperate with NATO. French military relations with the treaty organization measurably improved, resulting in practical collaboration in many areas.[221] While Nixon did not hit it off well with Pompidou, the latter's Foreign Minister Michel Jobert developed a close working relationship with Kissinger.[222] Distrustful of Chancellor Brandt's Ostpolitik, the Nixon administration increasingly looked to France as America's most like-minded ally in Europe. Kissinger even confided to Pompidou at the Azores summit in 1971 that if the United States entertained a special relationship with any country it was France.[223] British Prime Minister Edward Heath, in any case, who had succeeded Harold Wilson in 1970, would not have lost much sleep over this twist of sympathies. He was firmly committed to entering "Europe" and saw the Anglo-American special relationship as an obstacle to the hallowed goal of membership. "Indeed," Kissinger recalled, "he came close to *insisting* on receiving no preferential treatment."[224] (emphasis in original) This state of affairs between the great powers of the West greatly facilitated British membership of the Common Market in 1973.

The most important area of cooperation, however, was also the most undisclosed: nuclear weapons. Neither Nixon nor Kissinger had a strategic hang-up about the existence of multiple centers of atomic decisionmaking in the West. Nixon had told de Gaulle as early as 1963 that he would be in favor, as Eisenhower had been, of sharing nuclear secrets with France.[225] Kissinger had proven to be highly critical of the Kennedy and Johnson administration's campaign against national nuclear forces, which he believed had only soured the transatlantic relationship. In *The Troubled Partnership* (1965) he wrote: "We might ask ourselves how an American administration would respond if an allied government publicly and repeatedly insisted that one of our major programs was 'divisive,' 'dangerous,' and 'useless.'" In addition, he had suggested that "the nuclear forces of our Allies should not be viewed as an alternative to United States strategic power, but as a complement" and that the "most constructive avenue for Atlantic cooperation would be to build on the existing nuclear programs rather than bring a new force into being."[226]

Upon taking office, both Nixon and Kissinger undoubtedly realized that there was no better way of improving relations with Paris than by providing assistance to the French nuclear effort, provided that this assistance would remain secret.[227] In Paris, as we have seen, Nixon had privately told de Gaulle that – in Couve de Murville's words – "he had no objection to possession by France of an independent nuclear force," and that "on the contrary, he thought it useful."[228] A month-and-a-half later, on April 21, after de Gaulle had let pass without dissent the date on which the North Atlantic Treaty could be formally denounced, Nixon issued a top-secret directive to investigate military cooperation with France, including nuclear cooperation; in the subsequent five years, the White House issued directives to assist France in ensuring the security of its nuclear weapons, developing its missiles, and conducting underground testing.[229] For nearly two decades, the covert program of Franco-American nuclear collaboration was one of the best-kept secrets of American and French diplomacy. It was finally exposed in 1989 by Richard Ullman in an article in *Foreign Policy*. Ullman, a professor at Princeton University, revealed that the United States had provided substantial covert assistance to the French nuclear program from 1974 onwards.[230] The French historian Pierre Mélandri has suggested that nuclear cooperation commenced earlier and reached its apogee between 1971 and 1973, before the strains and suspicions surrounding Kissinger's proclamation of 1973 as the "Year of Europe" soured the bilateral relationship.[231] Of what is known of it, this cooperation covered a wide range of areas, such as the miniaturization of warheads, missile design, MIRVing, and solid fuel; it may also have included coordination of tactical nuclear weapons targeting.[232] What is certain is that, by 1974, the French *force de frappe* had moved from being an irritant in the Franco-American relationship to an asset of the Western alliance.[233] During the first Nixon administration, "relations between the United States and France flourished," Kissinger assessed.[234]

It is true that Franco-American relations improved considerably after 1968, in part because Paris found some value in the new administration's aloofness towards Europe. On July 23, 1969, for instance, President Pompidou told Ambassador Shriver that "wheat" was the "only outstanding issue between the U.S. and France."[235] But those who had helped to shape American policies towards Europe in the previous decades were anything but pleased. On the contrary, many American policymakers were deeply distraught at the new realism in American foreign policy. They were alarmed at the implications of Nixon's hard-boiled balance-of-power politics for the transatlantic relationship, the European integration movement, and even the moral stature of the United States. They dreaded the economic nationalism inherent in Nixon's "New Economic Policy" and embodied by his Secretary of the Treasury John Connally who said: "My philosophy is that all foreigners are out to screw us, and it's our job to screw them first."[236] And they lamented the administration's lack of interest in European affairs, despite Nixon's journey across the Atlantic early in the presidency. "No one in or out of authority is thinking much about Europe," J. Robert Schaetzel, still the American ambassador to the EEC until 1972, complained to Acheson in September 1969. "If they do think about it at all it is in a mood of irritation or outright anger."[237] Even NATO hardly occupied the minds of the Nixon White House, as was evident from the fact that the post of NATO ambassador was left vacant for nearly one year.

The mental world of the members of the Council on Foreign Relations was indeed a world away from that of Nixon, and while Kissinger had made his policy career with the help of the Council, which published a number of his books, there was a potent antipathy among its ranks toward the Harvard academic and his realpolitik views as well.[238] The secretive style of the Nixon-Kissinger team moreover sidelined a whole phalanx of public servants, reinforcing, in Stanley Hoffmann's words, "the splintering and demoralization, indeed the fading away, of the foreign policy elite."[239] These officials were abhorred by what they perceived as Nixon's and Kissinger's cynical world view and manipulative manners.[240] Dean Acheson seemed to be the exception, for he was surprisingly capable of establishing a working relationship with the new administration.[241] He agreed to be brought into the firing line when Nixon called on him in the spring of 1971 as the elder statesman to help defeat Senator Mike Mansfield's proposal to cut the

American troop commitment to NATO by half. Yet Acheson was equally unhappy with the Nixon administration's disregard for Europe. Deeply distrustful of Willy Brandt's Ostpolitik, which he felt was far too accommodating to the Soviets and threatened to undermine NATO, Acheson repeatedly pressed Nixon to re-energize his European policies "with a view to future joint action" among the allies. He had also backed a call in December 1968 on the president-elect to pursue a foreign policy geared towards the "development of Atlantic integration" which "would in the long run require new Atlantic political institutions of a federal character."[242] This sort of advice, however, which had been surrounded by a halo of respectability from the days of Truman to those of Johnson, fell on infertile ground in the Nixon years. "His role," Walter Lippmann observed of Nixon at the beginning of his second term in office in 1973,

> has been that of a man who had to liquidate, defuse, deflate the exaggerations of the romantic period of American imperialism and American inflation. Inflation of promises, inflation of hopes, the Great Society, American supremacy – all that had to be deflated because it was all beyond our power.

Reading Lippmann's remarks in a news summary, Nixon wrote: "A wise observation."[243]

De Gaulle Leaves the Scene

In late March 1969, de Gaulle flew to the United States to attend the funeral of his wartime comrade Dwight Eisenhower. "One had the sense that if he moved to a window the center of gravity might tilt everybody into the garden," Kissinger wrote about de Gaulle's "overwhelming" presence at the reception of world leaders.[244] Nixon spoke for an hour with the Frenchman on the Middle East, Vietnam, Franco-German relations, and American-Soviet relations, accompanied only by their interpreters.[245] It was their last meeting.

On April 27, de Gaulle abruptly resigned from the presidency upon having lost a double referendum on regionalization and Senate reform. "To resign over such matters raised the suspicion that the referenda had been arranged at least in part to provide de Gaulle with a pretext for leaving office," Kissinger observed in his memoirs.[246] The Nixon administration was hardly taken by surprise by de Gaulle's resignation, for his confidant André Malraux had informed Ambassador Shriver weeks in advance that he was secretly planning his resignation. The "financial, labor, social, and monetary situation," Shriver moreover reported, was "so fragile that any serious problem in any direction could bring on political troubles of major proportions for President de Gaulle. [...] The waves are rising."[247] Immediately upon hearing the news of de Gaulle's resignation, Nixon sent de Gaulle a handwritten personal message to express his "deep sense of personal loss," urging the Frenchman to pay a visit to the United States and assuring him that "scores of our cities and states would be honored if you could include them on your schedule." He added: "Putting it in blunt terms – in this age of mediocre leaders in most of the world – America's spirit needs your presence."[248] According to Vernon Walters, who hand-delivered Nixon's letter to Colombey-les-deux-Églises, de Gaulle was genuinely touched by Nixon's homage.[249] The General's instant reply was hardly any less flattering, as it stressed that "I have for you – with good reason – esteem, confidence, and friendship as great and as sincere as it is possible to have."[250]

De Gaulle had left in style by, in the words of his biographer Lacouture, "managing to transform a defeat into a withdrawal."[251] Ever since May 1968, he had been searching for a reaffirmation of his legitimacy. Failing that, he was determined to leave his duties with his image and historical reputation intact, perhaps haunted by the memories of the tragic degeneration of his former mentor Philippe Pétain and his war comrade Winston Churchill (both of whom had stayed on too long).[252] When de Gaulle left, he left without a word, never to appear in public again, resigned to his destiny, devoting himself to writing his memoirs in retirement at Colombey-les-deux-Églises. He simply withdrew into history. "I had a contract with France," de Gaulle explained to André Malraux in December 1969. "The contract has been broken. Therefore, it is no longer worth anything. [...] The French no longer have any national ambition. They don't want to do anything for France. I entertained them with banners, I persuaded them to be patient while waiting for – for what, if not for France?"[253] Now that the contract was broken, he had lost the zest to rule. France had grown tired of its imperious superintendent, who was, in addition, beginning to feel the strain of old age. Yet the mark he had left on his nation and its foreign policy was indelible. The French were just ready to continue Gaullism without de Gaulle. The General died on November 9, 1970, twelve days before his eightieth birthday.

Conclusion

Between the French withdrawal from NATO in 1966 and de Gaulle's resignation in April 1969, Franco-American relations experienced their lowest point as well as their greatest intimacy. The lowest point was in 1967 and early 1968, when de Gaulle opposed the United States at every turn – on monetary issues, Vietnam, nuclear strategy, the Middle East, and so forth. Its greatest intimacy came when Nixon and Kissinger took office in early 1969. Even if they did not fully embrace de Gaulle's vision, Nixon and Kissinger sympathized with the philosophy behind Gaullist foreign policy to such a degree that they can truly be seen as the personifications of some American version of Gaullism. Their predilection for a strong executive (in particular vis-à-vis Congress), their penchant for balance-of-power politics, their inclination towards traditional statecraft shaped by national interests – all of this meant that they operated on the same wavelength as le grand

Charles. They purposely sought to come to terms with de Gaulle's policy of independence and pursued a foreign policy, in particular with regard to Europe, that was inherently more accommodating of de Gaulle's views than that of any previous or subsequent administration. This was an important difference with the Franco-American rapprochement in Johnson's last year in office, which was of an overwhelmingly pragmatic nature as it was the byproduct of the serious domestic and international setbacks both Washington and Paris experienced in 1968.

Nixon's rise to power moreover marked the end of the era in American foreign policy that had been dominated by the bipartisan establishment. American foreign policy would henceforth be less orientated towards Europe and more susceptible to political swings. As a result, the exalted anticipation of what NATO and European integration might achieve for the transatlantic relationship faded into the past. "The Atlantic alliance was built on a reality and marketed on an illusion," Ronald Steel wrote in 1976.

> The reality was that the United States could not let Western Europe fall into Russian hands, and that the Europeans wanted American protection. The illusion was that the alliance would lead to a true partnership of equals with virtually identical interests. The illusion has dissipated. The reality remains.[254]

This was a pertinent synopsis of the American view of the transatlantic relationship at the end of de Gaulle's time in power. To what extent, however, had de Gaulle contributed to the shift towards realism in American policies toward Europe? It is important not to overstate this role. The shift was prompted above all by the relative decline of American power during the 1960s. At the end of the decade, the United States no longer occupied the same position of preeminence as in the first postwar decades. Economic adversity compelled the United States to concern itself more with protecting its own interests and less with shaping political and economic developments in Western Europe as part of any larger foreign policy design. This in itself greatly helped to improve Franco-American relations from early 1968 into the early 1970s. "As the United States distanced itself a little from Europe," Costigliola rightly concludes, "Paris found it somewhat easier to move closer to Washington while maintaining a measure of French independence."[255]

Yet the significance of the de Gaulle experience for the evolution of American policy toward Europe cannot be ignored. This significance amounts to more than the fact that de Gaulle provided a foreign policy paradigm that Nixon and Kissinger were to follow in many respects. It is equally important to note that de Gaulle, more than any other European leader, had exposed and even defined the limits of US power in Europe with his policy of independence. In addition, he had a determining influence over the course of European unity, rebuking the integrationary, Monnet-style method favored by the large majority of American policymakers, reasserting the position of the nation-state vis-à-vis the Commission, keeping Great Britain at bay for over a decade, and resuscitating the idea of "Europe" as a strategic entity separate from the United States and the Soviet Union. De Gaulle could not destroy NATO, but he was capable of preventing it from developing into something more than a military alliance. The generous and energetic role that the United States had played in Europe since the mid-1940s was hence reaching a spiritual dead end by the mid-1960s; with it, American approaches to NATO and European integration shifted from Atlantic idealism to realism even before the Nixon presidency.

This shift as well as de Gaulle's role in making it happen was illustrated by a discussion in the National Security Council on May 3, 1967. The State Department paper prepared for this meeting still reflected the optimistic and supportive attitude towards European integration of earlier days.[25] The ensuing discussion, however, revealed the growing bitterness about the direction in which the Common Market was developing and showed that European unity was no longer unambiguously desired in Washington. Secretary of the Treasury Henry Fowler directed his dismay in particular at France:

> France is trying either to expel us completely from Europe or at least to diminish our power there. The French may even use the Common Market to achieve this objective. We must face up to the problem of how to make a coordinated effort in which all U.S. departments and agencies participate to induce Germany and Italy to separate themselves from the French effort to use the Common Market against the United States.

When Johnson expressed his skepticism about the effectiveness of such a campaign, Fowler went on undeterred:

> The French have been trying to use the Common Market structure for the past five years in an effort to diminish our economic, political, and military influence. This French effort in Europe affects our ability to be effective in other parts of the world.

Others joined Fowler in censuring the European allies for their selfishness and resentment of American power. "Europeans have rejected the world after the loss of their colonies," Vice President Hubert Humphrey observed. "They resent U.S. power. Détente is what they want." The Europeans are "selfish" and should be pressured "to participate in the world outside their borders." The American ambassador to the United Nations, Arthur Goldberg, chimed in: "The Europeans are causing problems for us in the United Nations. We no longer have a solid bloc of western allies behind us." And Walt Rostow said: "Europe is neglecting the world. It is in an isolationist cycle." The meeting was not significant for the decisions that were made; Johnson, while "agreeing with the sentiment expressed," pressed his advisers to find practical ways to get the Europeans to make a larger contribution to NATO. But it revealed that the way in which American policy-makers viewed Europe was souring under the pressure of Vietnam, financial problems at home, and French politicking in Europe.[256]

Grand designs with lofty ends have a tendency of going bankrupt. This sobering reality made the Franco-American rapprochement in de Gaulle's last year in office possible: by 1968, both the United States and France were finding out that they could not claim to be exceptions to the rule. As the decade approached its conclusion, neither side would find that the state of the world reflected the aspirations it had had at the decade's beginning; in fact, each side had played an important – and underappreciated – role in denying the realization of the aspirations of the other. The 1960s had witnessed some of the most serious disputes in the history of the Franco-American relationship. More often than not, the Americans had been enveloped in a war of words with the General – about the value of NATO, about the nature of American leadership, about European integration, about nuclear weapons, about Germany, about dealing with the Soviet Union, about the international monetary system, about Vietnam. Differences of view between Washington and Paris would, of course, continue to trouble the relationship after de Gaulle had stepped down. New nadirs would be found. These differences are not likely to disappear. What it is unlikely, however, is that the United States will have to deal with another de Gaulle.

Conclusion

Atlantis Lost: The Reception of Gaullism in the United States

At the beginning of this study, we set out with three broad questions in mind. How did Americans *interpret* de Gaulle's policy of "independence" within the larger framework of their ideas about the transatlantic relationship? How did consecutive administrations actually *deal* with the challenges posed by de Gaulle's "independent" foreign policy from 1958 to 1969? And did de Gaulle's policy of "independence" *modify* American policies towards Europe and the Atlantic alliance? We will now attempt to answer these three questions on the basis of the foregoing.

De Gaulle – Hero of the Past

The Diversity of American Opinion

In respect of the first question, we should first of all observe that there was not *one* American evaluation of de Gaulle. Dean Acheson's and George Ball's condemnation of the General, for instance, differed greatly from the veneration exhibited by President Nixon and Henry Kissinger. President Eisenhower and his successor John F. Kennedy were – in different ways – tempted by de Gaulle's powerful vision and personality, and groped for common ground, but there was very little that connected President Johnson to his French counterpart (despite the Texan's unfailing restraint). Someone like McGeorge Bundy showed an understanding of de Gaulle that caused Ball to accuse him of being a "Gaullist"; while this charge was overdrawn, Bundy certainly tended to be less condemnatory and more pragmatic in his views of de Gaulle than most officials (including his successor Walt Rostow). Secretary of State Rusk meanwhile appears to have lost his legendary patience and equanimity only when it came to de Gaulle, whereas the factual mind of Secretary of Defense McNamara remained largely undisturbed by the Gaullist challenge (even as he strongly opposed the French nuclear program). Ambassador Charles Bohlen's influential advice that no American concession could alter de Gaulle's course contrasted sharply with that of his predecessor James Gavin, who pressed Washington – in vain – to be more forthcoming (in particular in the nuclear realm). In short, there were many interpretations of de Gaulle and his policies.

One might say that the American public, to begin with, generally entertained a favorable opinion of de Gaulle from his return to power in 1958 to his press conference of January 14, 1963, in which he torpedoed Kennedy's Grand Design by vetoing Great Britain's entry into the Common Market and rejecting the multilateral nuclear force. Before this press conference, he was most often portrayed as a hero from the war whose return to power had restored much-needed stability to French politics, who extricated his country from Algeria and other colonies in Africa, and who stood tall in the Cold War crises of Berlin and Cuba. Following his January 1963 press conference, however, popular admiration for de Gaulle as a statesman of high calibre turned into widespread damnation. The disenchantment was only deepened by the French withdrawal from NATO, de Gaulle's criticism of the Vietnam War, his attack on the US dollar, and his call for a free Quebec in the period from early 1966 to early 1968. During these years, de Gaulle transformed into a "mischief-maker" within the Western alliance whose policies were seen as incorrigibly anti-American and dangerously nationalistic.[1] De Gaulle's assault on US dominance within the Western alliance prompted American war veterans to return their medals, New York restaurant owners to pour French wine out on the street, and American women to return their French-made bags to department stores. From this period, the American public's appraisal of the bilateral relationship was never to recover completely. The French were to remain at best "bad-weather" friends: while they may be reliable when the chips are down (as de Gaulle had proven in the Cuban Missile Crisis), they were most often simply unbearable.

The views in Congress largely kept pace with the fluctuation in public opinion, but there were also always voices in support of a normalization of the bilateral relationship. De Gaulle's well-received address to a joint congressional session during his April 1960 visit – when the bilateral relationship still enjoyed the quiet before the storm – probably marked the high point of his standing among the representatives of the American people. By December 1967, however, Representative L. Mendel Rivers, a South Carolina Democrat, called de Gaulle "the most ungrateful man since Judas Iscariot betrayed his Christ."[2] There was, at the same time, also a sense in Congress – in particular within the Senate – that the Johnson administration shared part of the blame for alienating France and was losing the initiative in Europe by overreacting to de Gaulle's policies and being too rigid about NATO reform.[3] Johnson's attitude of calmness and reason in response to the NATO crisis of 1966 was thus also induced by a political requirement to fend off criticism that his administration was a part of the problem.[4]

Within America's foreign policy apparatus – and the circles of the foreign policy establishment that continued to be plugged in to this apparatus through Dean Acheson, John McCloy, and Averell Harriman – sympathy for de Gaulle indeed never ran very deep and recognition of his achievements was grudging at best. A stable France healed from its colonial sores was certainly seen as an asset to the Western world, but in most other respects de Gaulle's foreign policy views were regarded as too injurious to deserve support. De Gaulle was without doubt a formidable leader, but also one whose ways were seen as regrettably errant. Particularly in the State Department, traditionally a stronghold for the Atlantic idea and for the cause of European integration, sympathy for de Gaulle was hard to find. American diplomats were well aware of de Gaulle's long-standing aversion to NATO and European integration. They were continually apprehensive about the possibility of an attack on these landmarks of American postwar policy. They were also deeply disturbed by de Gaulle's high-profile determination to build an independent nuclear deterrent, because they principally opposed the proliferation of nuclear weaponry and because it risked whetting Germany's appetite for a nuclear force. Many diplomats were furthermore irritated with what they considered to be the *folie de grandeur* of French foreign policy – the gap between French means and de Gaulle's aspirations. De Gaulle's refusal to accept that France was at best a medium-sized power did not sit well with American policymakers who were preoccupied with managing the Western alliance as if it were only about devising an equitable division of labor in support of a common cause. They were certainly not prepared to accept de Gaulle's pretension to speak for Europe.

In particular, the "Europeanists" at the department preferred to treat Jean Monnet – whose vision of European integration and transatlantic cooperation they could easily associate with and who proved a master at cultivating a network of influential friendships in Washington – as their European equivalent. Gaullism truly became the private albatross around the neck of many American policymakers who dealt with Europe. Chastising him had become the name of the game. Not all American diplomats were of this anti-Gaullist mindset: Assistant Secretary of State for European Affairs William Tyler and the director of the department's Intelligence and Research Bureau, Thomas Hughes, were two examples of officials who took a more moderate view of Gaullism. But the daily conduct of America's foreign affairs with regard to Europe was usually managed by those who held a grudge against de Gaulle (until Nixon and Kissinger centralized foreign policy decisionmaking in the White House).

All the while, there was a small but notable minority of newspapermen and academics – some with connections in government – who exhibited a substantially higher degree of understanding of and intellectual sympathy for de Gaulle's policy of "independence" than either the State Department or general public opinion. Walter Lippmann, for one, was an ardent and self-professed admirer of de Gaulle and often defended him against American critics.[5] Other American journalists who took a relatively benevolent view of de Gaulle and his policies appeared to flock to the *New York Times*. Of these, Cyrus Sulzberger was probably the most prominent, as he was the newspaper's chief foreign correspondent in the 1950s and 1960s and a member of the family that owned the paper. Residing in Paris for many years, Sulzberger was also a privileged visitor of the Elysée and many of his columns for the *New York Times* were in fact based on private audiences with the General. Of the American academics who revealed an above-average appreciation for de Gaulle at the time, we have already examined the sympathizing views of Henry Kissinger. The other academic that deserves mention in this context is a fellow Harvard University professor: Stanley Hoffmann. In the course of the 1960s, Hoffmann's publications on French foreign policy constantly took issue with prevailing denunciations and revealed it to be a rational defense of the French national interest, not the upshot of a whimsical and anachronistic ruler.[6] He berated American policymakers for their deprecation and their crude views of de Gaulle. "Cursing de Gaulle is not a policy," he opined in *The Reporter* in January 1964.[7] Academic interpreters of de Gaulle's foreign policy such as Kissinger and Hoffmann made up a body of American scholarly opinion that presented a more benign view of Gaullism and felt that de Gaulle's criticism of the United States deserved merit for its acumen and for the sense of pride and independent judgment it conveyed.

American opinion about de Gaulle thus ranged from outright condemnation and indignation at his anti-American slights to admiration for his achievements for France and for the quality of his statesmanship. Merely noting this, however, is not sufficient. How Americans interpreted de Gaulle's policy of "independence" from 1958 to 1969 depended mainly on how they viewed the world at large and America's role in it – in particular in relation to Europe. Whether Americans condemned or appreciated de Gaulle's foreign policy generally depended on whether their foreign policy outlook was liberal or conservative. That de Gaulle invoked disturbing memories, earning him the reputation of an anachronism, has much to do with the historical ambivalence in the New World towards the Old. And de Gaulle's foreign policy distressed in particular those Americans who favored throwing America's weight in the scale of intra-European politics on the side of political and economic integration and reform; those who took a more distant view of America's role in Europe were generally less alarmed.

A Conservative Mind in a Liberal Age

American foreign policy during the early decades of the Cold War was an uneasy – albeit reasonably effective – synthesis of the internationalist strains of the two political traditions of liberalism and conservatism. This foreign policy synthesis induced the United States to unite the national interest with the ideology of the free world. This aspect of American foreign policy illuminates the American experience with de Gaulle as president of France in at least two ways.

First, it is important to recall that de Gaulle was a leader in the conservative tradition of European statecraft. His foreign policy outlook was, in the final analysis, that of a nationalist and a realist who adhered to the pre-ideological approach to balance-of-power politics typical of the French diplomacy of the *Ancien Régime*. One corollary was that de Gaulle disregarded the ideological – read: liberal – component in American foreign policy. In spite of its self-professed idealism, the United States was in his view no less engaged in power politics than any other country. World War II had, in his view, "readily manifested" the "United States' desire for hegemony, [...] which I had not failed to discern on every occasion."[8] De Gaulle's judgment that Roosevelt's "will to power cloaked itself in idealism"[9] was in fact pertinent to his judgment of American foreign policy as a whole. His criticism of American leadership in the Cold War was the perceptive criticism of a conservative realist who discarded with the rhetoric and was quick to identify the hegemon's self-serving motives. In this sense, his appreciation of the United States was not much different of his view of the Soviet Union. While this appreciation was not groundless, certainly not from the vantage point of the leader of the Free French who had been cold-shouldered by the Roosevelt administration, it was also one-dimensional. It ignored the fact that American policies in the Cold War were infused with genuinely pursued liberal ideals to a degree never before seen in a country – perhaps with the exception of Great Britain under William Gladstone. What is more, it encouraged de Gaulle to couch his challenge to American leadership, as Kissinger observed, "so woundingly" that it "spurred American self-righteousness rather than the objective reexamination of Atlantic relationships which the situation demands."[10] By denying Americans their idealism, de Gaulle thus made it more difficult to enter into a constructive dialogue.

Second, the distinction between political traditions in American foreign policy helps us to understand why different Americans reacted differently to de Gaulle as well as why most Americans at the time looked upon de Gaulle's foreign policy with disapproval.

American opinion about de Gaulle can be dissected along the liberal-conservative dividing line. Liberal-minded Americans who supported an active foreign policy, such as George Ball and his Europeanists at the State Department, objected to de Gaulle's foreign policy because of its emphasis on national sovereignty and its inclination to approach international affairs as a balance of power. They were afraid that de Gaulle's policy of national independence and grandeur was reintroducing the nationalist invective into European politics. They resented his vocal opposition to political and military integration, which they considered not only vital in harnessing the power of the free world against the Soviet Union but also unavoidable in a world of increasing interdependence. They objected to de Gaulle's view of the North Atlantic Treaty as merely a "classical" treaty in response to a transitory threat rather than as the harbinger of a more permanent bond between America and Europe. They distrusted his authoritarian style and disliked the Fifth Republic's presidential system.[11] And they suspected that French economic policies under de Gaulle were turning the Common Market into a protectionist bloc rather than a bulwark for the promotion of free trade. De Gaulle, in sum, ran opposite to the American liberal's deepest convictions.

Conservative internationalists, in contrast, were given to acknowledging the contemporary value of de Gaulle's foreign policy, for its motivating ideas were akin to their own. They were, at any rate, more tolerant of ideological diversity within the Western alliance than liberal internationalists. Conservative internationalists were also quite capable of comprehending de Gaulle's behavior as a rational defense of the French national interest. Eisenhower's sympathy for and understanding of the French nuclear program was a case in point. The ideological affinity between the Nixon administration and de Gaulle was, as we have seen, even quite remarkable. Neither Nixon nor Kissinger had any hangups about supporting the French nuclear program. The Republican president and his national security adviser welcomed de Gaulle's intergovernmental conception of Europe. They admired and emulated his conduct of foreign affairs, both in terms of its focus on the national interest and of its style and method. Nixon and Kissinger were, in sum, operating on de Gaulle's wavelength.

At the same time, even though postwar US foreign policy was a synthesis between the two political traditions, the overall tide in American politics during the early decades of the Cold War, from the 1940s until the late 1970s (with a respite in the 1950s), was decidedly liberal. The policies of the Kennedy and Johnson administrations in particular were informed by the liberal values of the age. But the two Republican administrations in this period also reflected this liberal frame of mind. Eisenhower, for one, was a fiscal and social conservative, but he was also a strong proponent of European political and economic integration, of NATO's integrated military command structure, and of decolonization; in addition, he was as much distressed as many liberals with the impact of high levels of defense spending on American society and with the pernicious influence of the "military-industrial complex." Both his secretaries of state, moreover, had Wilsonian inclinations. Nixon was considerably more conservative than Eisenhower, in particular in matters of foreign policy, but he too felt compelled to couch his foreign policy in idealistic terms. As Kissinger explained, "Nixon preferred to operate on two tracks simultaneously: invoking Wilsonian rhetoric to explain his goals while appealing to national interest to sustain his tactics."[12] De Gaulle was hence a conservative mind in an age that was in many ways dominated by American liberalism. The Franco-American conflict during these years was thus a clash between an American foreign policy steeped in liberal values and a French foreign policy steeped in the conservative European tradition in addition to one between the conception of an "Atlantic" Europe and a "European" Europe.

De Gaulle as the "Old" Europe Reincarnated
American political approaches to Europe have historically been prejudiced by an ambivalence in the New World towards the Old. This was the result of the fact

that America was both a departure from and a continuation of Europe. The idea of the United States' exceptionality hinged on being different from Europe. And while the American perspective on Europe can not be fully described in terms of either rejection and detachment or of veneration and affinity, the "old" Europe most often was "old" in a pejorative sense. This contrast between the New World and the Old World provides additional clues to understanding how Americans interpreted de Gaulle and his political persona.

First, majority American opinion came to view de Gaulle as a "narrow-minded" nationalist of the "old" European type whose policies harked back to the ill-conceived and destructive balance-of-power politics of the eighteenth and nineteenth centuries. This opinion became more pronounced when de Gaulle began to challenge openly American leadership within the Western alliance, which began with his January 1963 press conference. From a hero of the great war who had pulled France back from the brink of civil war, de Gaulle became the reincarnation of the "old" Europe that was supposed to make way for a "new" Europe – a Europe that would evolve beyond the nation-state, a Europe whose trail was blazen by such practical and eminently modern men as Jean Monnet, that would take on the economic dynamism of the New World, a Europe that would indeed have learned some valuable lessons from the United States.

There was always a strong tutorial bent to US policies towards postwar Europe. American policymakers, who were inclined to consider Europe as a whole rather than as the accumulation of national societies, had little understanding of or patience for the resilience of national outlooks. De Gaulle, however, defied their thesis that the European nation-state was growing obsolete. His dogmatic emphasis on the national interest appeared to them reminiscent of an unhealthy past. They regarded the Frenchman not as a Cold War revisionist, as his supporters did, but as a European reactionary; de Gaulle was, the American diplomat-writer Louis Halle judged, a "statesman swimming against the stream of history."[13] His authoritarian political style, too, was stripped of its contemporary significance; it became, instead, a holdover of the French Bonapartist tradition.

This is not to say that de Gaulle's nationalist policy of independence and grandeur was thought to have no future implications. On the contrary, American officials feared that de Gaulle *was* breathing new life into dangerous ghosts of the past: European nationalism and American isolationism. Gaullist foreign policy was reviving the old "European question" in American foreign policy: "how to protect the rest of the world – or at least their [the Americans'] own political and social experiment – from Europe's destructiveness, if not necessarily to save Europe from itself?"[14] By the same token, the rejection of Gaullism in the United States was an offshoot of the anti-Europeanism – or, more precisely, Europhobia – that had influenced American foreign policy from the outset.

Second, whereas de Gaulle deliberately sought to personify France in times of crisis, Americans exhibited a tendency to do exactly the opposite: to disconnect de

Gaulle from the French people. This tendency can be traced back to World War II: to the dubious legitimacy of de Gaulle's call of "June 18th" (in 1940) to continue the war against Germany, Roosevelt's stubborn refusal to recognize the Free French movement as the legitimate representative of the French people, and his penchant to regard America as the trustee of French sovereignty (at least until elections were held in France). The tendency was, however, not reserved to Roosevelt, for the period under examination here provides sufficient evidence of similar attitudes among Americans who dealt with de Gaulle. They often isolated de Gaulle from his environment, be it French or European, as if he was an aberration. The exclamation of one Kennedy administration official following de Gaulle's January 1963 press conference – that "one lonely, elderly ruler of a small country" was quelling the aspirations of "250 million other Europeans" – was just one case in point.[15] Ambassador Bohlen's reports from Paris were often peppered with assurances that – despite de Gaulle's anti-American slights – his contacts in the Quai d'Orsay and in the country at large revealed a matrix of enduring goodwill toward the United States. Johnson's letter of reply of March 1966 to de Gaulle's announcement of withdrawal from NATO, as we have seen, even deliberately distinguished between de Gaulle and France in order to "offer a golden bridge to the French nation" back to NATO (see Chapter Five).

This inclination to distinguish between a nation's leadership – which may be bad or seen to have erred – and its people, who are inherently good, is a common trait in American foreign policy. In the case of France in the 1960s, this distinction tapped into the historical ambivalence felt towards Europe: while de Gaulle was trying to restore French glory of the old days of European statecraft, the French people were believed to be interested above all in building a better life in the "new" Europe that was being constructed by the likes of Jean Monnet. Rejection of the "old" France exemplified by de Gaulle and affinity with the "new" France exemplified by Monnet reflected this ambivalence. De Gaulle may have been motivated by "une certaine idée de la France" that had been bequeathed by his patriotic upbringing and a national experience of centuries; the loyalty of the French, Americans hoped, was with the "new" France that had learned its lessons from the past and was moving away from the institutional framework of the nation-state. Most Americans were therefore never prepared to fully accept de Gaulle as the veritable spokesman of the French people, certainly not as its sole spokesman. Even if they did, they were inclined to do so without acknowledging the popularity of his challenge to American leadership. "It is a mistake for Americans to distinguish between the government and the people re[garding] foreign policy," Ernest Goldstein cabled to President Johnson from France in February 1968; "they collectively voted for the General knowing his foreign policy, but were willing to swallow it for his domestic policy."[16] Goldstein should have gone one step further: de Gaulle's challenge to the Americans was generally popular in France and his foreign policy served to strengthen domestic unity. If anything, de

Gaulle's domestic policies – not his foreign policy – were a source of unpopularity among the French (as the events of May 1968 were to show soon enough).

For most Americans, however, recognizing this was going one step too far: it involved admitting that US leadership was not universally wanted. The vehemence of American reactions to de Gaulle's verdicts on American leadership can only be fully understood if one recognizes that they chipped away at America's self-perception as a nation and a civilization. His portrayal of the United States as a hegemon and the co-author of the division of Europe – the "Yalta system" – grated many Americans, who cherished a rather more exalted view of the United States' international position. In particular, de Gaulle's propensity to put the United States on the same moral plane as the Soviet Union did not sit well with their view of the Cold War as a struggle between good and evil. De Gaulle was in fact attributing American foreign policy with the vices of the "old" Europe. De Gaulle's analysis that the United States was as motivated by "selfish" national interests as any other state – that "the will to power" was merely "cloaked in idealism" – was a denial of the American view that the United States was different from Europe. It thus went to the heart of the American self-image.

De Gaulle "The Ungrateful"

The third element in explaining American responses to De Gaulle is derived from the alternation in US policy toward Europe between geopolitical aloofness and engagement. Although after 1945 the terms of aloofness and engagement were redefined to reflect the abiding interest of the United States in a Europe that could never again pose a threat to the Western hemisphere, American foreign policy continued to be marked by shifts within these redefined terms. In de Gaulle's analysis, however, the United States simply suffered from the hegemonic affliction that comes with being the most powerful. This affliction was in his view an important part of the problem that he defined as the "Yalta system" or the "system of the blocs." De Gaulle did not give much credence to the possibility of a return to isolationism in American foreign policy. The problem was rather the opposite: a propensity on the part of Americans to act as "a universal judge and policeman."[17] De Gaulle was in favor of an alliance with the Americans in the Cold War, yet he was also determined to keep them at arms length in order to provide room for French independence and leadership in Europe. "I love the Anglo-Saxons," he later volunteered to his information minister Alain Peyrefitte, "on the condition that they do not aspire to dominate us."[18] French foreign policy under de Gaulle hence aimed to reduce American postwar predominance in Western Europe, undo the "Yalta system" through a policy of détente, and help bring about a European-wide equilibrium in which the United States would merely serve as an ally of ultimate recourse.

All of this was incompatible with almost any American interpretation of the United States' postwar involvement in Europe, which was based on the idea that the United States was responding to calls from severely weakened Western European democracies for American support and protection. The first political imperative in American politics after World War II had been to bring "the boys back home" and this imperative was overruled only after much hesitation. It had also taken the Truman administration much persuasion to get the Senate to ratify the North Atlantic Treaty of 1949. The United States did not seek hegemony after the war; instead, leadership was devolved to it by a combination of European consent, American resources, and Soviet expansionism. If it could be called an empire, it was – in the words of the historian Geir Lundestad – only an "empire by invitation."[19] The role of leader of the Western alliance was not of its own making, but thrust upon the United States by the political, moral, and financial bankruptcy of Europe. When de Gaulle criticized American involvement in Europe, it was often seen unbecoming of an ally that owed its continued existence as a sovereign state to this very involvement. He was seen as ungrateful. If anything, de Gaulle's attempts to reduce the American presence in Europe and the nationalism of his policies were counterproductive because they convinced American policymakers that Europe was far from ready to be freed from American tutelage and to be left to its own devices. De Gaulle's pursuit of French – and by extension European – "independence" from the United States thus paradoxically led to greater calls for strong American leadership in European affairs.

Second, whether Washington's relationship with de Gaulle was good or bad largely coincided with whether it pursued a strategy of aloofness or of engagement with respect to Europe. Because the gist of both Eisenhower's and Nixon's policies was towards aloofness from Europe (while maintaining the Cold War alliance), they were both in a reasonable position to develop something of an understanding with de Gaulle on the proper role and the degree of involvement of the United States in Europe. Both Eisenhower and Nixon – not coincidentally the two most conservative presidents of the period examined in this book – responded to America's relative decline by striving to reduce the burden of its international involvement. Both were also more tolerant of European autonomy and less concerned by the political implications of Gaullism for the future of Europe, and they were therefore less inclined to inject American power into intra-European politics. Eisenhower strongly favored more European self-sufficiency in defense matters, which helped to explain his support for the EDC as well as his willingness in the waning days of his presidency to consider aiding the French nuclear program. He moreover expressed sympathy for the notion of Europe as a "genuine third force comparable to the United States or to the Soviet Union."[20]

Nixon was above all concerned with conceptually adjusting US foreign policy to the decline in American power and prestige in the course of the 1960s and extricating the United States from Vietnam without giving the Soviet Union the edge in the Cold War. In the context of his view of a multipolar world, he went further than any other American president since World War II in permitting Europe an autonomous position. Nixon, in addition, reversed a bipartisan record of activist American support for European integration, focusing instead on maintaining and manipulating advantageous bilateral relationships.

The Kennedy administration's approach to Europe, by contrast, was unmistakably one of engagement in support of European integration within an Atlantic-oriented setting, and this policy of engagement carried over into the Johnson administration until it was toned down by Johnson's determination not to pick fights with de Gaulle and by the growing absorption in the quagmire of Vietnam. Kennedy's policies were also a response to the relative decline of the United States, but he aimed to offset this decline by actively shaping Europe into a more unified, active, and constructive partner of the United States. It was a policy aimed at sharing more of the burden without giving up much of the control. These policies were furthermore dominated by officials at the State Department who had personally contributed to the European integration movement earlier in their careers, such as George Ball and Robert Schaetzel. Their inclination to continue this stance in government was firmly supported by foreign policy wise men such as Dean Acheson and John McCloy, who believed strong American leadership in Europe continued to be necessary for political reasons. Their efforts were moreover intimately wound up with those of Jean Monnet, and they often directly involved "Mr. Europe" in shaping American policies.

The Kennedy administration's policy of engagement in Europe conflicted with de Gaulle's foreign policy aims in various ways. We have already noted that de Gaulle's rebuttal of Kennedy's design for an Atlantic partnership in early 1963 must be understood as a defensive move against an activist American foreign policy (see Chapter Three). To this notion one may add that the activism of the Kennedy administration was paradoxically much reinforced by the American perception that the threat of Gaullism was growing. De Gaulle's veto of the multilateral nuclear force (MLF), for instance, made it even more important to the American proponents of the MLF to realize it. Unease about de Gaulle's policy of independence was in fact a major determinant of many American policies towards Europe; in Walt Rostow's words, "a good deal of European and Atlantic policy was [...] taken up with coping with de Gaulle's enterprises in ways which permitted the EEC and NATO to survive."[21]

Both NATO and the Common Market did survive. But de Gaulle's opposition to American activism in Europe was not without effect. It contributed to the dismantling of Kennedy's strategy of forceful engagement. The evolution of Johnson's policies toward a more aloof stance toward Europe – a result of his decision in 1964 to let the MLF wither on the vine, the growing burden of Vietnam, the increasing domestic turmoil, and the emergence of the Common Market as an economic rival – was only temporarily interrupted by the need to show American leadership in the NATO crisis of 1966 and 1967. Even during this crisis, Johnson refused to place America's power behind a European crusade against de Gaulle, as Acheson and Ball had wanted. He understood that de Gaulle had exposed limits to what the engagement of American power in Europe could achieve. The postwar era of America's deep and often activist involvement in intra-European politics was coming to an end.

Dealing With De Gaulle: The Hegemon's Predicament

How did consecutive administrations actually *deal* with the challenges posed by de Gaulle's "independent" foreign policy from 1958 to 1969?

We have seen how Eisenhower and Kennedy genuinely tried to come to terms with de Gaulle's "tripartite" memorandum of September 1958, in particular by offering to expand the "special" relationship with Great Britain to France and by pledging that Washington would consult Paris prior to the use of nuclear weapons anywhere in the world barring emergency situations. Both, however, also had to take the views of the other European allies – Germany above all – into account, as they were highly sensitive to any notion of a "directorate" within the Western alliance. Discussions about de Gaulle's memorandum proposal lasted until the very end of Eisenhower's presidency and continued into the Kennedy presidency. In particular, Eisenhower's search for a compromise with de Gaulle preoccupied him more than is commonly understood. Neither did Kennedy thrust aside de Gaulle's memorandum proposal during his first year in office, even though the gist of his policies ran counter to de Gaulle's "tripartite" vision. De Gaulle's memorandum diplomacy finally reached a cul-de-sac in 1962, in part because of Kennedy's management of the Cold War (specifically his unilateral handling of the Cuban Missile Crisis) and evidence of the enduring Anglo-American affinity (exhibited above all at the Nassau meeting between Kennedy and Macmillan in December 1962).

The inconspicuous ending of de Gaulle's diplomatic drive for equal status with the Anglo-Saxons set the stage for the much more overt crisis within NATO that had been foreshadowed in de Gaulle's initial memorandum and that is analyzed in Chapter Five. The question remains, however, to what extent one can indeed speak of a crisis, as only the comprehensiveness and the briskness of the French withdrawal from NATO in 1966 had been a surprise to Washington. The Johnson administration had in fact anticipated this withdrawal and awaited – and used – the occasion to breathe new life into an alliance paralyzed by de Gaulle's obstructionism. If one can speak of a NATO crisis in 1966 and 1967, this is because the French withdrawal coincided with a desire across Europe for détente in the Cold War as well as with serious disagreements about financing the allied troop presence in Germany. It was, in addition, a crisis within American policymaking circles. Prominent members of the foreign policy establishment, led by the formidable Acheson and Ball, were greatly disenchanted by Johnson's refusal to stand up to the General and lead the forces of European and Atlantic integration. In their stead, pragmatic minds gained the decisive upper hand in the making of American foreign policy.

Under Johnson's self-possessed leadership, NATO showed more flexibility and resilience than many had supposed. But Johnson's measured response to the French withdrawal was also a reflection of the limited means with which the United States could stand up to de Gaulle by isolating him or France within Europe. There was little support among the European allies, least of all in all-important Germany, for an outright confrontation with de Gaulle. With regard to the organization of the Atlantic alliance, the United States was thus compelled to maneuver between Scylla and Charybdis: to withstand de Gaulle's unacceptable demands for a special status within the alliance while heeding a continual reluctance among the European allies to ostracize France over its policies toward NATO.

In particular, Kennedy and Johnson also felt that their hands were tied behind their backs with regard to France's nuclear efforts. The United States was unable to force France to halt its nuclear program. The story told in Chapter Four, moreover, underscores de Gaulle's ability to scuttle the American proposal for a multilateral nuclear force because he considered it detrimental to his foreign policy goals. In this realm, too, the options of the United States – the nuclear superpower – to impose its will on an intractable European ally therefore appear to have been limited.

The same could be said of the conflict with de Gaulle over the movement toward European unity. Many Americans had staked their hopes about Europe on this movement, which in their view was furthered by the supranational method pioneered by Jean Monnet rather than by de Gaulle's proposals for cooperation between Europe's nation-states. The end of the story, however, was that they were little more than restive bystanders as de Gaulle's intergovernmental approach to the Common Market gained the upper hand in the course of the 1960s. De Gaulle's veto of Kennedy's Atlantic "partnership" idea and the ensuing conclusion of the Franco-German Treaty of January 22, 1963, clearly exposed the limits of American power in Western Europe, even as Washington was successful in forcing Bonn to distance itself from the most objectionable features of de Gaulle's policies. After the clash of 1963, American policies would never again assume the measure of engagement in Europe's internal affairs that marked the early Kennedy years. The Common Market was increasingly seen as an economic rival to the United States. Nixon and Kissinger abandoned America's longstanding support for strengthening the position of the European institutions in relation to the nation-states. By the end of de Gaulle's tenure in 1969, American expectations about the transatlantic relationship had been shattered.

By 1968, the foreign policies of both the United States and France had reached a dead end, thus creating the conditions for a remarkable shift from divergence to accommodation in the bilateral relationship. This rapprochement was already underway in Johnson's final year in office, prompted by the domestic and international setbacks that both Washington and Paris experienced. It was given a significant further boost under Nixon and Kissinger, whose views of foreign policy coincided with those of de Gaulle to an unprecedented degree. Their duo stewardship marked not only the end of the era in American foreign policy that had been dominated by a liberally-bent bipartisan establishment; by the same token, it also symbolized the reemergence of the conservative foreign policy tradition in the United States. As such, this turn of events was a vindication of de Gaulle's views. The adjustment, first under Johnson and then under Nixon, was furthermore an indication that the hegemonic power of the United States within the Western alliance was subject to real and increasingly sharp limits.

This study illustrates how little leverage the United States actually had over de Gaulle's France. The United States was the natural leader within the Western alliance based on the preponderance of its power and the attractiveness of its idealism, but by the 1960s this no longer entailed the ability to force a wayward ally of France's calibre to follow suit. De Gaulle obviously believed that he was not risking the security of France by withdrawing French forces from NATO. He also knew that the French were generally supportive of his public stand against American supremacy. De Gaulle was equally aware that most European allies, in particular those who were also members of the Common Market, preferred a calm response to his transatlantic dissent; NATO could do without France, but the Common Market could not. Washington was able to contain the Gaullist heresy within the alliance by exploiting its leadership position, but it was unable to banish the heretic. What is more, under Nixon the heresy even reached Washington. If the United States was "imperial" at all, it was an emperor without clothes – and, like the child in Hans Christian Andersen's classic tale, de Gaulle was the little fellow to break the spell with his perceptive skills.

This history also shows that consecutive American presidents were aware of the scarcity of their options in dealing with de Gaulle. More than most American diplomats, they were on the whole more pragmatic, more determined to maintain a workable relationship with de Gaulle, and more tuned in to political realities in Europe – and in Germany in particular – that prohibited a policy of isolating France. Members of the White House staff in the turbulent Kennedy and Johnson years were almost as critical of the State Department's anti-Gaullism, which was often seen as part of the problem, as of de Gaulle. At the presidential level, moderation almost always prevailed in the face of de Gaulle's real or perceived slights against the United States. American hegemony within the Western alliance might no longer be perceived as universally accepted, as de Gaulle had withdrawn France's consent, but it was still accommodating.

One may conclude that the Franco-American relationship from 1958 to 1969 knew four distinct phases. In the first phase, from May 1958 to December 1962, the conflict between the United States and de Gaulle was still muted. The Cold

War was at its height. De Gaulle was busy extracting France from Algeria and establishing the Fifth Republic. The Franco-American disagreement about the organization of the Western alliance was still largely hidden from the public view. De Gaulle's opposition within the Western alliance was as yet subdued, allowing for a generally constructive relationship. By the spring of 1962, however, the incongruity between Washington and Paris about military-strategic issues (in particular nuclear policies) and the future of Europe was becoming increasingly obvious and already led to a deterioration in the relationship. By then, the crisis of 1963 was clearly in the offing.

The second phase began with de Gaulle's "thunderbolts" of January 1963 – his veto of Britain's membership of the Common Market, disavowal of the MLF, and the signing of the Franco-German Treaty – and lasted until Johnson decided in December 1964 against pressing the European allies on the MLF. This phase was one of open and often emotional discord, in particular over Germany. It was characterized by an assertive American reaction to de Gaulle's rebuke of Kennedy's Grand Design for an Atlantic partnership. In the third phase, from early 1965 to early 1968, there was hardly any room for constructive dialogue left between Paris and Washington. The Franco-American relationship had reached an impasse from which it seemed impossible to escape. This period was punctured by de Gaulle's acts of resistance to what he perceived as American domination, followed by ever so many holding actions led by Johnson. Following the French withdrawal from NATO in 1966, the relationship reached an all-time low in 1967 when de Gaulle opposed American policies at every turn. The fourth and final phase began in the spring of 1968, as the foreign policies of both Washington and Paris ran into domestic as well as international difficulty. This phase, which lasted until the end of de Gaulle's presidency in April 1969 and continued under Pompidou, was characterized by a shift from divergence to accommodation and rapprochement.

These phases were only loosely linked to the periodic transfers of presidential power in Washington. At the same time, however, there were marked differences between the American presidents and their respective working relationships with de Gaulle – and these differences unmistakably played a role in the development of the bilateral relationship from 1958 to 1969. Each of these transfers introduced a new personal dynamic in the relationship; in all cases except the transition from Kennedy to Johnson, they also introduced a new set of policies toward Europe.

Eisenhower, for one, could bank on the relationship of mutual respect with de Gaulle that had developed during World War II. He was the only one who could see eye to eye with de Gaulle in terms of political stature, as they had both proven their mettle during the war and both were statesmen who could draw on a wealth of experience. Although Eisenhower had repeatedly clashed with de Gaulle during the war, he had never conformed to Roosevelt's unreasonable antagonism and had always kept the lines of communication open. Moreover, as president he had become highly aggravated by the volatile "weakness" of the Fourth Republic; for this reason, too, he genuinely welcomed de Gaulle's return to power. Eisenhower was not devoid of criticism of his French colleague, but he valued his opinions as those of a fellow statesman and a steadfast ally in the Cold War. De Gaulle, meanwhile, appears to have genuinely liked the affable "Ike." Their congenial personal relationship helped to establish a cooperative ambiance in the Franco-American relationship that was open to dialogue, despite the differences of opinion discussed in earlier chapters.

Kennedy's relationship with de Gaulle, in contrast, was inevitably marked by the generation gap between the two. Their personal relationship was, as a result, from the outset imbalanced and awash with friction (which is not to say that it was bad). Kennedy was fascinated by de Gaulle and stood in awe of his historical record and leadership style; he was both deferential to de Gaulle – an attitude that may have been reinforced by his wife's French roots and her personal liking for de Gaulle – and irritated to the point of despair with his opposition to American policies. Kennedy's relationship with de Gaulle was hence the most complicated and incongruous of the four American presidents who dealt with de Gaulle from 1958 to 1969. This was reinforced by Kennedy's own unsettled views of Europe and the transatlantic relationship. His searching intellect might have produced an understanding with de Gaulle on some issues. De Gaulle meanwhile looked upon Kennedy as a novice, albeit a talented one for whom he moreover cherished a certain personal sympathy. Because of Kennedy's premature death, it remains an open question whether they might have been able to develop a more balanced personal relationship and a more constructive political relationship.

Compared with that of Eisenhower and Kennedy, Johnson's relationship with de Gaulle was notable for the absence of any personal rapport. Johnson lacked Eisenhower's wartime record or Kennedy's cosmopolitan East Coast outlook and worldly manners. As a Texan of provincial tastes and a politician who clearly felt more at home in Congress than among world leaders, he stood a world away from de Gaulle. There was no ideological affinity between the two either, as Johnson was also the most liberal president of the era. De Gaulle was unfailingly courteous in his – most often indirect – contacts with Johnson, but he clearly felt the absence of a rapport and he is known to have denigrated Johnson to his associates as a "cowboy" in politics.[22] Johnson's inability to establish a working relationship with de Gaulle was best illustrated by the fact that they could not agree on visiting each other even once, whether in France or in the United States, during the more than five years of his presidency (which took up nearly half of de Gaulle's period in office). The renowned "LBJ treatment" might have been highly effective in dealing with Congress, but it had no use for dealing with de Gaulle. Of all presidents, Johnson was moreover the least captivated by de Gaulle's ideas or personality.

At the same time, Johnson's conduct is notable for the unruffled manner in which he handled the French challenge. His unswerving restraint brought important psychological and political compensations for the United States and the alliance, reduced the symbolic appeal of de Gaulle's policies, and made the beginnings of Franco-American accommodation in 1968 possible. Amid howls of indignation [from his own bureaucracy/staff?], Johnson was able to see de Gaulle's defiance in perspective. He preserved NATO by reforming it with a soft hand. This study therefore supports the recent reappraisal among historians of Johnson as a foreign-policy president and corroborates the view that the Vietnam War did not decisively undermine his European policies.[23]

A meeting of minds, however, had to wait until Nixon's assumption of the presidency in January 1969. The overlap between Nixon and de Gaulle was only three months, but it was sufficient to establish the bilateral relationship on a different footing. American foreign policy in fact switched from Johnson's skillfully exercised holding action against de Gaulle to a mindful search for accommodation and collaboration. Indeed, in December 1971, Henry Kissinger confided to President Georges Pompidou that if the United States had a special relationship with any European country it was France.[24] Both Nixon and Kissinger clearly looked up to the General as a paragon of leadership. They shared many notions with de Gaulle about the proper conduct of foreign policy. De Gaulle was, at the end of his political life, thus finally presented with an American interlocutor with whom he could see eye to eye on most issues.

Atlantis Lost – The Paradigm Shift in American Views of Europe

The extent to which de Gaulle's policy of independence influenced American policies toward Europe is often overlooked. Conventional wisdom holds that the French challenge to American leadership within the Western alliance had little effect.[25] De Gaulle's Cold War revisionism certainly did not end the bipolar alignment or the American hegemonic position in Western Europe. NATO, too, survived the French withdrawal. De Gaulle furthermore failed in his effort to organize Europe around a Franco-German union led by France and independent of the United States. Washington's response to de Gaulle's actions had much to do with these failures. Neither was de Gaulle successful in eliminating the federalist inspiration behind the movement toward European unity. The "European" Europe of nation-states, stretching from the Atlantic to the Urals, did not materialize during his lifetime.

De Gaulle's policy of independence and grandeur nonetheless had an impact on American policies toward Europe in a number of important ways. First, as Walt Rostow admitted, the European policies of the Kennedy and the Johnson administrations in particular were to a considerable degree born out of a desire to contain de Gaulle's nationalist defiance.[26] This was, for instance, the case with

Kennedy's design for an Atlantic partnership and with the MLF proposal, both of which would not have occupied a central place in American foreign policy in the absence of the specter of Gaullism. It also holds true for Johnson's growing emphasis on détente from 1966 onwards, as this emphasis in part resulted from the need to regain the political initiative in response to the NATO crisis prompted by the French withdrawal and to de Gaulle's early overtures towards the Communist bloc. The crisis of 1966, as Andreas Wenger put it, was moreover "instrumental in the shift from the bilateral superpower détente of 1963 to the multilateral European détente of the 1970s."[27] De Gaulle's withdrawal from NATO thus gave occasion to the NATO-ization of détente.

Second, French policies forced the United States to face up to new strategic realities. The coming into being of the French nuclear force, for one, added a center of atomic decisionmaking in the alliance that introduced the prospect of the "French nuclear tail wagging the NATO dog."[28] American strategic thinkers such as Albert Wohlstetter were wrong to discount the military value of the French nuclear deterrent. Both Pierre Gallois's doctrine of proportional deterrence and André Beaufre's doctrine of multilateral deterrence had an irresistible military logic to them. Would not the slightest risk of French atomic bombs exploding over Kiev and Moscow make the Kremlin think twice before engaging in any large-scale aggression in Europe? Would not the existence of more than one center of decision in the West complicate Soviet decisionmaking and hence strengthen deterrence?[29] The first generation of the French nuclear force became partially operational in the fall of 1963 with the delivery of plutonium bombs to six Mirage IV bombers; by 1966, the planned force of fifty bombers was operational and scattered over nine airfields. This was a small but not negligible nuclear capability. "Although questions were raised in the 1960s about the planes' vulnerability to a first strike, and their ability to penetrate the Soviet air defense system, the likelihood that a few would survive to deliver their bombs could not be discounted," Michael Harrison judged.[30] Moreover, the next generations of the French nuclear force – in particular the missile-launched nuclear submarines – the first of which became operational in the early 1970s, were to be more effective.

Similarly, de Gaulle's policies with regard to European unity created unwanted realities from the American vantage point. De Gaulle twice vetoed British membership, reducing the opportunities for the United States to influence European affairs through the "special relationship." Although de Gaulle was unable to eliminate European federalism altogether, he *was* successful – through his "empty chair" policy – in imposing an intergovernmental approach that respected the principle of national sovereignty as well as the protectionist-minded common agricultural policy. French economic policies helped to transform the Common Market into an economic rival to the United States rather than the hoped-for bulwark of free trade. By the end of the 1960s, the Common Market had thus travelled a different road from the one that American supporters of European integration – the friends of Jean Monnet – had envisioned earlier. For this, de Gaulle was chiefly responsible.

De Gaulle's policy of independence thus revealed as well as defined the limits of American power in Europe. His return to power in 1958 heralded the end of easy American postwar predominance in Western Europe. One of de Gaulle's innovations was his exercise of "le pouvoir de dire non," in particular his ability to say "no" to the schemes of the more powerful United States. More than any other European leader, he brought fundamental differences within the Western alliance to light about the nature of the transatlantic relationship and the future of Europe. Instead of a gradually evolving Atlantic community, there was – as a committee of the House of Representatives concluded after a study mission to Europe in 1967 – "an increasing cleavage between the attitudes that prevail in the United States and those currently held by our European allies."[31] This brings us to our final observation.

As a result of the experience of dealing with de Gaulle and of the political and historical context in which Americans judged his policies, the Gaullist challenge to the United States put a stamp upon American perceptions and expectations of the transatlantic relationship. "Europe would never look to America with quite the same reverence after de Gaulle," the American historian William Hitchcock observed.[32] This study suggests that America would never look at Europe with quite the same affinity and sense of involvement.

We have already noted in the introduction to this study that the pervasive idea among American policymakers of an evolving Atlantic community – built on the Cold War nexus between North America and Europe and on the institutions that were being created in its wake – had the features of a foreign policy "paradigm."[33] Challenges to a ruling paradigm may result in a paradigm "crisis," in which case there may actually be competing paradigms. This in turn can lead to a paradigm "shift," which means that the original paradigm has undergone significant change or has been replaced with a new paradigm as a result of the crisis.

The same sequence can be observed in the Franco-American relationship from 1958 to 1969. Strengthening the Atlantic community was undeniably part of American conventional wisdom at the beginning of this period. This was the result of the requirements of the Cold War. The ambiguity inherent in the notion of an Atlantic community also served to wed liberal and conservative approaches to foreign policy and to reconcile longstanding ambivalences about Europe. Notwithstanding its inherent ambiguity, the goal of an Atlantic community presented a more or less coherent set of beliefs or assumptions about the transatlantic relationship that served as a guide for thought and action – and hence can described as a foreign policy paradigm. This paradigm was challenged by de Gaulle in various ways, leading to a crisis. American and French views of the transatlantic relationship were actually competing paradigms, each demanding its separate world view. American reactions to de Gaulle's policy statements were so vehement because many felt that the United States had given generously to enable Europe to recover from World War II and grow strong in unison with the United States. Yet now this very strength – under de Gaulle's leadership – appeared to threaten the alliance with Europe itself and to return Europe to the age of narrow-minded nationalism. From Washington's point of view, de Gaulle's "deviant" policies and frequent public disagreements put at risk the fundamental achievements of American policy in Europe since World War II. "We were not concerned at the prospect of Europe devoting its energies to its own genuine, political interests, for we were convinced that these interests would be identical with our own," Dean Rusk told a French journalist in 1964. "But we were concerned at the thesis that in order to be genuine, European interests would necessarily have to be different from those of the United States."[34]

De Gaulle's frequent clashes with the United States ultimately contributed to a paradigm shift in American perceptions of the transatlantic relationship. What became lost was the notion that the United States and Western Europe were part of a budding Atlantic community in which political and institutional ties were to become ever tighter. It also meant the ambition to assume a leadership role in strengthening either Atlantic or European integration was abandoned, the former because it no longer appeared realistic and the latter because it was no longer unequivocally perceived to be in the American national interest. The disenchantment with the pace and direction of European integration, which had begun under Johnson, was reflected in the policies of Nixon and Kissinger. By the late 1960s, the United States had clearly become of two minds about the objective of a united Europe. Even a stallwart supporter of European integration like J. Robert Schaetzel wrote in retrospect that "the excitement of the 1950s and '60s in a bold and exciting adventure has been lost as the [European] Community flounders in bewildering detail, endless national wrangling and shows little evidence of becoming the 'United States of Europe.'"[35] The United States still had overwhelming interests in Europe. However, it had lost interest in either Europe or the transatlantic relationship as a challenging building ground. What emerged from the Franco-American clash of the 1960s was a United States more attuned to the national interest as well as a Europe more aware of "European" interests. The American ability to read its national interest in the broadest possible terms diminished. The Europeanization of Europe, as Ralf Dahrendorf observed, was by the early 1970s reciprocated in the Americanization of America.[36] In the process, the liberal pipedream of an Atlantic community as a scaled-down world community vanished and made place for an Atlanticism grounded in realism.

It would be going too far to explain this shift in American transatlantic attitudes from de Gaulle's policy of independence alone. While the idea of an Atlantic community had been influential among American policymakers, it was inevitably blighted by the most often more pragmatic and short-term considerations customary at the top level of decisionmaking. At this level, where issues and crises had to be confronted squarely and without much time for reflection, national requirements often prevailed. "As a motivating ideal in Atlantic politics, the vision of an increasingly comprehensive and institutionalized political structure – an Atlantic commonwealth – was never quite plausible [...]," Francis Bator therefore wrote in hindsight. "Neither we nor the Europeans have been ready for it."[37] Developments in the Cold War, the tragedy of the Vietnam War, the United States' relative economic decline, the domestic turmoil in the second half of the 1960s – all of these also contributed to a lessening of interest among Americans in strengthening the transatlantic relationship. Underlying this shift, too, was the fading of the bipartisan foreign policy generation – the so-called Establishment that determined the gist of America's postwar policies – and the fragmentation of the foreign policy elite into opposing ideological camps.

Yet dealing with de Gaulle was an important and demoralizing experience for many American policymakers. There was a palpable sense of disillusionment among those who had spent their public careers strengthening the transatlantic relationship and supporting European integration. Dean Rusk voiced his disappointment as follows in 1969:

> My chief regret [...] is that Europe has drawn into itself and is not playing the role on the world scene that is waiting for Europe to play. The United States is too lonely as a world power. We need to have others associated with us, and we ought not to be the only ones who have some capability of action in all parts of the world. Now, a unified Europe could play that role. But a Europe of national states is not likely to be able to play a leading role as one of the great powers.[38]

Someone like Schaetzel ended his long diplomatic career on a similar note of disappointment and even bitterness. For a decade he had been in official positions of influence, first as deputy assistant secretary of state for Atlantic Affairs and then as ambassador to the European Communities, but it was a decade of precious little achievement in which the atmospherics of the transatlantic relationship had only deteriorated. "The soft-background music of Atlantic harmony and devotion to Europe cannot block out the public memories of years of errors and omissions, interrupted by sharp charges and angry responses," Schaetzel concluded in 1975. Neither did Great Britain's long hoped-for entry into the Common Market in 1973 bring new life to the European integration movement. "Britain turned from earnest new member into neo-Gaullist, obstructive, threatening withdrawal," Schaetzel felt. "Gaullism was alive and well in Brussels, only the language of obstruction was now English." These were the years of "Europessimism," marked by economic and political stagnation, the oil crisis after the Yom Kippur war of 1973, and Turkey's invasion of Cyprus in 1974. But, in Schaetzel's view, the problem lay in Washington, too. For Nixon's and Kissinger's conduct of diplomacy corresponded to "the instincts of the European pragmatists and the universal surge of nationalism."[39] Schaetzel's disappointment with the state of affairs in Europe was therefore also a disappointment with America itself.

Many American policymakers held de Gaulle's policies from 1958 to 1969 responsible for this state of affairs. De Gaulle had let the genie of European nationalism out of the bottle that America had made. "It is a great pity," wrote Ball in 1968,

> that General de Gaulle should have led that attack [the nationalist counterattack against rapid progress in European unity], that he should have put his extraordinary skills at the service of an outworn cause. For he – as no other man – had the charisma and authority and the iron will to lead Europe firmly and steadily toward unity. ... He could well have been the first president of some early form of European state."[40]

And in his memoirs, Ball judged that de Gaulle had been "one of the destructive elements in the larger chemistry of the West. [...] It is a tragedy [for the European people] not only for the breakage caused, but – what is even more poignant – because of the opportunity missed."[41]

In response to the French withdrawal from NATO, Harold van B. Cleveland explained the disenchantment as follows:

> What seems to trouble Americans [about the current state of Atlantic affairs] is that they expected something better – much better. They expected an Atlantic relationship in which conflicts of national interest, far from growing, would gradually give way to increasing cooperation and, in Western Europe's case, to supranational union. They were not prepared to find themselves involved in the seemingly indefinite exercise of power which is no longer unambiguously desired by their European allies.[42]

Acheson, of course, had never shunned the exercise of power. But he, too, sounded a note of disappointment at the end of the decade, holding de Gaulle's "nationalist separatism" accountable for sapping the life out of NATO and encouraging the return of American isolationism.[43] In his memoirs, which appeared in 1969 (and won the Pulitzer Prize in 1970), he pondered the results of his years at the helm:

> To the responsibilities and needs of that time the nation summoned an imaginative effort unique in history and even greater than that made in the preceding period of fighting. All who served in those years had an opportunity to give more than a sample of their best. Yet an account of the experience, despite its

successes, inevitably leaves a sense of disappointment and frustration, for the achievements fell short of both hope and need. How often what seemed almost within grasp slipped away. Alas, that is life. We cannot live our dreams.[44]

Acheson's words corresponded with the decline of the Establishment that had shaped American foreign policy since the late 1940s. President Nixon still turned to the elder statesman for advice despite their earlier animosity – and the latter felt it incumbent upon him to furnish it out of a reverence for the presidential office. But Acheson was no longer the towering presence over American foreign policy representing the illustrious postwar generation of diplomats. His death in October 1971, at the age of seventy-eight, marked the end of an era.

In 1963, three American supporters of the Atlantic community idea declared the following: "To the future historian, the unity and vitality of the North Atlantic Community, evoked by the challenges our time, may well appear to be the outstanding event of the twentieth century."[45] This statement rings hollow now. For many Americans, in the course of dealing with de Gaulle, Atlantis was lost.

Notes

Notes to Introduction

1. Ronald Steel, *Walter Lippmann and the American Century* (New York: Random House, 1981), 399.
2. Sulzberger's two volumes of published notes – *The Last of the Giants* (New York: Macmillan, 1970) and *An Age of Mediocrity* (New York: Macmillan, 1973) – give ample evidence of his high regard for de Gaulle.
3. *Time*, 5 January 1959.
4. Charles de Gaulle, "Discours prononcé a Washington devant les deux chambres réunis en Congrès," 25 April 1960, in *Discours et messages*, vol. 3, *Avec le renouveau* (Paris: Plon, 1970), 196-200.
5. *San Francisco Chronicle*, 29 April 1960.
6. Gallup poll in the *Washington Post*, 9 July 1966.
7. White House Central File, Subject File, France, box 31, Lyndon Baines Johnson Presidential Library (henceforth abbreviated as LBJL).
8. Etienne Burin des Roziers, a long-time aide of de Gaulle, rightfully disagreed with historians who emphasized the continuity between the Fourth and the Fifth Republic, observing that the instructions he received as a diplomat "changed completely as de Gaulle came back to power" and that this had far-reaching ramifications for France's relationship with the United States. Robert O. Paxton and Nicholas Wahl, eds., *De Gaulle and the United States: A Centennial Reappraisal*, (Oxford: Berg Publishers, 1994), 422-3.
9. Michael M. Harrison, *The Reluctant Ally: France and Atlantic Security* (Baltimore: Johns Hopkins University Press, 1981), 54. The governments of the Fourth Republic, to be sure, also had chafed under American postwar predominance and often resisted the roles assigned by Washington. In particular, the Suez Crisis of 1956 had a major impact on French foreign policy, and as French historian Maurice Vaïsse noted, "Gaullist France was already on the horizon in 1956." *Suez, 1956: The Crisis and its Consequences*, eds. Wm. Roger Louis and Roger Owen (Oxford: Oxford University Press, 1989), 335. For accounts of Franco-American relations under the Fourth Republic, see Irwin M. Wall, *The United States and the Making of Postwar France, 1945-1954* (New York: Cambridge University Press, 1991); William I. Hitchcock, *France Restored: Cold War Diplomacy and the Quest for Leadership in Europe* (Chapel Hill: University of North Carolina Press, 1998); John W. Young, *France, the Cold War and the Western Alliance, 1944-49: French Foreign Policy and Postwar Europe* (London: Leicester University Press, 1990); and Jean-Pierre Rioux, *The Fourth Republic, 1944-1958* (New York: Cambridge University Press, 1987).
10. Jean Baptiste Duroselle, *France and the United States: From the Beginnings to the Present* (Chicago: University of Chicago Press, 1976), 220.

11. De Gaulle, *Le fil de l'épée* 2d ed. (Paris: Berger-Levrault, 1944). The Dutch historian H.L. Wesseling has pointed out that de Gaulle's citation – which would translate into "to be great is to sustain a great argument" – was not entirely correct as it refers to the following passage in *Hamlet*: "Rightly to be great is not to stir without great argument, but greatly to find quarrel in a straw when honour's at stake." "De Gaulle en Hamlet," H.L. Wesseling, *NRC Handelsblad*, 22 May 1999.

12. Walt W. Rostow, *The Diffusion of Power: An Essay in Recent History* (New York: MacMillan, 1972), 394. Rostow served in the Kennedy White House staff and, from November 1961, as chairman of the Policy Planning Council at the State Department. In March 1966, he became President Johnson's National Security Adviser.

13. David Klein to McGeorge Bundy, memorandum, 3 April 1963, France-General, Country Series (henceforth abbreviated as CS), National Security Files (henceforth abbreviated as NSF), box 72, John F. Kennedy Presidential Library (henceforth abbreviated as JFKL). Bohlen revealed that one of de Gaulle's closest advisers served as an informant of the American embassy and "had him taped." The problem, however, was that de Gaulle very often did not apprise even his closest advisers and ministers of his next move. Bohlen quoted in Note C., page 41, file 4, box W-13, Arthur M. Schlesinger Jr. Papers, JFKL. François David, too, has suggested that the CIA had a confidential source of information within de Gaulle's cabinet. François David, "Les Etats-Unis et les débuts de la cinquième République. Mai 1958 - Janvier 1961" (Mémoire de maîtrise, Université de Paris-IV, 1992-1993).

14. The monograph that approaches this one the closest, because it likewise covers the bilateral relationship within the transatlantic framework from 1958 to 1969, is Frédéric Bozo's *Deux stratégies pour l'Europe. De Gaulle, les États-Unis et l'Alliance Atlantique, 1958-1969* (Paris: Plon and Fondation Charles de Gaulle, 1996), which has been translated as *Two Strategies For Europe: De Gaulle, the United States, and the Atlantic Alliance* (Lanham: Rowman and Littlefield, 2001). John Newhouse's *De Gaulle and the Anglo-Saxons* (New York: The Viking Press, 1970) may also be mentioned as such; while well-informed, he did not, however, have the important benefit of archival research. Frank Costigliola covers a much longer period in *France and the United States: The Cold Alliance Since World War II* (New York: Twayne Publishers, 1992), but his chapter on the period of de Gaulle's presidency equally deserves mention (pages 118-159). The same can be said of Charles Cogan's *Oldest Allies, Guarded Friends: The United States and France Since 1940* (New York: Praeger, 1994); however, although de Gaulle looms large throughout the book, only his chapter on the Multilateral Force falls within the scope of this study. Vincent Jauvert's readable *L'Amérique contre de Gaulle. Histoire secrète, 1961-1969* (Paris: Éditions du Seuil, 2000) makes no academic claims and is based on only a few documents. The contributions of scholars and "witnesses" in Paxton and Wahl, *De Gaulle and the United States*, are highly relevant to this study, but do not constitute a monograph. For other valuable accounts of the bilateral relationship in either a longer or shorter time frame, see Duroselle, *France and the United States*; Maurice Ferro, *De Gaulle et l'Amérique. Une amitié tumultueuse* (Paris: Plon, 1973); Jeffrey Glen Giauque, *Grand Designs and Visions of Unity: The Atlantic Powers and the Reorganization of Western Europe, 1955-1963* (Chapel Hill: University of North Carolina Press, 2002); Harrison, *The Reluctant Ally*; Richard F. Kuisel, *Seducing the French: The Dilemma of Americanization* (Berkeley and Los Angeles: Uni-

versity of California Press, 1993); Erin R. Mahan, *Kennedy, De Gaulle, and Western Europe* (New York: Palgrave Macmillan, 2002); and Marvin R. Zahniser, *Uncertain Friendship: American-French Relations Through the Cold War* (New York: John Wiley & Sons, 1975). Political scientist Stanley Hoffmann has not devoted a full-scale study to the topic, but he has written extensively on Franco-American relations during de Gaulle's hold on power; see in particular "De Gaulle, Europe and the Atlantic Alliance," *International Organization* 18 (Winter 1964): 1-28; "Perceptions, Reality and the Franco-American conflict," *Journal of International Affairs* 21, no.1 (1967): 57-71. The same applies to David Calleo, see in particular *Europe's Future: The Grand Alternative* (New York: Horizon Press, 1965) and *The Atlantic Fantasy: The United States, NATO, and Europe* (Baltimore: Johns Hopkins University Press, 1970). Henry Kissinger, too, has written perceptively on Franco-American relations under de Gaulle; see, e.g., chap. 2 in *The Troubled Partnership: A Re-appraisal of the Atlantic Alliance* (New York: McGraw-Hill for Council on Foreign Relations, 1965); chap. 24 in *Diplomacy* (New York: Simon & Schuster, 1994). William I. Hitchcock devoted a chapter to "the Gaullist temptation" in *The Struggle for Europe: The Turbulent History of a Divided Continent, 1945-2002* (New York: Doubleday, 2003), 221-241. Geir Lundestad has similarly included a chapter on de Gaulle's challenge in *"Empire" by Integration: The United States and European Integration, 1945-1997* (Oxford: Oxford University Press, 1998), 58-82. For a more complete listing of relevant works, see the bibliography.

15. John Dos Passos, *Journeys Between Wars* (New York: Harcourt, Brace & World, 1938), 334.
16. Bozo, *Two Strategies for Europe*, ix-xvii.
17. Costigliola, *France and the United States*, 7, 104, 121.
18. Philip G. Cerny, *The Politics of Grandeur: Ideological Aspects of de Gaulle's Foreign Policy* (Cambridge: Cambridge University Press, 1980), 213.
19. Louis J. Halle, *History, Philosophy, and Foreign Relations* (Lanham, MD: University Press of America, 1987), 117, 120. A State Department official who served at the Policy Planning Staff under Kennan, Halle turned his mind to political philosophy in the 1950s after a stint at the National War College.
20. Richard J. Barnet and Marcus G. Raskin, *After Twenty Years: The Decline of NATO and the Search for a New Policy in Europe* (New York: Vintage Books, 1965), 1. The authors worked at the State Department and the White House respectively during the Kennedy administration.
21. Geir Lundestad, *"Empire" by Integration*, 148.
22. For the importance of mental maps in diplomatic history, see Alan K. Henrikson, "Mental Maps," in *Explaining the History of American Foreign Relations*, eds, Michael J. Hogan and Thomas G. Patterson (Cambridge: Cambridge University Press, 1991), 177-192.
23. From a speech in Bordeaux on 25 September 1949. De Gaulle, *Discours et messages*, vol. 2, *Dans l'attente*, 307.
24. De Gaulle, *Memoirs of Hope: Renewal and Endeavor* (New York: Simon & Schuster, 1971), 11.
25. De Gaulle, *Dans l'attente*, 510-511.
26. From an address on 4 December 1954. De Gaulle, *Dans l'attente*, 625-626.

27. Sulzberger, *The Last of the Giants*, 60-61.

28. Ibid., 61.

29. Harrison, *The Reluctant Ally*, 68-69.

30. Press conference of 28 October 1966. *Major Addresses, Statements, and Press Conferences of General Charles de Gaulle, March 17, 1964 - May 16, 1967* (New York: Service de Presse et d'Information, 1967), 152.

31. André Malraux, *Felled Oaks: Conversation With de Gaulle* (New York: Holt, Rinehart and Winston, 1971), 33. Originally published in French as *Les chênes qu'on abat*.

Notes to Chapter One – Organizing the West

1. De Gaulle to Eisenhower, letter and memorandum, 17 September 1958, White House Memorandum Series, General Correspondence 1958 (2), box 6, John Foster Dulles Papers (henceforth abbreviated as JFD Papers), Dwight D. Eisenhower Library (henceforth abbreviated as DDEL). De Gaulle's memorandum was for a long time one of the most secret documents of the French government, giving occasion to wide speculation regarding its contents. It did not become publicly available until a copy was deposited in the Eisenhower Library in 1976 and was subsequently published in *Espoir* and *Le Monde*.

2. De Gaulle, *Memoirs of Hope*, 202-3.

3. Journalist David Schoenbrun was the first to consider de Gaulle's memorandum proposal in *The Three Lives of Charles de Gaulle* (New York: Atheneum, 1965), 295-303. John Newhouse is biased towards the "Anglo-Saxons," but his account is well-informed; see chapter 3 in *De Gaulle and the Anglo-Saxons*. Kohl analyzes the proposal within the framework of French nuclear diplomacy. Wilfrid L. Kohl, *French Nuclear Diplomacy* (Princeton, NJ: Princeton University Press, 1971), 70-81. Kolodziej and Harrison deal with the memorandum proposal in their excellent studies on French security policy. Edward A. Kolodziej, *French International Policy Under de Gaulle and Pompidou: The Politics of Grandeur* (Ithaca, NY: Cornell University Press, 1974), 71-86; Harrison, *The Reluctant Ally*, 16-20, 86-101. In particular, Harrison's analysis remains one of the most complete and penetrating. Maurice Vaïsse discusses the roots of the memorandum proposal in the Fourth Republic in "Aux origines du mémorandum de Septembre 1958," *Relations Internationales* 58 (Summer 1989): 253-263. See also "Un dialogue de sourds: les relations nucléaires franco-américaines de 1957 à 1960," *Relations Internationales* 68 (Winter 1991): 407-423. Cerny discusses the memorandum, which he explains from a miscalculation on de Gaulle's part instilled by his long absence from power, yet has no eye for de Gaulle's subsequent diplomacy. See Cerny, *The Politics of Grandeur*, chap. 7. Elizabeth Sherwood devotes a chapter to de Gaulle's memorandum diplomacy in her *Allies in Crisis: Meeting Global Challenges to Western Security* (New Haven: Yale University Press, 1990), 95-110. Costigliola discusses de Gaulle's memorandum proposal and the American response on the basis of a review of primary sources, but his discussion is cursive at best. Costigliola, *France and the United States*, 123-127. Bozo largely describes the issue from de Gaulle's perspective, although he has made use of both American and French primary sources. Bozo, *Two Strategies For Europe*, chap. 1 and 2.

4. Eisenhower's response to de Gaulle's letter was made public in the summer of 1966 by Senator Henry Jackson, then chairman of the Senate subcommittee on National Security and International Operations.

5. Kolodziej, *French International Policy Under de Gaulle and Pompidou*, 71-86.

6. Dwight D. Eisenhower, *The White House Years: Waging Peace, 1956-1961* (Garden City, NY: Doubleday, 1965), 430.

7. Irwin M. Wall, "The United States, Algeria, and the Fourth French Republic," *Diplomatic History*, 18, no.4 (Fall 1994): 489.

8. There was a pervasive sense of betrayal among army officers vis-à-vis a political class and its revolving door governments. The crisis over Algeria rose to a climax when, on May 13, 1958, Pierre Pflimlin presented a new cabinet to the National Assembly that was indeed generally expected to begin negotiations with the rebels. The prospect of a settlement that would abandon the idea of an *Algérie française* prompted massive demonstrations by the *colons* in Algiers, who ransacked government offices and seized control over the city. Importantly, they found the French army sympathetic to their side.

9. Lacouture, *De Gaulle: The Ruler*, 176. To be sure, de Gaulle has always denied that he explicitly endorsed the activities of his followers. See *Memoirs of Hope*, 17.

10. See in particular, Wall, "US, Algeria, and the Fourth French Republic," 491, 505. While Wall does not argue that the Eisenhower administration actively sought the downfall of the Fourth Republic, he does state that "the Americans appeared to have played a considerable role in undermining the very stability of the regime they had done so much since 1947 to help preserve" (489). The Franco-Tunisian crisis revolved around American and British arms deliveries to Tunisia which the French argued were being used by the rebels in Algeria. It did not help that Eisenhower had assigned Robert Murphy to head the so-called "good offices" mission with the British to solve the Franco-Tunisian crisis. Murphy had in World War II been picked by President Roosevelt to maintain relations with Vichy authorities in North Africa and had been a crucial player in the preparation of the allied invasion of French North Africa in 1942. In 1958, French military circles had not forgotten Murphy's role. See Alfred Grosser, *The Western Alliance: European-American Relations Since 1945* (New York: Continuum, 1980), 150-151. French suspicions that the United States moved to interfere in the Algerian crisis were not without substance, since by March 1958 Eisenhower, Dulles, Murphy, and Ambassador Houghton all believed that the question should be considered within NATO. Eisenhower and Dulles, memorandum of conversation, 1 March 1958, State Dept Subseries, Subject Series, White House Office, Office of the Staff Secretary (henceforth abbreviated as WHOSS), box 2, DDEL; Summary of Developments, "Good Offices in Franco-Tunesian Problem," 7 March 1958, Good Offices Mission (1), State Dept Subseries, Subject Series, WHOSS, box 5, DDEL.

11. Wall, *The United States and the Making of Postwar France, 1945-1954*, 111.

12. *France and the United States*, Costigliola, 91.

13. As for de Gaulle, he wrote in his memoirs that "the expedition which London and Paris undertook against Nasser had been mounted in such a way that the French forces of every kind and at every level were placed under the orders of the British, and

the latter had only to decide to recall theirs at the behest of Washington and Moscow for ours to be withdrawn as well." De Gaulle, *Memoirs of Hope*, 11.

14. *Oral history interview with Charles Yost*, no. 416, DDEL, 20. Yost served as minister at the American embassy in Paris from 1956 to 1958.

15. See Alfred Grosser, "France and Germany in the Atlantic Community," *International Organization*, 17 (Summer 1963): 550-573. The quote is on page 557.

16. Wall, "US, Algeria, and the Fourth French Republic," 493.

17. Eisenhower, diary note, 14 November 1957, President Dwight D. Eisenhower's Office Files (henceforth abbreviated as DEOF), International Series (henceforth abbreviated as IS), Roosevelt Study Center (henceforth abbreviated as RSC).

18. Dulles and Eisenhower, telephone conversation, 13 November 1957, White House Memos – Telcon, JFD Papers, box 10, DDEL.

19. Dulles to Bruce, Houghton, and Murphy, telegram, 2 April 1958, *Foreign Relations of the United States 1958-1960* (henceforth abbreviated as FRUS), vol. 7, part 2: Western Europe, 5.

20. Wall, *The United States and the Making of Postwar France, 1945-1954*; Young, *France, the Cold War and the Western Alliance*; Costigliola, *France and the United States*, chap. 2 and 3; Hitchcock, *France Restored*.

21. See William I. Hitchcock, "Reversal of Fortune: Britain, France, and the Making of Europe, 1945-1956," in *From War to Peace: Altered Strategic Landscapes in the Twentieth Century* eds. Paul Kennedy and William I. Hitchcock (New Haven: Yale University Press, 2000), 79-102.

22. Costigliola, *France and the United States*, 101. Dillon was ambassador to France from 1953 to 1959.

23. FRUS 1949, 3: 600-1. See also John L. Harper, *American Visions of Europe: Franklin D. Roosevelt, George F. Kennan, and Dean G. Acheson* (Cambridge: Cambridge University Press, 1994), 219, 289. Harper finds that Kennan at the time stood "virtually alone" in believing that Germany was bound to assume a leadership role.

24. Acheson was reported to have posed the question at a seminar at Princeton University. See Harper, *American Visions of Europe*, 327.

25. Truman to Eisenhower, letter, 15 February 1952; with attached letter from Eisenhower, 9 February 1952, Student Research File (B file), no. 34A, North Atlantic Treaty Organization, box 1, folder 3, Harry S. Truman Library (henceforth abbreviated as HSTL).

26. General Eisenhower to Secretary of Defense George C. Marshall, letter, 3 August 1951, Student Research File (B file), no. 34A, North Atlantic Treaty Organization, box 1, folder 2, HSTL.

27. Stephen E. Ambrose, *Eisenhower: Soldier, General of the Army, President-Elect, 1890-1952*, vol. 1 (New York: Simon & Schuster, 1983), 508.

28. See note 26 above.

29. Eisenhower and Spaak, memorandum of conversation, 24 November 1959, NATO (2), International Trips and Meetings, WHOSS, DDEL.

30. Winston S. Churchill to Dwight D. Eisenhower, letters, 7 December 1954 and 14 December 1954, DEOF, IS, RSC. Dwight D. Eisenhower to Emmet Hughes, letter, 11 January 1955, DEOF, Eisenhower Administration Series (henceforth abbreviated as EAS), RSC.

31. Eisenhower to Gruenther, letter, 26 April 1954, DEOF, EAS, RSC. Gruenther regularly informed Eisenhower of the mood among the French.

32. After their talks in Washington on October 25, 1957, Eisenhower and Macmillan issued a "Declaration of Common Purpose" that said that the British and American strategic forces would serve as "a trust for the defense of the free world." It furthermore stated that the Eisenhower administration would request Congress to amend the Atomic Energy Act of 1946 to enable closer nuclear cooperation between Great Britain, the United States, "and other friendly countries." See Paul E. Zinner, ed., *Documents on American Foreign Relations, 1957-58* (New York: Harper & Brothers, 1959), 132-136.

33. Eisenhower to CIA Director Allen W. Dulles, letter, 5 November 1957, DEOF, EAS, RSC.

34. *The Times*, 26 October 1957, as quoted in Andrew J. Pierre, *Nuclear Politics: The British Experience With an Independent Strategic Force, 1939-1970* (New York: Oxford University Press, 1972), 140-141.

35. Charles Yost, who served at the embassy in Paris from 1956 to 1958, recalled that "we were very disturbed by the instability of the French government – the constant changes, the time wasted in reconstructing a new government every few months, and the new government settling in. I personally, and some others in the embassy, thought that the probable solution was a de Gaulle government [...]. I maintained very close relations, for that reason [...], with Michel Debré, who was then very much on the outs but later of course was de Gaulle's prime minister." *Oral history interview with Charles Yost*, no. 416, DDEL, 20. See also Wall, "US, Algeria, and the Fourth French Republic," 492.

36. Schoenbrun, *The Three Lives of Charles de Gaulle*, 333-334.

37. As quoted in Ambrose, *Eisenhower*, 1:378. For this episode, see also Merle Miller, *Ike the Soldier: As They Knew Him* (New York: Perigee, 1987), 744.

38. Miller, *Ike the Soldier*, 683.

39. Schoenbrun, *The Three Lives of Charles de Gaulle*, 338.

40. David Eisenhower, *Eisenhower at War, 1943-1945* (New York: Random House, 1986), 163.

41. Raoul Aglion, *Roosevelt and De Gaulle, Allies in Conflict: A Personal Memoir* (New York: The Free Press, 1988), 194.

42. De Gaulle, *War Memoirs*, 435-7.

43. Truman to Eisenhower, letter, 20 March 1952, with attached letter from Eisenhower, 11 March 1952, Student Research File (B file), no. 34A, North Atlantic Treaty Organization, box 1, folder 3, HSTL.

44. Eisenhower to Gruenther, letter, 22 June 1953, DEOF, EAS, RSC.

45. Eisenhower to Gruenther, letter, 26 April 1954.

46. Wall, "US, Algeria and the Fourth French Republic," 501.

47. See for example Charles Williams, *The Last Great Frenchman: A Life of General de Gaulle* (London: Abacus, 1996), 363.

48. Houghton to Department of State, telegram, 1 June 1958, FRUS 1958-1960, vol. 7, part 2: Western Europe, 23-24. NATO Secretary General Paul-Henri Spaak was equally convinced that de Gaulle had lost touch with political and military realities during his 'desert' years and attributed to this some of his policy actions.

49. Elbrick to Dulles, memorandum, 26 June 1958, FRUS 1958-1960, vol. 7, part 2: Western Europe, 40-42; Elbrick to Acting Secretary of State Herter, memorandum, 27 May 1958, FRUS 1958-1960, vol. 7, part 2: Western Europe, 17-20.

50. Elbrick to Herter, memorandum, 27 May 1958, FRUS 1958-1960, vol. 7, part 2: Western Europe, 17-20; Elbrick to Dulles, memorandum, 5 June 1958, FRUS 1958-1960, vol. 7, part 2: Western Europe, 26-28. Houghton reported on the particular importance de Gaulle attached to acquiring a nuclear deterrent for France. Houghton to Department of State, telegram, 20 June 1958, FRUS 1958-1960, vol. 7, part 2: Western Europe, 36-37.

51. Dulles and Alphand, memorandum of conversation, 21 May 1958, FRUS 1958-1960, vol. 7, part 2: Western Europe, 10-13. Houghton to Department of State, telegram, 21 May 1958, FRUS 1958-1960, vol. 7, part 2: Western Europe, 13-15.

52. Elbrick to Herter, memorandum, 27 May 1958, FRUS 1958-1960, vol. 7, part 2: Western Europe, 17.

53. As cited in Wall, "US, Algeria, and the Fourth French Republic," 510.

54. Eisenhower made these remarks after reading a *Life* editorial by C.D. Jackson which stressed the need for stability in France and called for a positive American attitude toward de Gaulle. Ann C. Whitman to C.D. Jackson, letter, 5 June 1958, President Eisenhower's Office File (henceforth abbreviated as PEOF), EAS, RSC.

55. Eisenhower to Hoffmann, letter, 23 June 1958, DEOF, EAS, RSC.

56. De Gaulle, *Memoirs of Hope*, 167.

57. Originally, French strategic thinkers such as General Paul Ély and General Pierre Gallois had envisaged the French *force de dissuasion* as committed to the Atlantic alliance and strengthening its overall deterrent by forcing the adversary to worry about more nuclear centers of decision (multilateral deterrence); they had argued that the French nuclear force should be closely coordinated with the other allied nuclear forces in the context of NATO. Kohl, *French Nuclear Diplomacy*, 44-47, 54-61, 63-64, 82-84.

58. Lacouture, *De Gaulle: The Ruler*, 212.

59. De Gaulle's account of his talk with Adenauer appears in *Memoirs of Hope*, 173-179. His biographer Jean Lacouture calls this account "convincing" and the conversations themselves de Gaulle's "first great diplomatic success." Lacouture, *De Gaulle: The Ruler*, 215-216. See also chapter 6.

60. Hervé Alphand, *L'étonnement d'être. Journal, 1933-1973* (Paris: Fayard, 1977), 290.

61. Vaïsse, " Aux origines du mémorandum de septembre 1958," 257, 263-264, 267; Newhouse, *De Gaulle and the Anglo-Saxons*, 53-54.

62. Eisenhower et al., memorandum of conversation, 9 June 1958, DEOF, IS, RSC. During these meetings the Anglo-American agreement on nuclear weapons was discussed, with Admiral Strauss remarking that the Joint Committee report was "almost embarrassing in that it favored the UK so much in contrast to other countries."

63. Eisenhower and Dulles, memorandum of conversation, 4 June 1958, FRUS 1958-1960, vol. 7, part 2: Western Europe, 27, n. 4.

64. Dulles and Alphand, memorandum of conversation, 27 June 1958, FRUS 1958-1960, vol. 7, part 2: Western Europe, 42-45.

65. Houghton to Department of State, telegram, 30 June 1958, FRUS 1958-1960, vol. 7, part 2: Western Europe, 48-49.

66. Eisenhower et al., memorandum of conference, 3 July 1958, FRUS 1958-1960, vol. 7, part 2: Western Europe, 50-52. Parts of the document remain classified.

67. Elbrick to Dulles, memorandum, *Scope of your Meeting with de Gaulle*, 26 June 1958, FRUS 1958-1960, vol. 7, part 2: Western Europe, 40-42.

68. Text of the agreement in *Department of State Bulletin*, 28 July 1958, 157-164.

69. Newhouse, *De Gaulle and the Anglo-Saxons*, 57-58.

70. As quoted in Lacouture, *De Gaulle: The Ruler*, 213.

71. At this point, Dulles reaffirmed his earlier pledge from December 1957 to assist France in the development of atomic propulsion for French submarines. He then argued that Western policies should continue to aim at tying Germany closely to the West, not only to keep it out of the hands of the Soviets but also to contain German nationalism. De Gaulle responded at a later stage in the discussion that he shared the aim of integrating Germany into the West and foresaw no problems as long as the Germans had "no ambitions."

72. De Gaulle et al., memorandum of conversation, 5 July 1958, FRUS 1958-1960, vol. 7, part 2: Western Europe 53-64.

73. Dulles to Eisenhower, telegram, 5 July 1958, DEOF, IS, RSC. Also De Gaulle, *Memoirs of Hope*, 207-209.

74. Dulles to Eisenhower, telegram, 5 July 1958, DEOF, IS, RSC.

75. As quoted in Lacouture, *De Gaulle: The Ruler*, 214.

76. Alphand said that he had then warned de Gaulle that "the basic objective could be attained without formalization." Alphand and Elbrick, memorandum of conversation, 9 July 1958, FRUS 1958-1960, vol. 7, part 2: Western Europe, no. 39, 71-76.

77. As quoted in Lacouture, *De Gaulle: The Ruler*, 213.

78. Alphand and Elbrick, memorandum of conversation, 9 July 1958, FRUS 1958-1960, vol. 7, part 2: Western Europe, no. 39, 71-76.

79. Herter to McCone, letter, 16 September 1958, Chronological File, September 1958 (2), Christian A. Herter Papers (henceforth abbreviated as CAH Papers), box 5, DDEL.

80. Chamoun's position was threatened by what Eisenhower argued was communist-inspired unrest, but the real aim of the action was to prove to the Egyptian leader Nasser with a show of traditional gunboat diplomacy that he could not count on the Soviet Union. Nasser had been spreading propaganda for Arab unity and was getting increasingly close with Moscow; in January, Egypt had united with Syria in a new nation, the United Arab Republic (UAR); coups and semi-coups in Iraq, Saudi Arabia, and Jordan had brought pro-Nasser forces into power. Eisenhower, fearing that the Soviets by supporting Nasser and his Arab nationalism would gain control over the Middle East, publicly likened the situation in Lebanon with Greece in 1947, Czechoslovakia in 1948, China in 1949, and Korea in 1950. Indeed, if the bluster from Moscow was intense, the Soviet Union was unable to take any countermeasures on the ground. Ambrose, *Eisenhower*, 462-474.

81. Harrison, *The Reluctant Ally*, 87.

82. Vaïsse, "Aux origines du mémorandum de septembre 1958," 259.

83. Ambrose, *Eisenhower*, 482-485.

84. Harold Macmillan, *Riding the Storm 1956-1959* (London: Macmillan, 1971), 538-556.

85. *Espoir*, March 1979.

86. Dulles to Eisenhower, memorandum, 25 September 1958, Chronological Series, September 1958 (1), JFD Papers, box 16, DDEL.

87. Alphand, L'étonnement d'être, 292.

88. According to Harrison, neither the Quai d'Orsay nor the Council of Ministers were informed of the contents of the memorandum before it was delivered. See Harrison, *The Reluctant Ally*, 88. Bozo, however, provides evidence that Couve de Murville was involved in drafting the memorandum. See Bozo, *Two Strategies for Europe*, 15. The dating of de Gaulle's memorandum has been subject to confusion. De Gaulle curiously dates the memorandum 14 September in his *Memoirs of Hope*, 202. Others, such as Costigliola, have inaccurately dated it 25 September (see *France and the United States*, 123-127).

89. De Gaulle to Eisenhower, letter and memorandum,17 September 1958, White House Memorandum Series, General Correspondence 1958 (2), box 6, JFD Papers, DDEL. The text was publicly released by the Dwight D. Eisenhower Library in Abilene, Kansas, in 1976.

90. For an overview of tripartite designs during the Fourth Republic, see Harrison, *The Reluctant Ally*, 16-20. Also Hitchcock, *France Restored*, 122; Vaïsse, "Aux origines du mémorandum de septembre 1958," 253-268.

91. The French had been allowed to partake in the Standing Group in part because the United States did not want to legitimize an Anglo-American directorate. Lawrence S. Kaplan, *NATO and the United States* (Boston: Twayne Publishers, 1988), 38-39; Vaïsse, "Aux origines du mémorandum de septembre 1958," 264-265.

92. Although some French requests were conceded, the Standing Group was consistently outflanked by the SACEUR and debilitated by internal feuds. Harrison, *The Reluctant Ally*, 19; Vaïsse, "Aux origines du mémorandum de septembre 1958." For the perception of the French representative General Valluy on the inadequate workings of the Standing Group, see Grosser, *The Western Alliance*, 156-157.

93. In a speech in Lyon on 16 April 1950. FRUS 1950, 3: 54-58.

94. Dean Acheson, *Present At the Creation: My Years at the State Department* (New York: W.W. Norton & Co., 1969), 552. Acheson: "My difficulty was in getting from Pleven what he wanted the new body to do. What specifically did he want to coordinate? [...] The impression left with me was that the appearance of France on a worldwide tripartite body, rather than the functioning of the body, was what interested our guests."

95. Demands for a geographical extension of the Western alliance notably strengthened after the striking absence of collaboration during the Suez Crisis in 1956. The debacle also reinforced a French distaste for military integration, as the Anglo-French expeditionary force had then been under British command. Vaïsse, "Aux origines du mémorandum de septembre 1958," 257-261.

96. Pierre Mendès-France to Joseph Laniel, letter, 21 May 1954, Strictly Confidential, General Correspondence and Memorandum Series, JFD Papers, box 3, DDEL.

97. Cerny, *The Politics of Grandeur*, 165-166.

98. Alphand, Hood, and Murphy, memorandum of conversation, 4 December 1958, FRUS 1958-1960, vol. 7, part 2, 128-137. Eisenhower, who had dealt on a daily basis with the French leader as allied commander, similarly recognized this influence of de Gaulle's

wartime experience. Memorandum of discussion at the 390th meeting of the NSC, 11 December 1958, FRUS 1958-1960, vol. 4, part 1, 366-369.

99. Robert S. Jordan, *Political Leadership in NATO: A Study in Multinational Diplomacy* (Boulder, CO: Westview Press, 1979), 80.

100. Department of State to Embassy in UK, telegram, 8 October 1958, FRUS 1958-1960, vol. 7, part 2, 90-91; Joint Chiefs of Staff (henceforth abbreviated as JCS) 2278/5, 17 October 1958, in *Declassified Documents*, 1981, 301.

101. Dulles and Spaak, memorandum of conversation, 27 September 1958, FRUS 1958-1960, vol. 7, part 1: Western Europe, 359-360. On Spaak's reaction to de Gaulle's memorandum, see Jordan, *Political Leadership in NATO*, 76-81.

102. Eisenhower and Ambassador Manlio Brosio, memorandum of conversation, 6 October 1958, FRUS 1958-1960, vol. 7, part 2, 88-89.

103. Italian Prime Minister Fanfani, for instance, told Dulles that acceptance would have the "effect of an atom bomb on NATO." Embassy in Italy to Department of State, telegram, 18 October 1958, FRUS 1958-1960, vol. 7, part 2, 105-107.

104. David Bruce to Department of State, telegram, 9 October 1958, FRUS 1958-1960, vol. 7, part 1: Western Europe, 362-363.

105. Macmillan, *Riding the Storm*, 452-455.

106. Department of State to Embassy in UK, telegram, 8 October 1958, FRUS 1958-1960, vol. 7, part 2, 90-91.

107. Macmillan, *Riding the Storm*, 452-455; Dulles and Sir Harold Caccia, memorandum of conversation, 17 October 1958, FRUS 1958-1960, vol. 7, part 2, 101-103.

108. Before Houghton departed on leave for the US, on October 9, he bid good-bye to de Gaulle and the latter impressed upon him the seriousness he attached to the proposal. De Gaulle reiterated that discussions be initiated in Washington through Embassies and Standing Group. Houghton to Department of State, telegram, 9 October 1958, FRUS 1958-1960, vol. 7, part 2, 94. On October 25, Ambassador Alphand made clear that de Gaulle had no interest in withdrawing his proposal and that he hoped talks could begin soon. Dulles and Alphand, memorandum of conversation, 25 October 1958, FRUS 1958-1960, vol. 7, part 2, 109-110.

109. Eisenhower and Brosio, memorandum of conversation, 6 October 1958, FRUS 1958-1960, vol. 7, part 2, 88-89.

110. Department of State to Embassy in UK, telegram, 8 October 1958, FRUS 1958-1960, vol.7, part 2, 90-91.

111. Couve de Murville had stressed to Foreign Secretary Selwyn Lloyd that there was in the French view no connection between the Free Trade Area negotiations and de Gaulle's memorandum. Caccia to Dulles, letter, 7 November 1958, FRUS 1958-1960, vol. 7, part 2, 115-117. Dulles and Caccia, memorandum of conversation, 27 October 1958, FRUS 1958-1960, vol. 7, part 2, 111-112.

112. In a conversation with Dulles, for instance, Sir Harold Caccia, the ambassador in Washington, suggested the idea of a tripartite mobile force. However, Dulles immediately discarded it. Dulles and Caccia, memorandum of conversation, 9 October 1958, FRUS 1958-1960, vol. 7, part 2, 92-93.

113. Dulles oral history project, as cited in Richard Challener, "Dulles and De Gaulle," in Paxton and Wahl, *De Gaulle and the United States*, 159. Lucet had accompanied Alphand when he handed de Gaulle's memorandum to Dulles on 25 September 1958.

114. Dulles's testimony is printed in Senate Committee on Foreign Relations, *North Atlantic Treaty: Hearings before the Committee on Foreign Relations*, 81st Cong., 1st sess., 4 May 1949, 339-376.

115. Dulles and Eisenhower, memorandum of conversation, 1 May 1956, Eisenhower Papers, J.F. Dulles, White House Memos, box 4, DDEL.

116. Dulles's statement on 16 December 1957, printed in *Department of State Bulletin*, 6 January 1958, 10.

117. Richard Immerman, ed., *John Foster Dulles and the Diplomacy of the Cold War* (Princeton, NJ: Princeton University Press, 1990), 56-7.

118. Dulles and Caccia, memorandum of conversation, 9 October 1958, FRUS 1958-1960, vol. 7, part 2, 92-93.

119. Dulles to Spaak, letter, 10 October 1958, FRUS 1958-1960, vol. 7, part 1, 363-364.

120. Speech published in *Department of State Bulletin*, 20 October 1958, 607-611. Spaak spoke with Dulles on the same day. Dulles and Spaak, memorandum of conversation, 27 September 1958, FRUS 1958-1960, vol. 7, part 1: Western Europe, 359-360.

121. Paul-Henri Spaak, *The Continuing Battle: Memoirs of a European, 1936-1966* (Boston: Little, Brown, 1971), 182-185.

122. Jordan, *Political Leadership Within NATO*, 79.

123. Eisenhower and Brosio, memorandum of conversation, 6 October 1958, FRUS 1958-1960, vol. 7, part 2, 88-89.

124. Eisenhower to de Gaulle, letter, 2 October 1958, France, vol 1, IS, WHOSS, box 5, DDEL.

125. Deputy Assistant Secretary of State Jandrey to Dulles, memorandum, 9 October 1958, FRUS 1958-1960, vol. 7, part 2, 95-97.

126. Dulles and Eisenhower, memorandum of conversation, 13 October 1958, White House Memorandum Series, Meetings with President, JFD Papers, box 7, DDEL. (Emphasis in original.)

127. Dulles to Eisenhower, memorandum, 15 October 1958, France vol. 1, IS, WHOSS, box 5, DDEL. A typed notation at the end of the memorandum reads: "Foster, I agree we should not do this 3 power business unless we have to." See FRUS 1958-1960, vol. 7, part 2, editorial note, 100.

128. Dulles and Caccia, memorandum of conversation, 17 October 1958, FRUS 1958-1960, vol. 7, part 2, 101-103. Dulles's doubts were fanned by the resolute advice he received from former SACEUR Alfred Gruenther and John McCloy, then with the Chase Manhattan Bank, both of whom had voiced strong opposition to any discussions. Dulles and Elbrick, telephone conversation, 16 October 1958, Memoranda of Telcon – General, Telephone Calls, JFD Papers, box 9, DDEL.

129. De Gaulle, *Memoirs of Hope*, 203.

130. Eisenhower to de Gaulle, letter, 20 October 1958, France, vol. 1, IS, WHOSS, box 5, DDEL. In May 1964, the State Department deliberately leaked Eisenhower's letter of reply to James Reston of the *New York Times* in order to counter repeated statements that he had never replied at all. See Schoenbrun, *The Three Lives of De Gaulle*, 300. The

text was officially released in August 1966 through the offices of Senator Henry M. Jackson and Senator J. William Fulbright.

131. Robert Murphy appears frequently in de Gaulle's war memoirs as Roosevelt's personal representative in French North Africa. Based as consul general in Algiers, Murphy had proven himself far from sympathetic to de Gaulle's cause. Of this, the latter was very much aware. When Murphy told de Gaulle he was impressed with the large crowds that greeted de Gaulle upon his arrival in Algiers in July 1943, the Frenchman responded sarcastically that "those [...] are the ten per cent Gaullists that you reckoned on in Algiers." Murphy's final replacement by Edwin Wilson, de Gaulle noted, "produced an agreeable relaxation in our relations with the American embassy. For if the first incumbent scarcely appreciated the 'Gaullists'' success, the second, on the other hand, appeared to be greatly pleased by it. Mr. Wilson's visits were as agreeable and numerous as my interviews with Mr. Murphy had been infrequent and uncomfortable." De Gaulle, *War Memoirs*, 446, 540.

132. Robert Murphy, *Diplomat Among Warriors* (Garden City, NY: Doubleday, 1964), 182.

133. To make matters worse, French Ambassador Hervé Alphand was not well liked in Washington. See Harrison, *The Reluctant Ally*, 257, note 76.

134. On 25 October, for instance, Dulles explained to Alphand that his principal worry concerned not so much NATO reorganization as much as the concept of an extension of the NATO area to the Middle East, Africa, etc. Dulles and Alphand, memorandum of conversation, 25 October 1958, FRUS 1958-1960, vol. 7, part 2, 109-110.

135. Dulles and Alphand, memorandum of conversation, 28 October 1958, FRUS 1958-1960, vol. 7, part 2, 113-115; Herter, Joxe, and Alphand, memorandum of conversation, 20 November 1958, FRUS 1958-1960, vol. 7, part 2, 119-121.

136. Dulles and Murphy, telephone conversation, 8 November 1958, JFD Papers, box 9, DDEL. Supplementing a letter of October 20, Dulles wrote to Chancellor Adenauer: "We continue to be perplexed about the de Gaulle proposal. The French Ambassador has just left me and has presented the matter somewhat differently than heretofore. He now suggests that the French proposal really does not relate to NATO at all, but is designed to establish a relationship between the US, UK and France as regards world politics and military plans in non-NATO areas such as Africa, the Middle East and the Far East." Dulles to Adenauer, message, 31 October 1958, Chronological Series, JFD Papers, box 16, DDEL.

137. Dulles and de Gaulle, memorandum of conversation, 15 December 1958, FRUS 1958-1960, vol. 7, part 2, 146-153.

138. De Gaulle to Eisenhower, letter, 6 October 1959, FRUS 1958-1960, vol. 7, part 2, 287-288.

139. Tripartite talks among Alphand, Hood, Murphy, memorandum of conversation, 4 December 1958, FRUS 1958-1960, vol. 7, part 2, 128-137.

140. Tripartite talks among Alphand, Caccia, Murphy, memorandum of conversation, 10 December 1958, FRUS 1958-1960, vol. 7, part 2, 138-144.

141. Dulles and de Gaulle, memorandum of conversation, 15 December 1958, FRUS 1958-1960, vol. 7, part 2, 146-153.

142. Eisenhower to Dulles, telegram, 16 December 1958, FRUS 1958-1960, vol. 7, part 2, 155, n.5.

143. Memorandum of discussion at the 390th meeting of the NSC, 11 December 1958, FRUS 1958-1960, vol. 4, part 1, 366-369.

144. On 18 December, Dulles called Jean Monnet in Paris: "We are having some problems with M's chief here. It is a sort of sit-down strike on NATO at the moment." Dulles and Monnet, telephone conversation, 18 December 1958. Reporting his "most unsatisfactory meeting" with de Gaulle to Eisenhower, Dulles wrote: "I think we can make a greater effort at Washington to make them feel that they are in on important decisions and then see whether that in fact brings a dividend in terms of more cooperation with NATO." Dulles to Eisenhower, telegram, 15 December 1958, FRUS 1958-1960, vol. 7, part 2, 154-155.

145. Dulles and Alphand, memorandum of conversation, 7 January 1959, FRUS 1958-1960, vol. 7, part 2, 156-159.

146. Murphy and Alphand, memorandum of conversation, 9 January 1959, FRUS 1958-1960, vol. 7, part 2, 160-162. After receiving instructions from Paris, Alphand suggested that the United States designate a high military official from the JCS to such talks. Dulles, Murphy, and Alphand, memorandum of conversation, 22 January 1959, FRUS 1958-1960, vol. 7, part 2, 164-166.

147. Murphy and JCS, memorandum of conversation, 30 January 1959, FRUS 1958-1960, vol. 7, part 2, 168-169 (editorial note). The third trilateral meeting on February 3 discussed the Far Eastern situation merely in political terms, albeit in the presence of military representatives. Murphy, Alphand, Caccia, memorandum of conversation, 3 February 1959, FRUS 1958-1960, vol. 7, part 2, 169-180.

148. Dulles to Eisenhower, telegram, 6 February 1959, FRUS 1958-1960, vol. 7, part 2, 181-182. Dulles resigned on April 15 for health reasons and died on May 24, 1959.

149. Herter to Eisenhower, memorandum, 4 March 1959, NATO (1), International Trips and Meetings File (henceforth abbreviated as Int. T&M), WHOSS, DDEL.

150. Lyon to Department of State, telegram, 6 March 1959, FRUS 1958-1960, vol. 7, part 2, 184-186.

151. Burgess to Department of State, telegram, 9 March 1959, FRUS 1958-1960, vol. 7, part 1, 424-425.

152. Herter and Debré, memorandum of conversation, 1 May 1959, FRUS 1958-1960, vol. 7, part 2, 195-203. Responding to Debré's request for nuclear assistance, Herter had been relatively forthcoming by explaining that "once the French had effected their first atomic explosion, we would be in a different position, and could talk substance to them" and that "legislative restrictions [...] would be alleviated by this action." On April 28, in a "very tough" letter, Debré protested in strong terms that an FLN delegation has been admitted to the United States. He argued that France was fighting communism in Algeria in the interest of the Free World and was entitled to the support of its western allies. From this letter Herter derived that Debré believed Algeria was as important to the security of France as the solution to the Berlin Crisis. Debré to Houghton, letter, 28 April 1959, FRUS, vol. 13, 652-654.

153. De Gaulle to Eisenhower, letter, 25 May 1959, France – vol 1, IS, WHOSS, box 5, DDEL.

154. Department of State to Embassy in Paris, telegram, 6 March 1959, FRUS 1958-1960, vol. 7, part 2, 186-187.

155. Memorandum of conference with the president, 12 March 1959. Also Herter, memorandum of conference with the president, 2 May 1959, FRUS 1958-1960, vol. 7, part 2, 203-207; Herter to Ambassador Amory Houghton, letter, 2 May 1959, Chronological File, CAH Papers, box 7, DDEL.

156. Eisenhower and Norstad, memorandum of conference, 9 June 1959, NATO (2), Int. T&M, WHOSS, DDEL.

157. Memorandum of conference with the president, 12 March 1959, NATO (1), Int. T&M, WHOSS, DDEL.

158. Macmillan et al., memorandum of conference with the president, 27 March 1959, Macmillan Talks, Int. T&M, WHOSS, DDEL; Herter, memorandum of conference with the president, 2 May 1959, FRUS 1958-1960, vol. 7, part 2, 203-207; Eisenhower and Norstad, memorandum of conference, 9 June 1959 NATO (2), Int. T&M, WHOSS, DDEL.

159. Herter, memorandum of conference with the president, 2 May 1959, FRUS 1958-1960, vol. 7, part 2, 203-207.

160. Joint Chiefs of Staff, *Proposal on US policy toward France*, July 1959; memorandum of discussion NSC, "US Policy on France," 18 August 1959, FRUS 1958-1960, vol. 7, part 2, 243-253.

161. Eisenhower and Norstad, memorandum of conference, 9 June 1959, NATO (2), Int. T&M, WHOSS, DDEL.

162. Herter, memorandum of conference with the president, 2 May 1959, FRUS 1958-1960, vol. 7, part 2, 203-207. On 7 May 1958, France and the United States did, however, sign an agreement on "French-United States cooperation in the uses of atomic energy" which provided for the sale to France of a specified quantity of enriched uranium for the use in the development and operation of a land-based prototype submarine nuclear propulsion plant during a 10-year period. The signing of this agreement had been delayed because of the adverse congressional reaction to the French withdrawal of the Mediterranean Fleet in March 1959. Vaïsse, ed., *La France et l'atome. Études d'histoire nucléaire* (Bruxelles: Bruylant, 1994), 414-415.

163. Joint Chiefs of Staff, *Proposal on US policy toward France*, July 1959; memorandum of discussion NSC, "US Policy on France," 18 August 1959, FRUS 1958-1960, vol. 7, part 2, 243-253. Also Schoenbrun, *The Three Lives of Charles de Gaulle*, 335.

164. Eisenhower to de Gaulle, letter, 14 March 1959, France – vol. 1, IS, WHOSS, box 5, DDEL; Eisenhower to de Gaulle, letter, 19 March 1959, France – vol. 1, IS, WHOSS, box 5, DDEL; Eisenhower to de Gaulle, letter, 24 March 1959, Macmillan Talks, Int. T&M, WHOSS, box 6, DDEL; Eisenhower to de Gaulle, letter, 5 June 1959, France – vol. 1, IS, WHOSS, box 5, DDEL.

165. Second stage of tripartite talks, 16 - 21 April 1959, FRUS 1958-1960, vol. 7, part 2, 193-194, editorial note.

166. Dillon to American Embassy in Paris, telegram, 18 July 1959, France – vol. 1, IS, WHOSS, box 5, DDEL. Heavily sanitized document.

167. Eisenhower and de Gaulle, memorandum of conversation, 2 September 1959, 12pm, FRUS 1958-1960, vol. 7, part 2, 255-262; Eisenhower and de Gaulle, memorandum of conversation, 2 September 1959, 4pm. Also Lacouture, *De Gaulle: The Rebel*, 367-369; De

Gaulle, *Memoirs of Hope*, 210-215; Vernon A. Walters, *Silent Missions* (New York: Doubleday, 1978).

168. Eisenhower and Adenauer, memorandum of conversation, 27 August 1959, DDE Trip to Europe, Chronology (Bonn) (2), box 7, Int. T&M, WHOSS, DDEL; Eisenhower and Macmillan, memorandum of conversation, 29 August 1959, DDE Trip to Europe, Chronology (Bonn) (2), box 7, Int. T&M, WHOSS, DDEL; Herter et al., memorandum of conference with the president, 24 August 1959, State Department 1959, State Department Subseries, Subject Series, WHOSS, box 3, DDEL.

169. Eisenhower and de Gaulle, memorandum of conversation, 3 September 1959, FRUS 1958-1960, vol. 7, part 2, 271-272.

170. Eisenhower and de Gaulle, memorandum of conversation, 4 September 1959, FRUS 1958-1960, vol. 7, part 2, 273-274.

171. Lacouture, *De Gaulle: The Rebel*, 367-369.

172. Tripartite talks on military and economic assistance to Morocco and Tunisia were held at the Department of State on October 8 and 9, 1959. FRUS 1958-1960, vol. 7, part 2, 288-289, editorial note.

173. De Gaulle to Eisenhower, letter, 6 October 1959, FRUS 1958-1960, vol. 7, part 2, 287-288. On 20 December 1959, anticipating the explosion of the first French nuclear device a few months hence, de Gaulle similarly "intimated [to Secretary of State Herter] that he assumed following the explosion the United States would be in a position to cooperate with France." De Gaulle and Herter, memorandum of conversation, 20 December 1959, FRUS 1958-1960, vol. 7, part 2, 320-321. On 29 October, the National Security Council had to conclude – to Eisenhower's intense displeasure – that the explosion would not automatically qualify France for close atomic collaboration. Congress would not go along with a bilateral approach, upon which Eisenhower remarked that "the stupidity of Congress in this regard never ceased to amaze him." A study would be undertaken on whether it would be in the US interest to aid the French nuclear effort. The idea of a multilateral nuclear authority under NATO, in which France would be invited to participate, was also to be developed. Memorandum of discussion at NSC Meeting, 29 October 1959, FRUS 1958-1960, vol. 7, part 2, 290-295. The discussion reviewed American policy toward France and led to new guidelines. US Policy on France, report NSC 5910/1, 4 November 1959, NSC 5910/1 – US Policy Toward France, Foreign Policy Subseries, NSC Series, White House Office (henceforth abbreviated as WHO), Office of the Special Assistant for National Security Affairs (henceforth abbreviated as OSANA), box 27, DDEL.

174. De Gaulle to Eisenhower, letter, 6 October 1959, FRUS 1958-1960, vol. 7, part 2, 287-288. The exchange of letters between Eisenhower and de Gaulle in October 1959 was largely devoted to the possibility of a summit with Kruschev. Eisenhower urged the French president to concede to a summit meeting with the Soviet leader. De Gaulle was reluctant and expressed his reservations but on 26 October declared himself ready for a Western summit meeting in December to precede a summit with Kruschev in the spring of 1960. Eisenhower to de Gaulle, letter, 9 October 1959, DEOF, IS, RSC; Eisenhower to de Gaulle, letter, 16 October 1959, DEOF, IS, RSC; Eisenhower to de Gaulle, letter, 21 October 1959, Deptel 1703, DEOF, IS, RSC; De Gaulle to Eisenhower, letter,

26 October 1959; De Gaulle to Eisenhower, letter, 20 October 1959, FRUS 1958-1960, vol. 7, part 2, no. 63, 108-109.

175. De Gaulle and Herter, memorandum of conversation, 20 December 1959, FRUS 1958-1960, vol. 7, part 2, 320-321. In a memorandum to Eisenhower, Secretary of Defense Gates listed the evidence that the French government is "following a calculated policy of non-cooperation in defense matters." Gates to Eisenhower, memorandum, 17 December 1959, FRUS 1958-1960, vol. 7, part 2, 315-316.

176. France, Ambassade de France, *Major Addresses 1958-1964*, 61.

177. Eisenhower to de Gaulle, letter, 17 November 1959, France – vol. 1, IS, WHOSS, box 5, DDEL; De Gaulle to Eisenhower, letter, 24 November 1959, FRUS 1958-1960, vol. 7, part 2, 313-314.

178. Eisenhower to de Gaulle, letter, 21 September 1959, FRUS 1958-1960, vol. 7, part 2, 283-285.

179. In his reply to Eisenhower, de Gaulle played down the community-mindedness of the American troops in Europe by pointing out that they were under the command of an American general. De Gaulle to Eisenhower, letter, 6 October 1959, FRUS 1958-1960, vol. 7, part 2, 287-288.

180. Kohl, *French Nuclear Diplomacy*, 93-95; De Gaulle, *Memoirs of Hope*, 203-204. Oddly, de Gaulle misdated the speech on 16 September, when he delivered his address holding out self-determination to the Algerian people. The text of the speech appears in De Gaulle, *Avec le renouveau*, 126-127.

181. Macmillan's main concern, however, was clearly with the relations between the Common Market and the Outer Seven, and in the course of the conversations he even threatened a British withdrawal from NATO if an economic war developed between the two organizations. Eisenhower, de Gaulle, Macmillan, record of meeting, 20 December 1959, FRUS 1958-1960, vol. 7, part 2, 319. See also Schoenbrun, *The Three Lives of Charles de Gaulle*, 339.

182. Between January and March 1960, the foreign ministers corresponded about the establishment of tripartite talks. For a summary of the correspondence, which clearly evidenced the divergent outlooks, see FRUS 1958-1960, vol. 7, part 2, 326-327, editorial note.

183. Macmillan to Eisenhower, letter, 17 February 1960, FRUS 1958-1960, vol. 7, part 2, 328; Eisenhower to Macmillan, letter, 18 February 1960, FRUS 1958-1960, vol. 7, part 2, 328.

184. Eisenhower's press conference of 3 February 1960, in Kohl, *French Nuclear Diplomacy*, 107; Herter, Couve de Murville, Alphand, memorandum of conversation, 15 April 1960, FRUS 1958-1960, vol. 7, part 2, 336-339.

185. The main subject of the Eisenhower-de Gaulle conversations was the upcoming summit with Khrushchev. Herter, Dillon, Houghton, memorandum of conference with the president, 22 April 1960 (dated 27 April 1960); Eisenhower and de Gaulle, memorandum of conversation, 22 April 1960; Eisenhower and de Gaulle, memorandum of conversation, 24 April 1960, FRUS 1958-1960, vol. 7, part 2, 347-352; Eisenhower and de Gaulle, memorandum of conversation, 25 April 1960, IS, DEOF, RSC. Also De Gaulle, *Memoirs of Hope*, 242-247.

186. Herter, Bohlen, Houghton, memorandum of conference with the president, 16 May 1960, DEOF, IS, RSC.

187. On leaving Paris, Eisenhower sent a note of admiration for de Gaulle: "You and I have shared great experiences in war and in peace, and from those experiences has come, for my part at least, a respect and admiration for you that I have for few men." Eisenhower to de Gaulle, letter, 18 May 1960, DEOF, IS, RSC.

188. Eisenhower, Macmillan, de Gaulle, memorandum of conversation, 18 May 1960, FRUS, 1958-1960, vol. 9: Berlin Crisis, etc., 494-497; Eisenhower and de Gaulle, memorandum of conversation, 18 May 1960, DEOF, IS, RSC.

189. Ibid. Also Harold Macmillan, *Pointing the Way: 1959-1961* (London: Macmillan, 1980), 178-216, 236-284.

190. Eisenhower to Macmillan, letter, 4 June 1960, FRUS 1958-1960, vol. 7, part 2, 382-384.

191. De Gaulle to Eisenhower, letter, 10 June 1960, France, vol. 3, IS, WHOSS, box 5, DDEL. This letter was transmitted to Eisenhower in Manila on June 15. Dillon to Calhoun, telegram, 15 June 1960, France, vol. 3, IS, WHOSS, box 5, DDEL.

192. Macmillan to Eisenhower, letter, 25 May 1960, FRUS 1958-1960, vol. 7, part 2, 370-371.

193. State Department reports show that the depth and breadth of their opposition to tripartism was indeed growing. Dept of State (Dillon) to Embassy in France, telegram, 17 June 1960, FRUS 1958-1960, vol. 7, part 2, 386-388.

194. Kohler, Hood (Br. Embassy), memorandum of conversation, 20 June 1960, FRUS 1958-1960, vol. 7, part 2, 388-389; Embassy in France to Dept of State, telegram, 24 June 1960, FRUS 1958-1960, vol. 7, part 2, 392-394.

195. This was the thrust of Eisenhower's reply to de Gaulle's of June 10, 1960. Eisenhower to de Gaulle, letter, 18 June 1960, France, vol. 3, IS, WHOSS, box 5, DDEL.

196. Eisenhower and Herter, telephone conversation, 1 July 1960, FRUS 1958-1960, vol. 7, part 2, 395-396.

197. Eisenhower to Macmillan, letter, 30 June 1960, FRUS 1958-1960, vol. 7, part 2, 395-396. Macmillan, *Pointing the Way*, 245-247.

198. Eisenhower to de Gaulle, letter, 2 August 1960, France, vol. 3, IS, WHOSS, box 5, DDEL. Partly sanitized.

199. De Gaulle to Eisenhower, letter, 9 August 1960, FRUS 1958-1960, vol. 7, part 2, 401-402.

200. Macmillan recalled in his memoirs that de Gaulle "begged me (in almost passionate terms) to use all my influence with President Eisenhower to accept" a meeting in Bermuda. *Pointing the Way*, 247. In a letter to Eisenhower, the British prime minister expressed himself generally in favor of their tripartite meetings, particularly because "there are so many things in your affairs and ours on which de Gaulle can be difficult, and these meetings can sometimes bring him along." But he was reluctant to meet on such short notice. Macmillan to Eisenhower, letter, 13 August 1960, FRUS 1958-1960, vol. 7, part 2, 406-407.

201. Eisenhower and Herter, telephone conversation, 10 August 1960, FRUS 1958-1960, vol. 7, part 2, 402-405.

202. Eisenhower, memorandum for the files, 10 August 1960, FRUS 1958-1960, vol. 7, part 2, 405-406.

203. Merchant and Macmillan, memorandum of conference, 17 August 1960, FRUS 1958-1960, vol. 7, part 2, 408-412. Macmillan described his meeting with Livingston Merchant in *Pointing the Way*, 248.

204. Eisenhower to de Gaulle, letter, 30 August 1960, France, vol. 3, IS, WHOSS, box 5, DDEL.

205. De Gaulle's press conference, 5 September 1960, in France, Ambassade de France, *Major Adresses 1958-1964*, 84-98.

206. The meeting of foreign ministers on 23 September, which originally had to prepare the meeting of the heads of state, only exposed more clearly the gap between the French and the Americans and the British. Couve de Murville revealed the French attitude towards tripartitism at this time by noting that "there [is] no hurry in this regard ... now that the cold war is with us again... ." Herter, Couve de Murville, Lord Home, memorandum of conversation, 23 September 1960, State Department 1960, State Department Subseries, Subject Series, WHOSS, box 4, DDEL.

207. Eisenhower did, however, express interest in the idea of letting a European, probably a Frenchman, be the SACEUR. He did not see any qualified individual in the French military. Eisenhower and Macmillan, memorandum of conversation, 27 September 1960, [heavily sanitized]; Macmillan, *Pointing the Way*, 275. A report evaluating Franco-American relations in the context of official American policy as formulated in NSC 5910/1 (4 November 1959) similarly noted that the tactic to respond to de Gaulle's demands as far as possible had failed in mollifying him. *Report on France*, NSC 5910/1, 9 November 1960, NSC 5910/1 – US Policy Toward France, Foreign Policy Subseries, NSC Series, WHO, OSANA, box 27, DDEL.

208. Norstad, memorandum of conference with the president, 8 August 1960, NATO (3), Int. T&M, WHOSS, DDEL. The question of nuclear sharing figured prominently at several meetings. Eisenhower et al., memorandum of conversation, 3 October 1960, NATO (6), Int. T&M, WHOSS, DDEL; Eisenhower and Spaak, memorandum of conversation, 4 October 1960, NATO (6), Int. T&M, WHOSS, DDEL; FRUS 1958-1960, vol. 7, part 2, 412, editorial note. In a conversation with SACEUR General Norstad and Secretary General Spaak, Chancellor Adenauer's reaction to the idea was favorable: he very seriously declared that "Europe must have something" in the atomic field. Houghton to Secretary of State, telegram, 10 September 1960, NATO (3), Int. T&M, WHOSS, DDEL. On 6 December, Eisenhower told President-elect Kennedy that he believed the US should work more closely with the allies in the nuclear field and that "frankly, I see no need for the continuance of the Joint Committee on Atomic Energy." Robert H. Ferrell, ed., *The Eisenhower Diaries* (New York: W.W. Norton, 1981), 381-382.

209. Lyon to Rusk, Embtel 3323 (Paris), 17 February 1961, France-General, CS, NSF, box 70, JFKL.

210. Rusk and Alphand, memorandum of conversation, 28 February 1961, FRUS 1961-1963, vol. 13, 645-648. In addition, Alphand discussed tripartite cooperation in his first meeting with Kennedy after the presidential elections, clearly hoping to arouse an interest on the part of the new administration. See *Oral history interview with Hervé Alphand*, JFKL, 3.

211. Kennedy et al., memorandum of conversation, 10 March 1961, FRUS 1961-1963, vol. 13, 648-653. To illustrate his point that the West was bound to lose the Cold War without more effective policy coordination, Chaban-Delmas recalled that Khrushchev had once told him "in cold anger" that the Soviet Union "could always win against the West because there was no coordination between the policies of the Western nations and

he could play them one against the other." After Chaban-Delmas had reported to de Gaulle on his conversation with Kennedy, he repeated the gist of his message in Washington to the American embassy in Paris. De Gaulle would prove a "most cooperative and easy ally" if Kennedy worked towards closer working arrangements, he said. If, however, de Gaulle felt that there continued to be an "informing" rather than a "consulting" relationship, "the situation of West vis-à-vis East will continue to deteriorate." Lyon to Rusk, telegram, 22 March 1961, France-General, CS, NSF, box 70, JFKL. Lacouture gives the erroneous impression that de Gaulle had used Chaban-Delmas as a go-between primarily to warn Kennedy not to get deeply involved in Vietnam. Lacouture, *De Gaulle: The Ruler*, 371.

212. Acheson to Kennedy and Rusk, Embtel 4522 (Paris), 22 April 1961, France-General, CS, NSF, box 70, JFKL.

213. Kohler to Rusk, memorandum, 24 January 1961, FRUS 1961-1963, , vol. 13, 641-644.

214. Rusk and Alphand, memorandum of conversation, 28 February 1961, FRUS 1961-1963, vol. 13, 645-648.

215. See Chapter Two.

216. A *New Approach to France*, memorandum, 3 May 1961, France-General, CS, NSF, box 70, JFKL. Likewise, McGeorge Bundy advised Kennedy on the eve of the visit: "you can and should repeat to de Gaulle the basic assurance of nuclear weapons which Eisenhower gave to the British and which you have confirmed to them. The understanding is 'that the United States would, of course, in the event of increased tension or the threat of war take every possible step to consult with Britain and our other allies.' This is understood to mean consultation in advance to the use of nuclear weapons." Bundy to President, memorandum, 29 May 1961, France-General, CS, NSF, box 70, JFKL.

217. Alistair Horne, *Harold Macmillan, volume II: 1957-1986* (New York: Viking Penguin, 1989), 282-7.

218. Macmillan, *Pointing the Way*, 325.

219. Public Record Office, Prime Minister's Private Office (henceforth abbreviated as PRO/PREM) 11/3325, Memorandum by the Prime Minister, December 1960. The Macmillan Cabinet Papers, 1957-1963, can be consulted online through the website of the British National Archives (http://www.nationalarchives.gov.uk/).

220. Note from Macmillan's unpublished diaries, dated 29 January 1961, as quoted in Horne, *Harold Macmillan*, vol. 2, 286.

221. As quoted in Simona Toschi, "Washington-London-Paris: An Untenable Triangle (1960-1963)," *Journal of European Integration History* no. 2, (1995): 88-89.

222. Toschi, "Untenable Triangle," 89-90.

223. Macmillan's letter to Kennedy of 28 April 1961.

224. On 4 May, McGeorge Bundy had informed Sir Harold Caccia that Kennedy would not permit assistance to the French nuclear program. In the correspondence that followed, Macmillan tried to change Kennedy's mind, but to no avail. See Toschi, "Untenable Triangle," 90-91.

225. On 2 February 1961, Kennedy wrote de Gaulle about his views on the Congo, to which de Gaulle responded on 6 February. Kennedy's brief response on 10 February makes clear that their views on how to resolve the crisis were widely different. Both letters

can be found in France-Subjects, De Gaulle Correspondence, CS, NSF, NSF, box 73, JFKL. De Gaulle's letter is also published in *Lettres, notes et carnets, Janvier 1961- Décembre 1963* (Paris: Librairie Plon, 1986), 36-39.

226. *Oral history interview with Robert Lovett, JFKL, 38.*

227. For Macmillan's intense displeasure, see Horne, *Macmillan* 2:296, 300.

228. Kennedy and de Gaulle, memorandum of conversation, 2 June 1961, in FRUS, vol. 13, no. 230, 665.

229. Kennedy and de Gaulle, memorandum of conversation, FRUS, vol. 24, 214-220. See also de Gaulle's own recollection in *Memoirs of Hope*, 255-6.

230. Kennedy and de Gaulle, memorandum of conversation, 2 June 1961, in FRUS, vol. 13, no. 230; De Gaulle, *Memoirs of Hope*, 255, 259. De Gaulle's warning on military involvement in South East Asia did leave an impression on Kennedy, for in a discussion nearly two months later with his principal advisers he explained his own qualms by referring to their discussion. Memorandum of discussion on South East Asia, 28 July 1961, Meetings with the President, General, Meetings and Memoranda, NSF, box 317, JFKL.

231. Kennedy and de Gaulle, memorandum of conversation, 2 June 1961, in FRUS, vol. 13, no. 230, 666. In addition, de Gaulle proposed that a "small standing group" be established to develop the tripartite nuclear plan.

232. Kennedy's talking points for his meetings with de Gaulle stressed the United States' willingness to engage in tripartite discussions in the political as well as the military realm: "we certainly are willing and intend to consult with France bilaterally on problems on [the] same basis as with [the] British." *President's Visit to De Gaulle: Talking Points*, paper, 27 May 1961, President Kennedy's Office File (henceforth abbreviated as PKOF), part 5: Countries File (henceforth abbreviated as CsF), RSC.

233. McGeorge Bundy et al., memorandum of conversation, 8 May 1961, France-General, CS, NSF, box 70, JFKL. In this meeting, Alphand laid out the case for tripartite coordination in considerable detail. His exposition, however, caused Bundy to observe in an accompanying note that "it was not at all easy to tell where Alphand was presenting his own views, and where he was accurately describing de Gaulle's."

234. McGeorge Bundy to President, memorandum, 30 May 1961, France-General, CS, NSF, box 70, JFKL.

235. Kennedy and de Gaulle, memorandum of conversation, 2 June 1961, in FRUS, vol. 13, no. 230, 666. Before the Paris meetings, McGeorge Bundy had made it clear to Kennedy that he could extend these assurances "in the event of increased tension or the threat of war" and "in advance to the use of nuclear weapons." Bundy to President, memorandum, 29 May 1961, France-General, CS, NSF, box 70, JFKL. After the visit to Paris, Kennedy confirmed these guarantees in a letter to de Gaulle. Kennedy to de Gaulle, letter, 30 June 1961, France-Subjects, De Gaulle Correspondence, CS, NSF, box 73, JFKL (parts sanitized).

236. The quote is from notes by Arthur Schlesinger Jr. of the meeting. Berlin notes by A.M. S., Papers of Arthur M. Schlesinger Jr., box W-3, JFKL. In preparation of the visit, Walt Rostow in particular had been advocating an accommodating stance toward de Gaulle, pressing for "high level tripartite discussions of a Western strategy in Africa and Asia" and the establishment of a "tripartite group of the highest quality and

authority." Walt W. Rostow to McGeorge Bundy, *De Gaulle, Africa, and Southeast Asia,* memorandum, 13 May 1961, France-General, CS, NSF, box 70, JFKL.

237. *Oral history interview with Hervé Alphand,* 4.

238. Kennedy and de Gaulle, memorandum of conversation, 2 June 1961, in FRUS, vol. 13, no. 11 and no. 230, 23, 666-7. Bundy summarized the agreement somewhat later as follows in a memorandum to Kennedy: "The Paris agreement was that [a] machinery of consultation was needed and that ways and means would be worked out by the three foreign ministers. The military aspect was also agreed to be important (though we avoided any commitment to discuss strategic planning in any detail – as de Gaulle well knows) but the ways and means of military consultation were also left to the foreign ministers." Bundy to President, memorandum, 28 July 1961, PKOF, part 3: Departments and Agencies File (henceforth abbreviated as DAF), RSC.

239. Kennedy and de Gaulle, memorandum of conversation, 1 June 1961, in FRUS, vol. 13, no. 107, 314.

240. Kennedy and de Gaulle, memorandum of conversation, 2 June 1961, in FRUS, vol. 13, no. 11, 24-5.

241. In fact, even Kennedy expressed his personal disappointment at the lack of progress in a letter to de Gaulle. Kennedy to de Gaulle, letter, 30 June 1961, France-Subjects, De Gaulle Correspondence, CS, NSF, box 73, JFKL (parts sanitized). On 28 July, he made clear to Dean Rusk in an official note that he wanted "real improvements in our communications with the French on both political and military questions." *National Security Action Memorandum 64,* 28 July 1961, Meetings and Memoranda, NSF, box 330, JFKL.

242. Gavin to president and Secretary of State, Embtel 1811 (Paris), 4 October 1961, France-General, CS, NSF, box 70, JFKL.

243. De Gaulle to Kennedy, letter, 11 January 1962, PKOF, part 5, CsF, RSC. Kennedy was very annoyed to find that the contents of this correspondence were leaked to Sulzberger. Sulzberger column in the *New York Times,* 18 January 1962.

244. *Oral history interview with William Tyler,* JFKL, 11.

245. *Oral history interview with Roger Hilsman,* JFKL, 9-10.

246. *Oral history interview with Dean Acheson,* JFKL, 24-9. For a more extensive rendition of Acheson's visit to de Gaulle, see Brinkley, *Dean Acheson,* 164-8. After de Gaulle, Acheson travelled to Bonn to talk to Chancellor Adenauer.

247. Charles Bohlen to Dean Rusk, letter, 26 October 1962, France-General, CS, NSF, box 71a, JFKL.

248. Gavin to Rusk, Embtel 1200 (Paris), 2 September 1961, France-General, CS, NSF, box 70, JFKL.

249. Raymond L. Garthoff, *Reflections on the Cuban Missile Crisis* (Washington D.C.: Brookings Institution, 1989) rev. ed., 6-42; Thomas G. Paterson, "Fixation with Cuba: The Bay of Pigs, Missile Crisis, and Covert War Against Castro," in *Kennedy's Quest for Victory: American Foreign Policy, 1961-1963,* ed. Thomas G. Paterson (New York: Oxford University Press, 1989), 123-155.

250. When the withdrawal of these missiles occurred a few months later, this was widely interpreted in Europe as the result of a secret agreement between the White House and the Kremlin and taken as evidence that the new strategic doctrine of the United States was weakening the deterrent. This interpretation of the missile removal was, for

instance, reflected in a letter from Raymond Aron to McGeorge Bundy on 9 May 1963. France-General, CS, NSF, box 72, JFKL.

251. Anschuetz to Department of State, Airgram A-1170 (Paris), 15 November 1962, France-General, CS, NSF, box 71a, JFKL.

252. *Steering Group on Implementing the Nassau Decisions – Post Nassau Strategy*, 2 January 1963, NATO-weapons, Subgroup V, Post-Nassau Strategy, 1/63, Regional Security, NSF, box 230, JFKL.

253. Kennedy to Adenauer, letter, 12 January 1963, PKOF, part 5: Countries File (henceforth abbreviated as CsF), RSC.

254. Lyon to Rusk, Embtel 2595 (Paris), 24 December 1962, France-General, CS, NSF, box 71a, JFKL.

255. Sulzberger, *Last of the Giants*, 1040-1041.

256. Frédéric Bozo and Pierre Mélandri, "La France devant l'opinion américaine: le retour de de Gaulle début 1958 - printemps 1959," *Relations internationales* 58 (Summer 1989): 195-215.

257. *San Francisco Chronicle*, 29 April, 1960; as quoted in Gordon Wright, "Charles de Gaulle parmi les Américains," *De Gaulle et son siècle*. Acting Secretary C. Douglas Dillon, memorandum to the President *Report on President de Gaulle's trip*, 2 May 1960, France, vol. 3, IS, WHOSS, box 5, DDEL.

258. De Gaulle, *Memoirs of Hope*, 202.

259. In this regard, it should be noted that French communications were not entirely consistent. As we have seen, Ambassador Alphand – and later Chaban-Delmas in his conversation with Kennedy – often played down the institutional dimension of de Gaulle's proposal.

260. For similar assessments of the implications of de Gaulle's proposal for the Western alliance, see Harrison, *The Reluctant Ally*, 98-101, and Kolodziej, *French International Policy under De Gaulle and Pompidou*, 82-6.

261. Rusk to Kennedy and Ball, Secto 48 (Rome), 23 June 1962, PKOF, part 3: DAF, RSC.

262. Schoenbrun, *The Three Lives of Charles de Gaulle*, 339.

263. Kolodziej, for instance, remarks that "part of Anglo-American coolness to the French directorate proposal was attributable to their opposition to, and growing embarrassment over, France's Algerian policy." *French International Policy under De Gaulle and Pompidou*, 75; see also Harrison, *The Reluctant Ally*, 94.

264. From a secret note by Spaak dated 15 October 1958, as quoted in Sherwood, *Allies in Crisis*, 105.

265. Memorandum of discussion at the 390th meeting of the NSC, 11 December 1958, FRUS 1958-1960, vol. 4, part 1, 366-369.

266. Dulles' commitment to NATO was equally strong. A participant in the Paris Peace Conference of 1919 and competent most of all in European affairs, Dulles supported the alliance and its organization from a more Wilsonian and Atlanticist inspiration than Eisenhower. He was convinced that only integrated and supranational structures provided real solutions to Europe's problems. Dulles was notably concerned with the historical Franco-German relationship, which he described as the "suicidal strife," an "old cycle" of war and revenge, a "firetrap" that engulfed too many and that had to be replaced by the weaving of "a European fabric of mutual understanding and common

endeavour." Predictably, then, de Gaulle's design for a privileged French position in the Western alliance was also disagreeable to Dulles.

267. Eisenhower to Churchill, letter, 22 July 1954, DEOF, IS, RSC.

268. Eisenhower to Gruenther, letter, 26 April 1954, DEOF, EAS, RSC.

269. Eisenhower to Dulles, telegram, 16 December 1958, FRUS 1958-1960, vol. 7, part 2, 155, n.5.

270. Schoenbrun, The Three Lives of Charles de Gaulle, 338-339.

271. As reported by Sulzberger in Last of the Giants, 707-708.

272. Memorandum of conference with the president, 12 March 1959 and 2 May 1959, FRUS 1958-1960, vol. 7, part 2, 203-207.

273. US Policy on France, report NSC 5910/1, 4 November 1959, Foreign Policy Subseries, NSC Series, WHO, OSANA, box 27, DDEL.

274. Deputy Assistant Secretary of State Jandrey to Dulles, memorandum, 9 October 1958, FRUS 1958-1960, vol. 7, part 2, 95-97.

275. Schoenbrun, The Three Lives of Charles de Gaulle, 335.

276. Schoenbrun, The Three Lives of Charles de Gaulle, 339.

277. See for example Kohl, French Nuclear Diplomacy, 74-81; Newhouse, De Gaulle and the Anglo-Saxons, 61, 71-72; J.R. Tournoux, La Tragédie du Général (Paris: Plon, 1967). Their interpretation was supported by a reading of de Gaulle's Memoirs of Hope, which appeared shortly before his death in 1970. De Gaulle, Memoirs of Hope, 202-203.

278. Kohl, French Nuclear Diplomacy, 76-8.

279. Sherwood, Allies in Crisis, 104, 109.

280. Cerny, The Politics of Grandeur, 165.

281. Harrison, The Reluctant Ally, 100-101.

282. Schoenbrun, The Three Lives of Charles de Gaulle, 335-336; Robert Kleiman, The Atlantic Crisis: American Diplomacy Confronts a Resurgent Europe (New York: W.W. Norton & Co, 1964), 38-9, 44, 138-42. Alain Peyrefitte records that, after his press conference of January 14, 1963, de Gaulle said to him about his September 1958 memorandum: "Je cherchais [...] à trouver un moyen de sortir de l'OTAN et de reprendre ma liberté, que la IVe République avait aliénée. Alors, j'ai demandé la lune." Peyrefitte, C'était de Gaulle, vol. 1 (Paris: Fayard, 1994), 352.

Notes to Chapter Two – Whose Kind of Europe?

1. Eisenhower to Smith, letter, 3 September 1954, FRUS, 1952-1954, vol. 5, 1145.

2. The Rome Treaty called for the implementation in stages of a "common market" with common external tariffs for industrial and agricultural goods. It anticipated that the ECSC, the EEC, and EURATOM would ultimately be unified under a single administrative body and that an Assembly – later transformed into a European Parliament – and a Court of Justice would be developed in parallel. It furthermore charged a Brussels-based Commission of nine members, chosen by the national governments but pledged to independence, with the effective management of the EEC. The Rome Treaty became operational on 1 January 1958.

3. The EFTA treaty was signed on 4 January 1960 in Stockholm by Austria, Denmark, Norway, Portugal, Sweden, Switzerland, and the United Kingdom. Negotiations had

begun after the collapse in November 1958 of British-led efforts to create a European free trade zone which would dilute the Common Market. By 1966, EFTA had abolished tariffs and trade restrictions among its members. Today, only Iceland, Liechtenstein, Norway, and Switzerland are members of EFTA, which is headquartered in Geneva.

4. See Chapter Three.

5. Joseph Kraft, an American journalist close to the Kennedy administration, has earned credit for popularizing Kennedy's European policies with his book The Grand Design: From Common Market to Atlantic Partnership (New York: Harper & Brothers, 1962). The Belgian historian Pascaline Winand has probably rendered the most complete and detailed account of American policies toward European integration in the Eisenhower and Kennedy years in Eisenhower, Kennedy, and the United States of Europe (London: Macmillan, 1993). Erin R. Mahan, a historian at the State Department, emphasizes the links between security, economics, and politics in the Kennedy-de Gaulle relationship, using American, French, German, and British primary sources; see Kennedy, De Gaulle, and Western Europe. Oliver Bange, a German professor, takes issue with the predominant "Anglo-American" perspective that holds de Gaulle "solely" responsible for the crisis of 1963 and suggests that British and American moves at the end of 1962 forced the crisis by attempting to isolate de Gaulle politically, see The EEC Crisis of 1963: Kennedy, Macmillan, De Gaulle and Adenauer in Conflict (London: Macmillan Press, 2000). Of the autobiographies written by Kennedy's people, George W. Ball's is of particular interest: The Past Has Another Pattern: Memoirs (New York: W.W. Norton & Co., 1982). Biographies on Ball also contain a wealth of material; see in particular James A. Bill, George Ball: Behind the Scenes in US Foreign Policy (New Haven, CT: Yale University Press, 1997). Douglas Brinkley and Richard T. Griffiths have edited a helpful volume of articles on Kennedy's European policies: John F. Kennedy and Europe (Baton Rouge, LA: Louisiana State University Press, 1999). The same can be said of the volume edited by Thomas Paterson, Kennedy's Quest for Victory, although its scope is wider and its gist decidedly revisionist. For American supporters of Monnet and his goal of European unity, see Clifford P. Hackett, ed., Monnet and the Americans: The Father of a United Europe and his US Supporters (Washington DC: Jean Monnet Council, 1995). Denise Artaud is critical of Jean Monnet for acting as the European go-between for the Americans in "Le Grand Dessein de J.F. Kennedy: Proposition Mystique ou Occasion Manquée?" Revue D'Histoire Moderne et Contemporaine 29 (1982): 235-66. Frank Costigliola takes a revisionist – and therefore highly critical – view of Kennedy's Grand Design in "The Failed Design: Kennedy, De Gaulle, and the Struggle for Europe," Diplomatic History 8 (Summer 1984): 227-251. Frédéric Bozo pays relatively little attention to Kennedy's conflict with de Gaulle over the Common Market, blaming the failure of the Fouchet Plan largely on the United States; Two Strategies for Europe, 77-84. Other works of interest include Lundestad, "Empire" by Integration and Grosser, The Western Alliance, chap. 7.

6. See Chapter Three.

7. The story of Macmillan's agonizing over Europe is well told by Hugo Young, This Blessed Plot: Britain and Europe from Churchill to Blair (London: Macmillan/Papermac, 1999), 99-145. Young is particularly critical of the half-hearted nature of Macmillan's approach to the Common Market, which in his view was the real reason for failure of the membership negotiations: "... the British were not prepared to do more than ne-

gotiate and hesitate. They were not actually applying." (137) See also Horne, *Macmillan*, vol. 2, 256-262, passim.

8. In a speech in Zurich on 19 September 1946. See Young, *This Blessed Plot*, 16-17.

9. Young, *This Blessed Plot*, 5.

10. Carlo M. Cipolla, ed., *The Fontana Economic History of Europe: Contemporary Economies*, Part I (Glasgow: Collins/Fontana Books, 1976), 156, 164.

11. Britain declined two opportunities of joining the ECSC in its formative stage. The first opportunity arose in 1950-51, when Jean Monnet invited the British government to join; the second in 1953-54, when negotiations on an association agreement between Great Britain and the ECSC might have led to full membership. See Geoffrey Owen, "Britain and the European Coal and Steel Community," paper presented at Terni Conference on the European Coal and Steel Community, 16-17 May 2002. The Franks quote is from Young, *This Blessed Plot*, 68.

12. See Horne, *Macmillan*, vol. 2, 30.

13. De Gaulle, *Memoirs of Hope*, 188. While Macmillan did not mention the outburst in his own memoirs, de Gaulle's account deserves the benefit of the doubt according to his biographer Jean Lacouture. See Macmillan, *Riding the Storm*, 446-449; Lacouture, *De Gaulle: The Ruler*, 213.

14. Macmillan's plan would encompass all member states of the OEEC and the Common Market in a free trade zone. In November 1958, however, talks in Paris were suspended indefinitely following an open rift between France and Britain. De Gaulle and Adenauer subsequently agreed to oppose the British proposal in favor of a looser association of the Common Market with Britain and other OEEC countries.

15. From a Foreign Office memorandum of January 1960, quoted in Toschi, "Untenable Triangle," 83.

16. Herter, Dillon, Houghton, memorandum of conference with the president, 22 April 1960, State Department, 1960 (March-May) (4), State Department Subseries, Subject Series, box 4, WHOSS, DDEL (dated 27 April 1960).

17. Macmillan, *Pointing the Way*, 316.

18. For de Gaulle's views of the Common Market, see Edmond Jouve, *Le Général de Gaulle et la construction de l'Europe, 1940-1966*, 2 vols. (Paris: Librairie générale de droit et de jurisprudence, 1967); Kolodziej, *French International Policy Under De Gaulle and Pompidou*, 235-390; Alfred Grosser, *French Foreign Policy Under De Gaulle*, chap. 6; Mahoney, *De Gaulle*, chap. 7; Cohen, "De Gaulle and Europe Prior to 1958." Winand, too, includes a good discussion of de Gaulle's policies toward the Common Market in *Eisenhower, Kennedy, and the United States of Europe*, chap. 9.

19. See Chapter Two.

20. As reported by Charles Bohlen. *Continuing Elements of De Gaulle's Foreign Policy*, draft paper, 7 August 1963, France-General, CS, NSF, box 72, JFKL.

21. The Rome Treaty had indeed been a compromise between the French and German economies. French negotiators had agreed to concentrate on industrial products and the opening of the French market to German industrial goods in return for the promise that Germany would later agree to a common agricultural policy and open its markets to French agricultural products. The agricultural component of the Common Market was of capital importance to France. Twenty-seven percent of its population

was still employed in the agricultural sector, producing a surplus despite a relatively low efficiency. The French farm economy, which produced at the cheapest prices in Europe, would gain the most from such a policy. Given de Gaulle's antipathy towards the Common Market, Robert Marjolin posed the tantalizing hypothetical question: "if General de Gaulle had come to power two years earlier, in 1956, when the Rome Treaty negotiations were only beginning, would they have led to the outcome we know or would they have taken a different course?" Marjolin tentative response: "assuming the best, [...] it is almost certain [...] that the treaty would have been different in a number of important respects. The principle of unanimity would have been asserted without any limitation of duration. The Commission's role would have been reduced; it probably would have become merely a secretariat of the Council of Ministers. It is unlikely that France would have been content with the few articles in the treaty that laid the foundations of a common agricultural policy [...]. Would the other five countries have agreed to France's demands on these different points? No one can tell." Marjolin, "What Type of Europe?" in Brinkley and Hackett, *Jean Monnet*, 164.
22. De Gaulle, *Memoirs of Hope*, 169, 181-184, passim. Paris nevertheless sent top-flight officials and administrators to man and to dominate the EEC headquarters in Brussels. The staff of the Commission was French in organization, outlook, and management technique. It represented the French bureaucratic tradition which looked upon the state as the centralizing agent of modernization and progress.
23. De Gaulle, *Memoirs of Hope*, 135.
24. Kolodziej, *French International Policy Under De Gaulle and Pompidou*, 273-274.
25. Marjolin, for instance, stressed that "I personally was to find constant support in Paris for the completion of Europe's construction as defined in the Treaty of Rome." Marjolin, "What Type of Europe?" 164. In December 1958 and again in late 1959, de Gaulle's government ordered the accelerated implementation of the treaty's provisions. Paris also insisted that the Common Market had to be more than a customs union for industrial goods and had to include a common agricultural policy (CAP) and a gradual coordination of internal economic policies as well as trade policies. De Gaulle demanded progress on the CAP in return for each cut in external tariffs or internal industrial tariffs. To be sure, the French government displayed considerably less enthusiasm for EURATOM because it had no desire to share French advances in the area of atomic research with its partners on the basis of a supranational ideal.
26. See for example Kolodziej, *French International Policy Under De Gaulle and Pompidou*, 241. The term "systematic *rapprochement*" is used by de Gaulle in *Memoirs of Hope*, 171.
27. De Gaulle, *War Memoirs*, 873.
28. France, Ambassade de France, *Major Addresses 1958-1964*, 78-79.
29. Sulzberger, *Last of the Giants*, 45.
30. Jacques Bariéty, "Die Rolle der persönlichen Beziehungen zwischen Bundeskanzler Adenauer und General de Gaulle für die Deutsch-Französische Politik zwischen 1858 und 1963," in Hans-Peter Schwarz, ed., *Adenauer und Frankreich. Die deutsch-französischen Beziehungen 1958 bis 1969* (Bonn: Bouvier Verlag, 1985), 12-27. For other good discussions of de Gaulle's relationship with Adenauer, see Lacouture, *De Gaulle: The Ruler*, 334-344; Maillard, *De Gaulle und Deutschland. Der unvollendete Traum*, translated from the French by Hermann Kusterer (Bonn/Berlin: Bouvier Verlag, 1991), 181-285; Maurice

Vaïsse, "La reconciliation franco-allemande: le dialogue de Gaulle-Adenauer," *Politique Étrangère* (Winter 1993-4): 963-972; Willis, *France, Germany, and the New Europe*, 273-311.

31. On this meeting and its importance, see De Gaulle, *Memoirs of Hope*, 173-179; Adenauer, *Memoirs, 1955-1959*, vol. 3 (Stuttgart: Deutscher Verlags-Anstalt, 1967), 427-9; Lacouture, *De Gaulle: The Ruler*, 215-216; Maillard, *De Gaulle und Deutschland*, 181-211; Kolodziej, *French International Policy Under De Gaulle and Pompidou*, 260-264; Schoenbrun, *Three Lives of De Gaulle*, 297-298.

32. Max Schulze-Vorberg cited in Schwarz, *Adenauer und Frankreich*, 37.

33. Jacques Bariéty, "Die Rolle der persönlichen Beziehungen zwischen Bundeskanzler Adenauer und General de Gaulle," 17.

34. De Gaulle, *Memoirs of Hope*, 176. De Gaulle noted with satisfaction that "the Chancellor's pragmatism reconciled him to my position." Regarding the prospect of German unification, de Gaulle moreover "sensed in this Catholic Rhinelander [...] a feeling that, in the event, the present Federal Republic might experience some uneasiness in incorporating outright the Prussian, Protestant and socialist complex of the eastern territories." (177)

35. De Gaulle, *Memoirs of Hope*, 178. In this context, de Gaulle curiously speaks of "Britain's application for membership" of the Common Market, which would in fact not be in order until the summer of 1960.

36. De Gaulle, *Memoirs of Hope*, 177-178.

37. De Gaulle calculated that after their first meeting in Colombey-les-Deux-Églises until mid-1962, "Konrad Adenauer and I were to write to each other on some forty occasions. We saw each other fifteen times [...]. We spent more than a hundred hours in conversation, either in private, or with our ministers in attendance, or in the company of our families." *Memoirs of Hope*, 180. See also Maillard, *De Gaulle und Deutschland*, 213-262.

38. Kolodziej, *French International Policy Under De Gaulle and Pompidou*, 265. That Macmillan's free trade proposal otherwise could well have separated the French from the more free-trade oriented Germans and Dutch is argued by Miriam Camps, *Britain and the European Community, 1955-1963* (London: Oxford University Press, 1964), 127.

39. Adenauer's anxiety was caused in particular by the absence of any reference to Germany in Kennedy's inaugural address, the introduction of the flexible response strategy, and tentative proposals to discuss access rights to Berlin with the Soviet Union. See Frank A. Mayer, *Adenauer and Kennedy: A Study in German-American Relations 1961-1963* (New York: St. Martin's Press, 1996), 19-41; Kolodziej, *French International Policy Under De Gaulle and Pompidou*, 271. Acheson recalls that when he met with Adenauer in April 1961, the German chancellor was "worried to death" and "was not getting on well with this administration." Oral history interview with Dean Acheson, JFK Library, 16-17.

40. At a rally in Rodez on 21 September 1961, de Gaulle said that to negotiate on Soviet terms, "you start out giving your hat, then you give your coat, then your shirt, then your skin, and finally your soul." On 23-24 October 1961, de Gaulle and Adenauer sent personal letters to Kennedy, restating their opposition to any Western concessions on Berlin or the German problem. On 11-12 December 1961, the Western foreign minis-

ters failed to agree on a unified Western position on negotiating with the Soviet Union on Berlin because of France's refusal to accept such negotiations.

41. In October 1963, Adenauer recalled in an interview: "After the Berlin Wall began to go up [...] absolutely nothing yet happened [...] even though the Russians had broken their treaties and erected the Wall, the Americans put up with. [...] The Americans even tried to tell us that it was a good thing because the flow of refugees was stopped." As quoted in Mayer, *Adenauer and Kennedy*, 43.

42. See Jacques Bariéty, "De Gaulle, Adenauer et la genèse du traité de l'Elysée du 22 janvier 1963," in *De Gaulle et son siecle*, 6. To be sure, the intimacy between Paris and Bonn on Berlin was also instilled by a residual distrust between the two capitals about their long-term plans. As Adenauer told Rusk on 23 June 1962: "Diagramming the geographical relationship between the USSR, Germany and France, [...] Germany must do everything possible to prevent a Franco-Russian arrangement against Germany. Therefore complete intimacy between Germany and France was utterly fundamental." Rusk added: "This, incidentally, was Adenauer's reflection of the same underlying longer range Franco-German distrust which I saw from the other end in Paris." Rusk to Kennedy and Acting Secretary, Secto 48 (Rome), 23 June 1962, PKOF, part 3: DAF, RSC.

43. Guy de Carmoy, *The Foreign Policies of France, 1944-1968*; translated by Elaine P. Halperin (Chicago: University of Chicago Press, 1970), 382-383.

44. De Gaulle's meeting with Fanfani resulted in a French-Italian proposal to hold regular meetings of the foreign ministers of the Six.

45. It is unclear whether de Gaulle's timing was influenced by the changing position of the British government on the Common Market; de Gaulle makes no reference to it in his memoirs. It is interesting to note, however, that around the same time, in August 1960, de Gaulle made a passionate plea to Eisenhower and Macmillan to discuss his tripartite proposal of 1958, urging them to agree to a tripartite summit meeting in September. Such a meeting might have given legitimacy to France's claim to represent the Europe of the Six in the world councils of decision. See Chapter Three.

46. De Gaulle, *Memoirs of Hope*, 194.

47. France, Ambassade de France, *Major Addresses 1958-1964*, 93.

48. Kolodziej, *French International Policy Under De Gaulle and Pompidou*, 245.

49. De Gaulle, *Memoirs of Hope*, 194. In fact, the Italian government was deeply reluctant to go along with de Gaulle's plan as well.

50. See Albert Kersten's biographical sketch of Joseph Luns, the Dutch foreign minister, in *De Nederlandse ministers van Buitenlandse Zaken in de twintigste eeuw*, eds. Duco Hellema, Bert Zeeman, Bert van der Zwam (Den Haag: SDU uitgevers, 1999), 221.

51. Lacouture, *De Gaulle: The Ruler*, 213.

52. Winand, *Eisenhower, Kennedy, and the United States of Europe*, 262.

53. As quoted in Winand, *Eisenhower, Kennedy, and the United States of Europe*, 1.

54. For the history of early American support for European integration, see Winand, 1-63.

55. William Clayton to Undersecretary of State Robert A. Lovett, telephone conversation, as quoted in Michael J. Hogan, *The Marshall Plan: America, Britain, and the Reconstruction of Western Europe, 1947-1952* (New York: Cambridge University Press, 1987), 71.

56. Oral history interview with Ernst van der Beugel, HSTL, 13.

57. David W. Ellwood, *Rebuilding Europe: Western Europe, America, and Postwar Reconstruction* (London: Longman, 1992), 159.

58. Hogan, *The Marshall Plan*, 26-87, passim; Ellwood, *Rebuilding Europe*. As Hogan makes clear, in spite of the establishment of the OEEC, American pressure on European governments to accept supranational solutions ran into consistent opposition from European leaders to compromise national sovereignty.

59. Michael Hoffman in the *New York Times* of 24 June 1956, as quoted in Ellwood, *Rebuilding Europe*, 236.

60. Dean Acheson, "The Illusion of Disengagement," *Foreign Affairs* 36, no. 3 (April 1958): 371-382. Acheson had written this article in response to Kennan's calls for a super-power disengagement from Europe in his famous BBC Reith Lectures. On the Eisenhower administration's solid support for the Common Market and the Rome Treaty, especially over the rivaling EFTA, see Winand, *Eisenhower, Kennedy, and the United States of Europe*, 109-121.

61. Bowie, *The North Atlantic Nations Tasks For the 1960s: A Report to the Secretary of State*, August 1960. Bowie headed the State Department's Policy Planning Staff from 1953 and became assistant secretary of state for Policy Planning in 1955. Although he returned to Harvard University in late 1957, he continued to work for the Eisenhower administration as a consultant. Herter had asked Bowie to prepare a report following a ministerial meeting of the North Atlantic Council in December 1959. With the extensive help of administration officials and outside experts, it was completed in mid-August 1960. For discussions of the Bowie report, see also Winand, *Eisenhower, Kennedy, and the United States of Europe*, 160-166, 198-199.

62. Bowie, *The North Atlantic Nations Tasks For the 1960s*, 100-101.

63. Ibid., 98.

64. Most importantly, the Stevenson report, presented to Kennedy in November 1960, called for enhancing the authority of the executive branch in the field of trade policy and a fifty percent across-the-board tariff reduction within five years: "the authority of the President to change tariff rates must be substantially enlarged in order to give him the powers which may be essential to help him maintain the unity of the Atlantic Community concept." In addition, the report advocated the creation of a NATO strategic nuclear deterrent. Kennedy had requested the report from Adlai Stevenson, but Ball had done most of the work. The report left an impression on the presidential candidate. Bill, *George Ball*, 58-60; DiLeo, "George Ball and the Europeanists in the State Department, 1961-1963," in Brinkley and Griffiths, *John F. Kennedy and Europe*, 271-273; Ball, *The Past Has Another Pattern*, 159-162; Arthur M. Schlesinger, Jr., *A Thousand Days: John F. Kennedy in the White House* (London: Andre Deutsch Ltd., 1965), 140-145.

65. *Report to the Honorable John F. Kennedy by the Task Force on Foreign Economic Policy*, December 1960. See Bill, *George Ball*, 59-60. Robert Bowie was one of those who helped Ball to prepare this report.

66. *A Review of North Atlantic Problems for the Future*, March 1961, NATO, Acheson Report, 3/61, Regional Security, NSF, box 220, JFKL. See also FRUS, 1961-1963, vol. 13, West Europe and Canada, no. 100. Some of the most important contributors to Acheson's report, such as Robert Komer and Henry Owen, were involved in drawing up the Bo-

wie report as well. Bowie, too, served as a consultant. In a memorandum to President Kennedy, Komer commented that "from my experience on his task force, his [Acheson's] thinking seems quite similar to that of Mr. Bowie's earlier effort." Komer to Kennedy, memorandum, 6 March 1961, Staff Memoranda, Robert W. Komer, Meetings & Memoranda, NSF, box 321, JFKL.

67. J. Robert Schaetzel, *The Unhinged Alliance: America and the European Community* (New York: Harper & Row, 1975), 46.

68. Winand, *Eisenhower, Kennedy, and the United States of Europe*, 201.

69. Couve de Murville, Ball, and Gavin, memorandum of conversation, 21 May 1962, France-General, CS, NSF, box 71a, JFKL.

70. Ball, *The Past Has Another Pattern*, 220-221; Bill, *George Ball*, 109-110.

71. See for example George W. Ball, *The Discipline of Power: Essentials of a Modern World Structure* (Boston/Toronto: Little, Brown & Co., 1968), 57-58.

72. Ernst Van der Beugel, *From Marshall Aid to Atlantic Partnership* (Amsterdam: Elsevier, 1966), 246. See also Hackett, *Monnet and the Americans*. Together with Douglas Brinkley, Hackett also brings together a useful collection of essays about Monnet in Brinkley and Hackett, *Jean Monnet: The Path to European Unity* (New York: St. Martin's Press, 1991).

73. Jean Monnet, *Memoirs* (Garden City, NY: Doubleday, 1978), 42,44.

74. Monnet, *Memoirs*, 46.

75. Kai Bird, *The Chairman: John J. McCloy, the Making of the American Establishment* (New York: Simon & Schuster, 1992). Also Walter Isaacson and Evan Thomas, *The Wise Men: Six Friends and the World They Made* (New York: Simon & Schuster, 1986), 122.

76. Richard Mayne, "Jean Monnet: A Biographical Essay," in Hackett, *Monnet and the Americans*, 13.

77. Monnet was, in fact, the true author of Roosevelt's phrase in a famous fireside chat that the United States should function as "the arsenal of democracy." See Monnet, *Memoirs*, 160; Mayne, "Jean Monnet: A Biographical Essay," 14.

78. Costigliola, *France and the United States*, 51. The Monnet plan was moreover drawn up with the help of American economists, such as Robert Nathan and William Tomlinson. See Sherill Brown Wells, "Monnet and 'the Insiders': Nathan, Tomlinson, Bowie, and Schaetzel," in Hackett, *Monnet and the Americans*, 197-211.

79. As cited in Kuisel, *Seducing the French*, 205. Kuisel even calls Monnet an "ardent Americanizer." (202)

80. See Mayne, "Jean Monnet: A Biographical Essay." 19-20.

81. Monnet established the Action Committee in October 1955, after he had relinquished his post as president of the ECSC's High Authority; he finally dissolved it in May 1975. Based in Paris, the committee was composed of the political parties and trade unions of the six countries of the Common Market, with the exception of Communists, Gaullists, and neo-fascists. By involving trade unions, it helped to convert European social democratic parties to the cause of European integration. Monnet designed the Action Committee's name in part to help generate American support for his goal of a united Europe. Apart from gaining sympathy in influential circles across the Atlantic, the Action Committee received important financial support from the Ford Foundation. (See Douglas Brinkley, "Dean Acheson and Jean Monnet: On the Path to Atlantic Part-

nership," in Hackett, *Monnet and the Americans*, 87; Monnet, *Memoirs*, 407). There is little doubt that Monnet was inspired, too, by the example of American federalism. American journalist Don Cook, for instance, remembers how Monnet took great interest in a compromise Alexander Hamilton had struck with Thomas Jefferson about legislation enabling the federal government to assume all state debts, which was designed to give the central government control of the monetary system, and how Monnet tried to emulate the mechanism in Europe. Don Cook and Hackett, "Monnet and the American Press," in Hackett, *Monnet and the Americans*. 247-248.

82. John Gillingham, "Solving the Ruhr Problem: German Heavy Industry and the Schuman Plan," in Klaus Schwabe, ed., *The Beginnings of the Schuman Plan* (Baden-Baden: Nomos, 1988), 402.

83. According to Isaacson and Thomas, for instance, Monnet should even be seen as "the *eminence grise* to the Wise Men of American foreign policy." *Wise Men*, 122.

84. On Dulles's lifelong friendship with Monnet, see Winand, "Eisenhower, Dulles, Monnet, and the Uniting of Europe," in Hackett, *Monnet and the Americans*, 109-118. Dulles first met Monnet at the Paris Peace Conference in 1919; their lifelong friendship was so strong that Monnet was the only foreign pallbearer at Dulles's funeral in May 1959. Until 1921, Monnet served on the secretariat of the League of Nations as deputy to the League's British secretary-general, Eric Drummond. McCloy befriended Monnet in the mid-1920s as a young lawyer for the Cravath law firm based in Europe. Schwartz calls their relationship "one of the most fascinating and important examples of the transnational partnerships that sustained American and European cooperation in the years after 1945." See Thomas Schwartz, "The Transnational Partnership: Jean Monnet and Jack McCloy," in Hackett, *Monnet and the Americans*, 171-195.

85. On Monnet's vital role in wartime Washington, see Robert R. Nathan, "An Unsung Hero of World War II," in Brinkley and Hackett, *Jean Monnet*, 67-85. Nathan befriended Monnet during World War II while coordinating the United States' mobilization program. After the war, Nathan helped Monnet draw up his reconstruction plan for the French economy. See Wells, "Monnet and 'the Insiders,'" 198-204. For James Reston on Monnet, see *Deadline: A Memoir* (New York: Random House, 1991), 168-173.

86. Lawrence S. Kaplan, "Dean Acheson and the Atlantic Community," in Douglas Brinkley, ed., *Dean Acheson and the Making of US Foreign Policy* (New York: St.Martin's Press, 1992), 17. Acheson first met Monnet in 1927 as a young lawyer during a Washington dinner party, but they only developed a close working relationship during the war. See Brinkley, "Dean Acheson and Jean Monnet," 71-101.

87. Although Eisenhower became acquainted with Monnet during the war, their close cooperation began during Eisenhower's stint as NATO's first SACEUR. Monnet is, for instance, credited with persuading Eisenhower to support the EDC and the wider European integration movement. They remained in regular contact during Eisenhower's presidency. See Winand, "Eisenhower, Dulles, Monnet, and the Uniting of Europe," 103-135.

88. Wells, "Monnet and 'the Insiders,'" 211-216. Hogan points out that the shift in American policies in favor of European integration in 1947 began among junior officials in Washington. Hogan, *The Marshall Plan*, 35. A number of these, such as Walt W. Rostow (then at the State Department's German and Austrian Economic Division), would

later occupy senior positions in the Kennedy administration. George Ball had worked closely as a private citizen with Jean Monnet in late 1947 in the context of the CEEC (the precursor to the OEEC). Schaetzel became a supporter of European integration and a friend of Monnet while negotiating the US-EURATOM agreement in the mid-1950s.

89. Jacques Van Helmont, "Jean Monnet As He Was," in Brinkley and Hackett, *Jean Monnet*, 217. Van Helmont also writes that Monnet was "enchanted by the dynamism, the vast resources, and the spirit of organization of the Americans."

90. Van Helmont, "Jean Monnet As He Was," 214.

91. As quoted in Brinkley, "Dean Acheson and Jean Monnet," 78.

92. In the words of Van Helmont in "Jean Monnet As He Was," 214.

93. Monnet, *Memoirs*, 271.

94. Van Helmont, "Jean Monnet As He Was," 217.

95. See in particular François Duchêne, *Jean Monnet: The First Statesman of Interdependence* (New York: W.W. Norton, 1994), 27-28.

96. Van Helmont, "Jean Monnet As He Was," 211-212, 216-217. In addition, Van Helmont stressed that Monnet was "happy when he was on a journey" and "easily got into conversation with people of all conditions, in any country."

97. Monnet, *Memoirs*, 40.

98. As quoted in Schwartz, "Jean Monnet and Jack McCloy," 174.

99. Quoted in Kolodziej, *French International Policy Under De Gaulle and Pompidou*, 249.

100. Monnet, *Memoirs*, 524.

101. Duchêne, *Jean Monnet*.

102. Walt W. Rostow, "Kennedy's View of Monnet; and Vice Versa," in Brinkley and Griffiths, *Kennedy and Europe*, 281. It was Ball who took Monnet to see Kennedy, with whom he discussed his ideas about an Atlantic "partnership." See Winand, *Eisenhower, Kennedy, and the United States of Europe*, 148-149.

103. Duchêne, *Jean Monnet*, 326; Winand, *Eisenhower, Kennedy, and the United States of Europe*, 148.

104. Brinkley, "Dean Acheson and Jean Monnet," 91. Acheson joked that he knew he had returned to a position of influence "because Monnet was once again using him to advance his united Europe cause."

105. *The Economist*, 27 January 1962, 324.

106. Apart from Ball and Schaetzel, other names commonly associated with the Europeanist "gang" at the State Department include those of John Tuthill (the American representative to the OECD and the European Communities), David Bruce (Kennedy's ambassador to Great Britain), John Leddy (from 1962 ambassador to the OECD and from 1965 assistant secretary of state for European affairs) and Henry Owen (deputy chairman of the Policy Planning Council from November 1962). According to Ball's biographer James Bill, "beyond the secretariat, two dozen Ball boys were involved in substantive policymaking." Bill, *George Ball*, 69. For more detailed discussions of the views and careers of the Europeanists, see in particular Winand, *Eisenhower, Kennedy, and the United States of Europe*, 139-153; DiLeo, "George Ball and the Europeanists in the State Department, 1961-1963," in Brinkley and Griffiths, *Kennedy and Europe*, 263-280.

107. Ball, *The Past Has Another Pattern*, 168-169. On Rusk and Ball, see also Bill, *George Ball*, 72-74.

108. Schaetzel, *The Unhinged Alliance*, 41. Schaetzel adds that "Dean Acheson, who endorsed both European unity and the general goals of partnership, [...] gagged on the adjective 'equal'; his experience as a lawyer led him to insist that he had seen and been engaged in many partnerships, but never one that was equal."

109. Ball, *The Past Has Another Pattern*, 74. For Monnet's profound influence on Ball, see Bill, *George Ball*; Winand, *Eisenhower, Kennedy, and the United States of Europe*, 147, passim. Over the years, Ball had built an impressive network of relationships in the United States and Europe; he was, for instance, a leading participant in the Bilderberg conferences organized by dr. Joseph Retinger and Prince Bernhard of the Netherlands since 1952 in order to promote Atlantic consensus. Ball would maintain an intimate personal rapport with Monnet, up to the latter's death in 1979.

110. Brinkley, *Dean Acheson*, 101-103.

111. Brinkley, "Dean Acheson and Jean Monnet," 91.

112. *Oral history interview with Walt W. Rostow*, JFKL, 131. Also Winand, *Eisenhower, Kennedy, and the United States of Europe*, 156. Rostow was virtually alone in taking exception to this sequence. He argued that the nuclear question had to be dealt with simultaneously and from the outset pushed the idea of a multilateral nuclear force against this background.

113. *Key National Security Problems*, Policy Planning Council Paper, 10 February 1961, Policy Planning, Subjects, NSF, box 303, JFKL.

114. Ibid.

115. "Facts for America to Face," *Daily Telegraph*, 25 January 1963.

116. Marjolin, "What Type of Europe?" 169.

117. Ibid., 63.

118. See Duchêne, *Jean Monnet*, 98-125; Monnet, *Memoirs*, 195-200; Cogan, *Oldest Allies, Guarded Friends*, 39-44. Robert Murphy, the United States' official representative in North Africa, too, has credited Monnet for unifying the French resistance, although he mournfully notes that Roosevelt's support – through Harry Hopkins – had given Monnet "almost the status of a personal envoy of the President in North Africa." Murphy, *Diplomat Among Warriors*, 181.

119. Monnet's activities caused Alphand to note in his diaries in January 1944: "Jean Monnet amazes me. It is he who drafts the memoranda to the President of the United States, he who incites Eisenhower to send telegrams to shift the balance in our favor. [...] I will be the only Frenchman to know how much we owe him in this phase of the war." *L'étonnement d'être*, Alphand, 173. Monnet's most important contacts at this time included McCloy at the War Department and Acheson, who had become assistant secretary of state for economic affairs.

120. See Duchêne, *Jean Monnet*, 131-138.

121. In his memoirs, Monnet describes how he persuaded de Gaulle during their conversation in Washington that the French economy needed modernization, not merely reconstruction, if France wanted to be considered a great power. Monnet, *Memoirs*, 228-231. Also Duchêne, *Jean Monnet*, 145-146. Duchêne notes that their convergence on the need to modernize the French economy "was perhaps the purest note of harmony

Monnet and de Gaulle ever struck." In addition, the Plan helped Monnet to come "nearer to the heart of the French establishment than ever before or after," without which "he could hardly have proposed the Schuman Plan." (180)

122. See Duchêne, *Jean Monnet*, 123-125. Conversely, the United States' official representative in North Africa, Robert Murphy, looked upon Monnet's activities with equal distrust and imputed him with being "definitely out to gain every advantage for the French he possible can." See Schwartz, "The Transnational Partnership," 178.

123. In the words of John Tuthill, as quoted by Brinkley in "Dean Acheson and Jean Monnet," 87.

124. Peyrefitte, *C'était de Gaulle* 1:309.

125. As quoted in Duchêne, *Jean Monnet*, 81. Pleven worked closely with both Monnet and de Gaulle during the war. Monnet's memoirs, by contrast, are notably fair with regard to de Gaulle, even as he laments that de Gaulle called him "the inspirer" and offered nothing but words of derision to the European integration movement. De Gaulle, Monnet wrote, was a "mixture of a practical intelligence that could only command respect, and a disquieting tendency to overstep the bounds of common sense. He was by turns intimate, using his undoubted charm, and distant, impervious to argument when carried away by patriotic honour of personal pride." *Memoirs*, 198, 433-434, 440-441, passim.

126. *Oral history interview with W. Randolph Burgess*, no. 407, DDEL, 60. Randolph Burgess represented the United States on the North Atlantic Council from 1957 to 1961.

127. Acheson, *Present At the Creation*, 77.

128. Brinkley, "Dean Acheson and Jean Monnet," 77.

129. Cook and Hackett, "Monnet and the American Press," 246.

130. See for instance Bill, *George Ball*, 127-130.

131. *Oral history interview with George Ball*, LBJL, 17.

132. Dean Rusk, *As I Saw It* (New York: W.W. Norton & Co., 1990), 268.

133. Ball, *The Past Has Another Pattern*, 96-98.

134. David L. DiLeo, *George Ball: Vietnam and the Rethinking of Containment* (Chapel Hill: University of North Carolina Press, 1991), 140.

135. As relayed by Ball to his biographer. Bill, *George Ball*, 129.

136. Rusk et al., memorandum of conversation, 31 January 1961, FRUS, 1961-1963, vol. 13, no. 91, 250-252.

137. Rusk et al., memorandum of conversation, 1 February 1961, FRUS, 1961-1963, vol. 13, no. 93, 256-258.

138. Department of State to Embassy in Germany, telegram, 7 February 1961, FRUS, 1961-1963, vol. 13, no. 94, 258-260.

139. See Chapter Four.

140. De Gaulle, *Memoirs of Hope*, 195.

141. Department of State to Certain Missions in Europe, circular telegram, 24 March 1961, FRUS, 1961-1963, vol. 13, 4.

142. Monnet, *Memoirs*, 432-433. Monnet had to go to great lengths to persuade the federalist members of his Action Committee of the wisdom of searching for common ground with de Gaulle, arguing that "confederation would one day lead to a federation" and

would at least condition the Europeans to the idea that "they have joined an entity which is not only economic but political... ." (437)

143. See Winand, *Eisenhower, Kennedy, and the United States of Europe*, 257-258.

144. Ibid., 257.

145. Department of State to Certain Missions in Europe, circular telegram, 3 November 1961, FRUS, 1961-1963, vol. 13, no. 22, 49.

146. US Embassy in Belgium to Department of State, telegram, 29 November 1961, FRUS, 1961-1963, vol. 13, no. 24, 51-53.

147. Sulzberger, *Last of the Giants*, 42.

148. Georges-Henri Soutou, however, argues that de Gaulle did not intend to wreck the negotiations but only to up the ante. See Soutou, "Le général de Gaulle et le plan Fouchet," in *De Gaulle et son siècle*, vol. 5, (Paris: Plon, 1992).

149. Gavin to Rusk, Embtel 3973 (Paris), 21 February 1962, France-General, CS, NSF, box 71, JFKL. De Gaulle's handling of the Algerian crisis strengthened the suspicions about his long-term goals, because, as Gavin observed, it left one "impressed by his cleverness in moving inexorably towards his objective."

150. In a conversation with Ball a few months later, Couve de Murville explained the Dutch veto of the Fouchet Plan from its maritime tradition: "The Netherlands was an island in the same sense that the United Kingdom was an island. The Dutch had never really been interested in Europe; they had always been looking out over the waters at other areas of the world. As a consequence they had resisted the development of Europe at almost every point. The Dutch were, of course, in many ways the best of partners in the Community since they were the most honest and the most steady. But they were not Europeans – at least they were not Continental Europeans – as were the French and the Germans." Couve de Murville, Ball, and Gavin, memorandum of conversation, 21 May 1962, France-General, CS, NSF, box 71a, JFKL.

151. Rusk et al., memorandum of conversation, 28 May 1962, FRUS, 1961-1963, vol. 13, no. 253.

152. De Carmoy, *The Foreign Policies of France*, 383-391; Grosser, *The Western Alliance*, 202-204; Kolodziej, *French International Policy Under De Gaulle and Pompidou*, 292-309; Lacouture, *De Gaulle: The Ruler*, 348-351. Also de Gaulle, *Memoirs of Hope*, 171.

153. Schlesinger Jr., *A Thousand Days*, 729.

154. Amanda Smith, ed., *Hostage to Fortune: The Letters of Joseph Kennedy* (New York: Viking Penguin, 2001), xxxiv.

155. For Kennedy's youth experiences in Europe, see Robert Dallek, *An Unfinished Life: John F. Kennedy, 1917-1963* (Boston: Little, Brown and Company, 2003), 49-68. Europe also provided unforgettable experiences of a different nature to Kennedy. In Rome, he attended a unique private mass with Pope Pius XII at which his brother Edward received communion. On the French Riviera, during a summer time stay with his family, he socialized with German movie star Marlene Dietrich.

156. Dallek, *An Unfinished Life*, 61-66.

157. Rostow, "Kennedy's view of Monnet," 282.

158. Schlesinger, *A Thousand Days*, 480-509, 486.

159. George Ball recalls that, as president, Kennedy would stay in close contact with his father – whom he held in fearful regard – to get his advice, until the latter was hit by a

severe stroke in December 1961. Ball, *The Past Has Another Pattern*, 205. Also Reeves, *A Question of Character*, 310-311.

160. President Kennedy's State of the Union Address, January 1961, on http://odur.let.rug.nl/~usa/P/jk35/speeches/jfk61.htm (accessed October 2005).

161. *Oral history interview with Walt Rostow*, JFKL, 100.

162. In early 1963, for instance, Dillon calculated that "foreign countries and their nationals have acquired nearly $20 billion in dollar accounts ... which has allowed us to pursue policies over the years that would have been utterly impossible had not the dollar been a key currency." Dillon to Kennedy, memorandum, 11 February 1963, PKOF, part 3: DAF, RSC.

163. David P. Calleo, *The Imperious Economy* (Cambridge: Harvard University Press, 1982). For the statistics, see also Calleo's *The Bankrupting of America: How the Federal Budget is Impoverishing the Nation* (New York: Avon Books, 1992), chap. 3 and 6; and Borden, "Defending Hegemony: American Foreign Economic Policy," 57-85. Aside from military expenditures and foreign aid, the rise in the balance-of-payments deficit was caused by a substantial increase of American investments abroad.

164. Cipolla, *The Fontana Economic History of Europe, Part I*, 343-346. Paul Kennedy, *The Rise and Fall of the Great Powers: Economic Change and Military Conflict from 1500 to 2000* (New York: Random House, 1987), 420-437. During the 1950s, only the Japanese economy expanded faster than the economies of Western Europe. The German gold stock increased from $1566 million in January 1957 to $3015 million in January 1961; over the same period the French gold stock increased from $899 million to $1641 million. Source: *International Financial Statistics*, International Monetary Fund.

165. See for example Richard T. Griffiths, "'Two Souls, One Thought'? The EEC, the United States, and the Management of the International Monetary System," in Brinkley and Griffiths, *Kennedy and Europe*, 189-211.

166. Walter Heller, *Why Europe Grows Faster?*, memorandum to President, 5 May 1961, Council of Economic Advisers paper, NSF Departments and Agencies, box 270A, 5/24/1961, JFKL. Also Winand, *Eisenhower, Kennedy, and the United States of Europe*, 177.

167. *Department of State Bulletin*, 27 March 1961, 449-450. Ball also pressed Kennedy for a reform of the world payments system that would remove the American gold stock from "the mercy of European bankers and speculators" and relieve the United States of the constant fear of a flight from the dollar. In Ball's view, this reform would have to involve multilateral arrangements with the Western allies to avoid excessive American gold losses. However, this approach was not chosen during the Kennedy years, mostly because of the opposition of Secretary of the Treasury, C. Douglas Dillon. Such arrangements did finally come about with the creation of Special Drawing Rights in 1969. See Chapter Nine.

168. Bill, *George Ball*, 59, 64-68, 119-120; Schlesinger, *A Thousand Days*, 389. Kennedy's favorable opinion of Ball was reflected in his promotion to Undersecretary of State after the re-appointment of Chester Bowles in December 1962.

169. *Oral history interview with George W. Ball*, JFKL, 22. Ball, *The Past Has Another Pattern*, 165-168. On Ball's ambivalent personal relationship with Kennedy and his circle, see also DiLeo, "George Ball and the Europeanists," 270-271.

170. Ball, *The Past Has Another Pattern*, 205-207.

171. See Borden, "Defending Hegemony," 64-65.

172. Bill, *George Ball*, 119-120. Brinkley points out that Acheson, too, had a hand in arranging Monnet's meetings with Kennedy, "to remind Kennedy that de Gaulle spoke for only a fraction of Europeans... ." Brinkley, *Dean Acheson*, 187. In his memoirs, Monnet himself speaks highly of Kennedy following their first encounter, observing that Kennedy's "remarkable receptiveness rapidly gave him a political maturity that was exceptional in so young a man" and that "of all American Presidents, Kennedy was certainly the one whose education and upbringing best equipped him to understand the problems of Europe." Monnet, *Memoirs*, 464-465.

173. Duchêne, *Jean Monnet*, 327.

174. Rostow, "Kennedy's View of Monnet," 286.

175. On 30 March, Ball had already expressed strong support in a conversation with Heath. Ball later admitted that he had then taken a risk since he had not discussed the issue with Kennedy: "I was not sure whether I was making American policy or interpreting it." Ball, *The Past Has Another Pattern*, 211-213.

176. Rusk, *As I Saw It* , 267; *Oral history interview with Dean Rusk*, JFKL, 1:198.

177. Macmillan to Kennedy, letter, 28 April 1961 (top secret and personal). For a discussion of the contents of this letter, see also Chapter Three.

178. Ball, *The Past Has Another Pattern*, 210.

179. Ibid., 214.

180. Department of State to Embassy in UK, telegram, 23 May 1961, FRUS, vol. 13, no. 9, 20-21.

181. Ormsby-Gore in a message to the Foreign Office, PRO, FO 371/162578, "Annual Review for 1961," Sir David Ormsby-Gore to the Foreign Office, 2.1.1962.

182. Department of State to Embassy in UK, telegram, 23 May 1961, FRUS, vol. 13, no. 9, 20-21.

183. Kennedy and de Gaulle, memorandum of conversation, 2 June 1961, FRUS, vol. 13, no. 11, 24-25. See Chapter Three.

184. Mission at Geneva to Department of State, telegram, 24 May 1961, FRUS, vol. 13, no. 10, 21-23.

185. Winand, *Eisenhower, Kennedy, and the United States of Europe*, 267.

186. Macmillan to Kennedy, letter, 28 April 1961 (top secret and personal).

187. Department of State to Embassy in UK, telegram, 23 May 1961, FRUS, vol. 13, no. 9, 20-21.

188. Winand, *Eisenhower, Kennedy, and the United States of Europe*, 283.

189. Galbraith to Kennedy, letter, 25 July 1961, PKOF, part 1: Special Correspondence Files (henceforth abbreviated as SCF), RSC. Kennedy regularly consulted with Galbraith on economic issues and, according to Schlesinger, "was delighted by Galbraith's wit, effrontery and unabashed pursuit of the unconventional wisdom, and they were ... exceptionally good friends. Nor did the President appear to mind Ken's guerilla warfare against the icons and taboos of the Department of State." Schlesinger, *A Thousand Days*, 454, 544,720.

190. Kennedy to Ball, National Security Action Memorandum no. 76, 21 August 1961, PKOF, part 3: DAF, RSC. Also in FRUS, vol. 13, no. 15, 32. Kennedy also stated that "I have been informed that the effect [of British membership] will be extremely serious."

191. Ball to Kennedy, memorandum, 23 August 1961, FRUS, vol. 13, no. 16, 32-38.

192. The Trade Expansion Act was in fact anticipating that Britain – once admitted – would act as a proponent of free trade within the Common Market and would attempt to weaken the costly agricultural policy from which it stood little to gain. Moreover, without British entry, the effect of the authority granted by the TEA to eliminate all tariffs on products where the United States and the Common Market accounted for more than eighty percent of world trade would be limited to aircraft and margarine. Ynze Alkema, "European-American Trade Policies, 1961-1963," William Diebold, "A Watershed with Some Dry Sides: The Trade Expansion Act of 1962," and DiLeo, "George Ball and the Europeanists," all in Brinkley and Griffiths, *Kennedy and Europe*. Also Bill, *George Ball*, 123, n. 75; Winand, *Eisenhower, Kennedy, and the United States of Europe*, 169-188, passim. For Ball's own account, see *The Past Has Another Pattern*, 195-200, 203-207.

193. Ball, *The Past Has Another Pattern*, 218.

194. Miriam Camps, "Jean Monnet and the United Kingdom," in G. Majone, E. Noel, and P. Van den Bossche, *Jean Monnet et l' Europe d'aujourd'hui* (Baden-Baden: Nomos, 1989), 133.

195. *Department of State Bulletin*, 9 April 1962, 604.

196. President Kennedy's State of the Union Message, 20 January 1962, *Department of State Bulletin*, 29 January 1962, 162-163.

197. Rostow, "Kennedy's view of Monnet," 285.

198. *The Goal of an Atlantic Partnership*, address by President Kennedy, *Department of State Bulletin*, 23 July 1962, 131-133.

199. Prior to the Philadelphia speech, McGeorge Bundy (in December 1961) and George Ball (in February 1962) had already spoken publicly about the idea of an Atlantic "partnership" between the United States and an integrated Europe. Grosser, *The Western Alliance*, 201.

200. Walt Rostow, to be sure, has underscored that Kennedy's concern for the United States' balance of payments played a significant role in drafting this part of the speech, since the partnership idea fit Kennedy's belief that Europe should assume some of the burden of managing the world economy. Rostow: "In effect Kennedy was evoking a united Old World to restore the balance to the New." Rostow, "Kennedy's View of Monnet," 284-285.

201. Brinkley, *Dean Acheson*, 186-189. All, including Acheson, had had a hand in writing Kennedy's speech.

202. *Joint Declaration of the Action Committee for a United States of Europe*, 26 June 1962, on http://www.ena.lu/mce.cfm (accessed October 2005).

203. Lacouture registers that Couve de Murville called the Atlantic partnership an attractive and generous idea, but went on to express the objections of the Elysée. Lacouture, *De Gaulle: The Ruler*, 375.

204. Duchêne, *Jean Monnet*, 328.

205. Acheson, for instance, came to distrust Kennedy's motives for giving the Philadelphia speech, suspecting that it was a political ploy to increase support for the Trade Expansion Act rather than the expression of a profound policy vision on the part of the president. Brinkley, *Dean Acheson: The Cold War Years*, 188.

206. France's determination to have its way on the CAP had already been demonstrated on June 6, 1961, when the French Agriculture Minister Henri Rochereau announced that France would halt all tariff reductions after 1961 unless the Common Market adopted a farm policy. On 14 January 1962, an initial agreement between the Six was finally reached on the general shape and the mechanisms of the CAP; the CAP would be in large part financed by revenues from external tariffs on agricultural and industrial products. As a result, French agricultural products would be able to compete with the normally cheaper produce flowing to the European market from non-European suppliers, including American farmers. See for example Kolodziej, *French International Policy Under De Gaulle and Pompidou*, 272-291.

207. *Visions and Illusions of General de Gaulle*, memorandum, Sir Pierson Dixon (Paris) to Lord Home, 27 November 1961, PRO, PREM 11/3338.

208. Alastair Horne concludes that "throughout much of 1962, as a result of de Gaulle's inscrutability, Macmillan was to be found once again vacillating between optimism and downright pessimism, but coming down – usually in the strictest privacy of his diaries – more and more on the side of the latter." Horne, *Macmillan*, vol. 2, 326.

209. It is not clear how far Macmillan actually went in offering nuclear aid to de Gaulle and there was considerable confusion on both sides about this part of their discussions. See Horne, *Macmillan* 2:328-329; Lacouture, *De Gaulle: The Ruler*, 354.

210. Macmillan had given this report of his talks with de Gaulle to C.D. Jackson, the publisher of *Life* and *Time*, who communicated it to the White House. Jackson had frequently transmitted reports of his conversations with world leaders to Eisenhower, who had highly valued them, and continued this service under Kennedy. *Overseas Report from C.D. Jackson*, 25 June 1962, PKOF, part 5: CsF, RSC.

211. Peyrefitte, *C'était de Gaulle*, 1:299-303. In *Memoirs of Hope*, too, de Gaulle admits that Macmillans' plea "struck a sympathetic chord in me" (218).

212. *Overseas Report from C.D. Jackson*, 25 June 1962, PKOF, part 5: CsF, RSC. Macmillan appears to have made the same point to de Gaulle. See de Gaulle, *Memoirs of Hope*, 218.

213. Peyrefitte, *C'était de Gaulle*, 1:299-303.

214. Horne, *Macmillan*, 2:329.

215. Lacouture notes that Geoffroy de Courcel, the French ambassador to the United Kingdom, was confident that at the meeting at Château de Champs significant progress had been made in the direction of British membership of the Common Market. Lacouture, *De Gaulle: The Ruler*, 354.

216. President and the Congressional leadership, memorandum of conversation, 7 June 1961, France-General, CS, NSF, box 70, JFKL.

217. *Secretary's European Trip, June 18-29, 1962*, scope paper prepared in Department of State, 11 June 1962, FRUS, vol. 13, no. 44, 105-108.

218. Rusk to Department of State, telegram, 21 June 1962, FRUS, vol 13, no. 256, 725-727. Rusk had talked to de Gaulle, Pompidou and Couve de Murville. Couve de Murville had told Rusk that the only real difficulty to be resolved before British admission was the problem of the Commonwealth, making clear that this problem did not appear insurmountable, since "the British would go very far in the direction of the Six." Rusk to Department of State, telegram, 20 June 1962, FRUS, vol. 13, no. 45, 108-109. On 6 July, two days after the Philadelphia speech, Ambassador Gavin gave a similarly opti-

mistic analysis, arguing that the French leader was a "realist" who understood that Great Britain's entry would "fundamentally dilute" its special relationship with the United States. Gavin to Rusk, Embtel 86 (Paris), 6 July 1962, France-General, CS, NSF, box 71a, JFKL. Also FRUS, vol 13, no. 257, 727-730.

219. Rusk to President Kennedy and Acting Secretary, Secto 48 (Rome), 23 June 1962, PKOF, part 3: DAF, RSC.

220. Embassy in UK to Department of State, telegram, 26 June 1962, FRUS, vol 13, no. 395, 1077.

221. Rostow, "Kennedy's View of Monnet," 286-287.

222. The deal with the textile industry deeply dismayed Ball, who later wrote that negotiating with the textile barons caused him "more personal anguish than any other task I undertook during my total of twelve years in different branches of the government." *The Past Has Another Pattern*, 188. Another concession to Congress and business interests was to have the president's special representative for trade entrusted with the negotiation of all trade agreements instead of the State Department.

223. DiLeo, "George Ball and the Europeanists," 275.

224. *Oral history interview with Dean Rusk*, 1:190.

225. *Oral history interview with Charles Bohlen*, 36. See also Winand, *Eisenhower, Kennedy, and the United States of Europe*, 235.

226. Before the speech, Kennedy had also been discussing the issue with Walt Rostow, who recalls that Kennedy "would have no trouble transferring the special nuclear relationship from Britain to Europe" and that he considered it "perfectly viable in the Congress – if the British were to get out and the French were to get out" – to strike a nuclear deal with a politically integrated Europe prepared to carry more of the global burden alongside the United States. *Oral history interview with Walt W. Rostow*, 131-132. Also Rostow, "Kennedy's View of Monnet," 284-285.

227. News Conference Number 38, President John F. Kennedy, State Department Auditorium, Washington DC, 5 July 1962, see: http://www.jfklibrary.org/jfk_press_conference_620705.html.

228. In addition, Gavin offered his opinion that a "defense organization with coordination and pooling of material, scientific and industrial resources" would appear the logical corollary to European economic and political integration, and that it was "difficult to envisage any such defense organization encompassing two independent and uncoordinated nuclear forces." Gavin to Rusk, Embtel 86 (Paris), 6 July 1962, France-General, CS, NSF, box 71a, JFKL. Also FRUS, vol 13, no. 257, 727-730.

229. *Department of State Bulletin*, 22 October 1962, 604-605. Also McGeorge Bundy, *Danger and Survival: Choices about the Bomb in the First Fifty Years* (New York: Random House, 1988), 497.

230. *Department of State Bulletin*, 3 December 1962, 835.

231. Airgram from Paris on US presentation to the NAC on a NATO Multilateral Sea-based Force, 10/31/1962. In Paper, "Early history of the MLF," 17.

232. As quoted in Bill, *George Ball*, 112.

233. Rusk to Kennedy, memorandum, 16 October 1962, France-General, CS, NSF, box 71a, JFKL.

234. Rusk reported that his visit to Bonn "removed any doubt I might have had as to the inevitable growth of German pressure for nuclear weapons unless there are multilateral arrangements in NATO or Europe or unless there are significant steps toward disarmament in this field. The Chancellor asserted in the most positive terms that his 1954 declaration renouncing the production of nuclear weapons was made under and subject to then prevailing conditions (rebus sic stantibus)... ." Rusk to Kennedy and Ball, Secto 48 (Rome), 23 June 1962, PKOF, part 3: DAF, RSC.

235. De Gaulle, *Memoirs of Hope*, 180-181; Maurice Couve de Murville, *Une politique étrangère, 1958-1969* (France: Plon, 1971), 253-254; Lacouture, *De Gaulle: The Ruler*, 340-341; Maillard, *De Gaulle und Deutschland*, 220-222. To mark the symbolism, Adenauer was treated to an impressive military parade at Mourmelon, in which German troops participated alongside French units.

236. Embassy in France to Department of State, telegram, 20 September 1962, FRUS, vol. 13, no. 259, 736-737. De Gaulle also made clear to Gavin his elation about his recent visit to Germany. There had been "an explosion of goodwill" and he was "obviously tremendously impressed and pleased."

237. Monnet to Acheson, letter, 23 November 1962, as quoted in Brinkley, "Dean Acheson and Jean Monnet," 94. For Acheson's growing disenchantment with the Kennedy White House, see Brinkley, *Dean Acheson*, 196-202.

238. Winand, *Eisenhower, Kennedy, and the United States of Europe*, 295. Likewise, Monnet had given evidence of his inveterate optimism in a conversation with Hervé Alphand in early September. As Alphand noted in his diary: "Jean Monnet à l'antipode de de Gaulle. Pour lui, rien n'est 'bloqué', et d'abord pas la politique européenne... ." Alphand, in turn, tried to convince Monnet that "pour de Gaulle l'Europe avec l'Angleterre ne sera pas l'Europe, que l'Angleterre cherchera, par le dedans, à torpiller l'affaire, que son vieux rêve, séculaire, de diviser le Continent, revient sans cesse, sans même qu'elle en soit consciente, à la surface." However, "Monnet n'en croit rien et pense sincèrement que l'Angleterre d'aujourd'hui a change et veut coopérer loyalement." *L'étonnement d'être*, Alphand, 386.

239. *Oral history interview with Dean Rusk*, 1:189

240. Bohlen to Rusk, Embtel 2018 (Paris), 5 November 1962, France-General, CS, NSF, box 71a, JFKL.

241. Ball to Kennedy, memorandum, 10 December 1962, , FRUS 1961-1963, vol 13, no. 55, 138-139.

242. Couve de Murville, *Une politique étrangère*, 100.

243. Frank Costigliola, in particular, has overemphasized the Kennedy administration's penchant for hegemonic control in handling its European allies. See "The Failed Design: Kennedy, De Gaulle, and the Struggle for Europe," *Diplomatic History* 8 (Summer 1984): 227-251; "The Pursuit of Atlantic Community," in Paterson, *Kennedy's Quest for Victory*, 24-56; "Kennedy, De Gaulle, and the Challenge of Consultation," in Paxton and Wahl, *De Gaulle and the United States*, 169-194; "Kennedy, the European Allies, and the Failure to Consult," *Political Science Quarterly* (Spring 1995): 105-123.

244. Maillard, *De Gaulle und Deutschland*, 224-225.

245. Kennedy et al., memorandum of conversation, 25 May 1963, France-General, CS, NSF, box 72, JFKL.

246. Speaking before America's premier military academy, Acheson stated forcefully that "Great Britain had lost an empire and has not yet found a role" and that "the attempt to play a separate power role – that is, a role apart from Europe, a role based on a 'special relationship' with the United States, a role based on being the head of a 'commonwealth' [...] – this role is about to be played out." Acheson's speech created a huge uproar in Great Britain, much to his dismay. Brinkley, *Dean Acheson*, 176-182. See also Chapter Two.

247. Ball, *The Past Has Another Pattern*, 215-216, 217, 222.

248. Alan S. Milward, with the assistance of George Brennan and Frederico Romero, *The European Rescue of the Nation State* (London: Routledge, 1992).

249. "Meeting in the Cabinet Room, Friday, May 11, 1962, 4:30 pm," 11 May 1962, France-General, CS, NSF, box 71a, JFKL.

250. George M. Taber, *John F. Kennedy and a Uniting Europe: The Politics of Partnership* (Bruges: College of Europe, 1969), 96-98; Winand, *Eisenhower, Kennedy, and the United States of Europe*, 201; Douglas Brinkley, "Dean Acheson and Jean Monnet," 90.

251. Andrew J. Pierre, "Conflicting Visions: Defense, Nuclear Weapons, and Arms Control in the Franco-American Relationship During the De Gaulle Era," in Paxton and Wahl, *De Gaulle and the United States*, 291-2.

252. Miriam Camps, *European Unification in the Sixties: From Veto to Crisis* (New York: McGraw-Hill Book Company for the Council on Foreign Relations, 1966), 244.

253. Lacouture, *De Gaulle: The Ruler*, 355, 375.

254. Winand, *Eisenhower, Kennedy, and the United States of Europe*, 65, 75.

255. Schaetzel, *The Unhinged Alliance*, 41.

Notes to Chapter Three – The Clash

1. "Thoughts on Reading the Morning Papers," 9 May 1962, France-General, CS, NSF, box 71, JFKL.

2. Lippmann to Jackson, letter, 22 May 1962. Printed in John Morton Blum, ed., *Public Philosopher: Selected Letters of Walter Lippmann* (New York: Ticknor & Fields, 1985), 607.

3. From Ball, *The Past Has Another Pattern*, 269. Neustadt, too, used the word "thunderbolt" to describe de Gaulle's moves of January 1963.

4. T.C. Achilles to Acting Secretary, memorandum, 8 August 1961, Germany-Berlin, General, CS, NSF, box 82, JFKL.

5. This mindset was epitomized by Walt Rostow in a memorandum entitled *The Shape of the Battle*. Drawing a historical analogy with the change of fortunes in 1942 in the wake of a series of "defensive victories," Rostow tried to put the foreign policy setbacks early in the Kennedy administration in perspective, adding that "to turn the tide we must win our two defensive battles: Berlin and Viet-Nam." Rostow: "The crucial thing is to regard them as battles that must be won." Rostow to Kennedy, memorandum, 17 June 1961, PKOF, part 2: Staff Memoranda File (henceforth abbreviated as SMF), RSC. To be sure, this tendency irked some in the new administration. John Kenneth Galbraith, for instance, the liberal economist whom Kennedy had appointed as ambassador to India, expressed his irritation more than once in letters to the president. On 11 July 1961, he wrote, with characteristic wit, that the "two favorite absurdities [of the

new administration] consist (1) in reducing all matters to a choice between whether we win or lose and (2) to whether we are hard or soft." In the same vein, he wrote a few months later that "when I wake up at night I worry that in our first year in office we will be credited with losing Laos which we did not have, losing East Berlin which we did not have, losing East Germany which we did not have and (touchy point) with failing to persuade the world that Formosa is China. As an extreme idealist I am in favor of lost causes. But I wonder if we should lose our lost causes more than once." Galbraith to Kennedy, letter, 11 July 1961, PKOF, part 1: SCF, RSC; Galbraith to Kennedy, letter, 19 September 1961, PKOF, part 1: SCF, RSC. These letters are published in *Letters to Kennedy* ed. James Goodman (Cambridge, MA: Harvard University Press, 1998).

6. National Security Action Memorandum 62, 24 July 1961, Berlin, Meetings & Memoranda, NSF, box 330, JFKL.

7. Department of State to American embassy in Paris, Deptel 422, 20 July 1961, France-Subjects, De Gaulle Correspondence, CS, NSF, box 73a, JFKL. Kennedy sent similar letters to Macmillan and Adenauer.

8. Bundy to Kennedy, memorandum, 9 October 1962, France-General, De Murville Talks, CS, NSF, box 71a, JFKL.

9. "Memorandum: Talk With President Kennedy," 28 August 1961, President Kennedy, Robert H. Estabrook Papers, box 1, JFKL.

10. Department of State to American embassy in Paris, Deptel 422, 20 July 1961, France-Subjects, De Gaulle Correspondence, CS, NSF, box 73a, JFKL.

11. Kennedy to de Gaulle, letter, 24 August 1961, France-Subjects, De Gaulle Correspondence, CS, NSF, box 73a, JFKL.

12. Finletter to President Kennedy, Polto 240, 30 August 1961, France-Subjects, De Gaulle Correspondence, CS, NSF, box 73a, JFKL.

13. As Henry Kissinger had written to Kennedy in April 1961, "to talk to Adenauer about the wisdom of flexibility in the abstract is like telling a member of Alcoholics Anonymous that one Martini before dinner will not hurt him." Kissinger to Kennedy, memorandum, 6 April 1961, PKOF, part 5, CsF, RSC.

14. Rusk et al., memorandum of conversation, 10 August 1961, Germany, Berlin-General, CS, NSF, box 82, JFKL.

15. *Oral history interview with Barbara Ward Jackson*, JFKL, 17. Interestingly, Eisenhower was considerably more sympathetic to de Gaulle's view on negotiations over Berlin. As he told Allen Dulles in August 1961: "it is hard to negotiate with a man who is coming across your lawn armed with a club and ready to take possession of your house." Like de Gaulle, Eisenhower did not think that there would be a war and expressed reservations about sending American troops to Europe, arguing that this probably would not make an impression on Khrushchev and, if anything, should be the responsibility of the European allies. Dulles to Kennedy, memorandum, 22 August 1961, Germany, Berlin-General, CS, NSF, box 82, JFKL.

16. As typified by Stefan Collini in "Grand Illusion," *The Nation*, 28 February 2005.

17. "Meeting in the Cabinet Room, Friday, May 11, 1962, 4:30 pm," 11 May 1962, France-General, CS, NSF, box 71a, JFKL. Also FRUS, 1961-1963, vol. 13, no. 249, 695-701. Immediately after his meeting, he repeated his complaints about de Gaulle in a con-

versation with Henry Brandon, a British journalist of the *Sunday Times*. *Oral history interview with Henry Brandon, JFKL*, 6. Mahan suggests that Kennedy's dismay had also been fuelled by growing French conversions of US dollars into gold in the first two quarters of 1962, hence aggravating the balance-of-payments problem. Mahan, *Kennedy, De Gaulle, and Western Europe*, 120. The memorable dinner given in Malraux's honor at the White House is described in Letitia Baldrige, *In the Kennedy Style: Magical Evenings in the Kennedy White House* (New York: Doubleday, 1998), 103-117.

18. Gavin to Rusk, Embtel 5425 (Paris), 16 May 1962, France-General, CS, NSF, box 71a, JFKL.

19. Bundy to William H. Brubeck, memorandum, 18 May 1962, France-General, CS, NSF, box 71a, JFKL. Also FRUS, 1961-1963, vol. 13, no. 251. Apart from restating his opposition to "a series of national deterrents," Kennedy moreover resuscitated the ghost of American isolationism in an address on 17 May: "We cannot and do not take any European ally for granted and no one in Europe should take us for granted either [...]. American public opinion has turned away from isolation but its faith must not be shattered." Kennedy, *Public Papers of the Presidents: John F. Kennedy*, vol. 2 (Washington, DC: GPO, 1964), 400.

20. Embassy in France to Department of State, telegram, 28 May 1962, FRUS, 1961-1963, vol. 13, no. 252, 705-707.

21. Rusk to Department of State, telegram, 20 June 1962, FRUS, 1961-1963, vol. 13, no. 255, 718-724.

22. Lacouture describes how de Gaulle viewed his election victory primarily as one over the "party system" that had dominated the Fourth Republic. In a meeting of the Council of Ministers after the election, an elated de Gaulle observed: "We'll now have a bit of peace for several years. I wanted to smash the parties. I was the only one who could do it and the only one to believe that it was possible at the time I chose. I've been proved right against everybody. I declared war on the parties. I shall refrain from declaring war on the party leaders." Lacouture, *De Gaulle: The Ruler*, 494. David Klein of the White House staff argued that de Gaulle's election victory meant that he would be "more of a man with a mission than before, more determined to rearrange France's internal political life, and probably less compromising on the international scene." Klein to Bundy, memorandum, 27 November 1962, NSF, Countries, France, box 170a, JFKL.

23. While the British V-bomber force was capable of delivering British manufactured H-bombs, it was considered imperative that it had stand-off weapons to penetrate Soviet air defenses and to maintain an effective nuclear deterrent against the Soviet Union. On the early history of the Skybolt program, see *Into the Missile Age, 1956-1960*, Robert J. Watson, vol. 4, Office of the Secretary of Defense, Historical Office (Washington, DC: GPO, 1997) 373-374, 562-570.

24. *NATO and the Atlantic Nations*, Policy Directive, FRUS, 1961-1963, vol. 13, no. 100, 289.

25. *Implications for the United Kingdom of Decision to Abandon Skybolt*, Department of State Memorandum, 31 October 1962, FRUS, 1961-1963, vol. 13, no. 398, 1083-1085.

26. *Notes of Conversations Relating to Skybolt*, Robert S. McNamara, 9 November 1962, FRUS, 1961-1963, vol. 13, no. 399. McNamara's visit to Thorneycroft on 11 December nonetheless startled both men. McNamara gave his British equivalent an aide mémoire on

the technical weaknesses of Skybolt. To his surprise, Thorneycroft seemed wholly un-prepared. He insisted that the United States unambiguously support the independence of the British nuclear force, which McNamara refused. By that time, the decision to abort the Skybolt program had moreover been leaked to the press and British public opinion had been riled up by Acheson's West Point speech (see previous chapters in this book). McNamara returned from London without having reached agreement on the way forward. Ball thus had reason to call McNamara's voyage to London "a fore-gone disaster." Ball, *The Past Has Another Pattern*, 264. See also Richard E. Neustadt, Staff Memoranda, Skybolt and Nassau, 11/63, Meetings & Memoranda, NSF, box 322, JFKL, 1.

27. *Oral history interview with Peter Thorneycroft*, JFKL, 19. Rusk later claimed to have been surprised by the vehemence of the British reaction, believing it was purposely over-stated and that if Thorneycroft "had prepared the way, both in his own Cabinet and with the British public opinion, the cancellation of Skybolt would not have created quite the furor that it did." *Oral history interview with Dean Rusk* 1:185. See also Rusk, As I Saw It, 266.

28. *Oral history interview with Roswell Gilpatric*, JFKL, 89.

29. Harold Macmillan, At the End of the Day, 1961-1963 (London: Macmillan, 1973), 348.

30. Neustadt's report to Kennedy on Skybolt and Nassau includes an analysis of Macmil-lan's Rambouillet meeting with de Gaulle, based largely on British sources. He corro-borates that Macmillan told de Gaulle of his intention to ask Kennedy for Polaris mis-siles. While the meeting ended on a bad note, Neustadt concludes that Macmillan "had too much at stake to quit until the whistle blew." Neustadt Report, 80-84. On 29 December, Macmillan wrote to Heath that "my impression of de Gaulle is that he [...] does not want us now in the Community because he is in a mood of sulks about the future of Europe politically and would prefer to stay where he is with France dominat-ing the Five. At the same time I am not sure whether he wants this to be too public ...." As quoted in Horne, Macmillan 2:444. For de Gaulle's interpretation of the Ram-bouillet meeting, see Lacouture, De Gaulle: The Ruler, 355-356.

31. Ball, *The Past Has Another Pattern*, 265. Ball also felt that the crisis had been foisted upon Kennedy and Macmillan by McNamara's "doctrine of cost-effectiveness" which made it inconceivable to the American secretary of defense "to keep it [the Skybolt program] alive merely for political reasons." (264)

32. Rusk to McNamara, letter, 24 November 1962, FRUS, 1961-1963, vol. 13, no. 400. There was perceived to be an important difference between air-to-ground missiles such as the Hound Dog or the Skybolt and sea-based missiles such as Polaris because the latter were much less vulnerable to a first strike by the Soviet Union and had a longer range.

33. Memorandum of Conversation in the Oval Room, 16 December 1962, Meetings with the President, General, Meetings & Memoranda, NSF, box 317, JFKL. See also FRUS, 1961-1963, vol. 13, no. 401, 1088-1091.

34. "Last Conversation with President before NATO Meeting of December 1962," 13 De-cember 1962, Skybolt-Nassau Conference, folder 3, Richard E. Neustadt Papers, box 19, JFKL.

35. Records of Kennedy's three conversations with Macmillan at Nassau on Skybolt can be found in FRUS, 1961-1963, vol. 13, no. 402, 403, 406. Ball informed Rusk on 19 December of the progress of the talks and the proposed language of a public statement and of a private understanding with the British. Rusk's reply the next day put further pressure on the British to accept a multilateral solution. FRUS, 1961-1963, vol. 13, no. 404 and 405, 1106-1108.

36. The agreement was based on British acceptance of the American offer to provide Polaris missiles for a future British nuclear force which, together with equivalent American units, would be merged in the proposed NATO force. The United States offered five American-built Polaris submarines on the condition that they would be assigned to a NATO-wide nuclear force. Text of the joint communiqué issued on 21 December 1962, appears in *Department of State Bulletin*, vol. 48, no. 1229 (14 January 1963), 44.

37. Winand, *Eisenhower, Kennedy, and the United States of Europe*, 278-279, 317-318. Ormsby-Gore had become acquainted with Kennedy in the 1930s and, from 1954 onwards, stayed with the Kennedy family once a year. It was Kennedy who suggested to Macmillan to appoint his old friend as ambassador in Washington. In this capacity, Ormsby-Gore would often participate in the most secret deliberations of the Kennedy team. Arguably, the relationship between Kennedy and Ormsby-Gore should be likened to that between Alexander Hamilton and Captain Beckwith in the 1780s and Dean Acheson and Sir Oliver Franks in the 1940s (see Chapter One), for in all cases the British representative in Washington acted as a member of the American foreign policy team.

38. Richard E. Neustadt, Staff Memoranda, Skybolt and Nassau, 11/63, Meetings & Memoranda, NSF, box 322, JFKL , 101. See also Bange, *The EEC Crisis of 1963*, 80-85.

39. See for instance McGeorge Bundy's account of the conference in *Danger and Survival*, 490-495.

40. Richard E. Neustadt, Staff Memoranda, Skybolt and Nassau, 11/63, Meetings & Memoranda, NSF, box 322, JFKL, 1. {see note 294}

41. See for example Bange, *The EEC Crisis of 1963*, 50-51.

42. Bohlen had pressed for identical offers to London and Paris "for the bomber phase of nuclear development, with a definite commitment that at the missile stage both would agree to a multilateral solution." Paper by Charles Bohlen, 17 December 1962, Skybolt-Nassau (classified), folder 3, Richard E. Neustadt Papers, box 19, JFKL.

43. Tyler and Rostow to Rusk, memorandum, 17 December 1962, Skybolt-Nassau, (classified), folder 1, Richard E. Neustadt Papers, box 19, JFKL.

44. *Oral history interview with William Tyler*, 8-9. According to Ball, Tyler "saw more clearly the destructive implications of emerging events" and predicted that de Gaulle would be outraged by "Britain's incestuous ties to America." *The Past Has Another Pattern*, 268.

45. Delegation to the Heads of Government Meeting to Embassy in Paris, telegram, 20 December 1962, FRUS, 1961-1963, vol. 13, no. 407. On 29 December, Kennedy reiterated the offer to Alphand during the latter's visit to Palm Beach. See *Oral history interview with Hervé Alphand*, 6-7.

46. Ball, *The Past Has Another Pattern*, 268.

47. Rostow to Rusk, memorandum, 21 December 1962, Skybolt-Nassau (classified), folder 1, Richard E. Neustadt Papers, box 19, JFKL. Rostow had written the memorandum to urge Rusk to press McNamara on the multilateral idea, because the latter had "shown

some signs of wavering on this point." The differences between the Pentagon and the State Department regarding the manning of NATO force actually went back to the Eisenhower years. See Douglas, Gates, Irwin, Merchant, Kohler, Goodpaster, memorandum of conference with the President, NATO (6) [1959-1960] Int. T&M, WHOSS, DDEL.

48. Winand, *Eisenhower, Kennedy, and the United States of Europe*, 153, 224. Richard E. Neustadt, Staff Memoranda, Richard E. Neustadt, Skybolt and Nassau, 11/63, Meetings & Memoranda, NSF, box 322, JFKL, 70, 100.

49. *Nassau Follow-Up*, record of meeting, 28 December 1962, FRUS, 1961-1963, vol. 13, no. 410, 1116-1123.

50. The substantive differences of view between the State Department and the Pentagon, as well as the more detached view of the White House, were neatly summed up in a memorandum from the chairman of the Steering Group To Implement the Nassau Decision, Jeffrey C. Kitchen, to Dean Rusk on 4 January 1963. See FRUS, 1961-1963, vol. 13, no. 411, 1123-1128. These differences had become very clear in the various committees which were established in Washington to develop a post-Nassau strategy. The differences over the timescale of negotiations with France can also be found in *Meeting of Committee on Negotiations with the French*, 31 December 1962, Skybolt-Nassau (classified), folder 1, Richard E. Neustadt Papers, box 19, JFKL.

51. In his meeting with McNamara on December 28, Rusk had also expressed himself in this vein. Noting that there could now be envisaged three types of nuclear forces – (1) American forces outside NATO, (2) American, British, and possibly French forces assigned to NATO, and (3) a mixed-manned multilateral force under NATO – he said: "Ultimately, the first two types should whither away and the third type should become the basic force." *Nassau Follow-Up*, 1116-1123.

52. *Steering Group on Implementing the Nassau Decisions – Post Nassau Strategy*, 2 January 1963, NATO-weapons, Subgroup V, Post-Nassau Strategy, 1/63, Regional Security, NSF, box 230, JFKL.

53. Ibid.

54. Klein to Bundy, memorandum, 27 November 1962, France-General, CS, NSF, box 71a, JFKL. In a follow-up memorandum, Klein informed Bundy that Assistant Secretary of State for European Affairs, William R. Tyler, fully agreed with him and considered it "very urgent to end the isolation of de Gaulle." Klein to Bundy, memorandum, 6 December 1962, France-General, CS, NSF, box 71a, JFKL. The idea of a visit to the United States had been broached in September 1962 by de Gaulle himself in a personal letter to Alphand, although he did not yet think the time was right and saw too few prospects for agreement. Bundy to Kennedy, 17 September 1962, France-General, CS, NSF, box 71a, JFKL. On 8 November, Kennedy extended an informal invitation to de Gaulle to visit him after the elections in France on 25 November at Palm Beach "because I am already getting feelers from Macmillan for a December visit and I do not want such a visit to become definite and public ... without making it very clear to de Gaulle that I would value a chance to talk with him." Kennedy to Bohlen, Deptel 2494, 8 November 1962, France-Subjects, De Gaulle Correspondence, CS, NSF, box 73, JFKL.

55. John Steinbruner, *The Cybernetic Theory of Decision: New Dimensions of Political Analysis* (Princeton: Princeton University Press, 1974), 249-255.

56. The Mission to NATO and European Regional Organizations to Department of State, telegram, 11 January 1963, FRUS, 1961-1963, vol. 13, no. 164, 471-474.

57. Neustadt Report, 94.

58. Ibid., 101.

59. *Meeting with Secretary of State on Nassau follow-up*, memorandum for the record, 28 December 1962, Skybolt-Nassau (classified), folder 1, Richard E. Neustadt Papers, box 19, JFKL.

60. Lyon to Rusk, Embtel 2582 (Paris), 21 December 1962, France-Subjects, De Gaulle Correspondence, CS, NSF, box 73, JFKL. The next day Couve de Murville told Lyon that de Gaulle had been favorably impressed with the fact that Kennedy and Macmillan had communicated the results of their meeting before they became public. Lyon to Rusk, Embtel 2594 (Paris), 22 December 1962, France-General, CS, NSF, box 71a, JFKL. Burin des Roziers later confirmed that Kennedy's invitation, "contrary to what has been said, was not dismissed out of hand without any study" and that the French cabinet seriously studied it. Burin des Roziers in Paxton and Wahl, *De Gaulle and the United States*, 237.

61. Bundy to Kennedy, memorandum, 2 January 1963, France-Subjects, De Gaulle Correspondence, CS, NSF, box 73, JFKL.

62. Alphand, *L'étonnement d'être*, 389.

63. Lyon to Rusk, Embtel 2595 (Paris), 24 December 1962, France-General, CS, NSF, box 71a, JFKL. In conversations with American officials, French Ambassador Hervé Alphand, too, had reported a "very sour view of Nassau" from Paris. Bundy to Kennedy, memorandum, 29 December 1962, France-General, CS, NSF, box 71a, JFKL.

64. Burin des Roziers, 237. For the reception of the Nassau offer within the French Council of Ministers of 3 January 1963, see Peyrefitte, *C'était de Gaulle* 1:338-343.

65. Bundy to Kennedy, memorandum, 29 December 1962, France-General, CS, NSF, box 71a, JFKL.

66. Rusk to Kennedy, memorandum, 24 December 1962, France, CS, NSF, box 71a, JFKL.

67. Alphand, *L'étonnement d'être*, 390-391. Alphand recounts that he responded skeptically to Kennedy's explanations, but also that he did recommend to Paris not to abort the dialogue prematurely. He had strong doubts, however, that Paris would heed his advice. On Alphand's private visit with Kennedy, see also Bange, *The EEC Crisis of 1963*, 74-75.

68. Rusk to Bohlen, telegram, 1 January 1963, FRUS, 1961-1963, vol. 13, no. 262, 743-744.

69. Neustadt Report, 105.

70. Bohlen to Kennedy and Rusk, telegram, 4 January 1963, FRUS, 1961-1963, vol. 13, no. 263, 745-748.

71. See note 325 above.

72. Ball, *The Past Has Another Pattern*, 259-274.

73. France, Ambassade de France, *Major Addresses 1958- 1964*, 213-215.

74. It is important to note that de Gaulle did not exclude the possibility of future membership in his press conference. He told Peyrefitte that Great Britain could be ready for membership in four or eight years, in particular if the Labour Party would get a hold on power. But: "Elle n'entrera dans la Communauté européenne, que lorsqu'elle aura

repudié à la fois son rêve impériale et sa symbiose avec les Américains. Autrement dit, quand elle se sera convertie à l'Europe." Peyrefitte, *C'était de Gaulle* 1:355-356.

75. France, Ambassade de France, *Major Addresses 1958-1964*, 219.

76. The text of the treaty is in *Keesing's Contemporary Archives*, 19209.

77. Bange, *The EEC Crisis of 1963*, 112-116.

78. Newhouse, *De Gaulle and the Anglo-Saxons*, 237. Peyrefitte recalls that there were eight hundred journalists and guests, most of them from abroad, and that de Gaulle had been preparing the press conference intensively for three weeks (i.e. as he was being wooed by the Americans!), going over his message time and again: "Lectures; prome-nade; écriture d'un canévas détaillé; re-promenade; affinement de l'écriture; récita-tion; corrections. C'est pour lui une ascèse. Approfondir un sujet. [...] Tel et son jeu, [...], 'le jeu divin du héros.'" Peyrefitte, *C'était de Gaulle* 1:351-352. On the rehearsed but majestic quality of de Gaulle's press conferences, see also Lacouture, *De Gaulle: The Ruler*, 238-239.

79. Horne, *Macmillan* 2:446. Based on an interview with Philip de Zulueta.

80. Ibid., 449.

81. Macmillan, *At the End of the Day*, 367.

82. Duchêne, *Jean Monnet*, 329.

83. Horne, *Macmillan* 2:448.

84. In *Le Monde* of 24 January 1963, as quoted in Lacouture, *De Gaulle: The Ruler*, 359.

85. As recalled by Assistant Secretary of State for European Affairs William Tyler. Tyler to Bundy, memorandum, 12 March 1963, France, CF, NSF, box 169, LBJL.

86. As Theodore Sorensen wrote: "The angry initial reaction in the United States and Great Britain was due in part to surprise – not at de Gaulle's attitudes, which were old, but at his tactics, his willingness to act so abruptly, brazenly and brutally, and with so little notice to allies, when he might have blocked all the same efforts more subtly and gradually." *Kennedy*, Theodore C. Sorenson (New York: Harper & Row, 1965), 60.

87. Bohlen to Rusk, Embtel 2804 (Paris), 15 January 1963, France-Subjects, De Gaulle Press Statement, 1/14/63, part 2, CS, NSF, box 73, JFKL.

88. *Oral history interview with George Ball*, AC 88-3, LBJL, 18-19. See also Ball, *The Past Has Another Pattern*, 269-270. According to Ball, British EC negotiator Edward Heath had shared his optimistic mood and had gotten a similar innocuous message from Couve de Murville about the prospects of British membership.

89. Ball, *The Past Has Another Pattern*, 271.

90. Robert Schaetzel cabled the embassy in Paris that the White House concurred with James Reston of the *New York Times* who had made this point in the international edi-tion of the paper. Schaetzel to Embassy, Deptel 3539, 21 January 1963, France-Sub-jects, De Gaulle Press Statement, 1/14/63, part 3, CS, NSF, box 73, JFKL.

91. Adenauer defended himself by saying he had put the issue before Rusk in general terms in the summer of 1962, who at the time had not expressed any reservations. Brinkley, *Dean Acheson*, 191. The CIA analyzed that Adenauer felt the treaty was "West Germany's guarantee against a possible French move to seek a separate arrangement with the Soviets" and basically agreed with de Gaulle on the issue of British member-ship of the Common Market. *Adenauer's Attitude Toward De Gaulle*, CIA Intelligence Mem-

orandum, 4 February 1963, PKOF, part 3: DAF, RSC. On the Kennedy administration's initial reaction to the Franco-German treaty, see also Winand, *Eisenhower, Kennedy, and the United States of Europe*, 333-334, and Mayer, *Adenauer und Kennedy*, 91-94.

92. Monnet, *Memoirs*, 458.

93. For a detailed and colorful analysis of the host of contacts between capitals at the time and the proceedings of the Brussels meeting, see Bange, *The EEC Crisis of 1963*, 117-231.

94. Ball, *The Past Has Another Pattern*, 271. Although the French government categorically denied reports of a planned *entente* with the Soviet Union, Rostow did find these reports credible enough to believe that Paris had been engaging in talks with Moscow (without informing Bonn). He judged, however, that "the deal is premature by many years." Rostow to Ball, memorandum, 26 January 1963, France, CS, NSF, box 72, JFKL.

95. Kennedy to Bohlen, Deptel 3900, 14 February 1963, France-General, CS, NSF, box 72, JFKL.

96. *Questions to be settled by the United States in the coming months*, 31 January 1963, PKOF, part 2: SMF, RSC.

97. Kennedy for Dillon, memorandum, 19 January 1963, PKOF, part 3: DAF, RSC. Dillon stated in his reply that France had the ability to purchase $1.75 billion in gold in 1963, of which $750 million could be purchased immediately. The main risk of a French decision to convert dollars into gold would be the pressure this would put on countries such as Germany and Italy to follow suit: "if the French buy gold massively and thus deplete our gold to dangerous levels, only an approach on the highest political levels to other Continental countries may prevent a general degeneration of the world financial structure." However, Dillon noted that there were no signs of a French attack on the dollar. Dillon to Kennedy, memorandum, 24 January 1963, PKOF, part 3: DAF, RSC. A CIA report on French economic policies stated that "France's record of cooperation in assisting the US in its balance-of-payments difficulties during recent years is as good as that of any other European nation, and better than most." Examples are French prepayments of more than $400 million on long-term debts to the United States and participation in technical arrangements intended to stabilize the dollar and limit at least temporarily the outflow of American gold. *The Impact of French Economic Policy on US Interests*, CIA Special Report, 29 March 1963, France-General, CS, NSF, box 72, JFKL.

98. Alphand, *L'étonnement d'être*, 393-395. Neither Kennedy nor Bundy had a very high opinion of Alphand, about whom doubts often existed as to whether he was giving his government's opinions or his own.

99. *French Foreign Policy Outlook*, CIA Current Intelligence Memorandum, Europe, vol 4, Regional Security, NSF, box 213, NSF. This memorandum was included in Kennedy's weekend reading.

100. Tuthill to Rusk, Embtel (Brussels), 28 February 1963, PKOF, part 5: CsF, RSC.

101. *Impressions from My Trip to Europe*, Rostow to Kennedy, memorandum, 13 May 1963, PKOF, part 2: SMF, RSC.

102. Brinkley, *Dean Acheson*, 190.

103. See note 357 above.

104. *The Mess in Europe and the Meaning of Your Trip*, Ball to Kennedy, memorandum, 20 June 1963, FRUS 1961-1963, vol. 13, no. 79, 204-213.

105. Ibid.

106. *Reflections on the January Debacle*, Dean Acheson, 31 January 1963, 'State Department and White House Advisor, 1963: January-December,' Post-administration Files, Dean Acheson Papers, box 100, HSTL. Acheson wrote to his German friend Kurt Birrenbach in a similar vein: "Chancellor Adenauer made a mistake – and I think a serious one – in signing the French treaty when he did" and had committed "an act of singular imperception." Acheson to Birrenbach, letter, 19 February 1963, in David S. McLellan and Dean S. Acheson *Among Friends: Personal Letters of Dean Acheson* (New York: Dodd, Mead, 1980), 242-244. See also Brinkley, *Dean Acheson*, 192.

107. The link between Ball's presentation and de Gaulle's press conference had been suggested to Bohlen by André Malraux. See FRUS, 1961-1963, vol. 13, no. 266 and 270, 753-754, 762-769.

108. Bohlen to Kennedy, Embtel 3293 (Paris), 16 February 1963, France-General, CS, NSF, box 72, JFKL.

109. Bohlen to Bundy, letter, 2 March 1963, Correspondence with Ambassadors, Files of McGeorge Bundy, NSF, box 15-16, LBJL. Dean Rusk, too, appears to have favored a less high-profile response to de Gaulle than Acheson and Ball, although he was also personally irritated by de Gaulle. In his memoirs, for instance, Rusk professes that he believed "we'd just have to wait for de Gaulle to leave the scene ... ." Dean Rusk, *As I Saw It*, 268.

110. Neustadt to Schaetzel, letter, 15 May 1963, Richard E. Neustadt Papers, box 20, JFKL.

111. Schlesinger to Ball, memorandum, 12 February 1963, France, Papers of Arthur M. Schlesinger Jr., box WH-9, JFKL.

112. Schlesinger, *A Thousand Days*, 752-755. Schlesinger also notified Kennedy of his ideas and had a hand in drafting Kennedy's speeches for the European trip. Schlesinger: "In the long run, the most effective means of blocking de Gaulle's conquest of Europe will probably be the upsurge of democratic protest against his conception of a paternalistic-authoritarian Europe. By encouraging progressive tendencies, we can help counter the Gaullist idea of Europe without seeming to challenge de Gaulle directly." Schlesinger to Kennedy, memorandum, 10 April 1963, PKOF, part 2: SMF, RSC. Theodore Sorenson, who was Kennedy's main speech writer, confirms that "Kennedy's primary purpose [during the June 1963 trip] was not to negotiate with governments but to talk to their publics in the wake of de Gaulle's charges against the U.S." and that he had made the most of "the contrast between his youthful vitality and the weary pessimism of most older leaders." *Kennedy*, Sorenson, 652-653.

113. Acheson, "De Gaulle and the West," *New Leader*, 1 April 1963, 17-22. He also expressed this view in a letter to Kennedy on 20 February; see PKOF, part 1: SCF, RSC.

114. As cited in Brinkley, *Dean Acheson*, 195.

115. Evelyn Lincoln to McGeorge Bundy, memorandum, 1 February 1963, box 62, POF, JFKL.

116. As quoted in Bange, *The EEC Crisis of 1963*, 229-230.

117. McCloy to Adenauer, letter, 4 February 1963, PKOF, part 1: SCF, RSC.

118. While both Prime Minister Debré and Couve de Murville have stated that Monnet was the true author of the preamble, neither Monnet nor his biographer claim as much. Monnet did, however, try to "use the Bundestag ratification of the Franco-German treaty to stop the rot." *Jean Monnet*, Duchêne, 330-331.

119. Ball, *The Mess in Europe and the Meaning of Your Trip*, 208. Suspicions about the possibility of Franco-German nuclear collaboration were reinforced by reports in the spring of 1963 that France had asked Germany for financial and technical assistance under the scientific-technical provisions of the Franco-German Treaty for the completion of the gaseous diffusion plant at Pierrelatte – the plant that was designed to produce the weapons-grade highly enriched uranium for the French deterrent. Even as there was no evidence of joint nuclear weapons research and development, these reports sufficiently concerned Kennedy to request the CIA and the State Department to look into the matter. *Report on French Gaseous Plant*, National Security Action Memorandum 241, 7 May 1963, Meetings & Memoranda, NSF, box 342, JFKL.

120. In a letter to Belgian Foreign Minister Spaak, Rusk argued that the MLF would constitute a major step toward European integration and Atlantic partnership. It would bring the majority of EEC members and Great Britain together in an "enterprise of great moment" and at the same time associate the United States with this enterprise. Department of State to Brussels embassy, Topol 1667 (Paris), 8 May 1963, Subject File, box 23, #30c, NSF, LBJL.

121. Rostow to Tyler, memorandum, 19 February 1963, France-General, CS, NSF, box 72, JFKL.

122. Tuthill to Rusk, Ecbus 730 (Brussels), 22 January 1963, France-Subjects, De Gaulle Press Statement, 1/14/63, part 3, CS, NSF, box 73, JFKL.

123. L.J. Legere to Bundy, memorandum, 29 January 1963, Staff Memoranda, L.J. Legere, Meetings & Memoranda, NSF, box 322, JFKL.

124. See Winand, *Eisenhower, Kennedy, and the United States of Europe*, 338.

125. Kissinger, *The Troubled Partnership*, 138.

126. Arthur Schlesinger reports that the Merchant mission toured Europe in a chartered plane with a party of 32 and an elaborate itinerary, thus conveying a strong impression of activism. *A Thousand Days*, 747.

127. Steinbruner, *The Cybernetic Theory of Decision*, 249-255. Before the appointment of Livingston Merchant, the operational aspects were the responsibility of Gerard Smith and Admiral Lee, who carried less official authority.

128. Robert R. Bowie, "Strategy and Atlantic Alliance," *International Organization* 17 (Summer 1963): 709-732.

129. Bundy to Kennedy, memorandum, 15 June 1963, Memos to the President, McGeorge Bundy, NSF, box 2, LBJL.

130. Schlesinger, *A Thousand Days*, 754.

131. Couve de Murville, *Une politique étrangère*, 105-106.

132. Lacouture, *De Gaulle: The Ruler*, 343.

133. Lyon to Rusk, Embtel 830 (Paris), 21 August 1963, France, CS, NSF, box 72, JFKL. That there was also considerable irritation on the French side with the reversal of fortunes and with the American role was evidenced by a conversation between Couve de Murville and André Visson, which the latter reported to Washington. André Visson to

Kennedy, letter, 24 August 1963, France-General, CS, NSF, box 72, JFKL. A month later, Couve de Murville repeated the gist of his remarks of frustration to Bohlen, giving the American ambassador reason to observe that there existed a "profound French malaise" with the state of affairs. Bohlen to Rusk, Embtel 1465 (Paris), 25 September 1963, France-General, CS, NSF, box 73, JFKL.

134. Couve made these complaints in talks with both Bohlen and Rusk. Embassy in France to Department of State, telegram, 15 September 1963, FRUS, no. 274, 780-781; Klein to Bundy, memorandum, 7 October 1963, France-General, CS, NSF, box 73, JFKL.

135. Ball, *The Past Has Another Pattern*, 273. The preamble, to be sure, was not attached to the treaty itself but included in the German treaty of approval.

136. Lacouture, *De Gaulle: The Ruler*, 481.

137. Kennedy et al., memorandum of conversation, 18 February 1963, FRUS 1961-1963, vol. 13, no. 502, 502-506.

138. The instruction read that "you should not hesitate to press the concept of unanimity on the war issue as the tradition of NATO." Kennedy to Members of MLF Negotiating Delegation, memorandum, 21 February 1963, FRUS 1961-1963, vol. 13, no. 176, 509-511. A memorandum drawn up by McGeorge Bundy makes clear that Kennedy personally revised the instruction "to insure that it did not give an implication that the U.S. would necessarily be more flexible in later discussions." Memorandum for record (signed by McGeorge Bundy), 21 February 1963, FRUS 1961-1963, vol. 13, no. 175, 507-508.

139. Schlesinger, *A Thousand Days*, 745.

140. In the preceding months, Washington had strongly pressured the British government to join the MLF soon. See FRUS 1961-1963, vol. 13, no. 195, 197, 200. See also Lawrence S. Kaplan, "The MLF Debate," in Brinkley and Griffiths, *Kennedy and Europe*, 62-66.

141. Bundy to Kennedy, memorandum, 15 June 1963, Memos to the President, McGeorge Bundy, NSF, box 2, LBJL. Bundy later informed President Johnson that Kennedy had reacted very strongly and affirmatively to his memorandum. He told Hammond many years later that Kennedy even responded by pestering his national security adviser: "What took you so long?" See Paul Y. Hammond, *LBJ and the Presidential Management of Foreign Relations* (Austin, Texas: University of Texas Press, 1992), 114.

142. According to Steinbruner, the MLF proponents "hoped to tempt the President with visions of such an achievement [i.e., setting of a deadline for the establishment of the MLF] as a solid result of his trip, a dashing counterthrust to de Gaulle." Steinbruner, *The Cybernetic Theory of Decision*, 276.

143. Bundy to Rusk, memorandum, 11 July 1963, FRUS 1961-1963, vol. 13, no. 206, 603-604.

144. See Bundy, *Danger and Survival*, 328-334, 460-461. The Limited Test Ban Treaty prohibited tests in the earth's atmosphere, in outer space, and under water. Excluded were those tests carried out underground and considered by the West to be undetectable without inspection provisions unacceptable to the Soviet Union.

145. *Oral history interview with Theodore Sorenson*, JFKL, 104-105.

146. BAN to Harriman, cable, 19 July 1963, France-Subjects, De Gaulle Correspondence, CS, NSF, box 73, JFKL.

147. Kennedy to de Gaulle, letter, 24 July 1963, France-Subjects, De Gaulle Correspondence, CS, NSF, box 73, JFKL. Kennedy repeated this offer in September 1963. Ball to Rusk and Bohlen, *Highest Level Guidance for Your Conversation w/ General de Gaulle*, Deptel 1507, 25 September 1963, France-General, CS, NSF, box 73, JFKL. The State Department view was, predictably, less forthcoming. As Rostow wrote: "If we grant the French bilateral nuclear aid, we are in the impossible situation of asking Congress to accept a treaty in order to reduce proliferation in the long run while adding to proliferation in the short run [...]. It would not be tragic if the French were to sit outside the treaty for a while; it would be tragic if, in order to bring them in we were either to corrupt the possibility of getting the treaty through the Senate or further to distort the Alliance." Rostow to Rusk, memorandum, 22 July 1963, PKOF, part 4: CsF, RSC.

148. Bohlen to Rusk, Embtel 475 (Paris), 30 July 1963, France-General, CS, NSF, box 72, JFKL. In his semi-annual press conference on 29 July, de Gaulle confirmed that France would not sign the test ban treaty, but he stopped short of denouncing it altogether. On 5 September, France announced it would conduct H-bomb tests in the Pacific Ocean within the next few years. At various times, de Gaulle expressed understanding for the American refusal to aid the development of the French nuclear deterrent. In December 1963, for instance, he said to Sulzberger: "If I were in the position of the United States I would not do so either." Even if the Americans would, "they would obviously do it under conditions that would restrain the use of these devices. ... I never believed the United States would offer to help our nuclear military development and I never asked for such aid. And now it is very late. I cannot see what we would gain. We have now the certitude of being able to construct by ourselves our own nuclear and thermonuclear arsenal and we really would not save very much money if such aid were offered, even unconditionally." Sulzberger, *Last of the Giants*, 57. The French journalist Segonzac reported to Washington that French "sources close to the nuclear problems added that even if the United States offered France the same secrets as Britain, without any strings attached, it would probably be turned down because such a proposal would be considered as humiliating, France being quite capable of achieving alone the aim she is pursuing." See *Report from Paris*, Segonzac, 26 September 1963, France-General, CS, NSF, box 72, JFKL.

149. *Public Opinion About NATO and Nuclear Issues in Western Europe*, USIA Report, July 1963, Europe, Papers of Arthur M. Schlesinger Jr., box WH-9, JFKL.

150. Sulzberger, *Age of Mediocrity*, 55-56.

151. American diplomats primarily tried to work around the French by using bilateral channels with Great Britain and Germany. They also attempted to focus attention on perceived shortcomings in NATO's force posture while avoiding a divisive strategic debate. Department of State and Defense to Finletter, Topol 680, 24 November 1963; *NATO Force Planning; Chronology of Actions by Military Committee/Standing Group Concerning NATO Long Term and Force Planning;* and *Views Concerning NATO Force Planning;* background papers, undated, in *NATO Defense Policy Conference, 12/2/1963*, International Meetings and Travel File, NSF, box 33-34, LBJL. The background papers were prepared with a view to the NATO Ministerial Meetings in December 1963 and were discussed by Rusk and McNamara with President Johnson.

152. McNamara and Stikker, memorandum of conversation, 15 December 1963, NATO, General, volume 1, box 35, Agency File, NSF, #12, LBJL. On NATO's consideration of MC 100/1 and the French role, see also Jane E. Stromseth, *The Origins of Flexible Response: NATO's Debate Over Strategy in the 1960s* (New York: St. Martin's Press, 1988), 52-55. To be sure, France was not as isolated as many in Washington believed in its opposition to MC 100/1. British and German views on NATO's strategy were, in fact, closer to those of France than to those of the United States, since they too leaned towards a trip-wire strategy and depreciated the value of conventional forces. As Thomas Finletter, the American ambassador to NATO, reported, "France's position is not likely to appear much more on one end of the extreme, than the U.S.'s on the other." *Views Concerning NATO Force Planning*, background paper, undated, Volume: NATO Defense Policy Conference, 12/2/1963, International Meetings and Travel File, NSF, box 33-34, LBJL.

153. The costs associated with the French nuclear program amounted to approximately twenty-five percent of the French overall defense spending throughout the 1960s, and for part of the decade – from 1965 to 1968 – to approximately half of military equipment spending. At the same time, the defense budget was steadily declining, both as a share of the gross national product (from 5.5 percent in 1960 to 3.6 percent in 1969) and of the national budget (from 28.5 percent in 1960 to 17.9 percent in 1969). The Algerian "peace dividend" was thus funneled off for civilian purposes. Throughout the 1960s, French conventional force goals and equipment fell far behind schedule; in 1963, France had only two partially modernized divisions in West Germany and three light, and poorly equipped, divisions in France. See Gordon, *A Certain Idea of France*, 36-39.

154. *Continuing Elements of De Gaulle's Foreign Policy*, paper by Charles Bohlen, 7 August 1963, France-General, CS, NSF, box 72, JFKL.

155. *Remarks of President Kennedy to the National Security Council Meeting of January 22, 1963*, NSC Meetings 1963, NSF, box 314, JFKL; Mr Hilsman's remarks at directors' meeting on meeting of National Security Council with the President, 1/22/63, Personal Papers of Roger Hilsman, box 5, JFKL.

156. Acheson, for instance, was never quite sure whether Kennedy was sold on his policy report in the spring of 1963, even as it served as a basis of official policy. *Oral history interview with Dean Acheson*, 11.

157. Freeman to Kennedy, letter, 9 February 1963, PKOF, part 3: DAF, RSC.

158. *Oral history interview with Charles S. Murphy*, JFKL, 24.

159. Brinkley, *Dean Acheson*, 189.

160. De Gaulle to Debré, letter, 12 August 1963, in De Gaulle, *Lettres, notes et carnets, Janvier 1961- Décembre 1963* (Paris: Librairie Plon, 1986), 360.

161. *Report from Paris*, Segonzac, 26 September 1963, France-General, CS, NSF, box 72, JFKL. This report was handed to Kennedy as part of his "weekend reading." Segonzac noted that de Gaulle's advisers, such as Alain Peyrefitte, believed Germany was again turning to France as the euphoria of Kennedy's June visit to Berlin and the Rhineland was ebbing away and the United States was shifting its focus toward negotiating the test ban treaty with the Soviets (which reawakened fears that the Kennedy administration would be prepared to make concessions to Moscow against German interests). They also pointed out that once the Six had worked out the Common Agricultural

Policy, they were bound to present a united front against the United States in the Kennedy Round on trade – and that this meant Bonn would be moving closer to Paris.

162. Ball to Kennedy, memorandum, 1 March 1963, PKOF, part 5: CsS, RSC.

163. *Continuing Elements of De Gaulle's Foreign Policy*, paper by Charles Bohlen, 7 August 1963, France-General, CS, NSF, box 72, JFKL.

164. Rusk later wrote: "Rather quickly the Kennedy administration reached a point where we simply did not care what de Gaulle thought except on those matters over which he held a veto. We learned to proceed without him." Rusk, *As I Saw It*, 270-271.

165. *Possibilities and Limitations in Dealing with De Gaulle*, Thomas L. Hughes to Rusk, research memorandum, 6 April 1963, France-General, CS, NSF, box 72, JFKL.

166. De Gaulle, *Lettres, notes et carnets, Janvier 1961- Décembre 1963*, 396.

167. Sorenson, *Kennedy*, 560 -561.

168. James Gavin, "On Dealing With De Gaulle," *Atlantic Monthly* (June 1965): 49; Benjamin C. Bradlee, *Conversations with Kennedy* (New York: Pocket Books, 1976), 97.

169. *Oral history interview with Walt W. Rostow*, 100-101.

170. *Oral history interview with William Tyler*, 3-5.

171. William Tyler recalls how Kennedy during discussions would observe the German Chancellor, who was nearly twice his age and had the appearance of a sphinx with his immobile and vaguely Oriental facial expression, with a "certain feeling of bafflement." *Oral history interview with William Tyler*, 7.

172. Before this visit, Kennedy had been extensively briefed on de Gaulle as a leader, his reading habits, personality, and so on. CIA Briefing Packet, 18 May 1961, France-General, CS, NSF, JFKL.

173. In 1961, in particular, rumors of coup d'états and assassination plots against de Gaulle figured prominently in the reports from the American embassy in Paris. The April 1961 coup attempt by General Challe was also covered extensively. It was commonly believed that after this failed attempt the *pied-noirs* would increase their efforts to assassinate de Gaulle, because this now seemed the only way to stave off Algerian independence. On 8 September 1961, one of those attempts failed because of a faulty detonator in a bomb on the road.

174. In his first major foreign policy speech on 2 July 1957, Kennedy had called for American pressure on France to recognize Algerian independence. Kennedy's criticism of France's Algerian policy also figured prominently in *Strategy of Peace*, 66-81, 99-102, 212-215.

175. Kennedy's letter of support in the face of the insurrection was sent on 23 April 1961, and expressed sympathy for de Gaulle's Algerian policies. Rusk to Gavin, Deptel 4489, 23 April 1961, France-Subjects, De Gaulle Correspondence, CS, NSF, box 73, JFKL. A few weeks later, however, Assistant Secretary of Defense William P. Bundy reported that Kennedy's letter had not persuaded de Gaulle that the United States had played no role whatsoever in the events leading up to the coup attempt. There were reports that General Challe had been encouraged by his conversations with American officers at SHAPE prior to the coup attempt. These officers had reportedly been responsive to Challe's reasoning that an independent Algeria would "open the door to chaos and to Communist influence" and that a "government of pro-American generals would lead to acceptance of greater NATO integration and other US desires." De Gaulle had sup-

posedly already been concerned about these reports before the coup attempt. William P. Bundy to McNamara et al., memorandum, 6 May 1961, France-General, Excerpts from Paris Briefing Book, CS, NSF, box 70, JFKL.

176. *Oral history interview with John Jay Hooker*, JFKL, 29.

177. Sorenson, *Kennedy*, 323.

178. *Oral history interview with Charles Bohlen*, JFKL, 38. Jacqueline Kennedy often complained that American officials were "beastly to de Gaulle" and, according to Sorenson, served as the French ambassador's "pipeline to the White House." *Oral history interview with Peter Lisagor*, JFKL, 75; *Oral history interview with Theodore Sorenson*, JFKL, 107. Lisagor was a journalist who accompanied Kennedy on his trip to Paris and Vienna.

179. The comparison of Kennedy's White House to King Arthur's court was suggested to Theodore H. White by Jacqueline Kennedy. See Reeves, *A Question of Character*, 4.

180. Sorenson, *Kennedy*, 433.

181. McGeorge Bundy to Bohlen, letter, 29 November 1962, France-General, CS, NSF, box 71a, JFKL.

182. *Oral history interview with McGeorge Bundy*, JFKL, 4. Bundy and his staff were themselves instrumental in nurturing this attitude. When relations between Washington and Paris reached a low point in the spring of 1962, Bundy wrote: "I persist in thinking that if we could get the right means of communication we could get back in decent touch with the General – though we might still have disagreement with him on specific points." Bundy to Kennedy, memorandum, 28 May 1962, France-General, CS, NSF, box 71a, JFKL. This memorandum was accompanied by Averell Harriman's reminiscences of FDR's, Churchill's and Stalin's difficulties with de Gaulle, "to indicate to the President that presidential difficulties with de Gaulle did not start in 1961." David Klein emphatically disagreed with Bohlen's conclusion that a meeting of the minds with de Gaulle was not at all possible and argued in favor of an intensified dialogue with Paris. Klein to Bundy, memorandum, 19 August 1963, France-General, CS, NSF, box 72, JFKL.

183. Newhouse, *De Gaulle and the Anglo-Saxons*, 35. Newhouse's critical characterization of Kennedy's attitude is no doubt instilled by his even more critical analysis of de Gaulle's foreign policy.

184. *Oral history interview with Charles Bohlen*, 21. Bohlen recalls that Kennedy had a "curious fascination" with de Gaulle: "He was always trying to find out what made the man tick, why he acted the way he did, and what particular motivation he was working on... ." Every time he returned to the United States, Kennedy would invite him to Palm Beach to talk about de Gaulle: "he was obviously groping around, trying to get something to satisfy him as an explanation ... ."

185. Schlesinger, *A Thousand Days*, 744.

186. Ibid., 743.

187. Alphand, *L'étonnement d'être*, 389.

188. James Gavin, "On Dealing With De Gaulle," 50.

189. Embtel 2569 (Paris), 11/27/63, CF, box 169, NSF, LBJL.

190. Alphand, *L'étonnement d'être*, 389. According to Bohlen, de Gaulle agreed to meet Kennedy in the winter of 1964 "only because he felt it would be very awkward not to do it. De Gaulle clearly had no desire for the meeting ..." because "he felt there were no

subjects they could really reach any useful agreements on." *Oral history interview with Charles Bohlen*, 22.

191. Bundy to Johnson, memorandum, 1 December 1963, Memos to the President, McGeorge Bundy, NSF, box 1, LBJL.

192. *Oral history interview with Charles Bohlen*, 19, 22; Sorenson, *Kennedy*, 573.

193. Transcript of Voice of America Program "Press Conference USA" with Senator Fulbright, USIA, 30 November 1963, France, Country File, memos vol. I, National Security Files, box 169, LBJL. De Gaulle reportedly reacted angrily to Fulbright's statements.

194. *The Damnation of Charles de Gaulle: St. Peter's Advocate Presents the Defense*, paper by Dana Durand (research associate of the Washington Center of Foreign Policy Research), sent to McGeorge Bundy on 25 January 1964. WHCF, Subject File, CO 81, France, box 30, LBJL.

195. See for example Young, *This Blessed Plot*, 99-145.

196. In an interview with Hugo Young in 1994, Couve de Murville said that he thought "the end of the negotiation should have been announced in a softer way. The press conference is the basis for what is universally called de Gaulle's veto. Which is the wrong way to describe it. Everyone agreed that Britain wasn't ready, though only France said that she should wait. The right way to describe what happened is that the negotiations did not succeed." *This Blessed Plot*, 142-143.

197. Peyrefitte recounts de Gaulle as saying: "D'abord, je vais *vider* l'affaire de l'entrée de l'Angleterre dans le Marché commun. *Vider!* [...] Qu'après ça, on n'en parle plus de longtemps." See Peyrefitte, *C'était de Gaulle* 1:332-337.

198. In discussions with Macmillan, Kennedy, and Adenauer, de Gaulle would habitually emphasize the obstacles to British membership. In addition, Couve de Murville later informed Kennedy that as early as October 1962 he felt that Great Britain "would find itself unable to join the Common Market." Kennedy with Couve de Murville et al., memorandum of conversation, 25 May 1963, France-General, CS, NSF, box 72, JFKL.

199. "NATO ministerial meeting, Paris," 12/14/1962. In: Paper, "Early history of the MLF," 18.

200. Newhouse, *De Gaulle and the Anglo-Saxons*, 215.

201. In a conversation with a French embassy official, for instance, Schaetzel was unable to shed much light on the meaning of "a similar arrangement with France" and said that the offer "presumably" excluded assistance on the development of warheads. Schaetzel with Pierre Pelen, memorandum of conversation, 27 December 1962, Skybolt-Nassau (classified), folder 1, Richard E. Neustadt Papers, box 19, JFKL.

202. Kennedy and Macmillan, memorandum of conversation, 19 December 1962, FRUS, 1961-1963, vol. 13, nr. 402.

203. Alphand, *L'étonnement d'être*, 390-391.

204. Bange, *The EEC Crisis of 1963*, 49-51, 73-75.

205. Nassau Follow-Up, record of meeting, 28 December 1962, FRUS, 1961-1963, vol. 13, nr. 410, 1116-1123.

206. *Oral history interview with Dean Rusk*, 1:188.

207. Bundy, *Danger and Survival*, 492.

208. See for example Kolodziej, *French International Policy Under De Gaulle and Pompidou*, 280-281.

209. Richard H. Pells, *Not Like Us: How Europeans Have Loved, Hated, and Transformed American Culture Since World War II* (New York: Basic Books, 1997), 284.

210. De Gaulle, *Memoirs of Hope*, 254.

211. For a good survey of the literature on Kennedy's foreign policy, see Burton I. Kaufmann, "John F. Kennedy as World Leader: A Perspective on the Literature," in Michael J. Hogan, ed., *America in the World: The Historiography of American Foreign Relations Since 1941* (Cambridge: Cambridge University Press, 1991), 326-357. Apart from early eulogists of Kennedy, such as Arthur M. Schlesinger, Jr., and Theodore C. Sorensen, most historians have been very critical of Kennedy's conduct of foreign affairs. See in particular Paterson, *Kennedy's Quest for Victory*.

212. As James Gavin remarked in 1965: "Even though some of the top policy makers around the President shared his more detached and objective view of General de Gaulle, it is not surprising, when I recall the attitudes I found at operating levels of the State Department, that the past four years have been rather sterile of accomplishment in our dealings with France and the Common Market countries." James Gavin, "On Dealing With De Gaulle," *Atlantic Monthly* (June 1965): 51.

213. Couve de Murville, *Une politique étrangère, 1958-1969*, 106-107.

214. Spaak, *The Continuing Battle*, 406.

215. Monnet, *Memoirs*, 458.

216. Diebold, "A Watershed with Some Dry Sides," 259.

217. Flexible response was adopted as the Alliance's strategy only after the French withdrawal from NATO in 1966, and by then, this strategy had been transformed into something quite different from the strategy which originally had been proposed by McNamara.

218. As quoted in Alfred Grosser, "France and Germany in the Atlantic Community," *International Organization* 12 (Summer 1963): 566.

219. Klein to Bundy, memorandum, 27 November 1962, France-General, CS, NSF, box 71a, JFKL.

220. *The US and De Gaulle – The Past and the Future*, unsigned memorandum to Kennedy, 30 January 1963, PKOF, part 5: CsF, RSC.

Notes to Chapter Four – The Demise of the Last Atlantic Project

1. On Johnson's discomfiture with the vice presidency, see Robert Dallek, *Flawed Giant: Lyndon Johnson and His Times, 1961-1973* (New York: Oxford University Press, 1998), 4-53. Garner had been FDR's vice president from 1933 to 1941. On his colorful judgments on the vice presidency, see Jules Witcover, *Crapshoot: Rolling the Dice on the Vice Presidency* (New York: Crown, 1992), 400; Bascom N. Timmons, *Garner of Texas: A Personal History* (New York: Harper Brothers, 1948), 176, 178.

2. Lyndon B. Johnson, *Public Papers of the Presidents of the United States: Lyndon B. Johnson, 1963*, vol. x (Washington DC: GPO, xxxx), 8-10.

3. While there is still no monograph of the history of the MLF, there are many partial analyses. For those that consider the MLF in the framework of the Franco-American relationship, see Bozo, *Two Strategies for Europe*, 110-121; Cogan, *Oldest Allies, Guarded Friends*, 121-150; and Lloyd Gardner, "Johnson and De Gaulle," in Paxton and Wahl, *De*

Gaulle and the United States, 257-278. See also Winand, *Eisenhower, Kennedy, and the United States of Europe*, 203-243, 340-357, passim. Particularly helpful on the Johnson administration's MLF policies are Frank Costigliola, "Lyndon B. Johnson, Germany, and the 'End of the Cold War'," in Warren I. Cohen and Nancy Bernkopf Tucker, eds., *Lyndon Johnson Confronts the World: American Foreign Policy, 1963-1968* (Cambridge: Cambridge University Press, 1994), 173-210; Philip Geyelin, *Lyndon B. Johnson and the World* (New York: Frederick A. Praeger, 1966), chap. 7; Hammond, *LBJ and the Presidential Management of Foreign Relations*, 108-165; Thomas Schwartz, *Lyndon Johnson and Europe: In the Shadow of Vietnam* (Cambridge: Harvard University Press, 2003), 39-63, passim; and Steinbruner, *The Cybernetic Theory of Decision*, chap. 9. Also Bundy, *Danger and Survival*, 492-498, 503-504; Stromseth, *The Origins of Flexible Response*, 75-88, passim; Rostow, *The Diffusion of Power*, 392-394. For the British perspective, see Pierre, *Nuclear Politics*, 217-300. On the MLF and Germany, see Catherine McArdle Kelleher, *Germany and the Politics of Nuclear Weapons* (New York: Columbia University Press, 1975), 228-269; and George McGhee, *At the Creation of a New Germany: From Adenauer to Brandt. An Ambassador's Account* (New Haven: Yale University Press, 1989). Lawrence S. Kaplan focuses on the Kennedy administration in "The MLF Debate," in Douglas Brinkley and Clifford Hackett, eds., *Jean Monnet: The Path to European Unity* (New York: St. Martin's Press, 1991), 51-65. Alastair Buchan's contemporary treatment of the MLF remains informative, see *The Multilateral Force: An Historical Perspective*, Adelphi Papers No. 13 (London: The Institute for Strategic Studies, October 1964). For a critical point of view on the MLF, see Kissinger, *The Troubled Partnership*, chap. 5; for an analytical statement in support of the MLF, see Robert E. Osgood, *The Case for the MLF* (Washington: Washington Center for Foreign Policy Research, 1964).

4. Doris Kearns, *Lyndon Johnson and the American Dream* (New York: Harper, 1976), 170. See also Lyndon B. Johnson, *The Vantage Point: Perspectives of the Presidency, 1963-1969* (New York: Holt, Rinehard, Winston, 1971), 18; and Dallek, *Flawed Giant*, 54-62.

5. Both his Senate years and the vice presidency had initiated Johnson in the realm of diplomacy. As senator, he regularly traveled abroad. As vice president, he embarked on a summit trip every three months, visiting dozens of foreign countries and shaking hundreds of thousands of hands. President Kennedy, who realized that Johnson chafed inwardly at his subservient role as vice president, frequently enlisted him as personal emissary. In August 1961, Kennedy sent him to Berlin at the time the wall was being erected to manifest the United States' security commitment to the city. Johnson's diplomatic activities are chronicled by Elmer Plishke, "Lyndon Baines Johnson as a Diplomat in Chief," in Bernard J. Firestone and Robert C. Vogt, eds., *Lyndon Baines Johnson and the Uses of Power* (New York: Hofstra University, 1988), 257-286. For Johnson's vice presidential travels, see also Dallek, *Flawed Giant*, 12-20.

6. According to Walt Rostow, Eisenhower once told Johnson that he could not have conducted a "civilized" foreign policy without the cooperation of the Texan senator: "My man, the Republican in the Senate, was Bill Knowland, who was a dreadful, simple isolationist, and you boxed him out and we could work together." Walt W. Rostow, interview by the author, tape recording, Austin, TX, 27 November 1990.

7. As cited in Robert Kleiman, "Background for Atlantic Partnership," in Karl H. Cerny and Henry W. Briefs, eds., NATO in Quest of Cohesion (New York: Frederick A. Praeger, 1965), 457.

8. Speech by Vice President Johnson on 8 November 1963, in Department of State Bulletin, 2 December 1963, 852.

9. Rowland Evans and Robert Novak, Lyndon B. Johnson: The Exercise of Power. A Political Biography (London: George Allen and Union Ltd., 1966), 391.

10. Kearns, Lyndon Johnson and the American Dream, 175.

11. Louis Heren, No Hail, No Farewell: The Johnson Years (London: Weidenfeld and Nicolson, 1970), 157. When the new NATO Secretary General Manlio Brosio presented his credentials to Johnson in September 1964, he was disquieted to find that Johnson revealed very little knowledge and understanding of NATO issues. Instead, Johnson had insisted on explaining the charts that tracked his electoral campaign on a state-by-state basis, concentrating for the benefit of his NATO visitor on the situation in doubtful states. Sulzberger, Age of Mediocrity, 109.

12. George Ball, for one, recalls that his personal rapport with Johnson had been difficult because the new president was of "a breed I had known only from literature, legend, or at a distance." Ball, The Past Has Another Pattern, 316-317.

13. Kearns, Lyndon Johnson and the American Dream, 171.

14. Once he scolded an unfortunate aid in the presence of Prime Minister Nehru of India for failing to set up a press conference. Evans and Novak, Lyndon B. Johnson, 328-329. For Johnson's reputation, see also Schlesinger, A Thousand Days, 611.

15. Ball, The Past Has Another Pattern, 318.

16. Schlesinger, A Thousand Days, 646.

17. Rusk and de Gaulle, memorandum of conversation, 24 November 1963, "President's Meetings, 11/25-29/63," DSDUF, NSF, #49a, box 1, LBJL. See also Alphand's account of de Gaulle's awe-inspiring performance during Kennedy's funeral, in L'étonnement d'être, 414-416. Alphand also reveals that an anonymous death threat had been issued against de Gaulle while in Washington.

18. Oral history interview with George Ball, LBJL, 12. Ball had prepared Johnson for his reception of world leaders at Kennedy's funeral.

19. Some 220 of the world's leaders – representing 92 countries, five international organizations, and the Vatican – had gathered at the funeral ceremonies. See Plishke, "Lyndon Baines Johnson as Diplomat in Chief," 257.

20. "President's conversations with:", President's meetings, 11/25 - 29/63, DSDUF, NSF, box 1, #47, LBJL.

21. Bundy to President, memorandum, 20 December 1963, Memos to the President, McGeorge Bundy, NSF, box 1, LBJL.

22. Bohlen to Secretary of State, Embtel 2527 (Paris), 25 November 1963, Country File, NSF, box 169, LBJL. Johnson mentioned Bohlen's cable in his memoirs as well. See The Vantage Point, 23.

23. Johnson, The Vantage Point, 23.

24. "French-American relations," memorandum of conversation, 25 November 1963, DSDUF, NSF, box 1, LBJL.

25. See note 20 above.

26. See note 24 above.
27. This seems buttressed by the fact that Johnson excused himself directly after the meeting to an audience of some thirty state governors: "I am sorry I am late. General de Gaulle had to return to Paris. He has had a long day of it and he is flying back tonight. We talked a little longer than I anticipated. Even then we did not finish, so we have another meeting set up for early in the year when he comes back to this country." Johnson, *Public Papers*, 1963-1964:4.
28. Tyler and Alphand, memorandum of conversation, 26 November 1963, Country File, NSF, box 169, LBJL.
29. Bohlen to Secretary of State, Embtel 2544 (Paris), 27 November 1963, DSDUF, NSF, box 1, LBJL.
30. De Gaulle told Cyrus Sulzberger of the *New York Times* that he did not envision such a trip. Sulzberger, *Age of Mediocrity*, 57.
31. During the transition year 1964, Johnson would not leave the country for any extensive trips. As he told Sulzberger on 23 July 1964: "I have no plans to see him [de Gaulle] as of now. But after the elections, when there is a vice president and I can travel, I am not averse to meeting anyone, anywhere, older and younger than I. But many people are alarmed whenever I walk across the street. You can't take any chances with the thought of a man like [Speaker of the House John] McCormack moving into the White House." *Age of Mediocrity*, Sulzberger, 105.
32. The Johnson administration denounced the French move to recognize China in a short statement to newspaper correspondents on 27 January 1964: "We have repeatedly expressed to the Government of France the reasons why we consider that this would be an unfortunate step, particularly at a time when the Chinese communists are actively promoting aggression and subversion in Southeast Asia and elsewhere." *Atlantic Community Quarterly* 2, no. 1 (Spring 1964): 146.
33. Kearns, *Lyndon Johnson and the American Dream*, 195.
34. *Oral history interview with Charles Bohlen*, 18.
35. After Kennedy's funeral, as Peyrefitte reveals, he dismissed his American counterpart as a "cowboy-radical" and a "sergeant who's been crowned." Peyrefitte, *C'était de Gaulle* 2 :48. See also Lacouture, *De Gaulle: The Ruler*, 366, 379. There was also sufficient cause for Couve de Murville to mark the change of leadership in the White House in his memoirs: "Lyndon Johnson était aussi secret et énigmatique que son prédécesseur était ouvert et porté à la discussion." Couve de Murville, *Une politique étrangère*, 1958-1969, 121.
36. Editorials, books, stories, and articles in Stanley Hoffmann, "Cursing de Gaulle Is Not a Policy," *The Reporter*, 30 January 1964, 38-41. The engagement of American government officials in a campaign against de Gaulle was recognized and criticized by Dana Durand in a paper for the White House. Durand, "The Damnation of Charles de Gaulle."
37. Johnson, *The Vantage Point*, 23. As early as January 1964, the *New York Times* recognized the change of attitude at the highest levels in Washington with regard to de Gaulle: "Today the General is no longer viewed as a 10-foot-tall creator of obstacles, but rather as a peculiarly willful obstructionist. His notions of self-interest strike Washington as annoying and misguided where a year ago they seemed wholly defeating and malevo-

lent. President Johnson is setting the tone, and his equanimity is probably more conducive to composure than the simultaneous campaign of the Department of State to curb all forms of Francophobia." *New York Times*, 7 January 1964.

38. See for instance Geyelin, *Lyndon B. Johnson and the World*, 93; Sulzberger, *Age of Mediocrity*, 177. In a conversation with Paul Reynaud, Johnson used similar imagery in telling that whenever de Gaulle threw his "beanballs" at him, he had been ducking them. President and Paul Reynaud, memorandum of conversation, 25 May 1965, Country File, NSF, box 171, LBJL.

39. McGeorge Bundy wrote to Charles Bohlen: "We continue to make it a guideline here ... that the President will never be caught on picking a fight with General de Gaulle – or giving him the satisfaction of appearing to have pinked us." Bundy to Bohlen, letter, 25 July 1964, Files of McGeorge Bundy, NSF, box 15-16, LBJL.

40. Sulzberger, *Age of Mediocrity*, 177.

41. Ball, *The Past Has Another Pattern*, 336; *Oral history interview with Dean Rusk* 1:6, 4:17. David Bruce, the ambassador to London who frequently discussed de Gaulle's policies with Johnson, was struck by the president's temperateness: "I have never heard him say a critical word about the General; but there were some critical words about what he thought was his lack of judgment, his failure to view these affairs in a proper perspective, but always winding up with a tribute to General de Gaulle as a really great man." *Oral history interview with David Bruce*, LBJL, 7.

42. For a record of Johnson's meetings with Gaston Defferre, the socialist mayor of Marseille, see Department of State to Embassy Paris, Deptel 4868, 27 March 1964, Country File, NSF, box 169, LBJL; Rusk to President, memorandum, 18 March 1964, Country File, NSF, box 169, LBJL.

43. Dean Rusk: "He [Johnson] did not believe in personal vendettas among people carrying top political responsibility." *Oral history interview with Dean Rusk* 4:17.

44. Walt W. Rostow, interview.

45. Bohlen to President, memorandum, *Reflections on Current French Foreign Policy and Attitudes Toward the United States and Recommendations*, 11 March 1964, Country File, NSF, box 169, LBJL.

46. Taking issue with Bohlen's recommendation, Averell Harriman, for instance, guessed that de Gaulle was "amazed that he has gotten away with his disregard for American interests so far without strong reaction to him from us." Drawing on personal experience ("I have known de Gaulle since 1941, and I have seen him under many conditions"), Harriman advocated a firmer approach to de Gaulle. Harriman to Secretary of State, memorandum, 18 March 1964, Country File, NSF, box 169, #144a, LBJL.

47. Journalist Drew Pearson pressed Johnson to replace Bohlen – "a man can outwear his impact" – with General Omar Bradley, the man who liberated Paris in World War II but waited a day so de Gaulle could ride in at the head of the allied forces. Drew Pearson to President, memorandum, 27 September 1965, Country File, NSF, box 172, LBJL. Walter Lippmann, too, urged Johnson to replace Bohlen, believing that he was too hostile to de Gaulle. See Steel, *Walter Lippmann and the American Century*, 399, 555. Johnson probably never seriously contemplated Bohlen's dismissal, for he valued the advice of his ambassador. The first time he met with Bohlen, he leaned over, patted him on the knee, and said: "Chip, I am glad you're in the government. I want you to

know that you can stay in Paris as long as I'm in the White House." Sulzberger, *Age of Mediocrity*, 160.

48. Bohlen himself has claimed to have convinced Johnson that nothing could be done to change the direction of de Gaulle's policies. See Charles E. Bohlen, *Witness to History, 1929-1969* (New York: W.W. Norton & Co., 1973), 503. Bohlen's stance was moreover supported by McGeorge Bundy. Bundy's files show that he maintained close personal contact with Bohlen and shared the latter's basic assessment of de Gaulle. *Correspondence with Ambassadors*, Files of McGeorge Bundy, NSF, box 15–16, LBJL.

49. Geyelin, *Lyndon B. Johnson and the World*, 93.

50. Johnson and Reynaud, memorandum of conversation, 25 May 1965, Country File, NSF, box 171, LBJL.

51. Sulzberger, *Age of Mediocrity*, 178.

52. Johnson, *The Vantage Point*, 305. On Johnson's attitude towards de Gaulle, see also H. W. Brands, Jr., "Johnson and De Gaulle: American Diplomacy *Sotto Voce*," *Historian* 49 (1987): 482-485; and Gardner, "Johnson and De Gaulle," 257-278.

53. Geyelin, *Lyndon B. Johnson and the World*, 43; Kleiman, "Background for Atlantic Partnership," 456.

54. Alastair Buchan, "Is This NATO Crisis Necessary?" *The New Republic* 151 (August 1964): 19-21.

55. Bundy to President, memorandum, 6 December 1963, Memos to the President, NSF, box 1, LBJL. Bundy wrote that Kennedy had felt that the initiative should come from Europe, whereas the State Department ("not so much Dean Rusk") continuously urged strong American leadership and diplomatic pressure "on every front."

56. On 5 December, Acheson had sent Johnson a memorandum outlining the "do's and don'ts" of American policies toward Germany. Apart from the MLF, Acheson stressed the importance of continued support for European integration. See Brinkley, *Dean Acheson*, 207. Rostow, too, pressed the importance of forging ahead on the MLF with characteristic hyperbole: "If the multilateral solution is shot down now, as it was in 1932, the swing to the Right is all too likely to repeat itself." Rostow to Johnson, memorandum, 5 December 1963, Subject File, NSF, box 23, LBJL.

57. *Meeting on MLF at the White House, December 6, 1963*, memorandum of conversation, 18 December 1963, Subject File, NSF, box 22, LBJL.

58. *Briefing of General Eisenhower on MLF*, memorandum of conversation, 15 January 1964, Subject File, NSF, box 22, #24, LBJL; and *Briefing for the President*, paper, 6 December 1963, Subject File, NSF, box 22, #34, LBJL.

59. J.J. Lynch to Secretary of Navy, memorandum, 18 June 1964, Subject File, NSF, box 22, #40, LBJL.

60. Sulzberger, *Age of Mediocrity*, 63.

61. Thomas Finletter, for instance, the American ambassador at NATO who had been a staunch supporter of the project, decided to bend his steps to Washington after he had spoken with Harold Wilson. Wilson, who was widely expected to become British prime minister later that year, had told Finletter of his belief that "President Johnson is 'indecisive' about the support he intends to give to the Alliance in general and to this nuclear sharing idea … ." *Oral history interview with Thomas K. Finletter*, LBJL, 13-15.

62. Secretary General Stikker told Sulzberger at a lunch in February: "The Germans are trying a new approach on getting atomic weapons. They privately acknowledge that the MLF is a dead turkey and Heinrich Krone [of the so-called Gaullist wing in the CDU] came to Paris last month to ask de Gaulle for secret collaboration between the Germans and the French on nuclear weapons. He was specifically charged by Erhard ... and – I emphasize this word – Adenauer." Sulzberger, *Age of Mediocrity*, 63.

63. Rostow to Rusk, memorandum, 6 April 1964, Subject File, NSF, box 22, #62, LBJL.

64. Most American officials believed that de Gaulle was among the least interested to elevate Germany to nuclear status since he was determined to preserve France's nuclear monopoly in Western Europe. De Gaulle indeed never made any such offer. In August 1964, Bohlen asked Couve de Murville about persistent rumors that de Gaulle had suggested some form of nuclear cooperation with Germany in a visit to Bonn. The French foreign minister denied that nuclear matters had ever been discussed with the Germans, except in 1958 "when they were told [by de Gaulle] that there would be no discussions of nuclear matters between the two countries." Embassy to Secretary of State, Embtel 1132 (Paris), 28 August 1964, Country File, France, box 170, LBJL.

65. Rostow remembered that the episode caused "anxiety" at the highest level and that he had "never seen harder faces among officials of the United States." Walt W. Rostow, interview. See also Rostow's observations in *The Diffusion of Power*, 241-242.

66. Rostow to Rusk, memorandum, 6 April 1964, Subject File, NSF, box 22, #62, LBJL.

67. As recalled by Henry Owen. *Oral history interview with Henry Owen*, LBJL, 8.

68. *Discussion of the MLF at the White House*, memorandum of conversation, 10 April 1964, Subject File, NSF, box 22, #14, LBJL. Hammond also notes the importance of the April meeting, but he wrongly states that Bundy did not participate nor did he make use of the available documentary record for his account. Hammond, *LBJ and the Presidential Management of Foreign Relations*, 117.

69. Steinbruner, *The Cybernetic Theory of Decision*, 283.

70. Johnson's decision on the MLF was interpreted by some officials as a matter of loyalty to Kennedy. Walt W. Rostow, interview.

71. Four years later, Finletter said that Johnson expressed himself in "very categorical" terms at the meeting. He recalled Johnson as saying: "Well, ... I am tired of this nonsense. And we are going ahead with the MLF; it is to the interest of all concerned; and there is going to be no indecision about the United States on this; and I now give the following instructions: You, George Ball, you will see to it that Congress is apprised of all of this and that the necessary steps are taken there; and you (to me), Tom, you will see to it that our allies understand that we are backing this and we want their full support on it and so forth. And your instructions are to get the necessary documents ready for signature by the end of this calendar year." *Oral history interview with Thomas K. Finletter*, 15-16. Owen and Rostow have similar recollections. *Oral history interview with Henry D. Owen*, 8; Walt W. Rostow, interview. On Finletter's subsequent activities on behalf of the MLF in Europe, see McGhee, *At the Creation of a New Germany*, 137-138.

72. Klein to Bundy, letter, 20 June 1964, Subject File, NSF, box 22, #44a, LBJL.

73. Geyelin, *Lyndon B. Johnson and the World*, 160.

74. Only days after Johnson's decision, Walt Rostow wrote an article for *Die Welt*'s special issue on the fifteenth anniversary of NATO, in which he professed that the Johnson

administration was strongly committed to the MLF as "the best solution to a European desire for more responsibility in nuclear defense." *Die Welt*, 16 April 1964.

75. The administration's dealings with Congress were, however, poorly conceived. A number of the scheduled sessions with the involved committees were postponed and never rescheduled. Besides, Congress was preoccupied with other issues. Steinbruner, *The Cybernetic Theory of Decision*, 286. NSC staff member David Klein on Rusk's testimony before the Joint Committee on Atomic Energy: "The Committee pressed the point that the MLF was a Rube Goldberg military device conjured up for political purposes and the Secretary's responses were not as effective as they might have been. However, except for Senator Anderson, I would not characterize the atmosphere as hostile. The MLF is clearly short on avowed Congressional supporters." Klein to Bundy, letter, 20 May 1964, Subject File, NSF, box 22, LBJL.

76. *MLF Information Activities*, USIA memorandum, 1 June 1964, "Multilateral Force, Cables, vol.II", Subject File, NSF, box 22, LBJL.

77. As cited in Camps, *European Unification in the Sixties*, 13.

78. Rusk to Department of State, Embtel 11020 (The Hague), 14 May 1964, International Meeting and Travel File, NSF, box 33-34, LBJL.

79. Aldo Moro's coalition government in Italy was back on its feet after a crisis and indicated that it was prepared to sign an MLF agreement in 1964. Reports from London indicated that there had also been a thaw in British resistance. In Belgium and the Netherlands, there was a significant increase in top-level support for the MLF: "Spaak's persuasive rationale has [...] been centered around the MLF's capacity to prevent Franco-German nuclear cooperation rather than to satisfy German desires for a national nuclear force." J.J. Lynch to Secretary of Navy, memorandum, 18 June 1964, Subject File, NSF, box 22, #40, LBJL.

80. "Joint Statement Following Discussions with Chancellor Erhard of Germany," in Johnson, *Public Papers*, {vol#}:771-772.

81. *NATO Ministerial Meeting at the Hague, May 1964*, memorandum of conversation, 18 March 1964, International Meeting and Travel, NSF, box 33-34, LBJL.

82. Kelleher, *Germany and the Politics of Nuclear Weapons*, chap. 9 and 10.

83. *The Coming Crisis on the MLF*, paper by Alastair Buchan, 23 June 1964, Subject File, NSF, box 23, LBJL. To be sure, similar assessments appeared in the reporting from the American embassy in Germany. Hillenbrand to Department of State, Embtel 3540 (Bonn), 1 April 1964, Subject File, NSF, box 22, LBJL.

84. Ludwig Erhard, "European policy of the German federal government", address to the Christian Social Union Party State Convention in Munich, quoted in *The Atlantic Community Quarterly* 2, no.3 (Fall 1964): 377.

85. It was, for instance, hoped in both Washington and Bonn that the pledge of June 1964 to ready an agreement before the end of the year would help to galvanize the more diffident allies. Kelleher, *Germany and the Politics of Nuclear Weapons*, 245.

86. The best account of the British reaction to the MLF proposal remains Pierre, *Nuclear Politics*, chap. 9 and 10.

87. Hansard, 30 January 1963, vol. 670, no. 46, col. 961.

88. Paragraph 6 of the Nassau agreement mentioned the option of a multinational force. This option would resurface later in proposals for an Atlantic Nuclear Force (ANF) and an Interallied Nuclear Force (IANF).

89. See for instance Sir John Slessor's plea for a multinational force, "better than M.L.F.," in "Multilateral or multinational – an alternative to the M.L.F.," *The Atlantic Community Quarterly* 2 (Summer 1964): 285-291.

90. Pierre, *Nuclear Politics*, 249.

91. Sulzberger, *Last of the Giants*, 1036.

92. Neustadt to Bundy, memorandum, 6 July 1964, Subject File, NSF, box 23, #10, LBJL. Four years later, Neustadt's memorandum found its way to the press; see Andrew Kopkind, "The Special Relationship: The Neustadt Dossier," *New Left Review* 51 (September-October 1968): 11-21. On Neustadt's role, see also Hammond, *LBJ and the Presidential Management of Foreign Relations*, 118-119.

93. Reviewing the state of affairs in early November, Bundy informed Johnson that "the British Labour government has adopted a much more flexible and interested posture than it had taken in opposition." In addition, the American ambassador in London, David Bruce, strongly believed that a "tough" stance with the British on the MLF would eventually bring them on board. Bundy to Johnson, memorandum, 8 November 1964, FRUS, 1964-1968, vol. 13, Western Europe Region, #46. The British professor Alastair Buchan raised another possibility: "There is one other alternative [for a British government], namely to reject the whole train of reasoning which has led to the MLF and throw in her lot strategically with France. There is much to attract Britain's politicians, forced to accept a partnership with a Germany it has barely learnt to trust, and seeing its influence in Washington inevitably declining, to this course." Buchan, however, admitted that a Franco-British nuclear entente was unlikely to happen: "It would … call for such strong nerves, risking the hostility of the United States, Germany and probably the Soviet Union as well, as to be beyond the power, in my view, of the men who lead both the main British political parties of today." Alastair Buchan, *The Coming Crisis on the MLF*, paper, 23 June 1964, Subject File, NSF, box 23, LBJL, 9.

94. Neustadt to Bundy, memorandum, 6 July 1964, Subject File, NSF, box 23, #10, LBJL.

95. Buchan, *The Coming Crisis on the MLF*, 11. Buchan had close connections to Whitehall and was the founding head of the International Institute for Strategic Studies.

96. See also Pierre, *Nuclear Politics*, 251.

97. For a discussion of the ANF proposal, see Pierre, *Nuclear Politics*, 276-283.

98. For Ball's conversation with Wilson, see Ball to Department of State, telegram, 2 December 1964, FRUS, 1964-1968, vol. 13, Western Europe Region, #54. See also Harold Wilson, *A Personal Record: The Labour Government, 1964-1970* (Boston: Little, Brown and Company, 1971), 46; and Steinbruner, *The Cybernetic Theory of Decision*, 303.

99. Steinbruner, *The Cybernetic Theory of Decision*, 304.

100. The paper, dated 8 December 1964 and entitled US Comments on the UK Proposal of a Project for an Atlantic Nuclear Force, is printed in FRUS, 1964-1968, vol. 13, Western Europe Region, #61 (attachment). Besides restating the American position on the MLF, the paper stated that the United States would be willing to rename the force – if this would help to make the proposal acceptable to the British – but believed "a decision on the name should be reserved to later multilateral negotiations." Also Richard M. Moose to

Secretary of State et al., memorandum, 14 December 1964, Subject File, NSF, box 23, #27, LBJL.

101. Account of Johnson-Wilson conversation based on Johnson's debriefing to McGeorge Bundy: memorandum for the record, 7 December 1964, FRUS, 1964-1968, vol. 13, Western Europe Region, #58. For Wilson's slightly different recollection (in which he essentially claims to have killed off the MLF), see Wilson, A Personal Record, 47-51. See also Geyelin, Lyndon B. Johnson and the World, 173-174; and Steinbruner, The Cybernetic Theory of Decision, 307-308.

102. Department of State Bulletin, vol. VI, no. 1331, 28 December 1964, 902-904.

103. Bundy to President, memorandum, 10 December 1964, Memos to the President, McGeorge Bundy, NSF, box 2, LBJL.

104. Steinbruner, The Cybernetic Theory of Decision, 308.

105. After a meeting with Rusk on December 14 in Paris, Dutch Foreign Minister Joseph Luns commented that the American attitude on the MLF had become "rather flexible" after the Johnson-Wilson talks. Howe to Rusk, Embtel 440 (The Hague), 15 December 1964, International Meetings and Travel File, NSF, box 33-34, LBJL.

106. New York Times, 21 December 1964.

107. Johnson had shown NSAM 322 to Reston as the document came to his office for signature. See Geyelin, Lyndon B. Johnson and the World, 176; Steinbruner, The Cybernetic Theory of Decision, 309.

108. Pierre, Nuclear Politics, 279.

109. Kohl, French Nuclear Diplomacy, 240.

110. On de Gaulle's views of the MLF, see Kolodziej, French International Policy Under De Gaulle and Pompidou, 114-120; Bozo, Two Strategies for Europe, 110-121; Cogan, Oldest Allies, Guarded Friends, 128-131.

111. Bohlen, for instance, reported in January 1965: "Two years ago France told the United States that it would not participate presumably because all of its resources in this regard were fully utilized by its own force de dissuasion, but it had no objection to the project as outlined nor any objection to any other member of the alliance participating." Bohlen to Secretary of State, Embtel 3798, 5 January 1965, Committee File, Committee on Nuclear Proliferation, NSF, box 5, LBJL. German participation was condoned by Jacques Baumel, a prominent Gaullist politician, in a speech in Munich on 14 February 1964. Taylor to Department of State, Embtel 330 (Munich), 17 February 1964, Subject File, NSF, box 24, LBJL. And when Erhard paid a visit to Paris in February 1964, de Gaulle reportedly expressed "understanding" for Germany's interest in the MLF. McGhee to Rusk, Embtel 2929 (Bonn), 18 February 1964, Country File, France, NSF, box 169, LBJL.

112. Members of Erhard's cabinet were known to scorn de Gaulle's policies in private. Kelleher, Germany and the Politics of Nuclear Weapons, 267.

113. André François-Poncet in Le Figaro, 18 February 1964.

114. Articles by Theo Sommer in Die Zeit and Kurt Becker in Die Welt. As cited in Kelleher, Germany and the Politics of Nuclear Weapons, 239.

115. As quoted in Kelleher, Germany and the Politics of Nuclear Weapons, 240. Strauss had a consuming interest in gaining access to nuclear weapons and, as defense minister, had been the initiator of contacts to this effect with France in 1957.

116. Kelleher, *Germany and the Politics of Nuclear Weapons*, 64-74, 149, 239-240. On Strauss and the MLF, see also McGhee, *At the Creation of a New Germany*, 88.

117. The hidden weakness of Erhard's policy of support for the MLF was also recognized by Helga Haftendorn, a German professor, well before de Gaulle began his campaign to scuttle the force. "The position of Bonn remains particularly delicate ... vis-à-vis Washington and Paris as long as the United States and France do not see eye-to-eye with each other," Haftendorn observed. "It would become untenable if either side makes a conscious effort to force the Germans to a 'choice' between competing mystiques of a 'third force' and an 'Atlantic Community'." From a paper delivered by Helga Haftendorn of the German Society for Foreign Policy before the 2nd Arms Control and Disarmament Symposium in Ann Arbor. Mentioned in: Paper by John Newhouse, "Balancing the Risks in the MLF," 20 May 1964, Subject File, NSF, box 22, #45a, LBJL.

118. Durbrow to Secretary of State, Airgram POLTO A-65, 31 July 64, Country File, NSF, box 170, #65, LBJL.

119. McGhee, *At the Creation of a New Germany*, 149.

120. Kelleher, *Germany and the Politics of Nuclear Weapons*, 248; Newhouse, *De Gaulle and the Anglo-Saxons*, 268. The American embassy in Bonn reported on the following account making the rounds in Bonn. Erhard: "If I understand you correctly, you are asking for a political, economic, and military contribution to the French *force de frappe*. May I ask who would make the final decisions on the use of this weapon?" When de Gaulle replied that the *force de frappe* would remain under national control, Erhard stated: "Then you are asking me to choose between a small bang under French control and a large bang under American control." McGhee to Secretary of State, Embtel 284 (Bonn), 23 July 1964, Subject File, NSF, box 24, #27, LBJL.

121. In the same vein, *Die Zeit*'s editorial on the summit was entitled "Paris's shock therapy."

122. As reported from the American embassy in Bonn. McGhee to Secretary of State, Embtel 284 (Bonn), 23 July 1964, Subject File, NSF, box 24, #27, LBJL. The American embassy in Bonn moreover reported that it "would not find it implausible for de Gaulle, before it's too late, to step up his pressure on the FRG against participation [in the MLF]. This course is not dissimilar from de Gaulle's veto of UK entry, a step he was apparently compelled to take by the inner logic of his own view of Europe." Embassy to Department of State, Embtel 380 (Bonn), 30 July 1964, Country File, NSF, box 170, #60, LBJL.

123. France, Ambassade de France, *Major Addresses 1964-1967*, 23.

124. Johnson's moderate response to de Gaulle's press conference reflected the advice of his aides. While acknowledging that "the General really has given the President no option but to make it clear that he does not share many of the General's views," Klein recommended against meddling in Franco-German affairs: "the Germans will handle this their own way and anything from our side might complicate their lives." Klein to Bundy, memorandum, 23 July 1964, Country File, NSF, box 170, LBJL.

125. Thomas Hughes to Rusk, intelligence note, 7 October 1964, Subject File, NSF, box 23, #42, LBJL.

126. Erhard to Johnson, letter, 30 September, FRUS, 1964-1968, vol. 13, Western Europe Region, #36. Erhard's letter shows that he was also concerned with achieving agree-

ment on the MLF before the United Nations General Assembly could adopt resolutions opposing it and before any meeting he might have with Khrushchev. Grewe delivered the letter to Secretary Rusk on 2 October. He also talked extensively with Ball and other officials about how to have an agreement on the MLF ready by the end of the year. Ball et al., memorandum of conversation, 6 October 1964, FRUS, 1964-1968, vol. 13, Western Europe Region, #37.

127. Cited in Steinbruner, *The Cybernetic Theory of Decision*, 290. After the press conference, German spokesmen tried to repair the damage by denying that a bilateral deal was in the making. See Kelleher, *Germany and the Politics of Nuclear Weapons*, 248. On the Grewe "fiasco," see also Hammond, *LBJ and the Presidential Management of Foreign Relations*, 121-123.

128. Klein, citing the German embassy, stated that "...instead, he [Grewe] was given several [signals] and could pick and choose." Klein to Bundy, memorandum, 20 October 1964, Subject File, NSF, box 23, #35, LBJL.

129. Johnson to Erhard, letter, 7 October 1964, FRUS, 1964-1968, vol. 13, Western Europe Region, #38. See also Steinbruner, *The Cybernetic Theory of Decision*, 290-291. Dean Rusk conveyed a similar message at a press conference on 8 October. *New York Times*, 9 October 1964.

130. Department of State to American embassy in Rome, Deptel 955, 2 June 1964, "Multilateral Force, cables, vol. II," Subject File, NSF, box 22, LBJL.

131. Klein to Bundy, memorandum, 20 October 1964, Subject File, NSF, box 23, #35, LBJL.

132. The effect of the Grewe mission and Erhard's press conference on the French position regarding the MLF is corroborated by an analysis of the American embassy in Paris. Embassy in France to Department of State, telegram, 5 January 1965, FRUS, 1964-1968, vol. 12, Western Europe, #42.

133. Bohlen to Secretary of State, Embtel 2004 (Paris), 7 October 1964, Subject File, NSF, box 24, #116, LBJL.

134. On 23 October, Couve de Murville told Bohlen that French objections to the MLF had been reinforced by the emergence of the possibility of a bilateral agreement between the United States and Germany. Bohlen to Secretary of State, Embtel 2348 (Paris), 23 October 1964, Subject File, NSF, box 24, #114, LBJL. See also Bohlen to Secretary of State, Embtel 2496 (Paris), 28 October 1964, Subject File, NSF, box 24, #111, LBJL. In a circular to European embassies, the State Department requested their assessments on the French campaign against the multilateral force. Circular from Department of State to Embassies in Europe, 13 October 1964, Subject File, NSF, box 24, #4c, LBJL.

135. Department of State to all NATO capitals, Deptel 700, 21 October 1964, Subject File, NSF, box 24, #37, LBJL. De Leusse's call was followed up by Alphand on October 23, 1964. Department of State to Embassy in France, circular telegram, 23 October 1964, FRUS, 1964-1968, vol. 13, Western Europe Region, #42.

136. Camps, *European Unification in the Sixties*, 17.

137. Harrison, *The Reluctant Ally*, 84.

138. On the interrelationship between the MLF crisis and the cereal prices crisis in the Common Market, see Camps, *European Unification in the Sixties*, 16-22.

139. *Le Monde*, 22 October 1964.

140. *L'Année Politique 1964* (Paris: Presse Universitaire de France, 1965), 302.

141. As cited in Newhouse, *De Gaulle and the Anglo-Saxons*, 272-273.

142. A German official recalled that he "was told that unless we gave up the MLF, France would make common cause with those Eastern European states that feared a nuclear Germany in any form." In Kelleher, *Germany and the Politics of Nuclear Weapons*, 250.

143. France, Ambassade de France, *Major Addresses, 1964-1967*, 71-73.

144. Bohlen to Secretary of State, Embtel 2849 (Paris), 11 November 1964, Country File, NSF, box 170, #21, LBJL.

145. After talks with German politicians in Berlin and Bonn, Ball concluded that "the brutal French attack on the MLF [...] has become a major element in the bloody internecine fighting within the CDU" and there was evidence among the "Gaullist" wing of the party of "a considerable amount of anti-American feeling and a strong strain of resurgent German nationalism." Ball to Rusk, memorandum, 17 November 1964, FRUS, 1964-1968, vol. 13, Western Europe Region, #49. For Adenauer's criticism of the MLF as being anti-French, see also McGhee, *At the Creation of a New Germany*, 158.

146. Kelleher, *Germany and the Politics of Nuclear Weapons*, 250. Erhard's conversation with Ambassador McGhee on November 3 reveals the pressure de Gaulle had engendered, as a result of which the chancellor felt an agreement on the MLF could not be signed before early 1965. Embassy in Germany to Department of State, telegram, 4 November 1964, FRUS, 1964-1968, vol. 13, Western Europe Region, #45. On 11 December, Erhard made clear to Washington that his domestic position required that Johnson make a "big pitch personally" with de Gaulle before there could be an agreement on the MLF. Bundy to President, memorandum, 11 December 1964, Memos to the President, McGeorge Bundy, NSF, box 2, LBJL.

147. Hallstein, Ball, etc., memorandum of conversation, 17 November 1964, FRUS, 1964-1968, vol. 13, Western Europe Region, #48.

148. Schroeder informed Rusk that Bonn had taken a flexible approach to the grain price issue in order to bring France to resume its former position of disinterest in the MLF. MLF, memorandum of conversation, 14 December 1964, International Meeting and Travel File, NSF, box 33-34, LBJL. See also Camps, *European Unification in the Sixties*, 20-22.

149. Newhouse, *De Gaulle and the Anglo-Saxons*, 272.

150. This conclusion was also drawn by the Central Intelligence Agency at the time. *De Gaulle, Europe, and the MLF*, CIA Special Report, 27 November 1964, Country File, NSF, #103, LBJL.

151. Harrison, *The Reluctant Ally*, 138-139.

152. Helms to CIA Director, CIA memo, 1 July 1964, Country File, NSF, box 170, #25, LBJL.

153. Embassy in France to Department of State, telegram, 30 November 1964, FRUS, 1964-1968, vol. 13, Western Europe Region, #53.

154. Bohlen to Secretary of State, Embtel 2876 (Paris), 10 November 1964, Country File, NSF, box 170, LBJL. Tying the fate of NATO to the MLF, Couve de Murville moreover said that it was necessary to know "...whether this [MLF] force, far from strengthening the alliance, will not introduce ... a germ of division for which ... France is not responsible." *L'Année Politique 1964*, 302.

155. Department of State to all NATO capitals, Deptel 924, 15 November 1964, Subject File, NSF, #34, LBJL.

156. Bohlen to Secretary of State, Embtel 2791 (Paris), 6 November 1964, Subject File, NSF, box 24, #102, LBJL.

157. The Gaullist *La Nation*, for instance, wrote that the MLF would so degrade the importance of NATO's conventional forces that France would have no reason to keep her army in NATO and, furthermore, that the MLF would symbolize such a complete lack of agreement on NATO defense posture that the presence of allied bases in France would be jeopardized. See Harrison, *The Reluctant Ally*, 84.

158. *Outline for Congressional Briefings*, paper, 22 May 1964, Subject File, NSF, box 22, LBJL.

159. Jordan, *Political Leadership in NATO*, 116. See also Stikker, *Men of Responsibility*, 363-365. After his resignation, Stikker felt free to voice his disagreements with the French and loath their "guerilla" on his person: "On taking office, my initial request to pay my respects to President de Gaulle went unanswered for three months. I then saw him for 25 minutes, and never again, not even to pay a farewell call on my retirement. Prime Minister Debré I saw once for 15 minutes, Prime Minister Pompidou twice for 20 minutes, and Foreign Minister Couve de Murville once for 15 minutes. Only with the Minister of Defence, Messmer, did I have personal contact." Stikker, "France and its Diminishing Will to Cooperate," *Atlantic Community Quarterly* (Summer 1965): 198.

160. Stikker, *Men of Responsibility*, 353.

161. *NATO Ministerial Meeting at the Hague, May 1964*, memorandum of conversation, 18 March 1964, International Meeting and Travel File, NSF, box 33-34, LBJL. Rusk's response to Stikker's proposal had been standoffish at best; he told Stikker that he considered such a change in NATO's decisionmaking procedures unnecessary since the French were "perfectly willing" to let the MLF go ahead as long as they were not required to participate. On circumventing the French within NATO in relation to the MLF, see also Harlan Cleveland, *NATO: The Transatlantic Bargain* (New York: Harper & Row, 1970), 49.

162. On 21 April, Italy had officially proposed Brosio, who had also been a candidate when Stikker was selected. Two days later, the United Kingdom proposed Sir Harold Caccia. After consultations between Italy and the United Kingdom, the British withdrew Caccia's candidacy and Brosio was elected.

163. Jordan, *Political Leadership in NATO*, 171, 190.

164. Tyler to Rusk, memorandum, 26 September 1964, Subject File, NSF, Subject File, NSF, box 22, #35a, LBJL; Department of State to Certain Missions, circular airgram, 8 October 1964, FRUS, 1964-1968, vol. 13, Western Europe Region, #39. Brosio's visit to Washington on 28 and 29 September 1964 was attended with unusual fanfare. He was flown in a presidential plane from New York to Washington, given an honor guard, invited to a large luncheon by President Johnson, and invited along on a presidential visit to Strategic Air Command (SAC) in Omaha.

165. As reported by Edmond Taylor, "What Price MLF?", *The Reporter*, 3 December 1964, 12, 14. Brosio restated his views on NATO and the MLF to Rusk in December. Rusk and Brosio, memorandum of conversation, 13 December 1964, International Meeting and Travel, Subject File, NSF, box 33-34, LBJL.

166. Taylor, "What Price MLF?", 12.

167. Kissinger, *The Troubled Partnership*, 152.

168. Steinbruner, *The Cybernetic Theory of Decision*, 318.

169. *The Coming Crunch in European Policy*, Rostow to Rusk, memorandum, 12 October 1964, NSF, Subject File, #39, box 23, LBJL.

170. Rostow to Rusk, memorandum, 22 October 1964, Subject File, NSF, box 23, #34, LBJL.

171. *Summary of Discussion on MLF, Atlantic Defense and Related Matters*, memorandum of conversation, 31 October 1964, Subject File, NSF, box 25, #13c, LBJL. The meeting was held between Ball and Tyler of the State Department, John McNaughton of the Defense Department, and McGeorge Bundy of the White House staff (who was seconded by Richard Neustadt).

172. The American ambassador in Moscow, Foy Kohler, for instance, reported that Soviet objections to the MLF had to be taken seriously: "In opposing MLF, Moscow is reacting in familiar Pavlovian fashion to Western defense measure. I believe, however, that Soviets are also probably genuinely concerned that MLF will only hasten the day when FRG becomes a nuclear power." Embassy in Soviet Union to Department of State, telegram, 31 July 1964, FRUS, 1964-1968, vol. 13, Western Europe Region, #30.

173. ACDA's objections to the MLF were explicated by its director Adrian Fisher in the summer of 1964. Fisher to Rusk, memorandum, 15 June 1964, *Non-Proliferation and the MLF*, NSF, Subject File, MLF, box 22, #41, LBJL.

174. It should be noted, however, that the Pentagon never mounted an attempt to smother the MLF. Acquiescing in the State Department's lead, it had even carried out much of the planning for the fleet. Secretary Robert McNamara kept his skepticism of the project so private that he was known among MLF proponents as an ally. Ball, for instance, has recalled that "McNamara was very good on the MLF .... During most of the period, he and I sort of fought shoulder-to-shoulder for it." *Oral history interview with George Ball* 2:18.

175. Steinbruner, *The Cybernetic Theory of Decision*, 292; Hammond, *LBJ and the Presidential Management of Foreign Relations*, 113.

176. Klein, for instance, wrote in the margins of the State Department outline for Secretary Rusk's Congressional briefings on the MLF in the spring of 1964: "they have internal inconsistencies – and not a few overstatements and overcommitments" and "some of the stuff is sheer nonsense." Klein to Bundy, memorandum, 4 June 1964, Subject File, NSF, box 22, #2, LBJL.

177. Klein to Bundy, memorandum, 13 October 1964, Subject File, NSF, box 23, #38, LBJL. Klein also believed that the timetable for negotiating an MLF charter by the end of 1964 was unrealistic, since difficult issues of control and finance still had to be resolved and most participants in the MLF Working Group did not seem ready to commit themselves.

178. Klein to Bundy, memorandum, 10 October 1964, Subject File, NSF, box 23, #40, LBJL.

179. *The Future of Nuclear Defense of the Atlantic Alliance*, National Security Action Memorandum 318, President to Secretary of State and Secretary of Defense, 14 November 1964, Memos to the President, NSF, box 2, LBJL. There is little doubt that Bundy had come forward with NSAM 318 in order to wrest control from the lower levels of the State Department. A few days earlier he had written to Johnson that they are "still governed by an attitude of rigid hostility to the French, paternalistic domination of the Germans, and a serene conviction that if only Presidents will say what they tell them to,

all will be well. They also tend to believe, against all experience, that if Uncle Sam plays the firm nanny, the British can be forced out of the independent nuclear business for their own good." Bundy to Johnson, memorandum, 8 November 1964, FRUS, 1964-1968, vol. 13, Western Europe Region, #46.

180. On the Ball Committee, see Hammond, *LBJ and the Presidential Management of Foreign Relations*, 124-125; Steinbruner, *The Cybernetic Theory of Decision*, 292-294.

181. NSAM 318, *The Future of Nuclear Defense of the Atlantic Alliance*.

182. Department of State to all NATO capitals, Deptel 924, 15 November 1964, Subject File, NSF, box 24, #34, LBJL. This was also the gist of Rusk's conversation with de Gaulle on December 15. De Gaulle admitted that he had not taken the MLF seriously early on since he thought it was little more than a military staff study, and Rusk replied that Washington had genuinely believed France had no objection to the MLF per se. Rusk to Department of State, Secto 12 (Paris), 15 December 1964, Subject File, NSF, box 24, #127a, LBJL.

183. David E. Mark, *Considerations involving Germany and France which are pertinent to modifications of the US position on MLF*, paper, 4 November 1964, Subject File, NSF, box 23, #26a, LBJL, 4-5. (Emphasis added.) Mark served on the Test Ban Treaty delegation in Geneva, Switzerland in the late 1950s and at the State Department's Intelligence and Research Bureau in the 1960s.

184. *Summary of Discussion on MLF, Atlantic Defense and Related Matters*, memorandum of conversation, 31 October 1964, Subject File, NSF, box 25, #13c, LBJL.

185. With President Johnson's approval, Rusk gave the following instruction to Bohlen and Finletter on November 19, 1964, prior to a meeting with Couve de Murville: "Although we are firmly committed to creation of a mixed-manned nuclear force, we remain ready at all times to consider in terms of major present-day political and military factors, all other ideas relevant to dealing with the problem of nuclear forces within [the] NATO Alliance. We not only want [the] force to be as broadly based and comprehensive as possible; we are also anxious to insure that it will be closely tied in with all of other nuclear forces available to NATO member states, including those that will not be a part of MLF [it]self." Rusk to Bohlen and Finletter, Deptel 2765, 12 November 1964, Subject File, NSF, box 24, #100, LBJL.

186. Klein to Bundy, memorandum, 5 November 1964, #28; Bohlen to Secretary of State, Embtel 2727 (Paris), 4 November 1964, Subject File, NSF, box 23, #28a; *Possible Political Advantages to the US in the ANF Against the MLF*, paper, 8 December 1964, Subject File, NSF, box 23, #38; McBride to Secretary of State, Embtel 3505 (Paris), 11 December 1964, Subject File, NSF, box 24, #91. All documents are to be found in the LBJ Presidential Library.

187. When Rusk told de Gaulle that French Defense Minister Pierre Messmer's remarks in December about the possibility of coordinating nuclear forces had aroused McNamara's interest, de Gaulle replied that he had cleared Messmer's remarks in advance. He added, however, that such coordination would only become opportune once the *force de frappe* had achieved maturity in 1968 or 1969 – "si nous sommes toujours des alliées, comme je l'espère." De Gaulle also made clear that it would have to take place on a bilateral basis and not under NATO's auspices. Rusk to Department of State, Secto 26 (Paris), 16 December 1964, Subject File, NSF, box 24, #120, LBJL. See also

Bernard Ledwidge, *De Gaulle et les Américains: Conversations avec Dulles, Eisenhower, Kennedy, Rusk, 1958-1964* (Paris: Flammarion, 1984), 139-151.

188. Thomas Hughes, *Review of possible modifications in the MLF to take account of West European problems revealed during the MLF negotiations*, research memorandum, REU 61, 28 October 1964, Subject File, NSF, box 23, #31, iv, LBJL.

189. David E. Mark, *Considerations involving Germany and France which are pertinent to modifications of the US position on MLF*, paper, 4 November 1964, Subject File, NSF, box 23, #26a, LBJL.

190. Bohlen and Finletter to Secretary of State, Embtel 2768 (Paris), 5 November 1964, Subject File, NSF, box 24, #103, LBJL.

191. Rusk to Department of State, Secto 12 (Paris), 15 December 1964, Subject File, NSF, box 24, #127a, LBJL.

192. Undersecretary Tyler was charged with this responsibility. *Summary of Discussion on MLF, Atlantic Defense and Related Matters*, memorandum of conversation, 31 October 1964, Subject File, NSF, box 25, #25, LBJL.

193. Klein to Bundy, memorandum, 5 November 1964, Subject File, NSF, box 23, #28, LBJL.

194. As a result, there was considerable pressure on Washington to publish Eisenhower's reply of October 20, 1958. Walt Rostow and Dr. Fritz Zimmerman, memorandum of conversation, 16 April 1964, *De Gaulle Letter of 1958*, Country File, NSF, box 169, #53, LBJL. Particularly Bohlen thought it to be helpful to clear up some misunderstandings by publishing Eisenhower's letter. Bohlen to Secretary of State, Embtel 237 (Paris), 15 July 1964, Country File, NSF, box 172, LBJL. It was finally published after the French withdrawal from NATO in Senate Committee on Government Operations, *Atlantic Alliance: Hearings before the Subcommittee on National Security and International Operations*, 89th Cong., 2d sess., 1966.

195. Bohlen and Finletter to Secretary of State, Embtel 2768 (Paris), Subject File, NSF, box 24, #103, LBJL; Bohlen to Secretary of State, Embtel 2727 (Paris), 4 November 1964, Subject File, NSF, box 23, #28a, LBJL.

196. MLF, draft memorandum of conversation, 19 September 1964, Files of McGeorge Bundy, NSF, box 18-19, LBJL.

197. Sulzberger, *Age of Mediocrity*, 137-138.

198. The President's News Conference at the LBJ Ranch, 28 November 1964, in Johnson, *Public Papers*, 1963-1964:1616.

199. In June 1964, Rusk and McGeorge Bundy urged Johnson to make a short comment to the skeptical Congressional leadership on the MLF – "We do not want Congress to feel that the diplomats have stolen a march" – Johnson refused to follow up on the recommendation. Bundy to Johnson, memorandum, 15 June 1964, Memos to the President, McGeorge Bundy, box 2, LBJL.

200. Walt W. Rostow, interview by the author.

201. In all of this, the figure of Dean Rusk is strangely absent. He was certainly no die-hard advocate of the MLF. On April 17, 1964, he wrote Ball that he was "unable to make a personal commitment to support MLF with only Germany, Greece and Turkey" and that he considered "elementary [...] that the United States does not expose itself to a major prestige setback by pretending that the American Republic and NATO will come

crumbling down if at the end of the day Italy and Great Britain decide they want none of it." Rusk: "I do not know why we cannot deal with this matter in a businesslike fashion as a constructive worthwhile move without involving it with a second coming of Christ." Rusk to Department of State, telegram, 17 April 1964, FRUS, 1964-1968, vol. 13, Western Europe Region, #18. Yet there is little evidence that Rusk ever applied the brakes on the MLF enthusiasts.

202. For a record of Ball's conversation with Wilson, see Ball to Department of State, telegram, 2 December 1964, FRUS, 1964-1968, vol. 13, Western Europe Region, #54.

203. Ball to Johnson, memorandum, 5 December 1964, "McGeorge Bundy, 10/1-12/31/64," Memos to the President, box 2, LBJL. See also Steinbruner, The Cybernetic Theory of Decision, 302-304.

204. Kissinger to Bundy, letter, 27 November 1964, Files of McGeorge Bundy, Kissinger, box 15-16, LBJL.

205. Bundy to Rusk, McNamara, and Ball, memorandum, 25 November 1964, Memos to the President, McGeorge Bundy, NSF, box 2, LBJL. Apart from being "top secret," the document was classified as "Sensitive – Personal – Literally Eyes Only."

206. Geyelin, Lyndon B. Johnson and the World, 168.

207. Ibid., 162. On Acheson's generally strained personal relationship with Johnson, see Brinkley, Dean Acheson, 204-210.

208. Evans and Novak, Lyndon B. Johnson, 385.

209. The most extensive account of the 5 and 6 December meetings at the White House remains Geyelin, Lyndon B. Johnson and the World, 159-180. Geyelin based his account on interviews with those involved shortly thereafter. In the early 1970s, unnamed officials testified to the accuracy of Geyelin's account. See Steinbruner, The Cybernetic Theory of Decision, 305. David Bruce's diary notes are the only available documentary sources on the meetings of 5 and 6 December. Bruce, diary entry, 6 December 1964, FRUS, 1964-1968, vol. 13, Western Europe Region, #56.

210. On 13 November, Ankara had decided that it was "inappropriate" for the time being to join the MLF. The official reason was that the financial strains of the MLF would be too heavy for its economy. The State Department, however, was not satisfied with this explanation and instructed Ambassador Finletter to inquire with his Turkish colleague at NATO. Department of State to Finletter, Deptel 7112, 13 November 1964, "Multilateral Force, cables vol. 3," Subject File, NSF, LBJL. Four days later, Finletter reported that Turkey had decided "not to participate in the MLF at any time now or in the future" because of French opposition, but it had wanted to keep this secret in order not to embarrass the United States.

211. Rostow, Diffusion of Power, 392-393.

212. There was in particular increasing criticism that the MLF was at odds with the desire to halt proliferation. The National Committee for a Sane Nuclear Policy, for instance, supported by major figures in the scientific world and in public life, announced its opposition on such grounds. Sanford Gottlieb to Spurgeon Keeney, letter, 1 December 1964, Committee File, Committee on Nuclear Proliferation, NSF, box 5, LBJL. See also Steinbruner, The Cybernetic Theory of Decision, 300.

213. On 19 November, the situation on Capitol Hill had been discussed by Johnson and his advisers in similar ways. Since "the doubts [among senators] were uninformed

doubts," it was then concluded that a concerted effort, once the MLF was a more concrete proposition, would significantly improve the situation. MLF, draft memorandum of conversation, 19 November 1964, Files of McGeorge Bundy, NSF, box 18-19, LBJL.

214. As cited in Steinbruner, *The Cybernetic Theory of Decision*, 307.

215. As cited in Geyelin, *Lyndon B. Johnson and the World*, 169.

216. Bundy to Kennedy, memorandum, 15 June 1963, Memos to the President, McGeorge Bundy, NSF, box 2, LBJL. See also Chapter Four.

217. Bundy furthermore listed opposition to the MLF from the Soviet Union, professional military men such as Norstad, American commentators such as Lippmann and Kennan, and members of Congress. Bundy to Johnson, memorandum, 6 December 1964, FRUS, 1964-1968, vol. 13, Western Europe Region, #57.

218. Ibid.

219. Existence and content of this cable are reported in Rostow, *The Diffusion of Power*, 312; Geyelin, *Lyndon B. Johnson and the World*, 171-172. See also *LBJ and the Presidential Management of Foreign Relations*, 127; and Steinbruner, *The Cybernetic Theory of Decision*, 172. Hammond moreover points out that McGhee's candid report had been solicited by David Klein on 30 November. It is also noteworthy that McGhee did not favor the MLF and later said that it was "very badly conceived." *Oral history interview with George McGhee*, LBJL, 8; McGhee, *At the Creation of a New Germany*, 87.

220. Steinbruner, *The Cybernetic Theory of Decision*, 306.

221. According to Bruce's diary. Bruce, diary entry, 6 December 1964, FRUS, 1964-1968, vol. 13, Western Europe Region, #56. Acheson was not present at this meeting.

222. "For the first time in my life," George Ball later recalled, "I really got very angry at Mac Bundy, because the President started to read a paper that Mac had written which Mac had not sent me in advance." *Oral history interview with George Ball* 2:21.

223. Walt W. Rostow, interview.

224. Providing a contrast to Geyelin's glowing account of Johnson's mastery, Bruce even wrote about the December 6 meeting that "Johnson [...], telling Texan or other stories, picturesque in language, confused us as to how he might negotiate. [...] What he will say to Wilson tomorrow is wrapped in mystery. [...] I was disappointed, for I do not know where we stand." Bruce, diary entry, 6 December 1964, FRUS, 1964-1968, vol. 13, Western Europe Region, #56.

225. For the documentary record of Johnson's conversations with Wilson on 7 and 8 December 1964, see FRUS, 1964-1968, vol. 13, Western Europe Region, #58, #59, #60.

226. Johnson had directed Bundy to make clear in no uncertain terms through the British Ambassador Lord Harlech that Wilson should resist any "temptation" of claiming to have "'won a victory' over Washington" in the upcoming debates in the House of Commons. Bundy's words were not devoid of intimidation: "[...] a man in the Prime Minister's position would be extremely ill-advised to run any risks of this sort with a sensitive and determined man like President Johnson, since the President has plenty of cards to play if this becomes a public contest. I shall tell Lord Harlech that the President has shown great restraint in these last days because of his concern to avoid any appearance of running a power play against a weak opponent. But if his generosity is misunderstood, I doubt if it is likely to last." Bundy to Bruce, memorandum, 9 Decem-

ber 1964, FRUS, 1964-1968, vol. 13, Western Europe Region, #62. See also Steinbruner, *The Cybernetic Theory of Decision*, 308.

227. The communiqué stated that Johnson and Wilson had "discussed existing proposals for this purpose [strengthening the unity of the Atlantic Alliance in its strategic nuclear defense] and an outline of some new proposals presented by the British government. They agreed that the objective in this field is to cooperate in finding the arrangements *which best meet the legitimate interests of all members of the Alliance*, while maintaining existing safeguards on the use of nuclear weapons, and preventing their further proliferation. A number of elements of this problem were considered during this *initial exchange of views* as a *preliminary to further discussions* among interested members of the Alliance." *Department of State Bulletin*, vol. 51, no.1331, 28 December 1964, 902-904. (Emphasis added.)

228. Bundy to President, memorandum, 10 December 1964, Memos to the President, NSF, box 2, LBJL.

229. Geyelin, *Lyndon B. Johnson and the World*, 174.

230. An Anglo-German accord, albeit unlikely, was not entirely impossible. Wilson still might feel pressured by the Labour Party's left wing to seek an alliance framework that would enable the disposal of the independent British nuclear deterrent. Furthermore, the Erhard government was not as insistent on the formula of a surface fleet as the State Department proponents had argued. Steinbruner, *The Cybernetic Theory of Decision*, 308-309.

231. Ambassador Bohlen had reported that despite the "amicable nature" of Rusk's conversations with de Gaulle and Couve de Murville in Paris on 15 and 16 December 1964, French opposition to the MLF remained just as strong and had to be kept in mind with a view to any future plans for a nuclear force within NATO. Bohlen to Secretary of State, Embtel 3798 (Paris), 5 January 1964, Committee File, Committee on Nuclear Proliferation, NSF, box 5, LBJL.

232. Geyelin, *Lyndon B. Johnson and the World*, 162-163.

233. NSAM 322, 17 December 1964, FRUS, 1964-1968, vol. 13, Western Europe Region, #65.

234. For an assessment of the reasons why Johnson showed NSAM 322 to Reston, see Steinbruner, *The Cybernetic Theory of Decision*, 321-326. Reston's memoirs contain no reconstruction of the episode.

235. *New York Times*, 21 December 1964.

236. Having first censured the United States for being overbearing by pushing the MLF, European press circles now took Johnson's change of position as a sign of reawakening isolationism. Geyelin, *Lyndon B. Johnson and the World*, 176.

237. John A. Bovey to Department of State, Airgram A-2121 (Paris), 23 March 1965, Subject File, NSF, box 25, #33, LBJL. This report is corroborated by Alphand in his published diary. His diary entry of 3 January 1965 gives an account of a conversation in late December 1964, during which de Gaulle said: "Si le project voit le jour, cela nous donnera une belle occasion de sortir de l'O.T.A.N. [...] puisqu'une autre autorité interalliée, dont nous refusons de faire partie, aura été créée." De Gaulle also told Alphand that he intended to withdraw France from NATO before 1969: "Nous annoncerons

avant 1969 notre décision de ne plus y être associés." Alphand, *L'étonnement d'être*, 443-444.

238. Bundy to President, memorandum, 12 January 1964, Memos to the President, McGeorge Bundy, NSF, box 2, LBJL, On 7 January, Ambassador McGhee found Schroeder "at a loss as to how next to proceed with the MLF." Embassy in Germany to Department of State, telegram, 9 January 1965, FRUS, 1964-1968, vol. 13, Western Europe Region #67.

239. For the full transcript of Johnson's press conference, see Johnson, *Public Papers*, Book 1, 54-60. Prior to the press conference, an explanation of America's MLF stance was sent to all embassies in Europe and, in personal letters from Dean Rusk, to the foreign ministers of Great Britain (Gordon Walker) and Germany (Gerhard Schroeder). Denying that the American MLF position had changed, Rusk said Johnson had only directed that "the United States should conduct itself so that what emerges will truly represent the views of the major potential European participants and cannot plausibly be challenged as resulting from United States pressure upon unwilling European allies." Rusk to Schroeder, letter, 13 January 1965, FRUS, 1964-1968, vol. 13, Western Europe Region, #68.

240. Bundy to President, memorandum, 11 December 1964, Memos to the President, McGeorge Bundy, NSF, box 2, LBJL.

241. Klein to Bundy, memorandum, 1 March 1965, Subject File, NSF, box 23, #9, LBJL.

242. Johnson transmitted the content of his conversation with Erhard on a collective nuclear force in a personal letter to Harold Wilson. Johnson to Wilson, letter, 23 December 1965, Confidential File, WHCF, box 58, LBJL.

243. Kissinger's report was transmitted to Johnson by McNamara. Califano to President, memorandum, 23 March 1966, WHCF, CF, box 8, LBJL.

244. Humphrey and Spinelli, memorandum of conversation, 15 January 1965, Name File, *Vice President*, NSF, box 4, LBJL.

245. Bundy, *Danger and Survival*, 495.

246. Ibid.

247. Tyler to Rusk, memorandum, 8 March 1965, FRUS, 1964-1968, vol. 13, Western Europe Region, #75.

248. Alphand, *L'étonnement d'être*, 445.

249. As cited in Brinkley, *Dean Acheson*, 223.

250. *Never Mind the Flak*, Neustadt to Bundy, memorandum, 8 January 1965, Neustadt Memos, Name File, NSF, box 7, LBJL.

251. Bundy to President, memorandum, 10 December 1964, FRUS, 1964-1968, vol. 13, Western Europe Region, #63.

252. In November 1965, Bundy wrote: "I find my colleague Francis Bator [who had succeeded David Klein in the fall] fully persuaded that we have been unreasonably rigid with the French in recent years, and I have asked him to do some homework on this for submission to you." Bundy to President, memorandum, 16 November 1965, Confidential File, WHCF, box 8, LBJL.

253. Steinbruner, *The Cybernetic Theory of Decision*, 332.

254. Finletter, *Interim Report*, 92.

255. *Oral history interview with Thomas K. Finletter*, 17.

256. Ibid.

257. Steinbruner, *The Cybernetic Theory of Decision*, 310.

258. Walt Rostow became National Security Adviser in 1966, and Henry Owen was consequently promoted to head of the Policy Planning Council. George Ball stayed on the job until 1966 and claimed to have played a modest role in protecting the advocates from becoming "fair game" in the administration. *Oral history interview with George Ball* 2:21.

259. Bundy to President, memorandum, 2 February 1965, Memos to the President, McGeorge Bundy, NSF, box 2, LBJL. McGeorge Bundy served as Johnson's principal watchdog until his departure from the White House staff in early 1966. It was Bundy, for instance, who was quick to counter attempts by the State Department to take the MLF "off the ice" after the elections in Germany in September 1965. In response to a George Ball paper to this effect, Bundy restated the case against the MLF in a memorandum for Johnson. As late as 1966, he felt compelled to exercise vigilance. In response to a paper by Walt Rostow, Bundy expressed annoyance with the stubborn persistence of the MLF supporters. "These enthusiasts for a collective force have been a zealous lobby within the government for five years, and it was always quite a job to keep a proper eye on them. Dean Rusk does not do it, so the job has fallen to me in the last year or two, and I hope they won't trap anyone into another unmanageable idea like the MLF after I get out of here." Ironically, Rostow would become Bundy's successor as national security adviser (after a short interregnum by Robert Komer). Bundy to President, memorandum, 28 January 1966, Memos to the President, McGeorge Bundy, box 6, #47, LBJL.

260. *Oral history interview with Thomas K. Finletter*, 17.

261. Ball, *The Past Has Another Pattern*, 274.

262. As cited in David Dimbleby and David Reynolds, *An Ocean Apart: The Relationship between Britain and America in the Twentieth Century* (New York: Random House, 1988), 263. On Ball's support for the MLF, see Bill, Ball, 114-119.

263. Hammond, *LBJ and the Presidential Management of Foreign Relations*, 142.

264. Bundy, *Danger and Survival*, 498.

265. Camps, *European Unification in the Sixties*, 16, 117-118.

266. McCloy to Chairman of the ACDA, memorandum, 8 January 1965, *McCloy Memorandum on Non-Proliferation*, Committee File, Committee on Nuclear Proliferation, NSF, box 6, LBJL.

Notes to Chapter Five – The Gaulle Throws Down the Gauntlet

1. For other academic treatises on the French withdrawal from NATO, see Bozo, *Two Strategies for Europe*, 143-218; Costigliola, *France and the United States*, 144-149; Harrison, *The Reluctant Ally*, 134-163; Michael M. Harrison and Mark G. McDonough, *Negotiations on the French Withdrawal From NATO* (Washington, DC: SAIS Foreign Policy Institute, 1987); Kohl, *French Nuclear Diplomacy*, 251-259; Schwartz, *Lyndon Johnson and Europe*, 92-139; Samuel F. Wells Jr., "Charles de Gaulle and the French Withdrawal from NATO's Integrated Command," in Lawrence S. Kaplan, ed., *American Historians and the Atlantic Alliance* (Kent: Kent State University Press, 1991); Andreas Wenger, "Crisis and Oppor-

tunity: NATO's Transformation and the Multilateralization of Détente, 1966-1968," *Journal of Cold War Studies* 6, no. 1 (2004): 22-74; and the contributions of Helga Haftendorn, Frédéric Bozo, and Thomas Schwartz in Helga Haftendorn et al., eds, *The Strategic Triangle: France, Germany, and the United States in the Shaping of the New Europe* (Washington DC/Baltimore: Woodrow Wilson Center Press/Johns Hopkins University Press, 2006), 77-145. For a thorough examination from a legal perspective, see Eric Stein and Dominique Carreau, "Law and Peaceful Change in a Subsystem: 'Withdrawal' of France from the North Atlantic Treaty Organization," *American Journal of International Law* 62 (July 1968): 577-640. On Johnson's attitude towards de Gaulle, see also Brands, Jr., "Johnson and De Gaulle: American Diplomacy *Sotto Voce*," 482-485; and Gardner, "Johnson and De Gaulle," 257-278.

2. Military integration within NATO consisted of three elements: 1) the existence of command headquarters with integrated military staffs (the most important of which was SHAPE); 2) the agreement of NATO member states to place their forces under an integrated command, instead of keeping them under national command, in time of military action; and 3) the planning in peacetime undertaken by the integrated command headquarters. Integration did not involve the command of national units in peacetime under an integrated headquarters. Nor would the integrated command assume authority over a member state's armed forces without its concurrence. As Stein and Carreau concluded, "it is impossible to identify in this complex 'integration' machinery any ironclad commitment that would draw a member state into a war against its will." See "Law and Peaceful Change in a Subsystem," 594.

3. De Gaulle, *War Memoirs*, 873.

4. For a detailed and far more complete account of French partial withdrawals from NATO and other acts of non-cooperation from 1958 to 1965, see Harrison, *The Reluctant Ally*, 134-140.

5. Bohlen to Rusk, Embtel 3802, 5 January 1965, Country File, France, box 170, cables vol. 5, NSF, LBJL.

6. These reports were plausibly fed by the highlevel French diplomat at the Quai d'Orsay singled out by Vincent Jauvert in *L'Amérique contre de Gaulle*, 144-156. According to Jauvert, this unnamed diplomat served as a mole ("*une taupe*") for the United States out of spite with de Gaulle's foreign policy and repeatedly leaked confidential information through the American embassy in Paris.

7. Bohlen to Rusk, Embtel 6238, 4 May 1965, Country File, France, box 171, memos vol. 6, NSF, LBJL.

8. Bohlen to Rusk, Embtel 6843, 3 June 1965, Country File, France, box 171, cables vol. 6, NSF, LBJL. On 30 May 1965, Bohlen offered the same analysis to Sulzberger. See Sulzberger, *Age of Mediocrity*, 180. In a conversation at the Elysée, de Gaulle confirmed his intention to proceed against NATO along these lines to Sulzberger himself. Bohlen to Rusk, Embtel 51, 2 July 1965, Country File, France, box 171, cables vol. 7, NSF, LBJL.

9. Bohlen to Rusk, Embtel 6802, 2 June 1965, Country File, France, box 171, cables vol. 5, NSF, LBJL. There were also indications that de Gaulle was seriously contemplating eventually denouncing or significantly amending the Treaty itself and that the Quai d'Orsay had been ordered to prepare drafts for this purpose. Bohlen to Rusk, Embtel 6181, 4 May 1965, Country File, France, box 171, cables vol. 6, NSF, LBJL.

10. Finletter to Rusk, Polto 1701, 25 May 1965, Country File, France, box 171, cables vol. 6, NSF, LBJL.
11. Sulzberger, *Age of Mediocrity*, 134-135.
12. "Faut-il réformer l'Alliance atlantique?" *Politique Étrangère* 3 (1965); *New York Times*, 17 October 1965.
13. As Director of Intelligence and Research at the State Department, Thomas L. Hughes devoted a number of analyses to the article. For instance Hughes to Rusk, research memorandum (REU 41.3), 30 November 1965, Country File, France, memos vol. 8, NSF, box 172, LBJL.
14. Alphand, *L'étonnement d'être*, 452-453, 461.
15. In his memoirs, de Gaulle put it this way: "My aim [...] was to disengage France, not from the Atlantic alliance, which I intended to maintain by way of ultimate precaution, but from the integration realized by NATO under American command; to establish relations with each of the States of the Eastern bloc, first and foremost Russia, with the object of bringing about a *détente* followed by understanding and cooperation; to do likewise, when the time was ripe, with China; and finally, to provide France with a nuclear capability such that no one could attack us without running the risk of frightful injury." De Gaulle, *Memoirs of Hope*, 202.
16. Schwartz rightfully points out that historians have generally underestimated "the degree to which he [Johnson] was determined to reduce the threat of nuclear war with the Soviet Union." Schwartz, *Lyndon Johnson and Europe*, 17.
17. De Gaulle, *Discours et messages*, vol. 4, *Pour l'effort*, 155.
18. Wolfram Hanrieder, *The Stable Crisis* (New York: Harper and Row, 1970), 102.
19. In the words of Jean de la Chevadière de la Grandville, chief of the Treaty Section of the French foreign ministry, vis-à-vis Henry Kissinger. McNamara to President, memorandum, 23 March 1966, WHCF, Confidential File, box 8, France, LBJL
20. The American embassy from Paris assessed that the fact that a majority of French voters did not consider de Gaulle first choice for president would not have any softening effect on his foreign policies. On the contrary, it would be more in character for him to "demonstrate his force of will." McBride (Paris) to Department of State, Embtel 3186, 7 December 1965, Country File, France, cables vol. 8, NSF, box 172, LBJL.
21. Richard Helms to Director of CIA, memorandum, 30 June 1964, NATO, General, vol. 1, box 35, Agency File, NSF, #20, LBJL.
22. *NATO and France*, paper, Department of State Policy Planning Council, 6 May 1964, NATO, General, vol. 1, Agency File, NSF, #26a, box 35, LBJL.
23. Ibid.
24. Bohlen to President, *Reflections on Current French Foreign Policy and Attitudes Toward the United States and Recommendations*, memorandum, 11 March 1964, Country File, France, memos vol. 1, NSF, box 169, LBJL; *Franco-American Differences – Their Origins and Developments*, memorandum, 27 October 1964, Files of McGeorge Bundy, box 15-16, LBJL.
25. For Harriman's views, see Chapter Five. On 16 March 1965, Ball had assailed de Gaulle in a speech for attempting to restore the traditional European system of alliances which had led to two world wars and to exclude the United States from European affairs, and for "weakening or dismantling organizations and arrangements through

which America and Europe cooperate." Ball, "The Dangers of Nostalgia," printed in *The Atlantic Community Quarterly* 3, no. 2 (Summer 1965): 167-176.

26. Tyler to Bundy, letter, 12 March 1964, Country File, France, memos vol. 1, box 169, NSF, LBJL.

27. *The EEC and the NATO Crises*, paper prepared for Bundy, 22 October 1965 (undated), LBJL, 3.

28. Ball, *The Past Has Another Pattern*, 331-333. Ball's rendition of his meeting with de Gaulle on 31 August is corroborated by his report from Rome to Rusk. Embassy in Italy to Department of State, telegram, 1 September 1965, FRUS 1964-1968, vol. 13, #101. De Gaulle repeated this message to Bohlen during a lunch at Rambouillet, saying that the Alliance could be preserved under various guises and even "without a treaty." After Bohlen had stated that from an American perspective the North Atlantic Treaty was a "quasi-sacred obligation," de Gaulle argued that in international affairs, treaties themselves were less important than their interpretation: "He said that history was actually the history of wars and that periods between wars were merely politics, which I gathered to mean that great events and great decisions were made in time of war whereas in time of peace there was nothing but political intrigue." Bohlen to Rusk, Embtel 2337, 28 October 1965, cables, vol. 8, Country File, France, box 172, NSF. Thomas L. Hughes suggested that de Gaulle's assertion that the Alliance would survive even without a treaty was based on the conviction that in response to a Soviet attack the French nuclear force could trigger an escalation that would ultimately unavoidably involve American strategic forces. Hughes to Rusk, research memorandum (REU 41.1), 30 September 1965, memos vol. 6, Country File, France, NSF, box 172, LBJL.

29. Ball/Bohlen to Rusk, Secun 3 (Paris), 6 September 1965, cables vol. 8, Country File, France, box 172, LBJL.

30. McBride to Rusk, Embtel 3513, 11 December 1965, Country File, France, box 170, cables vol. 5, NSF, LBJL.

31. The result of this interagency discussion was encapsulated in a long, secret policy paper. *France and NATO*, paper, 25 September 1965, Country File, France, memos vol. 8, box 172, NSF, #220, LBJL.

32. *France and NATO*, memorandum of conversation, 26 August 1965, Country File, France, memos vol. 7, box 171, NSF, LBJL.

33. American Embassy in Paris to Department of State, Airgram 784, *Annual Review of US Military Installations in France*, 19 October 1965, Country File, France, cables vol. 8, box 172, NSF, LBJL..

34. As reported by General David A. Burchinal in a final report on the relocation of US troops from France (page 6). *Fast Relocation of US Forces from France*, report, Headquarters United States European Command, 12 October 1967, NATO-General, vol. 5, box 35, Agency File, NSF, #6b, LBJL.

35. *France and NATO*, paper, 25 September 1965, LBJL, 10. The withdrawal costs were tentatively estimated in this paper at more than $750 million.

36. Klein to Bundy, memorandum, 5 May 1965, Memos, vol. 6, Country File, France, box 171, NSF. See also Schwartz, *Lyndon Johnson and Europe*, 96-97.

37. As reported by Ball to LBJ. Ball to President, memorandum, 14 November 1965.

38. Bohlen to Rusk, Embtel 6843, 3 June 1965, Country File, France, cables vol. 6, NSF, box 171, LBJL.
39. *France and NATO*, 25 September 1965, LBJL, 21.
40. Bundy to President, memorandum, 3 June 1965, McGeorge Bundy, vol. 11, June 1965, box 3, MtP, NSF, #109, LBJL.
41. *France and NATO*, 25 September 1965, LBJL, 15.
42. Ball/Bohlen to Rusk, Secun 3 (Paris), 6 September 1965, cables vol. 8, Country File, France, box 172, LBJL.
43. *France and NATO*, 25 September 1965, LBJL, 4.
44. See in particular Brian VanDeMark's detailed study of the Americanization of the war in 1965. *Into the Quagmire: Lyndon Johnson and the Escalation of the Vietnam War* (New York: Oxford University Press, 1991).
45. Acheson to Erik Bohemen, letter, 7 July 1965, in McLellan and Acheson, *Among Friends*, 272.
46. *France and NATO*, 25 September 1965, LBJL, 22.
47. Bohlen to Rusk, Embtel 6282, 6 May 1965, Country File, France box 171, cables vol. 4, NSF, LBJL.
48. Cleveland to Rusk, Embtel 3131, 5 December 1965, cables vol. 8, Country File, France, NSF, box 172, LBJL.
    The Allied Command Europe Mobile Force (AMF), based in Heidelberg, was created in 1960 as a small multinational force that could be sent at short notice to any threatened part of allied territory in Europe. The AMF was not deployed in a crisis role until January 1991, when part of its air component was sent to southeast Turkey during the first Gulf War to demonstrate NATO's collective solidarity.
49. Ball, *The Past Has Another Pattern*, 334.
50. The "*select* committee" was sometimes also referred to as the "*special* committee" or the "McNamara Committee." We will henceforth refer to it as the Select Committee. McNamara had proposed a similar consultative mechanism at the Athens meeting of NATO in Mary 1962, but there had then been little response.
51. Durbrow to Rusk, Polto 92, 22 July 1965, Country File, France, box 171, cables vol. 7, NSF, LBJL.
52. The Paris embassy, for instance, assessed that de Gaulle, although averse to the McNamara Committee, would probably not as vigorously oppose it as he did the MLF because it would isolate him much more in Europe and France. Richard Funkhouser to Department of State, Airgram 580, 18 September 1965, Country File, NSF, box 172, LBJL.
53. Funkhouser to Department of State, Airgram 580, 18 September 1965, Country File, NSF, box 172, LBJL.
54. Finletter to Rusk, Polto 1742, 1 June 1965, Country File, France, cables vol. 6, box 171, NSF, LBJL.
55. Funkhouser to Department of State, Airgram 580, 18 September 1965, Country File, NSF, box 172, LBJL.
56. In 1964, India commissioned a reprocessing facility at Trombay, which was used to separate the plutonium produced by the Cirus research reactor. This plutonium was used in India's first nuclear test on May 18, 1974.

57. For the Gilpatric Report, dated 21 January 1965, see FRUS 1964-1968, vol. 11, Arms Control and Disarmament, #64.

58. Johnson's interest was further heightened when his rival Robert Kennedy used his maiden speech in the Senate in June 1965 to advocate a nuclear nonproliferation treaty and censured the administration for not having done enough. See Schwartz, *Lyndon Johnson and Europe*, 55-56.

59. Bundy to President, memorandum, 10 October 1965, McGeorge Bundy, vol. 15, box 5, Memos to the President, NSF, #16, LBJL. On Johnson's interest in a nuclear non-proliferation treaty, see Schwartz, *Lyndon Johnson and Europe*, 53-59.

60. Bundy to President, memorandum, 12 September 1965, Memos to the President, McGeorge Bundy, NSF, box 4, LBJL; *The Case For a Fresh Start on Atlantic Nuclear Defense (With No Mixed Manned Forces or Plans for Such Forces)*, paper, 18 October 1965, Memos to the President, McGeorge Bundy, NSF, box 5, LBJL. McGeorge Bundy also noted that the shift to nuclear consultation would be "more constructive in relation to the French and British deterrents."

61. Bundy to President, memorandum, 25 November 1965, Memos to the President, McGeorge Bundy, NSF, box 5, LBJL.

62. Cleveland to Rusk and McNamara, Polto 784, 16 November 1965, Country File, France, cables vol. 8, NSF, box 172, LBJL.

63. Cleveland to Rusk, Polto 918 (Paris), 29 November 1965, Country File, France, cables vol. 8, NSF, box 172, LBJL.

64. Cleveland to Rusk, Embtel 3444, 16 December 1965, Country File, France, cables vol. 8, NSF, box 172, LBJL.

65. Johnson to Wilson, letter, 23 December 1965, Confidential File, IT 34 NATO, White House Central Files, box 58, LBJL.

66. Bundy to President, memorandum, 6 January 1966, Memos to the President, McGeorge Bundy/Robert Komer, NSF, box 6, LBJL. Bundy added: "I happen to think he [Wilson] is right, but I doubt if George Ball will."

67. Cleveland to Rusk, Embtel 3491, 18 December 1965, Country File, France, cables vol. 8, NSF, box 172, LBJL.

68. National Security Action Memorandum 336, 6 August 1965, FRUS 1964-1968, vol. 12, Western Europe, #51. This NSAM directed the addressed Departments and Agencies to "provide a complete catalogue of activities with respect to France being undertaken or planned to be undertaken by the United States, whether covert, clandestine, or overt, that could be regarded as illegal or that could cause embarrassment to the United States if the French decided to make an issue out of them."

69. Alphand, *L'étonnement d'être*, 461.

70. Bohlen to Rusk, Embtel 482, 27 July 1965, cables, vol. 7, Country File, France, box 171, NSF, LBJL.

71. Embassy in Paris to Department of State, Airgram 1701 (Paris), 2 February 1964, Country File, NSF, box 170, (64), LBJL, 4.

72. Finletter to Rusk, Polto 1871, 29 June 1965, cables, vol. 8, Country File, France, box 171, NSF, LBJL. It should be noted, however, that Bohlen at times also gave evidence of a more nuanced view. In one cable, upon observing that the opposition to NATO was largely confined to Gaullists and Communists and that embassy officials were often

accosted with expressions of friendly sentiment, he admitted to confusion: "There is no question but that the nationalistic policies of the Fifth Republic have aroused more of a sentiment of association than did the more European and Atlantic forces of most of the governments of the Fourth Republic. Thus while on the surface there are many protestations of pro-American sentiment and dislike of Gaullist policies, fundamentally there is sympathy for much of the attitude of independence so carefully cultivated, and this may be increasing with time. [...] We can only conclude that French fundamental sentiments on these issues are very divided but that a layer of nationalism has been added to the French cake by the General which tastes better and better to many Frenchman." Bohlen to Rusk, Embtel 1051, 27 August 1965, cables, vol. 7, Country File, France, box 171, NSF, LBJL.

73. There are many indications that de Gaulle peeved the usually bland Rusk as few others could. According to Cyrus Sulzberger, for instance, Rusk "revealed an alarming tendency to oversimplify his analysis of the General" and expressed serious doubts about his readiness to fight on the side of the allies in the case of a war with the Soviet Union in Europe. See Sulzberger, *Age of Mediocrity*, 222-225. In the fall of 1965, Ball, a known critic of de Gaulle, volunteered to James Reston of the *New York Times* that France was presenting more problems to American foreign policy than the Soviet Union. Ball and Reston, telephone conversation, 21 September 1965, vol (General) US and Europe, box 6, Papers of George W. Ball, #36, LBJL.

74. Dallek, *Flawed Giant*, 100.

75. See for example Schwartz, *Lyndon Johnson and Europe*, 105.

76. Ball and Dillon, telephone conversation, 6 November 1965, France II, box 3, Papers of George W. Ball, #89, LBJL.

77. Douglas Dillon, *Some Thoughts on US Policy and Gaullist France*, paper, #89a, submitted with memorandum, Bundy to President, 3 January 1966, Memos to the President, McGeorge Bundy and Robert Komer, box 6, #89, LBJL.

78. Excerpts from de Gaulle's press conference, February 21, 1966, as reprinted in Senate Committee on Foreign Relations, *United States Policy Toward Europe (and Related Matters)*, 89th Cong., 2d sess., 1966, 422–425.

79. Ibid.

80. See Jauvert, *L'Amérique contre de Gaulle*, 148.

81. Bator to President, memorandum, 3 March 1966, vol. 1, France-NATO Dispute, box 177, CF, NSF, #262, LBJL. Assistant Secretary of State for European Affairs John Leddy later confirmed the existence of these indications during a hearing before Congress on March 22. ,House Committee on Foreign Affairs, *The Crisis in NATO: Hearings before the Subcommittee on Europe of the House Committee on Foreign Affairs*, 89th Cong., 2d sess., 1966, 14-15.

82. During a hearing before Congress on March 17, 1966, Bohlen admitted that even as the French withdrawal from NATO had been expected, there was an "element of surprise in the suddenness of it and the fact that he did it at one fell swoop..." In House Committee, *The Crisis in NATO*, 5. Likewise, Leddy stated that after de Gaulle's press conference of February 21 that "we had reason to believe, partly because of the tone of the language that he used in this press conference, that he would probably not

move soon, that perhaps he would delay matters until after the French parliamentary elections [in March 1967]...." Ibid., 15.

83. Leddy and Ball, telephone conversation, 7 March 1966, vol. France II, box 3, Papers of George W. Ball, #96, LBJL. Bohlen's judgment was relayed to Johnson. See memorandum, Bator to President, 7 March 1966, vol. 1, France-NATO Dispute, box 177, CF, NSF, #257d, LBJL. That de Gaulle's note was tougher than the position the Quai d'Orsay had been preparing is corroborated by Kissinger's report of a conversation with de la Grandville in January. De la Grandville, who was chief of the Treaty Section of the French foreign ministry, had implied that American troops would be allowed to stay under a regime which would nominally restore French sovereignty over American bases on French soil. McNamara to President, memorandum, 23 March 1966, WHCF, Confidential File, box 8, France, LBJL. For a similar rendition, see Jauvert, L'Amérique contre de Gaulle, 149. This leaves the reader with the tantalizing suggestion that de la Grandville was in fact the mole who remains nameless in Jauvert's book.

84. De Gaulle's letter appears in FRUS 1964-1968, Western Europe, #137.

85. Aide mémoire, as reprinted in Department of State Bulletin, 18 April 1966, 617-618. The aide mémoire was dated 10 March and was delivered to the American embassy in Paris on 11 March. The same text was delivered to other allies.

86. French aide mémoire of 29 March 1966. In Department of State Bulletin, 2 May 1966, 702-703.

87. In a telephone conversation with journalist Chalmers Roberts in the evening of 7 March, for instance, Ball scolded the French for thinking that "they can have their cake and eat it too." He told Roberts that "we do not agree with de Gaulle's assumption that he can stay in the treaty and not assume any responsibilities." Ball and Roberts, telephone conversation, 7 March 1966, vol. France II, box 3, Papers of George W. Ball, #124, LBJL.

88. Ball handed Johnson's letter to French Ambassador Lucet in the evening of 7 March. Letter appears in Senate Committee, Atlantic Alliance, 288.

89. Senate Committee, Atlantic Alliance, 32-33. For a discussion of the significance to be attached to the word "unprovoked," see also Harrison, The Reluctant Ally, 131-132. Harrison concludes that "Vietnam and unchecked American global activism were evidently important factors behind the General's NATO decisions." (131)

90. On Bundy's departure from the White House, see Bird, The Color of Truth, 347-349. While Bundy saw eye to eye with Johnson on dealing with de Gaulle, he had remained very much a Kennedy man and a representative of the Establishment who never hit it off with the Texan.

91. Bator had joined the staff of the National Security Council in April 1964 and had been appointed Deputy National Security Adviser in 1965. His areas of responsibility included European affairs and foreign economic policy.

92. Bator to President, memorandum, 7 March 1966, vol.1, France-NATO Dispute, box 177, CF, NSF, #259, LBJL.

93. Bator to President, memorandum, 8 March 1966, vol. 1, France-NATO Dispute, box 177, CF, NSF, #258, LBJL. The documentary record shows that Ball was indeed hardly reticent in his conversations with prominent newspaper men like James Reston, Eric Sevareid, and Chalmers Roberts.

94. Rostow to President, memorandum, 7 March 1966, CF, CO 81 (France), WHCF, box 8, LBJL.
95. Senate Committee, *Atlantic Alliance*, 288.
96. Ball and Cleveland, telephone conversation, 8 March 1966, vol. France II, box 3, Papers of George W. Ball, #101, LBJL. Such a declaration was considered indispensable in order to create a "sense of isolation." Ball, Cleveland, and Leddy, telephone conversation, 11 March 1966, vol. France II, box 3, Papers of George W. Ball, #106, LBJL.
97. Joint Declaration Agreed Upon by the Fourteen Member Nations, 18 March 1966, in Senate Committee, *Atlantic Alliance*, 291.
98. Ball and Collins, telephone conversation, 10 March 1966; Ball and Sevareid, telephone conversation, 15 March 1966; Ball and Reston, telephone conversation, 15 March 1966 in vol. France II, box 3, Papers of George W. Ball, #105, #116 and #45, LBJL.
99. A transcript of this interview appeared in *Department of State Bulletin*, 18 April 1966, 614-616.
100. "Dean Acheson's Word for De Gaulle: 'Nonsense'," US *News and World Report* 60, 18 April 1966, 79.
101. Senate Committee, *Atlantic Alliance. Hearings*, 78.
102. Acheson to President, memorandum, 31 March 1965, Memos to the President, McGeorge Bundy, NSF, box 3, LBJL. Acheson's study would have reviewed the policy paper he had prepared for Kennedy in early 1961. Bundy, however, opposed Acheson's proposal for a policy review and informed Johnson that he did "not at all share his [Acheson's] view that he should be the man to do it. [...] He has extremely firm and well-developed ideas which do not really fit the current state of Europe and which you have already had to overcome." Bundy to President, memorandum, 18 March 1965, Memos to the President, McGeorge Bundy, NSF, box 3, LBJL. On Bundy's advice, Johnson kept Acheson at bay by promising that his views would be taken into account in the interagency study coordinated by George Ball. Johnson to Acheson, letter, 1 April 1965.
103. This policy statement was presented to Johnson by General Lauris Norstad. Norstad to President, letter, 8 December 1965, Subject File, EX IT 26/A, WHCF, box 6, LBJL.
104. EKH to Francis Bator, memorandum, 13 December 1965, Subject File, EX IT 26/A, WHCF, box 6, LBJL.
105. "Dealing with De Gaulle: Dean Acheson Tells How," US *News and World Report*, 25 March 1966, 22.
106. President Appointment File, Diary Backup, box 31. No official record of these meetings was made. However, Komer's files contain some handwritten notes of these meetings as well as their agendas. In Files of Robert W. Komer, box 1-2, #1a, #4, #5, #9, LBJL. LBJ had already discussed the situation with Rusk and McNamara during the Tuesday lunch of 8 March. Tuesday Lunch Agenda, 8 March 1966, Files of Robert W. Komer, box 1-2, #98, LBJL.
107. Handwritten note (undated), Files of Robert W. Komer, box 1-2, #9, LBJL.
108. Bohlen was – "as one of the individuals involved in the creation of NATO" – livid about de Gaulle's note of March 7, forcing Couve de Murville to admit that it amounted to a "denunciation" and suggesting that it was "a step in the direction of neutrality." Embassy in France to Department of State, telegram, FRUS 1964-1968,

Western Europe, #136. For Bohlen's response to the French withdrawal from NATO, see also Schwartz, *Lyndon Johnson and Europe*, 100-101, 103.

109. Handwritten note (undated), Files of Robert W. Komer, box 1-2, #9, LBJL.

110. Komer to President, memorandum, 16 March 1966, FRUS 1964-1968, Western Europe Region, #143.

111. Bill Moyers to President, memorandum, 17 March 1966, vol. 1, France-NATO Dispute, box 177, CF, NSF, #243, LBJL; Bator to President, memorandum, 17 March 1966, Files of Robert W. Komer, box 1-2, #1, LBJL.

112. Ball and Bator, telephone conversation, 18 March 1966, vol. France II, box 3, Papers of George W. Ball, #125, LBJL.

113. Bator to President, memorandum, 18 March 1966, IT 34 NATO, Confidential File, White House Central Files, box 58, LBJL.

114. Ball and Lucet, memorandum of conversation, 22 March 1966, memos, vol. 9, Country File, France, NSF, LBJL.

115. Beginning in 1965, Johnson often requested Eisenhower's views, particularly with regard to Vietnam, and between 1963 and 1966 he paid the former president nine visits. General Andrew Goodpaster, *Phone conversation with General Eisenhower*, memorandum for the record, 21 March 1966; Komer to President, memorandum, 21 March 1966; Bromley Smith to President, memorandum, 11 June 1966 in Name File, *President Eisenhower*, box 3, NSF, LBJL.

116. Texts of letter appear in Senate Committee, *Atlantic Alliance Hearings*, 287-290.

117. Addressing the Foreign Service Institute on March 23, for instance, Johnson spoke about Atlantic affairs much along the lines of his letter without even once mentioning de Gaulle. See Johnson, *Public Papers*, {vol. #}:351-354.

118. J. Robert Schaetzel to Walt Rostow, memorandum, 3 May 1966, vol. 3, France-NATO Dispute, box 177, CF, NSF, #114, LBJL.

119. Ball, *The Larger Meaning of the NATO Crisis*, *Department of State Bulletin* 54, 16 May, 1966, 762-768.

120. President to Secretary of State and Secretary of Defense, memorandum, 4 May 1966, vol. 3, France-NATO Dispute, box 177, CF, NSF, #110, LBJL.

121. Ball used these words to describe his situation within the Johnson administration by the summer of 1966. While he referred in particular to his lonely opposition to escalating America's involvement in the Vietnam War, they may also be applied to Ball's waning influence on the administration's policies toward Europe. Ball, *The Past Has Another Pattern*, 424.

122. Rostow/Bator to President, memorandum, 18 May 1966, Walt Rostow, memos to the President, box 7, #72a, LBJL. Rostow had assumed his new position on 31 March 1966.

123. French Aide Mémoire of 29 March 1966. In *Department of State Bulletin*, 2 May 1966, 702-703. The French government only made exceptions for the depots of the American army at Deols-La Martinerie and the petroleum pipeline. Whereas a longer time limit could be considered for the depots, Paris was willing to consider special provisions for the continued operation of the pipeline.

124. NATO Session, handwritten note, 17 March 1966, Files of Robert W. Komer, box 1-2, #5, LBJL. Rusk, moreover, suggested that France could be made to pay for the relocation costs.

125. McNamara to President, memorandum, 25 May 1966, memos vol. 9, Country File, France, NSF, box 172, LBJL.

126. Ball and Leddy, telephone conversation, 5 April 1966, vol. France II, box 3, Papers of George W. Ball, #132, LBJL.

127. Rusk, As I Saw It, 271.

128. Rostow to President, memorandum, 25 May 1966, memos vol. 9, Country File, France, NSF, box 172, LBJL.

129. Rostow, interview by the author.

130. Bromley Smith to President, Summary Notes of 566th NSC Meeting, December 13, 1966, NSC Meetings File, NSF, box 2, LBJL. At this meeting McNamara lowered the estimated withdrawal costs to a range of $175 million to $275 million. These costs, moreover, would be partially offset by foreign exchange savings amounting to $75 million a year.

131. Harrison and McDonough, Negotiations on the French Withdrawal from NATO, 31-32. The Pentagon used the evacuation to reduce the number of American military and civilian personnel and dependents serving abroad by 39,000. Most American military installations and the headquarters of American forces in Europe (USEUCOM) in St. Germain-en-Laye near Paris were moved to Germany; most air force units were relocated to Great Britain. The home port of the Sixth Fleet was moved to Italy. Negotiations with France on a financial claim to offset the costs of the evacuation dragged on for years before they were finally settled in 1974 at $100 million.

132. Report, "Fast Relocation of US Forces from France" by Headquarters United States European Command, 12 October 1967, NATO-General, vol. 5, box 35, Agency File, NSF, #6b, LBJL. {see FN page 321}

133. Senate Committee, United States Policy Toward Europe (and Related Matters), 8.

134. Department of State Bulletin, 18 April 1966, 617-618.

135. Ball to President, memorandum, 10 April 1966, plus attached Memorandum for Guidance of Mr. McCloy in his Discussion of French Forces in Germany (dated 9 April), vol. [NATO], McCloy Talks, box 21, SF, NSF.

136. Bator to President, memorandum, 16 March 1966, vol. 1, France-NATO Dispute, box 177, CF, NSF, #247, LBJL.

137. Rostow/Bator to President, memorandum, 18 May 1966, Memos to the President, Walt Rostow, box 7, #72a, LBJL. On 18 March, Ambassador McGhee had reported from Bonn that in the Bundestag "no one felt that French troops could remain as occupation rather than NATO forces." McGhee to Rusk, Embtel 2902 (Bonn), 18 March 1966, vol. 1, France-NATO Dispute, box 177, CF, NSF, #212, LBJL.

138. On his trip to Germany in January 1966, Kissinger had already encountered a "mixture of exasperation, fear and unhappiness about the deterioration of Franco-German relations." McNamara to President, memorandum, 23 March 1966, WHCF, Confidential File, box 8, France, LBJL.

139. See note 135. (Emphasis added.)

140. McGhee to Rusk, Embtel 3166 (Bonn), 6 April 1966, vol. 2, NATO-France Dispute, box 177, CF, NSF, #181, LBJL.

141. These agreements, which were reached to facilitate the accession of West Germany to NATO, were: the Final Act of the London Conference of 3 October 1954; the implementing resolutions of the NATO Council of Ministers of 22 October 1954; and the Convention on the presence of foreign forces in the Federal Republic of Germany of 23 October 1954.

142. "Reply of the Federal German Republic to the Memorandum of the French Government of March 29," in The Atlantic Community Quarterly 4, no. 2 (Summer 1966): 289-292.

143. Hillenbrand to Rusk, Embtel 3312 (Bonn), 16 April 1966, vol. [NATO] McCloy Talks, box 21, SF, NSF, #12, LBJL.

144. McCloy to Rusk, Embtel 3321 (Bonn), 17 April 1966, vol. [NATO] McCloy Talks, box 21, SF NSF, #5, LBJL.

145. On McCloy's involvement in these talks, see Bird, The Chairman, 587-596.

146. Rostow/Bator to President, memorandum, 18 May 1966, Memos to the President, Walt Rostow, box 7, #72a, LBJL.

147. McCloy to Rusk, Embtel 3305 (Bonn), 15 April 1966, vol. [NATO] McCloy Talks, box wi, SF, NSF, #3, LBJL. Acheson was also of this mind, as he told the British that he wanted Bonn to take a "firm line" and that the departure of French troops from Germany would be "no great loss." As cited in Schwartz, Lyndon Johnson and Europe, 107.

148. Bator to President, memorandum, 16 March 1966, vol. 1, France-NATO Dispute, CF, NSF, box 177, #247, LBJL

149. Rostow/Bator to President, memorandum, 18 May 1966, Memos to the President, Walt Rostow, box 7, #72a, LBJL. This tough position was based on negotiating instructions given to McCloy. Ball to President, memorandum, 10 April 1966, plus attached "Memorandum for Guidance of Mr. McCloy in his Discussion of French Forces in Germany" (dated 9 April), vol. [NATO], McCloy Talks, box 21, SF, NSF.

150. "Reply of the French Government to the Memorandum of the Government of Germany dated May 3, 1966," in The Atlantic Community Quarterly 4, no. 2 (Summer 1966): 292.

151. Bohlen to Rusk, Embtel 8672, 13 June 1966, Memos to the President, Rostow, NSF, box 8, #1, LBJL.

152. Harrison, "France and the Atlantic Alliance," 454.

153. The State Department unwisely still believed it had leverage over Paris by threatening to expel French forces from Germany. Rusk, for instance, reported after a meeting of NATO foreign ministers in early June: "my guess is that we will only be able to get satisfactory arrangement on French troops in Germany by playing a very tough diplomatic game [...] and [by] making it very clear that we (together with the Germans and the British) are prepared to face the prospect that the French might end by pulling their forces out of Germany." Rusk to President, Acting Secretary and Secretary McNamara, Secto, 9 June 1966, Memos to the President, Rostow, NSF, box 8, #19a, LBJL.

154. Harrison, "France and the Atlantic Alliance," 455-457.

155. Cleveland (Paris) to Rusk, Embtel 1461, 29 July 1966, Country File, France, cables vol. IX, box 172, LBJL.

156. French forces in Germany, background paper, 6 December 1966, International Meeting and Travel File, NSF, box 35, LBJL. The Lemnitzer-Ailleret agreement of 1967 served

as the basis for French participation in the defense of Germany and contained detailed arrangements for the involvement of French forces in case of a Soviet attack.

157. Harrison and McDonough, *Negotiations on the French Withdrawal from NATO*, 33-35.

158. *US-French Bilaterals on Withdrawal of US Forces*, background paper, 14 November 1966, NATO-Visit of SG Manlio Brosio, box 39, Agency File, NSF, #13, LBJL.

159. Rostow/Bator to President, memorandum, 18 May 1966, Memos to the President, Walt Rostow, box 7, #72a, LBJL.

160. Bohlen to Rusk, Embtel 8716, 14 June 1966, cables, vol. 9, Country File, France, box 172, NSF, LBJL.

161. Bohlen to Rusk, Embtel 8211, 26 May 1966, cables vol. 9, Country File, France, box 172, NSF, LBJL.

162. *France-NATO: The Constitutional Question*, background paper, 14 November 1996, NATO-Visit of SG Manlio Brosio, box 39, Agency File, NSF, #11.

163. As Bator informed Johnson: "I am very much afraid that the MLF-ites will once again start pushing for some form of nuclear sharing involving hardware. They will argue that French objections are no longer relevant, and that it is even more important now, following de Gaulle's attack, to give the Germans a sense of security. [...] I am afraid nothing will increase de Gaulle's support more, throughout Europe (Germany in-cluded) than an American initiative to push some kind of a hardware solution down reluctant European throats – and nothing will be more divisive of the Alliance." Bator to President, memorandum, 16 March 1966, vol. 1, France-NATO Dispute, CF, NSF, box 177, #247, LBJL.

164. Bator feared that any indulgence on Johnson's part would be interpreted by "the MLF-ites in State as a full-speed ahead from the White House." Bator to President, memor-andum, 22 March 1966, vol. 1, France-NATO Dispute, box 177, CF, NSF, #235, LBJL. Although Johnson impressed on Wilson the importance of involving Germany "in a meaningful partnership" and of "avoiding the rankling discrimination that has caused so much grief in the past," he stopped short of forcing the issue. Johnson to Wilson, letter, 23 March 1966, White House Central Files, CF, box 58, IT34 NATO, LBJL.

165. National Security Action Memorandum 345, FRUS 1964-1968, vol. 13, #159. It was, ironically, Dean Acheson, a consistent supporter of the MLF, who was asked to chair the working group of State Department and Pentagon officials that would develop proposals.

166. "The Special Committee" position paper, 8 December 1966, International Meetings and Travel File, NSF, box 35, LBJL.

167. Bromley Smith to President, "Summary Notes of 566th NSC Meeting, December 13, 1966," NSC Meetings File, NSF, box 2, LBJL.

168. Stromseth, *The Origins of Flexible Response*, 80.

169. Kissinger's notes of his conversations with German politicians and officials as trans-mitted to Johnson by McNamara in March 1966. McNamara to President, memoran-dum, 23 March 1966, WHCF, Confidential File, box 8, France, LBJL.

170. Bator to President, memorandum, *A Nuclear Role for Germany: What Do the Germans Want?*, 4 April 1966, Bator Papers, box 3, LBJL.

171. According to the Hallstein Doctrine, the Federal Republic of Germany (or West Ger-many) had the exclusive right to represent the entire German nation, and with the

exception of the Soviet Union, it would not establish or maintain diplomatic relations with any state that recognized the German Democratic Republic (or East Germany). The doctrine was first applied to Yugoslavia in 1957. Walter Hallstein was state secretary at the foreign ministry when he devised the policy in September 1955, though much of the work formulating this is said to have been done by his deputy Wilhelm Grewe.

172. Brandt's policy of "change through rapprochement" had been foreshadowed most clearly by his close adviser Egon Bahr in a speech on 15 July 1963, before the Evangelical Academy in Tutzing. For the original German text of this speech, see Bernhard Pollmann, ed., *Lesebuch zur Deutschen Geschichte*, vol. 3, *Vom deutschen Reich bis zur Gegenwart* (Dortmund: Chronik Verlag, 1984), 247-49. As McGhee's memoirs make clear, the United States had actively encouraged Brandt to develop his ideas about uniting Germany through a policy of "small steps." McGhee, *At the Creation of a New Germany*, 175-176.

173. Rusk to President, Cable 9261 (Paris), 16 December 1966, Country File, France, NSF, box 173, #24, LBJL.

174. Stromseth, *The Origins of Flexible Response*, chap. 9. The operational aspects of the strategy were subsequently elaborated in Military Committee document 14/3 (MC 14/3), dated 16 January 1968, which replaced the strategy of massive retaliation encapsulated in MC 14/2.

175. *France, the USSR, and European Security (Part I: Problems and Prospects for the Soviet-French Rapprochement)*, CIA Intelligence Memorandum, 20 May 1966, memos vol. 9, Country File, France, NSF, box 172, LBJL.

176. Bohlen to Rusk, Embtel 8672, 13 June 1966, Memos to the President, Rostow, NSF, box 8, #1, LBJL.

177. *France, the USSR, and European Security Part I*, CIA Intelligence Memorandum, 20 July 1966, memos vol. 9, Country File, France, NSF, box 172, LBJL.

178. Rostow to President, memorandum, 24 June 1966, memos vol. 9, Country File, France, NSF, box 172, LBJL.

179. Schwartz, *Lyndon Johnson and Europe*, 17, 20.

180. Rostow, *The Diffusion of Power*, 390.

181. National Security Action Memorandum 304, 3 June 1966, FRUS 1964-1968, vol. 17, Eastern Europe, #4.

182. National Security Action Memorandum. 345, 22 April 1966, FRUS 1964-1968, vol. 13, #159.

183. Ball and Rostow, telephone conversation, 17 May 1966, vol. (General), US and Europe, box 6, Papers of George W. Ball, #47, LBJL; Rostow to President, memorandum, 20 June 1966, Memos to the President, Rostow, NSF, box 8, #1, LBJL.

184. National Security Action Memorandum 352, FRUS 1964-1968, vol. 17, Eastern Europe, #15.

185. Rostow to President, memorandum, 6 October 1966, Speech File, NSF, box 5, LBJL.

186. For this address, see Johnson, *Public Papers*, vol. 2, 1125-1130. For another analysis of the speech, see Schwartz, *Lyndon Johnson and Europe*, 133-139.

187. Rostow to President, memorandum, 10 June 1966, Memos to the President, Rostow, box 8, #6, LBJL.

188. *NATO Strategic Concepts and NATO Force Levels*, report, 16 September 1966, NATO-General, vol. 4, Agency File, NSF, box 35, #16a, LBJL.

189. Ibid.

190. Cleveland to Rusk etc., memorandum, 17 November 1966, NATO-General vol. 4, box 35, Agency File, NSF, #12, LBJL.

191. Andreas Wenger, "Crisis and Opportunity: NATO's Transformation and the Multila-teralization of Détente, 1966-1968," *Journal of Cold War Studies* 6, no. 1 (2004): 22-74.

192. For Canada's proposals in 1964, see Anna Locher and Christian Nuenlist, "Reinvent-ing NATO: Canada and the Multilateralization of Détente, 1962–66," *International Jour-nal* 58, no. 3 (Spring 2003): 283–302.

193. Department of State to Embassy in Belgium, telegram, 26 November 1966, FRUS, 1964–1968, vol. 13, #221; Rusk to Department of State, telegram, 14 December 1966, FRUS, 1964–1968, vol. 13, #228.

194. Future Tasks of the Alliance, Council Ministerial Session, 13 December 1967, in NATO Archives, NISCA 4/10/6, Item 67, C-R(67) 51, 15; and Secretary's Statement in the North Atlantic Council, 6 December 1966, Lot Files, Conference Files, NSF, box 432, LBJL.

195. *Oral history interview with Dean Rusk* 4:18.

196. In 2004, NATO placed 250 documentary records relating to the Harmel Report on the internet: http://www.isn.ethz.ch/php/collections/coll_Harmel.htm. For detailed stud-ies of the Harmel Report, see Wenger, "Crisis and Opportunity"; Andreas Wenger, Anna Locher, Christian Nünlist, *The Future Tasks of the Alliance: NATO's Harmel Report 1966/67* (Parallel History Project on NATO and the Warsaw Pact, July 2004); Helga Haftendorn, "Entstehung und Bedeutung des Harmel-Berichts der NATO von 1967," *Vierteljahrshefte für Zeitgeschichte* 40, no. 2 (April 1992): 169–220; and Helga Haftendorn, "The Adaptation of the NATO Alliance to a Period of Détente: The 1967 Harmel Re-port," in Wilfried Loth, ed., *Crises and Compromises: The European Project, 1963–1969* (Ba-den-Baden: Nomos, 2001), 285–322. The above account also relies on a critical con-temporary assessment of the Harmel exercise by the Central Intelligence Agency: *The Harmel Study – NATO Looks to its Future*, CIA Intelligence Memorandum, 7 December 1967, NATO-General, vol. 5, Agency File, NSF, box 35, #4, LBJL.

197. CIA Intelligence Memorandum, *The Harmel Study – NATO Looks to its Future*, 7 December 1967, Agency File, NSF, box 35, #4, LBJL.

198. Record of Meeting between the Secretary General and the German Foreign Minister at the Foreign Office, Bonn, 9 October 1967, in NATO Archives, NISCA 4/10/6, Item 03, 6. Available on: http://www.isn.ethz.ch/php/documents/collection_Harmel/docu-ments/volume9/03-V9.pdf.

199. The Harmel Report – officially called *The Future Tasks of the Alliance, Report of the Council* – is available on NATO's website at http://www.nato.int/docu/comm/49-95/c671213b. htm.

200. CIA Intelligence Memorandum, *The Harmel Study – NATO Looks to its Future*, 7 December 1967, Agency File, NSF, box 35, #4, LBJL.

201. The paper was entitled "The Ideological Basis and the Unity of the Alliance." Available on: http://www.isn.ethz.ch/php/documents/collection_Harmel/documents/volume5/ 25-V5.pdf.

202. Haftendorn, "The Adaptation of the NATO Alliance," 304.

203. CIA Intelligence Memorandum, *The Harmel Study – NATO Looks to its Future*, 7 December 1967, Agency File, NSF, box 35, #4, LBJL.

204. Haftendorn, "The Adaptation of the NATO Alliance," 308-310.

205. Final Harmel Report, "The Future Security Policy of the Alliance: Report of the Rapporteur Sub-Group 3, Mr. Foy D. Kohler, USA," available from: http://www.isn.ethz.ch/php/collections/coll_Harmel.htm#4/10/4/3.

206. Haftendorn, "The Adaptation of the NATO Alliance," 305-308. The Mutual and Balanced Force Reduction (MBFR) negotiations between NATO and the Warsaw Pact about a reduction of conventional military forces in Central Europe to equal but significantly lower levels would not formally begin until October 1973.

207. Haftendorn, "The Adaptation of the NATO Alliance," 287.

208. *The Harmel Study*.

209. Brosio, Rostow, Cleveland, 10 September 1967, in NATO Archives, NISCA 4/10/5, Item 44. Available on: http://www.isn.ethz.ch/php/documents/collection_Harmel/documents/volume8/44-V8.pdf.

210. Memorandum of conversation, 27 September 1967, FRUS, 1964–1968, vol. 13, 618.

211. Meeting of Rapporteurs of Sub-Groups for Study on Future Tasks of the Alliance, 11 October 1976, in NATO Archives, NISCA 4/10/6, Item 4, 5. Available on: http://www.isn.ethz.ch/php/documents/collection_Harmel/documents/volume9/04-V9.pdf.

212. *The Harmel Study*, 6. Frustration with the French only increased when, on 6 November, de Gaulle disapproved of the Quai d'Orsay's comparatively accommodating position. See Haftendorn, "The Adaptation of the NATO Alliance," 315.

213. CIA Intelligence Memorandum, *The Harmel Study – NATO Looks to its Future*, 7 December 1967, Agency File, NSF, box 35, #4, LBJL.

214. Department of State to the Posts in the NATO Capitals, circular telegram, 16 November 1967, FRUS, 1964–1968, vol. 13, 640–641; and Intelligence Note No. 904, 9 November 1967, FRUS, 1964–1968, vol. 13, 637–639.

215. Memorandum for Rapporteurs, Future of the Alliance Study, 18 July 1967, in NATO Archives, NISCA 4/10/5, Item 29, 6. Also available on: http://www.isn.ethz.ch/php/documents/collection_Harmel/documents/volume8/33-V8.pdf.

216. Wenger, "Crisis and Opportunity," 71.

217. Ibid, 72.

218. *The Harmel Report*, available on http://www.nato.int/docu/comm/49-95/c671213b.htm.

219. See note 209.

220. *The Harmel Report*.

221. Memorandum of conversation, 25 September 1967, FRUS, 1964–1968, vol. 13, #266; Meeting of Rapporteurs of Sub-Groups for Study on Future Tasks of the Alliance, 11 October 1966, in NATO Archives, NISCA 4/10/6, Item 4, 5 (http://www.isn.ethz.ch/php/documents/collection_Harmel/documents/volume9/04-V9.pdf).

222. Record of Meeting between the Secretary General and the German Foreign Minister at the Foreign Office, Bonn, 9 October 1967, in NATO Archives, NISCA 4/10/6, Item 03, 6. Available on: http://www.isn.ethz.ch/php/documents/collection_Harmel/documents/volume9/03-V9.pdf. {same as FN 198}

223. For text of the Mansfield resolution (S. Res. 300), 31 August 1966, see *The Congressional Record, 1966, Senate,* 21442.

224. Bromley Smith to President, *Summary Notes of 566th NSC Meeting, December 13, 1966,* NSC Meetings File, NSF, box 2, LBJL.

225. Bator to President, memorandum, 23 August 1966, NATO-General, vol. 4, box 35, Agency File, NSF, #23b, LBJL.

226. The concept of "dual-basing" was very helpful in reducing the size of the problem: it enabled a reduction of foreign exchange costs as a result of troop deployments abroad while maintaining the commitment of these forces to the defense of Western Europe. In Rusk's proposal it meant that one of the three brigades would remain in Germany at all times while the other two would be based in the US. The three brigades would be rotated periodically by military air transport. Similarly, one-fourth of the aircraft in an air wing would remain in Germany at all times while the remaining three-fourths would be based in the United States. The units returned to the United States would remain committed to NATO and would be returned to Europe quickly in case of need.

227. Rostow/Bator to President, memorandum, 22 November 1966, NATO-Report to the President: US Forces for the NATO Central Region, box 39, Agency File, NSF, #3c, LBJL.

228. *Oral history interview with Eugene Rostow,* LBJL, 29. As Under Secretary of State for Political Affairs, Eugene Rostow was closely involved with the tripartite negotiations.

229. Bird, *The Chairman,* 587-596.

230. McCloy to Rostow, letter, 17 February 1967, NATO, General, vol. 4, Agency File, NSF, #7 and #7a, box 35, LBJL.

231. Report by John McCloy, 21 November 1966, Memos to the President, Rostow, NSF, box 11; Rostow/Bator to President, memorandum, 22 November 1966, NATO-Report to the President: US Forces for the NATO Central Region, box 39, Agency File, NSF, #3c, LBJL.

232. Bromley Smith to President, *Summary Notes of 566th NSC Meeting, December 13, 1966,* NSC Meetings File, NSF, box 2, LBJL. {same as FN 224}

233. For instance, in anticipation of Erhard's visit to the United States in late September 1966, Rostow noted that a letter he had received through Henry Kissinger from the influential German industrialist Kurt Birrenbach reflected loneliness among the Germans and a sense of being badly treated that is beginning to worry me." Rostow to President, memorandum, 2 September 1966, Memos to the President, Rostow, NSF, box 10, LBJL.

234. *President's Conversation with John McCloy Concerning US Position in Trilateral Negotiations,* memorandum for the record, 2 March 1967, vol. Trilaterals, box 18, Papers of Francis M. Bator, #1, LBJL. During this conversation, Johnson also expressed his irritation with the German unwillingness to be forthcoming. "I know my Germans. You know I lived in Fredericksburg grew up in Fredericksburg; they are great people; but by God they are stingy as Hell…"

235. A history of the trilateral negotiations can be found in an undated paper entitled "The Trilateral Negotiations and NATO," in Trilateral Negotiations and NATO, Book I, box 50, National Security Council History, NSF, #1a, LBJL. This history served as a basis for part of Johnson's memoirs: *The Vantage Point,* 306-311.

236. Senate Committee, *Atlantic Alliance. Hearings*, 248.

237. House Committee on Foreign Affairs, *The Crisis in NATO*, 6.

238. Senate Committee, *Atlantic Alliance*, 67. Underscoring in the original.

239. In May 1965, Hughes suggested that de Gaulle "might be willing to stay in NATO – on a somewhat different basis from the present one – if he thought he could nevertheless pursue his European policies with hope of success." He suggested that measures to enhance the status of France and to reduce the preponderance of American officers and the emphasis on military integration within NATO, in combination with "some form of nuclear coordination and possibly cooperation," might persuade de Gaulle to "leave the Alliance alone." Hughes to Rusk, research memorandum, 4 May 1965, Country File, France, memos vol. VI, box 171. LBJL.

240. McNamara's appraisal of NATO during one Senate hearing, for instance, might as well have been drafted in Paris: "... the national governments have not played a sufficiently direct role in Alliance military planning, and have left the primary responsibility to achieve an effective and efficient force posture to military authorities who did not have the political or financial responsibility. Specifically, I think there has been a tendency for governments to entrust many planning and 'thinking' jobs to NATO's international military commanders, and then forget about them. It is, of course, desirable and even imperative that we have 'integrated' commanders and integrated staffs who take a NATO-wide view, and who owe their allegiance not to any one nation but to the Alliance as a whole. [...] But its indispensable counterpart is a continuing, intense involvement of *nationally* responsible governmental leaders, civilian and military, in these vital planning activities." Senate Committee, *Atlantic Alliance*, 249-250.

241. In early April 1966, Richard Neustadt, for instance, censured the "quasi-independence" of the SACEUR and the emphasis placed within NATO on military integration, arguing that the United States had a "real *negative* stake" in its continuance: "For my money SACEUR is the Quemoy of Europe!" Neustadt to John McNaughton, letter, 4 April 1966, France-NATO, 1963-1967, Personal Papers of Adam Yarmolinski, box 32, JFKL.

242. Poirier to Rostow, letter, 23 April 1966, Subject File, WHCF, box 7, LBJL.

243. Senate Committee, *United States Policy Toward Europe (and Related Matters)*, 8.

244. Kissinger's notes of his conversation with de la Grandville as transmitted to Johnson by McNamara in March 1966. Robert McNamara to President, memorandum, 23 March 1966, WHCF, Confidential File, box 8, France, LBJL. Interestingly, de la Grandville suggested a compromise along the following lines: SHAPE would be moved to Luxembourg as a forward headquarters; French forces stationed in Germany would continue to be assigned to SHAPE; French territory, however, would fall in the same category as British territory, meaning that the SACEUR would have to obtain approval from the French government for any military operation on French soil ("except perhaps for some border districts in the northeast"). It is nonetheless doubtful that de Gaulle would have accepted any infringement on national sovereignty, least of all any foreign control over any French forces in wartime.

245. House Committee on Foreign Affairs, *The Crisis in NATO*, 21. The historian Samuel Wells Jr. similarly concludes that the United States could not have succeeded in keeping de Gaulle inside NATO. Wells, "Charles de Gaulle and the French Withdrawal

from NATO's Integrated Command," 90-93. Harrison and McDonough also conclude that "on matters of high principle such as defense sovereignty, de Gaulle was simply unwilling to bargain incessantly and behave like a cooperative friend and ally." Harrison and McDonough, *Negotiations on the French Withdrawal From NATO*, 44.

246. The House Republican Committee on NATO, chaired by Congressman Paul Findley, for instance, urged Johnson to "break the ice" by paying a visit to Paris for a "man-to-man discussion" with de Gaulle. Findley criticized the administration for dismissing de Gaulle's views as lacking significant public support in Europe and even in France. In June 1965, the Findley Committee paid a visit to Paris and on 30 June published a report which put responsibility for Franco-American differences squarely with the Johnson administration. The report was labeled as partisan in nature, but nonetheless prompted Bohlen to state his opposition to a presidential visit to Paris during an election year in France. Bohlen to Rusk, Embtel 7401, 29 June 1965, Country File, France, cables vol. VII, box 171, LBJL. The text of the Findley Report is contained in Deptel 6713, Rusk to Bohlen/Finletter, 29 June 1965, Country File, France, box 171, cables vol. 7, NSF, LBJL.

247. In December 1964, when Sulzberger asked him whether the time was ripe for a meeting with LBJ, de Gaulle "raised his eyebrows, looked sceptical, spread his long arms, shrugged his shoulders, and said, 'That depends. What do you expect? Would it only be a contact between chiefs of state to talk together amiably ….'" Asked about the report of the Findley Committee, he sniffed: "That is meaningless, that is politics." Sulzberger, *Age of Mediocrity*, 146, 185-190.

248. Kissinger's notes of conversations with French and German officials were given to LBJ for night reading. McNamara to President, memorandum, 23 March 1966, WHCF, Confidential File, box 8, France, LBJL.

249. Rostow to President, memorandum, 7 March 1966, CF, CO 81 (France), WHCF, box 8, LBJL.

250. Bozo, *Two Strategies for Europe*, 190.

251. Couve de Murville, *Une politique étrangère*, 82.

252. In particular, Thomas Schwartz has made a valuable contribution to Johnson's rehabilitation as a foreign policy president on the basis of his accomplishments in the European arena and in improving relations with the Soviet Union. Schwartz, *Lyndon Johnson and Europe*, 92-186.

253. Senate Committee, *Atlantic Alliance*, 153-154. Schelling had earned fame in 1960 with *The Strategy of Conflict*, which pioneered the study of bargaining and strategic behavior. Schelling's economic theories about war were extended in *Arms and Influence* (1966). In 2005, he was awarded the Nobel Prize together with Robert Aumann for "having enhanced our understanding of conflict and cooperation through game-theory analysis."

254. George W. Ball, "The Larger Meaning of the NATO Crisis," *Department of State Bulletin* 54, 16 May 1966, 766.

255. Senator Mike Mansfield, Under Secretary Eugene Rostow and Assistant Secretary Douglas MacArthur, memorandum of conversation, 9 December 1966, FRUS 1964-1968, vol. XIII, #224.

256. Acheson to Eden, letter, 29 June 1966, as printed in McLellan and Acheson, *Among Friends*, 279.

257. Bruce, diary entry, FRUS 1964-1968, vol. 13, #166. After this spat, according to Bruce, "Acheson visibly seethed in silence; LBJ looked like a human thundercloud." Acheson himself recorded that "Rusk and McNamara dove for cover while Ball and I slugged it out with Mr. Big." See note 256.

258. Johnson to Rusk and McNamara, memorandum, 4 May 1966, FRUS 1964-1968, vol. 13, #161.

259. Acheson to Truman, letter, 3 October 1966, as printed in McLellan and Acheson, *Among Friends*, 281-282. Acheson's rueful mood of unfulfilled expectations was possibly also induced by the fact that he was writing his memoirs at the time, which were published in 1969 as *Present at the Creation*.

260. As cited in Schwartz, *Lyndon Johnson and Europe*, 143.

261. Ball, *The Past Has Another Pattern*, 425.

Note to Chapter Six – Grand Designs Go Bankrupt

1. Embassy in France to Department of State, telegram, 11 July 1967, FRUS, 1964-1968, vol. 12, Western Europe, #73.

2. *France and the Atlantic Alliance*, CIA Intelligence Memorandum, 6 October 1967, vol. 14, CF, NSF, box 174, LBJL. Such analyses were corroborated by information from contacts within the French government. In August 1967, the American embassy had sent a secret message to Washington informing Johnson that its source at the Quai d'Orsay was convinced France would leave the Atlantic Alliance in 1968 and that all his policies were geared toward this end. Jauvert, *L'Amérique contre de Gaulle*, 168.

3. As quoted in Brinkley, *Dean Acheson*, 235.

4. Ibid., 235-236.

5. In early 1968, a Gallup poll indicated that less than half (49 percent) of all Americans still had a favorable opinion of France, down from 68 percent in 1957, ranking it among only six nations with ratings of under 50 percent. The other five countries were Egypt (39%), the Soviet Union (19%), North Vietnam (7%), Cuba (6%), and Communist China (5%). According to this poll, Great Britain (85%) and West Germany (75%) had become notably more popular over the same decade. Fred Panzer to President, memorandum, 6 February 1968, CO 81, WHCF, box 30, LBJL.

6. For instance, when Johnson read in the gossip pages of *The Washington Post* in the fall of 1967 that Secretary Fowler, who was having gallbladder problems, had responded to a question about his health that he was allright "except for my de Gaulle bladder," he made sure to reprimand his secretary of the treasury. *Oral history interview with E. Ernest Goldstein* 5:4-6.

7. A report of their brief and insubstantial conversation is printed in FRUS, 1964-1968, vol. 12, Western Europe, #73.

8. Johnson to Eisenhower, letter, 29 April 1967, CO 81, WHCF, box 30, LBJL.

9. mbassy Bonn to Department of State, Embtel 3054 (Bonn), , WHCF, box 30, LBJL.

10. *New York Times*, 26 April 1967.

11. On de Gaulle's views of Israel and the Arab-Israeli war, see Lacouture, *De Gaulle: The Ruler*, 434-446.

12. Johnson did put pressure on Israel to refrain from going to war with its Arab neighbors, but he was ultimately unable to prevent the Israeli attack. The State Department's first reaction to the outbreak of the war was moreover hardly a statement of unqualified support, since it declared the United States "neutral in thought, word, and deed." American-Israeli relations plummeted upon the Israeli attack on the USS *Liberty* on 8 June, which cost the lives of 34 American sailors. Tel Aviv insisted it was a military mistake, but Johnson and his advisers remained skeptical. Only when faced with the consternation of the American Jewish community at the United States' neutral stance did Johnson grudgingly strike a somewhat more pro-Israeli note. See Dallek, *Flawed Giant*, 425-432; William B. Quandt, "Lyndon Johnson and the June 1967 War: What Color Was the Light?" *Middle East Journal* 46 (1992): 177-197; and Warren I. Cohen, "Balancing American Interests in the Middle East: Lyndon Baines Johnson vs. Gamal Abdul Nasser," in Cohen and Tucker, *Lyndon Johnson Confronts the World*, 279-309.

13. Embassy in France (Bohlen) to Department of State, telegram 12 July 1967, FRUS, 1964-1968, vol. 12, Western Europe, #74. Bohlen: "It is disconcerting to say the least to see the head of an important and traditionally friendly country conduct its foreign policy on such a series of subjective and relatively trivial prejudices as de Gaulle seems to be doing in France. [...] His supposition, and it is certainly no more than that, that if the U.S. had really given a flat warning to Israel we could have prevented the war is ridiculous on the face of it."

14. For text of the press conference, see Charles de Gaulle, *Discours et messages*, vol. 5, *Vers le terme*, 227-247. To be sure, de Gaulle cannot be labeled an anti-Semite. He was stunned at the spin given to his words, for he had meant them as an expression of admiration. See Lacouture, *De Gaulle: The Ruler*, 434-446.

15. See for example Peyrefitte, *C'était de Gaulle* 3:303-380 (the quote appears on page 332); Lacouture, *De Gaulle: The Ruler*, 447-464.

16. Peyrefitte, *C'était de Gaulle* 3:338-339.

17. Bohlen to Rusk, Embtel 9412 (Paris),23 January 1968, vol. 13, CF, NSF, #78, box 174, LBJL.

18. On de Gaulle and Quebec, see Lacouture, *De Gaulle: The Ruler*, 447-464. The quote appears on page 452 (emphasis added).

19. John Francis Bosher, *The Gaullist Attack on Canada 1967-1997* (Montreal: McGill-Queen's University Press, 1999), 29. Also Peyrefitte, *C'était de Gaulle* 3:307.

20. In a press conference on 27 November 1967, de Gaulle stated that "cet État du Québec aurait à régler librement et en égal avec le reste du Canada, les modalités de leur coopération pour maîtriser et exploiter une nature très difficile sur d'immenses étendues et pour faire face à l'envahissement des Etats-Unis [...]." The Johnson administration, to be sure, had watched Argus-eyed the strengthening of bonds between France and Quebec for some time. In June, Henry Fowler had expressed the administration's concern with the possible implications of de Gaulle's visit to Quebec to his Canadian colleague Mitchell Sharp. The State Department assessed that de Gaulle was determined to support the separatist movement in Quebec in order to create an independent state in North America less amenable to the United States than Canada. Jauvert, *L'Amérique contre de Gaulle*, 165-166.

21. Charles Ailleret, "'Défense dirigée' ou 'défense tous azimuts,'" *Revue de défense nationale* 23 (December 1967): 1,923-1,927. A translation into English was published a few months later as "Defense in All Directions," *The Atlantic Community Quarterly* (Spring 1968): 17-25. Ailleret's article was based on a directive that de Gaulle himself had drafted earlier that year. De Gaulle also gave final approval to the text. See Lacouture, *De Gaulle: The Ruler*, 428-429; Gordon, *A Certain Idea of France*, 64; Bozo, *Two Strategies for Europe*, 203-205. It should be noted that de Gaulle had expressed similar ideas about the purposes of the French nuclear force in his legendary speech for the École militaire of 3 November 1959, as he stated that "since France could be destroyed on occasion from any point in the world, it is necessary that our force be designed so that it can act anywhere in the world." *Avec le renouveau*, 126.

22. Ailleret, "Defense in All Directions," 17-25.

23. French fear of American military action was not as far-fetched as it seemed. The United States' Ambassador to NATO, Harlan Cleveland, for instance, told Sulzberger that "if the French were to remain neutral or hostile in any war with Russia," the United States should "seize such installations as we require on French soil even if [...] [this meant] 'fighting a two front war.'" Sulzberger, *Age of Mediocrity*, 218. As for Ailleret, he was highly conscious of such a scenario because of his personal involvement in negotiating the terms of France's withdrawal from NATO. See Jauvert, *L'Amérique contre de Gaulle*, 170.

24. Lacouture, *De Gaulle: The Ruler*, 434. For a similar contemporary assessment, see the diary notes of Hervé Alphand, dated 12 August 1967, in *L'étonnement d'être*, 493.

25. Harrison, *The Reluctant Ally*, 166-167.

26. *Time*, 17 August 1962.

27. Bundy to Johnson, memorandum, 11 November 1964, MtP, NSF, box 2, LBJL.

28. Steel, *Lippmann*, 555.

29. Embassy in France to Department of State, telegram, 24 November 1966, FRUS, 1964-1968, vol. 12, Western Europe, #76.

30. Bohlen to Department of State, Airgram 1405 (Paris), 9 February 1968, as reprinted in Jauvert, *L'Amérique contre de Gaulle*, 250-253.

31. Henry Tanner, "The Ire Over De Gaulle," *New York Times*, 12 January 1968.

32. Statement before the Council of Ministers on 3 April 1968, in France, Ambassade de France, *French Foreign Policy*, 1968, 149.

33. For de Gaulle's policies toward American involvement in the Vietnam conflict in the 1960s, see Marianna P. Sullivan, *France's Vietnam Policy: A Study in French-American Relations* (Westport, CT: Greenwood Press, 1978); Fredrik Logevall, "De Gaulle, Neutralization, and American Involvement in Vietnam, 1963-1964," *Pacific Historical Review* 1, no.1 (February 1992): 69-102; Anne Sa'adah, "Idées Simples and Idées Fixes: De Gaulle, the United States, and Vietnam," in Paxton and Wahl, *De Gaulle and the United States*, 295-315.

34. See Chapter One.

35. Lawrence J. Bassett and Stephen E. Pelz, "The Failed Search for Victory: Vietnam and the Politics of War," in Paterson, *Kennedy's Quest for Victory*.

36. De Gaulle's criticism was nonetheless still muted. In December 1963, he impressed on Rusk that his comments on a neutralization of Vietnam upon Diem's assassination

had been "misunderstood" as an attack on the United States' Vietnam policies and that he "was merely giving the general direction for the future." Rusk to Johnson, Secto 25, 16 December 1963, vol. 5, box 170, CF, NSF, #133, LBJL.

37. Bohlen to Rusk, Embtel 6234 (Paris), 4 May 1965, vol. 6, box 171, CF, NSF, #218b, LBJL.

38. Logevall, "De Gaulle, Neutralization, and American Involvement in Vietnam, 1963-1964," 69-102. In December 1963, Henry Cabot Lodge, the American ambassador to Vietnam, reported that "some [Vietnamese] generals are seriously concerned that US secretly favors neutral solution for South Vietnam and that there is even suspicion that my stop-over in Paris on the way back to Saigon was for the purpose of talks with [the] French in this vein." Lodge to Rusk, Embtel 1135 (Saigon), 10 December 1963, Vietnam cables vol. 1, CF, NSF, #57, LBJL.

39. Lodge to Harriman, Embtel 1398 (Saigon), 25 January 1964, Vietnam cables, vol. 2, CF, Vn, NSF, #97, LBJL.

40. Lodge to Rusk, Embtel 1413 (Saigon), 28 January 1964, Vietnam cables, vol. 2, CF, Vn, NSF, #107, LBJL. One day later, Lodge added that "we have many reports from particularly responsible sources about [a] French neutralist plot, French money, and French agents" and that "we suspect a secret agreement between him and the CHI-COMS [Chinese communists]." Lodge to Rusk, Embtel 1431 (Saigon), 29 January 1964, Vietnam cables, vol. 2, Memos & Misc., CF, Vnam, NSF, #110, LBJL. In February, Lodge made a similar appeal to President Johnson. Lodge to Johnson, Embtel 1606 (Saigon), 22 February 1964, McGeorge Bundy, vol. 3, box 1, MtP, NSF, #38g, LBJL. Bohlen, however, resisted Lodge's call to approach de Gaulle, believing it would do nothing to change his opinion. Bohlen to Bundy, letter, 12 March 1964, vol. 1, box 169, CF, NSF, #142, LBJL. On 21 March, Johnson nonetheless instructed Bohlen to have a "frank" discussion with de Gaulle on Vietnam. Johnson to Bohlen, Deptel 4793, 21 March 1964, McGeorge Bundy, vol. 3, box 1, MtP, NSF, #38e, LBJL. Rumors of a French-sponsored neutralist coup were fed constantly by General Nguyen Khanh, leader of the South Vietnamese military junta.

41. Mansfield to Johnson, letter, 1 February 1964, vol. 1, box 1, Memos to the President, NSF, #17b, LBJL.

42. McNamara to Johnson, memorandum, 13 March 1964, vol. 2, Memos to the President, NSF, #28, LBJL.

43. Johnson to Ball, memorandum, 4 June 1964, Memo, vol. 3, box 170, CF, NSF, #68, LBJL.

44. Ball to Johnson and Rusk, Secun 3 (Paris), 5 June 1964, Southeast Asia, vol. 2, Memos A, box 52, CF, Vnam, NSF, #70, LBJL.

45. Sullivan, France's Vietnam Policy, 93.

46. Ball, The Past Has Another Pattern, 377-379. Ball: "My selection for that mission was no accident; in Lyndon Johnson's mind, the very fact that I opposed the war made me the best advocate of the administration's position." On Ball's views on Vietnam, see also DiLeo, George Ball.

47. Rostow to Johnson, memorandum, 6 June 1964, Southeast Asia, vol. 2, memos A, box 52, CF, Vnam, NSF, #95b, LBJL.

48. Ambassador Bohlen's plea from Paris to "deal with French on equal basis with other allies" on Vietnam, after he had been instructed not to inform the French government of the initiation of air strikes against North Vietnam in early February 1965, was illustrative. Bohlen to Rusk, Embtel 4503 (Paris), 9 February 1965, vol. 5, CF, NSF, #34, box 170, LBJL. Costigliola aptly described this incident as "an ironic footnote to de Gaulle's directorate proposal [...]." *France and The United States*, 141.

49. Bohlen to Rusk, Embtel 5168 (Paris), 12 March 1965, vol. 6, box 171, CF, NSF, #154, LBJL.

50. Bohlen to Rusk, Embtel 6234 (Paris), 4 May 1965, vol. 6, box 171, CF, NSF, #218b, LBJL.

51. Bundy to Johnson, memorandum, 19 February 1965, France, Couve de Murville Visit 2/65, CF, NSF, #1, box 175, LBJL.

52. "American Foreign Policy: The Twenty-Five Year Record and the Achievement of 1964," 19 December 1964, McGeorge Bundy, vol. 7, MtP, NSF, box 2, LBJL.

53. Rusk and Alphand, memorandum of conversation, 1 July 1964, Memo, vol. 3, box 170, CF, NSF, #71b, LBJL. For Rusk's irritation with de Gaulle over Vietnam, see also Schoenbaum, *Waging Peace and War*, 396.

54. Bundy to Johnson, memorandum, "France in Vietnam, 1954, and the U.S. in Vietnam, 1965 – a useful analogy?" 30 June 1965, McGeorge Bundy, vol. 11, June 1965, box 3, MtP, NSF, #10, LBJL. See also Joseph A. Califano, *The Triumph and Tragedy of Lyndon Johnson: The White House Years* (New York: Simon & Schuster, 1991), 34.

55. Sullivan, *France's Vietnam Policy*, 89.

56. CIA Report to Department of State, 2 August 1965, TDCS – 314/10763-65, LBJL. In particular, Etienne Manac'h, director of the Asian Division of the French Foreign Ministry, had excellent contacts with Hanoi through Mai Van Bo, the North Vietnamese delegate general to France, and would play a crucial role in preparing for the Paris peace talks beginning in 1968. Sullivan, *France's Vietnam Policy*, 105-107.

57. For the text of this speech, see De Gaulle, *Vers le terme*, 76. On his way to Cambodia, during a stop-over in Ethiopia, de Gaulle had apprised the American ambassador in Addis Ababa of his intentions, saying "with a twinkle that the route to Cambodia did not go by Washington." Embassy in Ethiopia to Department of State, telegram, 27 August 1966, FRUS, 1964-1968, vol. 12, Western Europe, #65.

58. Hughes to Rusk, research memorandum, 26 February 1965, vol. 6, box 171, CF, NSF, #232a, LBJL.

59. Bohlen to Rusk, Embtel 6690 (Paris), 25 May 1965, vol. 6, box 171, CF, NSF, #136, LBJL; Bohlen to Rusk, Embtel 6582 (Paris), 19 May 1965, vol. 6, box 171, CF, NSF, #138, LBJL.

60. Sullivan, *France's Vietnam Policy*, 106.

61. See Dallek, *Flawed Giant*, 538; Johnson, *The Vantage Point*, 501-505.

62. FRUS, 1964-1968, vol. 6, Vietnam, January-August 1968, #221, note 2.

63. Notes of Meeting, 30 April 1968, Foreign Relations, 1964-1968, vol. 6, Vietnam, January-August 1968, #216.

64. *Significance of Paris as Site for Vietnamese Negotiations*, CIA Intelligence Memorandum, 6 May 1968, vol. 75, May 6-8, 1968, MtP, NSF, #40a, box 33, LBJL.

65. Lacouture, *De Gaulle: The Ruler*, 474.

66. Sullivan, *France's Vietnam Policy*, chap. 5.

67. Ibid., 117.

68. From the memoirs of François Flohic (entitled *Souvenirs d'outre-Gaulle* (1979)), as quoted in Charles G. Cogan, "The Break-Up: General De Gaulle's Separation from Power," *Journal of Contemporary History* 27, no.1 (January 1992): 177.

69. *Le Monde*, 15 March 1968.

70. Lacouture, *De Gaulle: The Ruler*, 536.

71. Rostow to Johnson, Embtel 15183 (Paris), 30 May 1968, vol. 13, CF, NSF, #111, box 174, LBJL.

72. De Gaulle's possible resignation was the first item discussed at a luncheon meeting with President Johnson on 29 May. "Lunch meeting with the President, Wednesday, May 29, 1968 – 1.30 pm," vol. 79, May 25-31, 1968, MtP, NSF, #22, box 35, LBJL.

73. Katzenbach to President (at the LBJ Ranch), cable, 30 May 1968, vol. 13, box 174, CF, NSF, #112, LBJL.

74. *The French Crisis*, CIA Intelligence Memorandum, 31 May 1968. vol. 13, CF, NSF, #158, box 174, LBJL.

75. De Gaulle, *Vers le terme*, 292-293.

76. *France's Student-Labor Crisis: Causes and Consequences*, CIA Intelligence Memorandum, 25 May 1968, vol. 13, CF, NSF, #180b, box 174, LBJL.

77. William F. Buckley Jr., "Smile Turns Serious on De Gaulle," *Evening Star*, 24 May 1968.

78. "Ferment in France," *New York Times*, 19 May 1968.

79. Scott Stossel, *Sarge: The Life and Times of Sargent Shriver* (Washington: Smithsonian Books, 2004), 502, 510-511. On Shriver's views of the student movement, see also Jauvert, *L'Amérique contre de Gaulle*, 173-174. "I knew Sarge Shriver was a dynamic fellow," Rostow joked to Johnson, "but I didn't think all of this would come from sending him to Paris." Rostow to Johnson, memorandum, 24 May 1968, LBJL. More than any previous ambassador, Shriver would travel around the country to meet with the French. Being "*un Kennedy à Paris*," he was able to project a more idealistic image of the United States and soon became, according to *Paris Match*, one of the most popular people in France. Ernest Goldstein "argued long and hard for someone who would be young and dynamic, and who would serve as a rallying point for the very fundamental pro-American feeling that exists in 99 percent of the French people, really. And when Sarge Shriver got it, I was very happy; and he and I had had several long talks about the way to carry on." *Oral history interview with E. Ernest Goldstein*, LBJL, 24.

80. Walters, *Silent Missions*, 459. On this disposition of American diplomats, see also Jauvert, *L'Amérique contre de Gaulle*, 172.

81. Embassy in France to Department of State, telegram 28 May 1968, FRUS, 1964-1968, vol. 12, Western Europe, #79.

82. Shriver to Rusk, Embtel 2568 (Paris), 4 June 1968, vol. 13, CF, NSF, #42a, box 174, LBJL.

83. Katzenbach to Johnson, memorandum, 29 May 1968, vol. 13, CF, NSF, #162a, box 174, LBJL.

84. Gavin, *Gold, Dollars, and Power*, 183. The May crisis had strongly encouraged speculators to expect a devaluation sooner or later of the franc, which had already been considered the weakest currency in the Common Market before the crisis. In May and

June, they were beginning to exchange huge numbers of francs in hopes of forcing such a devaluation (after which they could buy back francs at a much cheaper rate).

85. Fowler to Johnson, memorandum, 6 June 1968. See FRUS 1964-1968, vol. 8, International Monetary and Trade Policy, #199.

86. Rostow to Johnson, memorandum, 4 June 1968, vol. 80, June 1-6, 1968, MtP, NSF, #45, box 35, LBJL.

87. White House to Embassy in Germany, telegram, 18 November 1968, FRUS 1964-1968, vol. 8, International Monetary and Trade Policy, #208. For Fowler's report of his ensuing conversation with Kiesinger, see #209.

88. Johnson to Wilson, telegram, 19 November 1968, FRUS 1964-1968, vol. 8, International Monetary and Trade Policy, #210.

89. Rostow to Johnson, telegram, 20 November 1968, FRUS 1964-1968, vol. 8, International Monetary and Trade Policy, #213.

90. De Gaulle, *Discours et messages* 5:354-357. By denouncing devaluation, de Gaulle actually ignored the advice of Finance Minister François Ortoli to accept a limited devaluation. See Lacouture, *De Gaulle: The Ruler*, 564-565.

91. Cook, *Charles de Gaulle*, 413.

92. Rostow, paper, 22 November 1968, FRUS 1964-1968, vol. 8, International Monetary and Trade Policy, #220.

93. For the messages exchanged between Johnson and de Gaulle on 24 November, see *Department of State Bulletin*, 16 December 1968, 628.

94. Johnson, *The Vantage Point*, 319.

95. Rostow to Johnson, memorandum, 25 November 1968, vol. 14, CF, NSF, #46 and #46a, box 174, LBJL.

96. Lacouture, *De Gaulle: The Ruler*, 564.

97. Embassy in Germany to White House, telegram, 22 November 1968, FRUS 1964-1968, vol. 8, International Monetary and Trade Policy, #219.

98. The Bonn communiqué of 22 November 1968, *Department of State Bulletin*, 16 December 1968, 627-628.

99. Memorandum for the Record, 23 November 1968, FRUS 1964-1968, vol. 8, International Monetary and Trade Policy, #221.

100. Record of Meeting of the National Security Council, 25 November 1968, FRUS 1964-1968, vol. 8, International Monetary and Trade Policy, #222.

101. Johnson, *The Vantage Point*, 486-490.

102. Schwartz, *Lyndon Johnson and Europe*, 214-215.

103. Notes of Meeting, 24 July 1968, FRUS 1964-1968, vol. 17, Eastern Europe, #72.

104. Summary of Meeting, Johnson, Ambassador Dobrynin, and Rostow, 20 August 1968, FRUS 1964-1968, vol. 17, Eastern Europe, #80. Diplomatic old-hand Bohlen, however, was considerably more concerned as he wrote to Rusk: "I find the military preparations somewhat excessive for a war of nerves, and it could be that in addition to making final preparation for a move into Czechoslovakia the Soviets are preparing for any eventuality which might arise." Bohlen to Rusk, memorandum, 26 July 1968, FRUS 1964-1968, vol. 17, Eastern Europe, #73.

105. Notes of Cabinet Meeting, 22 August 1968, FRUS 1964-1968, vol. 17, Eastern Europe, #84.

106. Kolodziej, *French International Policy Under De Gaulle and Pompidou*, 371, 374-375.

107. De Gaulle, *Vers le terme*.

108. Lacouture, *De Gaulle: The Ruler*, 471.

109. As cited in Lacouture, *De Gaulle: The Ruler*, 472.

110. Katzenbach to Department of State, telegram, 29 July 1968, FRUS, 1964-1968, vol. 12, Western Europe, #81.

111. Lacouture, *De Gaulle: The Ruler*, 473.

112. Kolodziej, *French International Policy Under De Gaulle and Pompidou*, 375.

113. The Council of Ministers' statement on the Soviet intervention is printed in Lacouture, *De Gaulle: The Ruler*, 472.

114. Text of Governor Harriman's interview with Radio Luxembourg, 11 September 1968, vol. 93, Sept 1-11, 1968, MtP, NSF, #11 and 11a, box 39, LBJL.

115. Embassy in France to Department of State, telegram, 2 September 1968, FRUS, 1964-1968, vol. 12, Western Europe, #83.

116. Article by Henry Tanner in the *New York Times*, as quoted in Shriver to Rusk, Embtel 6951 (Paris), 11 October 1968, vol. 14, CF, NSF, #80, box 174, LBJL.

117. Embassy in France to Department of State, telegram, 10 October 1968, FRUS, 1964-1968, vol. 12, Western Europe, #84.

118. "Possibilities for Accommodation between the US and France," CIA Memorandum, 28 August 1968, vol. 14, CF, NSF, #163a, box 174, LBJL.

119. "French Foreign Policy in the Wake of the Czechoslovak Crisis," CIA Intelligence Memorandum, 10 October 1968, vol. 14, CF, NSF, #155a, box 174, LBJL; Hughes to Rusk, research memorandum, 27 November 1968, REU-66, vol. 14, CF, NSF, #62a, box 174, LBJL. French approach to détente did in fact change, to the effect that a resumption of political contacts with Moscow was made contingent on its willingness to accept the sovereignty of the countries of Eastern Europe.

120. Werner Lippert, for instance, concludes that "U.S. détente and German Ostpolitik were some very distinct policies, both in quality and in purpose" and even posits that the "unilateralism of Ostpolitik" has resulted in "rifts within the NATO community [that] continue to this day." Werner Lippert, "Richard Nixon's Détente and Willy Brandt's Ostpolitik: The Politics and Economic Diplomacy of Engaging the East," dissertation submitted to the faculty of the Graduate School of Vanderbilt University, August 2005, 249-251.

121. Peter Merseburger, *Willy Brandt, 1913-1992: Visionär und Realist* (München: Deutscher Taschenbuch Verlag, 2004) (2002), 525-527. Brandt, however, recalls that de Gaulle did not show his pique. At a next dinner meeting, "ließ er mich besonders gut bedienen und Verführte mich, mehr zu essen, als mir der Hunger vorschrieb."

122. Rostow to Johnson, cable, 23 September 1968, telegram to LBJ Ranch, vol. 95, box 39, MtP, NSF, #43, LBJL. On de Gaulle's reproaches toward Germany in the aftermath of the Soviet crackdown in Czechoslovakia, see also Bozo, *Two Strategies for Europe*, 225-226; Couve de Murville, *Une politique étrangère, 1958-1969*, 282.

123. Bohlen to Rusk, Embtel 9412 (Paris), 23 January 1968, vol. 13, CF, NSF, #78, box 174, LBJL.

124. Communiqué of 16 November 1968, in *NATO: Facts and Figures* (Brussels: NATO Information Service, 1971), 369-371.

125. This was not immediately clear from Shriver's own account of this conversation, but a CIA memorandum cited an official from the Quai d'Orsay who stated that this had been the gist of de Gaulle's comments. Rostow to Johnson, telegram, 23 September 1968, telegram to LBJ Ranch, vol. 95, Sept. 19-25, 1968, MtP, NSF, #43, box 39, LBJL; "French Foreign Policy in the Wake of the Czechoslovak Crisis," CIA Intelligence Memorandum, 10 October 1968, vol. 14, CF, NSF, #155a, box 174, LBJL.

126. Johnson et al., memorandum of conversation, 11 October 1968, FRUS, 1964-1968, vol. 12, Western Europe, #85.

127. Hughes to Rusk, research memorandum, 27 November 1968. On the revival of tripartitism in French diplomacy in late 1968, see also Bozo, Two Strategies for Europe, 227-229.

128. In the words of Lacouture, De Gaulle: The Ruler, 474.

129. On de Gaulle's discussion with Soames, see Lacouture, De Gaulle: The Ruler, 475-477; Wilson, A Personal Record, 610-611; Bozo, Two Strategies for Europe, 232-234; Ledwidge, De Gaulle et les Américains, 392-397; Young, This Blessed Plot, 200-207.

130. Eugene Rostow and Lucet, memorandum of conversation, 25 November 1968, FRUS 1964-1968, vol. 12, Western Europe, #86. The Entente Cordiale was based on a series of Franco-British agreements signed on 8 April 1904, and was at least in part designed to counter growing German power in the late nineteeth and early twentieth century. Along with the Anglo-Russian Entente and the Franco-Russian Alliance, it later became part of the Triple Entente between Great Britain, France, and Russia.

131. For Wilson's account of the so-called Soames Affair, which is highly critical of his Foreign Office, see The Labour Government 1964-1970, 610-612. The Foreign Office also availed other allies, including the United States, of the gist of de Gaulle's remarks to Soames, after which "word spread like wildfire through NATO." See Henry A. Kissinger, White House Years (Boston: Little, Brown and Co., 1979), 87-88.

132. De Gaulle's adviser Bernard Tricot, the Elysée's secretary-general, for instance, said that "de Gaulle was ready to make real changes in his policy in order to bring [the] UK into [a] closer relationship with Europe" but that as a result of the affair would "not be willing to make [a] serious move [to] help [the] British as long as [the] Labour government is in power." Sargent Shriver to Secretary of State Rogers, telegram, 7 March 1969, NSC Files, Country Files-Europe, France, vol. I (20 Jan – 11 Apr, 1969), [1.62], box 674, NPMP. In addition, Pompidou informed the American embassy in Paris that de Gaulle was convinced that the Conservatives would win the next elections and that "he will be able to strike a bargain soon after those elections which will bring [the] UK into [the] European framework in a way which will be mutually satisfactory both to [the] French and [the] English." Shriver to Rogers, telegram, 5 March 1969, NSC Files, Country Files-Europe, France, vol. I (20 Jan – 11 Apr, 1969), [1.62], box 674, Nixon Presidential Materials Project (henceforth abbreviated as NPMP), National Archives and Records administration (henceforth abbreviated as NARA).

133. Rusk to Johnson, memorandum, 17 September 1968, vol. 94, Sept. 12-18, 1968, MtP, NSF, #12 and #12a, box 39, LBJL.

134. Department of State to Embassy in Paris, Deptel 255361, 15 October 1968, vol. 14, CF, NSF, #115, box 174, LBJL. It was Ernest Goldstein who recalled Debré's words to

Johnson. *Oral history interview with E. Ernest Goldstein*, LBJL, 5:2-3. A report of the conversation is printed in FRUS, 1964-1968, vol. 12, Western Europe, #85.

135. Nixon had 43.4 percent of the popular vote against Vice President Hubert Humphrey's 42.7 percent and Governor George Wallace's 13.5 percent. In the electoral college, however, his victory was clear cut: Nixon (301 votes), Humphrey (191), and Wallace (46).

136. For Nixon's recollection of this meeting, see Richard Nixon, *Leaders* (New York: Simon Schuster, 1990) (1982), 42-43, 61.

137. De Gaulle, *Memoirs of Hope*, 244.

138. De Gaulle, *Lettres, notes et carnets* (Paris: Librarie Plon, 1986), 35.

139. Richard M. Nixon, *RN: The Memoirs of Richard Nixon* (New York: Simon & Schuster, 1990), 248.

140. Stephen E. Ambrose, *Nixon: The Education of a Politician, 1913-1962*, vol. 1 (New York: Simon & Schuster, 1987), 671.

141. Peyrefitte, *C'était de Gaulle* 2:51.

142. Nixon, *Leaders*, 44.

143. C. L. Sulzberger, *The World and Richard Nixon* (New York: Prentice Hall Press), 6. Nixon, too, surmised that this played a role. See *Leaders*, 62.

144. *Le Monde*, 4 March 1969.

145. Nixon recalled, for instance, that when he visited France as a congressman in 1947, "virtually all the French and American officials I met reinforced the negative image I had of de Gaulle." Nixon, *Leaders*, 42.

146. Nixon, *Leaders*, 62.

147. Richard M. Nixon, *In the Arena: A Memory of Victory, Defeat and Renewal* (New York: Simon & Schuster, 1990), 142. Nixon told Sulzberger that he considered de Gaulle's book a "handbook for anyone going into politics in the communication age." Sulzberger, *The World and Richard Nixon*, 160.

148. Nixon, *Leaders*, 72.

149. Wicker, *One of Us*, 420-421. Also Stephen A. Ambrose, *Nixon: The Triumph of a Politician, 1962-1972*, vol. 2 (New York: Simon & Schuster, 1989), 268.

150. Nixon's speech is reprinted in FRUS 1969-1976, vol. 1, Foundations of Foreign Policy, 1967-1972, #2. In his memoirs, he writes that this speech "gave me the most pleasure and satisfaction in my political career... ." Nixon, *Memoirs*, 284.

151. For a similar assessment, see William Bundy, *A Tangled Web: The Making of Foreign Policy in the Nixon Presidency* (London/New York: I.B. Tauris, 1998), 517. The riots of May 1968 had probably enhanced Nixon's empathy for de Gaulle, and he seems to have shared both the latter's puzzlement as to the causes of discontent among the young and his conviction that there was a communist hidden hand behind it all. Shortly upon taking office, news of clashes in Paris between authorities and students in January 1969 – the worst in France since May 1968 – prompted Nixon to request a CIA analysis "in depth" of worldwide common factors of youth discontent. Annotated news summary, 24 January 1969, News Summaries - January 1969, Annotated News Summaries, President's Office Files, Special Files, box 30, NPMP, NARA. Ambrose records that Nixon was convinced that the rioting in the streets of Paris and Pittsburgh were part of a worldwide communist strategy. Ambrose, *Nixon: Triumph of a Politician*, 262.

152. Richard M. Nixon, *Six Crises* (New York: Doubleday, 1968) (1962), xvii.

153. Jon Roper, "Richard Nixon's Political Hinterland: The Shadows of JFK and Charles de Gaulle," *Presidential Studies Quarterly* 28, no. 2 (Spring 1998): 422-434. Roper argues, on the basis of an analysis of his writings, that Nixon was deeply influenced by the "heroic" leadership of Kennedy and de Gaulle.

154. Kissinger, *Diplomacy*, 706.

155. First Annual Report to the Congress on United States Foreign Policy for the 1970s, 18 February 1970, in *Nixon Papers*, 1970, 119.

156. Kissinger, *Diplomacy*, 712. On page 731, Kissinger slightly amends this assessment by stating that "Nixon was the first president *since Theodore Roosevelt* to conduct American foreign policy largely in the name of the national interest." (Emphasis added). One had indeed to go back to Theodore Roosevelt and Henry Cabot Lodge at the turn of the century, John Quincy Adams in the early nineteenth century, and Alexander Hamilton in the founding days of the American republic to find a similar dedication to the national interest. George Kennan may have been the only other postwar thinker about international relations who fit the conservative realist mold.

157. Nixon, *In the Arena*, 207.

158. William Safire, *Before the Fall: An Inside View of the Pre-Watergate White House* (New York: Ballantine Books, 1975, 1977), 889; Bundy, *A Tangled Web*, 55, 517; C. L. Sulzberger, *The World and Richard Nixon*, 154-167. Safire served as Nixon's speech writer. The quote is Bundy's. Sulzberger describes Nixon as "an avid courtier" who was "sincerely respectful of the General's techniques and studied these with more than a little profit to his own ideas of governance." (163)

159. Arthur Schlesinger Jr., *The Imperial Presidency* (New York: Popular Library, 1974), 247-248.

160. Kissinger, *Diplomacy*, 705.

161. *Time*, 3 January 1972, 15. Nixon had made similar remarks on 6 July 1971, to Midwestern News Media Executives in Kansas City, Missouri; see Richard M. Nixon, *Public Papers of the Presidents of the United States: Richard Nixon, 1971*, vol. x (Washington DC: GPO, 1972), 806.

162. Kissinger, *Diplomacy*, 714.

163. Nixon, *Memoirs*, 344. On the Nixon administration's policies towards the Soviet Union, see John Lewis Gaddis, *Strategies of Containment: A Critical Appraisal of Postwar American National Security Policy* (Oxford: Oxford University Press, 1982), chap. 9 and 10; Robert Litwak, *Détente and the Nixon Doctrine: American Foreign Policy and the Pursuit of Stability, 1969-1976* (Cambridge: Cambridge University Press, 1984).; Joan Hoff-Wilson, "'Nixingerism,' NATO, and Détente," *Diplomatic History* 13, no. 4 (Fall 1989): 501-525.

164. This aspect of the Nixon administration's thinking, the historian John Lewis Gaddis pointed out, actually amounted to a return to Kennan's original conception of containment. Gaddis describes the Nixon-Kissinger readjustment of American foreign policy as a return to Kennan's views in the late 1940s. He explains that, although "there is no evidence that Kissinger consciously drew on Kennan's ideas in planning policy during the Nixon administration," the similarity of their conceptual approaches was striking and "seem to have grown out of a shared commitment to the 'realist' tradition in American foreign policy, an intellectual orientation solidly grounded in the study of

European diplomatic history." Gaddis, *Strategies of Containment*, chap. nine, 308, passim.

165. Just days before Nixon's trip to China in February 1972, for instance, Kissinger said in a preparatory meeting in the Oval Office: "For the next 15 years we have to lean toward the Chinese against the Russians. We have to play this balance of power game totally unemotionally. Right now, we need the Chinese to correct the Russians, and to discipline the Russians." In FRUS 1969-1976, vol. 1, Foundations of Foreign Policy, 1967-1972, #105.

166. FRUS 1969-1976, vol. 1, Foundations of Foreign Policy, 1967-1972, #2.

167. Address by President Nixon to the North Atlantic Council, 10 April 1969, in Nixon, *Public Papers*, {vol#}: 272-276. Nixon expressed dismay with the lack of follow-up by his administation on this speech, adding that "during the past 8 years Kennedy or Johnson could burp and the whole administration establishment went into action saying what a 'great and imaginitive proposal' this was." Nixon to Secretary of State et al., memorandum, 14 April 1969, Special Files, Presidents' Personal File, Memoranda from the President, 1969-1974, box 1, NPMP, NARA.

168. Shortly before his trip to Europe, for instance, upon reading a Sulzberger column suggesting that it is time to have a European Commander of NATO, Nixon posed the question whether he should indeed consider that possibility. Nixon to Kissinger, memorandum, 13 February 1969, Special Files, Presidents' Personal File, Memoranda from the President, 1969-1974, box 1, NPMP. Kissinger had in fact already made the argument in his 1968 essay: "It is in our interest that Europeans should assume much greater responsibility for developing doctrine and force levels in NATO, perhaps by vitalizing such institutions as the West European Union (WEU), perhaps by alternative arrangements. The Supreme Allied Commander should in time be a European." Essay by Henry A. Kissinger, "Central Issues of American Foreign Policy," reprinted in FRUS 1969-1976, vol. 1, Foundations of Foreign Policy, 1967-1972, #4.

169. Annotated news summary, 10 April 1969, News Summaries – April 1969, Annotated News Summaries, President's Office Files, Special Files, box 30, NPMP, NARA.

170. "This isolationism is a troublesome trend," Nixon said in a meeting in April 1969. "The people are saying now 'Why don't we cut the military budget? Why not bring home the divisions in Europe?' The next step could be 'Let the rest of the world go hang.'" Report on Meeting of the Cabinet Committee on Economic Policy, 10 April 1969, in FRUS 1969-1976, vol. 1, Foundations of Foreign Policy, 1967-1972, #19. Nixon attacked "new isolationists" in an address in March 1971, equating proposals to cut the military budget and overseas commitments with "weakness." Address reprinted in FRUS 1969-1976, vol. 1, Foundations of Foreign Policy, 1967-1972, #87.

171. Nixon, *Memoirs*, 343.

172. Nixon's remarks to the press during a visit to Guam were on a background basis only but quickly stirred great interest since they seemed to imply an American withdrawal from Asia. They were subsequently refined into a policy that became known as the Nixon Doctrine. It held that, while the United States would continue to honor its treaty obligations and to extend its nuclear protection to allies, it would encourage Asian nations to be responsible for their own defense and intervene only when its interests were at stake. It not only cleared the ground for the Vietnamization of the Vietnam

War, but it also encouraged the notion of increasing regionalization. The full text of Nixon's remarks is printed in Nixon, *Public Papers*, {vol. #}:544-556.

173. Bruce Mazlish, *Kissinger: The European Mind in American Foreign Policy* (New York: Basic Books,1976).

174. Kissinger, *The Troubled Partnership*, 63. Likewise, Nixon believed that de Gaulle "was capable of working on a far bigger canvas than he had in his country." Sulzberger, *The World and Richard Nixon*, 160.

175. Kissinger: "By evoking so many memories of authoritarian rule, de Gaulle has polarized the discussion within Europe in a manner that makes it next to impossible to come to grips with the substance of his thought. A strong Europe was bound to present a challenge to American leadership. But by couching this challenge so woundingly, de Gaulle has spurred American self-righteousness rather than the objective reexamination of Atlantic relationships which the situation demands." Kissinger, *The Troubled Partnership*, 61-63.

176. Kissinger, *The Troubled Partnership*, 48.

177. Ibid., 238

178. Ibid., 244.

179. Ibid., 243-247. In Kissinger's view, this committee would have to consist of six members: the United States, Great Britain, France, Germany, Italy, and one rotating member representing the smaller countries.

180. Ibid., 232.

181. Ibid., 41.

182. Ibid., 44.

183. Kissinger, "Dealing with De Gaulle," in Paxton and Wahl, *De Gaulle and the United States*, 335. In *White House Years*, Kissinger similarly assessed that the United States had been "extraordinarily insensitive to the psychological problems of a country like France" (see page 106).

184. After de Gaulle's decision to withdraw France from NATO, for instance, Kissinger gave a speech at the University of Texas which contained the same ideas and proposals. See James R. Roach, ed., *The United States and the Atlantic Community: Issues and Prospects* (Austin, TX: University of Texas Press, 1967), 9-17.

185. Essay by Henry A. Kissinger, "Central Issues of American Foreign Policy," reprinted in FRUS 1969-1976, vol. 1, Foundations of Foreign Policy, 1967-1972, #4. The essay was first published in *Agenda for a Nation* (Washington, DC: The Brookings Institution, 1968) and subsequently in Kissinger's *American Foreign Policy: Three Essays* (New York: W. W. Norton, 1969), 51-97.

186. Ibid.

187. Ibid.

188. Kissinger, *White House Years*, 88.

189. Handwritten notes of President Nixon, 20-21 Jan 1969, Special Files, President's Office Files, President's Handwriting, box 1, NPMP, NARA.

190. Shriver to Undersecretary of State Elliot L. Richardson, letter, 26 March 1969, CF France, Subject Files: Confidential Files, White House Central Files, Special Files, box 6, NPMP; Shriver to Nixon, letter, 20 June 1969, Countries, Subject Files, WHCF, box 27, NPMP, NARA.

191. Nixon, *Memoirs*, 370.

192. *Washington Post*, 3 March 1969.

193. Arthur F. Burns to President, memorandum, 23 April 1969, WHCF, SuF, Europe [1969-1970], box 5, NPMP, NARA.

194. See also Nixon's own judgment to this effect: Nixon, *Memoirs*, 371.

195. Charged with planning the trip, Nixon's aides Bob Haldeman and John Ehrlichman had visited the Shrivers' residence prior to Nixon's visit. They had been horrified with the clutter in the house, the Catholic paraphernalia, the "psychedelic" dining room, and the fact that the residence was a "veritable shrine" to the Kennedys. Every time they "saw a picture of President Kennedy, they would recoil, as if to say, 'Ahhh! Monster!" All the Kennedy photographs were subsequently taken down and the residence was completely refurnished with movie-prop furniture from MGM studios. Nixon even brought his "own food," sidelining Shriver's French chef. See Stossel, *Sarge*, 545-546.

196. Nixon, *Leaders*, 73. Of the three meetings, two were held at de Gaulle's office in the Elysée and one at the Grand Trianon Palace in Versailles.

197. Richard Nixon and de Gaulle, memorandum of conversation, Paris, 28 February 1969, National Security Council Files (NSCF), box 1023, NPMP, NARA.

198. Richard Nixon and de Gaulle, memorandum of conversation, 1 March 1969, NSC Files, Presidential/HAK memcons, Memcons The President-General de Gaulle, 2/28-3/2/69, box 1023, NPMP, NARA.

199. In his conversation with Nixon in Washington on 31 March 1969, de Gaulle likewise expressed irritation with an Anglo-German agreement to produce enriched uranium for civilian purposes, since it might bring Germany once step closer to producing a nuclear weapon. "The French knew the Germans well. This is why they were prudent in dealing with them. They realized all of the tremendous vitality, drive, and capacity of the Germans. They knew that they had a certain bonhomie, but they also had a driving ambition which, when it became uncontrolled, had led to bitter experience in the past." Nixon, de Gaulle, Andronikov, General Walters, memorandum of conversation, 31 March 1969, NSC Files, Presidential/HAK Memcons, Memcon The President and General de Gaulle, box 1023, NPMP, NARA.

200. Nixon and de Gaulle, memorandum of conversation, 2 March 1969, NSC Files, Presidential/HAK memcons, Memcons The President - General de Gaulle, 2/28-3/2/69, box 1023, NPMP, NARA. "For any private matters below the Chief of State level," Nixon added, "General de Gaulle could have his people communicate with Dr. Kissinger."

201. Nixon and de Gaulle, memorandum of conversation, Paris, 28 February 1969, National Security Council Files (NSCF), box 1023, NPMP, NARA.

202. Sulzberger, *The World and Richard Nixon*, 11. Kissinger, incidentally, does not believe that he left behind a favorable impression, as he wittily recalls in his memoirs: "Nixon had the amazing idea of asking me [in front of the General] what I thought of de Gaulle's views of Europe. And I had the extraordinarily poor judgment to respond to Nixon's request. De Gaulle considered this invitation so astonishing that in preparing himself for the impertinence of my opinion he drew himself up to an even more imposing height. 'I found it fascinating,' I said. 'But I do not know how the President will keep Germany from dominating the Europe he has just described.' De Gaulle, seized by profound melancholy at so much obtuseness, seemed to grow another inch

as he contemplated me with the natural haughtiness of a snowcapped Alpine peak toward a little foothill. 'Par la guerre,' he said simply ('through war'). [...] I do not believe I made a lasting impression on the great French leader." Kissinger, *White House Years*, 110.

203. Shriver to Rogers, telegram, 6 March 1969, NSC Files, Country Files-Europe, France, vol. I (20 Jan – 11 Apr, 1969), [1.62], box 674, NPMP, NARA.

204. Shriver to Rogers, telegram, 7 March 1969, NSC Files, Country Files-Europe, France, vol. I (20 Jan – 11 Apr, 1969), [1.62], box 674, NPMP, NARA.

205. Nixon and de Gaulle, memorandum of conversation, 2 March 1969.

206. Nixon, *Memoirs*, 374.

207. Ibid., 370.

208. Sulzberger, *The World and Richard Nixon*, 157. In their 1 March 1969 meeting, de Gaulle indeed said that "the French already had relations with the Chinese and it would be better for the U.S. to recognize China before they were obliged to do it by the growth of China." See FRUS 1969-1976, vol. 1, Foundations of Foreign Policy, 1967-1972, #14.

209. Nixon and de Gaulle, memorandum of conversation, Paris, 28 February 1969.

210. Kissinger, *White House Years*, 765-766, 768. Kissinger writes that "between August 1 and the end of September we exchanged more messages [through Paris] than we had in the previous twenty years." (768) Kissinger also had secret meetings in Paris with the Chinese ambassador in Paris, Huang Chen. Many of the instructions to and reports from Walters are published in FRUS, 1969-1976, Documents on China, 1969-1972, Volume E-13.

211. Seymour M. Hersh, *The Price of Power: Kissinger in the Nixon White House* (New York: Summit Books, 1983), 352.

212. George C. Herring, *America's Longest War: The United States and Vietnam, 1950-1975* (New York: John Wiley & Sons, 1979), 219.

213. Safire, *Before the Fall*, 150.

214. Sulzberger, *The World and Richard Nixon*, 158-159.

215. Nixon and de Gaulle, memorandum of conversation, 2 March 1969. See also Nixon, *Memoirs*, 374.

216. Nixon, for instance, confirmed de Gaulle's influence to Sulzberger: "Did de Gaulle influence me in developing the policy of withdrawal trying to have what we call peace with honor, the answer is yes." Sulzberger, *The World and Richard Nixon*, 158-159. De Gaulle's withdrawal from Algeria may also have served as a model for Kissinger; see Mazlish, *Kissinger*, 244.

217. Herring, *The Longest War*, 221.

218. In addition, Nixon asked de Gaulle to transmit to the North Vietnamese that the United States was prepared "once a settlement was reached [to] make a major effort to assist them in rebuilding their cities and give them economic assistance [...]." Nixon and de Gaulle, memorandum of conversation, 2 March 1969.

219. Nixon, de Gaulle, Andronikov, General Walters, memorandum of conversation, 31 March 1969. During this conversation, de Gaulle reiterated that while he felt the United States should end the war "this did not mean [...] that such a departure should be precipitate" but "be organized and planned."

220. Nixon, *Leaders*, 76.

221. Harrison, *The Reluctant Ally*, 169-170.

222. Cogan, *Oldest Allies, Guarded Friends*, 153-154.

223. Quoted from a French report of a discussion between Kissinger and Pompidou on 13 December 1971, in Mélandri, "Aux origines de la cooperation nucléaire Franco-Américaine," in Maurice Vaïsse, *La France et l'Atome*, 236.

224. Kissinger, *White House Years*, 933.

225. Ambrose, *Nixon: The Triumph of a Politician*, 24.

226. Kissinger, *The Troubled Partnership*, 119, 166, 167.

227. On 14 June 1968, French Foreign Minister Debré had declared that the development of the French nuclear force would be delayed for one to two years as a result of economic problems caused by the month-long national strike. And in early January 1969, *Le Monde* reported that French army officers had recommended that the United States be asked to help in developing France's atomic weapons. The secrecy of the cooperation allowed France to uphold the icon of an independent deterrent, avoided recriminations in Germany, and averted opposition in the American Congress.

228. Couve de Murville, *Une politique étrangère*, 155. French Defense Minister Pierre Messmer likewise declared that Nixon "made it known to General de Gaulle that he accepted the de-facto reality of the new French nuclear capability." Messmer, "De Gaulle's Defense Policy and the United States from 1958-69," in Paxton and Wahl, *De Gaulle and the United States*, 355.

229. Jauvert, *L'Amérique contre de Gaulle*, 180-182.

230. Richard Ullman, "The Covert French Connection," *Foreign Policy* no. 75 (Summer 1989): 3-33. Ullman's article turned into a controversy in the United States as well as France. It suggested that consecutive American administrations had violated the Atomic Energy Act by providing asssitance to France. In France, it undermined the image of French nuclear independence. Pompidou's successor, Valéry Giscard d'Estaing, confirmed the existence of Franco-American nuclear collaboration in the second volume of his memoirs, *Le pouvoir et la vie. L'affrontement* (Paris: Compagnie 12, 1991), 183-192.

231. Mélandri, "Aux origines de la coopération nucléaire franco-américaine," 235-254. Kissinger's "Year of Europe" speech on 23 April 1973, to Associated Press irked Europeans because it portrayed them as parochial and suggested that Washington expected them to give in on economic issues because the United States carried much of the defense burden. As Schaetzel noted, "Europeans detected nothing less than an administration attack on the European Community." J. Robert Schaetzel, "Some European Questions for Dr. Kissinger," *Foreign Policy* 12 (Fall 1973): 67.

232. Philip Gordon writes that "one former French military leader of the highest authority" once confirmed to him that the nuclear collaboration with the United States was "very important" and saved France much time and money. There are contradictory statements as to whether this cooperation included the coordination of tactical nuclear targeting. Gordon, *A Certain Idea of France*, 216, endnote 37. The Joint Chiefs of Staff had suggested discussions with Paris on target coordination between the French *force de frappe* and the United States' Strategic Air Command as early as the spring of 1965. Bohlen and others, however, had then recommended against it since it would amount to a "political victory for de Gaulle." Bohlen to Rusk, Embtel 5745 (Paris), 24 April

1965, Country File, France, cables, vol. 6, 2/65-6/65, NSF, box 171, LBJL; Klein to Bundy, memorandum, 13 April 1965, Country File, France, memos, vol. 6, 2/65-6/65, NSF, box 171, LBJL.

233. The Ottawa communiqué of the North Atlantic Council of June 1974 acknowledged for the first time that it contributed to the deterrent of the Western alliance. Declaration on Atlantic Relations issued by the North Atlantic Council, 19 June 1974, see: http://www.nato.int/docu/basictxt/b740619a.htm (accessed October 2006). According to Duval and Mélandri, this declaration was largely written by French officials (in particular François de Rose). Marcel Duval and Pierre Mélandri, "Les Etats-Unis et la prolifération nucléaire: le cas français," *Revue d'histoire diplomatique* (1995), 209.

234. Kissinger, *Years of Upheaval*, 129.

235. C. Fred Bergsten of the National Security Council Staff to Kissinger, memorandum, 2 August 1969, FRUS, 1969-1976, vol. 4, Foreign Assistance, International Development, Trade Policies, 1969-1972, #401. Pompidou was referring to the breaching of the price minimums for wheat contained in the International Grains Arrangement (IGA), which the United States argued was started by the EC but which the French claimed was begun by the United States.

236. Hersh, *Price of Power*, 462, footnote.

237. As cited in Costigliola, *France and the United States*, 173.

238. Nixon "hated the world of the Council, with its smooth patrician manner and aura of inherited wealth and status," while he remained to the American foreign policy establishment "an aloof outsider, a strange bird." Leonard Silk and Mark Silk, *The American Establishment* (New York: Basic Books, 1980), 207, 208, passim.

239. Stanley Hoffmann, *Primacy or World Order: American Foreign Policy Since the Cold War* (New York: McGraw-Hill, 1978), 52.

240. Someone like George Ball, for instance, intensely disliked Nixon, whom he regarded a cynical and amoral manipulator, and clashed with Kissinger "at almost every turn," stating that "his [Kissinger's] guiding purpose is, by constantly tinkering with the mechanism, to maintain a shifting balance of power – an act which, unrelated to any body of basic principles, becomes a tour de force with no meaning beyond the virtuousity of the achievement." *Diplomacy for a Crowded World* (Boston: Atlantic Monthly Press, 1976), 306. On Ball's antagonistic relationship with Kissinger, see Bill, *Ball*, 212-224.

241. Acheson had loathed Nixon more than anyone else during the 1950s and 1960s, but learned to appreciate Nixon's ostensible command of foreign policy issues and was more than a little susceptible to Nixon's – and Kissinger's – calculated flattery. He also nurtured a friendly relationship with Kissinger, whose bright intellect and sense of realism he respected. On Acheson's incongruous relationship with Nixon and Kissinger, see Brinkley, *Dean Acheson*, 263-302; and Chace, *Acheson*, 429-436.

242. Livingston Merchant et al., to President-elect Nixon, "Strengthening Atlantic Relations", letter and paper, 23 December 1968, WHCF, SuF, CO 1-5, Europe [1969-1970], box 6, NPMP, NARA.

243. As quoted in Ambrose, *Nixon: Triumph of a Politician*, 251-252.

244. Kissinger, *White House Years*, 104.

245. Nixon, de Gaulle, Andronikov, General Walters, memorandum of conversation, 31 March 1969.
246. Kissinger, *White House Years*, 387.
247. Shriver to Rogers, telegram, 7 March 1969, Nixon Papers, National Archives.
248. Nixon to de Gaulle, letter, 28 April 1969, Special Files, Presidents' Personal File, Name/Subject File, 1969-1974, box 7, NPMP, NARA.
249. Walter, *Silent Missions*, 500-501.
250. Nixon's letter to de Gaulle is reprinted in his memoirs. Nixon, *Memoirs*, 386.
251. Lacouture, *De Gaulle: The Ruler*, 577.
252. Cogan, "The Break-Up: General De Gaulle's Separation from Power," 178.
253. Malraux, *Felled Oaks*, 16-17.
254. Ronald Steel, "The Abdication of Europe," in James Chace and Earl C. Ravenal, eds., *Atlantis Lost: US-European Relations after the Cold War* (New York: New York University Press, 1976), 47.
255. Costigliola, *France and the United States*, 161.
256. Summary notes of 569th NSC Meeting, 3 May 1967, Papers of Bromley K. Smith, box 31, LBJL. In a memorandum a few weeks later, Fowler repeated his conviction that the "principal menace to our position in Western Europe [...] is the desire of the French, under de Gaulle, to expel us as a practical matter from Europe." To that end, Paris was "blocking measures to achieve a better multilateral sharing of responsibilities by the Common Market partners while the U.S. follows a course which it cannot afford much longer." Fowler to Johnson, memorandum, 25 May 1967, Papers of Bromley K. Smith, box 31, LBJL.

Notes to Conclusion

1. James Chace and Elizabeth Malkin, "The Mischief-Maker: The American Media and De Gaulle, 1964-1968," in Paxton and Wahl, *De Gaulle and the United States*, 359-376.
2. *New York Times*, 8 December 1967.
3. In 1965, for instance, Senator Henry Jackson – a Democrat from Washington State – concluded that the situation had not been improved by "the tendency of some American policymakers to treat psychological and political problems as though they were primarily technical and to try to solve political problems with technical expedients." Senate Committee, *Atlantic Alliance*. Beginning on 17 March 1966, the House Committee on Foreign Affairs also held hearings in response to the crisis in NATO. *The Crisis in NATO: Hearings before the Subcommittee on Europe of the House Committee on Foreign Affairs*.
4. In May 1966, for instance, Johnson assured Senator Church that he had no desire to pick fights with de Gaulle and that he intended to use the relocation of NATO to modernize it. Johnson to Church, letter, 23 May 1966, Subject File, France, WHCF, box 30, LBJL. Johnson's response to the NATO crisis of 1966 moreover gave him favorable marks in public opinion polls at a time when other parts of his foreign policy were subject to mounting criticism. A Harris survey in early June 1966 indicated that 73% of the American population strongly supported keeping NATO alive and Johnson received favorable marks for the way he handled the crisis. *The Washington Post*, 6 June 1966.

5. On Lippmann's admiration for de Gaulle, see also Steel, *Walter Lippmann and the American Century*, 396-403, and Steel's contribution in Paxton and Wahl, *De Gaulle and the United States*, 377-390. Also Steel, "Walter Lippmann et Charles de Gaulle," *De Gaulle et son siècle* (Journées Internationales organisées par l'Institut Charles de Gaulle, Novembre 1990), 19-24. In *The Past Has Another Pattern*, George Ball described Lippmann as an "ardent Gaullist" with whom he could never agree on the question whether Monnet or de Gaulle was the greater Frenchman; see page 96.

6. Stanley Hoffmann, "De Gaulle's Memoirs: The Hero as History," *World Politics* 13, no. 1 (October 1960): 140-155; "De Gaulle, Europe, and the Atlantic Alliance," *International Organization* 18 (Winter 1964): 1-28; "Europe's Identity Crisis: Between the Past and America", *Daedalus* (Fall 1964); "Perceptions, Reality, and the Franco-American conflict," *Journal of International Affairs* 21, no. 1 (1967): 57-71. Some of these articles were later published in *Decline or Renewal?* (1974).

7. Stanley Hoffmann, "Cursing De Gaulle is Not a Policy," *The Reporter*, 30 January 1964: 38-41.

8. De Gaulle, *War Memoirs*, 875.

9. Ibid., 573.

10. Kissinger, *Troubled Partnership*, 62-3.

11. George Ball, for instance, typically judged that while the Constitution of 1958 restored stability to France, "de Gaulle tarnished that achievement in 1962 by amendments providing for the direct election of a President and the popular referendum – a dubious engine that could someday invite dictatorial abuse in a political system lacking America's checks and balances." Ball, *The Past Has Another Pattern*, 97.

12. Kissinger, *Diplomacy*, 706.

13. Halle, *History, Philosophy, and Foreign Relations*, 256.

14. Harper, *American Visions of Europe*, 1.

15. See Chapter Three.

16. Goldstein to Johnson, Embtel 10199 (Paris), 12 February 1968, vol. 13, CF, NSF, #141a, box 174, LBJL.

17. De Gaulle, *Memoirs of Hope*, 244.

18. Peyrefitte, *C'était de Gaulle* 2:50.

19. Geir Lundestad, "Empire by Invitation? The United States and Western Europe, 1945-1952," *Journal of Peace Research* 23 (September 1986): 263-77.

20. Memorandum of conversation with President, 1 May 1956, Eisenhower Papers, DDE, J. F. Dulles, White House Memos, box 4, DDEL.

21. Rostow, *The Diffusion of Power*, 394.

22. Peyrefitte, *C'était de Gaulle* 2:47-48.

23. For such a reappraisal, see in particular Schwartz, *Lyndon Johnson and Europe*. In his memoirs, Johnson insisted that European affairs "absorbed much more of my time and attention than most people realized." Johnson, *The Vantage Point*, 306. Likewise, Johnson was livid when German Chancellor Kiesinger in a speech implied that the United States did not consult his government enough: "If I had a dollar for every time I consulted the Germans, I'd be a millionaire." Memorandum for the Record, 2 March 1967, vol. Trilaterals, box 18, Papers of Francis M. Bator, #1, LBJL.

24. From a French report on a conversation between Pompidou and Kissinger at the Azores meeting of December 1971, as cited in Mélandri, "Aux origines de la coopération nucléaire franco-américaine," 236.

25. This wisdom was, for instance, formulated by Anton DePorte, who described the French challenge as a "failed" challenge to the postwar European system and de Gaulle's resignation in April 1969 as "from the point of view of foreign policy, an anticlimax." See DePorte, *Europe Between the Superpowers*, 188, 229-242.

26. Rostow, *The Diffusion of Power*, 394.

27. Wenger, "Crisis and Opportunity," 72.

28. As put by a NATO planner, quoted in Ullman, "The Covert French Connection," *Foreign Policy*, 27.

29. On the undervalued deterrent potential of the French nuclear force, see also Gordon, *A Certain Idea of France*, 43.

30. Harrison, *The Reluctant Ally*, 121. See also Kohl, *French Nuclear Diplomacy*, 182-183.

31. House Committee on Foreign Affairs, *Our Changing Partnership with Europe*. H.R. Report no. 26, 90th Cong., 1st sess., 1967, 11.

32. Hitchcock, *The Struggle for Europe*, 222.

33. The concept of a paradigm originates in the philosophy of science, where it was developed by Thomas Kuhn as a way to explain scientific development as the succession of scientific revolutions, but it has been used as well in order to elucidate significant shifts in foreign policy. In Kuhn's definition, paradigms are "universally recognized scientific achievements that for a time provide model problems and solutions to a community of practitioners." Thomas S. Kuhn, *The Structure of Scientific Revolutions*, 2d ed. (Chicago: University of Chicago Press, 1970), viii. For a definition of a paradigm in the realm of international relations, see Evans and Newnham, *The Penguin Dictionary of International Relations*, 416-7. For the use of the paradigm concept in understanding changes in American foreign policy, see Michael Roskin, "From Pearl Harbor to Vietnam: Shifting Generational Paradigms and Foreign Policy," *Political Science Quarterly* (Fall 1974): 563-588.

34. Rusk and Alfred Max, memorandum of conversation, 30 December 1964, memos vol. V, Country File, France, box 170, NSF, LBJL.

35. Robert J. Schaetzel, "The Americans' Image of Europe," in Karl Kaiser and Hans-Peter Schwarz, eds., *America and Western Europe: Problems and Prospects* (Lexington, MA.: Lexington Books, 1977), 40.

36. Ralf Dahrendorf, in Andrew J. Pierre, *A Widening Atlantic: Domestic Change and American Foreign Policy* (New York: Council of Foreign Relations, 1986), 5-11.

37. Francis M. Bator, "The Politics of Alliance: The United States and Europe," in Kermit Gordon, ed., *Agenda for the Nation* (New York: Doubleday & Co., 1968), 344.

38. *Oral history interview with Dean Rusk* 1:194.

39. Schaetzel, *The Unhinged Alliance*, 175-176.

40. Ball, *The Discipline of Power*, 148.

41. Ball, *The Past Has Another Pattern*, 97.

42. Cleveland, *The Atlantic Idea and its European Rivals*, 164.

43. Acheson, *This Vast External Realm*, 167.

44. Acheson, *Present At the Creation*, 725.

45. Robert Strausz-Hupé, James E. Dougherty, and William R. Kintner, *Building the Atlantic World* (New York: Harper & Row, 1963), 1.

Bibliography

Archival collections

Harry S Truman Presidential Library, Independence (Missouri)

I reviewed the Student Research Files on NATO and on European integration (which includes material on proposals for a European Defence Force and for an Atlantic Union). I also reviewed Truman's Office Files regarding France (OF 203). Student Research Files from the Truman Library on the Truman Doctrine, the Marshall Plan, and the Decision to Drop the Bomb are moreover available on the internet: *www.trumanlibrary.org*. They are compiled by the staff of the Truman Library and contain copies of original documents from various files.

Dwight D. Eisenhower Library, Abilene (Kansas)

Manuscripts

Burgess, W. Randolph. Papers, 1951-62.

Dulles, John Foster. Papers, 1951-1959.

Eisenhower, Dwight D. Papers, pre-presidential, 1916-52.

Eisenhower, Dwight D. Papers as President of the US, 1953-61 (Ann Whitman File).
    Dulles-Herter Series
    International Series
    International Meetings Series
    National Security Council Series
    Name Series

Eisenhower, Dwight D. Records as President of the US, White House Central Files, 1953-1961.
    Official File
    Confidential File

Gray, Gordon. Papers, 1946-76.

Herter, Christian A. Papers, 1957-61.

Jackson, C.D. Papers, 1931-1967.

McCone, John A. Papers, 1958-61.

McElroy, Neil H. Papers, 1948-62.

Norstad, Lauris. Papers, 1930-87.

Randall, Clarence B. Journals, 1953-1961.

White House Office, National Security Council staff. Papers, 1948-1961.

White House Office, Office of the Special Assistant for National Security Affairs (Robert Cutler, Dillon Anderson, and Gordon Gray). Records, 1952-61.

White House Office, Office of the Staff Secretary, Paul T. Carrol, Andrew J. Goodpaster, L. Arthur Minnich, and Christopher H. Russel. Records, 1952-1961.

Oral Histories

Bohlen, Charles
Bowie, Robert R.
Burgess, W. Randolph
Dillon, Clarence Douglas
Eisenhower, Dwight D.
Gates, Thomas S.
Goodpaster, Andrew J.
Houghton, Amory
Lacy, William S. B.
Lemnitzer, Lyman

McCloy, John J.
McCone, John A.
McElroy, Neil H.
Merchant, Livingston
Murphy, Robert D.
Norstad, Lauris
Strauss, Lewis L.
Wilcox, Francis O.
Yost, Charles

John F. Kennedy Library, Boston (Massachussetts)

National Security File

These constitute the working files of McGeorge Bundy, Special Assistant to the President for National Security Affairs. It is the primary foreign policy file of the Kennedy White House and consists of the following series:

Countries
Regional Security
Trips and Conferences
Departments and Agencies
Subjects
Meetings and Memorandums
Staff files of Chester V. Clifton, Carl Kaysen, William H. Brubeck, Henry Kissinger, and Robert W. Komer.

White House Central File

Designed as a reference service for the President and his staff and to document White House activities.

White House Central Subject File
White House Central Name File

White House Staff Files

McGeorge Bundy
Christian Herter
Walt W. Rostow

Personal Papers

Papers of George W. Ball, 1961-63
Papers of McGeorge Bundy, 1963-65
Papers of (James) Harlan Cleveland, 1961-69
Papers of C. Douglas Dillon, 1957-65
Papers of Robert H. Estabrook, papers
Papers of Roger Hilsman, 1961-65
Papers of William Kaufmann, 1953-83
Papers of Richard Neustadt, 1949-72
Papers of Arthur M. Schlesinger jr., 1939-83

President's Office File
See listing below under Roosevelt Study Center.

Oral Histories

Acheson, Dean
Alphand, Hervé
Bohlen, Charles E.
Bundy, McGeorge
Cleveland, (James) Harlan
Cooper, Chester L.
Couve de Murville, Maurice
Dillon, C. Douglas
Douglas-Home, Sir Alec
Finletter, Thomas K.
Fischer, Adrian S.
Forrestal, Michael V.
Foster, William C.
Grewe, Wilhelm
Harriman, W. Averell
Hillenbrand, Martin J.
Hilsman, Roger
Johnson, U(ral) Alexis
Kennedy, Robert F.
Knight, William E.
Kohler, Foy D.
Komer, Robert W.

Lemnitzer, Lyman L.
Lippmann, Walter
Lovett, Robert A.
Luns, Joseph M.A.H.
Mansfield, Mike
McGhee, George C.
McNamara, Robert S.
Merchant, Livingston
Nitze, Paul H.
Reilly, Sir (D'Arcy) Patrick
Rickover, Hyman G.
Rostow, Walt W.
Rusk, Dean
Schlesinger, Arthur M.
Sorenson, Theodore
Stikker, Dirk U.
Sullivan, William H.
Taylor, Maxwell D.
Thompson, Llewellyn E.
Thorneycroft, Lord Peter
Tyler, William R.
Yarmolinski, Adam

Lyndon B. Johnson Library, Austin (Texas)

National Security File
Country File (box 169-178)

Subject File (box 18, 21-22, 39, 51)
Agency File (box 35-40, 56)
Name File (box 1, 7)
National Security Council Histories (box 24, 38-39, 50-51, 53)
Memos to the President (box 1-39)
Files of Mc George Bundy (box 1-14)
Files of R. Komer (box 1-2)
Files of Walt W. Rostow (box 1-5)
National Security Action Memorandums (box 1-9)
National Security Council Meetings (box 2)
Committee File, Committee on Nuclear Proliferation (box 5-6)
International Meetings and Travel File (box 33-35)
Speech File (box 5)

White House Central Files
Subject File (box 6-7, 30-31)
Confidential File (box 8, 58)

Personal Papers
Papers of George W. Ball (box 1-7)
Papers of Francis M. Bator
Papers of Fred Panzer
Papers of Walt W. Rostow
Papers of Dean Rusk
Papers of McGeorge Bundy

Office Files of the White House Aides
Goldstein, E. Ernest (box 4, 8, 15)
Panzer, Fred (box 181, 343, 423)

Oral Histories

Ackley, Gardner	Leddy, John M.
Anderson, Robert B.	Lee, Philip R.
Beech, Keyes	Lemnitzer, Lyman
Bohlen, Charles E.	McCloy, John J.
Bruce, David K. E.	McCone, John A.
Cleveland, Harlan	McGhee, George
Deming, Frederick L.	McPherson, Harry
Finletter, Thomas K.	McNamara, Robert S.
Fisher, Adrian S.	Mundt, Karl Earl
Gilpatric, Roswell	Murphy, Charles S.
Goldberg, Arthur J.	Owen, Henry D.
Goldstein, E. Ernest	Pearson, Drew
Goodpaster, Andrew J.	Reedy, George E.
Katzenbach, Nicholas B.	Reynolds, William

Roosa, Robert V.
Rostow, Eugene V.
Rostow, Walt W.

Rusk, Dean
White, William S.

Nixon Presidential Materials – National Archives and Records Administration, College Park (Maryland)

The National Archives and Records Administration (NARA) is the custodian of the historical materials of the Nixon administration created and received by the White House during the administration of President Richard M. Nixon (1969-1974).

National Security Council Files
President's Trip Files
Country Files – Europe
Presidential Correspondence
Name Files
Presidential/HAK Memcons

Special Files
Alexander M. Haig
　　Speech Files (box 44)
President's Office Files
　　President's Handwriting (box 1-8)
　　Annotated News Summaries (box 30-32)
　　President's Meetings File (box 77, 80, 83)
　　Chronological File (box 100)
President's Personal Files
　　Memoranda from the President (box 1-2)
　　Name/Subject File (box 5, 7, 9-12, 15-17)
　　Foreign Affairs File (box 166-167)
John A. Scali
　　Subject Files (box 1-8)
Staff Secretary
　　Memoranda Files (box 42-52)
Central Files
　　Subject Files: Confidential Files (box 6, 14-15, 18, 36, 66)

White House Central Files
Subject Files
　　Countries (box 5-6, 27-28)
　　Federal Government
　　Central Intelligence Agency
　　National Security Council

Department of State
Department of Treasury
Department of Defense
Foreign Affairs
International Organizations
Trips

Roosevelt Study Center, Middelburg (The Netherlands)

The Roosevelt Study Center is a research institute on twentieth-century American history located in Middelburg, the Netherlands. It owns a large collection of microfiche copies of American archives. For this book, I have reviewed the following collections.

Dwight D. Eisenhower

Eisenhower, Dwight D. Papers as President of the United States, 1953-61 (Ann Whitman File), in particular:
international series
administration series

John F. Kennedy

President's Office Files
These are the working files of President Kennedy as maintained by his personal secretary, Mrs. Evelyn Lincoln, in the White House. The files include:
correspondence
staff memorandums
departments and agencies
subjects
countries
special events through the years

North Atlantic Treaty Organization (NATO)

In 2004, NATO placed 250 documents relating to the 1967 Harmel Report on the internet: http://www.isn.ethz.ch/php/collections/coll_Harmel.htm.

Macmillan Cabinet Papers, U.K. National Archives

The Macmillan Cabinet Papers, 1957-1963, can be consulted online through the website of the British National Archives (http://www.nationalarchives.gov.uk/). It provides a complete coverage (nearly 12,000 pages) of the Cabinet Conclusions [Minutes] (CAB 128) and Memoranda (CAB 129), including recently released material, and access to 165 files (over 16,000 pages) from the records of the Prime Minister's Private Office (PREM 11).

Published documents

Bowie, Robert R. *The North Atlantic Nations Tasks For the 1960s: A Report to the Secretary of State, August 1960.* Nuclear History Program Occasional Paper 7. College Park: Center for International Security Studies, University of Maryland, 1991.

Council on Foreign Relations. *United States Documents on American Foreign Relations.* (annual) New York: Harper and Brothers for the Council on Foreign Relations.

Dallek, Robert, ed. *The Dynamics of World Power: A Documentary History of United States Foreign Policy, 1945-1973,* vol. 1, part 1 and 2: Western Europe. New York: Chelsea House, 1983.

De Gaulle, Charles. *Discours et messages, 1940-1946.* vol. 1. Paris: Berger-Levrault, 1946

—. *Discours et messages,* vol. 2, *Dans l'attente, Février 1946-Avril 1958.* Paris: Plon, 1970.

—. *Discours et messages,* vol. 3, *Avec le renouveau, Mai 1958-Juillet 1962.* Paris: Plon, 1970.

—. *Discours et messages,* vol. 4, *Pour l'effort.* Paris: Plon, 1970.

—. *Discours et messages,* vol. 5, *Vers le terme, Février 1966-Avril 1969.* Paris: Plon, 1970.

De Gaulle, Charles. *Lettres, notes et carnets, vol. 2, 1919-Juin 1940.* Paris: Plon, 1980.

—. *Lettres, notes et carnets, vol. 3, Juin 1940-Juillet 1941.* Paris: Plon, 1981.

—. *Lettres, notes et carnets, vol. 4, Juillet 1941- Mai 1943.* Paris: Plon, 1982.

—. *Lettres, notes et carnets, vol. 5, Juin 1943 – Mai 1945.* Paris: Plon, 1983.

—. *Lettres, notes et carnets, vol. 6. Mai 1945- Juin 1951.* Paris: Plon, 1984.

—. *Lettres, notes et carnets, vol. 7, Juin 1951- Mai 1958.* Paris: Plon, 1985.

—. *Lettres, notes et carnets, vol. 8, Juin 1958 - Décembre 1960.* Paris: Plon, 1985.

—. *Lettres, notes et carnets, vol. 9, Janvier 1961- Décembre 1963.* Paris: Plon, 1986.

—. *Lettres, notes et carnets, vol. 10, Janvier 1964- Juin 1966.* Paris: Plon, 1986.

—. *Lettres, notes et carnets, vol. 11, Juillet 1966- Avril 1969.* Paris: Plon, 1987.

—. *Lettres, notes et carnets, vol. 12, Mai 1969- Novembre 1970.* Paris: Plon, 1988.

France, Ambassade de France. *French Foreign Policy, 1966.* New York: Service de Presse et d'Information, 1967.

—. *Major addresses, statements, and press conferences of General de Gaulle, May 19, 1958-January 31, 1964.* New York: Service de Presse and d'Information, 1964.

—. *Major addresses, statements, and press conferences of General de Gaulle, March 17, 1964-May 16, 1967.* New York: Service de Presse and d'Information, 1967.

Geelhoed, Bruce E., and Anthony O. Edmonds. *The Macmillan-Eisenhower Correspondence, 1957-1959.* New York: Palgrave Macmillan, 2005.

Graebner, Norman A.. *Ideas and Diplomacy: Readings in the Intellectual Tradition of American Foreign Policy.* New York: Oxford University Press, 1964.

Herter, Christian A., and William L. Clayton. *A New Look at Foreign Economic Policy (in Light of the Cold War and of the Common Market in Europe.* Report prepared for the Subcommittee on Foreign Economic Policy of the Joint Economic Committee, 87th Cong., 1st sess., 1961.

United States. *Public Papers of the Presidents of the United States.* (annual) Washington, DC: US Government Printing Office.

US Congress. House. Committee on Foreign Affairs. *The Crisis in NATO: Hearings before the Subcommittee on Europe.* 89th Cong., 2nd sess., March-June, 1966.

—. House. Committee on Foreign Affairs. *Our Changing Partnership with Europe.* H.R. Report no.26, 90th Cong., 1st sess., 1967

—. Joint Committee on Atomic Energy, *Amending the Atomic Energy of 1954. Hearings* before the Subcommittee on Agreements for Cooperation on the Exchange for Cooperation on the Exchange of Military Information and Material with Allies, 85th cong., 2nd sess., 1958

—. Subcommittee on Foreign Economic Policy of the Joint Economic Committee, *A New Look at Foreign Economic Policy in Light of the Cold War and the Extension of the Common Market in Europe*. Report by Christian A. Herter and William L. Clayton, 87th Cong., 1st sess., 1961.

—. Senate. Committee on Foreign Relations. *Problems and Trends in Atlantic Partnership I*. Senate Doc. no. 132, 87th Cong., 2d. sess., 1962.

—. Senate. Committee on Foreign Relations. *Problems and Trends in Atlantic Partnership II*. Senate Doc. no. 21, 88th Cong., 1st sess., 1963.

—. Senate. Committee on Foreign Relations. *United States Policy Toward Europe (and Related Matters)*. 89th Cong., 2d sess., 1966.

—. Senate. Committee on Government Operations. *Atlantic Alliance: Hearings before the Subcommittee on National Security and International Operations*, 89th Cong., 2d sess., 1966.

—. Senate. Foreign Relations Committee. *Executive Sessions 1963*. Washington, DC: GPO, 1986.

United States Department of Defense. *The Pentagon Papers: The Defense Department History of United States Decisionmaking on Vietnam*. Edited by Senator Gravel. Boston, 1991.

United States Department of State. *Department of State Bulletin*. Washington, DC: GPO.

United States Department of State. *Foreign Relations of the United States*. Washington, DC: GPO. In particular:

1958-1960, Dwight D. Eisenhower
vol. 3. National Security Policy (1996)
vol. 4. Foreign Economic Policy (1992)
vol. 7, part 1. Western European Integration and Canada (1993)
vol. 7, part 2. Western Europe (1993)
vol. 8. The Berlin Crisis, 1958-1959; Foreign Ministers Meeting, 1959 (1993)
vol. 9. The Berlin Crisis, 1959-1960; Germany; Austria (1993)

1961-1963, John F. Kennedy
vol. 1. Vietnam, 1961 (1988)
vol. 2. Vietnam, 1962 (1990)
vol. 3. Vietnam, January-August 1963 (1991)
vol. 4. Vietnam, August-December 1963 (1991)
vol. 5. Soviet Union (1998)
vol. 7. Arms Control and Disarmament (1995)
vol. 8. National Security Policy (1996)
vol. 9. Foreign Economic Policy (1995)
vol. 11. Cuban Missile Crisis and Aftermath (1997)
vol. 13. Western Europe and Canada (1994)
vol. 14. Berlin Crisis, 1961-1962 (1994)
vol. 15. Berlin Crisis, 1962-1963 (1994)

1964-1968, *Lyndon B. Johnson*

vol. 1. Vietnam, 1964 (1992)

vol. 2. Vietnam, January-June 1965 (1996)

vol. 3. Vietnam, July-December 1965 (1996)

vol. 4. Vietnam, 1966 (1998)

vol. 5. Vietnam, 1967 (2002)

vol. 6. Vietnam, 1968 (2002)

vol. 7. Vietnam, 1968 (2003)

vol. 8. International Monetary and Trade Policy (1998)

vol. 10. National Security Policy (2002)

vol. 11. Arms Control (1997)

vol. 12. Western Europe (2001)

vol. 13. Western Europe Region (1995)

vol. 14. Soviet Union (2001)

vol. 15. Berlin; Germany (1999)

vol. 17. Eastern Europe (1996)

vol. 18. Arab-Israeli Dispute, 1964-1967 (2000)

vol. 19. Arab-Israeli Crisis and War, 1967 (2004)

vol. 20. Arab-Israeli Dispute, 1967-1968 (2001)

1969-1976, *Richard M. Nixon*

vol. 1. Foundations of Foreign Policy, 1969-1972 (2003)

vol. 3. Foreign Economic Policy; International Monetary Policy, 1969-1976 (2002)

vol. 6. Vietnam, January 1969-July 1970 (2006)

vol. 17. China, 1969-1972

vol. E-13. Documents on China, 1969-1972 (2006)

An increasing number of volumes of the Foreign Relations of the United States can be accessed through the website of the Department of State (http://www.state.gov/r/pa/ho/frus/) or the digital collections of the University of Wisconsin (http://digicoll.library.wisc.edu/FRUS/).

United States Department of State. *Strengthening the Forces of Freedom: Selected Speeches and Statements of Secretary of State Acheson, February 1949-April 1950.* Washington, DC: GPO, 1950.

United States Information Agency. *The Atlantic Community.* Information Center Service, Subject Bibliography no. 35, 25 November 1957.

Books authored by de Gaulle (in chronological order of first appearance)

La discorde chez l'ennemi. Paris: Berger-Levrault, 1924. Translated as *The Enemy's House Divided.* Chapel Hill: University of North Carolina Press, 2002.

Le fil de l'épée. 2d ed. Paris: Berger-Levrault, 1944. Originally published in 1932. Translated as *The Edge of the Sword.* New York: Criterion, 1960.

Vers l'armée de métier. Paris: Presses Pocket, 1963. Translated as *The Army of the Future.* London: Hutchinson, 1945.

La France et son armée. Paris: Plon, 1938. Translated as *France and her Army*. London: Hutchinson, 1945.

Trois Études. Paris: Berger-Levrault, 1945.

Mémoires de guerre. Vol. 1 *L'Appel*, 1940-1942; Vol. 2. *L'Unité*, 1942-1944; Vol. 3 *Le Salut*, 1944-1946. Paris: Plon, 1954, 1956, and 1959. Translated as *The Complete War Memoirs of Charles de Gaulle*. New York: Simon & Schuster, 1964.

Mémoires d'espoir. Vol. 1, *Le renouveau*, 1958-1962; Vol. 2 *L'effort*, 1962. Paris: Plon, 1970 and 1971. Translated as *Memoirs of Hope: Renewal and Endeavor*. New York: Simon & Schuster, 1971.

Memoirs, correspondence, conversations, and diaries

Acheson, Dean. *Present at the Creation: My Years in the State Department*. New York: W.W. Norton & Co., 1969.

Adenauer, Konrad. *Memoirs 1945-1953*. Chicago: Henry Regnery Co., 1966.

—. *Erinnerungen 1959-1963*. Stuttgart: Deutscher Bücherbund, 1969.

Aglion, Raoul. *Roosevelt and De Gaulle, Allies in Conflict: A Personal Memoir*. New York: The Free Press, 1988.

Alphand, Hervé. *L'étonnement d'être. Journal, 1933-1973*. Paris: Fayard, 1977.

Ball, George W. *The Past Has Another Pattern: Memoirs*. New York: W.W. Norton & Co., 1982.

Beschloss, Michael, ed. *Taking Charge: The Johnson White House Tapes*. New York: Simon and Schuster, 1997.

Billotte, Pierre. *Le passé au futur*. Paris: Stock, 1979.

Blum, John Morton, ed. *Public Philosopher: Selected Letters of Walter Lippmann*. New York: Ticknor & Fields, 1985.

Bohlen, Charles E. *Witness to History, 1929-1969*. New York: W.W. Norton & Co., 1973.

Churchill, Winston S. *The Second World War*. London: Penguin Books, 1990.

Couve de Murville, Maurice. *Une politique étrangère, 1958-1969*. Paris: Plon, 1971.

Dobrynin, Anatoly. *In Confidence: Moscow's Ambassador to America's Seven Cold War Presidents*. New York: Random House, 1995.

Eisenhower, Dwight. *Mandate for Change, 1953-1956*. Garden City: Doubleday, 1963.

—. *Letters to Mamie*. Garden City: Doubleday, 1977.

Ferrell, Robert H., ed. *The Eisenhower Diaries*. New York: W.W. Norton, 1981.

Galbraith, John Kenneth. *Ambassador's Journal: A Personal Account of the Kennedy Years*. London, 1969.

—. *Letters to Kennedy*. Cambridge: Harvard University Press, 1998. Edited by James Goodman.

Harriman, Averell, and Elie Abel. *Special Envoy to Churchill and Stalin, 1941-1946*. New York: Random House, 1975.

Johnson, Lyndon B. *The Vantage Point: Perspectives of the Presidency 1963-1969*. New York: Holt, Rinehart and Winston, 1971.

Kennan, George F. *Memoirs 1925-1950*. New York: Pantheon Books, 1967.

— *Sketches From a Life*. New York: Pantheon Books, 1989.

Kimball, Warren F. *Churchill and Roosevelt: The Complete Correspondence*. 3 vols. Princeton: Princeton University Press, 1984.

Kissinger, Henry A. *White House Years.* Boston: Little, Brown and Co., 1979.

—. *Years of Upheaval.* Boston: Little Brown, 1982.

Ledwidge, Bernard. *De Gaulle et les Américains: Conversations avec Dulles, Eisenhower, Kennedy, Rusk, 1958-1964.* Paris: Flammarion, 1984.

Macmillan, Harold. *Riding the Storm, 1956-1959.* London: Macmillan, 1971.

—. *Pointing the Way, 1959-1961.* London: Macmillan, 1972.

—. *At the End of the Day, 1961-1963.* London: Macmillan, 1973.

Malraux, André. *Antimemoirs.* Translated by Terence Kilmartin. New York: Holt, Rinehart and Winston, 1968.

—. *Felled Oaks: Conversation With de Gaulle.* New York: Holt, Rinehart and Winston, 1971.

—, and James Burnham. *The Case for De Gaulle: A Dialogue Between André Malraux and James Burnham.* New York: Random House, 1948.

May, Ernest R. and Philip D. Zelikow. *The Kennedy Tapes: Inside the White House During the Cuban Missile Crisis.* Cambridge: Harvard University Press, 1997.

McGhee, George. *At the Creation of a New Germany: From Adenauer to Brandt. An Ambassador's Account.* New Haven: Yale University Press, 1989.

McLellan, David S., and David S. Acheson. *Among Friends: Personal Letters of Dean Acheson.* New York: Dodd, Mead, 1980.

Murphy, Robert. *Diplomat Among Warriors.* Garden City: Doubleday, 1964.

Monnet, Jean. *Memoirs.* Translated from the French by Richard Mayne. Garden City: Doubleday, 1978.

Nixon, Richard M. *RN: The Memoirs of Richard Nixon.* New York: Simon & Schuster, 1990.

—. *Leaders.* New York: Simon Schuster, 1990.

—. *In the Arena: A Memory of Victory, Defeat and Renewal.* New York: Simon & Schuster, 1990.

Peyrefitte, Alain. *C'était de Gaulle.* 3 vols. Paris: Fayard, 1994.

Roosevelt, Eleanor. *The Autobiography of Eleanor Roosevelt.* New York: Da Capo Press, 1992.

Reston, James. *Deadline: A Memoir.* New York: Random House, 1991.

Rueff, Jacques. *De l'aube au crépuscule.* Paris: Plon, 1977.

Rusk, Dean. *As I Saw It.* New York: W.W. Norton & Co., 1990.

Spaak, Paul-Henri. *The Continuing Battle: Memoirs of a European, 1936-1966.* Boston: Little, Brown, 1971.

Stikker, Dirk U. *Men of Responsibility: A Memoir.* New York: Harper & Row, 1965.

Smith, Amanda. *Hostage to Fortune: The Letters of Joseph Kennedy.* New York: Viking Penguin, 2001.

Walters, Vernon A. *Silent Missions.* New York: Doubleday, 1978.

—. *The Mighty and the Meek: Dispatches from the Front Line of Diplomacy.* London: St Ermins Press, 2001.

Wilson, Harold. *A Personal Record: The Labour Government, 1964-1970.* Boston: Little, Brown and Company, 1971.

Other books and articles by American officials

Acheson, Dean. *An American Vista.* London: Hamish Hamilton, 1956.

—. *Power and Diplomacy.* Cambridge: Harvard University Press, 1958.

—. *This Vast External Realm.* New York: W.W. Norton & Co., 1973.

—. "Dealing with de Gaulle: Dean Acheson tells how." *US News and World Report* 54, 25 March 1963: 22.

—. "Dean Acheson's Word for de Gaulle: 'Nonsense'." *US News and World Report* 60, 18 April 1966: 79.

Ball, George. *The Discipline of Power: Essentials of a Modern World Structure.* Boston: Little, Brown & Co., 1968.

—. *Diplomacy for a Crowded World.* Boston: Atlantic Monthly Press, 1976.

—. "The Larger Meaning of the NATO Crisis." Address on 29 April 1966 in *Department of State Bulletin* 54, 16 May 1966: 762-768.

—. "Toward an Atlantic Partnership." Address on 6 February 1962 in *Department of State Bulletin* 46, 5 March 1962: 364-370.

—. "Developing Atlantic Partnership." Address on 2 April 1962 in *Department of State Bulletin* 46, 23 April 1962: 666-673.

—. "NATO and World Responsibilities." Address on 7 May 1964 in *Department of State Bulletin* 50, 25 May 1964: 823-828.

—. "Undersecretary Ball departs for meetings at London and Paris." Statement on 27 November 1964 in *Department of State Bulletin* 51, 14 December 1964: 847-848.

—. "George Ball: Talking tough to de Gaulle." Excerpts from an address, *US News and World Report* 58, 29 March 1965.

—. "Mr. Ball discusses U.S. relations with Europe on BBC." Interview edited by A. Burnet, 2 October 1965 in *Department of State Bulletin* 53, 25 October 1965: 653-660.

—. "Undersecretary Ball discusses US views on Vietnam and NATO." Interview edited by André Fontaine in *Department of State Bulletin* 54, 18 April 1966: 613-616.

—. "US Policy on the Atlantic Union." Statement on 20 September 1966 in *Department of State Bulletin* 55, 17 October 1966: 613-615.

—. "US policy towards NATO." in *NATO in Quest for Cohesion.* Edited by Karl H. Cerny and Henry W. Briefs. New York: Frederick A. Praeger, 1965.

—. "The dangers of nostalgia." Address on 16 March 1965 in *The Atlantic Community Quarterly* (Summer 1965): 167-176.

Bator, Francis M. "The Politics of Alliance: The United States and Europe." In Kermit Gordon, *Agenda for the Nation.* New York: Doubleday & Co., 1968: 335-372.

Bohlen, Charles E. *The Transformation of American Foreign Policy.* New York: W.W. Norton & Co., 1969.

Bowie, Robert R. "Strategy and the Atlantic Alliance." *International Organization* 17 (Summer 1963): 709-732.

Bundy, McGeorge. *Danger and Survival: Choices about the Bomb in the First Fifty Years.* New York: Randon House, 1988.

Bundy, William. *A Tangled Web: The Making of Foreign Policy in the Nixon Presidency.* London/New York: I.B. Tauris, 1998.

Cleveland, Harlan. *NATO: The Transatlantic Bargain.* New York: Harper & Row, 1970.

—. "Golden Rule of Consultation." Address on 20 June 1967 in *Department of State Bulletin* 57, 31 July 1967: 141-146.

Finletter, Thomas K. *Interim Report on the U.S. Search for a Substitute for Isolation.* New York: W. W. Norton & Co., 1968.

Gavin, James. "On Dealing With de Gaulle." *Atlantic Monthly* (June 1965): 49-54.

Halle, Louis J. *History, Philosophy, and Foreign Relations.* Lanham: University Press of America, 1987.

—. *The Nature of Power: Civilization and Foreign Policy.* London: Rupert Hart-Davis, 1955.

Herter, Christian A. *Toward an Atlantic Community.* New York: Harper & Row, 1963.

—. "Atlantica." *Foreign Affairs* 41, no. 2 (January 1963): 299-309.

— and William L. Clayton, *A New Look at Foreign Economic Policy.* Washington, DC: GPO, 1961.

Kennan, George F. *American Diplomacy, 1900-1950.* Chicago: University of Chicago Press, 1951.

—. *Russia, the Atom, and the West.* The BBC Reith Lectures. New York: Harper & Brothers, 1958.

—. *At a Century's Ending: Reflections 1982-1995.* New York: W.W. Norton & Co., 1996.

Kennedy, John F. *The Strategy of Peace.* Edited by Allan Nevins. New York: Harper & Brothers, 1960.

—. *Profiles in Courage.* New York: Perennial Library, 1964. Memorial edition.

Kissinger, Henry A. *A World Restored: Metternich, Castlereagh and the Problems of Peace 1812-22.* Boston: Houghton Mifflin, 1957.

—. *Nuclear Weapons and Foreign Policy.* New York: Harper & Brothers for the Council on Foreign Relations, 1957.

—. *The Troubled Partnership.* New York: McGraw-Hill for the Council on Foreign Relations, 1965.

—. *Diplomacy.* New York: Simon and Schuster, 1994.

—. "Illusionist: Why We Misread De Gaulle." *Harper's Magazine* (March 1965): 69-77.

—. "Coalition Diplomacy in a Nuclear Age." *Foreign Affairs* (July 1964).

—. "For a New Atlantic Alliance." *The Reporter* 14 July 1966.

McCloy, John J. *The Atlantic Alliance: Its Origin and Its Future.* New York: Columbia University Press, 1969.

McNamara, Robert S. "Defense Arrangements of the North Atlantic Community." *Department of State Bulletin* 9 July 1962: 64-69.

Neustadt, Richard E. "Memorandum on the British Labour Party and the MLF Prepared by Richard Neustadt, July 6, 1964." *New Left Review* 51 (Sept-Oct 1968): 11-21.

Rostow, Eugene V. "Prospects for the Alliance." *The Atlantic Community Quarterly* 3 (Spring 1965): 35-42.

—. "New challenges to American foreign policy, 1963-1968." *The Atlantic Community Quarterly* 7 (Summer 1969): 118-124.

Rostow, Walt W. *View from the Seventh Floor.* New York: Harper & Row, 1964.

—. *The Diffusion of Power: An Essay in Recent History.* New York: MacMillan Co., 1972.

Safire, William. *Before the Fall: An Inside View of the Pre-Watergate White House.* New York: Ballantine Books, 1977.

Schaetzel, Robert J. *The Unhinged Alliance: America and the European Community.* New York: Harper & Row for the Council on Foreign Relations, 1975.

—. "Some European Questions for Dr. Kissinger."*Foreign Policy* 12 (Fall 1973): 66-74.

—. "The Americans' Image of Europe." in Karl Kaiser and Hans-Peter Schwarz, eds. *America and Western Europe: Problems and Prospects.* Lexington: Lexington Books, 1977.

Schlesinger, Arthur M., Jr. *A Thousand Days: John F. Kennedy in the White House*. London: Andre Deutsch Ltd., 1965.

Sorenson, Theodore C. *Kennedy*. New York: Harper & Row, 1965.

Taylor, Maxwell. *The Uncertain Trumpet*. New York: Harper & Row, 1959.

Wohlstetter, Albert. "The Delicate Balance of Terror." *Foreign Affairs* (January 1959): 355-387.

—. "Nuclear Sharing, NATO, and the N + 1." *Foreign Affairs* (April 1961).

Biographies

Abramson, Rudy. *Spanning the Century: The Life of Averell Harriman, 1891-1986*. New York: William Morrow & Co., 1992.

Ambrose, Stephen E. *Eisenhower: Soldier, General of the Army, President-Elect, 1890-1952*. Vol. 1. New York: Simon & Schuster, 1983.

—. *Eisenhower: The President*. Vol. 2. New York: Simon & Schuster, 1984.

—. *Nixon: The Education of a Politician, 1913-1962*. Vol. 1. New York: Simon & Schuster, 1987.

—. *Nixon: The Triumph of a Politician, 1962-1972*. Vol. 2. New York: Simon & Schuster, 1989.

Beisner, Robert L. *Dean Acheson: A Life in the Cold War*. Oxford: Oxford University Press, 2006.

Bill, James A. *George Ball: Behind the Scenes in U.S. Foreign Policy*. New Haven: Yale University Press, 1997.

Bird, Kai. *The Chairman: John J. McCloy, the Making of the American Establishment*. New York: Simon & Schuster, 1992.

—. *The Color of Truth: McGeorge Bundy and William Bundy – Brothers in Arms*. New York: Simon and Schuster, 1998.

Bornet, Vaughn Davis. *The Presidency of Lyndon B. Johnson*. Lawrence: University of Kansas, 1983.

Brinkley, Douglas. *Dean Acheson: The Cold War Years, 1953-71*. New Haven: Yale University Press, 1992.

Califano, Joseph A. *The Triumph and Tragedy of Lyndon Johnson: The White House Years*. New York: Simon & Schuster, 1991.

Chace, James. *Acheson: The Secretary of State Who Created the American World*. New York: Simon & Schuster, 1998.

Chernow, Ron. *Alexander Hamilton*. New York: Penguin Press, 2004.

Cogan, Charles A. *Charles de Gaulle: A Brief Biography with Documents*. New York: St. Martin's Press, 1996.

Cohen, Warren I. *Dean Rusk*. Totowa: Cooper Square Publishers, 1980.

Conkin, Paul. *Big Daddy from the Pedernales*. Boston: Twayne, 1986.

Cook, Don. *Charles de Gaulle: A Biography*. New York: Perigee Books, 1983.

Crawley, Adrian. *De Gaulle*. London: Collins, 1969.

Crozier, Brian. *De Gaulle*. Norwalk: Easton Press, 1990.

Dallek, Robert. *Flawed Giant: Lyndon Johnson and His Times, 1961-1973*. New York: Oxford University Press, 1998.

—. *An Unfinished Life: John F. Kennedy, 1917-1963*. Boston: Little, Brown and Company, 2003.

DiLeo, David L. *George Ball: Vietnam and the Rethinking of Containment*. Chapel Hill: University of North Carolina, 1991.

Duchêne, François. *Jean Monnet: The First Statesman of Interdependence*. New York: W.W. Norton, 1994.

Dugger, Ronnie. *The Politician*. New York: W.W. Norton & Co., 1982.

Eisenhower, David. *Eisenhower at War, 1943-1945*. New York: Random House, 1986.

Evans, Rowland and Robert Novak. *Lyndon B. Johnson: The Exercise of Power. A Political Biography*. London: George Allen and Union Ltd., 1966.

Hersh, Seymour M. *The Price of Power: Kissinger in the Nixon White House*. New York: Summit Books, 1983.

Hoopes, Townsend. *The Devil and John Foster Dulles: The Diplomacy of the Eisenhower Era*. Boston: Little, Brown & Co., 1973.

Horne, Alistair. *Harold Macmillan, Volume II: 1957-1986*. New York: Viking Penguin, 1989.

Isaacson, Walter. *Kissinger. A Biography*. London: Faber and Faber, 1992.

— and Evan Thomas. *The Wise Men: Six Friends and the World They Made*. New York: Simon & Schuster, 1986.

Kearns, Doris. *Lyndon Johnson and the American Dream*. New York: Harper & Row, 1976.

Lacouture, Jean. *De Gaulle: The Rebel, 1890-1944*. Translated from the French by Patrick O'Brian. New York: W.W. Norton & Company, 1990.

—. *De Gaulle: The Ruler, 1945-1970*. Translated from the French by Alan Sheridan. New York: W.W. Norton & Company, 1992.

McCullough, David. *Truman*. New York: Simon & Schuster, 1992.

Merseburger, Peter. *Willy Brandt, 1913-1992: Visionär und Realist*. München: Deutscher Taschenbuch Verlag, 2004.

Miller, Merle. *Ike the Soldier: As They Knew Him*. New York: Perigee, 1987.

Miller, Nathan. *Theodore Roosevelt: A Life*. New York: William Morrow & Co., 1992.

Parmet, Herbert S. *Jack: The Struggles of John F. Kennedy*. New York: Dial Press, 1980.

Pogue, Forrest C. *George C. Marshall: Statesman, 1945-1959*. New York: Viking, 1987.

Reeves, Richard. *President Kennedy: Profile of Power*. New York: Simon & Schuster, 1993.

Reeves, Thomas C. *A Question of Character: A Life of John F. Kennedy*. New York: Macmillan, 1991.

Ruddy, Michael T. *The Cautious Diplomat: Charles E. Bohlen and the Soviet Union, 1929-1969*. Kent: Kent State University Press, 1986.

Schoenbaum, Thomas J. *Waging Peace and War: Dean Rusk in the Truman, Kennedy and Johnson years*. New York: Simon & Schuster, 1988.

Schoenbrun, David. *The Three Lives of Charles de Gaulle*. New York: Atheneum, 1966.

Schulzinger, Robert D. *Henry Kissinger: Doctor of Diplomacy*. New York: Columbia University Press, 1989.

Steel, Ronald. *Walter Lippmann and the American Century*. New York: Random House, 1981.

Stossel, Scott. *Sarge: The Life and Times of Sargent Shriver*. Washington, DC: Smithsonian Books, 2004.

Talbott, Strobe. *Master of the Game: Paul Nitze and the Nuclear Game*. New York: Vintage Books, 1988.

Taubman, William. *Khrushchev: The Man, His Era*. London: The Free Press/Simon & Schuster, 2003.

Werth, Alexander. *De Gaulle: A Political Biography*. New York: Simon & Schuster, 1966.

Williams, Charles. *The Last Great Frenchman: A Life of General de Gaulle*. (1993) London: Abacus, 1996.

Books on the bilateral relationship between France and the United States

Blumenthal, Henry. *France and the United States: Their Diplomatic Relations, 1789-1914*. Chapel Hill: University of North Carolina Press, 1970.

—. *Illusion and Reality in Franco-American Diplomacy, 1919-1945*. Baton Rouge: Louisiana State University Press, 1986.

Bozo, Frédéric. *Deux stratégies pour l'Europe. De Gaulle, les États-Unis et l'Alliance Atlantique, 1958 - 1969*. Paris: Plon and Fondation Charles de Gaulle, 1996.

—. *Two Strategies for Europe: De Gaulle, the United States, and the Atlantic Alliance*. Translated by Susan Emanuel. Lanham: Rowman and Littlefield, 2001.

Cogan, Charles G. *Oldest Allies, Guarded Friends: The United States and France Since 1940*. New York: Praeger, 1994.

Costigliola, Frank. *France and the United States: The Cold Alliance Since World War II*. New York: Twayne Publishers, 1992.

Cresswell, Michael. *A Question of Balance: How France and the United States Created Cold War Europe*. Cambridge: Harvard University Press, 2006.

Dickie, Robert B. *Foreign Investment: France, A Case Study*. Leyden: A.W. Sijthoff, 1970.

Duroselle, Jean-Baptiste. *France and the United States: From the Beginnings to the Present*. Translated by Derek Coltman. Chicago: University of Chicago Press, 1978.

Ferro, Maurice. *De Gaulle et l'Amérique. Une amitié tumultueuse*. Paris: Plon, 1973.

Gallup, George H. *The Gallup International Public Opinion Polls: France, 1939, 1944-1975*. New York: Random House, 1976.

Hess, John L. *The Case for De Gaulle: An American Viewpoint*. New York: William Morrow & Co., 1968.

Hurstfield, Julian G. *America and the French Nation*. Chapel Hill: University of North Carolina Press, 1986.

Jauvert, Vincent. *L'Amérique contre de Gaulle. Histoire secrète, 1961-1969*. Paris: Éditions du Seuil, 2000.

Kaplan, Lawrence S., Denise Artaud, and Mark R. Rubin, eds. *Dien Bien Phu and the Crisis of Franco-American Relations, 1954-1955*. Wilmington, DE: SR Books, 1990.

Kersaudy, François. *De Gaulle et Roosevelt. Le duel au sommet*. Paris: Perrin, 2006.

Kuisel, Richard F. *Seducing the French: The Dilemma of Americanization*. Berkeley: University of California Press, 1993.

Langer, William L. *Our Vichy Gamble*. Hamden: Archon, 1965.

Mahan, Erin R. *Kennedy, De Gaulle, and Western Europe*. New York: Palgrave Macmillan, 2002.

Newhouse, John. *De Gaulle and the Anglo-Saxons*. New York: The Viking Press, 1970.

Paxton, Robert O. and Nicholas Wahl, eds. *De Gaulle and the United States: A Centennial Reappraisal*. Oxford: Berg Publishers, 1994.

Servan-Schreiber, Jean-Jacques. *The American Challenge*. New York: Atheneum, 1968.

Sullivan, Marianna P. *France's Vietnam Policy: A Study in French-American Relations*. Westport: Greenwood Press, 1978.

Viorst, Milton. *Hostile Allies: FDR and Charles de Gaulle*. New York: MacMillan, 1965.

Wall, Irwin M. *The United States and the Making of Postwar France, 1945-1954*. New York: Cambridge University Press, 1991.

—. *Les États-Unis et la guerre d'Algérie*. Paris: Soleb, 2006.

Zahniser, Marvin R. *Uncertain Friendship: American-French Relations Through the Cold War*. New York: John Wiley & Sons, 1975.

Books on French politics and foreign policy

Adamthwaite, Anthony P. *Grandeur and Misery: France's Bid for Power in Europe, 1914-1940*. London and New York: St. Martin's Press, 1995.

Andrews, William G. and Stanley Hoffmann, eds. *The Impact of the Fifth Republic on France*. Albany: State University of New York Press, 1981.

Beloff, Nora. *The General Says No: Britain's Exclusion from Europe*. London: Penguin Books Ltd, 1963.

Bosher, John Francis. *The Gaullist Attack on Canada 1967-1997*. Montreal: McGill-Queen's University Press, 1999.

Cerny, Philip G. *The Politics of Grandeur: Ideological Aspects of de Gaulle's Foreign Policy*. Cambridge: Cambridge University Press, 1980.

Cobban, Alfred. *A History of Modern France, vol 3: 1871-1962*. London: Penguin Books, 1984.

de Carmoy, Guy. *The Foreign Policies of France, 1944-1968*. Translated by Elaine P. Halperin. Chicago: University of Chicago Press, 1970.

DePorte, A. W. *De Gaulle's Foreign Policy, 1944-1946*. Cambridge: Harvard University Press, 1968.

Diamond, Robert A. *France Under De Gaulle*. New York: Facts on File, Inc., 1970.

Doise, Jean, and Maurice Vaïsse. *Diplomatie et outil militaire. Politique étrangère de la France, 1871-1969*. Paris: Imprimerie nationale, 1987.

Draus, Franciszek. *History, Truth, Liberty: Selected Writings of Raymond Aron*. Chicago: University of Chicago Press, 1985.

Dreyfus, François-G. *De Gaulle et le Gaullisme*. Paris: Press Universitaires de France, 1982.

Gallois, Pierre. *The Balance of Terror: Strategy for the Nuclear Age*. New York: Houghton Mifflin, 1961.

Gladwyn, Lord. *De Gaulle's Europe or Why the General Says No*. London: Secker & Warburg, 1969.

Gordon, Philip H. *A Certain Idea of France: French Security Policy and the Gaullist Legacy*. Princeton: Princeton University Press, 1993.

Gough, Hugh, and John Horne, eds. *De Gaulle and Twentieth-Century France*. London: Edward Arnold, 1994.

Grosser, Alfred. *French Foreign Policy Under De Gaulle*. Translated by Lois Ames Pattison. Boston: Little, Brown, 1965.

Guichard, Jean-Pierre. *De Gaulle face aux crises, 1940-1969*. Paris: Le cherche midi, 2000.

Harrison, Michael M. *The Reluctant Ally: France and Atlantic Security*. Baltimore: Johns Hopkins University Press, 1981.

Hitchcock, William I. *France Restored: Cold War Diplomacy and the Quest for Leadership in Europe*. Chapel Hill: University of North Carolina Press, 1998.

Hoffmann, Stanley. *Decline or Renewal? France Since the 1930s*. New York: Viking Press, 1974.

Isenberg, Irwin. *France Under de Gaulle*. New York: H.W. Wilson Company, 1967.

Funk, Arthur. *Charles de Gaulle: The Crucial Years 1943-1944*. Norton: University of Oklahoma, 1959.

Jouve, Edmond. *Le Général de Gaulle et la construction de l'Europe, 1940-1966*. 2 vols. Paris: Librairie générale de droit et de jurisprudence, 1967.

Kohl, Wilfrid L. *French Nuclear Diplomacy*. Princeton: Princeton University Press, 1971.

Kolodziej, Edward A. *French International Policy Under de Gaulle and Pompidou: The Politics of Grandeur*. Ithaca: Cornell University Press, 1974.

Lacouture, Jean. *Citations du président de Gaulle*. Paris: Éditions du Seuil, 1968.

Macridis, Roy C. *De Gaulle: Implacable Ally*. New York: Harper & Row, 1966.

Mahoney, Daniel J. *De Gaulle: Statesmanship, Grandeur, and Modern Democracy*. New Brunswick: Transaction Publishers, 2000.

Maillard, Pierre. *De Gaulle und Deutschland. Der unvollendete Traum*. Translated from French by Hermann Kusterer. Bonn/Berlin: Bouvier Verlag, 1991.

May, Ernest R. *Strange Victory: Hitler's Conquest of France*. New York: Hill and Wang, 2000.

McMillan, James F. *Dreyfus to de Gaulle: Politics and Society in France, 1898-1969*. London: Edward Arnold, 1985.

Melton, George. *Darlan: Admiral and Statesman of France 1881-1942*. Westport: Praeger, 1998.

Mendl, Wolf. *Deterrence and Persuasion: French Nuclear Armament in the Context of National Policy, 1945-1969*. New York: Praeger, 1970.

Michel, Henri. *Darlan*. Paris: Hachette, 1993.

Oudin, Bernard. *Aristide Briand. La paix: une idée neuve en Europe*. Paris: Éditions Robert Laffont, 1987.

Paxton, Robert O. *Vichy France: Old Guard and New Order*. New York: Norton, 1973.

Rioux, Jean-Pierre. *The Fourth Republic, 1944-1958*. New York: Cambridge University Press, 1987.

Serfaty, Simon. *France, De Gaulle, and Europe: The Policy of the Fourth and Fifth Republics Toward the Continent*. Baltimore: The Johns Hopkins University Press, 1968.

Soutou, Georges-Henri. *The French Military Program For Nuclear Energy, 1945-1981*. Nuclear History Program Occasional Paper 3. College Park: Center for International Security Studies, University of Maryland, 1989.

—. *L'alliance incertaine. Les rapports politico-stratégiques franco-allemands, 1954-1996*. Paris: Fayard, 1996.

Tournoux, Jean-Raymond. *La tragédie du General*. Paris: Plon, 1967.

Willis, F. Roy. *France, Germany and the New Europe*. Stanford: Stanford University Press, 1968.

—. *De Gaulle: Anachronism, Realist, or Prophet*. New York: Holt, Rinehart and Winston, 1967, 1978.

Young, John W. *France, the Cold War and the Western Alliance, 1944-49: French Foreign Policy and Postwar Europe*. London: Leicester University Press, 1990.

Vaïsse, Maurice. *La Grandeur. Politique étrangère du general de Gaulle, 1958-1969*. Paris: Fayard, 1998.

—. ed. *La France et l'atome. Études d'histoire nucléaire*. Brussels: Bruylant, 1994.

—. ed. *De Gaulle et la Russie*. Paris: CNRS Éditions, 2006.

—, Pierre Mélandri and Frédéric Bozo. *La France et l'OTAN, 1949-1996*. Paris, 1996.

Velthoven, Paul van. *Raymond Aron. Het verantwoorde engagement*. Soesterberg: Aspekt, 2005.

Wahl, Nicholas. *The Fifth Republic: France's New Political System*. New York: Random House, 1959.

Wesseling, H.L. *Certain Ideas of France: Essays on French History and Civilization*. Westport: Greenwood Press, 2002.

—. *Franser dan Frans*. Amsterdam: Bert Bakker, 2004.

—. *Frankrijk in oorlog, 1870-1962. De meest dramatische eeuw uit de Franse geschiedenis*. Amsterdam: Bert Bakker, 2006.

White, Dorothy Shipley. *Seeds of Discord: de Gaulle, Free France, and the Allies*. Syracuse: Syracuse University Press, 1964.

Books on American politics and foreign policy

Adrianapoulos, Argyris G. *Western Europe in Kissinger's Global Strategy*. London: Macmillan Press, 1988.

Ambrose, Stephen E. *Rise to Globalism: American Foreign Policy Since 1938*. New York: Penguin Books, 1988.

Anderson, David L. *Trapped by Success: The Eisenhower Administration and Vietnam, 1953-1961*. New York: Columbia University Press, 1991.

Aron, Raymond. *The Imperial Republic: The United States and the World, 1945-1973*. Translated by Frank Jellinek. Eaglewood Cliffs: Prentice-Hall Inc., 1974.

Artaud, Denise. *La fin de l'innocence. Les Etats-Unis de Wilson à Reagan*. Paris: Armand Colin, 1985.

Ashton, Nigel. *Kennedy, Macmillan and the Cold War: The Irony of Interdependence*. Basingstroke: Palgrave Macmillan, 2002.

Ausland, John C. *Kennedy, Khruschev, and Berlin: The 1961-1964 Berlin Crisis*. Oslo: Scandinavian University Press, 1967.

Bailyn, Bernard. *To Begin the World Anew: The Genius and Ambiguities of the American Founders*. New York: Random House, 2003.

Berding, A.H. *Dulles on Diplomacy*. Princeton: D. van Norstrand, 1975.

Berman, Larry. *Lyndon Johnson's War: The Road to Stalemate in Vietnam*. New York: W.W. Norton & Company, 1989.

Beschloss, Michael. *The Crisis Years: Kennedy and Khrushchev, 1960-1963*. New York: Harper Collins, 1991.

Blum, John Morton. *Years of Discord: American Politics and Society, 1961-1974*. New York: W.W. Norton & Co., 1991.

Bradlee, Benjamin C. *Conversations with Kennedy*. New York: Pocket Books, 1976.

Brands, H.W. *Cold Warriors: Eisenhower's Generation and American Foreign Policy*. New York: Columbia University Press, 1988.

—. *The Devil We Knew: Americans and the Cold War*. Oxford: Oxford University Press, 1993.

Brinkley, Douglas. *Dean Acheson and the Making of U.S. Foreign Policy*. New York: St. Martin's Press, 1993.

— and Richard T. Griffiths, eds. *John F. Kennedy and Europe*. Baton Rouge: Louisiana State University Press, 1999.

Brown, Seyom. *The Faces of Power: Constancy and Change in United States Foreign Policy from Truman to Johnson*. New York: Columbia University Press, 1968.

Burman, Stephen. *America in the Modern World: The Transcendence of American Hegemony*. Hemel Hempstead: Harrester Wheatsheaf, 1991.

Burns, Edward McNall. *The American Idea of Mission: Concepts of National Purpose and Destiny*. New Brunswick: Rutgers University Press, 1957.

Calleo, David P. *The Imperious Economy*. Cambridge: Harvard University Press, 1982.

—. *The Bankrupting of America: How the Federal Budget is Impoverishing the Nation*. New York: Avon Books, 1992.

—. *Beyond American Hegemony: The Future of the Western Alliance*. New York: Basic Books, 1987.

Catlin, George. *Kissinger's Atlantic Charter*. Gerrards Cross: Van Duren Press, 1974.

Catudal, Honoré M. *Kennedy and the Berlin Wall Crisis: A Case Study in U.S. Decisionmaking*. Berlin: Berlin-Verlag, 1980.

Chafe, William H. *The Unfinished Journey: America Since World War II*. New York: Oxford University Press, 1986.

Cohen, Warren I., and Nancy Bernkopf Tucker, eds. *Lyndon Johnson Confronts the World: American Foreign Policy, 1963-1968*. Cambridge: Cambridge University Press, 1994.

Cunningham, Noble E. Jr. *Jefferson vs. Hamilton: Confrontations That Shaped the Nation*. Boston/New York: Bedford/St.Martin's, 2000.

Dallek, Robert. *The American Style of Foreign Policy: Cultural Politics and Foreign Affairs*. New York: Alfred A. Knopf, 1983.

Davids, Jules. *The United States in World Affairs, 1964*. New York: Harper & Row for the Council of Foreign Relations, 1965.

Freedman, Lawrence. *Kennedy's Wars: Berlin, Cuba, Laos, and Vietnam*. New York: Oxford University Press, 2000.

Fromkin, David. *In the Time of the Americans: FDR, Truman, Marshall, MacArthur - The Generation That Changed America's Role in the World*. London: Papermac Macmillan, 1996.

Gaddis, John Lewis. *Strategies of Containment: A Critical Appraisal of Postwar American National Security Policy*. Oxford: Oxford University Press, 1982.

—. *Surprise, Security, and the American Experience*. Cambridge: Harvard University Press, 2004.

Geyelin, Philip. *Lyndon B. Johnson and the World*. New York: Frederick A. Praeger, 1966.

Goetzmann, William H. *New Lands, New Men: America and the Second Great Age of Discovery*. New York: Viking Penguin, 1986.

Halberstam, David. *The Best and the Brightest*. New York: Fawcett Crest Books, 1972.

Hammond, Paul Y. *LBJ and the Presidential Management of Foreign Relations*. Austin: University of Texas Press, 1992.

Harper, John L. *American Visions of Europe: Franklin D. Roosevelt, George F. Kennan, and Dean G. Acheson*. Cambridge: Cambridge University Press, 1994.

—. *American Machiavelli: Alexander Hamilton and the Origins of U.S. Foreign Policy*. Cambridge: Cambridge University Press, 2004.

Hartz, Louis. *The Liberal Tradition in America: An Interpretation of American Political Thought Since the Revolution*. New York: Harcourt, Brace and Company, 1955.

Heald, Morrell, and Lawrence S. Kaplan. *Culture and Diplomacy: The American Experience*. Westport/London: Greenwood Press, 1977.

Heren, Louis. *No Hail, No Farewell: The Johnson Years*. London: Weidenfeld and Nicolson, 1970.

Herring, George C. *America's Longest War: The United States and Vietnam, 1950-1975*. New York: John Wiley & Sons, 1979.

Hoffmann, Stanley. *Gulliver's Troubles or the Setting of American Foreign Policy*. New York: McGraw-Hill for the Council on Foreign Relations, 1968.

—. *Primacy or World Order: American Foreign Policy Since the Cold War*. New York: McGraw-Hill, 1978.

Hogan, Michael J. *The Marshall Plan: America, Britain, and the Reconstruction of Western Europe, 1947-1952*. New York: Cambridge University Press, 1987.

— and Thomas G. Patterson, eds. *Explaining the History of American Foreign Relations*. Cambridge: Cambridge University Press, 1991.

—. *America in the World: The Historiography of American Foreign Relations Since 1941*. Cambridge: Cambridge University Press, 1995.

Immerman, Richard. *John Foster Dulles and the Diplomacy of the Cold War*. Princeton: Princeton University Press, 1990.

Johnson, Richard A. *The Administration of United States Foreign Policy*. Austin: University of Texas Press, 1971.

Jonas, Manfred. *Isolationism in America, 1935-1941*. Ithaca: Cornell University Press, 1966.

Kaplan, Lawrence S. *Thomas Jefferson: Westward the Course of Empire*. Wilmington: Scholarly Resources Books, 1999.

Kaplan, Lawrence S. *American Historians and the Atlantic Alliance*. Kent: Kent State University Press, 1991.

Kaufmann, William. *The McNamara Strategy*. New York: Harper & Row, 1964.

Kraft, Joseph. *The Grand Design: From Common Market to Atlantic Partnership*. New York: Harper & Brothers, 1962.

Kunz, Diane. *Butter and Guns: America's Cold War Economic Policy*. New York: Free Press, 1997.

Lerner, Max. *America as a Civilization: The Basic Frame*. Vol. 1. New York: Simon and Schuster, 1957.

Lineberry, William P. *The United States in World Affairs, 1970*. New York: Simon & Schuster for the Council on Foreign Relations, 1972.

Lippmann, Walter. *The Cold War: A Study in U.S. Foreign Policy*. New York: Harper, 1947.

—. *United States Foreign Policy: Shield of the Republic*. Boston: Little, Brown and Company, 1943.

—. *US War Aims*. Boston: Little, Brown and Company, 1944.

—. *Western Unity and the Common Market*. London: Hamish Hamilton, 1962.

Litwak, Robert. *Détente and the Nixon Doctrine: American Foreign Policy and the Pursuit of Stability, 1969-1976*. Cambridge: Cambridge University Press, 1984.

Lundestad, Geir. *"Empire" by Integration: The United States and European Integration, 1945-1997*. Oxford: Oxford University Press, 1998.

Mace, George. *Locke, Hobbes, and the Federalist Papers: An Essay of the Genesis of American Political Heritage*. Carbondale: Southern Illinois University Press, 1979.

MacGregor Burns, James. *Roosevelt 1940-1945*. New York: Harcourt Brace Jovanovich, 1970.

Mazlish, Bruce. *Kissinger: The European Mind in American Foreign Policy*. New York: Basic Books, 1976.

McAuliffe, Mary S. *CIA Documents on the Cuban Missile Crisis, 1962.* Washington, DC: Central Intelligence Agency, 1991.

McDougall, Walter A. *Promised Land, Crusader State: The American Encounter with the World Since 1776.* New York: Houghton Mifflin, 1998.

McNay, John T. *Acheson and Empire: The British Accent in American Foreign Policy.* Columbia: University of Missouri Press, 2001.

Minnen, Cornelis van, and John F. Sears, eds. *FDR and His Contemporaries: Foreign Perceptions of an American President.* New York: St. Martin's Press, 1992.

Morris, Richard B. *The Forging of the Union, 1781-1789.* New York: Harper & Row, 1987.

Nash, Philip. *The Other Missiles of October: Eisenhower, Kennedy, and the Jupiters, 1957-1963.* Chapel Hill: University of North Carolina Press, 1997.

Niebuhr, Reinhold. *The Irony of American History.* New York: Charles Scribner's Sons, 1952.

Osgood, Robert Endicott. *Alliances and American Foreign Policy.* Baltimore: Johns Hopkins University Press, 1968.

—, et al. *America and the World: From the Truman Doctrine to Vietnam.* Baltimore: Johns Hopkins University Press, 1970.

—. *Ideals and Self-Interest in America's Foreign Relations.* Chicago: University of Chicago Press, 1953.

Paterson, Thomas G. *Kennedy's Quest for Victory: American Foreign Policy, 1961-1963.* New York: Oxford University Press, 1989.

Patterson, James T. *Grand Expectations: The United States, 1945-1974.* New York/Oxford: Oxford University Press, 1996.

Raeymaker, Omer De and Albert H. Bowman, eds. *American Foreign Policy in Europe: A Colloquium.* Louvain: Nauwelaerts Publishing House, 1969.

Reyn, Sebastian. *Allies or Aliens? George W. Bush and the Transatlantic Crisis in Historical Perspective.* Den Haag: Atlantische Commissie, 2004.

Roman, Peter J. *Eisenhower and the Missile Gap.* Ithaca: Cornell University Press, 1996.

Schlesinger, Arthur M., Jr. *The Imperial Presidency.* New York: Popular Library, 1974.

—. *The Cycles of American History.* Boston: Houghton Mifflin, 1986.

Schulzinger, Robert D. *The Wise Men of Foreign Affairs: The History of the Council on Foreign Relations.* New York: Columbia University Press, 1984.

—. *American Diplomacy in the Twentieth Century.* New York: Oxford University Press, 1984.

Schwartz, Thomas. *Lyndon Johnson and Europe: In the Shadow of Vietnam.* Cambridge: Harvard University Press, 2003.

Robert E. Sherwood. *Roosevelt and Hopkins: An Intimate History.* New York: Harper & Brothers Publishers, 1948.

Silk, Leonard and Mark Silk. *The American Establishment.* New York: Basic Books, 1980.

Steel, Ronald. *The End of Alliance: America and the Future of Europe.* New York: Viking, 1964.

—. *Pax Americana.* New York: The Viking Press, 1967.

Steinbruner, John. *The Cybernetic Theory of Decision: New Dimensions of Political Analysis.* Princeton: Princeton University Press, 1974.

Stebbins, Richard P. *The United States in World Affairs.* (annually from 1956 to 1963 and 1965 to 1967) New York: Council on Foreign Relations.

Sulzberger, C. L. *The World and Richard Nixon.* New York: Prentice Hall Press, 1987.

Taber, George M. *John F. Kennedy and a Uniting Europe.* Bruges: College of Europe, 1969.

Theoharis, Athan G. *The Yalta Myths: An Issue in U.S. Politics, 1945-1955.* Columbia: University of Missouri Press, 1970.

Thompson, Kenneth W., ed. *The Kennedy Presidency: 17 Intimate Perspectives of John F. Kennedy.* Lanham: University Press of America, 1985.

Thornton, Richard C. *The Nixon-Kissinger Years: The Reshaping of American Foreign Policy.* 2d ed. St. Paul: Paragon, 2001.

Tocqueville, Alexis de. *Democracy in America and Two Essays on America.* London: Penguin Books, 2003.

Tucker, Robert W. *Nation Or Empire? The Debate Over American Foreign Policy.* Baltimore/London: Johns Hopkins University Press, 1968.

VanDeMark, Brian. *Into the Quagmire: Lyndon Johnson and the Escalation of the Vietnam War.* New York: Oxford University Press, 1991.

Watson, Robert J. *Into the Missile Age, 1956-1960.* History of the Office of the Secretary of Defense, vol. 4. Washington DC: Historical Office, Office of the Secretary of Defense, 1997.

Weisband, Edward. *The Ideology of American Foreign Policy: A Paradigm of Lockian Liberalism.* London: Sage Publications, 1973.

Williams, William Appleman. *The Tragedy of American Diplomacy.* New York: W.W. Norton & Co., 1972.

Winand, Pascaline. *Eisenhower, Kennedy, and the United States of Europe.* London: Macmillan, 1993.

Wittkopf, Eugene R. *Faces of Internationalism: Public Opinion and American Foreign Policy.* Durham and London: Duke University Press, 1990.

Books on the transatlantic relationship (including NATO)

Amme, Carl H. *NATO Without France: A Strategic Appraisal.* Stanford: The Hoover Institution on War, Revolution, and Peace at Stanford University, 1967.

Bailyn, Bernard. *Atlantic History: Concept and Contours.* Cambridge: Harvard University Press, 2005.

Ball, M. Margaret. *NATO and the European Union Movement.* New York: Frederick A. Praeger, 1959.

Bange, Oliver. *The EEC Crisis of 1963: Kennedy, Macmillan, de Gaulle and Adenauer in Conflict.* London: Macmillan Press, 2000.

Barnet, Richard J. *The Alliance.* New York: Simon & Schuster, 1983.

Beaufre, André. *NATO and Europe.* New York: Alfred A. Knopf, 1966.

Beer, Francis A. *Integration and Disintegration in NATO.* Columbus: Ohio State University Press, 1969.

Beloff, Max. *The United States and the Unity of Europe.* Westport: Greenwood Press, 1963.

Berthon, Simon. *Alllies at War.* London: HarperCollins, 2001.

Birrenbach, Kurt. *The Future of the Atlantic Community: Toward an European-American Partnership.* New York: Frederick A. Praeger, 1963.

Boorstin, Daniel J. *America and the Image of Europe: Reflections on American Thought.* New York: Meridian Books, 1960.

Calleo, David P. *The Atlantic Fantasy: The United States, NATO and Europe*. Baltimore: Johns Hopkins University Press, 1970.

Catlin, George. *The Atlantic Community*. Wakefield: Coram Publisher Ltd., 1959.

Cerny, Karl H. and Henry W. Briefs, eds. *NATO in Quest of Cohesion*. New York: Frederick A. Praeger, 1965.

Chace, James and Earl C. Ravenal, eds. *Atlantis Lost: US-European Relations after the Cold War*. New York: New York University Press, 1976.

Cleveland, Harold B. van. *The Atlantic Idea and its European Rivals*. New York: McGraw-Hill, 1966.

Cook, Don. *Forging the Alliance: NATO, 1945 to 1950*. London: Secker & Warburg, 1989.

Cromwell, William C. ed. *Political Problems of Atlantic Partnership: National Perspectives*. Bruges: College of Europe, 1969.

Dahrendorf, Ralf and Theodore C. Sorenson. *A Widening Atlantic? Domestic Change and Foreign Policy*. New York: Council on Foreign Relations, 1986.

DePorte, A. W. *Europe Between the Superpowers: The Enduring Balance*. New Haven: Yale University, 1979.

Deutsch, Karl W.. et.al. *Political Community and the North Atlantic Area: International Organization in the Light of Historical Experience*. Princeton: Princeton University Press, 1957.

Ellwood, David W. *Rebuilding Europe: Western Europe, America, and Postwar Reconstruction*. London: Longman, 1992.

Evans, J. Martin. *America: The View From Europe*. San Francisco: San Francisco Press, 1976.

Fedder, Edwin H. *NATO: The Dynamics of Alliance in the Postwar World*. New York: Dodd, Mead & Co., 1973.

Fox, Annette Baker and William T.R. Fox. *NATO and the Range of American Choice*. New York: Columbia University Press, 1967.

Furniss, Edgar S. *The Western Alliance: Its Status and Prospects*. Columbus: Ohio University Press, 1965.

Giauque, Jeffrey Glen. *Grand Designs and Visions of Unity: The Atlantic Powers and the Reorganization of Western Europe, 1955-1963*. Chapel Hill: University of North Carolina Press, 2002.

Goodman, Elliot R. *The Fate of the Atlantic Community*. New York: Praeger, 1975.

Grosser, Alfred. *The Western Alliance: European-American Relations Since 1945*. Translated by Michael Shaw. New York: Continuum, 1980.

Hackett, Clifford P. *Monnet and the Americans: The Father of a United Europe and his U.S. Supporters*. Washington DC: Jean Monnet Council, 1995.

Haftendorn, Helga et al., eds. *The Strategic Triangle: France, Germany, and the United States in the Shaping of the New Europe*. Washington D.C./Baltimore: Woodrow Wilson Center Press/ Johns Hopkins University Press, 2006.

Hahn, Walter F., and Robert L. Pfaltzgraff, Jr., eds. *Atlantic Community in Crisis: A Redefinition of the Transatlantic Relationship*. New York: Pergamon Press, 1979.

Harrison, Michael M., and Mark G. McDonough. *Negotiations on the French Withdrawal From NATO*. Washington, DC: SAIS Foreign Policy Institute, 1987.

Hartley, Livingston. *Atlantic Challenge*. New York: Oceana Publications Inc., 1965.

Heller, Francis H., and John R. Gillingham. *NATO: The Founding of the Atlantic Alliance and the Integration of Europe*. New York: St.Martin's Press, 1992.

Hunt, K. *NATO Without France: The Military Implications*. Adelphi Paper no. 32. London: Institute for Strategic Studies, 1966.

Jordan, Robert S. *Political Leadership in NATO: A Study in Multinational Diplomacy*. Boulder: Westview Press, 1979.

Joseph, Franz M. *As Others See Us: The United States Through Foreign Eyes*. Princeton: Princeton University Press, 1959.

Kaiser, Karl, and Hans-Peter Schwarz, eds. *America and Western Europe: Problems and Prospects*. Lexington: Lexington Books, 1977.

Kaplan, Lawrence S. *NATO and the United States*. Boston: Twayne Publishers, 1988.

—. *The United States and NATO: The Formative Years*. Lexington: University Press of Kentucky, 1984.

Kleiman, Robert. *Atlantic Crisis: American Diplomacy Confronts a Resurgent Europe*. New York: W. W. Norton & Co, 1964.

Koht, Halvdan. *The American Spirit in Europe: A Survey of Transatlantic Influences*. Philadelphia: University of Pennsylvania Press, 1949.

Kraus, Michael. *The Atlantic Civilization: Eighteenth Century Origins*. New York: Russel & Russel, 1961.

Lerner, Daniel, and Morton Gorden. *Euratlantica*. Cambridge: MIT Press, 1969.

Lundestad, Geir. *No End to Alliance: The United States and Western Europe: Past, Present and Future*. New York/Houndmills: St Martin's Press/Macmillan Press, 1998.

Mead, Robert O. *Atlantic Legacy: Essays in American-European Cultural History*. New York: New York University Press, 1969.

Mendershausen, Horst. *From NATO to Independence: Reflections on De Gaulle's Secession P-3334*. Washington, DC: Washington Center of Foreign Policy, March 1966.

—. *Unrest and Cohesion in the Atlantic Alliance: NATO and the German Question*. Memorandum RM-4936-PR. Santa Monica: Rand Corporation, April 1966.

Middleton, Drew. *The Atlantic Community: A Study in Unity and Disunity*. New York: David McKay Company Inc., 1965.

Munk, Frank. *Atlantic Dilemma: Partnership or Community?*. New York: Oceana Publications, Inc., 1964.

Neustadt, Richard E. *Alliance Politics*. New York: Columbia University Press, 1970.

Osgood, Robert Endicott. *NATO: The Entangling Alliance*. Chicago: University of Chicago Press, 1962.

Pells, Richard H. *Not Like Us: How Europeans Have Loved, Hated, and Transformed American Culture Since World War II*. New York: Basic Books, 1997.

Pfaltzgraff, Robert L., Jr. *The Atlantic Community: A Complex Imbalance*. New York: Van Nostrand Reinhold Co., 1969.

Reid, Escott. *Time of Fear and Hope: The Making of the North Atlantic Treaty, 1947-1949*. Toronto: McClelland and Stewart, 1977.

Roach, James R. *The United States and the Atlantic Community: Issues and Prospects*. Austin: University of Texas Press, 1967.

Sherwood, Elisabeth. *Allies in Crisis: Meeting Global Challenges to Western Security*. New Haven: Yale University Press, 1990.

Spaak, Paul-Henri. *The Crisis of the Atlantic Alliance*. Columbus: Ohio State University Press, 1967.

Strausz-Hupé, Robert, James E. Dougherty, and William R. Kintner. *Building the Atlantic World*. New York: Harper & Row, 1963.

Streit, Clarence. *Freedom's Frontier: Atlantic Union Now, the Vast Opportunity the Two American Revolutions Offer Sovereign Citizens*. New York: Harper & Brothers, 1961.

—. *Union Now: A Proposal for an Atlantic Federal Union of the Free*. New York: Harper & Brothers, 1940.

—. *Union Now With Britain*. New York: Harper & Brothers, 1941.

Stromseth, Jane E. *The Origins of Flexible Response: NATO's Debate Over Strategy in the 1960s*. New York: St. Martin's Press, 1988.

Stuart, Douglas, and William Tow. *The Limits of Alliance: NATO Out-of-Area Problems Since 1949*. Baltimore: Johns Hopkins University Press, 1990.

Trachtenberg, Marc. *Between Empire and Alliance: America and Europe during the Cold War*. Lanham: Rowman and Littlefield, 2003.

Van der Beugel, Ernst. *From Marshall Aid to Atlantic Partnership*. Amsterdam: Elsevier, 1966.

Vandevanter, E. *Some Fundamentals of NATO Organization*. Memorandum RM-3559-PR. Santa Monica: Rand Corporation, April 1966.

—. *Studies on NATO: An Analysis of Integration*. Memorandum RM-5006-PR. Santa Monica: Rand Corporation, Augustus 1966.

Wampler, Robert A. *Nuclear Weapons and the Atlantic Alliance: A Guide to U.S. Sources*. Nuclear History Program Occasional Paper Series. College Park: Center for International Security Studies, University of Maryland, 1989.

Wilcox, Francis O., and H. Field Haviland, Jr., eds. *The Atlantic Community: Progress and prospects*. New York: Frederick A. Praeger, 1963.

Other books

Adams, Henry. *The Education of Henry Adams*. Boston: Houghton Mifflin, 1973.

Armstrong, Hamilton Fish. *Fifty Years of Foreign Affairs*. New York: Praeger Publishers for the Council on Foreign Relations, 1972.

Aron, Raymond. *The Great Debate: Theories of Nuclear Strategy*. Garden City: Doubleday & Company, 1965.

Bald, Detlef. *Die Atombewaffnung der Bundeswehr. Militär, Öffentlichkeit und Politik in der Ära Adenauer*. Bremen: Temmen, 1994.

Brinkley, Douglas, and Clifford Hackett. *Jean Monnet: The Path to European Unity*. New York: St. Martin's Press, 1991.

Buchan, Alastair. *The End of the Postwar Era: A New Balance of World Power*. London: Weidenfeld and Nicolson, 1974.

Calleo, David P. *Europe's Future: The Grand Alternative*. New York: Horizon Press, 1965.

Camps, Miriam. *Britain and the European Community, 1955-1963*. London: Oxford University Press, 1964.

—. *European Unification in the Sixties: From Veto to Crisis*. New York: McGraw-Hill Book Company for the Council on Foreign Relations, 1966.

Carr, Edward Hallett. *The Twenty Years' Crisis, 1919-1939: An Introduction to the Study of International Relations*. London: Macmillan, 1939.

Cipolla, Carlo M. *The Fontana Economic History of Europe: Contemporary Economies, Part I*. Glasgow: Collins/Fontana Books, 1976.

Cowley, Robert. *The Cold War: A Military History*. New York: Random House, 2005.

Deutsch, Karl W., Roy C. Macridis, Lewis J. Edinger, and Richard L. Merritt, *France, Germany and the Western Alliance: A Study of Elite Attitudes on European Integration and World Politics*. New York: Charles Scribner's Sons, 1967.

Dimbleby, David, and David Reynolds. *An Ocean Apart: The Relationship Between Britain and America in the Twentieth Century*. New York: Random House, 1988.

Eichengreen, Barry. *Global Imbalances and the Lessons of Bretton Woods*. NBER Working Paper Series no. 10497, May 2004.

Gaddis, John Lewis. *We Now Know: Rethinking Cold War History*. New York: Oxford University Press, 1997.

—. *The Landscape of History: How Historians Map the Past*. New York: Oxford University Press, 2002.

—, et al. *Cold War Statesmen Confront the Bomb: Nuclear Diplomacy Since 1945*. Oxford/New York: Oxford University Press, 1999.

Garthoff, Raymond L. *Reflections on the Cuban Missile Crisis*. Revised edition. Washington, DC: Brookings Institution, 1989.

Gavin, Francis J. *Gold, Dollars, and Power: The Politics of International Monetary Relations, 1958-1971*. Chapel Hill: University of North Carolina Press, 2004.

Hanrieder, Wolfram F., and Graeme P. Auton. *The Foreign Policies of West Germany, France and Britain*. New Jersey: Prentice-Hall, 1980.

—. *Germany, America, Europe: Forty Years of German Foreign Policy*. New Haven: Yale University Press, 1989.

Harris, Ian. *The Mind of John Locke: A Study of Political Theory in Its Intellectual Setting*. Cambridge: Cambridge University Press, 1994.

Hitchcock, William I. *The Struggle for Europe: The Turbulent History of a Divided Continent, 1945-2002*. New York: Doubleday, 2003.

Hobbes, Thomas. *Leviathan*. Oxford: Oxford University Press, 1996.

Kelleher, Catherin McArdle. *Germany and the Politics of Nuclear Weapons*. New York: Columbia University Press, 1975.

Kennedy, Paul. *The Rise and Fall of the Great Powers: Economic Change and Military Conflict from 1500 to 2000*. New York: Random House, 1987.

Kennedy, Paul, and William I. Hitchcock. *From War to Peace: Altered Strategic Landscapes in the Twentieth Century*. New Haven: Yale University Press, 2000.

Kersaudy, François. *Churchill and de Gaulle*. New York: Atheneum, 1983.

Kimball, Warren F. *Forged in War: Roosevelt, Churchill and the Second World War*. New York: William Morrow & Co., 1997.

Krugman, Paul R., and Maurice Obstfeld. *International Economics: Theory and Policy*, 3rd edition.. New York: Harper Collins, 1994.

Larres, Klaus. *Churchill's Cold War: The Politics of Personal Diplomacy*. New Haven: Yale University Press, 2002.

Macridis, Roy C. *Modern European Governments: Cases in Comparative Policy Making*. Eaglewood Cliffs: Prentice-Hall Inc., 1968.

Mastny, Vojtech. *The Cold War and Soviet Insecurity: The Stalin Years*. New York: Oxford University Press, 1996.

Mayer, Frank A. *Adenauer and Kennedy: A Study in German-American Relations 1961-1963*. New York: St. Martin's Press, 1996.

Milward, Alan S. *The Reconstruction of Western Europe, 1945-1950*. Berkeley: University of California Press, 1984.

Morgan, Roger. *West European Politics Since 1945: The Shaping of the European Community*. London: B.T. Batsford Ltd, 1972.

Pierre, Andrew J. *Nuclear Politics: The British Experience With an Independent Strategic Force, 1939-1970*. New York: Oxford University Press, 1972.

Roberts, Owen J., John F. Schmidt, and Clarence K. Streit. *The New Federalist, by Publius II*. New York: Harper & Brothers, 1950.

Rockefeller, Nelson A. *The Future of Federalism*. Cambridge: Harvard University Press, 1963.

Rogow, Arnold A. *Thomas Hobbes: Radical in the Service of Reaction*. New York: W.W. Norton & Co., 1986.

Schick, Jack M. *The Berlin Crisis 1958-1962*. Philadelphia: University of Pennsylvania Press, 1971.

Schlusser, Robert M. *The Berlin Crisis of 1961: Soviet-American Relations and the Struggle for Power in the Kremlin, June-November 1961*. Baltimore: Johns Hopkins University Press, 1973.

Schwarz, Hans-Peter. *Adenauer und Frankreich. Die deutsch-französischen Beziehungen 1958 bis 1969*. Bonn: Bouvier Verlag, 1985.

Slusser, Robert M. *The Berlin Crisis of 1961*. Baltimore: 1973.

Solomon, Robert. *The International Monetary System, 1945-1981*. New York: Harper & Row, 1982.

Sommerville, Johann P. *Thomas Hobbes: Political Ideas in Historical Context*. London: Macmillan, 1992.

Stützle, Walter. *Kennedy und Adenauer in der Berlin Krise 1961-62*. Bonn: Verlag Neue Gesellschaft, 1973.

Sulzberger, C. L. *The Last of the Giants*. New York: MacMillan, 1970.

—. *An Age of Mediocrity*. New York: MacMillan, 1973.

—. *Seven Continents & Forty Years*. New York: Quadrangle, 1977.

Thornton, Richard C. *Odd Man Out: Truman, Stalin, Mao, and the Origins of the Korean War*. Washington, DC: Brassey's, 2000.

Trachtenberg, Marc. *History and Strategy*. Princeton: Princeton University Press, 1991.

—. *A Constructed Peace: The Making of the European Settlement, 1945-1963*. Princeton: Princeton University Press, 1999.

Triffin, Robert. *Gold and the Dollar Crisis*. New Haven: Yale University Press, 1960.

Urwin, Derek W. *The Community of Europe: A History of European Integration*. London: Longman, 1991.

Weil, Gordon L., and Ian Davidson. *The Gold War*. New York: Holt, Rinehart, and Winston, 1970.

Young, Hugo. *This Blessed Plot: Britain and Europe from Churchill to Blair*. London: Macmillan/Papermac, 1999.

Zubok, Vladislav, and Constantine Pleshakov. *Inside the Kremlin's Cold War: From Stalin to Khrushchev*. Cambridge: Harvard University Press, 1996.

Zwerdling, Alex. *Improvised Europeans: American Literary Expatriates and the Siege of London.* New York: Basic Books, 1998.

Articles

Adenauer, Konrad. "Adenauer talks about Johnson: exclusive interview with the former Chancellor of West Germany." *US News and World Report* 55, 16 December 1963: 44-47.

Ailleret, Charles. "The Strategic Theory of 'Flexible Response'." *The Atlantic Community Quarterly* (Fall 1964): 413-428.

—. "'Défense dirigée' ou 'défense tous azimuts.'" *Revue de défense nationale* 23 (December 1967): 1,923-1,927.

—. "Defense in All Directions." *The Atlantic Community Quarterly* (Spring 1968): 17-25.

Alexandre, Marc. "Le Dollar et la France." *La Nef* 26 (1966): 119-138.

Artaud, Denise. "Le Grand Dessein de J.F. Kennedy. Proposition mystique ou occasion manquée?" *Revue D'Histoire Moderne et Contemporaine* 29 (1982): 235-66.

Bagnato, Bruna. "France and the Origins of the Atlantic Pact." In *The Atlantic Pact Forty Years Later: A Historical Appraisal,* Ennio di Nolfo, 79-110. Berlin: Walter de Gruyter, 1991.

Barbier, Colette. "La force multilatérale." *Relations Internationales* no. 69 (Spring 1992).

Barclay, Daniel. "Cyclical Behavior and Ideological Change in American Politics." *Michigan Journal of Political Science* 2, issue iii (Fall 2004): 4-38.

Bariéty, Jacques. "La perception de la puissance française par le chancelier K. Adenauer de 1958 à 1963." *Relations Internationales* 58 (Summer 1989): 217-225.

—. "De Gaulle, Adenauer et la genèse du traité de l'Elysée du 22 janvier 1963." in *De Gaulle et son siecle,* Journées internationales organisées par l'Institut Charles de Gaulle, 19-24 November 1990, Paris.

Barrett, David M. "The Mythology Surrounding Lyndon Johnson, his Advisers, and the 1965 Decision to Escalate the Vietnam War." *Political Science Quarterly* 103 (Winter 1988-1989): 637-663.

Baum, Keith W. "Two's Company, Three's a Crowd: The Eisenhower Administration, France, and Nuclear Weapons." *Presidential Studies Quarterly* 20 (Spring 1990): 315-328.

Birrenbach, Kurt. "Partnership and consultation in NATO." *The Atlantic Community Quarterly* (Spring 1964): 62-71.

Jean-Paul Bled. "L'image de l'Allemagne chez Charles de Gaulle avant juin 1940." *Études gaulliennes,* no. 17 (1977).

Bozo, Frédéric and Pierre Melandri. "La France devant l'opinion américaine: le retour de de Gaulle début 1958-printemps 1959." *Relations Internationales* 58 (Summer 1989): 195-215.

Brandon, Henry. "Report from Washington: Watching De Gaulle." *Saturday Review* 47, 22 February 1964: 14 ff.

Brands, H.W., Jr. "Johnson and de Gaulle: American Diplomacy Sotto Voce." *Historian* 49 (1987): 482-485.

Brenner, Philip. "Kennedy and Khrushchev on Cuba: two stages, three parties." *Problems of Communism* 41 (Spring 1992): 24-27.

Brodie, Bernard. "How Not to Lead an Alliance." *The Reporter* 9 March 1967: 18-24.

Buchan, Alastair. "The multilateral force: an historical perspective." *Adelphi Papers* no. 13. London: Institute for Strategic Studies, October 1964.

Buffet, Cyril. "La politique nucléaire de la France et la seconde crise de Berlin, 1958-1962." *Relations Internationales* 59 (Autumn 1989): 347-358.

Cate, Curtis. "Charles de Gaulle: The Last Romantic." *The Atlantic Monthly* 206, no. 5 (November 1960): 56-63.

Cogan, Charles G. "The Break-Up: General de Gaulle's Separation from Power." *Journal of Contemporary History* 27, no.1 (January 1992): 167-199.

—. "Integrated Command...or Military Protectorate." *Diplomatic History* 26, Issue 2 (April 2002): 309-315.

Cohen, William B. "De Gaulle and Europe Prior to 1958." *French Politics and Society* 8, no. 4 (Fall 1990): 1-12.

Costigliola, Frank. "The Failed Design: Kennedy, de Gaulle, and the Struggle for Europe." *Diplomatic History* 8 (Summer 1984): 227-251.

—. "Kennedy, the European Allies and the Failure to Consult." *Political Science Quarterly* (Spring 1995): 105-123.

—. "Culture, Emotion and the Creation of an Atlantic Identity, 1948-1952." in *The United States and Western Europe: Cooperation and Conflict*, Geir Lundestad. Oslo: Scandinavian University Press, 1998.

—. "The Nuclear Family: Tropes of Gender and Pathology in the Western Alliance." *Diplomatic History* 21, Issue 2 (April 1997): 163-183.

Couve de Murville, Maurice. "Why De Gaulle is challenging the US." Interview with Couve de Murville in *US News and World Report* 50, 16 March 1964: 70-75.

—, Hervé Alphand, and Etienne Burin des Roziers. "Les Relations franco-américaines au temps du général de Gaulle: dossier." *Espoir* 26 March 1979: 37-78.

Crabb, Cecil V., Jr. "The Gaullist Revolt against the Anglo-Saxons." *The Atlantic Community Quarterly* (Spring 1964): 35-44. Reprinted from *The Annals of the American Academy of Political and Social Science*, January 1964.

Creswell, Michael, and Marc Trachtenberg. "France and the German Question, 1945-1955." *Journal of Cold War Studies* 5, no. 3 (Summer 2003): 5-28.

de Carmoy, Guy. "Force de Frappe: A Triple Debate." *The Atlantic Community Quarterly* (Summer 1964): 278-184.

DePorte, Anton W. "De Gaulle's Europe: Playing the Russian Card." *French Politics and Society* 8, no. 4 (1990): 25-40.

Duval, Marcel, and Pierre Mélandri. "Les Etats-Unis et la prolifération nucléaire: le cas français."*Revue d'histoire diplomatique* (1995): 193-220.

Fontaine, André. "The ABC of MLF." *The Reporter* 31 December 1964: 10-14.

—. "What is French policy?" *Foreign Affairs* 45 (October 1966): 58-76.

Gaddis, John Lewis. "The Tragedy of Cold War History: Reflections on Revisionism." *Foreign Affairs* (January/February 1994): 142-154.

Gavin, Francis J. "The Gold Battles Within the Cold War: American Monetary Policy and the Defense of Europe, 1960-1963." *Diplomatic History* 26, no. 1 (Winter 2002): 61-94.

Gillingham, John. "Turning Weakness into Strength: France's Post-World War II Diplomacy." *Diplomatic History* 24, Issue 3 (July 2000): 543-546.

Goodman, Elliot R. "Five nuclear options for the West." *Forensic Quarterly* (August 1964).

—. "de Gaulle's NATO policy in perspective." *Orbis* 10 (Fall 1966): 690-723.

Griffiths, Richard T. "Dank U mijnheer Monnet; ik zal ervoor zorgen." In *Met de Franse slag, Opstellen voor H.L. Wesseling*, edited by M. Ph. Bossenbroek, M.E.H.N Mout, and C. Musterd, 107-122. Leiden: Centrum voor Moderne Geschiedenis, Rijksuniversiteit Leiden, 1998.

Grigg, John. "In defense of Charles de Gaulle." *New York Times Magazine* 23 February 1964.

Grosser, Alfred. "France and Germany in the Atlantic Community." *International Organization* 17 (Summer 1963): 550-573.

—. "France and Germany: divergent outlooks." *Foreign Affairs* 44 (October 1965): 26-36.

Helga Haftendorn. "Entstehung und Bedeutung des Harmel-Berichts der NATO von 1967." *Vierteljahrshefte für Zeitgeschichte* 40, no. 2 (April 1992): 169–220.

—. "The Adaptation of the NATO Alliance to a Period of Détente: The 1967 Harmel Report." In *Crises and Compromises: The European Project,1963–1969*, by Wilfried Loth, 285-322. Baden-Baden: Nomos, 2001.

Hamilton, Lee H., André Fontaine, and Brian U. Post. "Internationalist America: An Exchange." *Foreign Policy* (Winter 1986-87): 29-42.

Hitchcock, William I. "France, the Western Alliance, and the Origins of the Schuman Plan, 1948–1950." *Diplomatic History* 21, Issue 4 (October 1997): 603-630.

Hoffmann, Stanley. "de Gaulle, Europe, and the Atlantic Alliance." *International Organization* 18 (Winter 1964): 1-28.

—. "Heroic leadership: the case of modern France." In *Political leadership in industrialized societies: studies in comparative analysis*, Lewis J. Edinger, 108-154. New York: John Wiley & Sons, 1967.

—. "Perceptions, Reality, and the Franco-American conflict." *Journal of International Affairs* 21, no. 1 (1967): 57-71.

—. "de Gaulle's Memoirs: The Hero as History." *World Politics* 13, no. 1 (October 1960): 140-155.

—. "Cursing de Gaulle is Not a Policy." *The Reporter* 30 January 1964: 38-41.

—. "Gaullism by any other name." *Foreign Policy* no. 57 (Winter 1984-1985): 38-57.

—. "Europe's Identity Crisis: Between the Past and America." *Daedalus* (Fall 1964).

—. "Discord in Community: The North Atlantic Area as a Partial International System." In *The Atlantic Community: Progress and Prospects*, edited by Francis O. Wilcox and H. Field Haviland, Jr., 3-31. New York: Frederick A. Praeger, 1963.

Hoffmann, Inge and Stanley Hoffmann. "The will to grandeur: de Gaulle as an artist." In *Philosopher and Kings: Studies in Leadership*, Dankwart Rustow, 248-316. New York: George Braziller, 1970.

Hoff-Wilson, Joan. "'Nixingerism,' NATO, and Détente." *Diplomatic History* 13, no. 4 (Fall 1989): 501-525.

Hughes, Thomas L. "The Twilight of Internationalism." *Foreign Policy* 61 (Winter 1985-86).

Humphrey, David C. "Tuesday Lunch at the Johnson White House: A Preliminary Assessment." *Diplomatic History* 8, no. 1 (Winter 1984): 81-101.

Johnson, Douglas. "The Political Principles of General de Gaulle." *International Affairs* 41, no. 4 (Oct., 1965): 650-662.

—. "Barricades of yesteryear...Charles de Gaulle and the events of 1968." *History Today* 38 (June 1988): 6-8.

Kleiman, Robert. "Background for Atlantic Partnership." In *NATO in Quest of Cohesion*, edited by Karl H. Cerny and Henry W. Briefs, 431-460. New York: Frederick A. Praeger, 1965

Klingberg, Frank L. "The Historical Alternation of Moods in American Foreign Policy." *World Politics* 4, no. 2 (January 1952): 239-273.

—. "Cyclical Trends in American Foreign Policy Moods and Their Policy Implications." in *Challenges to America: United States Foreign Policy in the 1980s*, edited by Charles W. Kegley, Jr. and Patrick J. McGowan, 37-55. Beverly Hills: Sage Publications, 1979.

Kohl, Wilfrid L. "Nuclear sharing in NATO and the multilateral force." *Political Science Quarterly* 80 (March 1965): 88-109.

Kolodziej, Edward A. "de Gaulle, Germany, and the Superpowers: German Unification and the End of the Cold War." *French Politics and Society* 8, no. 4 (Fall 1990): 41-61.

Krakau, Knud. "American Foreign Relations: An American Style?" In *Oceans Apart? Comparing Germany and the United States*, Erich Angermann and Marie-Luise Frings, 121-145. Stuttgart: Klett-Cotta, 1981.

Kuisel, Richard F. "De Gaulle's Dilemma: The American Challenge and Europe." *French Politics and Society* 8, no. 4 (Fall 1990): 13-24.

Kunz, Diane B. "Lyndon Johnson's Dollar Diplomacy." *History Today* 42 (April 1992): 45-51.

Lafeber, Walter. "The 'Lion in the Path': The U.S. Emergence As a World Power." *Political Science Quarterly* 5 (1986): 705-718.

Leffler, Melvyn. "Inside Enemy Archives: The Cold War Reopened." *Foreign Affairs* (July/August 1996): 120-135.

Locher, Anna, and Christian Nuenlist. "Reinventing NATO: Canada and the Multilateralization of Détente, 1962-66." *International Journal* 58, no. 3 (Spring 2003): 283–302.

Logevall, Fredrik. "De Gaulle, Neutralization, and American Involvement in Vietnam, 1963-1964." *Pacific Historical Review* 1, no. 1 (February 1992): 69-102.

Lowi, Theodore J., and Martin A. Schain. "Conditional Surrender: Charles de Gaulle and American Opinion." *Political Science and Politics* 25 (September 1992): 498-506.

Maggiotto, Michael, and Eugene R. Wittkopf. "American Public Attitudes Toward Foreign Policy." *International Studies Quarterly* (December 1981).

Masters, Roger D. "The Lockean Tradition in American Foreign Policy." *Journal of International Affairs* 21, no. 2 (1967): 253-277.

Mastny, Vojtech. "Was 1968 a Strategic Watershed of the Cold War?" *Diplomatic History* 29, Issue 1 (January 2005): 149-177.

Mélandri, Pierre. "The Troubled Friendship: France and the United States, 1945-1989." In *No End to Alliance: The United States and Western Europe: Past, Present and Future*, Geir Lundestad, 112-133. New York/Houndmills: St Martin's Press/Macmillan Press, 1998.

Monnet, Jean, Maurice Delarue, Jacques Putman, Claude Julien, Michel Mohrt, Paul-Marie de la Gorce, J.A. Fieschi, André Philip, Pierre Uri, Gilbert Gantier, Marc Alexandre, Serge Mallet, and Gaston Deferre. "Les Américains et nous." *La Nef* 26 (February-April 1966): 7-159.

Morgenthau, Hans J. "The Founding Fathers and Foreign Policy: Implications for the Late Twentieth Century." *Orbis* (Spring 1976).

Moulin, Leo "Anti-Americanism in Europe: A Psychoanalysis." *Orbis* (Winter 1958).

Mueller, John D. "Jacques Rueff: Political Economist for the 21st Century?" January 2000, (available on http://www.eppc.org/publications/pubID.2261/pub_detail.asp) (accessed July 2006).

Nouailhat, Yves-Henri. "Nixon-de Gaulle: un épisode original des relations franco-américaines." Revue Française d'Études Américaines no. 32 (April 1987): 309-318.

Pfaltzgraff, Diane K. "The Atlantic Community: A Conceptual History." In Atlantic Community in Crisis: A Redefinition of the Transatlantic Relationship, Hahn, Walter F., and Robert L. Pfaltzgraff, Jr. New York: Pergamon Press, 1979.

Plishke, Elmer. "Lyndon Baines Johnson as a Diplomat in Chief." In Lyndon Baines Johnson and the uses of power, edited by Bernard J. Firestone and Robert C. Vogt, 257-286. New York: Hofstra University Press, 1988.

Pohlmann, Marcus D. "Constraining Presidents at the Brink: the Cuban Missile Crisis." Presidential Studies Quarterly 19 (Spring 1989): 337-346.

Porch, Douglas. "Military 'Culture' and the Fall of France in 1940." International Security 24, no. 4 (Spring 2000): 157-180.

Roobol, W.H. "In Search of an Atlantic Identity." In Yearbook of European Studies 4 (1991): 1-14.

Roper, Jon. "Richard Nixon's Political Hinterland: The Shadows of JFK and Charles de Gaulle." Presidential Studies Quarterly 28, no. 2 (Spring 1998): 422-434.

Rosenau, James N., and Ole R. Holsti. "U.S. Leadership in a Shrinking World: The Breakdown of Consensuses and the Emergence of Conflicting Belief Systems." World Politics 3 (1983): 368-392.

Roskin, Michael. "From Pearl Harbor to Vietnam: Shifting Generational Paradigms and Foreign Policy." Political Science Quarterly (Fall 1974): 563-588.

Russet, Bruce. "The Mysterious Case of Vanishing Hegemony; Or, Is Mark Twain Really Dead?" International Organization 39, no. 2 (Spring 1985): 207-232.

Schlesinger, Arthur, Jr. "Onward and Upward from the Missile Crisis." Problems of Communism 41 (Spring 1992): 5-7.

—. "Foreign Policy and the American Character." Foreign Affairs (Fall 1983).

Scowcroft, Brent. "Eisenhower and a Foreign Policy Agenda." Presidential Studies Quarterly 22 (Summer 1992): 451-454.

Serfaty, Simon. "Atlantic Fantasies." Washington Quarterly (Summer 1982).

Slessor, John. "Multilateral or Multinational: An Alternative to the MLF." The Atlantic Community Quarterly (Summer 1964): 285-291.

Sommer, Theo. "How Many Fingers on How Many Triggers?" The Atlantic Community Quarterly 4 (Winter 1963-64): 556-560.

—. "For an Atlantic Future." The Atlantic Community Quarterly (October 1964): 600-613. Reprinted from Foreign Affairs October 1964.

Soutou, George-Henri. "Les problèmes de sécurité dans les rapports franco-allemands de 1956 à 1963." Relations Internationales 58 (Summer 1989): 227-251.

Spaak, Paul-Henri. "NATO and the Communist Challenge." Address before the Atlantic Treaty Association, 27 September 1958, published in United States Department of State, Department of State Bulletin, 652-4. Washington, DC: US GPO, 20 October 1958.

Steel, Ronald. "Walter Lippmann et Charles de Gaulle." De Gaulle et Son Siècle. Journées Internationales organisées par l'Institut Charles de Gaulle, 19-24 Novembre 1990.

—. "In Place of NATO." *The New Republic*, 14 November 1964.

Stein, Eric and Dominique Carreau. "Law and Peaceful Change in a Subsystem: 'Withdrawal' of France from the North Atlantic Treaty Organization." *American Journal of International Law* 62 (July 1968): 577-640.

Stikker, Dirk U. "NATO – The Shifting Alliance." *The Atlantic Community Quarterly* 3 (Spring 1965): 7-17.

—. "France and its Diminishing Will to Cooperate." *The Atlantic Community Quarterly* 3 (Summer 1965): 197-205.

—. "Effect of Political Factors on the Future Strength of NATO." *The Atlantic Community Quarterly* 6 (Fall 1968).

Taylor, Edmond. "What Price MLF?" *The Reporter* 3 December 1964: 12, 14.

—. "The Long NATO crisis." *The Reporter* 21 April 1966: 16-21.

Toschi, Simona. "Washington-London-Paris: An Untenable Triangle. 1960-1963)." *Journal of European Integration History* no 2 (1995): 81-109.

Trachtenberg, Marc. "Reparation at the Paris Peace Conference." *Journal of Modern History* (March 1979). Republished in part in *The Legacy of the Great War: Peacemaking, 1919*, William R. Keylor. Boston: Houghton Mifflin, 1998.

Ullmann, Richard H. "The Covert French Connection." *Foreign Policy* 75 (Summer 1989): 3-33.

Vaïsse, Maurice. "Aux Origines du Mémorandum de Septembre 1958." *Relations Internationales* 58 (Summer 1989): 253-263.

—. "Un dialogue de sourds: les relations nucléaires franco-américaines de 1957 à 1960." *Relations Internationales* 68 (Winter 1991): 407-423.

—. "La réconciliation franco-allemande: le dialogue de Gaulle-Adenauer." *Politique Étrangère* (Winter 1993-4): 963-972.

Verheyen, Dirk. "Beyond Cowboys and Eurowimps: European-American Imagery in Historical Context." *Orbis* (Spring 1987): 55-73.

Wall, Irwin M. "The United States, Algeria, and the Fall of the Fourth French Republic." *Diplomatic History* 18, no. 4 (Fall 1994): 489-511.

Warner, Geoffrey. "The Anglo-American Special Relationship." *Diplomatic History* 13, no. 4 (Fall 1989): 479-499.

Watt, Donald Cameron. "Britain and the Historiography of the Yalta conference and the Cold War." *Diplomatic History* 13 (Winter 1989): 67-98.

Weber, Eugen. "European Reactions to American Policies." *International Journal* (Spring 1956).

Weigall, David. "British Ideas of European Unity and Regional Confederation in the Context of Anglo-Soviet Relations, 1941-5." in *Making the New Europe: European Unity and the Second World War*, 156-168. London: Pinter, 1990.

Wells Jr., Samuel F. "Charles de Gaulle and the French Withdrawal from NATO's Integrated Command." In *American Historians and the Atlantic Alliance*, Lawrence S. Kaplan. Kent: Kent State University Press, 1991.

Wenger, Andreas. "Crisis and Opportunity: NATO's Transformation and the Multilateralization of Détente, 1966-1968." *Journal of Cold War Studies* 6, no. 1 (2004): 22-74.

—, Anna Locher, Christian Nünlist. *The Future Tasks of the Alliance: NATO's Harmel Report 1966/67*. Parallel History Project on NATO and the Warsaw Pact, July 2004), available on the internet: http://www.isn.ethz.ch/php/collections/coll_Harmel.htm.

Wesseling, H.L. "Had de Gaulle gelijk?" in *Alles naar wens. Tien voordrachten over cultuur, geschiedenis en politiek*. Amsterdam: Bert Bakker, 1998.

Wightman, David R. "Money and Security: Financing American Troops in Germany and the Trilateral Negotiations of 1966-67." *Rivista di Storia Economica* 1 (1988): 26-77.

Wolfers, Arnold. "Integration in the West: the conflict of perspectives." *International Organization* 17 (Summer 1963): 753-770.

"Faut-il reformer l'Alliance Atlantique?" *Politique Étrangère* no.4-5 (1965): 230-244.

"Faut-il reformer l'Alliance Atlantique? Examen critique," *Politique Étrangère* (1965): 324-329.

Dissertations, theses, and unpublished papers

Arenth, Joachim. "Von West-Berlin bis Sudvietnam: die Berlin-Krise und der Vietnam-Krieg als Problemfelder der amerikanisch-westeuropaischer Beziehungen von 1958 bis 1969 in Spiegel amerikanischer Quellen." Ph.D. diss., Ludwig Maximilians Universitat, Munich, Germany, 1991.

David, François. "Les Etats-Unis et les débuts de la cinquième République. May 1958 - Janvier 1961." Mémoire de maîtrise 1992-1993, Université de Paris-IV.

Kaplan, Larry. "Dean Acheson and the Atlantic Community." Paper delivered at a conference at the Johns Hopkins University on 6 April 1996.

Klein Bluemink. "Kissingerian Realism in International Politics: Political Theory, Philosophy and Practice." Ph.D. diss., University of Leiden. the Netherlands, 2000.

Kunz, Diane B. "Lyndon Johnson's Dollar Diplomacy: The Security Connection." Paper presented at the annual meeting of the Organization of American Historians, Louisville, KY, April 1991.

Lippert, Werner. "Richard Nixon's Détente and Willy Brandt's *Ostpolitik*: The Politics and Economic Diplomacy of Engaging the East." Ph.D. diss., submitted to the faculty of the Graduate School of Vanderbilt University, August 2005.

May, Richard. "LBJ and Nuclear Weapons: A Man of Sight, Guided by Politics, Blinded by his Generation." Paper for the University of Texas, 13 May 1987.

Montpas, David. "The Trilateral Negotiations: The Johnson Administration and the Necessity of Compromise." Paper for the University of Texas, Spring 1991.

Owen, Geoffrey. "Britain and the European Coal and Steel Community." Paper presented at Terni Conference on the European Coal and Steel Community, 16-17 May 2002.

Pautsch, Ilse Dorothee. "The multilateral force and the cohesion of NATO." MA thesis, University of Texas, 1981.

Reyn, Sebastian. "Dealing With de Gaulle: or How the General Raised the Price of the MLF and LBJ Refused to Pay It." MA thesis, University of Leiden, the Netherlands, 1991.

Reyna, Michael M. "Foreign Economic Decisionmaking in the Johnson Administration: the Gold Crisis." Draft report for the LBJ School of Public Affairs, Austin, TX, July 1982.

Stanley, James G. "United States foreign policy vis-à-vis Western Europe during the Johnson Administration: a change in priorities?" Ph.D. diss., American University, 1976. University Microfilms 7707769.

Useful weblinks

Lyndon B. Johnson Presidential Library (http://www.lbjlib.utexas.edu)
NARA Nixon Presidential Materials (http://nixon.archives.gov)
Roosevelt Study Center (http://www.roosevelt.nl/en/)
Department of State (http://www.state.gov/r/pa/ho/frus/)
University of Wisconsin digital collection (http://digicoll.library.wisc.edu/FRUS/).

Abbreviations

References to sources

CAH Papers	Christian A. Herter Papers
CF	Country File
CS	Country Series
CsF	Countries File
DAF	Departments and Agencies File
DDEL	Dwight D. Eisenhower Library
DEOF	President Dwight D. Eisenhower's Office Files, 1953-1961
EAS	Eisenhower Administration Series
FRUS	Foreign Relations of the United States
Int. T & M	International Trips and Meetings File
IS	International Series
JFD Papers	John Foster Dulles Papers
JFKL	John F. Kennedy Presidential Library
[mf]	[microform University Publications of America]
HSTL	Harry S Truman Presidential Library
LBJL	Lyndon B. Johnson Presidential Library
MtP	Memos to the President
NARA	National Archives and Records Administration
NPMP	Nixon Presidential Materials Project
NSCH	National Security Council History
NSF	National Security Files
OSANA	Office of the Special Assistant for National Security Affairs
PEOF	President Eisenhower's Office File
PKOF	President Kennedy's Office File
PRO/PREM	Public Record Office, Prime Minister's Private Office
RSC	Roosevelt Study Center
SCF	Special Correspondence Files
SF	Subject File
SMF	Staff Memoranda File
SsF	Subjects File
WHCF	White House Central Files
WHO	White House Office
WHOSS	White House Office, Office of the Staff Secretary

Other

ACDA	Arms Control and Disarmament Agency
AFCENT	Allied Forces Central Europe
ANF	Atlantic Nuclear Force
AEC	Atomic Energy Commission
BOAR	British Army on the Rhine
CAP	Common Agricultural Policy
CEEC	Committee on European Economic Cooperation
CFLN	Comité Français de Libération Nationale
CIA	Central Intelligence Agency
CDU	Christian Democratic Union (Germany)
DAC	Democratic Advisory Council
DPC	Defense Planning Committee
ECSC	European Coal and Steel Community
EDC	European Defense Community
EEC	European Economic Community
EFTA	European Free Trade Association
ERP	European Recovery Program
Euratom	European Atomic Energy Agency
GATT	General Agreement on Tariffs and Trade
IAEA	International Atomic Energy Agency
IMF	International Monetary Fund
JCAE	Joint Committee on Atomic Energy
JCS	Joint Chiefs of Staff
MC	Military Committee
MLF	Multilateral Force
MRBM	Medium Range Ballistic Missile
NAC	North Atlantic Council
NDAC	Nuclear Defense Affairs Committee
NADGE	NATO Air Defense Ground Environment
NATO	North Atlantic Treaty Organization
NPG	Nuclear Planning Group
NPT	Nuclear Nonproliferation Treaty
NSAM	National Security Action Memorandum
NSC	National Security Council
OECD	Organization for Economic Cooperation and Development
OEEC	Organization for European Economic Cooperation
SACEUR	Supreme Allied Commander in Europe
SDR	Special Drawing Rights
SHAPE	Supreme Headquarters, Allied Powers, Europe
SPD	Social Democratic Party (Germany)

TEA	Trade Expansion Act
UN	United Nations
USIA	United States Information Agency

Index of persons

Acheson, Dean, 28, 66, 72, 101-102, 104, 108, 113, 115-116, 132, 165, 167, 170, 180, 196, 201, 203, 234, 260, 270, 272, 304, 307, 341, 349, 355-356, 365, 384, 388, 400, 406, 408-413, 416-417, 420-421, 425, 428-430, 434, 443, 455, 458, 467, 471, 478, 494; Acheson Report, 97, 103, 109, 146, 197; commitment to Atlantic community, 193; the crisis of 1963, 165, 167, 170-71, 180; and de Gaulle, 66, 72, 170, 355, 356; French withdrawal from NATO, 257, 260, 270, 272-73, 275, 294, 300, 304-305; as Johnson's adviser, 203, 234, 235, 244, 245, 257, 260, 272-73, 275, 304-305, 366; as Kennedy's adviser, 72, 97, 109, 115, 117, 124, 132, 165, 167, 170-71, 174, 180, 182, 186-87, 191, 342, 365; and Monnet, 101-105, 107, 116, 125, 132, 191; multilateral force, 196, 203, 234, 235, 244-47; and Nixon, 341-42, 349-50, 377; as Truman's secretary of state, 28-29, 42

Adams, John Quincy, 488

Adenauer, Konrad, 35, 44, 51, 56, 64, 73-75, 78, 90-93, 108-110, 117-119, 126-129, 131-132, 134-135, 138, 142-144, 148, 152, 158, 161-163, 167, 169-171, 173-184, 200, 208, 215, 220, 238, 251, 254, 284, 301, 308, 328, 343, 386, 391, 394, 397, 400-401, 403-407, 420, 422, 428-430, 439, 444, 450

Aglion, Raoul, 32, 385

Ailleret, Charles, 280, 310, 480

Alsop, Joseph, 34, 36, 39, 41, 43, 51-52, 56, 59, 65-67, 70-71, 111, 157, 158, 164, 186, 190, 200, 218, 221, 228, 241, 244, 253, 386-392, 395, 397-401, 412, 420, 425-427, 429, 436-437, 440-441, 449, 457-458, 461, 464, 480, 482

Aron, Raymond, 401

Ball, George, 97-98, 103-104, 107-108, 110, 115-119, 121-122, 125, 127, 131, 133, 135-136, 148-151, 153, 156-157, 159, 162-163, 166, 168-174, 181-182, 186-187, 191, 193, 196, 198-199, 205, 208, 211, 227-228, 231-236, 238, 242, 244, 246-247, 257-259, 263, 266, 268, 271-276, 303-305, 314-316, 319, 333, 339, 355, 359, 365-366, 376, 401, 403, 408-409, 411-417, 419, 420-421, 424-425, 427-433, 435, 440, 442, 444, 446, 449-450, 452-456, 459, 461-464, 466-470, 472, 477-478, 481, 494, 496-497; influence of Monnet, 103-104; and Johnson, 198-99, 205, 211, 227-28, 231, 232-36, 238, 242, 244, 246, 247, 257-59, 263, 266, 268, 271-76, 303-305, 314-315, 316; and Kennedy, 115-119, 121-123, 125, 136, 149-151, 153, 156-157, 159, 162-163, 166-174, 181-82, 186-87, 191, 193; views on de Gaulle, 107-108, 153

Bange, Oliver, 190, 403, 425, 427-430, 437

Bator, Francis, 270, 271, 273-275, 277, 279, 282-283, 375, 458, 465-471, 475, 496-497

Baumel, Jacques, 216, 447

Tuthill, John, 165, 172, 411, 413, 429, 431

Tyler, William, 153, 184, 205, 243, 257, 357, 400, 425-426, 428, 431, 435, 441, 451-452, 454, 458, 462

Vance, Cyrus, 273, 276

Viviani, René, 99

Von Hassel, Kai-Uwe, 264

Wahl, Nicholas, 379-380, 390, 420-421, 427, 438, 480, 490, 493, 495-496

Walters, Vernon, 321-322, 346, 351, 394, 483, 491-492, 495

Wesseling, Henk, 380

Wilson, Harold, 210-212, 217, 227, 229, 231-236, 238-246, 264, 282, 296-297, 323, 330, 348, 443, 446-447, 455, 457-458, 464, 471, 484, 486

Wilson, Woodrow; 100; Wilsonianism, 19, 102, 334-335, 360, 401

Winand, Pascaline, 94, 98, 403-404, 407-412, 414-417, 419-421, 425-426, 429, 431, 439

Wohlstetter, Albert, 372

Curriculum vitae

Dr. Sebastian Reyn (1967) is a top-level policymaker and strategist at the Netherlands' Ministry of Defense and a member of the Dutch Civil Service (the top level of public administration). He has worked on a broad range of policy issues, including the Balkan wars, NATO, nuclear policy and missile defense, the fight against terrorism after 9/11, Afghanistan and Iraq. He has co-authored a number of major policy reviews regarding the Netherlands' armed forces and served as a speech writer to the Minister of Defense. From 2008 to 2010 he directed a wide-ranging Future Policy Survey for the Dutch Armed Forces involving five ministries. For this, the Minister of Defence awarded him a golden medal of merit.

In 1991, Reyn graduated with honours from the University of Leiden in The Netherlands with an M.A. degree in history. His M.A. thesis on President Lyndon Johnson's policy vis-à-vis Charles de Gaulle in the framework of the multilateral nuclear force MLF received a total of three awards.

In 1994, Reyn graduated from the Johns Hopkins School of Advanced International Studies (SAIS) in Bologna, Italy, with a degree in international relations. In 2007, Reyn received his Ph.D. cum laude from the University of Leiden. This book is based on his Ph.D. dissertation.

Reyn has published widely on academic and policy issues. He is the author of Allies or Aliens? George W. Bush and the Transatlantic Crisis in Historical Perspective (Netherlands Atlantic Association, 2004), which received wide acclaim and is used by various universities in the Netherlands and the United States as a college text book.